W9-CXN-567

Fundamental Illustrator 7

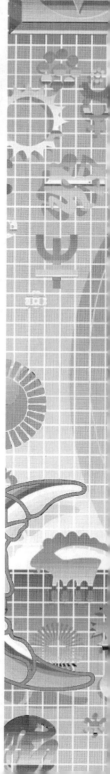

About the Author...

Steve Bain is an award-winning technical illustrator, author and writer. He has worked in the print and communication industry for nearly two decades, and has been using digital-based software since the early 1980s. He was one of the first digital artists to use early Macintosh and Windows-based illustration and publishing software.

Steve continues illustrating and writing for communication, print, and the World Wide Web. He is author of *Special Edition, Using CorelDRAW! 6* and *Looking Good Online*. He is also a monthly contributor to *Canada Computes*, *Corel Magazine*, *The CorelDRAW! Journal*, *The Illustrator Journal*, and *Applied Arts Magazine, and several technology and illustration-related publications in North America and Europe.*

Fundamental Illustrator 7

Steve Bain

Osborne **McGraw-Hill**

Berkeley   New York   St. Louis   San Francisco
Auckland   Bogotá   Hamburg   London
Madrid   Mexico City   Milan   Montreal   New
Delhi   Panama City   Paris   São Paulo
Singapore   Sydney   Tokyo   Toronto

Osborne/**McGraw-Hill**
2600 Tenth Street
Berkeley, California 94710
U.S.A.

For information on translations or book distributors outside the U.S.A., or to arrange bulk purchase discounts for sales promotions, premiums, or fund-raisers, please contact Osborne/**McGraw-Hill** at the above address.

Fundmental Illustrator 7

1234567890 AGM 901987654321098

ISBN 0-07-882415-X

Publisher: Brandon A. Nordin
Editor-in-Chief: Scott Rogers
Acquisitions Editor: Megg Bonar
Project Editor: Jennifer Wenzel
Associate Project Editor: Heidi Poulin
Editorial Assistant: Gordon Hurd
Technical Editor: Walter Arnold
Copy Editor: Ann Spivack
Proofreader: Sally Engelfried
Indexer: Valerie Robbins
Computer Designer: Michelle Galicia
Illustrator: Lance Ravella
Cover Illustration: Gary Priester
Cover Design: Regan Honda

The effort made in writing this book is first dedicated to my wife Wendy,
whose unwavering support and constant encouragement,
are the reason you are holding this book in your hands. An equal
dedication goes to our three-year-old son David, whose endless
enthusiasm to do utterly ungrown-up-like things provides constant
inspiration. This dedication also includes those extended
family members who stepped in for me to join him in some of
those ungrown-up things.

This book is also dedicated to you - the reader. Without your inquisitive
mind, patronage and thirst for knowledge, books such as this just
wouldn't be written. It's for you that the high-quality information and
creative tutorials found in *Fundamental Illustrator 7* have been written,
designed, and structured, and for whom the ideas and creativity have
been prepared. I trust you'll enjoy the drawing adventures you are
about to embark on.

CONTENTS AT A GLANCE

CONTENTS

PART II
Working with Illustrator 7's Tools

PART III

Beyond Basic Tools

PART V
Reference

Producing a book such as *Fundamental Illustrator 7* is the collaborative effort of many creative and technical professionals. In this regard, I'd like to extend my thanks to specific members of the Osborne/McGraw-Hill team, whom I can comfortably say are one of the most capable and professional group I have encountered in the book-publishing industry. Most credit must go to a key player of this team, acquisitions editor Megg Bonar, who has proven to be a driving force behind the writing and production of this book. And, to her trusty right hand Gordon Hurd whose knowledge of the secret ins and outs of publishing administration provide much-needed support. I would also like to extend thanks and give credit to project editor Jennifer Wenzel and copy editor Ann Spivack for their due diligence and strict attention to detail. Arlette Crosland deserves thanks for her help on last minute art rendering. And last, I extend thanks to publisher Brandon Nordin and Scott Rogers for their flexibility and understanding toward this complex and creative effort.

I'd also like to acknowledge the efforts of Gary Priester, Donald V. Phillips, Jim Cook, and John M. Stafford who have contributed their expertise to selected portions of Fundamental Illustrator 7 and to whom a generous helping of acknowledgment and credit is well due. While some are accomplished designers and illustrators who have a natural gift for writing, others are writers with exceptional talents for illustrating.

I'd also like to acknowledge the efforts of our diligent technical reviewers. Walter Arnold provided technical insight from a Windows platform perspective, while Kelly Dolan ensured accuracy for Macintosh-specific issues. In addition, Eric Hess of Adobe Systems provided a clear account of Illustrator 7 from a developer's viewpoint and contributed his own unique expertise into program operation. All involved have added to the high degree of quality and accuracy you'll see in the explanation, reference information and exercises to follow.

Let me also take this opportunity to thank Adobe's public relations specialist, Thérèse Bruno, for her effort and support in providing the vital information which make books such as these possible. And, of course let's not forget to acknowledge the efforts of Adobe's largely-anonymous software engineers who have put obvious considerable thought, endless enthusiasm and careful consideration into the design of Adobe Illustrator over the years.

ACKNOWLEDGMENTS

Fundamental Illustrator 7 is a book for all levels of user who are using (or contemplating using) Adobe Illustrator 7. Concepts and features of the program have been explained using common, everyday language and many of the creative exercises are easy to follow and quick to perform. Fundamental Illustrator is also supported by a comprehensive glossary and index to help locate and define the not-so-common terms you might encounter. A 32-page color insert provides tutorial overviews and color support where needed and has been designed in such a way to stimulate creative ideas. The information, reference and examples in this book have been structured and organized in a logical and natural learning progression.

Fundamental Illustrator 7 has been written with value for the reader in mind. It has been structured as both a drawing teacher, reference manual, and learning tool. Information and step-by-step lessons have been written in easily-understood terms, and topics feature complete cross-referencing to related subjects contained in the book.

Who Should Have this Book

On the creative side of business, Fundamental Illustrator 7 will be of interest to art and design students, digital artists, illustrators, professional designers, Internet artists, art directors, and desktop publishers — regardless of which platform they work on. But, while Fundamental Illustrator 7 is focused toward creative aspects of the program's use, it will also be invaluable to professionals not entirely familiar with drawing techniques such as those working in the technical-related industries such as engineering and architecture or service-based industries such as multimedia and service bureaus.

Fundamental Illustrator 7 will be a valuable reference and illustration guide for you if you currently use Adobe Illustrator or are upgrading from a previous version, and work in one of the following occupations:

- Graphic illustrator
- Technical illustrator
- Graphic designer
- Web designer
- Multimedia designer

- Digital artist
- Service bureau operator
- Media communicator
- Engineering
- Drafting
- Architecture
- Adobe Illustrator upgrader

What's so Great About this Book?

Where other illustration program books often do well at providing technical information and/or program feature reference they often lack a degree of reader instruction and learning. And, where some how-to illustration books often excel in providing drawing techniques, they often fall short when it comes to complete program reference. This is where Fundamental Illustrator 7 has the advantage.

Not only does Fundamental Illustrator 7 provide complete program operational reference and comprehensive feature use, it also fully explores drawing techniques specifically geared toward Adobe Illustrator 7. Plus, through the inclusion of chapter drawing tutorials, this book provides a wealth of creative stimulation and a wealth of illustration ideas to draw on.

While bridging the reference-and-technique gap found in other books, Fundamental Illustrator 7 also delivers in these areas:

- Explains program operation and feature use without technical jargon
- Covers and addresses both Macintosh and Windows platforms
- Loaded with tips, tricks, and Illustrator 7 shortcuts
- Teaches illustration techniques
- Covers comprehensive Adobe Illustrator 7 features
- Covers print and World Wide Web issues

About the Contributors

Gary W. Priester is a designer, illustrator and an author in his own right. He is also a partner in The Black Point Group, a ten-year old graphic design firm located in Northern California. Gary's knack for color is showcased not only in parts of *Fundamental Illustrator 7*, but also in his own book *Looking Good in Color*. Some of Gary's design and illustration work can also be viewed monthly in *Corel Magazine* and *The CorelDRAW Journal*. He is also host of *The Trompe L'Oeil Room* on the World Wide Web at URL http://trompe.i-us.com.

Don Phillips is an illustrator in Marietta, Ohio. Although his technical background is in drafting and design technology, Don is an illustrator at heart. And, although his professional life involves illustrating, he's actually a full-time ordained ministry pastor. Don is also an occasional contributor to Corel Magazine.

Jim Cook is a freelance illustrator, cartoonist, and writer in Collinsville, Illinois. Jim's professional background includes eight years creating information graphics for news media and he has also spent considerable time designing World Wide Web sites. Jim also writes a monthly internet column found at URL http://home.stlnet.com/~jcook/writing/oti.

John M. Stafford is a freelance illustrator and an Adobe certified instructor in Alexandria, Virginia. His certification includes Illustrator, Photoshop, and Acrobat. John comes from a professional background in information graphics for print and news media.

About the Cover

The *Fundamental Illustrator 7* cover design and images seen embellishing key pages was created using Illustrator 7, by Gary Priester. The aim was to create an illustration that highlighted Illustrator's strengths as well as its new features. The sun theme conveys the concept of warmth and other elements were transformed using Illustrator 7's new availability of Photoshop filters and compatible plug-ins. Mosaic and Plastic Wrap filters were used on the right side of the big sun while the small metal spheres in the upper left came as inpirations from the chapter on working in color. The illusion of transparency and drop shadows was engineered using Illustrator 7's ability to match patterns. The white grid with objects in front and back were employed to create a feeling of space and depth.

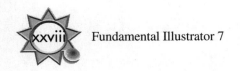

Conventions Used

In order to cover multi-platform use, you'll encounter command and shortcut notations which may seem confusing at first. Because of the slight differences in keyboard and shortcut identification across Macintosh and Windows platforms, you'll generally see textual reference such as CTRL/COMMAND and/or ALT/OPTION used to identify certain key combinations. The CTRL (short for Control) and ALT (short for Alternate) keys pertain to Windows platform users, while the COMMAND and OPTION keys pertain to Macintosh users.

Where multiple keys are pressed to accomplish a command, a "+" joins the key strokes. Where menu and sub-menu access is referred to – all of which are common to all platforms – commands are separated by a vertical stroke in this way: File|Open. Where single keys can be pressed to select tools the shortcut is noted in this way: (X).

The order of these keyboard notations remains constant and consistent throughout *Fundamental Illustrator 7*. However, you'll also encounter instances where these platforms deviate from typical commonality. In these instances, both Macintosh and Windows users are addressed separately, and we have our technical reviewers to thank for their combined effort and accuracy.

Tips, Cautions, Notes, and Shortcuts

Fundamental Illustrator 7 is fully-loaded with relevant Tips, Cautions, and Notes as they relate to the tools and features being used. The perspective offered by these value-added considerations are combined together in the text with extensive coverage of the keyboard shortcuts implemented in Adobe Illustrator 7. And, in case you need a complete reference of all available Illustrator 7 shortcuts (both obvious and hidden), Appendix B covers them all.

Complete Subject Cross-Referencing

As you'll also discover on your exploration of the chapters to come, reference duplication has been avoided by integrating complete subject cross-referencing to optional related ideas and concepts you may wish to explore further. In this unique way, *Fundamental Illustrator 7* enables you to focus your reading and learning efforts and avoid the need to hunt-and-pick for related information.

Chapter Tutorials

As you thumb the pages of this book, you'll notice chapters 5 through 13 detail use of specific Illustrator 7 tools. And, while simply reading about their capabilities can provide you with the necessary groundwork and background information for using these tools, putting this knowledge into practice can be another story indeed. This is where the tutorials provide you with value few other books deliver.

Each of these chapters end in one or more tutorials designed to guide you through practical projects of the tools covered in a comprehensive, step-by-step learning exercise. Some tutorials address basic issues, while others excel to take you into areas of illustration techniques which take years to master. Where color reproduction enhances the illustration and drawing effects achieved, certain steps (indicated by color palette symbols) are showcased in the color insert of this book.

Color Support

Where other books simply depict what can be done by showcasing completed illustrations, they often lack the information needed to understand how the illustrations were produced. *Fundamental Illustrator 7* provides you with a color guide to how illustrations are actually *produced* via a full-color overview. The 32-page color section found in this book is integrated with the detailed step-by-step practical tutorials found at the end of chapters 5 through 13.

How this Book is Organized

Fundamental Illustrator 7 has been organized into five parts containing 18 chapters supported by two appendices. While each chapter is designed to guide you through use of Adobe Illustrator 7's tools, the four organized parts have been structured in a sequence logical to learning the program.

Part 1: Welcome to Illustrator 7

Whether you're just getting acquainted with Illustrator 7 as a first-time user or you're revisiting this latest version, Part 1: Welcome to Illustrator 7 is designed to cover the basics. **Chapter 1: Getting Started** is designed to have you quickly using the tools and producing drawings.

Chapter 2: Managing Illustrator 7 Files provides you with an understanding of Illustrator 7's basic file operations so that you can begin managing and working with the material you are producing. In an effort to maximize your productivity, you'll also learn how to fine-tune program functions and drawing preferences to suit the way you work *before* you actually begin drawing in **Chapter 3: Making Illustrator Easy to Use.**

And, if you're a seasoned Adobe Illustrator user and just loading up this latest release, **Chapter 4: What's New in Illustrator 7** will take you quickly through all that has changed since the previous release to save you time spent familiarizing yourself with what's new this time around.

Part 2: Working with Illustrator 7's Tools

As you become more comfortable with working in Adobe Illustrator 7, you will naturally demand to know more about intermediate and advanced drawing techniques. Part 2: Working with Illustrator 7's Tools covers use of all tools and effects Illustrator is capable of and you'll begin your practical journey through all of the capabilities of the program by following along with the step-by-step tutorials.

Part 2 begins with one of the most common demands made on drawing programs by providing all you need to know about working with type in **Chapter 5: Working with Type**. In a natural progression toward integrating type into your drawings and illustrations, **Chapter 6: Type Options and Effects** enables you to continue this exploration by providing complete reference for controlling and enhancing type effects.

Following exploration of text and type options, the next three chapters in Part 2 involve learning the powerful capabilities of Illustrator's object-creation tools. In **Chapter 7: Creating and Editing Drawing Objects**, you'll begin to discover how to create simple and complex shapes, and manipulate, transform and distort those shapes to fit your drawing needs. **Chapter 8: Selecting and Arranging Objects**, enables you to capitalize on objects you've created by detailing exactly how to manage those objects and their optional properties. In **Chapter 9: Object Transform Tools**, you'll also discover some of the more powerful transformation techniques and learn how to use Illustrator's automated Pathfinder commands.

Part 2 closes with two chapters on learning how to apply basic fill and stroke properties to the objects you have created including some slightly-advanced techniques for achieving realistic-looking effects in **Chapter 10: Setting Fills and Strokes. Chapter 11: Working in Color** explains the ins and outs of working in color including print and World Wide Web issues and provides a comprehensive understanding of how Illustrator 7's color tools behave.

Part 3: Beyond Basic Tools

Part 3 has been structured to cover advanced operation of Illustrator 7 including use of filters, masks, and bitmap tools. **Chapter 12: Mastering Filter Effects** details use of the enormous number of both vector and Photoshop plug-in filters, and provides you with an exploration of real-life, practical uses for using these effects. **Chapter 13: Working with Masks** details use of one of the least-understood, but more useful features of Illustrator used by experts who know their true illustration benefit.

    Chapter 14: Working with Bitmap Tools, explains some of the intricacies of working with imported and created bitmaps, and details where some of the related Illustrator tools can be found. **Chapter 15: Getting the Most Out of Illustrator** summarizes some of the more advanced techniques used by Illustrator experts to squeeze the most benefit they can from the program.

Part 4: Creating Print, Web, and File Images

Once your drawings have been created, Part 4: Creating Print, Web, and file images provides the critical information required to properly prepare your images for mass reproduction and use online. **Chapter 16: Importing and Exporting from Illustrator 7** covers all of the various file format filters now available in Illustrator and details all their options and capabilities. If you're printing drawings to desktop printers or preparing them for offset reproduction **Chapter 17: Printing from Illustrator 7** will provide you with the necessary background for successful output and provides troubleshooting strategies for complex documents. If you're like many who are making the transition to online artwork, **Chapter 18: Illustrator 7 and the Web** clear up much of the mystery surrounding preparing images for the World Wide Web.

Part 5: Reference

Finally, Part 5: Reference provides back-end support by defining some of the more uncommon terminology encountered throughout this book in **Appendix A: Glossary of Terms**. In a comprehensive and thorough collection, **Appendix B: Summary of Keyboard Shortcuts** details the extensive shortcuts engineered into Adobe Illustrator 7.

PART
I

Welcome to Illustrator 7

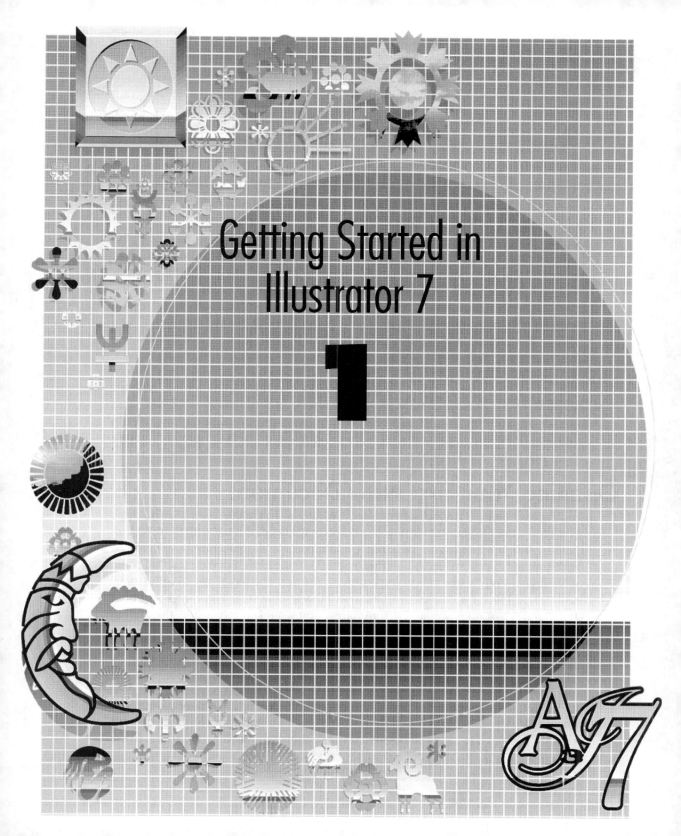

Getting Started in
Illustrator 7

1

If you've just arrived at this chapter with the intention of learning the basics, then congratulations are in order. You've chosen to start at the *very* beginning—which is always a good choice. This chapter will help you to develop a basic understanding of using Illustrator 7.

You're about to enter into a drawing adventure that will open your eyes to the benefits of using electronic illustration technology together with the power of your computer to produce single images or thousands of reproductions. On this journey, you'll discover ways to create simple drawings or complex illustrations and get the most out Adobe Illustrator 7. You'll also learn that you don't need to be a fine arts graduate to create simple diagrams or realistic, true-to-life images.

Whether you're a long-time dedicated Adobe Illustrator fan or a first-time user, this chapter will help to get you up and running quickly and point you in the right direction for getting more detailed descriptions further on in this book. This chapter guides you through opening your first new document, creating simple objects, navigating your document through view controls, and the basics of moving and transforming objects. You'll also find some valuable information on how to help yourself if you get stuck and some secrets on using dialog box shortcuts within Illustrator 7's interface controls.

Opening Your First New Document

For the experienced Adobe software user, gazing at Illustrator 7 for the first time won't seem unfamiliar. But for new users who may not be familiar with the program, there may be a small degree of panic. Certain parts of the interface have changed since previous versions, including menu options, the addition of palettes, and some of the higher-end capabilities of the program. But don't be too alarmed—Illustrator has been designed for ease of use, and with a few simple steps you can get yourself started quickly. Under normal circumstances, you would simply follow this step to open a new document:

- With Illustrator 7 launched, choose File|New (CTRL/COMMAND+N). Notice that a new document opens.

By default, Illustrator 7 automatically opens a new untitled art document each time it is launched. So, if you've just launched the program, what you'll see on your screen is a brand new unsaved document containing nothing but white space. In the document title bar, you'll notice that the name of the document is displayed for identification, as shown in Figure 1-1.

Note   *For newer Windows platform Illustrator 7 users, the appearance of more than one window may be confusing. In fact, there are really two types of windows showing: the main window, which is Illustrator 7's program window, and the drawing document window. Both appear to be nearly identical. On the other hand, Macintosh users see only individual document windows while files are open.*

Illustrator 7 employs an automatic-naming function for newly-created, unsaved documents and, as you'll discover, it supports a multiple-document interface—meaning you can have more than one document opened at one time. In fact, you

Name of document   Close box

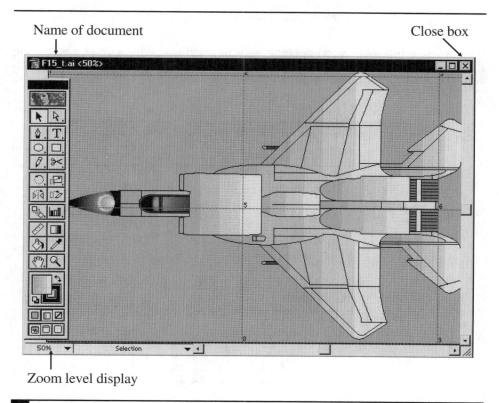

Zoom level display

FIGURE 1-1   Opening a new Illustrator 7 document

can have as many documents opened as your system's RAM restrictions will allow. As you open more new documents, Illustrator names them sequentially as *Untitled Art 1*, *Untitled Art 2*, and so on. This numbering system continues for as long as the program is open regardless of whether the new documents are saved or not, and it resets itself once you quit the program and relaunch it.

If you wish to save your document, you will need to give it a logical name and location on your system. To save a new document, follow these steps:

1. With your new Untitled document open, choose File|Save As (CTRL/COMMAND+SHIFT+S). Notice the Save As dialog box opens as shown below.

2. Enter a name in the File Name box and set a location to save the file.

3. Select the appropriate Illustrator version file format. Version 7.0 is the default.

4. Click OK. Your document is saved.

For more information on opening, closing, saving, saving copies, and saving your documents to previous versions of Illustrator, see **Chapter 2: Managing Illustrator 7 Files**.

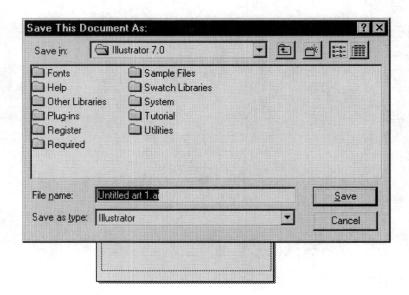

Tip *If you have more than one document open at a time, you can bring the one you would like to save to the forefront by choosing it from the bottom of the Window menu where all open documents are listed.*

Once you have saved your new document, closing it (or quitting the program altogether) is likely the next most logical operation on your learning list. You can close your Illustrator document a number of different ways. The most straightforward way to close a document is to click the close box in the upper-right corner of your document window. By default, Illustrator will automatically ask you if you would like to save any recent unsaved changes before it closes the document. If no other documents are opened, what remains will be the program window, as shown in Figure 1-2 (Windows) and Figure 1-3 (Macintosh).

Note *If you find that the Save option under the File menu is grayed out and unavailable, you are probably trying to save a document that contains no recent changes. Only documents that have been changed in some way may be saved using the Save command. On the other hand, the Save As and Save a Copy As commands will both be available.*

Beside the name of each new document you'll also notice a percent value in brackets, as in "Untitled art 1 <33.3%>". This value indicates the view magnification you are currently seeing your document through. In Illustrator 7, the view magnification can be changed to values ranging from 6.25 percent (low magnification) to 1600 percent (highly magnified). To quickly change the view magnification of what you are seeing, click the Zoom Level Display menu in the lower-left corner of the Illustrator screen.

Tip *To Zoom directly to a specific object in your document, select the Zoom Tool in the main Toolbox palette and click directly on the object you wish a closer view of. Zoom views increase gradually in magnification each time the Zoom Tool is clicked on the screen. To Zoom out again, click again while holding the ALT/OPTION key.*

For more information on using zoom controls and other document viewing features available in Illustrator 7, see the "View Commands" section in **Chapter 3: Making Illustrator Easy to Use**.

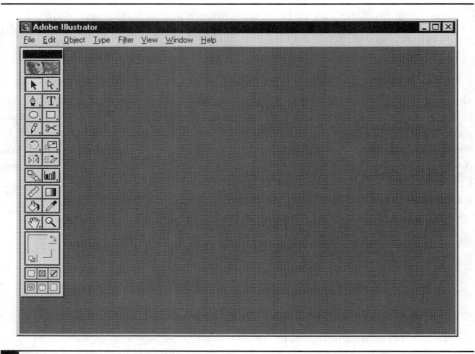

FIGURE 1-2   Illustrator 7's Windows version program window

Helping Yourself to Illustrator Help

Even though Fundamental Illustrator 7 is your best source for reference information, program tips, tutorials, and drawing techniques, one of the most valuable things anyone can learn is how to help themselves. And, even though Fundamental Illustrator 7 guides you carefully through all aspects of real-life use of all program features, there may be some exploration you wish to do on your own.

 For instant help in identifying Toolbox, palette, and screen interface elements in Illustrator 7, activate the Show Tool Tips option found in the File\Preferences\General dialog box. Tool Tips behave like pop-up flags which identify program parts when your cursor is held above certain areas. By default, Tool Tips are selected after initial installation of Adobe Illustrator 7.

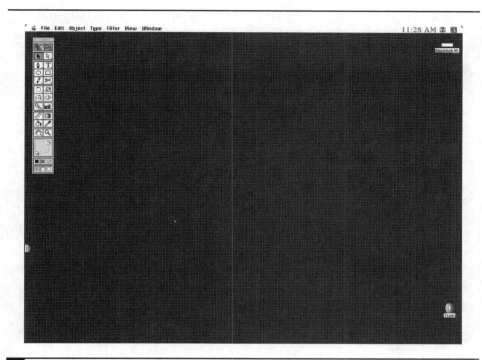

FIGURE 1-3   Illustrator 7's Macintosh version program window

After opening, saving, and closing a new document for the first time, you're probably going to have a million questions you'll need to have answered. The good news here is that Illustrator 7 features a comprehensive collection of Help information. And, as with many other operations, you can access Illustrator 7's online Help feature a number of ways, the quickest of which is to press the F1 key on your keyboard. But if you're using the Windows version, you can choose either Contents, Search, or Keyboard from the Help menu for topics specific to Illustrator 7 or How to Use Help for general questions regarding using the Help feature. Mac users may press COMMAND? or launch the QuickHelp application to access help.

For Windows users, Illustrator 7's Help feature comes in the form of three tabbed areas: Contents, Index, and Find. The Contents help, shown below, lists query areas which can be expanded through double-clicks to show more detailed pages connected through hypertext links. Double-clicking on a topic causes Help to display a hypertext page of related information.

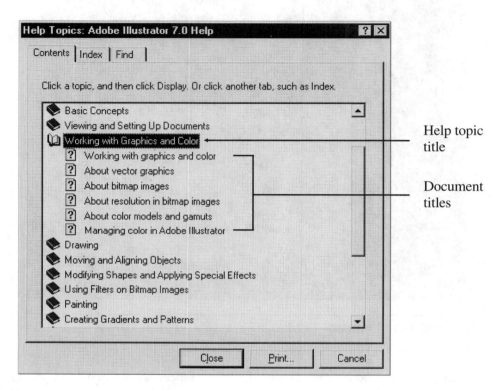

Both the Index and Find functions only accept single-word queries. Entering more than one word will not locate a multiword term.

To locate preset cross references in the Help hypertext documents, use the Index feature. The Index has been organized like any index in a book, whereby you can look up specific references to keywords by entering the word in the box numbered 1 as shown here. Illustrator's Help index provides quick access to related topics which have been marked with entries matching your query. Once a keyword has been entered, the Help feature will display a listing of indexed topics in the box below. To view the page, double-click on its corresponding entry in this box.

Enter keyword here

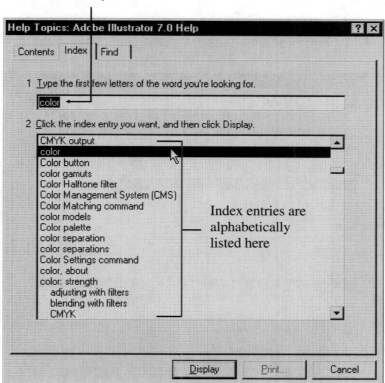

Index entries are alphabetically listed here

Last on the list of Help features is the Find feature. The Find function queries a text database compiled by Adobe. Using this feature is slightly different between Windows and Macintosh versions. In the Windows version, if you're using the Find function for the first time following installation of Illustrator 7, you may notice that an Install Wizard asks if you would like to install the minimized or maximized search database. As a general rule, the minimized database is usually comprehensive enough for most queries. Once in the Find feature, enter a keyword of the subject you would like to research to have Help display a list of relevant matching words in box 2. Narrow your query by clicking on the result which most closely matches your query in box 2 to display more focused results in box 3. Then, double-click the one that most closely matches your query as shown next. If you wish to customize the Find command further than the default settings, explore the other settings available by clicking the Options button.

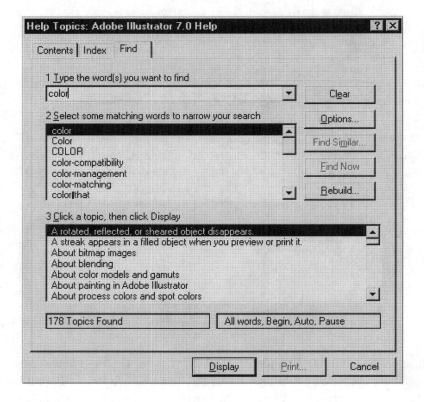

The difference for Macintosh version users is that they do not have to click the Find tab to search Illustrator's Help feature they just type in the specific words or combinations they're looking for. Mac users have additional tools to include or exclude certain terms during their search as shown next. Once a search is complete, users may click the More Choices button to expand the search by including Boolean operators and additional search criteria.

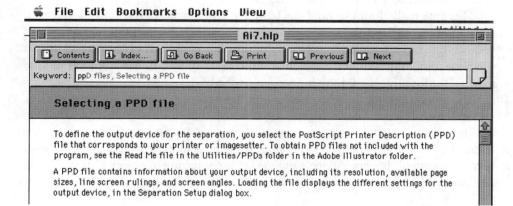

Tip   *Unfortunately, Help topics are usually quite general and generic in nature, and, although many of the facts and figures about features in Illustrator are included in the Help documents, little information exists on their real-life use. While some simple topics can be easily found, others can send you on a wild goose chase wasting valuable time in a fruitless effort. On the bright side, you have* Fundamental Illustrator 7 *in hand, which will take you through step-by-step illustration techniques, provide tips, and reveal nearly everything you need to know about creating drawings with Illustrator 7.*

Creating Simple Objects

Creating your very first drawing object can be a frustrating and/or intimidating task if you aren't familiar with the drawing tools available. However, creating an object is a relatively uncomplicated task—especially if you're not too particular about details such as size, color, position on the page, and so on. And, as with any drawing program, these details can be changed as your drawn object or drawing begins to take shape. In other words, don't worry too much about details so long as you actually *begin* your drawing process. All objects in Illustrator are created using the basic tools available in the Toolbox and the mouse.

There are really four essential and basic types of objects in Illustrator 7 you need to be familiar with at this point: rectangles, ellipses, paths, and text. Of course, as you become more familiar with Illustrator you'll probably want to find out all you can about other types of objects such as bitmaps or hybrids of basic objects such as masks. But for now, we'll remain focused on the basics.

The objects you are going to create with these tools are sometimes referred to as *vector-based* objects. Vector objects are created using points joined by lines. In Illustrator these points are known as *anchor points* while the lines that join them are referred to as *paths*. Other programs refer to these object parts differently, so don't become confused. It's just Adobe's unique way of referring to object parts created in Illustrator.

Create a Rectangle

A rectangle in its natural state is the name given to any closed object which is created from four straight sides and has four corners, each measuring 90 degrees. Sound like elementary school? You won't think so once you see what you can do with a simple rectangle. There are actually four Rectangle tools to choose from within the main Toolbox palette, including the usual rectangle as well as rounded, centered, and rounded-centered. Clicking and holding your mouse on the Rectangle tool will display the entire collection, but for learning purposes, we'll stick to the usual tool.

To create a simple rectangle, follow these steps:

1. With a new or existing document open, select the Rectangle tool from the main Toolbox palette. Notice your cursor changes to four crosshair marks with a dot in the center.

2. Click and drag with the Rectangle tool anywhere on your page using a diagonal-style motion (usually from upper-left to lower-right) and release the mouse.

3. That's it, you're done!

Notice that as you dragged the mouse, the corner of a blue rectagonal outline appeared and grew in the direction you dragged the cursor, as shown in Figure 1-4. And, as the rectagonal outline grew, a mark in the center of the shape—referred to as a center point—followed along. And finally, once you released the mouse, four markers appeared at the corners of the rectangle. While the rectangle remains in its natural state, these markers are sometimes referred to as anchor points.

The handles that appear in the corner of the rectangle serve several purposes. First, they are anchor points which determine the size and shape of the object. Next, they enable you to alter the shape by altering their properties. And last, they provide a visual reference for the corners of the rectangle shape itself, as does the center point.

For more information on creating other types of rectangles, see the "Rectangle Tools" section in **Chapter 7: Creating and Editing Drawing Objects**.

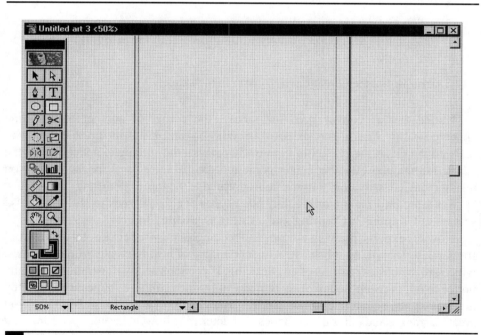

FIGURE 1-4   Creating a simple rectagonal shape with the Rectangle tool

Create an Ellipse

Ellipse objects are quite similar to rectangles in that they feature the same number of anchor points and a center point and are created in much the same way. An ellipse can be defined as any closed object created featuring four anchor points connecting four curve paths in a symmetrical and concentric shape around a center point. Or in plain language, a circle—round or not.

As with the Rectangle tool, there is more than one ellipse tool to choose from, comprising the usual Ellipse and Centered Ellipse tools. Both Ellipse tools are capable of creating centered, rounded, or rounded-centered ellipses. To see the Ellipse tools, click and hold the Ellipse tool displayed in the main Toolbox palette using your mouse.

To create an ellipse object using the usual Ellipse tool, follow these steps:

1. With a new or existing document open, select the Ellipse tool from the main Toolbox palette. Notice your cursor changes to four crosshair marks with a dot in the center.

2. Click and drag with the Ellipse tool anywhere on your page using a diagonal-style motion (usually from upper-left to lower-right) and release the mouse.

3. You're finished creating your first ellipse shape.

Notice that as you dragged the mouse, the corner of another blue outline appeared—this time in the shape of an ellipse—and grew in the direction you dragged the cursor, as shown in Figure1-5. As with the rectangle, notice that as the ellipse outline grew, another center point appeared in the new shape, and once you released the mouse button, four markers appeared at the top, bottom, and sides of it.

For more information on creating other types of ellipses, see the "Ellipse Tools" section in **Chapter 7: Creating and Editing Drawing Objects**.

Now for experts, drawing ellipses and rectangles may seem like child's play, but for new users it will establish a root understanding of how to create primary shapes, which are the basic elements of any drawing. If you look at any illustration, you may notice that it is composed of arrangements of hybrids of these shapes whether they are rectangles, squares, ellipses, circles, triangles, polygons, or so on. How you create, arrange, and color these shapes will determine how accurately your drawing portrays your ideas or real life itself.

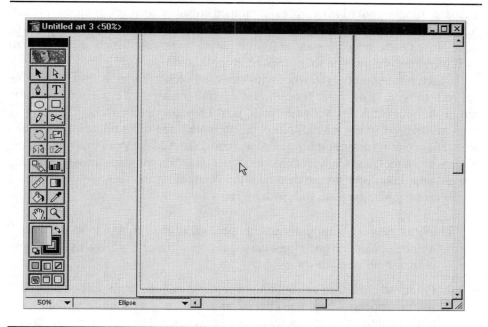

FIGURE 1-5   Creating a simple ellipse object with the Ellipse tool

Create a Path

For Adobe Illustrator users, the term *path* refers to any line which joins two anchor points. In fact, you could simply call them lines, but because a line usually joins only two points, that term may not be entirely accurate. Paths can be straight or curved and can contain multiple anchor points. They can also be described as *closed* or *open*. For example, the rectangle and ellipse shapes you've just created are both closed paths, while two anchor points joined by a simple path are considered open. This may at first seem like overcomplicating a simple subject, but understanding how paths work in combination with anchor points is the key to creating them.

Paths can contain two or more anchor points, and the shape of a path is determined by the properties set out in the anchor points they contain. Each anchor point contains two shaping handles called *direction points,* and the individual paths that join each anchor point are referred to as *segments*. Segments may be curved or straight, referred to in Illustrator as *curve segments* and *line segments*.

Paths may also be simple or compound. For example, two anchor points joined by a straight line would be considered a simple path, or an ellipse shape is considered a closed simple path. Two ellipses combined together to form a single unit are considered a compound path. In other words, a compound path may contain two or more closed paths which appear to form separate shapes but which are considered by Illustrator to be a single shape. Sound complicated?

In fact, once you begin to work with elements such as these, it may seem quite natural to you. For now though, let's concentrate on creating ordinary, run-of-the-mill paths. For your first path, you'll be using the Pen tool. The Pen tool lives in harmony in the main Toolbox palette with three other related tools which are used for editing or fine-tuning paths, including the Add Anchor Point tool, Delete Anchor Point tool, and Convert Direction Point tool. You can view these by clicking and holding down your mouse button on the Pen tool symbol.

To create your first path, follow these steps:

1. With a new or existing document open, select the Pen tool from the main Toolbox palette. Notice your cursor changes to a calligraphy-style ink pen with a small *x* beside it.

2. Point and click the Pen tool once anywhere on your page. Notice a blue marker appears where you clicked, and while you were clicking the Pen tool, it changed momentarily to an arrow cursor. This indicates you have created the first anchor point of your path.

3. Click a second time anywhere on your page. This is the second anchor point of your path. Notice a blue line appears on your page to represent the path you are creating and your tool appears without the small *x* symbol attached, as shown in Figure 1-6.

4. Now, select the Selection tool from the main Toolbox palette to end the session.

5. You're finished creating your first path.

*Options exist within Illustrator to control the appearance of tool cursors, which in some cases may alter what is being described in the steps you follow in this book. The File\Preferences\General command provides access to a number of options including the ability to set an option to use "precise" cursors. In the case of the Pen tool, this cursor changes to a small + style cursor to increase the accuracy of the placement of anchor points. For more information on setting advanced options for using some of the tools in Illustrator 7, see "Setting Preferences," **Chapter 3: Making Illustrator 7 Easy to Use**.*

Holding the CAPS LOCK *key while using tools will change the cursor state to precise.*

Clicking on a different tool in the Toolbox is a sign to Illustrator that you have finished drawing your object and wish to do something else. Notice that when you clicked the Selection tool, both the path and the anchor points it contains remained selected and highlighted in blue. Undoubtedly, you'll want to try this again and again. Don't worry—as you move through Fundamental Illustrator 7, you'll be creating plenty of these, some infinitely more complex than what you have just created.

Before moving on to the final object tool, try experimenting a little by repeating the steps you just followed, only this time continue adding points. Try click-dragging on some of the points instead of directly clicking to see how the line shape behaves. End your session by clicking the Selection tool once again.

For more information on creating other types of ellipses, see the "Working with Pen Tools" section in **Chapter 7: Creating and Editing Drawing Objects**.

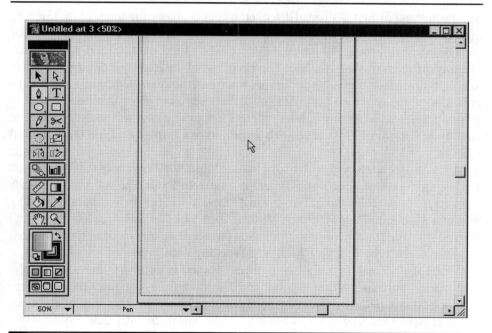

FIGURE 1-6   Creating your first path

Create Type

While the preceding three tools create closed or open paths, the Type tool creates something entirely different—characters and words based on the fonts currently installed on your computer's system. To put it simply, fonts represent collections of characters and symbols mapped to corresponding keys on your keyboard.

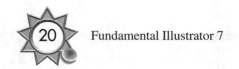

One of the most confusing issues about using software that enables you to enter letters or words in your document surrounds use of the terms text *and* type. *From program to program, you'll see these terms used both differently and interchangeably. Unfortunately, there are no terminology police, and so we just have to live with the ambiguity. For the record and in the context of a discussion of Illustrator tools, this book refers to letters and words as type.*

Individual letters are actually outlines of objects that have been designed using simple or compound closed paths. For example, the outline of the letter *T* is a closed path and in certain font styles can be as simple as two rectangles joined together. Other letters containing cutout shapes, such as the letter *O* or the letter *P*, are considered compound paths, because they are composed of two shapes: the outline and the hole cut from it. As you'll discover in later chapters, the shape of these letters may be changed, transformed, or altered should the need arise.

The interesting thing about type is that it can be edited, manipulated, and adjusted in many different ways in Illustrator 7, regardless of the font style or size you select to use. In Illustrator, individual letters are referred to as characters, while collections of letters are referred to as type. But you'll discover more about that later. In fact, if working with text is nothing new to you, feel free to skip over this section and move directly to **Chapter 5: Working with Type** and/or **Chapter 6: Type Options and Effects**.

Type can be created with a myriad of tools in Illustrator 7—some of them new, some not. Clicking and holding down the Type tool in the main Toolbox palette actually reveals that six type tools reside there. The "normal" Type tool is first in line and followed by the Area Type tool, Path Type tool, Vertical Type tool, Vertical Area Type tool, and Vertical Path Type tool. For more information on using Illustrator's other type tools, see "Hybrids of the Type Tool" in **Chapter 5: Working with Type**.

While the normal Type tool is used for creation of ordinary lines of type, the others offer more specialized capabilities. Illustrator 7 now features the capability to attach type to paths or objects. And Illustrator 7 now includes the capability of working in various languages that orient themselves differently than Roman-style English language characters, for instance, Japanese character sets.

For learning purposes in the steps that follow, you'll be using the Type tool. If this seems overwhelmingly complicated, persevere. It'll all become clear in a few moments. To create your first type object, follow these steps:

1. With a new or existing document open, select the Type tool from the main Toolbox palette. Notice your cursor changes to what is referred to as an *I-beam* cursor. The *I* in I-beam is the point of entry for your first character.

2. Click the I-beam cursor of the Type tool once anywhere on your page. Notice that a blinking cursor appears. This indicates where your first character of type will appear.

3. Type a character or word using your keyboard as shown in Figure 1-7. Notice that as you enter your characters, the cursor continues to blink, following along with you. Finish entering your character or word.

4. Now, choose the Selection tool from the main Toolbox palette to end the Type tool session. Notice that the type now features a blue line aligned

FIGURE 1-7   Creating a simple type object using the Type tool

with the bottom of the characters. In typographic terminology this is known as the *baseline* of the type.

5. You've just created your first type object.

Now that you've created your first type object, chances are you may wish to change the letters through editing. To edit the characters you've just entered, follow these steps:

1. With the Type tool selected once again from the main Toolbox palette, click and drag either left-to-right or right-to-left across the character you would like to change, as shown in Figure 1-8. Notice that as you drag your mouse across the letters, they become highlighted in reverse color. To simply add a letter, click to create an insertion point where you'd like to enter the new letter.

2. Type the new letters as you did before.

3. Click the Selection tool once again to end the editing session.

FIGURE 1-8   Select to edit your type for dragging across the letters

Type can feature any of the characteristics of other objects such as size and color, but type can also be controlled in other ways, including setting a certain typeface, style, line spacing (leading), word and letter spacing (tracking), kerning, alignment, indentation, and hyphenation. These characteristics are set either through menu commands, keyboard shortcuts, or by using Illustrator's Character and Paragraph palettes. For more information on using setting type characteristics, see "Setting Character and Paragraph Attributes" in **Chapter 5: Working with Type**.

For more information on working with palettes, see "Working with Tool Palettes" in **Chapter 4: What's New in Illustrator 7?** and "About Toolboxes, Palettes, and Text Boxes" in **Chapter 3: Making Illustrator 7 Easy to Use**. As you advance in your use of type characteristics, you can top your list by consulting the Character Attributes shortcuts in **Appendix B: Summary of Keyboard Shortcuts**.

Selecting, Zooming, and Viewing Your Work

To work efficiently, knowing Illustrator 7's methods for selecting the objects you are creating and working with, and controlling how you see those objects, will help a great deal. Several essential tools exist within Illustrator to enable you to do this. For the most part, these operations will form the basis for your work habits in the program.

Selecting Objects

In order to change an object in any way in Illustrator, it must first be selected. When you select an object, your actions are telling Illustrator that you are about to do something, whether that something is changing the object's size, position, or color. You can select an object with the Selection tool (which is the first tool listed in the main Toolbox, for a good reason). Although it doesn't perform any special tricks, it is always the first (and also often the last) tool used in any operation. The Selection tool has only one mode—selection mode—unlike other tools in Illustrator.

The act of selecting an object can also be done in a number of different ways. You can select objects by clicking directly on them or you can *marquee* select them. The marquee method simply means that you have clicked your mouse and dragged diagonally in an action to surround or encompass all or part of the object or objects you would like to select. You can also use the Selection tool in combination with the SHIFT key to "multiple select" more than one object. You may also use a Selection tool-SHIFT key combination to deselect an object from a collection of selected objects.

To select all the objects on and off your page, press CTRL/COMMAND+A or deselect all of the objects you have selected by pressing CTRL/COMMAND+SHIFT+A.

The SHIFT key works in combination with the Selection tool in a toggle-style manner. In other words, pressing the SHIFT key with the Selection tool enables you to select or deselect objects as you wish. To select an object and experiment a little with using Selection tool and SHIFT key combinations, follow these steps:

1. If you haven't already done so, open a new or existing document.

2. Create several objects such as a rectangle, ellipse, path, and type object as shown in Figure 1-9, using the steps described in previous sections of this chapter.

3. Choose the Selection tool from the main Toolbox palette.

4. One at a time, click on these objects and notice how they become highlighted with blue markings each time they are selected.

5. Now, while holding down the SHIFT key, click on them one at a time again until they are all selected. Notice that each one is highlighted individually, but they are all selected.

6. With the SHIFT key still held, click each of them again and notice how they become deselected and their highlighting disappears.

7. Release the SHIFT key and click anywhere on the page to deselect any objects selected.

8. Now, using the marquee-select method, drag diagonally from upper-left to lower-right to come in contact with all of the objects and release the mouse. Notice they are all selected once again, as shown in Figure 1-10.

9. Next, hold the SHIFT key and perform the same action in step 8. Notice they all become deselected.

 To delete an object from your drawing, select it using the Selection tool and press DELETE.

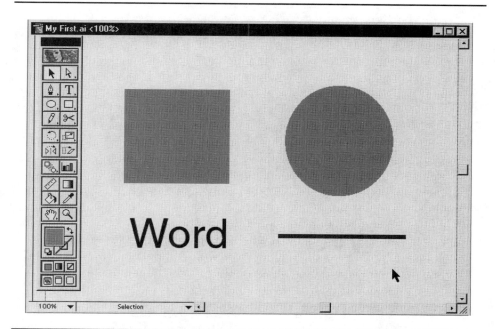

FIGURE 1-9   Create four new objects using steps described in previous sections

Your method of selection may also be dependent on how your document is being viewed at the time. Illustrator 7 features two main view modes: Artwork and Preview. Artwork view displays only a wireframe outline of the objects on your page, while Preview displays the objects including all their assigned color attributes. You'll find these options located at the top of the View menu. While in Artwork view, objects may only be selected by clicking the Selection tool on their outlines or object markers; while in Preview mode, objects may be selected by clicking anywhere on the object itself.

Note   *If you're having difficulties selecting an object that has no assigned color, try clicking on its outline instead of within its center. Objects which do not include fill colors cannot be selected with the Selection Tool by clicking on their interior shape area.*

Objects may also be selected by the attributes or properties assigned to them and without using the Selection tool at all, which for some users will be considered

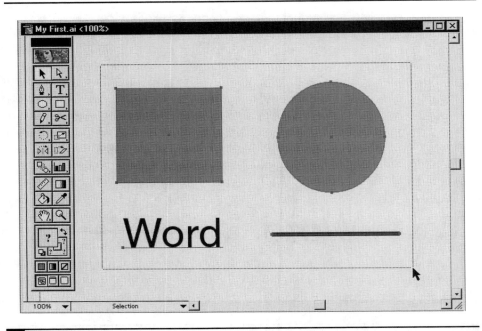

FIGURE 1-10   Multiple selection can be done using either the marquee or SHIFT key selection methods

advanced selection. For more information on using Illustrator 7's selection commands, see "Object Selection Methods," **Chapter 8: Selecting and Arranging Objects.**

Using Zoom Controls

Zooming in and out is how Illustrator enables you to see more or less of the objects you've created on your page. It's reminiscent of how I once heard an airline pilot's classic description of the use of his aircraft's control stick: "Pull it back and the houses get smaller, and push it forward to make them bigger." In reality it's a little more complicated than that (hopefully), but not in the case of Illustrator 7. This operation is referred to as *zooming*.

Illustrator features two main controls for zooming into or out of your arrangement of objects. First, the simplest method of zooming involves selecting a magnification view from the Zoom Level Display feature found in the lower-left corner of your document window. To change the zoom level using this feature, click on it to display a list of magnification values as shown below. The higher the value selected, the closer your view will be to the page.

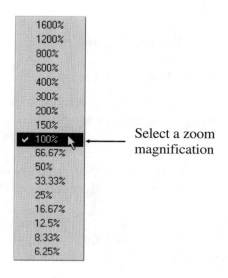

Select a zoom magnification

> *Zoom Level Display may also be changed through use of keyboard commands by pressing CTRL/COMMAND+Plus key to increase page magnification or CTRL+Minus key to decrease page magnification. Plus and minus keys on either your main or numeric keyboard may be used.*

Unfortunately, while the Zoom Level Display enables you to increase or decrease magnification of your drawing, it offers little control over exactly where you are zooming to. This is where the next tool provides invaluable zooming freedom. In the main Toolbox palette, you may have already noticed the symbol of a magnifying glass referred to in Illustrator as the Zoom tool. This is likely the tool you'll use most of the time as you become comfortable with working in Illustrator.

Although the Zoom tool features no companion Zoom tools, it's versatile enough to be used in a number of different ways, including zooming into or out of your drawing to exactly where you specify or marquee zooming for viewing a magnification of an exact area of your drawing. By default, the Zoom tool's natural state is used for increasing magnification, but that's not all it can do. By holding down the ALT/OPTION key, the Zoom tool will also decrease magnification based on the magnifications listed in the Zoom Level Display.

You can switch your cursor temporarily to become the Zoom tool at any time by pressing both the CTRL/COMMAND and SPACE BAR keys on your keyboard to increase magnification or CTRL/COMMAND+ALT/OPTION+SPACE BAR to decrease magnification.

To become familiar with Zoom tool operations, follow these steps:

1. If you haven't already done so, open a new or existing document.

2. As in previous sections, create some objects to experiment on such as a rectangle and an ellipse, using steps described in the "Creating Simple Objects" section of this chapter.

Choose the Zoom tool from the main Toolbox palette. Notice that it automatically features a "plus" symbol, indicating it is ready to increase your view magnification.

1. Click on the center of one of the objects you have created. Note that your zoom magnification has increased. Click several times if you wish, and notice each time that the magnification increases.

2. Now, hold the ALT/OPTION key down and click again. Notice that a "minus" symbol now appears in the center of your Zoom Tool and your magnification has decreased as you clicked the page.

3. Next, zoom out using the ALT/OPTION key combination until you can see both objects on your screen again.

4. Using the marquee method, surround the other object by dragging the Zoom tool from the upper-left corner to the lower-right corner and release the mouse, as shown in Figure 1-11. Notice that your magnification increased to display the area you selected.

 You can fit your entire drawing quickly into view by using the View\Fit in Window command (CTRL/COMMAND+0) or quickly view your objects at 100 percent magnification by using the View\Actual Size command (CTRL/COMMAND+1).

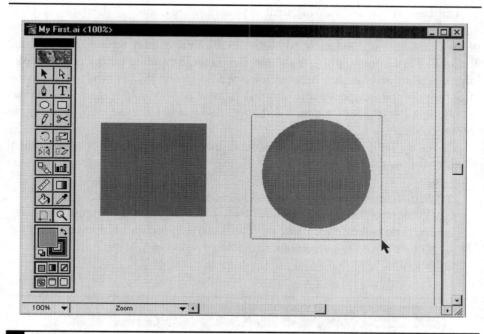

FIGURE 1-11   The Zoom tool can be used to increase the magnification of a specific area of your drawing

Note   *For a quick reference of your current zoom setting, check the value currently displayed in the Zoom Level Display in the lower-left corner of your document window.*

Viewing Your Drawing

Illustrator also provides you with a variety of ways to view your drawing. View controls include how your objects are displayed and which part of your drawing you see. As mentioned in the previous section, Artwork and Preview display options enable you to view whether your objects are drawn on your screen as wireframe outlines or in full color. But you can also set how your drawing is viewed using window features.

One basic method of viewing areas of your drawing is through the use of multiple document windows. Illustrator 7 enables you to open more than one viewing window of the same drawing, and each may be set to different display settings and different sections of your drawing. For example, if you were creating enhanced detail of a large diagram and needed to work on specific minor details while still paying attention to the scope of the overall drawing, you could open two views simultaneously: one for the detailed changes and one to view the entire drawing, as shown in Figure 1-12.

To set up for viewing your Illustrator drawing in more than one document window, follow these steps.

1. With an existing document opened and saved, choose Window|New Window. Notice a new document automatically named *filename:2* (where filename is the actual name of your Illustrator document) appears. At the moment, your two document windows overlap so you can only see one at a time.

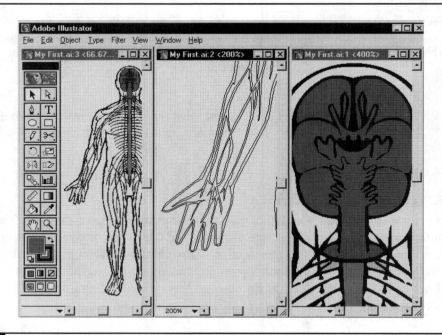

FIGURE 1-12 Working with multiple document window views of the same drawing

2. To set your window sizes to see both document windows at once, manually size the windows above and below each other (Macintosh) or choose Window|Tile (Windows). Using the Window|Tile command on the Windows platform arranges opened documents to exactly fit the dimensions of your screen.

3. To change the view settings in each of the document windows, click the title bar of the window to make it the active window, and use the Zoom and Preview commands discussed earlier in this chapter to set your view and magnification preferences.

Note *When closing multiple document views of the same drawing, Illustrator will only prompt you to save changes to your document when you try to close the last open document window of the drawing.*

For more information on controlling the views of your drawing, see the "View Commands" section in **Chapter 3: Making Illustrator 7 Easy to Use.**

Note *Illustrator 7 also includes Toolbox palette options for changing the view of your document in a certain sense. At the bottom of the main Toolbox palette are three buttons for changing the appearance of your Illustrator 7 screen, including Standard Screen Mode, Full Screen Mode with Menu Bar, and Full Screen Mode. Essentially, using these options enables you to maximize your work space unencumbered by scroll bars or program menus. For more information on using these modes, see "Customizing Windows and Display" in **Chapter 3: Making Illustrator 7 Easy to Use**.*

Moving, Scaling, and Rotating Objects

Illustrator 7 features specialized tools for changing the position, size, and orientation of the objects in your drawing as well as some more advanced operations. For expert Illustrator users, these tools form the basis for adjusting and assembling drawing objects. For newer users, as you become more familiar with working in Illustrator, these types of operations will almost seem to become second nature to you.

Moving Objects

Objects may be moved through a number of different methods depending on how accurate the position of your object needs to be on your page or in your drawing.

Moving objects is done directly through the use of the Selection tool. To move an object, simply click directly on the object with the Selection tool and drag it to the desired position.

 As is the case with selecting objects, when using Illustrator's Preview view, you'll be able to select and move an object by clicking either on its perimeter or interior area. In Artwork view however, you may only select objects by clicking on their outline.

You may also move objects through the use of "nudges" using the UP, DOWN, LEFT, and RIGHT ARROW keys on your keyboard. Each time you press an arrow key, Illustrator moves the object a specified measure. This increment can be set through the File|Preferences|Keyboard Increments command dialog box, as shown below.

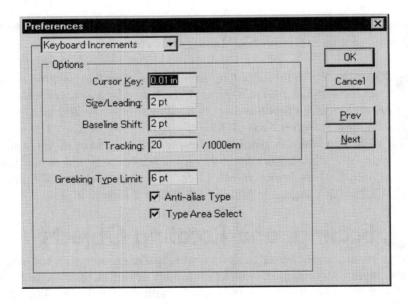

Simply put, dragging objects using the Selection tool is the best method for roughly placing objects, while moving objects using the arrow keys offers more precision but is also more tedious for moving objects great distances on your page. A third method exists for moving objects through use of the Move command. To use this command, first select the object you wish to move and choose Object| Transform|Move to access the Move command dialog box shown below. Move command options enable you to reposition an object vertically and/or horizontally, relative to its current position by a specified measure.

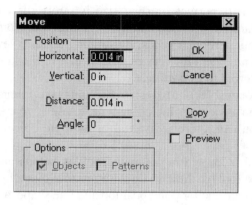

To quickly move an object using either the Selection tool or arrow keys, follow these steps:

1. If you haven't already done so, choose the Selection tool from the main Toolbox palette.

2. Select an object to move by clicking on it.

3. Click and hold the Selection tool directly on the object and drag it to a new location and release. Notice that while you were moving the object, a blue outline representation was displayed to indicate the object's current position.

4. Now, with the object still selected, press either the UP, DOWN, LEFT, or RIGHT ARROW keys on your keyboard and observe the objects movements. Notice that each time you press an arrow key, the object moves a preset amount.

 Holding the SHIFT key while dragging an object with the Selection tool constrains the movement of your object on either a vertical or horizontal plane. To use the SHIFT key movement constraint, press and hold the SHIFT key after clicking on it with your Selection tool.

For more information on moving objects including advanced use of the Transform palette, see the "Moving, Scaling, and Rotating Objects" and the "Transform Palette" sections in **Chapter 9: Object Transform Tools**.

Changing an Object's Size

Unless you're extremely well-organized or working with pen and paper, drawing a shape or object at its perfect finished size is rarely the case when using most illustration software. And the advantage of using your computer to create your drawing. To fit your particular needs, Illustrator 7 features several methods—some for rough sizing and others for very precise sizing. In Illustrator, changing the size of an object is referred to as *scaling*.

First, Illustrator enables you to resize objects using a unique Scale tool. The Scale tool can be used on any object, including type, to adjust your elements to their exact required size. You can resize individual or multiple objects, depending on your selection.

The Scale tool is located in the main Toolbox palette along with the Reshape tool. The Reshape tool has little to do with resizing overall object size but instead enables you to change anchor point position and line shape, and, for the purposes of getting started, could be considered a tool for slightly more advanced. For more information on using the Reshape tool, see "Editing Paths with the Reshape Tool" in **Chapter 7: Creating and Editing Drawing Objects**.

The Scale tool is also one of those tools in Illustrator that appears quite simplistic at first glance but features a multitude of capabilities. Not only can you scale an object to any width or depth, but through the use of keyboard combinations you may also constrain scaling vertically or horizontally, maintain the aspect ratio of the original object, or set the center origin which your object is scaled around. For the purposes of quickly using this tool though, let's focus on simple scaling of an object.

To resize an object using the Scale tool, follow these steps:

1. If you haven't already done so, create and select an object to resize on your page.

2. With the object selected, click the Scale tool in the main Toolbox palette. Notice that your cursor changes to a crosshair and your object now includes a center point mark.

3. Click your cursor on your screen and drag it either toward or away from the center point of the object to reduce or enlarge its size. Notice as you drag the cursor a blue outline representation appears to reflect the scaling results as shown in Figure 1-13. Notice also that your object changes shape both vertically and horizontally.

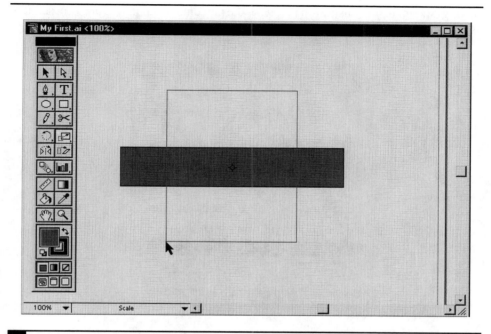

FIGURE 1-13   Scaling a rectangle using the Scale tool

4. To jump slightly ahead in advancement now, click once again inside the object's boundaries and hold down the SHIFT key using the same resizing motion. Notice as you drag to resize the object, its shape remains constrained either vertically, horizontally, or proportionately, depending on the direction of your mouse movement.

5. Release the mouse button once you are satisfied with the object's new size.

While the Scale tool enables you to quickly change the size of an object, you may wish to change its size with more precision. For this, Illustrator features the Scale command, found by selecting an object to scale and choosing Object| Transform|Scale. The Scale command operates by way of dialog box options which enable you to enter precise vertical and horizontal dimensions for non-uniform scaling, shown in the illustration below, or the percentage values for uniform scaling, as shown in the second illustration below.

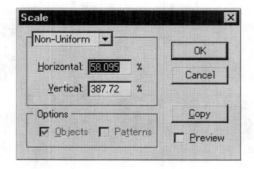

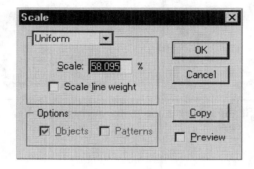

For more information on resizing objects and further options when using the Scale command, see "Scaling Objects," **Chapter 9: Object Transform Tools**.

Rotating an Object

The ability to rotate an object from its original angle is especially useful for quickly creating shapes which can't otherwise be created using the rectangle or ellipse tools, or any object, for that matter. For example, drawing a diamond shape can't be done using only the Rectangle tool in its natural state due to the fact that the rectangle's sides are automatically aligned vertically and horizontally.

As with object Move operations, rotating an object can be done several ways. First, Illustrator features the Rotate tool found in the main Toolbox palette. The Rotate tool enables you to roughly turn objects around a specified rotation point. By default, this point is aligned with the center of your object, but you can reposition it if you wish.

The Rotate tool resides in the main Toolbox palette along with Illustrator 7's new Twirl tool which (if you happen to choose it in error) you'll find operates quite differently from the Rotate tool. For more information about the Twirl tool, see "Using the Twirl Tool" in **Chapter 9: Object Transform Tools**.

To rotate an object using the Rotate tool, follow these steps:

1. If you haven't already done so, select an object to rotate by clicking on it with the Selection tool.

2. Choose the Rotate tool from the main Toolbox palette. Notice that the object now features a center point of rotation and your cursor has changed to a crosshair cursor.

3. Click and drag anywhere around the object in a circular motion around the center point as shown in Figure 1-14. Notice as you drag to rotate the object that a blue representation is displayed indicating the current rotation of the object.

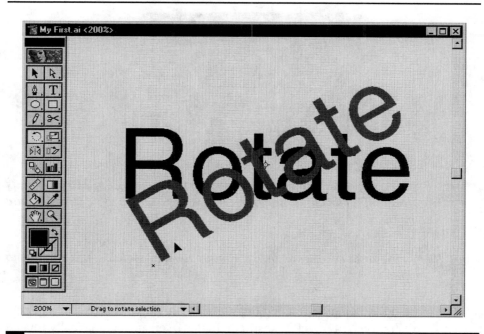

FIGURE 1-14 Rotating a type object with the Rotate tool

4. Release the mouse button to complete the rotation command.

5. Now, click your cursor to set the rotation point away from its original position with your mouse and rotate the object once more using the same circular motion. Notice that the object now rotates around the new center position.

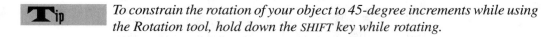 *To constrain the rotation of your object to 45-degree increments while using the Rotation tool, hold down the SHIFT key while rotating.*

Rotating objects may also be done to precise measures using the Object| Transform|Rotate command. Objects may be rotated to exact degree measures entered in the Angle box of the Rotate dialog box shown below. The angle of rotation values are based on the fact that there are 360 degrees in a circle. Other options within this dialog box enable you to preview or make a copy of your rotated object before proceeding. And if your object features special attributes such as pattern colors, you can choose to rotate them along with your selected object.

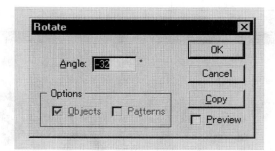

Entering negative values in the Rotate command dialog box causes objects to rotate clockwise, while positive values cause objects to rotate counterclockwise.

Entering a value of zero in the Rotate command dialog box causes no rotation to occur.

For more information on rotating objects see "Moving, Scaling, and Rotating Objects" in **Chapter 9: Object Transform Tools**. To create automatically rotated objects using the Preferences command, see "Setting Keyboard Increment Preferences" in **Chapter 3: Making Illustrator 7 Easy to Use**.

Adding Color to Objects

Adding color to an object is one of the key attributes you can apply in Illustrator 7. You can use any color you see in the rainbow, as well as some you don't—including black or white. In Illustrator 7, color is applied through use of the Swatch and Color palettes. There are all sorts of ways to color an object and all *types* of colors in Illustrator 7, and if you've ever spent time with people who make color their business, you may already know that they can talk about color for days on end.

For the purposes of getting started though, we'll concentrate on applying simple colors to objects and point you in the right direction for more detailed information about working in color and using Illustrator 7's color tools.

The Swatch palette contains all of the colors currently existing in your Illustrator 7 program. First, a swatch is defined as a collection of color "recipes," while the swatch itself simply displays a color representation or *chip*. Color recipes can be based on four-color process CMYK (cyan, magenta, yellow, black), RGB (red, green, blue), or HSB (hue, saturation, brightness) values.

Color recipes may also be based on third-party color ink specification models such as Pantone, Trumatch, Focoltone, DIC Color, or optimum World Wide Web color palettes for preparing Internet images. For more information on Illustrator 7's color models, see the section "Understanding Color Models." Or, for more information on working with third-party color swatches, see the section "Using Other Swatch Libraries." Both of these sections are found in **Chapter 11: Working in Color.**

Adobe's Fill and Stroke Concept

Before you begin coloring your objects, perhaps a little background information on how Illustrator handles object colors is in order. To Illustrator, all objects are made up of two basic parts: a *fill* and an outline, or *stroke*. An object's fill can be thought of as any area within a closed object or any area created by joining the first and last anchor points of a path. An object's stroke is its outline path. These two object parts may be colored and controlled independently of each other while remaining attached.

Controlling the characteristics of the fill and stroke properties of objects is done through the main Toolbox palette, which is also characteristic of interface aspects in other Adobe programs such as PageMaker and Photoshop. At the bottom of the

Toolbox you'll notice an area containing fill and stroke mode buttons. Each mode button sets Illustrator to either one mode or the other. While in Stroke mode, all color changes made to an object will affect the stroke of the object you have currently selected. And, while in Fill mode, the same applies. This is perhaps one of the most critical but commonly confused features for newcomers to Illustrator.

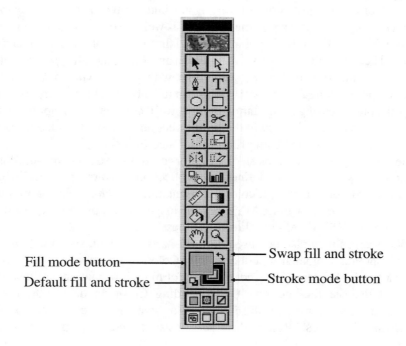

Fill mode button —————————————— Swap fill and stroke

Default fill and stroke ————— Stroke mode button

Setting Fill Colors

You may choose any of the color recipes discussed previously and apply them to your newly created objects as your drawing requires. Whichever you choose, applying color to your objects is a quick operation using the Swatch palette.

To add color to your object, you must first determine whether you wish to color the object's fill or stroke and click the corresponding button. For demonstration purposes, we'll assign a fill color. To add a fill color to an object, follow these steps:

 By default, Illustrator automatically assigns the last fill and stroke colors selected to newly created objects, including stroke thickness and styles.

1. If you haven't already done so, create an object to apply color to and choose the Fill button in the main Toolbox palette.

2. Choose Window|Show Swatches to display the Swatches palette.

3. Select the object using the Selection tool from the main Toolbox palette.

4. Click any color in the Swatches palette. Notice your object is immediately assigned the color you clicked.

5. Now jump ahead slightly and use the Color palette. Choose Window|Show Color to display the Color palette, as shown in Figure 1-15.

6. If it isn't already displayed, choose CMYK from the Color palette's flyout menu. Notice that four color bars are shown, each labeled C, M, Y, or K, as well as a horizontal bar composed of various blended colors referred to as the *CMYK Spectrum*.

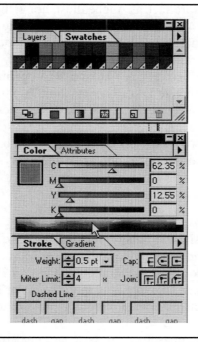

FIGURE 1-15   Assigning a fill color to an object using the Swatches and Colors palettes

7. Place your cursor inside this area and click on a color. Notice your cursor changes to an eyedropper tool while inside the CMYK Spectrum area. Notice also that your object now features the color you chose and its CMYK color values appear in the Color palette.

In order to demonstrate how quickly colors can be assigned to objects using various color settings and color models, we jumped ahead slightly—but it's likely that you know now there's much more to choosing a color than simply using the Swatches palette. In fact, there are several ways to create, organize, and access whichever color collection you choose to work with.

Stroke colors can be assigned to objects in the same way as fill colors, as long as the Stroke button is selected in the main Toolbox palette.

Get to Know the Shortcuts

In most progressive software such as Adobe Illustrator 7, there is usually more than one way to accomplish a task. This often boils down to one of two strategies: easy-but-tedious commands or quick-but-mysterious shortcuts. In order to get you started on the road to working efficiently in Illustrator 7, you should be aware that some nifty shortcuts have been engineered into the program to help you work more quickly and be more productive as you become more familiar with Illustrator's use. Some overlap to general interface use, while others are specific to Illustrator 7 itself.

This book includes a comprehensive summary of Illustrator's keyboard, dialog box, and tool-related shortcuts categorized by usage. To browse the shortcuts list, turn to **Appendix B: Summary of Keyboard Shortcuts**.

Conclusion

This chapter has been designed to answer most of the first questions new users have about using Illustrator and is geared toward answering queries such as "How do I create type?" or "How do I select several objects at once?" By following through this chapter, you have been able to gain a quick beginner's perspective into basic Illustrator 7 operations and have been pointed to areas of this book where you can get more information.

While many of these questions can be considered basic or elementary, the remaining chapters of *Fundamental Illustrator 7* help flesh out how to use each and every tool contained in the program. Each of the tool and effect chapters have been integrated with procedural steps sequences and also include illustration-related step-by-step tutorials which cover typical illustration methods, with added consideration given to expert users. Each of these tutorials has been reproduced in full color to provide you with exact color representations of illustration steps.

To continue on your beginner's quest for information, the next chapter provides detailed information on opening, closing, saving, and working with Illustrator 7 files and includes insights into more effective ways to manage your drawing files.

Managing Illustrator 7 Files

2

Creating, opening, saving and retrieving the drawings you create using Adobe Illustrator 7 (or any program, for that matter) are perhaps the most critical operations you will learn. If you can't save and retrieve your work, what use is any of this fancy technology? Learning the correct and efficient ways to perform these operations will no doubt make using the software a whole lot easier and more productive.

In this chapter, you'll discover some obvious (and some not-so-obvious) file management operations, which for experienced users might fall under the heading "common sense" but for others will provide a solid foundation for working with Adobe Illustrator 7 files, previous version Illustrator files, and files created using other platforms and software programs. You'll gain an understanding of how forming good file-management habits will not only help you stay organized while using Illustrator 7 but maximize the capabilities of the system you are using.

Opening New Files

The best place to start is at the beginning—by creating a brand-new file. After you launch Illustrator 7, a new untitled drawing file is automatically opened and waiting for you to begin drawing. You can open additional new files by choosing File|New (CTRL/COMMAND+N). In fact, Illustrator opens the new file with unprecedented eagerness—and no questions asked. That means it's up to you to answer questions such as "How big do you want your page to be?" or "How would you like to see this document?" or "What's it for?" and so on. These are answers you'll have to come up with on your own and set up for later. In fact, later in this chapter, you'll discover how to set these options for yourself even before the file opens by customizing your Illustrator 7 startup file. To skip to this section now, see "Customizing Your Startup File."

Each time you open a new document, the newly opened and as yet unsaved file is automatically named in sequence as *Untitled art 1*, *Untitled art 2*, and so on. Closing these new files doesn't affect the sequence of their creation, and they continue following this numbering scheme whether they are used or not. As you may have guessed from this information, Adobe Illustrator 7 supports what is referred to in the software industry as a *multiple document interface* or *MDI*. In English, this means that you can have more than one file open at a time, the limit of which is set by the available memory on your system.

 Memory requirements for running Illustrator 7 efficiently vary by platform. For Macintosh and Power Macintosh users, Adobe recommends a minimum 68030 processor using System 7.5.1 or later and at least 25 megabytes of random-access memory (RAM), 8 of which should be dedicated solely to Illustrator 7. Ideally, Adobe says the PowerPC processor works best running on a system equipped with at least 32 megabytes of RAM. For Windows 95 and NT users, they recommend a minimum 486 processor system (but ideally a Pentium) equipped with at least 16 megabytes of RAM (ideally equipped with 32). All platforms are recommended to have at least 25 megabytes of free hard drive space as an absolute minimum. In reality though, a typical install will occupy roughly 70 megabytes. Oh, and don't forget to allow room for your drawing files.

Each new document conceals the one behind it, so it won't be obvious that several different files are opened at once. These facts won't be surprises for veteran computer users. But for newer users, having more than one file open at a time can be daunting and confusing. How do you change document windows?

The answer can be found under the Window menu. If you happen to have multiple files opened (or even if you don't), at the bottom of this menu you'll see all open files listed as shown in the illustration below. To bring one of these files to the forefront, select it from the Window menu.

Opening Existing Files

Apart from opening brand-new files, the ability to retrieve previously worked-on files is the bare minimum anyone can expect a software program to be capable of. But opening files can be a nightmare if you're not quite sure what it is you're opening. Sharing or trading files can be hazardous if you aren't sure who the file came from or where it's been.

There are a number of issues to be aware of when opening a file, the stickiest of which involve opening previous version files, opening documents containing strange fonts, opening documents which may contain linked files, and file formats native to other programs or platforms. Who said the desktop was a safe place to work?

Opening Native Illustrator Files

The term *native* refers to a file created by Illustrator in a current or previous version of your software. Wouldn't it be nice if all programs could read all files—no matter how or where they were created? In fact, while Adobe Illustrator 7 can open files created using its own special file format, to a limited extent it can also open files created by other software programs, such as bitmap, vector software, and some competitors' files, such as native files created using Amiga, Kodak, Pixar, and Corel software.

If you work on multiple platforms, don't worry too much about compatibility issues, because Illustrator 7 works on multiple platforms as well. Files created on both Macintosh and Windows platforms will port seamlessly. In other words, a file created on a Mac can be opened on both Windows 95 and/or Windows NT platforms.

When a file from another creator is opened, Illustrator 7 uses specially prepared import filters to read the information contained in the file. Choosing files in the Open command dialog box shown below automatically sets the filter to be used, provided that the file is in a format compatible with Illustrator 7's import filters.

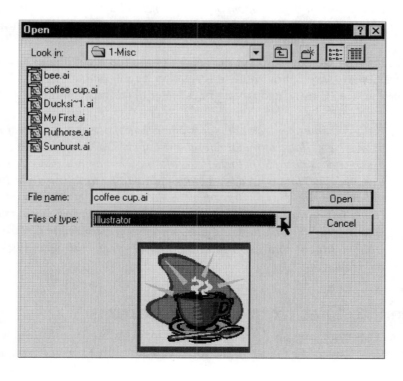

To open any of the compatible file formats in Illustrator 7 using the File|Open (CTRL/COMMAND+O) command, follow these steps:

1. With Illustrator 7 currently running, Choose File|Open to display the Open command dialog box.

2. If you know which program was used to create the file (Illustrator, for example), choose the file type from the Files of Type drop-down menu.

3. Locate the folder containing the file you wish to open and click on it in the display window. Notice that the file name automatically appears in the File Name box and a color representation of the file appears in the Preview window at the bottom and center.

4. Click OK to open the file. Notice that a progress bar appears on your screen as the file is read by Illustrator 7's import filter.

Tip *For Windows users, to open files you last worked on quickly, use the "recent files" shortcut at the bottom of the File menu. Illustrator 7 lists the last four files opened at the bottom of this menu in order from most recent to least recent.*

The Preview window displays the header of the file according to how the file was previously saved. For more information about saving files with header information, see "Closing and Saving Files" later in this chapter.

Note *If the file you open contains fonts other than those currently available on your system, Illustrator will refer to the SuperATM feature to automatically assign and substitute a font. If an alternative has not been defined, the system default font is used in its place—which isn't usually a desirable thing to have happen. This terrible phenomena is referred to as* font substitution. *If you notice that the file happens to include characters formatted in the your system's default font and you're pretty sure it shouldn't, close the file without saving changes, install the missing font onto your system, and reopen the file.*

Opening Files from Other Programs

Opening files from programs other than Illustrator or Adobe is performed using the same Open command as for native file formats. The ability to open other formats is extremely valuable when you consider the wealth of images created using other software and other platforms. The most useful and common of these types of images comes in the form of clip art, which in recent years has grown into a market all its own. Many new users find that clip art is a cheap resource for cutting production and drawing time.

Note *If you attempt to open a file that contains type formatted using a font not available on your system, Illustrator 7 displays a warning dialog box, as shown below. You have the option of either opening the file regardless of the warning or closing and installing the missing font. This warning only appears for native Illustrator documents and not for other file formats opened in Illustrator 7. Instead, fonts in non-Illustrator documents are automatically substituted using your system's default font. If necessary, you can use Illustrator 7's Find Font command to permanently replace any uninstalled fonts. For more information, see "Finding and Replacing Fonts," Chapter 6: Type Options and Effects.*

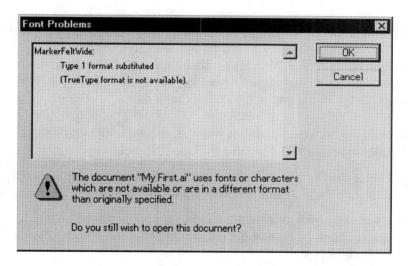

After you open a file that has been prepared in another program's native code, the original is automatically displayed in Illustrator 7's document title bar, including any applicable file extensions. And you may notice that although you can open, view, and amend this file, it cannot be saved in its native format again using Illustrator's Save command. Instead, Illustrator 7 enables you to save the document as an Illustrator file.

The following list of non-Illustrator file types shows formats compatible with Illustrator 7's File|Open command:

Adobe Acrobat PDF	Kodak Photo CD
Amiga IFF	Macintosh PICT
BMP	MacPaint
CGM	Microsoft RTF
Corel CMX	Microsoft Word
CorelDRAW! Version 5	PCX
CorelDRAW! Version 6 and 7	Photoshop 4 and earlier versions
Adobe Photoshop	Pixar
Adobe Photoshop Filmstrip	PixelPaint
GIF 89A and 87A	PNG
Adobe Illustrator	Targa
Adobe Illustrator EPS	Text
JPEG	Windows Metafile
	Corel WordPerfect

This format list is essentially identical to the formats available for import using the Place command, although the procedure and result are slightly different. For more information on Illustrator 7's import file formats, see "Importing with the Place Command" in Chapter 16: Importing and Exporting from Illustrator 7.

To open a file in Illustrator 7, follow these steps:

1. With the Illustrator 7 already running, choose File|Open or press CTRL/COMMAND-O. Note that the Open dialog box appears.

2. Locate the file you wish to open in the file display window and click on it. Notice the file name you selected now appears in the File Name box.

3. (In the Windows version, if you wish to narrow the file types which appear, click the type of file you would like to open in the Files of Type drop-down box.)

4. Click OK to open the file.

Opening Older Illustrator Files

Adobe is fully backward-compatible. In other words, you can open files prepared using the program back when it was called Illustrator 1.1, as well as versions 1.0 to 6.0 and all versions between.

Tip *When a file created using an older version of Illustrator is opened in Illustrator 7, it isn't automatically updated to the current version. Instead, the file must be saved using Illustrator 7's Save, Save As, or Save a Copy commands and specified as version 7.*

When an older version file is opened in Illustrator 7, Illustrator will not provide the user with a warning that it is opening a previous-version file unless the file contains missing linked images or missing fonts. Illustrator simply opens it directly, without hesitation.

Opening Files versus Placing Them

In terms of procedure, placing a file into your currently opened Illustrator document is slightly different than opening the file as a separate document. Placing files into your document enables you to combine multiple images instantly in a single file. The list of compatible files available for placing is nearly identical to those files you can *open* in Illustrator 7, with the exception of any native Adobe files.

Essentially the Place command is Illustrator 7's import function and operates by reading and filtering data from other file formats into Illustrator 7. Placed files may also be linked to your Illustrator 7 document without the data describing them being stored in your drawing file. Illustrator 7 documents containing linked files merely contain visual representations of linked files while the original file remains a separate document. Linked files may also be embedded into your Illustrator document where you'll have the freedom to apply filters and make changes to the images.

For more information on linking and files in your Illustrator 7 document, refer to "Working with Links" in **Chapter 16: Importing and Exporting from Illustrator 7**.

Caution *One disadvantage involved with "Placing" files from other non-Adobe programs—as opposed to opening them—has to do with fonts used in those documents. If the file you are placing uses fonts that are not installed currently on your system, Illustrator 7 does not provide a warning nor does it identify missing fonts or store their names with associated font objects. Instead, your system's default font is automatically substituted without any warning screens. On the Macintosh platform, this means fonts are often replaced with Helvetica, while Windows users will see Arial as the replacement font.*

Drag-and-Drop Opening

Illustrator 7 files may also be opened from the desktop through what is referred to as *drag-and-drop* actions. Drag-and-drop opening, while slightly advanced in operation, has several advantages and one or two disadvantages. Advantages include the ability to open more than one file at a time, which isn't an option using simply the File|Open command. For users who wish to view, print, and/or work on multiple files at a time, this feature will be invaluable and adopting its use will save time and increase your productivity.

But the disadvantages in using the drag-and-drop method are also worth taking into consideration before using this feature. For example, the files you wish to open must all be contained in the same folder, which can be slightly inconvenient organizationally. Seldom are working files for different projects stored in the same folder.

Plus, should your files contain missing elements such as linked files or fonts not installed, Illustrator ceases the file-opening operation while it displays a warning dialog box. The remaining files stand waiting to be opened until you have responded and, once you have done so, the opening process continues.

Note *Files opened using the drag-and-drop method are opened in alphabetical order.*

Using Windows platform versions of Illustrator 7, users may drag multiple files directly from Windows 95 or the NT file manager program Explorer. To drag-and-drop using Windows, follow these steps:

1. First, launch both Adobe Illustrator 7 and Explorer.

2. Position the Illustrator 7 program window in the background and bring the Explorer window to the forefront of your screen.

3. With the folder located and your files in view, hold down the SHIFT key and click on the files to multiple select the ones you wish to open.

4. Once selected, release the SHIFT key, click on one of the selected files, and drag it to the Illustrator 7 program window as shown in Figure 2-1. The progress bar will indicate the files are being opened.

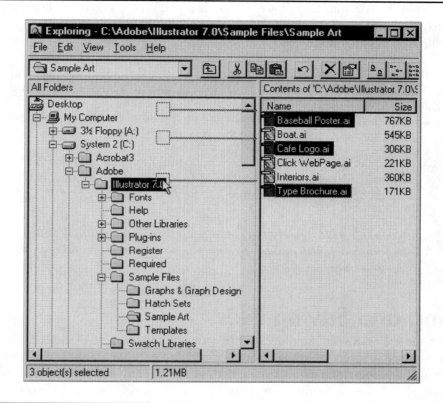

FIGURE 2-1   Drag-and-drop opening is the fastest method for opening multiple files

> *You may also drag-and-drop files directly onto an Illustrator 7 shortcut icon if you have set one up on your Windows 95 or Windows NT desktop to launch Illustrator 7 and open multiple files.*

> *It isn't necessary to close other open Illustrator 7 files in order to open files using the drag-and-drop method.*

Using the Macintosh or Power Macintosh platform versions of Illustrator 7, nearly the same operation applies. To open multiple files using the drag-and-drop on the Mac, follow these steps:

1. Position the Illustrator 7 program window in the background and open the folder containing the files you wish to open from the Macintosh desktop.

2. With the folder located and open and your files in view, hold down the SHIFT key and click file icons to multiple-select them.

3. Once your files are selected, release the SHIFT key, click on one of the selected files, and drag it into the Illustrator 7 program window in the background. The progress bar will indicate the files are being opened.

 You may also drag-and-drop files directly onto an Illustrator 7 shortcut icon on your Macintosh desktop to both launch the program and open the files simultaneously.

Closing and Saving Files

With the previous section on opening Illustrator 7 files, you've discovered there's often more that meets the eye when it comes to file command functions. Saving files is equally as important as opening and working in them, and closing them is an eventuality. Expert computer users familiar with file saving operations might think that defining these commands is second nature. But newer users in uncertain territory will need to pay close attention to Illustrator 7's Save functions. You'll discover there's more than one way to save and close a file, and you may even pick up a shortcut or two.

Saving Files

Perhaps the most straightforward file command is the Save command. Saving a file is no more complex that choosing File|Save (CTRL/COMMAND+S) to secure the work you have just done. Saving should be done as often as you possibly can and at least every ten minutes while you are drawing. As a precaution, you should also be saving your files before any major file operation such as Placing, Exporting, or any feature-intensive operation. The same goes for any other program you happen to have open, regardless of what the program does or how stable you happen to think it is.

 When saving a file in Illustrator 7 using Windows versions, the file extension for the selected file format is added automatically.

The first time you save an untitled art file in Illustrator, the main Save command dialog box opens, as shown below. Within this dialog box are a number of options which enable you to set basic file characteristics, including name and location of your file, or you can save to a specific type of file comprising native, Adobe EPS (encapsulated PostScript), or Adobe PDF (portable document format). In reality, this is also the Save As dialog box and contains the same options.

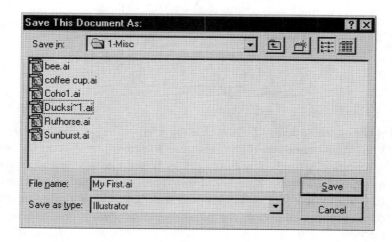

Save operations are a two-step process for two of the three file formats. In each case, the first dialog box shown above will appear, enabling you to name and save your document to a specific location. But three formats exist, and depending on which you choose, a second dialog box will appear with more options.

 To save all your open documents with their current names, locations, and formats hold the ALT/OPTION key and click the close button in the upper-right corner of your first visible document.

Choosing to save to Illustrator 7's native and EPS file formats will cause a second dialog box to appear, as shown below. Here you may choose to save to a previous version of Illustrator reaching as far back as the very first version of the program. File versions include 7.0 (by default for all newly created files), 6.0, 5.0/5.5, 4.0, 3.0/3.2/, 88, and 1.0/1.1 formats.

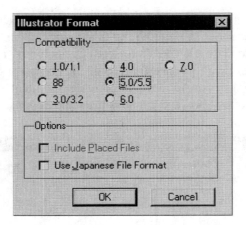

Note   *When working with files which were created using previous versions of Illustrator—but opened and amended in Illustrator 7—the file version is automatically tracked by Illustrator 7. When it comes time to save the file, by default Illustrator 7 saves to the original version the file was created in. If you wish the file to be updated to a more recent version, click the corresponding option in the Save command dialog box. If some of the features or options you have used are not applicable to the earlier version of Illustrator, a warning box will appear.*

When saving to Adobe's EPS format, you have the same version options to save to as for native Illustrator files, including additional header preview options, as shown below. You may save a file with 8-bit or 1-bit preview or "display headers," or no header preview (None). Most programs can import EPS file formats, but placing, resizing, or visually identifying them can be difficult if the file contains no preview.

The more detailed the header preview is, the easier it will be to work with in these programs. 1-bit previews are less detailed than 8-bit previews. Depending on the version you select, you may also choose to include any placed (imported) files which have been linked and include document thumbnails. The Include Place Documents option will only be available if you have placed files into Illustrator 7 using the Place command; otherwise it will be unavailable. Document thumbnails enable Illustrator 7 to display a small image of the file in the Open dialog preview box if and when the file is reopened in Illustrator 7.

Preview headers for EPS files saved on Illustrator 7 Windows platform versions use TIFF headers, while EPS files prepared using the Macintosh version use PICT headers.

Further options enable you to choose Use Japanese File Format to save the document as a Japanese Language document, which is only supported by Illustrator versions 3.0 or later.

And, for documents which feature fonts not installed on the destination program you are creating the EPS for, you may choose to include your Illustrator document fonts with the EPS file by choosing Include Document Fonts.

Choosing to include headers, placed files, and document fonts will increase the file size of your EPS file. If file size is a concern, you may be wise to choose the header preview option None and leave the option Include Document Thumbnails unselected. Neither of these options affect the eventual appearance of the EPS file when printed.

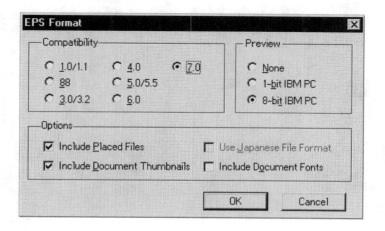

Save As and Save a Copy As Commands

The ability to save a file under a different name is more of a convenience than rocket science. The Save As (CTRL/COMMAND+SHIFT+S) And Save a Copy As (CTRL/COMMAND+ALT/OPTION+S) commands in Illustrator 7 *do* save time for the user, but for the most part they are simply hybrids of the main Save command. Save As enables you to save your current file under a different name and/or file type including any changes that you have made to the document since opening it. The Save As command can be used in cases where you wish to preserve the original document but saves the amendments you recently made to the file under a new name.

 After using the Save As command, the newly saved version of your drawing becomes the active open document.

The Save a Copy As command enables you to literally save a *copy* of your current drawing, including any current changes you have made to it. Saving a copy will not affect the state of your original document. The copy is simply saved to disk using a naming convention which adds the characters *copy* to the end of your original file name, as shown below. Once saved, you are returned to your original unsaved drawing file. In other words, the Save a Copy As command saves the copy without opening it.

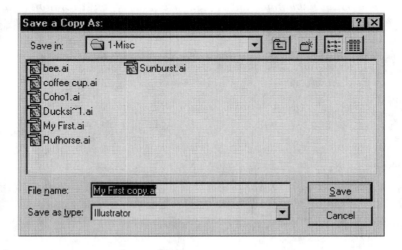

Both the Save As and Save a Copy As command dialog boxes are followed by the usual file format options as with Illustrator 7's main Save command, including the native, EPS, and PDF file formats.

Using the Revert Command

If you find that the things you have done to your drawing since last saving it are completely wrong, or you wish to discard all that you have recently done to your drawing, there's always the Revert command. Select the Revert command from the File menu to have Illustrator 7 return the state of your drawing to what it was after you last saved it. Be warned, though: only one warning dialog box will appear before all your recent changes are deleted, as shown next.

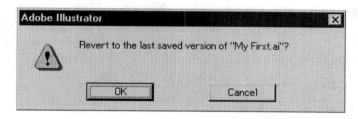

The Revert command is essentially a macro command which automatically closes your file without saving any changes and reopens the very same file. Because this is a macro-type command involving closing the file without saving, it cannot be undone using any conventional methods.

Looking for a way to undo the Revert command? No such luck. There is no hidden Undo feature for this command. Once you have chosen to discard your recent changes they are gone forever.

Saving to Previous Illustrator Versions

As more and more people begin to use Adobe Illustrator, and with each additional version hitting the marketplace, the demand on the engineers at Adobe increases to provide what is referred to as *backward compatibility* capabilities in the software. Backward compatibility refers to the ability of the software to save to previous versions. While some software programs provide tools for saving files to formats which were readable a couple of versions back, Adobe has provided options for saving to all versions of Illustrator since the program was first released.

A number of issues surround the ability of saving to previous versions. The main one, of course, is native drawing features such as attaching type to a path or an object or linking imported files. As Illustrator has evolved throughout the years, some features have been added and some eliminated or changed. This makes saving files to previous versions difficult due to the fact that older versions of Illustrator usually don't support some of the newer features engineered into Illustrator.

The version you are saving your file to will determine which features will be available to you. Features that might be in question when saving to previous versions of Illustrator include:

- Gradients

- Layers

- Text on paths

- Text attached to object paths

- Vertical text

- URL links to objects

- Linked images

- Object URL and text annotation

Tip *Saving files to Illustrator versions 6.0 or earlier offers the option of choosing the Japanese File Format option—all except for the Illustrator 1.0/1.1 version. The Japanese File Format is built into Adobe Illustrator 7 native files.*

Note *By default, when Illustrator opens previous file versions 1.0/1.1, 88, 3.0/3.2, the files automatically display at 100 percent magnification as opposed to the default setting stored in your startup file (by default, 33.33 percent).*

Closing Files

Once you are finished working in your file and before you exit Illustrator 7, you won't be able to avoid the "Do you want to Save your changes to . . ." question, which is by default an automatic query that appears before you can close each and every drawing file you've made changes in. Thankfully, these queries prevent you from losing any of your work by accident. To close a file, choose File|Close (CTRL/COMMAND+W) or click the close box in the upper-right corner of your document window.

 To close all open documents, hold down your ALT/OPTION key and click the close box in the upper-right corner of the first visible document window.

Each time a file is closed, Illustrator 7 checks for any recent unsaved changes that have been made to the file. If your opened files haven't undergone any changes, the files simply close. If they've changed, Illustrator stops and asks whether you would like to save the changes. If you're using the Close All command described in the previous tip, this slightly defeats the advantages of being able to close all files at once; hence, this next user tip.

 To smooth the process of closing all files when using the Close All command, precede it with the Save All command to avoid Illustrator's automatically generated Save queries. To save changes made to all open documents, hold down the ALT/OPTION key and click the Close button in the upper-right corner of your first visible document window.

Backing Up Files

It's interesting to note that Illustrator 7 users essentially work without a net. In other words, where other drawing programs include built-in file backup features, Illustrator doesn't: a tribute to the engineers who develop the program. Because of the program's inherent stability, users can use the program free from worries, corrupted files from IPFs (illegal program functions) on Windows platforms, or software bombs on the Mac.

Having said that, though, working without file backups is hazardous in practice if you're prone to losing files or if you work on a system used by multiple users. It's always a good habit to save a backup copy of your working files somewhere, whether that's on floppy, Zip, optical, or network drives. Backups should be made, at the very minimum, once per day they are worked on.

 Making a backup copy of your working files can quickly be done by using the File\Save a Copy (CTRL/COMMAND+ALT+S) command after your final Save (CTRL/COMMAND+S).

Conclusion

In this chapter, you have seen how to carry out Illustrator 7's basic file command operations, which are critical to using the program effectively. You've also discovered the hidden shortcuts of some of these functions and how there's much more than simply opening, saving, and closing files in Adobe Illustrator 7.

Now that you have a basic understanding of these functions, you're ready to start tackling some of the more challenging aspects of Illustrator's features by exploring one of the *Fundamental Illustrator 7*'s tutorials. But, if you'd like to be more fully prepared for your experiences, you may want to continue studying your own potential for productivity improvements in the next chapter, **Making Illustrator 7 Easy to Use.**

Making Illustrator 7 Easy to Use

3

If you've arrived at this chapter seeking ways to beef up your productivity and speed while using Adobe Illustrator 7, then you've come to the right place. This chapter not only bridges the gap between basic and advanced users but reveals Illustrator 7's hidden features for reducing tedium and increasing efficiency. Let's face it—time is money, and to repeat a very tired old saying, a penny saved is a penny earned.

This chapter will show you how to work easily with many of Illustrator 7's interface components such as toolbars, palettes, dialog boxes, and screen modes. You'll also discover how to customize certain aspects of your drawing and how it appears to you on your screen. And, to make drawing easier, you'll learn to control measuring and measurement tools and set program preferences to suit the way you work. Along the way, you'll see all the related keyboard and mouse shortcuts that Illustrator 7 has to offer.

Setting Document Options

When Illustrator is first launched, the default page size, letter, is oriented *portrait style*. To beginning users, this may sound like a secret, mysterious language, and if you happen to be one of those you may want to use the following section as a guide to better understand how to format your document to suit your drawing and/or printing needs.

If you're preparing your drawing to be reproduced on a printer down the hall, down the street, or in another city, it's always wise to set these options so that they will match your final needs. Correct formatting will reduce the confusion level for other people working with your drawing, and it may even save you time and money.

The size, orientation, and proportional properties of the drawing you're creating are critical to processes such as printing. For example, take a typical business card design scenario. Standard North American business cards measure three and a half inches wide and two inches deep (tall). But more often than not, new users simply begin working with whatever is in front of them and proceed to create their business card design either *on* the letter-sized page or *to fit* the proportions of the page. Neither approach is correct.

The correct approach is to set the physical *artboard* size to two inches by three inches in portrait orientation using the options found in Illustrator 7's Document

Setup dialog box, as shown below. To access these options, choose File|Document Setup. There are also a few other options you may want to define in your drawing with the aim of clarifying specifications for yourself and anyone else who works with your document.

 To access Document Setup options quickly, use the keyboard shortcut CTRL/COMMAND+SHIFT+P.

3

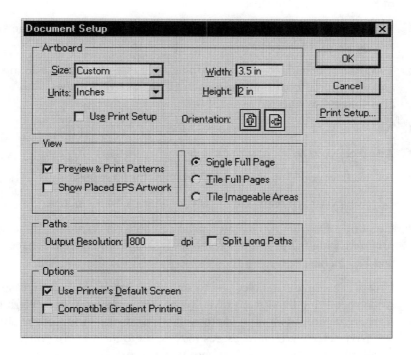

Specifying Artboard Sizes

In an effort to reduce user confusion surrounding the terms for printed page and document page sizes, Adobe coined the term *artboard* to describe the plane on which your drawing is actually being created. For example, although you may be creating a drawing that is 4 inches by 6 inches, the page you are printing it onto may be 8.5 by 11 inches in size.

Fiddling with terminology may at first seem like overcomplication of a fairly simple concept, but if you work in the digital printing world, where the term *page* can refer to document page size, output page size, final printed page size, and so on,

the likelihood for confusion is high—especially for new users unfamiliar with service bureau or printing industry jargon.

The *artboard size* sets the physical size of your drawing page to sizes determined by the type of printer you currently have set in your Document Setup, PPD options. Page sizes often include the following standard page measures:

- **Letter**   The term *letter* refers to the common North American page size of 8.5 inches by 11 inches.

- **Legal**   The term *legal* refers to the common legal document page size of 8.5 inches by 14 inches.

- **Tabloid**   This older term is used in news or circular format printing sizes and sets your artboard dimensions to 11 inches by 17 inches. This term is also sometimes referred to as *tab* size.

- **A4**   Sets your artboard size to 8.27 inches by 11.69 inches.

- **A3**   Sets your artboard size to 11.69 inches by 16.54 inches.

- **B5**   Sets your artboard size to 7.17 inches by 10 inches.

- **B4**   Sets your artboard size to 10.12 inches by 14.33 inches.

- **Custom**   Enables you to enter any size you wish within the limits of the programs height and width parameters which fall in a range between 2 and 120 inches.

- **Units**   This option enables you to set your preference of unit measure when specifying the dimensions of your artboard size. When entering measure values, Illustrator 7 automatically adds the suffix for the units you have selected. Unit measures may be set to inches (in), points @pt = , picas (p), millimeters (mm), or centimeters (cm). Points and picas are generally used by the printing industry, whereby one inch equals 6 picas and 1 pica equals 12 points. The pica measure format includes both picas and points in combination with each other. For example, a measure of "6p3" denotes 6 picas plus 3 points.

- **Width**   Value must be between 2 and 120 inches. In standardized page-measuring terminology, width is always the first measure indicated. For example, a sheet measuring 8.5 by 11 inches specifies the width as 8.5 inches.

- **Height**   Value must also be between 2 and 120 inches.

■ **Orientation** These two buttons enable you to set how your page is oriented. Pages may be set to either portrait or landscape, meaning that the page is either aligned tall or wide. These two terms may be confusing for newer users not familiar with printing terminology, and in an effort to reduce confusion, Adobe has set the portrait and landscape orientation buttons to simply swap the measures you have set in the Width and Height boxes.

■ **Selecting the Use Print/Page Setup option** Selecting this option automatically sets the dimensions of your artboard size to match the Paper Size option currently selected in your Print Setup, as shown next. Macintosh version users may click the Page Setup button from within the Document Setup dialog box to access the printer driver option.

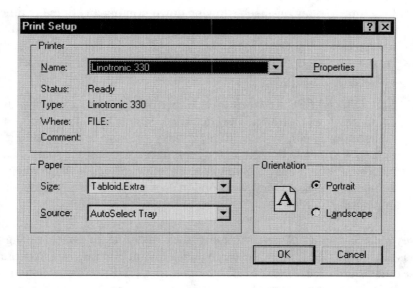

For more information on controlling printer options, see "Print Setup Options," **Chapter 17: Printing from Illustrator 7**. The remaining options in the Document Setup dialog have more to do with how Illustrator 7 handles the physical printing of your document rather than how you work with it, and setting these now will have little effect on how you prepare your document. However, if you're searching specifically for more information on choosing these options, turn to "Document Setup Printing Options" in **Chapter 17: Printing from Illustrator 7**. There, you'll discover more detailed information about options controlling how Illustrator converts, prints, and exports long and complex object paths and path resolution and

printing of screens and gradients. You'll also find out more about the Print Setup shortcut, as seen above.

Setting Document View Options

Illustrator 7 features a number of view options in the Document Setup dialog box, which enable you to see things you wouldn't normally see under default circumstances. The ability to control these options enables you to fine-tune screen redraw time and placement of objects.

- **Preview and Print Patterns** Under preview mode this option sets whether or not patterns appear on your screen and your printed output. Some of the tile patterns you can use in Illustrator 7 can sometimes take a long time to draw onscreen, slowing down printing and drawing time. Opting not to show these patterns in Preview mode will enable you to concentrate on the actual shape of the object under both circumstances. By default, this option is selected active and all patterns will print and display.

- **Show Placed EPS Artwork** Under normal circumstances, viewing your drawing in Artwork view displays a simple bounding box around the area occupied by placed EPS files in your drawing. By selecting this option, you enable Illustrator 7 to reproduce a crude 1-bit image of all placed EPS files, enabling you to visually identify their shape when composing your drawing. This option does not affect the Preview display of placed EPS files.

Beyond the display of patterns and placed EPS files in your drawing, View options also enable you to show onscreen indications of printing results for drawings whose dimensions exceed those of the maximum page size of your printer. Illustrator 7 is capable of printing individual pieces of large drawings to match the output size of your page, enabling you to assemble the pages again to see a physical proof of your entire drawing. This printing method is referred to as *tiling*.

The ability to print tiles of your drawing is one of the more useful and innovative printing resources of any drawing program, but few programs do it well. Illustrator 7 goes the extra mile here by enabling you not only to print tiles, but to actually see the tiles directly in your drawing. The ability to see the tile seams in your drawing enables you to plan for the eventual reassembly of your drawing and minimize any unfortunate splits in objects.

- **Single Full Page**   This option (the default) displays only a single page at a time. Tiles are represented by two rectangles: the printed page size and the printable page size.

- **Tile Full Pages**   This option enables you to display only "whole" tiles of pages and omits pages which are destined to feature only portions of tiles of your drawing.

- **Tile Imageable Areas**   Choosing this option enables you to print all tiled pages of your drawing regardless of whether the tile occupies an entire page or not. This option is also the only tile viewing option which automatically numbers all pages of the tiling sequence directly on your screen, as shown in Figure 3-1. Where space does not enable the page numerals to appear, they simply don't display but are always counted.

 You can actually control the placement of the tiles displayed using Illustrator 7's tile-viewing options using the Page tool and printing tiles manually. For more information on positioning tiles using the Page tool, see the section called "Printing Tiled Documents," in **Chapter 17: Printing from Illustrator 7**.

About Toolboxes, Palettes, and Text Boxes

Nearly all of the properties assigned to objects in Illustrator 7 are assigned through options available in palettes and dialog boxes. In an effort to enable users to customize the way they work, Adobe has implemented the capability to "tear off" and separate individual parts of palettes and reassemble them to suit your most common requirements. This next section covers many of the methods of using and fine-tuning these features and will be of interest to users who want to capitalize on the increased productivity benefits of using keyboard shortcuts.

As you select and use the various interface features in Illustrator 7 such as the main Toolbox and other palettes, you may notice that continually accessing the menu bars at the top of the program window quickly becomes quite tedious. The good news is that many such palettes can be displayed via keyboard shortcuts which can

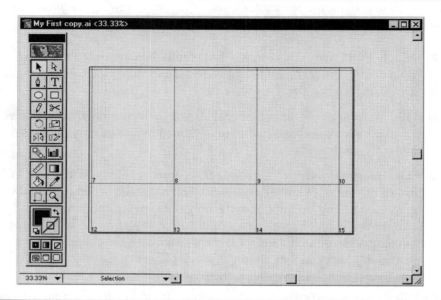

FIGURE 3-1   Using the Tile Imageable Areas option, tiles display complete with page numbers

save you an immense amount of time. And, while a few of the shortcuts are indicated beside the menu bar commands themselves, most are not.

 *For a summary of all keyboard shortcuts available when using toolboxes and palettes, see the complete shortcut listing in **Appendix B: Summary of Keyboard Shortcuts**.*

Toolbox Options

The main toolbox, shown next, contains many more tools than can be displayed at any one time. Accessing the hidden tools can be done by clicking and holding your mouse pointer, but Adobe has implemented a much quicker and simpler way through keystroke access. Each tool class has been assigned a specific keyboard letter which enables you to cycle through the various tools.

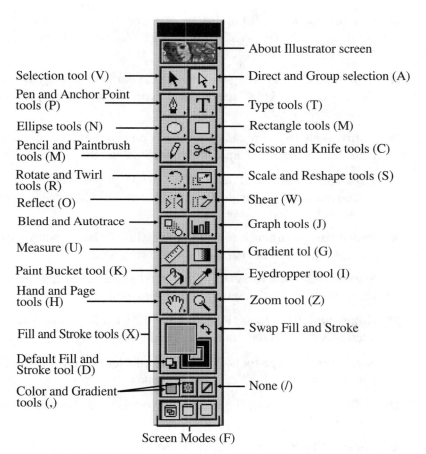

About Illustrator screen
Selection tool (V)
Direct and Group selection (A)
Pen and Anchor Point tools (P)
Type tools (T)
Ellipse tools (N)
Rectangle tools (M)
Pencil and Paintbrush tools (M)
Scissor and Knife tools (C)
Rotate and Twirl tools (R)
Scale and Reshape tools (S)
Reflect (O)
Shear (W)
Blend and Autotrace
Graph tools (J)
Measure (U)
Gradient tol (G)
Paint Bucket tool (K)
Eyedropper tool (I)
Hand and Page tools (H)
Zoom tool (Z)
Fill and Stroke tools (X)
Swap Fill and Stroke
Default Fill and Stroke tool (D)
Color and Gradient tools (,)
None (/)
Screen Modes (F)

The following is a summary of the tools found in Illustrator 7's toolbox and a brief description of their function:

- **About Illustrator screen**   This shortcut button causes the Adobe Illustrator 7 screen to display, which identifies licensing, version, developer credit, and copyright information.

- **Selection tool (V)**   Pressing the letter *V* on your keyboard instantly selects the Selection tool.

- **Direct and Group selection (A)**   Pressing the letter *A* on your keyboard alternates between the Direct Selection and Group Selection tools.

- **Pen and Anchor Point tools (P)**   Pressing the letter *P* on your keyboard cycle-selects the Pen, Add Anchor, Delete Anchor, and Convert Direction Point tools.

- **Type tools (T)**   Pressing the letter *T* on your keyboard cycle-selects the Type, Area Type, Path Type, Vertical Type, Vertical Area Type, and Vertical Path Type tools.

- **Ellipse tools (N)**   Pressing the letter *N* on your keyboard cycle-selects the Ellipse, Centered Ellipse, Polygon, Star, and Spiral tools.

- **Rectangle tools (M)**   Pressing the letter *M* on your keyboard cycle-selects the Rectangle, Rounded Rectangle, Centered Rectangle, and Centered Rounded Rectangle tools.

- **Pencil and Paintbrush tools (Y)**   Pressing the letter *Y* on your keyboard alternates between the Pencil and Paintbrush tools.

- **Scissor and Knife tools (C)**   Pressing the letter *C* on your keyboard alternates between the Scissors and Knife tools.

- **Rotate and Twirl tools (R)**   Pressing the letter *R* on your keyboard alternates between the Rotate and Twirl tools.

- **Scale and Reshape tools (S)**   Pressing the letter *S* on your keyboard alternates between the Scale and Reshape tools.

- **Reflect (O)**   Pressing the letter *O* on your keyboard instantly selects the Reflect tool.

- **Shear (W)**   Pressing the letter *W* on your keyboard instantly selects the Shear tool.

- **Blend and Autotrace (B)**   Pressing the letter *B* on your keyboard alternates between the Blend and Autotrace tools.

- **Graph tools (J)**   Pressing the letter *J* on your keyboard cycle-selects Column, Stacked Column, Bar, Stacked Bar, Line, Area, Scatter, Pie, and Radar Graph tools.

- **Measure (U)**   Pressing the letter *U* on your keyboard instantly selects the Measure tool.

- **Gradient tool (G)**   Pressing the letter *G* on your keyboard instantly selects the Gradient tool.

- **Paint Bucket tool (K)**   Pressing the letter *K* on your keyboard instantly selects the Paint Bucket tool.

- **Eyedropper tool (I)**   Pressing the letter *I* on your keyboard instantly selects the Eyedropper tool.

- **Hand and Page tools (H)**   Pressing the letter *H* on your keyboard alternates between the Hand and Page tools.

- **Zoom tool (Z)**   Pressing the letter *Z* on your keyboard instantly selects the Zoom In tool. Holding the ALT/OPTION switches this to the Zoom Out tool.

- **Fill and Stroke tools (X)**   Pressing the letter *X* on your keyboard alternates between Fill and Stroke modes for assigning fill and stroke colors and properties to objects.

- **Default Fill and Stroke tool (D)**   Pressing the letter *D* sets the fill and stroke mode colors and thicknesses to Illustrator 7's default settings.

- **Color and Gradient tools (,)**   Pressing the *Comma* key on your keyboard selects the Color palette.

- **Gradient palette (.)**   Pressing the *Period* key on your keyboard selects the Gradient palette.

- **None (/)**   Pressing the **Slash** key on your keyboard sets the currently displayed fill or stroke settings to None, depending on which mode is selected.

- **Screen modes (F)**   Pressing the letter *F* on your keyboard cycle-selects between Standard Screen Mode, Full Screen Mode with Menu Bars, and Full Screen Mode.

Note   *Shortcut keys for the Toolbox palette are not case-sensitive.*

Tip   *For more information on using specific tools in the Toolbox, see the related chapters in **Part II: Working with Illustrator 7's Tools**.*

Along with these keyboard shortcuts for selecting tools, you may also temporarily switch from any currently selected tool to other specific tools by holding down certain keyboard combinations as follows:

- **Hand tool**   Hold down the SPACE BAR while any tool is selected.

- **Selection tool**   Hold down the CTRL/COMMAND key while any tool is selected.

- **Zoom In tool**   Hold down CTRL/COMMAND+SPACE BAR while any tool is selected.

- **Zoom Out tool**   Hold down CTRL/COMMAND+ALT/OPTION+SPACE BAR while any tool is selected.

- **Centered Mode of tool**   (Ellipses and Rectangles): Hold down ALT/OPTION key.

- **Access Precise Dimensioning dialog boxes**   Click anywhere on your drawing page (without dragging) while using any Ellipse, Rectangle, or Graph tool.

- **Add Anchor Point**   Hold down ALT/OPTION key with Scissors tool selected.

- **Alternate Add and Delete Anchor Point tools**   Hold down ALT/OPTION key with either Add or Delete Anchor Point tools selected.

- **Alternate Between Pen and Convert Anchor Point tools**   Hold down ALT/OPTION key.

If memorizing these last few pages seems like an impossible task, don't worry—you'll be reminded whenever the tool comes up when you're reading chapters discussing the use of specific tools and when you're working through the tutorials that accompany those chapters. However, if the keystroke shortcuts for accessing tools in the Main Toolbox palette appear useful to you, try making a photocopy of the page they appear on and taping it near your monitor until you're familiar with them.

Palette Shortcuts

In one form or another, palettes have been in existence for years in Adobe Illustrator and other Adobe products, but there never have been so many—until now. Palettes in the past have remained static or floating collections of icons as convenient shortcuts to certain program features. But now, in their various states and conditions, palettes make up the very heart of features. In fact, the palettes *themselves* have become program features which may be accessed through menus or keyboard commands.

There are 13 main palettes in Illustrator 7, including the main Toolbox. Palettes may be selected a number of different ways: the simplest of which is through menu access. Most palettes, however, allow access via a keyboard shortcut. Table 1 shows a listing of available palette shortcuts.

Note   *At least ten more color-specific palettes exist in Illustrator 7, which must be specifically selected using the Windows\Swatch Libraries command, as shown in Figure 3-2. Extra libraries include ink catalogs for companies such as Pantone, Focoltone, Trumatch, Toyo, and so on. For more information on using these color swatches, see the section called "Using Other Swatch Libraries," in **Chapter 11: Working in Color.***

Palette	Shortcut	Menu access
Toolbox and palettes	TAB	Window\Show/Hide Tools
Swatches	F5	Window\Show/Hide Swatches
Color	F6	Window\Show/Hide Color
Layers	F7	Window\Show/Hide Layers
Info	F8	Window\Show/Hide Info
Gradient	F9	Window\Show/Hide Gradient
Stroke	F10	Window\Show/Hide Stroke
Attributes	F11	Window\Show/Hide Attributes
Character	CTRL/COMMAND+T	Type\Character
Transform	None	Object\Transform
Align	None	Window\Show/Hide Align
Paragraph	CTRL/COMMAND+M	Type\Paragraph
MM Design	None	Type\MM Design

■ **TABLE 3-1**   Palette Shortcuts

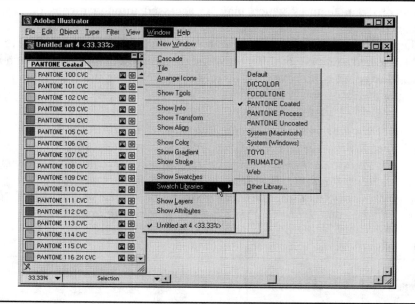

FIGURE 3-2   To access certain color swatches containing specific color collections, use the Swatch Libraries command

Hiding and Displaying Palettes

A number of shortcuts have also been engineered into the palette controls themselves to expand or reduce their current display conditions. Palettes can be selected and maximized or minimized to reveal main or more detailed features via mouse clicks and double-clicks. When a palette is selected, by default it appears on your screen in the last state it was used.

Palettes that display on your screen grouped with other palettes may be selected through single-clicking on their respective palette tab, while palettes that appear featuring only their title bar and/or title *tabs* can be maximized to show all features by double-clicking once on their title tabs. Double-clicking on the palette tab a second time minimizes the palette to show only brief, commonly used features. This can also be done by clicking on the Zoom box (Macintosh) or Maximize/Minimize button (Windows) button in the upper-right corner of the palette's title bar beside the Close button.

For example, when working with the Color palette, which by default is grouped with the Attributes, Stroke, and Gradient palettes, as shown next, follow these steps to maximize or minimize its features:

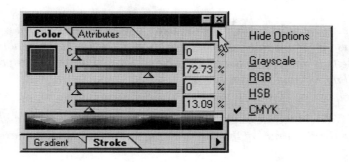

1. With Illustrator 7 launched and a new or existing drawing file opened, choose the Color palette by selecting Window|Show Color (F6).

2. To see more or fewer of the features, double-click on the palette name (Color) tab. Notice that the palette either grows or shrinks, depending on its current display condition.

3. Double-click a second time on the Color tab to further reduce or expand the features it contains.

4. To select one of the other palettes in the group, click once on its palette tab name to bring it to the forefront of the group. If the palette you selected remains minimized, double-click its name tab to expand the display.

You may also show or hide a palette's full set of features by clicking the flyout (black triangle) directly to the right of the palette name and selecting Show/Hide Options. This flyout button may also include certain palette options specific to the palette tool itself, as shown above.

Resizing Palettes

While some palettes are capable of being resized, others are not. Resizable palettes feature a resizing box (Macintosh) or tab (Windows) which can be dragged in the

direction you would like the palette to expand. Resizing certain palettes can make viewing their options and preview characteristic much more detailed, as in the case of the Gradient or Swatch palettes. Table 2 shows a guide to which palettes are resizable and how they may be resized.

 A resizable palette cannot be resized when docked or grouped with another palette which is not resizable. For example, while the resizable Gradient palette is docked to the nonresizable Color and/or Attributes palettes, you will not be able to alter its size.

 To change the dimensions of a resizable palette, grab and drag the lower-right corner of the palette in the direction you wish to expand it.

Palette	Resizable
Toolbox	No
Swatches	Yes, vertically and horizontally
Color	No
Layers	Yes, vertically and horizontally
Info	No
Gradient	Yes, horizontally only
Stroke	No
Attributes	No
Character	No
Transform	No
Align	No
Paragraph	No
MM Design	No

TABLE 3-2   Palette resizing capabilities

Moving, Docking, and Grouping Palettes

Palettes may also be organized and reorganized to suit the way you work. You can move them around your working screen by dragging their title bars or separate them from a group by dragging their title tabs, and certain palettes are resizable—meaning that you can resize the dimensions of the palette itself as covered in the previous section.

By default, Illustrator 7's tool palettes have been organized into palette *groups* which inherently reside together. For example, the Color and Attributes palettes have been grouped together to compose a single palette unit, as well as the Stroke and Gradient palettes; the Character, Paragraph, and MM Design palettes; and so on. Illustrator 7 enables you to separate and reassemble these palette groups as you see fit. For instance, the Color palette can be ungrouped from the Attributes palette. To separate a grouped palette, click and drag its title tab to a position outside of the current palette, as shown in Figure 3-3.

Drag title tab out of current group

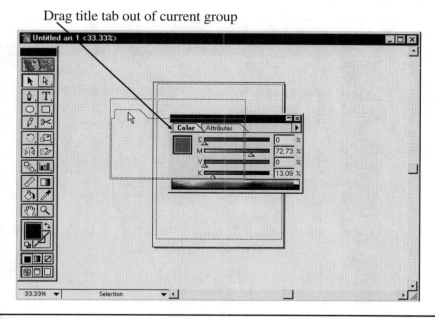

■ FIGURE 3-3   To separate a palette from its current grouping, drag its title tab outside of the group

While ungrouping palettes can be valuable if you need to work with only one at a time, palettes can also be recombined in any combination of groups. If your current project demands that you access only two or three palettes consistently, you can maximize your working screen space by grouping them together. To group two palettes together, drag the title bar of the first into the tab area of the second, as shown in Figure 3-4.

Note *Palette grouping and docking is not a function that can be reversed using the Undo (CTRL/COMMAND+Z) command. To ungroup or undock a palette you must drag it from its current grouped or docked position.*

The term *docking* refers not to grouping palettes with each other, but to attaching palettes to the bottoms of other palettes so that the two behave as a single unit when moved. Docking also enables you to view both docked palettes simultaneously when both are maximized. The procedure for docking palettes together is similar to

Drag to here to combine palettes

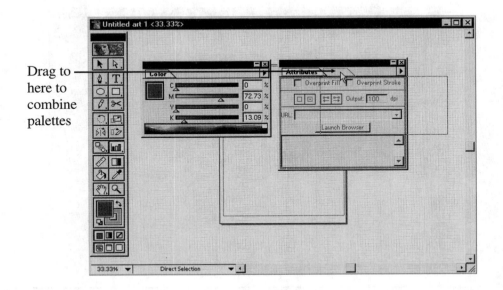

FIGURE 3-4   Combining individual palettes maximizes your screen real estate

grouping, but the point to which you drag the first palette to the second is different. To dock two palettes together, drag the title tab of the first palette to the very bottom of the second palette, as shown in Figure 3-5. To undock the palette, simply drag its title tab to a point outside of the palette to which it is docked.

Dialog Box Shortcuts

When you're working in tool palettes and dialog boxes—or wherever you find yourself entering numeric values—a number of conveniences have been built into Illustrator 7. These conveniences are what set Illustrator 7 apart from many other drawing programs, and Adobe has gone that extra mile to implement them.

To go that extra mile though, Adobe has included so many that it would be nearly impossible to list all instances. Instead, this section will provide you with the common threads and principles on which these niceties are based in order to give you a basic understanding of their wider functions. Once you grasp their

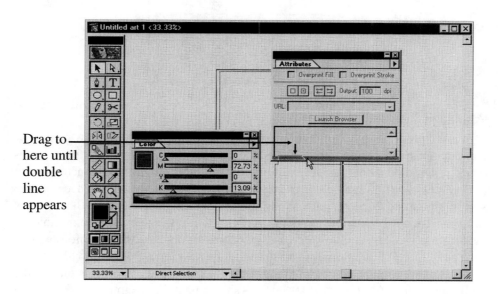

Drag to here until double line appears

FIGURE 3-5   Docking palettes together causes the two palettes to become attached vertically

functionality, you'll be able to explore their implementation to suit the way in which you work and the tools and features you most commonly use.

First, when entering values into any dialog box or palette where numerical entries are required, press the TAB key, which enables you to cycle through the available options in the order that they appear, usually left-to-right and top-to-bottom. To cycle through these same entry boxes in reverse order, hold the SHIFT key while pressing the TAB key. For example, in the illustration below, the Character palette (CTRL/COMMAND+T) features a number of options for setting the size, width, leading, etc. of selected type. After selecting and entering values in the Font Size box, you can move quickly to enter values in the Leading box by pressing the TAB key once. The next value becomes immediately highlighted and ready for reentering a new value.

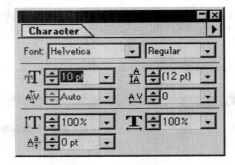

For more information on using the Character palette and working with type, see "Setting Character Attributes," **Chapter 5: Working with Type**.

Next, pressing the SHIFT key together with the UP and DOWN ARROW combinations enables you to increase or decrease values in numeric entry boxes quickly, based on default values built into Illustrator 7. Using the Character palette (CTRL/COMMAND+T) again as an example, you may wish to increase or decrease the size of type more than one point at a time. Where a single click on an UP or DOWN *spinner* beside the value increases or decreases the font size by one point, holding the SHIFT keys while clicking increases or decreases the value by default font sizes such as 8, 12, 16, 20, 24 points, and so on.

This convention behaves identically with other Illustrator 7 features such as the Paragraph palette (CTRL/COMMAND+M), as shown next. For example, after clicking the first entry box, which sets character indent measure, a single click on either the UP or DOWN ARROWS will cause the value to change by one point, and a SHIFT-click on either button causes the value to change in increments of six points.

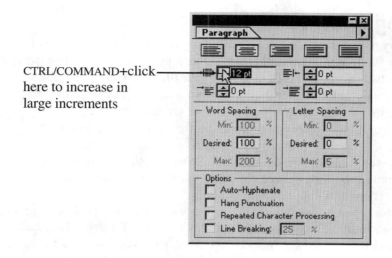

CTRL/COMMAND+click
here to increase in
large increments

For more information on using Paragraph Palette features, see "Setting Paragraph Attributes," **Chapter 5: Working with Type**.

Finally, you may also use your keyboard UP and DOWN ARROW keys to change values quickly in numeric option boxes. For example, clicking inside the Font Size box of the Character palette and pressing the UP ARROW key three times changes 10-point type size to 13 points. This may not seem like rocket science, but it will enable you to change numeric values quickly without having to reach for your mouse and position it inside one of those tiny boxes.

Getting Information

Although opening and viewing a drawing might very well reveal how it looks, there's a lot you won't be able to figure out from simply looking at a drawing. In the past, as with other programs, to find out detailed information about a drawing or document you were forced to explore specific dialog boxes, which usually meant using pen and paper to record what you found.

The very fact that you have a computer sitting in front of you makes this method quite ridiculous. Nevertheless, that's how countless documents were scrutinized regarding their page size, font information, colors used, and complexity. Now that any type of property can be measured in Illustrator 7, documents can provide all sorts of useful information about themselves without forcing users to go hunting for it. This is a true innovation for any drawing program.

Getting Document Info

The ability to summarize information about your document can serve many useful purposes. First, you can record and include the information with your file in electronic text format and include it with your Illustrator 7 drawing file wherever it goes. Anyone needing information about your document can simply read the text file—and won't need to own Illustrator 7 or go through the effort of opening and viewing your drawing file. The potential for time saving is enormous. A text of your drawing could also accompany your Illustrator file for archiving purposes, so you wouldn't even have to open the file yourself to refresh your memory on its details. The potential grows even more for this feature if you employ outside vendors to print your file.

The Document Info command in Illustrator summarizes nine key aspects of your drawing, including Document, Objects, Spot Colors, Patterns, Gradients, Fonts, Linked Images, Embedded Images, and Font Details. This information may be selected and viewed while your drawing file is opened and, if you desire, saved to a separate text file. To obtain highly detailed information about a drawing, deselect any currently selected objects and choose File|Document Info to access the Document Info dialog box, as shown below.

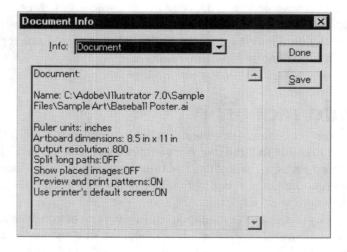

In order to access the Document Info command, be sure that all objects in your drawing are deselected. To deselect all objects, use the shortcut CTRL/COMMAND+SHIFT+A. If any objects in your drawing are selected, this menu item changes to Selection Info instead, in an effort to enable you to obtain details about specific drawing objects.

The Document Info command provides detailed information on various aspects of your drawing as follows:

- **Document**   Includes file name and location, ruler units, artboard dimensions, output resolution, and currently set optional conditions comprising split long paths, show placed images, preview and print patterns, and use printer's default screen.

- **Objects**   Lists the total number of paths, masks, and compound paths; the number of objects which feature RGB, CMYK, and grayscale colors; and the numbers of objects including spot colors, patterns, and gradients.

- **Spot Colors**   If your document features objects with spot colors, they are individually listed.

- **Patterns**   If your document features objects assigned with patterns, they are individually listed.

- **Gradients**   Lists total number of objects with gradient fills and their color space, such as CMYK, RGB, or mixed.

- **Fonts**   Provides a detailed listing of all fonts used in your drawing whether they are presently loaded on the host system or not.

- **Linked Images**   Lists the number, name, type, and location of all externally linked files including channels, size, dimension, and resolution.

- **Embedded Images**   Lists details about any embedded images in your drawing comprising type, channels, size, dimension, and resolution.

- **Font Details**   Includes a detailed listing about the fonts used in your document include the PostScript name, Windows font name, language, font, and Tsume type.

Getting Object Information

Along with document information, you may also obtain detailed information about a specific objects or group of objects in the drawing you are viewing through use of the Selection Info command. The same advantages apply as with Document Info when finding and/or saving specific information about an object in your drawing.

And, as with Document Info, the Selection Info command reveals information regarding object characteristics such as colors, patterns, gradients, fonts, linked images, embedded images, and font details. In fact, if your drawing contains objects prepared in other programs such as an image editor or another drawing program, this will be Illustrator 7's only available method for scrutinizing them, as shown below.

To obtain information about an object or group of objects, first select the object using the Selection tool from the main toolbox and choose File|Selection Info.

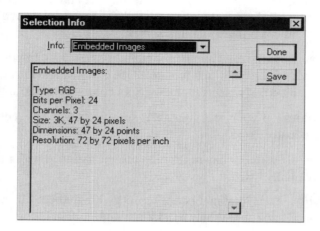

Saving Info to Text Files

Illustrator provides you with the ability to save a text summary of either your drawing or your selected objects by clicking the Save button from either the Selection Info or Document Info dialog boxes. From there a dialog box is generated, enabling you to name and save the text file (shown next), which can then be opened in any text editor such as MacWrite (Macintosh) or NotePad (Windows).

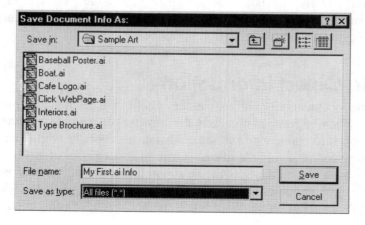

The following example was generated from one of the sample files included on the Adobe Illustrator 7 program disc:

```
Document Info - Weekday, Month, Day, Time, Year
----------------------------------------------------------------
--
Document:
Name: C:\Adobe\Illustrator 7.0\Sample Files\Sample Art\Baseball Poster.ai
Ruler units: inches
Artboard dimensions: 8.5 in x 11 in
Output resolution: 800
Split long paths: OFF
Show placed images: OFF
Preview and print patterns: ON
Use printer's default screen: ON
----------------------------------------------------------------
--
Objects:
Paths: 1701
Masks: NONE
Compounds: 57
RGB Objects: NONE
CMYK Objects: 1652
Grayscale Objects: 53
Spot Colors: NONE
Patterns: NONE
Gradients: NONE
Fonts: 2
Linked Images: NONE
Embedded Images: 1
----------------------------------------------------------------
--
Spot Colors:
NONE
----------------------------------------------------------------
--
Patterns:
NONE
```

```
---------------------------------------------------------------
--
Gradients:
NONE
---------------------------------------------------------------
--
Fonts:
Helvetica(Type 1)
Helvetica-Bold(Type 1)
---------------------------------------------------------------
--
Linked Images:
NONE
---------------------------------------------------------------
--
Embedded Images:
Type: RGB
Bits per Pixel: 24
Channels: 3
Size: 3K, 47 by 24 pixels
Dimensions: 47 by 24 points
Resolution: 72 by 72 pixels per inch
---------------------------------------------------------------
--
Font Details:
Helvetica
     PostScript Name: Helvetica
     Windows Font Name: Helvetica
     Language: Roman
     Font Type: Type 1
     Tsume Type: N/A
Helvetica-Bold
     PostScript Name: Helvetica-Bold
     Windows Font Name: Helvetica
     Language: Roman
     Font Type:  Type 1
     Tsume Type: N/A
```

Customizing Windows and Display

As is characteristic of Adobe Illustrator 7, you are able to maximize complete use of your screen with ultimate and total control. Users have the choice through either keyboard or Toolbox palette shortcuts of choosing to work with or without menus, with or without toolboxes and palettes, in full color or in a wireframe display mode, and any combinations therein. Few other drawing programs offer this level of control over what you are able to see on your screen.

Cycle Screen Modes

The three main display modes are controlled through buttons on the Toolbox palette comprised of Standard Screen, Full Screen with Menu Bar, and Full Screen modes described as follows:

- **Standard Screen Mode**   This is the default display mode and enables you to work with all menus, screen interface features, and tool palettes accessible and visible, as shown in Figure 3-6.

- **Full Screen Mode with Menu Bar**   Switching to this mode enables you to see only Illustrator 7's command menus, Toolbox, and palettes. The program and document window, scroll bars, Zoom and Status Bar display, and program title bar each become invisible, as shown in Figure 3-7.

- **Full Screen Mode**   Using this display mode, only the Toolbox and palettes are visible, as seen in Figure 3-8. To use this mode you must be quite familiar with Illustrator 7's commands and keyboard shortcuts in order to remain productive and efficient. Otherwise, you will constantly be reverting to Standard Screen Mode in order to change views or access menus.

Setting Status Bar Display

Compared to other drawing programs, Adobe Illustrator 7 includes a very brief set of onscreen information providers, including time, date, system resources, number of undos and redos, current tool selections, and keyboard modes. This display of information can be set to whichever is most critical at the time you are drawing.

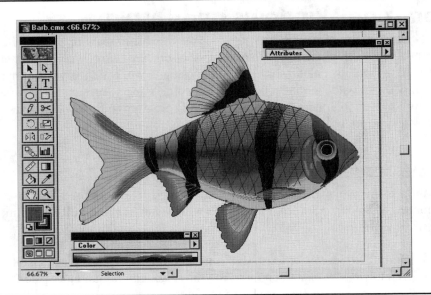

FIGURE 3-6   Standard Screen Mode is the default display and shows all
visible interface tools

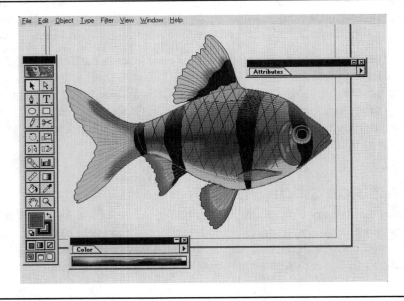

FIGURE 3-7   Full Screen Mode with Menu Bar increases your working
space dramatically

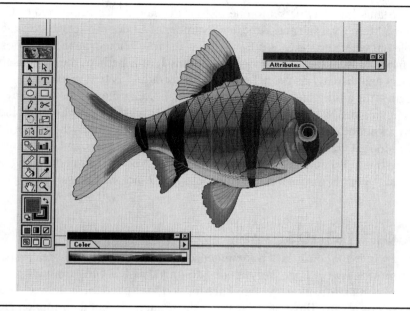

FIGURE 3-8   Full Screen Mode enables you to work unencumbered by your screen boundaries

 To hide the main Toolbox and all other palettes while in any screen mode, press the TAB key once. To bring them back again, press the TAB key a second time.

For example, if you are on the verge of running out of system resources such as random access memory (Macintosh) or virtual memory (Windows), you may choose to keep a close eye on it using the Status Bar. Or, if you are constantly wondering what effect certain keyboard combinations have on the state of your chosen tool, you may choose the Current Tool display mode shown below.

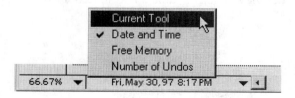

The Status Bar may be set to one of four display modes comprised of Current Tool, Free Memory, Date and Time, and Number of Undos. To set the display, click and hold anywhere on the Status Bar to show the four-choice menu and choose one of the modes. Of all the display modes, Current Tool is perhaps the most useful for new users and displays as the default when Illustrator 7 is first installed.

Finally, for a little on-screen entertainment, holding the ALT/OPTION key down while clicking on the Status Bar offers some humorous display options, including a mysterious phone number, Eyes (which follow your cursor around the screen), Moon Phases, Mouse Clicks, National Debt ($U.S.), Random number, and Shopping Days Till Christmas. Whether or not the engineers at Adobe intended these comical options to appear in the final release of Illustrator 7, no one knows.

View Commands

Drawing within the confines of a computer screen can be a limiting ordeal, especially if your drawing is very large, very small, or highly detailed. Most drawing programs offer similar magnification tools in order for you to expand the little world on your screen. In this regard, Illustrator 7 features the usual tools, but their implementation and use are slightly different.

Zooming Shortcuts

The most common technique for changing the view you see on your screen is through use of the Zoom tool found in the main Toolbox palette. The Zoom tool can be used in two modes: increasing and decreasing magnification. Illustrator 7 is capable of magnification views of within a range of 1600 percent (highly increased magnification) to 6.25 percent (highly decreased magnification), with 100 percent as the "actual size" of the measured objects on your screen.

The Zoom tool can be selected from the main Toolbox palette, or you can temporarily access it by holding keyboard combinations. You can control the Zoom tool with keyboard combinations, clicks, and double-clicks to change the magnification of your view quickly. Table 3 lists the Zoom Tool's hidden shortcuts.

To do this	Do this
Zoom in (temporary)	Hold down CTRL/COMMAND+SPACE BAR
Zoom out (temporary)	Hold down CTRL/COMMAND+ALT/OPTION+SPACE BAR

To do this	Do this
Zoom out (with Zoom tool)	Hold down ALT/OPTION with Zoom tool selected
Set view to 100 percent	Double-click Zoom tool in Toolbox
Marquee Zoom in	Drag Zoom tool to surround objects
Adjust Marquee Zoom area	Drag Zoom tool to surround objects, then press SPACEBAR to move the marquee prior to releasing the mouse button

Hand Tool Shortcuts

The Hand tool can also come into play when you are changing views but is not as commonly used as the Zoom tool. The Hand Tool is essentially capable of quickly changing the scroll bar position of your Illustrator 7 document window. This is a more interactive way of navigating your drawing, because you receive instant feedback as to the screen position of your drawing objects.

The Hand tool has only one mode: scrolling mode. To use the Hand tool, select it from the main Toolbox palette or use keyboard shortcuts to change your cursor tool into the Hand tool temporarily. Once in Hand tool mode, drag the objects on your screen to change your view in the direction of your drag. Table 4 shows a list of keyboard shortcuts for selecting and using the Hand tool.

To do this	Do this
Hand Tool (temporary)	Hold down SPACEBAR
Fit artwork in window	Double-click Hand tool in the Toolbox

Opening Multiple Windows

Introducing Illustrator 7's ability to open multiple documents in past versions has created some interesting and valuable working methods. As with other programs, you can open more than one document at a time in Illustrator 7.

While that may be no surprise, you may also (read this slowly) open more than one copy of a document window. In other words, you can work simultaneously on *multiple* areas of a drawing. Plus, Illustrator 7 has a set of simple features under the Window menu that can organize your work this way, including the New Window and Cascade and Tile (Windows version only) window commands.

To set up multiple document windows of the same drawing, follow these steps:

1. With Illustrator 7 launched, open one new or existing document.

2. If you haven't already done so, create some sample drawing elements for yourself to see.

3. Select the Window|New Window command three times in succession, waiting for each window to be created between commands. Notice that each new window features the filename followed by a colon and number. These numbers enable you to identify and select your new windows.

4. With at least four windows of your document opened (the original, now with the suffix :1 added to its window name), plus three additional numbered windows, choose the Window menu without selecting any commands. Notice that your multiple windows are listed at the bottom of this menu.

5. Now, manually resize your document windows (Macintosh) or choose Window|Cascade (Windows) to stagger the windows of all your open documents, as shown in Figure 3-9. To select any of the document windows you see, click on its document title bar.

6. Now, manually resize your document windows (Macintosh) or choose Window|Tile (Windows) to view all the windows and their currently showing contents. Try selecting each of the windows and changing views or magnification, as shown in Figure 3-10. Use the Zoom or Hand tool shortcuts to change views.

7. To return to viewing your drawing as a single document, click the close button for any three of the numbered windows. Notice that the last one automatically becomes your original and Illustrator 7 does not prompt you to save changes to additional windows of the same document.

Creating and Saving Views

Illustrator 7 includes a View feature, which enables you to save certain drawing views and positions with your drawing file. This View feature is capable of saving up to 25 specific views. The ability to save views lets you recall zoom level, scroll position, layer options, and Artwork or Preview settings instantly.

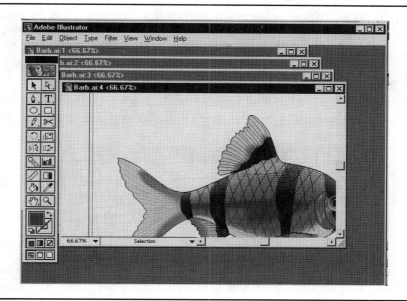

FIGURE 3-9   The Cascade command enables you to stack all open windows neatly

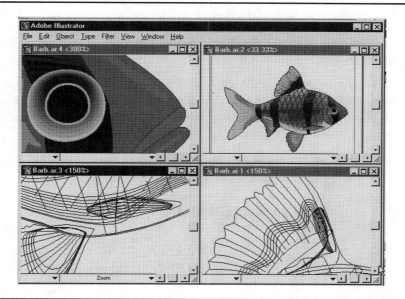

FIGURE 3-10   The Tile command enables you to see all opened windows in a grid

There's a slight trick to using this feature. Before you plunge ahead and create a new view, you must first set up all of its parameters *before* saving it. To save a view setup, follow these steps:

1. With your current document opened and set to a certain position, magnification, and artwork or preview, choose View|New View. A dialog box appears, enabling you to enter a name for your view as shown below.

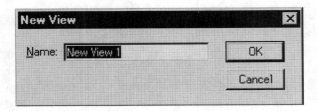

2. Once named, click the OK button to save the view and its name. Notice that the new named view now appears at the bottom of the View menu. If you wish, change the parameters of your drawing view and, each time, create a new named view using the same procedure. Each new view name is saved to the View menu. By default, each new view is named New View 1, New View 2, and so on.

3. To recall one of the views, choose it from the View menu. Notice your drawing view is instantly recalled.

4. To rename or delete a view, choose View|Edit Views. Notice the Edit Views dialog box appears, as shown next. Select a saved view by clicking on its name in the list Edit View and enter a new name in the Name box or click Delete to eliminate it.

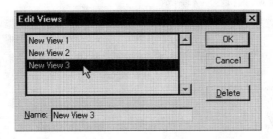

5. Click OK.

Tip   *When each view is created, Illustrator 7 automatically adds shortcut hot keys to each new view and places them at the bottom of the View menu. For example, CTRL/COMMAND+ALT/OPTION+SHIFT+1 is assigned to the first view created, CTRL/COMMAND+ALT/OPTION+SHIFT+2 to the second, and so on.*

Note   *Illustrator 7's View feature does not record screen mode settings which globally apply to program viewing.*

Using Rulers, Grids, and Guides

Working on a computer screen for many new users can be a mystery when it comes to getting a sense of the size of your objects or your artwork dimensions. This is where Illustrator 7's onscreen grid and ruler display options can help. Rulers can be displayed by choosing the View|Show Rulers option (CTRL/COMMAND+R), and while active can provide you with a general indication of object or drawing element size. Rulers appear at the top and left of your document window and change as you navigate your drawing.

Grids can also be used to measure and align objects visually or simply to get an idea of the proportions of objects in relation to each other. To display Illustrator 7's grid feature, choose View|Show Grid (CTRL/COMMAND+"). Grids align with your ruler markings and remain as a fixed reference on your screen. With both Rulers and Grids showing on your screen, visually aligning objects can be accomplished quickly, as shown in Figure 3-11.

Guides are essentially user-defined horizontal and vertical reference or ruler lines. Guides can be positioned anywhere on your screen by dragging them from your onscreen Ruler and may also be repositioned by dragging them from their original position to a new position on your screen. To see your guides, choose View|Show Guides (CTRL/COMMAND+;).

Tip   *While dragging a guide from your Ruler, hold the ALT/OPTION key to toggle the guide between a vertical guide or horizontal guide.*

Guides appear on your screen in Artwork view as dashed green lines (dashed blue when selected) and in Preview view as dashed blue lines. While guides are showing, you delete a guide by clicking once on it and pressing the DELETE key. You may also delete a guide by dragging it back into the Ruler. And you may globally lock or unlock guides so that they cannot be moved by choosing View|Lock Guides or View|Unlock Guides (CTRL/COMMAND+ALT/OPTION+;).

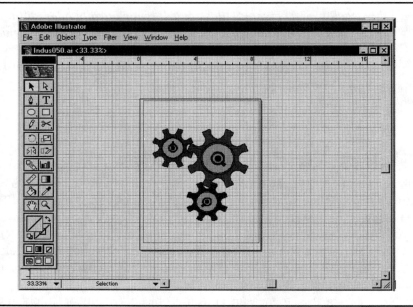

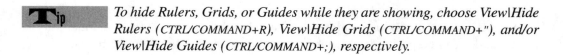

FIGURE 3-11   Illustrator's Rulers and Grids enable you to arrange objects visually with higher accuracy

> **Tip** *To hide Rulers, Grids, or Guides while they are showing, choose View\Hide Rulers (CTRL/COMMAND+R), View\Hide Grids (CTRL/COMMAND+"), and/or View\Hide Guides (CTRL/COMMAND+;), respectively.*

> **Tip** *Onscreen display colors of guides and grids may be set to any color you wish using the File\Preferences\Guides and Grid options (CTRL/COMMAND+K).*

To make it faster to align objects in your drawing, Illustrator 7 features *snap to* options which cause objects dragged close to or near them to be attracted almost magnetically. To cause objects to snap to grid lines in your drawing, choose View\Snap to Grid (CTRL/COMMAND+SHIFT+"). By default, objects snap to guides automatically when dragged within two pixels of a guide.

While guides themselves are limited to vertical or horizontal alignment, objects themselves may also be used as guides in your drawing. Once an object is made into a guide, you can set other objects to snap to the object. To make an object into a guide, select the object and choose View|Make Guides (CTRL/COMMAND+5). An object that has been made into a guide appears on your screen as a dashed green line in Artwork view (blue when selected) and a dashed blue line in Preview, as shown in Figure 3-12.

 As with many of the commands in Illustrator 7, you may also access ruler, guide, and grid options through right mouse button pop-up menus (Windows) or COMMAND+Click (Macintosh).

To transform an object which has been made into a guide back to its original state, select the guide object and choose View|Release Guides (CTRL/ COMMAND+ALT/OPTION+5).

Setting Ruler Units

Different drawing types and various types of illustrators usually require—or prefer—using their own specific measuring increments. Where print-based illustrators use points and picas, engineers and architects often use inches or millimeters. You can set the incremental measure of your ruler markings to suit the way you work or the type of drawing you are creating through the File| Preferences|Units and Undo Levels (CTRL/COMMAND+K) command.

For more information, see the section called "Units and Undo Levels" (later in this chapter.)

Changing Ruler Origin

The origin of your ruler is the point at which vertical and horizontal zero is located. Illustrator 7 enables you to set this point to anywhere on your screen, making it easier to measure distances and objects in your drawing. By default, Illustrator positions the zero point of the ruler at the upper-left corner of your artboard.

To change the zero origin of your ruler, first make sure the Ruler is showing (CTRL/COMMAND+R) and drag from the upper-left corner of your screen where the vertical and horizontal ruler marks intersect to the point on your screen or page where you would like to begin measuring. To reset this point to another position, drag again from where the vertical and horizontal display ruler marks intersect to your new zero origin position.

Guides   Ruler   Grid lines

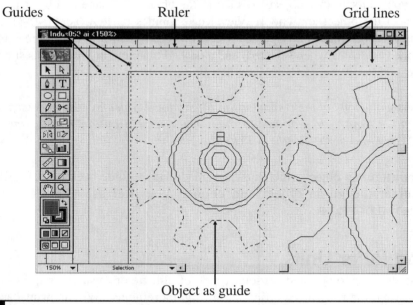

Object as guide

FIGURE 3-12   Making objects into guides enables you to "snap" other objects to them

    To reset the zero origin of your ruler quickly back to its default position at the upper-left corner of your artboard, double-click on the point where the vertical and horizontal markings intersect on the ruler display.

Using the Measuring Tool

Illustrator 7's Measure tool is a nifty little innovation that provides a quick, interactive method of finding the linear dimensions of an object, section, or area of your drawing without having to use rulers or grids. The Measure tool works in combination with the Info palette to measure and display vertical, horizontal, or slope (angle) values.

    Holding the SHIFT key while dragging constrains movement of the Measure tool to either vertical, horizontal, or 45-degree increments of slope when measuring objects or distances.

To measure objects interactively using the Measure tool, follow these steps:

1. With a new or existing drawing open, choose the Measure tool from the main Toolbox palette. Notice the Measure tool cursor by default is a "+" style crosshair cursor.

2. Click the Measure tool cursor at the start point and drag it to the end point of the area or object you wish to measure. Notice that as soon as you click the Measure tool on your page, the Info palette appears.

3. As you drag the Measure tool cursor the distance, the Info palette displays the X, Y, W, H, D, and the slope angle is displayed, as shown in Figure 3-13.

The values indicated by **X** and **Y** show the actual reference points on your page. Values measured by **W** (width) and **H** (height) show the difference between the vertical and horizontal start and end point positions, indicating both dimensions of the space. The **D** (distance) value records the measured distance between the start and end points, and the *slope* value denoted by the angle measure symbol records the angle of the slope created between the start and end points.

After your measurement has taken place, the values remain in view until the next measurement is taken, and the Info Palette remains in view until closed by the user. The Info palette is also capable of being used by a number of tools in Illustrator 7, including the Selection, Pen, Text, Rectangle, Ellipse, Scale, Rotate, Reflect and Shear tools. For more information on using the Info palette with other tools, see "Using the Info Palette," **Chapter 9: Object Transform Tools**.

Setting Preferences

The Preferences settings in Illustrator 7 set overall program functions as well as how certain core features perform. Default settings established by Adobe, which are set when the program is first installed, take into consideration how most illustrators use the tools, based on user input throughout the versions.

You do not need to have any documents opened in order to access Illustrator 7's Preferences command.

Start point   End point

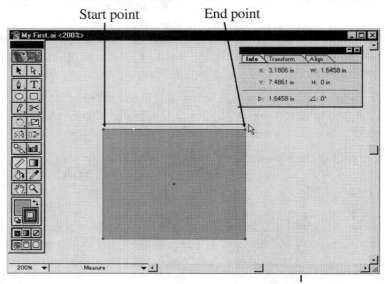

Records measures and distances

FIGURE 3-13   Using the Measure tool to measure objects and distances

In many cases, average users will simply leave the program operating at these established settings and default options. But, if you happen to be a specialist at what you do, you may wish—or need—to optimize these settings to suit your working habits. Preferences have been loosely categorized under General, Keyboard Increments, Units and Undo Levels, Guides and Grid, Hyphenation Options, Plug-ins, and Scratch Disk groupings. Preference settings are stored in a file named AI Prefs located in your system folder (Macintosh), Adobe/Illustrator 7.0 folder (Windows 95), or in the Win32app/Illustrator 7.0 (Windows NT). Each time Illustrator 7 is closed, the changed Preference settings are saved in this file.

To access the preferences settings, choose File|Preferences (CTRL/COMMAND+K) and choose the specific group from the drop-down menu in the Preferences dialog box according to your needs. This section defines what these options do and how to take advantage of their powers.

General

The General category, shown next, features overall tool settings and a hodgepodge of options which set a variety of program behaviors.

Tool Behavior

Under the heading of Tool Behavior you may set the Constrain Angles of all objects created in Illustrator 7. This includes inherently vertically or horizontally created objects such as lines, ellipses, and rectangles. Setting this value to anything but 0 causes all objects to be created at the angle entered here.

- **Corner Radius**   Corner radius determines the curve radius for newly created ellipse and rectangle objects which feature rounded corners. The default setting for a corner radius is 0.17 inches.

- **Curve Fitting Tolerance**   Curve fitting is a function of the Pencil tool when you are drawing lines. The value may be set within a range of 1 to 10. The lower the value, the more detailed and closer the curve fit; and the higher the value, the less detailed and smooth the curve. The curve fitting tolerance default setting is 2 pixels.

- **Autotrace Gap**   This is a function of the Autotrace tool, which enables you to create traced paths based on the contours of shapes in a bitmap image. Bitmap images often contain gaps between pixels which can cause poorly created Autotraced paths. Autotrace Gap may be set to 0, 1, or 2 pixels. Lower settings cause longer and more detailed trace paths, while higher settings create less detailed but faster traces. The autotrace gap default setting is 0 pixels.

Options

- **Snap to Point**   When creating paths, this option enables Illustrator to allow anchor points to join when positioning anchor points within 2 pixels of each other, which can cut the drawing time of closed paths dramatically. By default, this option is selected. If the work you do is highly detailed and you don't wish anchor points to join automatically, deselect this option.

- **Transform Pattern Tiles**   If you wish patterns that you have assigned to fill objects to be transformed along with object transformations, select this option. By default, this option is deselected.

- **Use Precise Cursors**   The precise cursor option enables you to change the appearance of certain cursors to crosshairs instead of their natural icon-based symbols, such as the Pen tool. Precise cursors, however, are excellent for drawing operations such as tracing bitmap images. By default, this option is deselected.

- **Paste Remembers Layers**   When copying objects between drawings using clipboard commands, you may want Illustrator 7 to include the layering information featured in the source document and move it to the destination document. Copying layer information takes longer than regular copy operations and so, by default, this option is selected inactive.

- **Disable Warnings**   This option is for the truly gifted and enables you to bypass Illustrator 7's series of warnings associated with adding or deleting anchor points using the Scissors and Blend tools. By default, this option is deselected.

- **Area Select**   While this option is selected, clicking on an object's fill selects the object. When disabled, objects must be selected by clicking on their outline path. By default, the Area Select option is selected.

- **Scale Line Weight**   Whenever an object is transformed, Illustrator uses this setting to scale the thickness of the object's outline. If selected, this option enables Illustrator to calculate a new thickness for the outline based on the transformation. By default, this option is deselected.

■ **Show Tool Tips**   Tool Tips are those little flags that appear when you hold your cursor over any of Illustrator 7's features and help to identify what they are. It's a great feature for new users but quickly becomes tedious after you're pretty sure you know what you're looking at. By default, this option is selected.

■ **Japanese Crop Marks**   Japanese and North American crop marks are different in appearance. If you're accustomed to using the Japanese style markings, select this feature. By default, this option is deselected.

■ **Use Adobe Illustrator 6.0 Tool Shortcuts (Macintosh only)**   Select this option to enable Illustrator 7.0 to use the same shortcuts available in the version 6.0 release of Illustrator.

 To navigate between preference screens in the Preference dialog box, click the Next and Back buttons.

Keyboard Increments

Keyboard increments have been organized into options and type greeking limits, as shown next.

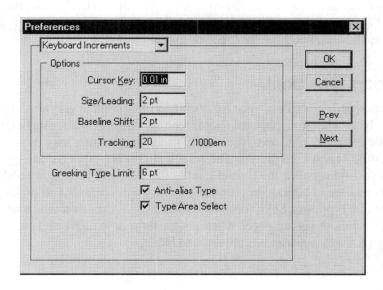

Options

- **Cursor Key**   The Cursor Key option sets the physical distance an object is moved when your keyboard arrow keys are used to "nudge" an object. The default setting is 0.01 inches but may be set within a range of 0 and 18 inches.

- **Size/Leading**   When you use your keyboard shortcut commands to increase or decrease type size or type leading values, this setting is used. It may be set within a range of 0.1 points and 72 points. The default setting is 2 points.

- **Baseline Shift**   When you use your keyboard shortcut commands to increase or decrease baseline shift above or below the baseline of your text, this setting is used. It may be set within a range of 0.1 points and 72 points. The default setting is 2 points.

- **Tracking**   Tracking has the effect of spacing your text either tighter or looser, depending on your particular needs and/or the type style used. Tracking is measured in *em* spaces which is an extremely small amount of space. When you use your keyboard shortcut commands to increase or decrease the tracking of your text, this setting is used. Tracking may be set within a range of -1,000 ems and 10,000 ems. The default setting is 20/1000 ems. An em is a unit of measure representing a width of space equal to the height of the typeface you are using.

Greeking Type Limit

In order to speed screen draw time for documents that contain very small type sizes, type may be *greeked* to display as a simple representative gray line roughly matching the physical size of your text. The Greek Type Limit setting may be set within a range of 1 point and 1,296 points. The default setting is 6 points, meaning any type which is to display below the 6 point limit will appear as a rough gray outline. You may also set type to display on your screen without the default *Anti-aliasing* effect or the default Type Area Select option. Anti-aliasing is the effect which allows type to "blend" without jagged edges when it is rasterized. Rasterizing is an operation whereby vector objects can be converted to bitmaps.

Units and Undo levels

Units and Undo Level settings of the Preferences command enable you to specify how Illustrator displays unit measures for things such as dialog box values for type and measures, including Ruler increments, as shown next.

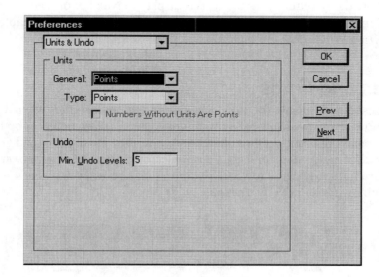

Units

The General Units box sets the measure of rulers and dialog options which measure objects properties other than type sizes. Units may be specified as points, picas, inches, centimeters, or millimeters from the drop-down menu. The Type box sets the indicated measure of any Type (font) objects in Illustrator. While the General units are set to picas, which are measured in formats such as *3P4* (which equates to a measure of 3 picas plus 4 points), unspecified unit values entered into numeric value boxes may be set to points only by selecting the Numbers Without Units Are Points option.

Undo

As you work and use the Undo command, Illustrator 7 is capable of tracking and/or reversing any number of commands up to 200. If your system is limited in resources, however, tracking and storing all these commands can quickly drain resources, and it's possible to run out of memory if the minimum Undo setting is excessive. This may be one reason Adobe has set the default Minimum Undo Levels default setting to only five.

You may also visually monitor the number of Undos and Redos you have used in your drawing by setting your Status Bar display to Number of Undos. For more information on setting Status bar display, see the section earlier in this chapter called "Customizing Windows and Display."

Guides and Grids

Preferences settings enable you to set the colors of guides and grids when displayed using the Preview view as shown below. Similar options are available for both guides and grids, enabling you to set the color and style of lines. Both guides and grids may be set to one of nine preset colors or a custom color, while styles may be set to lines or dots. Gridlines may be set to appear within a range between .01 inches and 13.88 inches with subdivisions between 1 and 1,000.

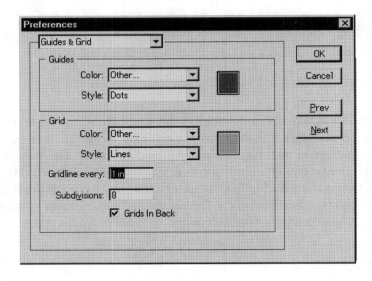

Hyphenation Options

Hyphenation options enable you to specify the language Illustrator 7 uses to hyphenate words in text, as shown in the illustration below. In Illustrator 7, the language you choose to hyphenate text may be based on any of the following languages: U.S. English, U.K. English, French, German, Spanish, Dutch, Italian, Swedish, Norwegian, Finnish, Danish, or Hungarian. Select the language you require from the Default Language drop-down menu.

   If you need to customize you hyphenation dictionary, you may enter new hyphenation examples in the New Entry box and click on the Add button, or delete existing entries using the Delete button.

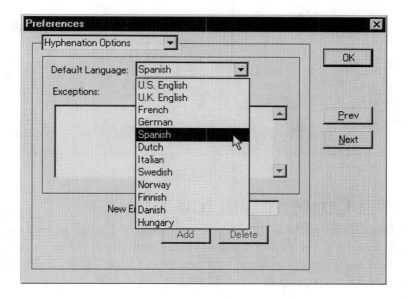

Plug-ins & Scratch Disks

Finally, the long list of Preferences options ends with Plug-ins & Scratch Disks options. Use the Choose button shown next to locate the folder where Plug-ins are stored on your system, and use the Primary and Secondary drop-down menus to set locations for temporary files. Illustrator 7 uses temporary files to store information when working on drawings in which not enough RAM is present to serve its needs. Temporary files can be stored on either the Primary disk or Secondary disk locations

(should the Primary become full). Primary scratch disks, by default, are the disks where the program and system files reside and, ideally, the fastest of the scratch disk drives.

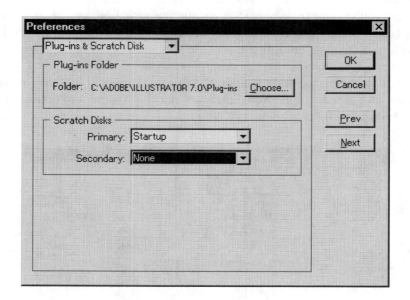

Creating a Custom Startup File

Startup files feature all the information your Illustrator 7 program needs to know when it is launched. The Startup file includes information about how you last left the program, such as custom colors you may have created, zoom levels, window sizes, document and page setup settings, program preferences, viewing preferences, and so on.

The Startup file is located in the Plug-ins folder in the main Adobe Illustrator folder (Macintosh) or the Adobe/Illustrator 7.0/Plug-ins folder (Windows). If you like, you may create a custom Startup file of your own containing your own set of document preferences and so on. A Startup file is actually an Adobe Illustrator 7 drawing file which contains all the associated settings, colors, and custom preferences embedded into it. When Illustrator launches, it is automatically set to search for this exact file in an exact location. Whichever settings are set in the Startup file are the launch settings of the program.

To create a custom Startup file of your own, follow these steps:

1. First, back up your current default Startup file by making a copy and saving it using the same name but in a different location (or vice-versa).

2. Open your existing Startup file and use it as a template on which to build a new Startup file, as shown in Figure 3-14.

3. Customize any existing colors, patterns, or gradients to suit the ones you normally use when you work. To delete any colors, you must delete them from the color and swatch palettes and the Startup document artboard.

4. Save any graph designs that you want available in your documents using the Graph Design dialog box.

5. Select the options you want as default settings using the Page Setup, Document Setup (CTRL/COMMAND+SHIFT+P), and Preferences (CTRL/COMMAND+K) commands.

6. Once you have saved your changes, save (CTRL/COMMAND+S) the new document as Adobe Illustrator Startup (Macintosh) or Startup.ai (Windows) to the Plug-ins folder.

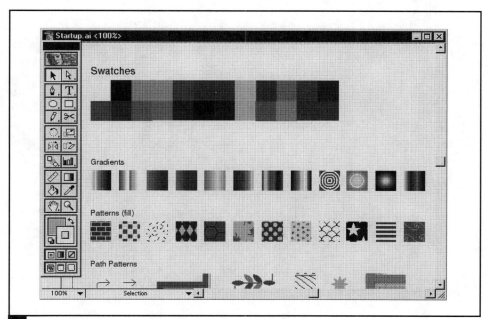

FIGURE 3-14   Creating your own custom Startup file

Conclusion

If any of the chapters in *Fundamental Illustrator 7* are a must-read, this is the one. This chapter has covered roughly intermediate-level topics geared toward forming a solid foundation of knowledge on which you can build better work habits. The features covered in this chapter have been selected as the most valuable in helping you become more productive in your Illustrator 7 drawing techniques and illustration methods. You've also probably discovered that it's much better to begin reaping the benefits of these techniques now rather than waiting a few months or even years before using them.

If you're an experienced user and you've come across some never-before-seen features in this chapter, now is the time to check out the next chapter. **Chapter 4: What's New in Illustrator 7** reveals features that have been implemented since the last version, as well as the concepts behind many of them.

What's New in Illustrator 7?

4

I f you've just completed the previous chapter, "Making Illustrator 7 Easy to Use," you're probably not too interested in what's been revamped in the program, as long as you know how to use the features. However, if you've just arrived here to learn what's changed since you used a previous version of the program, you'll find this chapter a quick read, as it provides you with an overview of what's new and what's been updated.

Regardless of which platform version you use, you'll learn that some of Illustrator 7's changes are cosmetic while others are quite extensive, altering some of the very roots of Illustrator 7's inner workings. You'll also find references to sections in this book where the features are covered in detail—so you don't have to waste valuable drawing time hunting them down.

A Slick New Interface

Illustrator 7's new interface (the stuff you see on your screen) has been beefed up considerably. It now struts a three-dimensional look and employs tabbed palettes, which benefit you in two ways: Tabbed palettes take up much less screen space while still providing access to more features. In many regards, palettes have also replaced commands that have previously been found in Illustrator's program menus, freeing space on the menus for access to lesser-used features and some new functions of the program.

Plus, Illustrator 7's new interface has been engineered to match that of Photoshop, to provide users working in both programs a high degree of familiarity and interface "comfort." Many of the common tools, buttons, and palettes appear similar or identical between the two programs. If you have access to the Adobe Tour and Training CD, you'll find the interface changes discussed in detail. Adobe has prepared a Macromedia Director movie to guide you through Illustrator's new interface parts.

A Helping Hand Online

Users who are upgrading from previous versions of Illustrator on either Macintosh or Windows platforms may notice that online help exists via the Balloon Help menu

(Macintosh) or the Help menu (Windows). Full retail and competitive upgrade versions of Illustrator 7 also ship with a Print Publishing Guide, which details technical issues surrounding working with Illustrator in the prepress and offset printing industries.

Note   *Much of the information covered in the guide is detailed in real terms in* Fundamental Illustrator 7.

Tool Tips

The new Tool Tips feature in Illustrator 7 can be compared to using training wheels when learning to ride a bike, only without the embarrassing connotations. If you're new to Illustrator, Tool Tips provide an invaluable service in identifying all visible tool, palette, and status bar features while you work in the program—without making you leave your screen or access a Help menu.

To display a Tool Tip, position your cursor over a feature and watch for an identifying "flag" to automatically appear. If none appears within a second or two, the feature may be deactivated. To reactivate it, choose File|Preferences (CTRL/COMMAND+K), select the General preferences group, click the Show Tool Tips option as shown here, and click OK to exit the dialog box.

For more information on using help features in Illustrator 7, see the section called "Getting Help" in **Chapter 1: Getting Started**.

Context-Sensitive Help for the Mac

With the Macintosh version, you may also access Illustrator 7's online help features directly onscreen using context-sensitive features. Context-sensitive help means you are able to get more information about any screen feature, tool, or palette by holding the COMMAND key and clicking on a program feature.

Extended Color, Web, and Printing Support

Developments in the color reproduction industry have made it possible to achieve more accurate color when printing and creating images for the Web. Illustrator 7 now features extended support for RGB (red, green, blue) color models (these are common when producing color images in Web pages, interface design, and multimedia productions), color management, and printing color separations with the following new and revamped features.

Color Management

Illustrator 7 now supports the international color profiles set by the International Color Consortium (ICC) in an effort to achieve color matching from monitor and scanning hardware through to printed reproduction. While Macintosh users have long enjoyed the accuracy of the ColorSync system built into the Apple system software, Windows users now enjoy the equivalent with Kodak's PC version. With the ICC engine built into Adobe Illustrator 7 software (and also Photoshop 4.0), users may now accurately convert between RGB and CMYK (process colors cyan, magenta, yellow, and black) through CIELAB color conversions. Process color is now accurately displayed using this system in an effort to have Illustrator show (as closely as hardware allows) what the printed image will look like.

Users may also convert accurately between spot and process colors when performing color separations for print. Gradient and pattern colors are also displayed accurately using this same method. For more information on using Illustrator 7's color management features, see the section called "Illustrator 7's Color Management System" in **Chapter 11: Working in Color**.

Link Objects to the Web

Objects in your drawing may now be assigned individual URLs, (uniform resource locators) enabling users to link drawing objects directly to the World Wide Web. (Some users believe that this feature alone brings Illustrator 7 into mainstream Web usefulness.) Giving users the ability to assign URLs to objects opens the doors for creating image maps (commonly used for designing interactive objects), interface buttons, or clickable information graphics in Web page design. Drawings may be exported to Web image formats and set to retain their linking information.

Objects may also be selected to launch your Internet Web browser directly from within Illustrator 7. This feature is managed through use of the Attributes palette. For more information on using Illustrator 7's Web linking features, see "Preparing Images for the Web" in **Chapter 18: Illustrator 7 and the Web**.

Raster Image-Linking Support

In cases where users are working with large bitmap or EPS graphic images, Illustrator 7 now supports raster image linking. Image linking enables you to create a link to externally stored image files in an effort to incorporate the images into your Illustrator 7 drawings without having to store the image's data in the drawing. The ability to link images to your Illustrator 7 drawing is especially useful when creating drawings for offset printing.

When importing files into your Illustrator 7 drawing through the Place command, the Place dialog box offers an option to create the link to the external file. By default, this link feature is active, meaning that all imported images are automatically linked unless the Link option is deselected. The next illustration shows the Link option selected.

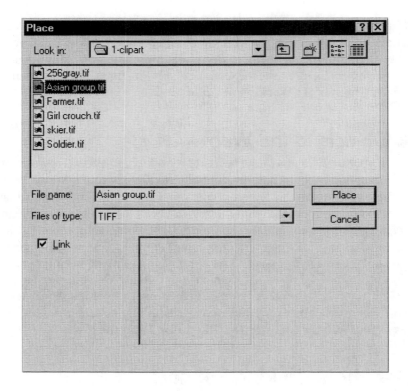

For more information on using Illustrator 7's image linking features, see the "Linking Large Images" section in **Chapter 15: Getting the Most out of Illustrator 7**. For information on working with imported bitmap images see the "Linking Bitmaps" section in **Chapter 14: Working with Bitmap Tools**.

Printing Color Separations

Illustrator 7 includes the color separation capabilities previously available in Adobe Separator. Illustrator's print engine now includes all the necessary tools for producing film separations from spot, RGB, or process color illustrations, as well as the ability to automatically trap objects using the Pathfinder Trap filter.

For information on using the print engine, see **Chapter 17: Printing from Illustrator 7** or for information on using the Trap filter, see the "Working with Pathfinder Filters" section in **Chapter 9: Object Transform Tools**.

New and Updated Tools

What would the new release of a drawing program be without a few time-saving new tools? Illustrator 7 now includes enhanced type tools, as well as new Reshape, Ellipse, Rectangle, and Graph tools, comprising 11 new tools in total.

The Reshape Tool

The Reshape tool enables users to alter the shape of objects based on the relative position of selected anchor points. Anchor points may be positioned and reshaped globally instead of requiring that you reposition each anchor point individually. For information on using the new Reshape Tool, see the "Editing Paths with the Reshape Tool" section in **Chapter 7: Creating and Editing Drawing Objects**.

Type Tools

Three new type tools in Illustrator 7 include support for Asian character sets comprised of Japanese, Chinese, and Korean language characters. New type tools are comprised of the Vertical, Vertical Area, and Vertical Path tools. Vertical type may have the same type properties, font style, alignment, color, and so on as other type tools while flowing text from top to bottom and left to right, conforming to Asian publishing standards.

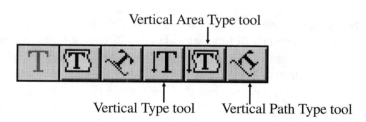

Vertical Area Type tool

Vertical Type tool   Vertical Path Type tool

The Ellipse and Rectangle Tools

The Ellipse and Rectangle tool sets include four new tools, which are essentially hybrids of the regular tools. These hybrids—Centered Rectangle, Rounded Rectangle, Rounded-Centered Rectangle and Centered Ellipse—can also be selected using tool-and-keyboard combinations of the regular tools.

Graphing Tools

Three new graphing tools in Illustrator 7 combine the ability to create data sets and apply them graphically to variations of line, column, bar, area, pie, scatter, or radar style charts as shown here:

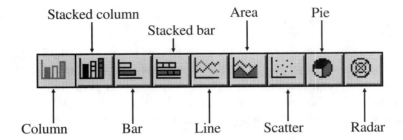

New and Improved Palettes

New and updated tool palettes include the main Toolbox palette, plus the Character, Layers, Align, Transform, Stroke, Color, Gradient, Swatches, and MM Design palettes, many of which have been designed specifically to work with each other. Palettes also may be grouped, ungrouped, attached, or detached from each other according to your working preferences. The following is a brief summary of palette changes in Illustrator 7, including references to further information within this book:

- **Toolbox palette** The main Toolbox palette holds all the interactive-type tools available in Illustrator. The Toolbox now includes improved Fill and Stroke controls for selecting and changing fill and stroke attributes. Three new shortcut buttons have been added: the Color, Gradient, and None buttons. The palette has also been revamped to include ten additional tools as well as re-engineered to work with assigned hot keys for specific tool sets. Tools may now be selected by pressing a single keystroke. For information on using these hot keys, see the "Toolbox Hot Keys" section in **Appendix B: Summary of Keyboard Shortcuts**.

- **Character palette** The Character palette has been expanded to support Korean, Chinese, and Japanese language fonts, as well as to offer Japanese text-layout rules, rotated text, and proportional fonts for some double-byte fonts. For information on working with this palette, see "Using the Character Palette" in **Chapter 5: Working with Type**.

■ **Layers palette** Updated for Illustrator 7, the Layers palette enables users to organize and manage the layering, appearance, printing, and layer-locking features of drawing objects. It now includes buttons for creating and deleting layers. For information on using the Layers palette, see the "Working in Layers" section in **Chapter 8: Selecting and Arranging Objects**.

■ **Align palette** The Align palette enables users to line up drawing objects based on the shape of their bounding boxes. Options include vertical alignments to the left, center, or right edges of objects and horizontal alignments to top, center, or bottom alignments of objects. For information on using the Layers palette, see the "Aligning Objects" section in **Chapter 8: Selecting and Arranging Objects**.

■ **Transform palette** The Transform palette, formerly called the Control palette, has gone through a transformation of its own. Transform displays information about selected objects including width, depth, slope, angle, and page position based on nine object reference points. It enables you to apply transformations to objects by entering new values for these properties. For information on working with the Transform palette, see the section called "The Transform Palette" in **Chapter 9: Object Transform Tools**.

■ **Stroke palette** The new Stroke palette enables you to assign thickness, miter, and end-point behavior, and to customize dashed-line patterns. Strokes may feature a maximum thickness of 1,000 points. For more information on working with the new Stroke palette, see the "Using the Stroke Palette" section in **Chapter 10: Setting Fills and Strokes**.

■ **Color, Gradient, and Swatches palettes** The new Color palette features an interface innovation in selecting colors called the Color Spectrum Ramp. It features a color spectrum pick tool directly on the palette itself. An updated Gradient palette works in combination with the Color palette to create custom linear or radial fills. And the new Swatches palettes provides access to all color libraries and enables you to manage and create your own. For more information on working with the Color, Gradient, and Swatches palettes, see **Chapter 10: Setting Fills and Strokes**, and **Chapter 11: Working in Color**.

- **MM Design palette**   A new MM Design palette enables you to edit multiple master fonts for your drawing. For information on working with the new MM Design palette, see the "Working with MM Design" section in **Chapter 6: Type Options and Effects**.

General Program Changes

The remaining improvements and changes to Illustrator 7 come in the form of a potpourri of features. Although some of these changes are new to the Windows version, they have previously been implemented on recent Macintosh versions of Illustrator (such as version 6.0). The following brief overview summarizes these changes and lists references to help you further explore their capabilities:

- **Pathfinder filters**   Pathfinder commands enable users to create new objects based on the shape and arrangement of existing object through use of specialized filters. The Pathfinder capabilities are very powerful, allowing you to perform object creation through combining, overlapping, and excluding object shapes with ten new filters: Unite, Intersect, Exclude, Minus Front, Minus Back, Divide, Outline, Trim, Merge, and Crop. You may also create new objects using Hard, Soft, and Trap filters. For more about working with the Pathfinder filters, see the "Working with Pathfinder" section in **Chapter 9: Object Transform Tools**.

- **Multiple levels of Undo**   Illustrator 7 is capable of undoing recent commands. This ability is limited only by the memory restrictions of the system you are working on.

- **Photoshop and vector filters**   With the introduction of color, bitmap conversion, and rasterize commands, Illustrator 7 now features an enormous number of Photoshop filters to help you work with bitmap-based objects. Illustrator 7's filters let you apply effects to both vector and bitmap objects. For more information about working with these filters, see **Chapter 12: Mastering Filter Effects**.

- **Editable EPS files**   Illustrator 7 fully supports editing imported or opened PostScript level 1 EPS (encapsulated PostScript) files, regardless of which program was used to create them.

- **Adobe PDF support**   Illustrator 7 is capable of opening, editing, and saving to Adobe's portable document format (PDF), opening the doors for use of this increasingly popular format in applications such as the World Wide Web. For background information on capitalizing on use of PDF with the World Wide Web, see the "Preparing PDF Files" section in **Chapter 18: Illustrator 7 and the WWW**.

- **Drag-and-drop functionality**   To a certain extent, Illustrator 7 supports drag-and-drop operations between other Adobe products such as Photoshop, PageMill, PageMaker, Dimensions, and Streamline.

Conclusion

If you've just upgraded to Illustrator 7 from a previous version on Macintosh or Windows platforms, you may be overwhelmed by the changes to Illustrator, depending on the last version you used. This chapter's brief overview of the new and improved features in Illustrator 7 helps you to quickly familiarize yourself with new program features—and tells you where to go for more detailed information.

PART
II

Working with Illustrator 7's Tools

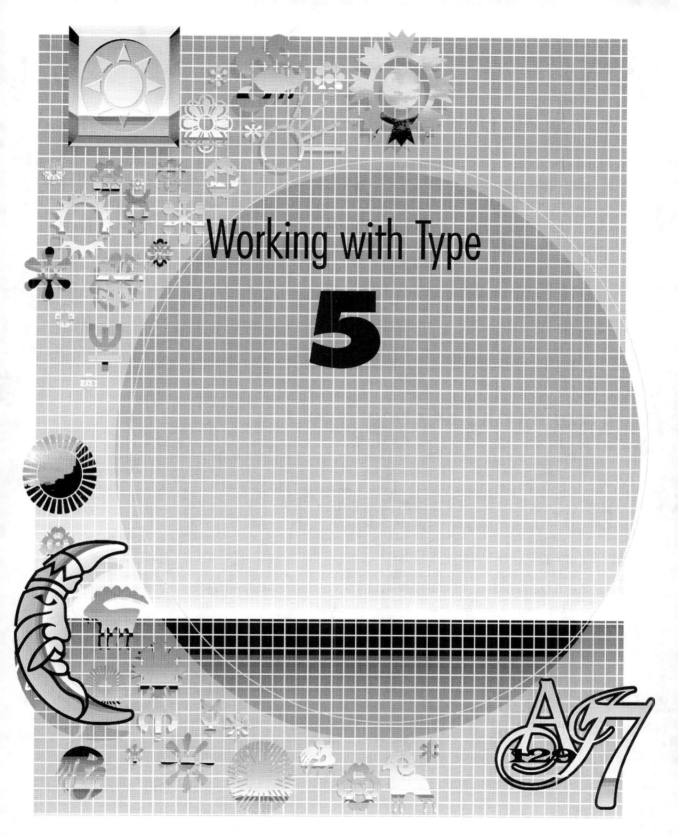

Working with Type

5

Y ou're probably used to thinking of type in terms of concepts such as characters, words, and paragraphs. To understand how to use type effectively in Adobe Illustrator, it helps to add the additional concept of the type object. A type object is simply an object a point, path, or shape containing text. Like other objects in Illustrator, type objects can be skewed, resized, and otherwise manipulated with the program's drawing tools. In addition, the text within type objects can be formatted with powerful typographic tools like the ones you're used to finding in page layout and word processing programs.

In this chapter you'll learn to create type objects, enter and edit text, and format type. You'll also learn how to apply a couple of Illustrator's "special effects" to your type.

Creating and Entering Type

Type objects are created with the Type tool, which is selected when you click on the T button in the main Toolbox or when you type **T** on your keyboard. As with most of Illustrator's tools, the Type tool has several variations, shown in Figure 5-1. View these by clicking and holding on the Type button. The first half of this chapter will emphasize Illustrator's basic Type tool which, as you'll see later, combines almost all the functionality of the other Type tools.

With the Type tool selected, you'll notice the cursor changes to something resembling an I-beam in a dashed rectangle when it is moved over the artboard. This indicates you are ready to create a type object. As you explore type in Illustrator you will notice several other variations of the type cursor, as shown in Figure 5-2. These other shapes are necessary because the Type tool performs different functions depending upon the object on which it is acting. The cursor changes to inform the user what functionality is available.

The simplest way to enter type into an Illustrator document is to create type on a point, as shown in Figure 5-3, by clicking the Type tool on the artboard. This creates a flashing insertion point at the location of the click. Whenever an insertion point is present in a document, any text you enter will appear at that point. In addition to typing, you can also enter type by pasting (Edit|Paste or CTRL/COMMAND+V) text or by placing (File|Place) a text file at an insertion point.

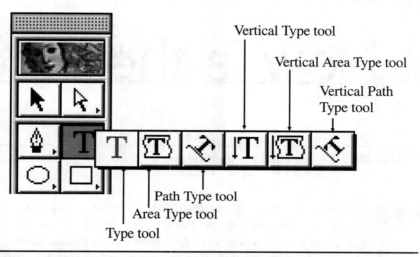

5

FIGURE 5-1   The main Toolbox showing the variations of the Type tool

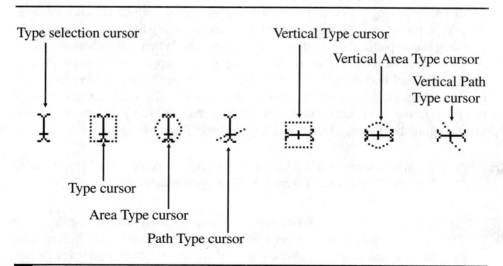

FIGURE 5-2   Variations of the type cursor

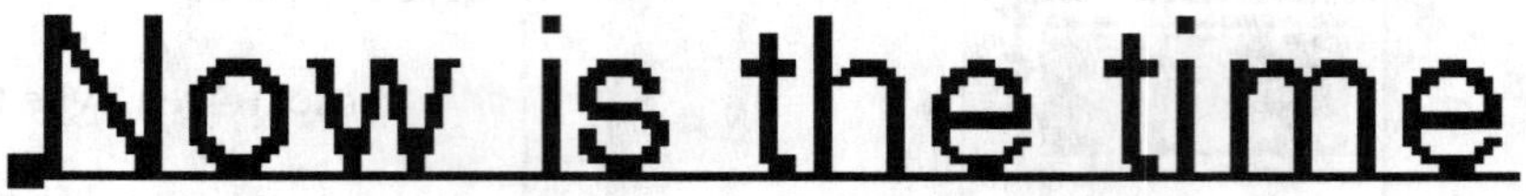

Now is the time

FIGURE 5-3   The flashing insertion point

    *To place a text file, choose File\Place while an insertion point is active. Locate your file and press the Place button. Illustrator allows you to place ASCII text, Rich Text Format (RTF), Microsoft Word, and Word Perfect files. Placed files retain most of their character and paragraph formatting. For additional information on placing text files see the section on "Type From Other Sources" in **Chapter 6: Type Options and Effects**.*

If your text consists of more than a few words, it is useful to enter it into a box rather than allowing it to scroll off your page. A *text box*, which is really a simple Area Type object, can be created by clicking and dragging the basic Type tool. As you drag the Type tool, the outline of a box appears. When you're happy with its dimensions, release the mouse. An insertion point will appear at the top of the box and as you enter text it will wrap to fill the box. Notice that if you have more text than the box can hold, a small "+" appears in the lower-right-hand corner to indicate that some of the text is not being displayed. You can solve this problem by clicking and dragging the bottom of the box with the Direct Selection tool.

    *To learn more about modifying the shape of type containers, see "Transforming Type and Containers," **Chapter 6: Type Options and Effects**.*

    You cannot create a new Type object while the cursor is in the text editing mode (in other words, if an insertion point is flashing or text is selected). To deactivate the insertion point or selection, hold down the CTRL/COMMAND key (which temporarily changes the cursor to the Selection tool) and click in an empty area of the artboard. When you release the command key, the cursor will return to the basic Type tool and you are ready to create a newType object.

Selecting and Editing Type

If you're familiar with a word processing or page layout program, you'll find selecting and editing type in Illustrator a familiar process.

Selecting Type for Editing

With the Type tool selected the cursor changes to a simple I-beam (the type selection cursor) whenever it passes over an existing type object. This indicates that the text tool is in editing mode. In editing mode you can make selections of text within type objects in a number of ways, as shown in Table 5-1.

Modifying Selections

After you have made a text selection, you may modify it in the ways shown in Table 5-2.

Editing Type

Once type is selected it may be edited using the familiar Cut (CTRL/COMMAND+X) and Copy (CTRL/COMMAND+C) commands in the Edit menu. The selection can also

Action	Result
Single-click	Places insertion point at location of click
Single-click and drag	Selects multiple characters
Double-click	Selects a single word
Double-click and drag	Selects multiple words
Triple-click	Selects a single paragraph
Triple-click and drag	Selects multiple paragraphs
Edit, Select All (CTRL/COMMAND+A)	Selects all text within a text object with an active insertion point

TABLE 5-1   Different Ways of Selecting Text Within Type Objects

be replaced by typing in new text or pasting (Edit|Paste or CTRL/COMMAND+V) in text from the clipboard. If you simply wish to delete the selected text, select Edit|Clear or hit the BACKSPACE/DELETE key.

Action	Result
SHIFT+LEFT or RIGHT ARROW	Moves end of selection left or right by one character
CTRL/COMMAND+SHIFT+LEFT or RIGHT ARROW	Moves end of selection left or right by one word
SHIFT+UP or DOWN ARROW	Moves end of selection left or right by one line
CTRL/COMMAND+SHIFT+UP or DOWN ARROW	Moves end of selection left or right by one paragraph
SHIFT Click	Moves end of selection left or right to point of the click
LEFT or RIGHT ARROW	Moves cursor one character left or right, previously selected text is deselected
CTRL/COMMAND+LEFT or RIGHT ARROW	Moves cursor left or right one word, previously selected text is deselected
UP or DOWN ARROW	Moves cursor up or down one line, previously selected text is deselected
CTRL/COMMAND+UP or DOWN ARROW	Moves cursor up or down one paragraph, previously selected text is deselected
Click	Moves cursor to point of the click, previously selected text is deselected

TABLE 5-2   Ways of Modifying Selections

Selecting Type Objects

It is also possible to select Type objects by clicking directly on the type with any one of the selection tools. This selects both the type and its container. The type and container may then be cut, copied, or deleted as well as modified (moved, resized, skewed, etc.) using Illustrator 7's transformation tools and commands.

Painting Type

You can paint selected type by applying a stroke and/or fill just as you would paint any other object in Illustrator 7.

However, there is one case where the stroke and fill are applied in a manner that may be unexpected. When an entire Type object type and its associated path or container is selected and a stroke or fill is applied, only the type and not the path or container is painted. This allows you to select a type object or multiple type objects and paint all the associated type at once rather than being forced to select each bit of type individually with the type tool.

Note   *Painting objects is discussed in detail in **Chapter 10: Setting Fills and Strokes**. The subject is introduced here because of the special considerations involved in working with color in type.*

Character Attributes

Character attributes are changes to the type, including font and size, that can be applied to one or more type character. Character attributes may be applied to sections of type within a text object or to all the type within one or more selected text objects. In addition, you can set character attributes with no type selected and the attributes apply to any new type entered.

Figure 5-4 will help you familiarize yourself with the character attributes that can be set within Adobe Illustrator.

Now take a look at Figure 5-5 which shows the Character palette (Type|Character or CTRL/COMMAND+T) where the attributes of your type can be set. The small symbols to the left of the text entry boxes are designed to help you understand what each of these Illustrator options do. If you hold your mouse over one of the symbols, its pop-up help text will appear with the name of the tool.

Setting Character Attributes

To the right of each attribute in the Character palette is a pop-up menu that allows you to select from a range of settings for each attribute. To the left of each attribute (except Font) are UP and DOWN ARROWS that allow you to adjust these settings in small increments. The amount of the increment is set in the Keyboard Increments Preferences dialog box (File|Preferences|Keyboard Increments) as described in "Setting Preferences," **Chapter 3: Making Illustrator 7 Easy to Use**. You can adjust the settings by larger increments by holding down the SHIFT key while clicking on one of the arrows.

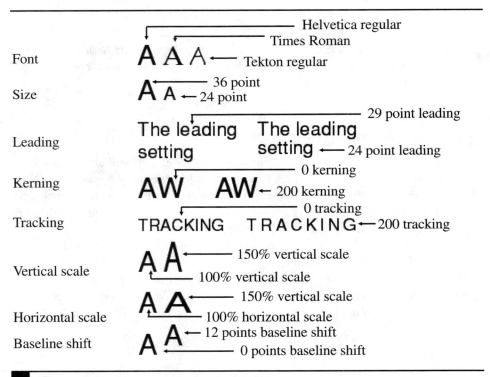

FIGURE 5-4   Character attributes

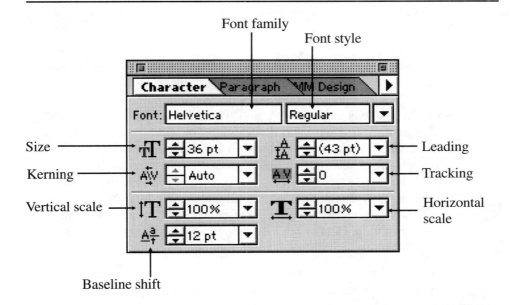

Font family

Font style

Size

Kerning

Vertical scale

Baseline shift

Leading

Tracking

Horizontal scale

FIGURE 5-5   The Character palette can be accessed through the TypeICharacter (CTRL/COMMAND+T) command

It is also possible to type your desired character attribute settings directly into the text box associated with that attribute. When any text box is highlighted, you may jump to the next by pressing the TAB key.

Now let's take a look at each attribute individually.

■ **Font family and style**   The font attribute includes both the font family (such as Helvetica) and the font style (such as bold or italic). You can select a font from the pop-up menu in the Character palette or by typing your choice directly into the Font text boxes at the top of the Character palette. The text box on the left is for the font family, the one on the right is for font style. As you type in the font family text box, Illustrator will attempt to guess your choice from the available fonts. When the name of the desired font family appears, use the TAB key to navigate to the style text box and enter your choice for font style.

Note *Illustrator will not let you type the name of a font that is not available in your system.*

It is also possible to set the font from the submenu that appears when you select the Font command from the Type menu, as shown in Figure 5-6.

- **Size** Type size is measured in points which, in PostScript, are equal to 1/72 of an inch. But don't choose 72-point type and expect all your letters to be one inch tall. Type size is the total vertical space allowed for all the characters in a type family including ascenders (the up stroke on letters such as b and d), descenders (the down stroke of letters such as g and j) (see Figure 5-7) and, optionally, a small amount of space above and below the characters. Therefore, the visual size of type from different font families can vary widely even though they are the same point size, as Figure 5-7 shows.

You can select type size in a variety of ways, from within the Character palette using the options described above, from the submenu of the Type|Size command, or using the keyboard shortcuts as follows:

To reduce the size of selected type press CTRL/COMMAND+SHIFT+< or press CTRL/COMMAND+SHIFT+> to increase its size.

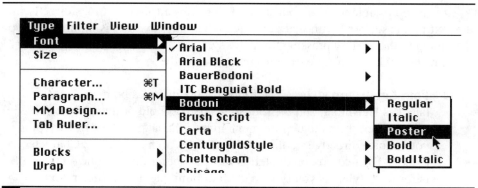

FIGURE 5-6 Setting the font from the Type menu

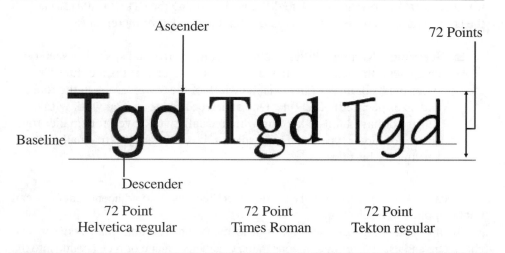

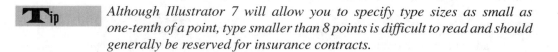

FIGURE 5-7   The visual size of different typefaces displayed can vary even when all are the same point size

Although Illustrator 7 will allow you to specify type sizes as small as one-tenth of a point, type smaller than 8 points is difficult to read and should generally be reserved for insurance contracts.

■ **Leading**   Leading is the distance in points between the baseline of one line of type and the baseline of the line above it, as shown in Figure 5-4. Although leading can be set for individual characters, the leading for an entire line of type will be determined by the largest amount of leading specified for any character within that line.

There are several ways to set leading. If you have not previously set the leading manually, Illustrator will set it for you automatically based upon the font size. In this case, the numeric value in the leading text box in the Character palette will be displayed in parentheses.

To specify a value for leading other than the automatic one, adjust the number in the Leading text box in the Character palette using the standard options. Alternatively, use ALT/OPTION+DOWN ARROW to increase the leading of selected

text and ALT/OPTION+UP ARROW to decrease it. Adding the CTRL/COMMAND key to the combination increases and decreases leading by a larger increment.

- **Kerning**   Kerning allows you to adjust the horizontal space between two characters. In Illustrator 7 the amount of the adjustment is measured in thousandths of an em (an *em* is the width of the lowercase *m* in the font and size specified). The Type One and TrueType fonts you work with in Illustrator have built-in kerning which usually works well for smaller font sizes. For larger type, such as headlines, it is necessary to manually adjust kerning for best results.

Because kerning applies only to the space between two adjacent letters, it can not be applied to a selection.

To apply kerning, use the Type tool to create an insertion point between two characters and use the kerning options in the Character palette or type a value into the Kerning text box in the Character palette. Positive kerning inserts additional space between characters, negative kerning reduces the space between characters. You can also use the ALT/OPTION+LEFT or RIGHT ARROW shortcut respectively to decrease or increase the kerning between two characters. To decrease/increase kerning by a larger amount use CTRL/COMMAND+ALT/OPTION+LEFT or RIGHT ARROW.

- **Tracking**   Tracking is similar to kerning, except that it allows you to adjust the horizontal space between many characters at once. When you modify the tracking of a text selection, an equal amount of space is added or subtracted between each pair of characters in the selection. The amount of the adjustment is measured in thousandths of an em.

To apply tracking, use the Type tool to select multiple characters and use the tracking options in the Character palette or type a value into the Tracking text box in the Character palette. Positive tracking inserts additional space between selected characters, negative tracking reduces the space between the selected characters. You can also use the ALT/OPTION+LEFT or RIGHT ARROW shortcut respectively to decrease or increase tracking among selected characters. To decrease/increase tracking by a larger amount use CTRL/COMMAND+ALT/OPTION+LEFT or RIGHT ARROW.

Setting Optional Character Attributes

The Show Options command in the pop-up menu at the upper-right corner of the Character palette allows you to alternately display and hide options for scaling type horizontally and vertically and shifting it above or below the baseline. Because these attributes are reset less frequently than other character attributes, their options are generally hidden to save space.

■ **Vertical and horizontal scale**   Vertical and horizontal scaling increases or decreases the height and width of selected type. These values can only be set in the Character palette, although use of the Scale tool (see "Moving, Scaling, and Rotating Objects," **Chapter 9: Object Transform Tools**) on a text object may change the value of the horizontal scale.

Tip   *The sound you hear when you scale type is the type's designer screaming. She spent months slaving to balance the proportions of her font and with one click of the mouse you're changing them. If you find yourself scaling type by more than 10 to 15 percent, you'll have more aesthetically pleasing results by choosing a typeface originally designed to those proportions. You'll also be making a contribution to the mental health of type designers everywhere.*

■ **Baseline shift**   The baseline shift setting, which moves selected type above or below the baseline, is useful in creating fractions, footnotes, and other special effects. It can be set in the Character palette or with the SHIFT+ALT/OPTION+UP or DOWN ARROW shortcut. To increase or decrease the baseline shift by a larger amount use the CTRL/COMMAND+SHIFT+ALT/ OPTION+UP or DOWN ARROW combination.

Tip   *You can apply all of the character attributes (except kerning) to selected Type objects even while other non-Type objects are selected. The type attributes will have no effect on the non-Type objects.*

Setting Paragraph Attributes

Paragraph attributes apply to entire paragraphs rather than individual characters. When you set a paragraph attribute it applies to any paragraph that is at least partially selected or has an active insertion point within it.

Paragraph attributes can be set from the Paragraph palette, shown in Figure 5-8 or, in some cases, through keyboard shortcuts. The Paragraph palette can be accessed through the Type|Paragraph command (CTRL/COMMAND+M).

- **Alignment** The five buttons at the top of the Paragraph palette represent the five text alignments available in Illustrator. The lines are representative of how your type will align when each option is selected. If you are unsure of what each button does, hold your cursor over the button and help text will appear. The keyboard shortcut to Align Left is CTRL/COMMAND+SHIFT+L; for Align Center, it's CTRL/COMMAND+SHIFT+C; for Align Right, it's CTRL/COMMAND+SHIFT+R; for Justify Full Lines, it's CTRL/COMMAND+SHIFT+J; and for Justify All Lines, it's CTRL/COMMAND+SHIFT+F.

Note   *Justify and Justify All Lines are only applicable to area type (see "Working with Area Type" later in this chapter.)*

- **Left and right indentation** These settings option the amount of offset from the left and right side of a text container. As with other character attribute settings, values may be entered directly into the corresponding text boxes or the existing values may be adjusted with the UP and DOWN ARROWS to the left of the text box. It is possible to make area type extend beyond the border of its container by entering a negative value for the indentation setting.

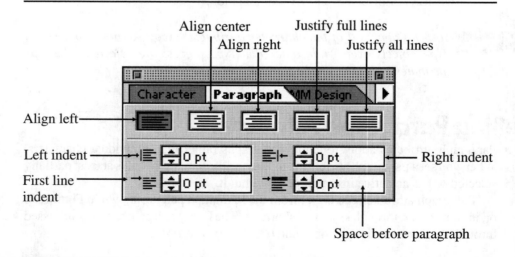

FIGURE 5-8   The Paragraph palette

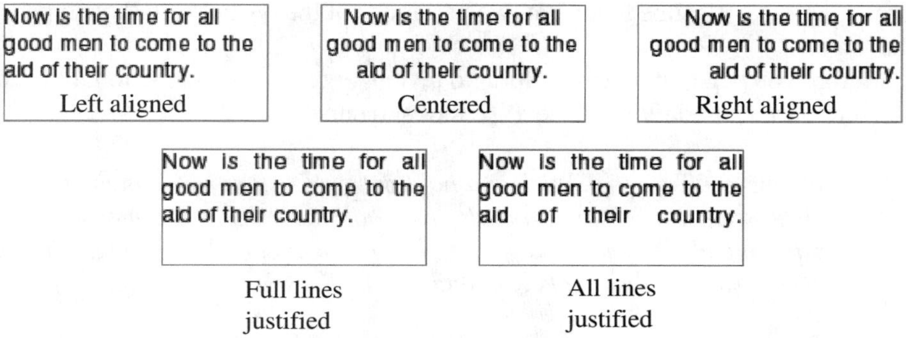

Now is the time for all
good men to come to the
aid of their country.

Left aligned

Now is the time for all
good men to come to the
aid of their country.

Centered

Now is the time for all
good men to come to the
aid of their country.

Right aligned

Now is the time for all
good men to come to the
aid of their country.

Full lines
justified

Now is the time for all
good men to come to the
aid of their country.

All lines
justified

FIGURE 5-9   Text formatted with Align Left, Align Center, Align Right,
Justify Full Lines, and Justify All Lines

■ **First line left indent**   This setting controls by how much space the
opening line of a paragraph is offset. A positive value offsets the left
margin of the first line to the right. A negative value will offset the left
margin of the first line to the left (beyond the margin).

Tip   *To leave the first line of a paragraph flush left and indent the succeeding
lines, set the left indent to a positive number and the first line indent to the
negative value of the same number.*

Note   *Indentation settings apply only to area type (see "Working with Area Type"
later in this chapter.)*

■ **Space before paragraph**   This attribute adds additional space beyond
the existing leading before the selected paragraph(s). It can be set by
entering a value directly in the text box or adjusted using the arrows to the
left of the text box.

Hybrids of the Type Tool

Now that you have a basic understanding of creating, selecting, editing, and formatting type, it's time to look at two variations of the type object: Area type and Path type.

Before you begin, it may be helpful to review Figures 5-1 and 5-2 to familiarize yourself with the variations of the Type tool and cursor.

 *To select a Type tool, click and hold the type button in the main Toolbox. Then drag the cursor to the desired tool and release the mouse button. Alternatively, type the **T** key to select the type tool and then toggle through the alternative Type tools with additional clicks of the T key.*

Working with Area Type

Area type is simply type in a container. The container can be a closed path such as a rectangle, oval, or more complex shape or an open path (for a discussion of open and closed paths see "Working with the Pen Tool," **Chapter 7: Creating and Editing Drawing Objects**). When text is pasted or placed into an area type object, it wraps to fill the container, as shown in Figure 5-10.

Now is the time for all good men to come to the aid of their country.

Now is the time for all good men to come to the aid of their country.

Now is the time for all good men to come to the aid of their country.

FIGURE 5-10   Examples of Area type

The simplest way to create an Area Type object is by clicking and dragging the basic Type tool as described earlier in this chapter. In addition, two methods exist for converting existing objects into area type objects:

■ Select the basic or Area Type tool and move the cursor over the outline of an existing closed path. The Area Type cursor should now be active. Click on the path to convert it into an Area Type object. An active insertion point will appear at the top of the object.

■ Select the area Type tool and click on an open path to convert it into an Area Type object.

 When a drawing object is converted to an area type object, the new object is unfilled and unstroked and therefore will not be visible in Preview mode.

Working with Path Type

Path type is, logically enough, type that follows the contours of a path. Path type is created by converting an existing path to a path type object as follows:

1. Select the basic or Path Type tool and move the cursor over an existing open path. The Path Type cursor should now be active. Click on the path to convert it into a Path Type object. An active insertion point will appear at the point of the click.

2. Select the Path Type tool and click on a closed path to convert it into an Path Type container.

 When you click on a path to create a Path Type object, the path will no longer be visible in the Preview mode. The point of the click becomes the reference point for aligning type (right, left, or centered) along the path. **Chapter 6: Type Options and Effects** *will discuss working with type along a path in more detail.*

Tip *On Macintosh computers, to access the Path Type tool while the Area Type tool is selected or vice versa hold down the OPTION key.*

Working with Vertical Type

With vertical type, each character entered appears below the previous one rather than to its right side. In the case of Path type, this results in characters with their axes parallel to the path rather than perpendicular to it. Figure 5-11 shows examples of vertical type on a point, Vertical Area type, and Vertical Path type. Notice also that new paragraphs appear to the left of the preceding paragraph.

 Paragraph alignment for vertical type occurs along the vertical rather than the horizontal axis. In other words, left-aligned type aligns with the top of its container and right-aligned type with the bottom.

The method used to create Vertical Type objects exactly parallels the method described previously for creating regular or "Horizontal" Type objects with the exception that the vertical variations of the Type tool are used.

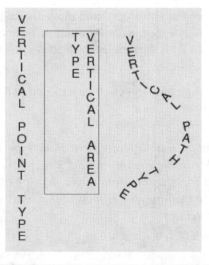

FIGURE 5-11   Examples of Vertical type

It is possible to access the vertical equivalent of the selected Type tool by holding down the SHIFT key. For example, with the basic Type tool selected, move the cursor over an empty area of the artboard and hold down the SHIFT key. Notice that the cursor changes to indicate the vertical Type tool is active. Click while holding the SHIFT key to create vertical type on a point or release the SHIFT key to returns to the basic text cursor.

The simplest method of creating vertical type is to create vertical type on a point by clicking on an open area of the artboard with the vertical Type tool selected.

Working with Vertical Area Type

Create vertical area type objects in one of the following ways:

- Select the Vertical Type tool and click and drag to create a rectangular Vertical Type object.

- Select the Vertical Type tool or Vertical Area Type tool and move the cursor over the outline of an existing closed path. The vertical area Type cursor should now be active. Click on the path to convert it into a Vertical Area Type object. An active insertion point for vertical type (a flashing horizontal line) will appear at the upper right of the object.

- Select the Area Type tool and click on an open path to convert it into an Area Type object.

Working with Vertical Path Type

Vertical Path type is created by converting an existing path to a Vertical Path Type object in one of the following ways:

- Select the Vertical Path Type tool or Path Type tool and move the cursor over an existing open path. The Vertical Path Type cursor should now be active. Click on the path to convert it into a path type object. An active insertion point will appear at the point of the click.

- Select the Vertical Path Type tool and click on a closed path to convert it into a Path Type container.

After you have created a type object, you can change the orientation of the type it contains by selecting the Type\Type Orientation\Vertical or Type\Type Orientation\Horizontal menu command.

Converting Type to Outlines

Occasionally you may need to modify your type in ways that cannot be accomplished using the formatting options already discussed. You may, for example, wish to create a distinctive logo by modifying the shape of certain letters with one or more of Illustrator's drawing tools. This is accomplished by converting the type within an object into outlines. This turns each character of the type into a drawing object that can be reshaped and manipulated with the Object Transform tools. (Discussed in **Chapter 9: Object Transform Tools.)**

The down side of this process is that, once type has been converted into outlines, it can no longer be selected and edited as text.

To convert type to outlines, select a type object and its type by clicking on the type with the Selection tool. Then select the Type\Create Outlines (CTRL/COMMAND+SHIFT+O) menu option. The letters will be converted into drawing objects. To understand the process better, view the transformation in Artwork mode (View\Artwork) or use the CTRL/COMMAND+Y combination to toggle between Artwork and Preview modes.

 *When type is converted into an outline, it becomes a compound object (see the section "Working with Compound Paths," **Chapter 6: Type Options and Effects**). If you wish to use a converted character as a container for other type, you must first release the compound path (Objects\Compound Paths\Release) or CTRL/COMMAND+ALT/OPTION+8.*

Chapter 5 Tutorial:
Creating, Editing, and Formatting Type

As a practical exploration of the features and effects discussed in this chapter, follow through in this step-by-step tutorial. As you do so, you may notice that some of these steps are accompanied by a "Color palette" symbol. This symbol indicates that the step has also been illustrated in full color in the *Fundamental Illustrator* 7 color insert. The purpose of the color insert is to provide you with a brief overview of the tutorial and act as an overall reference for the practical use of color throughout these tutorials.

Watch for this symbol:

Water Works, a local water park, is introducing their newest attraction, a virtual reality surfing simulator known as The Big Kahuna. They want to send a flyer to their customers and include a coupon for one free ride. The grand opening is next week, so you don't have much time.

You can create the flyer using what you've learned about working with type in Illustrator 7 by following these steps:

1. Set the General Units and Type Units options in the Units and Undo Preferences dialog box (select File|Preferences|Units and Undo) to points.

2. With the page in portrait mode, choose Show Rulers (CTRL/COMMAND+R) from the View menu to display the rulers if they are not already visible. Click and drag a vertical guideline from the ruler on the left side of the drawing window. When it is 144 points to the right of the left edge of the page, release the mouse to set the guide. Create a second guideline 36 points to the left of the right edge of the page in the same manner.

3. Select the Type tool from the main Toolbox palette and click near the upper-left corner of the page to create a point type object. Enter the text **WATER WORKS** at the point. If necessary, press CTRL/COMMAND+ SHIFT+L to left-align the type.

4. Select the type by clicking and dragging across it with the Type tool.

5. Choose the Character command (CTRL/COMMAND+T) from the Type menu to display the Character palette. In the Character palette, set the font to Times Roman using the pop-up menu to the right of the Font text boxes and set the size to 60 points using the Size pop-up menu. The WATER WORKS headline should now look like this:

WATER WORKS

6. On second thought, WATER WORKS would look better set vertically. Change the orientation by choosing the Type|Type Orientation|Vertical menu command while the type is selected.

7. Position the Type tool below the W in WATER. The cursor will change to a horizontal I-beam. Click and drag the cursor upward across the W to select it.

8. With the W selected, change its font to Times Bold and size to 100 points in the Character palette (CTRL/COMMAND+T). Because 100 points is not one of the sizes available in the size menu, you will need to enter **100** directly into the Size text box.

9. Resizing the W has made the spacing between the W and A awkward. Create an active insertion point by clicking the Type tool once between the two letters. Decrease the kerning between the letters by using the ALT/OPTION+UP ARROW shortcut until the letters appear as shown here:

10. If necessary, use the Selection tool to click and drag the WATER WORKS type into the position shown in Figure 5-12.

11. Select the Pen tool and, near the top of the page, create a wavy path between the two guidelines you created in step 2, as shown in Figure 5-13. For more information on drawing paths, see the section "Creating Paths and Shapes," **Chapter 7: Creating and Editing Drawing Objects.**

12. Convert the path to a Path Type object by clicking near its left end with the type tool.

FIGURE 5-12   WATER WORKS in proper position on the flyer

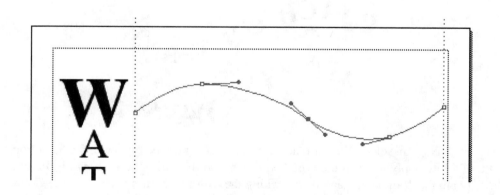

FIGURE 5-13   The wavy path

13. As you can see from the size of the flashing insertion point, the type size is still set to 100 points. With the insertion point still active and before entering any type, change the point size to 48 points by choosing 48 from the Size pop-up menu in the Character palette.

14. Enter **CATCH THE WAVE** at the insertion point. Because the last type you set was left-aligned, the type will flow to the right as you enter it.

15. Depending upon the shape of the path, it may be necessary to increase or decrease the size of CATCH THE WAVE to fit the path. Select all the type in the headline by clicking on the type with the Selection tool. Then use the up or down Size spinner in the Character palette to increase or decrease the type until the headline fits the path.

16. As the type follows the path, the spacing between several of the letters becomes awkward (the spaces around the letter A, for instance). To kern between the C and the A, click the type tool between the two letters to create an active insertion point. Decrease the kerning between the letters using the ALT/OPTION+LEFT ARROW shortcut. When you are satisfied with the spacing, kern the other letter pairs as necessary. Here you see the headline before and after kerning:

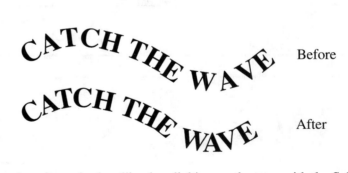

Before

After

Once again, select the entire headline by clicking on the type with the Selection tool. Now apply a fill to the type by clicking on the Fill button (shown in Figure 5-14) in the Tool palette and then clicking the Color (,) button to activate the Color palette. Choose a bright blue color for the fill by clicking on the color in the Color Spectrum bar in the Color palette, shown in Figure 5-15.

Draw a container for the text of the brochure immediately below the headline and between the two guidelines you created in step 2. Leave about four inches at the bottom of the page for the coupon.

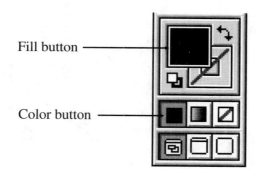

Fill button

Color button

FIGURE 5-14 The Fill and Color buttons in the main Toolbox palette

Because the left guideline is near the WATER WORKS type, the cursor may change to the Vertical Type Selection cursor when you place it over the guideline. In that case, when you click and drag you will end up selecting letters in WATER WORKS instead of creating a type container. To correct the situation, begin by placing the Type tool over the right guideline and then click and drag down and to the left to create the type container, as shown in Figure 5-16.

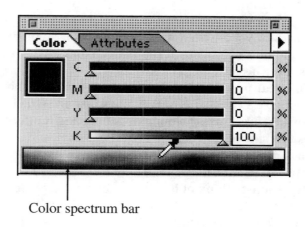

Color spectrum bar

FIGURE 5-15 The Color Spectrum bar in the Color palette

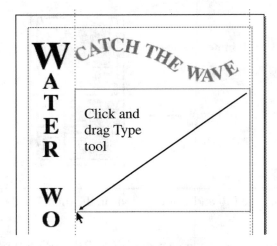

FIGURE 5-16   Clicking and dragging the type tool to create the type container

19. Before entering the text, set the font to Helvetica regular and the size to 14 points in the Character palette.

20. Enter the following text into the container:

Dear Wet Head,

   We know you've been waiting all year for summer to return so you could hit the beaches at the Water Works. Well, the wait is almost over because we reopen June 1.
   This year promises to be our biggest, best, and most exciting ever because THE BIG KAHUNA has just arrived. That's right, the world's first surfing simulator is here and it offers the best waves this side of Hawaii.
   So come on in and join the fun! Bring in the coupon below and hang ten on the house.
   Hey, come to think of it, why not bring the whole family and hang 40!
   The Water Works staff
   P.S. Don't forget to sign up for the first ever Kansas State Surfing Championships coming in August.

NOTE: *If, at any point in this process, the text should overflow the container, you can enlarge the container by clicking and dragging its bottom line with the Direct Selection tool.*

21. Select all the type in the container by clicking on the type with the Selection tool. Display the Paragraph palette by choosing Paragraph (CTRL/COMMAND+M) from the Type menu. Enter **9** into the Space Before Paragraph text box.

22. Select the first paragraph (Dear Wet Head) by placing the Type tool within the paragraph and triple-clicking. In the Character palette, set the font to Helvetica Bold and the size to 18.

23. Paint the selected type by clicking the Fill button in the main Toolbox palette, then clicking the Color button to display the Color palette, and finally clicking on a blue shade in the Color Spectrum bar of the Color palette to apply it to the selected type.

24. Select the next four paragraphs by placing the Type tool within the first paragraph of the group ("We know…") and triple-clicking to select the paragraph. On the third click, hold the mouse button and drag the cursor across the next three paragraphs to add them to the selection. When all four paragraphs are selected, release the mouse button.

25. Set the indent of the first line of the selected paragraphs to 18 points by entering **18** into the First Line Indent text box in the Paragraph palette.

26. Select the next paragraph ("The Water Works staff") by placing the Type tool within the paragraph and triple-clicking.

27. In the Character palette, set the font to Helvetica Bold and the size to 18.

28. Paint the selected type blue as described in step 23.

29. Select the words THE BIG KAHUNA. Make the selection by placing the Type tool over the word THE. Double-click on the word to select it and hold the mouse button down. Drag the mouse over the other words to add them to the selection. When the selection is complete, release the mouse button.

30. In the Character palette, set the font to Helvetica Bold and the size to 18.

5

31. If the Baseline Shift options are not visible in the Character palette, access them by selecting Show Options from the flyout menu in the upper-right corner of the palette. Enter the value -2 in the Baseline Shift text box to move the selected type down two points relative to the baseline.

32. Paint the selected type as you did in step 23, this time selecting a red color from the Color Spectrum bar in the Color palette.

33. Changing the size of the words THE BIG KAHUNA has altered the leading between its line and the one above it. To restore the original leading, triple-click within the paragraph containing the words to select it. In the Leading text box in the Character palette enter **17** to override Illustrator 7's automatic setting.

34. The text should now look like this:

Dear Wet Head,

We know you've been waiting all year for summer to return so you could hit the beaches at the Water Works. Well, the wait is almost over because we reopen June 1.

This year promises to be our biggest, best and most exciting ever because **THE BIG KAHUNA** has just arrived. That's right, the world's first surfing simulator is here and it offers the best waves this side of Hawaii.

So come on in and join the the fun! Bring in the coupon below and hang ten on the house.

Hey, come to think of it, why not bring the whole family and hang 40!

The Water Works staff

P.S. Don't forget to sign up for the first ever Kansas State Surfing Championships coming in August.

35. Using the Rectangle tool, click and drag to draw the outline of the coupon. Begin about 36 points below the text of the letter and allow about 18 points between the sides of the rectangle and the guidelines, as shown in Figure 5-17.

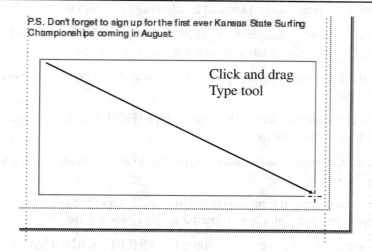

P.S. Don't forget to sign up for the first ever Kansas State Surfing
Championships coming in August.

Click and drag
Type tool

FIGURE 5-17 Drawing the coupon box

36. Convert the rectangle to a text path by clicking in the middle of the bottom line of the rectangle with the Path Type tool.

37. Before entering text along the path enter the following settings into the Character palette: Font - Helvetica Bold, Size - 18 points, Leading - Auto, Baseline Shift - 0.

38. Repeatedly type the word "FREE" (feel free to Cut and Paste) followed by a space and let the type flow around the coupon box. Stop just before the type begins to overlap.

39. With the insertion point still active on the path, choose Select All (CTRL/COMMAND+A) from the Edit menu to select all the type on the path.

40. Paint the selected type blue as in step 23.

41. Click the Type tool in the middle of the coupon box to create a point type object and enter the following text:

> **Good for one**
> **FREE RIDE**
> **on the**
> **BIG KAHUNA**

42. Select the type you just created by clicking on it with the Selection tool.

43. In the Character palette, set the font to Times Bold (Times New Roman Bold on Windows platform versions) and the size to 24 points.

44. In the Paragraph palette, click on the Center Align button to center the type.

45. Select the second line of the coupon type (FREE RIDE) by triple-clicking on it with the Type tool.

46. In the Character palette, set the type size to 36 points and the leading to 36 points.

47. Paint the selected type as you did in step 23, this time selecting a red color from the Color Spectrum bar in the Color palette.

48. Select the last line of the coupon type (THE BIG KAHUNA) by triple-clicking on it with the Type tool.

49. In the Character palette, set the type size to 48 points and the leading to 48 points.,

50. Paint the selected type as you did in step 23, this time selecting a red color from the Color Spectrum bar in the Color palette.

51. If necessary, click and drag the coupon type to center it in the coupon outline. The coupon should now look like this:

Now it's time to add a little interest to the layout. You'll do this by distorting the CATCH THE WAVE headline so it will look as if it's being viewed through water.

52. Select the headline by clicking on the type with the Selection tool.

53. Convert the type into drawing objects by choosing the Create Outlines (CTRL/COMMAND+SHIFT+O) command from the Type menu.

54. With the headline still selected, choose the Roughen filter from the Distort submenu of the Filters menu. In the Roughen dialog box, enter **5** in the Size text box, **1** in the Detail text box, and select the Smooth Points option. Click OK to apply the filter.

55. All the elements of the flyer are complete. If any elements are out of place, move them into position by clicking and dragging them with the Selection tool. Your completed flyer should look like this:

5

Dear Wet Head,

We know you've been waiting all year for summer to return so you could hit the beaches at the Water Works. Well, the wait is almost over because we reopen June 1.

This year promises to be our biggest, best and most exciting ever because **THE BIG KAHUNA** has just arrived. That's right, the world's first surfing simulator is here and it offers the best waves this side of Hawaii.

So come on in and join the the fun! Bring in the coupon below and hang ten on the house.

Hey, come to think of it, why not bring the whole family and hang 40!

The Water Works staff

P.S. Don't forget to sign up for the first ever Kansas State Surfing Championships coming in August.

Good for one
FREE RIDE
on the
BIG KAHUNA

Conclusion

This chapter has covered many of the basic operations involved in working with type objects. While Illustrator 7 features some powerful tools for formatting, composing, editing type objects, and applying type attributes, much more can be accomplished through further manipulation. To complete your exploration of Illustrator 7's full type capabilities, continue on now to **Chapter 6: Type Options and Effects** following this chapter.

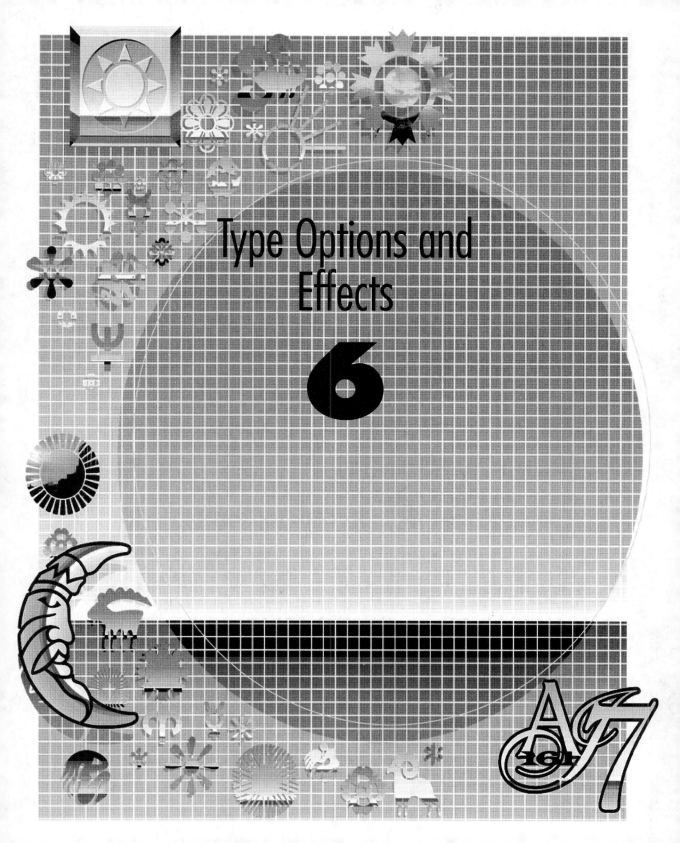

Type Options and Effects

6

In this chapter you'll be introduced to the tools and controls that make it possible to create sophisticated typographic projects—such as flyers, brochures, and newsletters—in Illustrator 7. You'll learn how to set type in columns, wrap it around pictures, and flow it from one object to another. You'll use Illustrator 7's Object Transform tools to apply special effects to your type. And you'll discover how to add special typographic bells and whistles to your documents to give them a finished, professional appearance.

Working with Type Effects

This section outlines the principles of making selections within type objects and introduces you to the techniques used to apply special effects to those selections with Illustrator 7's many tools and commands.

Selections Within Area Type and Path Type Objects

In Illustrator 7, how a type object is selected and the kind of object (Type on a point, Area Type, or Path Type) it is, play large roles in determining how a given tool or command affects both the object and the type it contains. These various kinds of type objects can be defined as follows: Type on a point is type which is oriented on a given anchor point. This point indicates to Illustrator the vertical and horizontal position of the type on your page. Area Type is type is applied to type which essentially resides inside of a container. Area Type is capable of flowing with the horizontal and vertical dimensions of the container boundaries. Path type is essentially Type on a Point whose baseline has been set to follow the contours of a path. Therefore, it is critical to understand selections within type objects before you begin applying special effects.

To understand selections in type objects, recall that a type object is composed of both type *and* a drawing object—point, container, or path—that defines the position of the type on the page.

In the case of Area and Path Type, the container or path may be selected and manipulated independently from (or in conjunction with) its associated type. Table 6-1 outlines how selections are made within Area and Path Type objects. The results of these selections are shown in Figure 6-1.

Note   *Certain Illustrator commands apply only to type. Others apply only to containers and paths. When these functions are used while both a container or path and its type are selected, only the relevant part of the selection will be acted upon. For example, applying a type style will change the type but leave the container undisturbed. Likewise, applying a Distort filter will change the shape of the container but not affect the type.*

Manipulating Area and Path Type

Now you are ready to look at how various selections can be used with Illustrator 7's commands and tools to modify type objects. In general, selections within type objects are used in the following ways:

■   A partial selection of a container or path is used to reshape the object. When an object is reshaped in this way, the type is unaffected except that it wraps to conform to the new shape.

To Select	Use This Tool	and Click on or Click and Drag Across
Part of the container or path	Direct Selection tool	The line segment(s) or point(s) you wish to select (but not the type)
The entire container or path but not its type	Group Selection tool	The outline of the container or path
The container or path and its type	Any selection tool	The type
	or use	
	Selection tool	The outline of the container or path

TABLE 6-1   Making Selections Within a Path or Area Type Object.

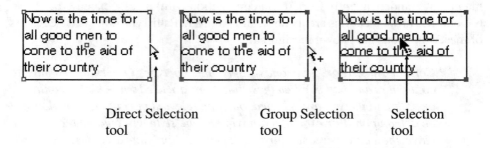

Direct Selection   Group Selection   Selection
tool   tool   tool

FIGURE 6-1   Selections within area and path type objects. From left the
                 selections are being made with the Direct Selection tool, the
                 Group Selection tool, and the Selection tool.

■ A selection of an entire container or path (but not the associated text) is
  used to transform the object with Illustrator 7's Object Transform tools
  and commands. Again, the type is unaffected except that it wraps to
  conform to the new shape.

■ A selection that includes either a container or path and its type is used to
  transform both the type and object using Illustrator 7's Object Transform
  tools and commands.

Transforming Type and Containers

The following examples outline various ways of manipulating Area and Path Type objects.

Note   *Although the examples use area type, the same procedures also apply to*
           path type.

■ **Moving area type**   Moving a type container also moves the type within it.
  Move a container by clicking on the type with any of the selection tools and
  holding down the mouse button while dragging the type and container.
  Release the mouse button when you are happy with the new location.

■ **Reshaping a container with the Direct Selection tool**   Remember the
  overflowing text box in Chapter 5? Wouldn't it be nice to be able to
  stretch the box to accommodate all the type? You can.

Create a rectangular text container by clicking and dragging the Type tool and then enter enough type to overflow the container. The small **+** at the lower-right corner of the container indicates it contains more type than can be displayed.

Click and hold the Direct Selection tool on the bottom line of the container and drag the line downward. When you release the mouse, the type that was hidden will flow into the enlarged container, as Figure 6-2 shows.

You can also reshape an area type object by clicking and dragging on single or multiple points and/or single or multiple line segments along the outline of the container. To select multiple points or line segments, hold down the SHIFT key and click on each of the various elements with the Direct Selection tool or drag the Direct Selection tool over the elements to be selected.

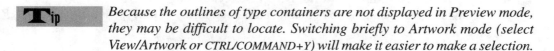

Because the outlines of type containers are not displayed in Preview mode, they may be difficult to locate. Switching briefly to Artwork mode (select View/Artwork or CTRL/COMMAND+Y) will make it easier to make a selection.

- **Transforming a container with Illustrator's Object Transform tools**
  Now look at a simple transformation scaling (see "Moving, Scaling, and Rotating Objects," **Chapter 9: Object Transform Tools**), as it applies to a selected container.

Create a rectangular text container by clicking and dragging with the Type tool (T) and enter some text.

Select only the container by clicking on its outline with the Group Selection tool.

Scale the container with the Scale tool (S) by clicking and dragging away from the Point of Origin (see "Illustrator's Point of Origin Concept," **Chapter 9: Object**

FIGURE 6-2 Stretching a type container by clicking and dragging on a line segment with the Direct Selection tool

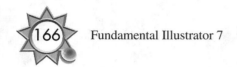

Transform Tools). When you are satisfied with the new dimensions of the container, release the mouse. The type will wrap to conform to the new dimensions of the container but is otherwise unchanged, as Figure 6-3 shows.

Note   *Although the Scale tool is used in this and the succeeding example, the concepts involved in selecting and transforming containers and type apply to the use of the other transformation tools, to the commands found in the submenu of the Object/Transform menu item, and to some filters. As you work through these exercises, experiment with other transformations and filters to become familiar with how they affect type objects.*

■ **Reshaping a container with the Direct Selection tool**   Create a rectangular type container by clicking and dragging with the Type tool and enter some text.

Select the type and container by clicking on the type with the Selection tool (V) and scale it as before with the Scale tool. Notice that the container and the type are both scaled.

When you are satisfied with the new size of the container and type, release the mouse.

Note   *Because the previous examples apply to both area and path type, you may want to revisit the exercises on moving, reshaping, and scaling using path type instead of area type. Simply substitute paths for containers in the exercises.*

Now is the time for
all good men to
come to the aid of

Drag

Now is the time for all
good men to come to the
aid of their country.

FIGURE 6-3   Scaling a container with the Scale tool

Painting Type Containers and Paths

Illustrator 7's paint tools apply to selected type objects somewhat differently than the Transformation tools. As you saw in the preceding chapter (see "Painting Type," **Chapter 5: Working with Type**), when an entire type object is selected and a stroke or fill is applied, only the type is painted. Although this may seem counterintuitive, it is actually a convenience. Because containers and paths holding type are rarely painted, it is simpler to be able to select a type object or multiple type objects and paint all the associated type than to have to select each bit of type individually with the Type tool. Besides, if the type and container were both painted, you would no longer be able to see the type.

There are times, however, when you will want to paint the container or path. In those cases, simply select the container or path but not the type by clicking on its outline with the Direct Selection tool and apply the desired stroke and fill.

Note   *Painting objects is discussed in detail in **Chapter 10: Setting Fills and Strokes**. The subject is introduced here to illustrate special considerations involved in working with color in type.*

Working with Type Along a Path

Now let's look at a few concepts that apply only to path type.

■   **Repositioning type on a path**   The Left Align (CTRL/COMMAND+ SHIFT+L), Centered (CTRL/COMMAND+SHIFT+C), and Right Align (CTRL/COMMAND+SHIFT+R) paragraph attributes are applied to path type relative to the I-beam that is visible when both the type and path are selected (see Figure 6-4). Initially, the I-beam is located at the point on the path where the Type tool was clicked to convert the path into a type object.

Note   *Justify (CTRL/COMMAND+SHIFT+J) and Justify Last Line (CTRL/COMMAND+ SHIFT+F) commands do not apply to path type objects. If they are used on path type, the type will appear left-aligned relative to the I-beam.*

To reposition the I-beam, select the path and its type by clicking on the type with the Selection tool. Then click and drag the I-beam parallel to the path. When you

Left aligned type on a path

Center aligned type on a path

Right aligned type on a path

FIGURE 6-4   Type on a path aligned left, centered, and aligned right. The alignment is in reference to the I-beam.

are satisfied with the new position, release the mouse. The type will realign to the new position of the I-beam (see Figure 6-5).

■   **Flipping type direction on a path**   To flip the direction type flows along a path, use the Selection tool to click and drag the I-beam from one side of the path to the other, as shown in Figure 6-6.

 *You can flip the type direction and reposition the I-beam at the same time by dragging the I-beam both along the path and across it with the same motion.*

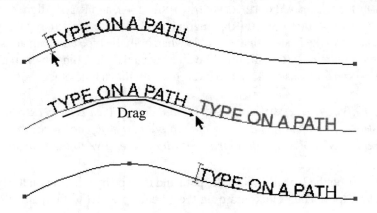

FIGURE 6-5   Repositioning type on a path by dragging the I-beam parallel to the path

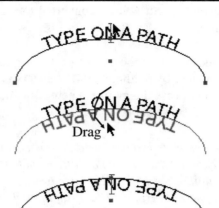

■ **FIGURE 6-6**   Flipping the direction of type on a path by dragging the
I-beam across the path (see center example)

Linking and Unlinking Area Type

Earlier you learned to reshape or resize a text container to accommodate overflowing
text. Another solution to this problem is to create a second object and link it to the
first so that the excess type flows into the second object.

Note   *Only area type objects can be linked. Path type and type on a point cannot
be linked.*

Creating Linked Text Containers

To create linked type containers, click and drag the Type tool to create a rectangular
text container. Enter text until the small + appears indicating the text has overflowed
the container.

Next, create a container linked to the first in one of the following ways:

1. Create a second object, either a type container created with the Type tool
   or a drawing object created with one of the drawing tools (see **Chapter 7:
   Creating and Editing Drawing Objects**). Select all or part of both
   objects and choose the Type|Blocks|Link menu command or the CTRL+3
   keyboard shortcut.

If necessary, the second object will be converted to a type container and the excess type will flow into it.

2. Click and hold the cursor on the outline of the original container. Now duplicate the container by holding the ALT/OPTION key and dragging the outline. When you release the mouse, a new container will be created and the excess type will flow into it.

Note   *It is interesting and useful to note what happens when you select both the container and type (click on the type with one of the selection tools) before ALT/OPTION dragging the object. In this case, the container and all of its type (even the type not displayed) are duplicated and the two containers are not linked.*

Object Arrangement and Type Flow Between Linked Objects

Alternatively you could have pasted the second object behind the first object using Edit/Paste Behind or CTRL/COMMAND+B. In this case the type would have reflowed, filling the pasted-in object first and the original container next. This is because type in linked containers flows from the backmost container to the frontmost container.

Note   *In general, the first object you draw will be the farthest back. Each succeeding object created is located in front of all previously created objects. This stacking order can be rearranged using the commands in the submenu of the Object/Arrange menu item or by using the Paste In Front (CTRL/COMMAND+F) and Paste In Back (CTRL/COMMAND+B) commands. Stacking order can also be affected by the use of layers (see the section on "Working in Layers," **Chapter 8: Selecting and Arranging Objects**).*

Working with Multiple Linked Containers

You can repeat the process of linking containers indefinitely. As you create multiple linked text containers, it is important to realize how the type flow is affected by the different methods of creating links and the different types of selections that can be made on type objects.

Table 6-2 outlines how type and containers can be selected within linked type objects, and Figure 6-7 shows the results of duplicating the various selections by ALT/ OPTION dragging them.

Note   *You can also select and edit portions of the text within linked containers with the Type tools. Such a selection can extend between multiple containers, as shown in Figure 6-7.*

To Select	Use This Tool	and Click on or Drag Across
All type and containers in a linked group	the Selection tool	Any text or container in the linked group
A single container and its type	the Group Selection tool	The type in the container
A single container only	the Group Selection tool	The outline of the container
Part of a container	the Direct Selection tool	The point(s) and/or line segment(s) to be selected

With This Selected	ALT/OPTION Dragging Duplicates	These Links Are Created
All linked containers and their type	The containers and type	The new group is not linked to the original
A single container and its type	The selected container and type are duplicated	The new container and type are inserted into the linking sequence immediately after the original

TABLE 6-2   Selecting Containers and Type Within Linked Text Objects

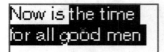

FIGURE 6-7   A text selection can extend between two or more containers

You'll see the results of all these efforts here:

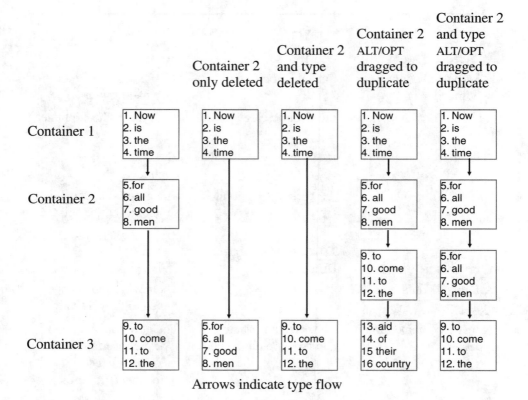

		Container 2 only deleted	Container 2 and type deleted	Container 2 ALT/OPT dragged to duplicate	Container 2 and type ALT/OPT dragged to duplicate
Container 1	1. Now 2. is 3. the 4. time	1. Now 2. is 3. the 4. time	1. Now 2. is 3. the 4. time	1. Now 2. is 3. the 4. time	1. Now 2. is 3. the 4. time
Container 2	5.for 6. all 7. good 8. men			5.for 6. all 7. good 8. men	5.for 6. all 7. good 8. men
				9. to 10. come 11. to 12. the	5.for 6. all 7. good 8. men
Container 3	9. to 10. come 11. to 12. the	5.for 6. all 7. good 8. men	9. to 10. come 11. to 12. the	13. aid 14. of 15 their 16 country	9. to 10. come 11. to 12. the

Arrows indicate type flow

Unlinking Text Containers

To unlink a group of text containers, select the group by clicking the Selection tool on the type in one of the containers. Select the Type|Blocks|Unlink menu command or CTRL+ALT+3.

When containers are unlinked, the type in each container remains the same, but it is no longer connected to the type in the other containers.

Setting Type in Rows and Columns

The previous section suggests one somewhat clumsy way to set type in newspaper-style columns. Fortunately Illustrator 7 offers a much more elegant approach to creating columns and rows of type.

Suppose that you need to flow type into three equally sized columns. Instead of drawing three containers and linking them, Illustrator 7 makes it possible to draw one box large enough to accommodate the three columns and then convert the box to three columns with the Type|Rows & Columns menu command. Follow these steps:

1. With the Type tool, draw a text container large enough to accommodate three columns of type.

2. Select the box and choose the Type|Rows & Columns menu command. The Rows & Columns dialog box will appear, as shown in Figure 6-8.

3. Ignore the other settings for now and type **3** in the Number text box below the heading Column and click OK. Your original rectangle will be converted into three linked text boxes occupying the same space as the original object.

Now take another look at the Rows & Columns dialog box shown in Figure 6-8. You'll see that it offers several controls grouped under the headings of Rows, Columns, and Options.

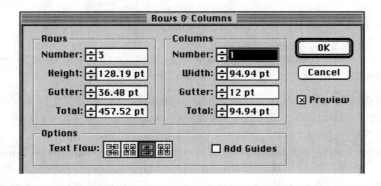

FIGURE 6-8   The Rows & Columns dialog box

The Rows and Columns settings—Number, Height or Width, Gutter, and Total—are set by typing values into the corresponding text boxes or by using the up or down arrows to the left of the text boxes. The settings for Rows and Columns are as follows:

- **Number** sets the number of rows or columns to be created.

- **Height (rows only)** sets the height of the boxes in each row.

- **Width (columns only)** sets the width of the boxes in each column.

- **Gutter** sets the vertical space between rows or the horizontal space between columns.

- **Total** sets the overall height or width of the group of rows and columns.

Note   *Checking the Preview box beneath the OK and Cancel buttons will allow you to view how changing these setting affects your drawing as you set them.*

All the settings are interactive, which means changing one setting will also change one or more of the other settings.

Tip   *If you want to create a grouping of rows and columns to fit an exact dimension, it is not necessary to draw the original object to those dimensions. Simply create an object of any size and use the Total settings to adjust the overall dimensions of the grouping. Similarly, you can use the Total settings to adjust the dimensions of an existing rectangular object. To do so, select the object, choose the Type/Rows & Columns menu command and adjust the Total settings to the desired new dimensions.*

In addition, there are two options settings available.

- **Text Flow** controls the sequence in which type flows from one box to another within the linked group, as shown in Figure 6-9.

- **Add Guides**, when checked, adds a grouping of horizontal and vertical guides defining your rows and columns, as shown in Figure 6-10.

Note   *Illustrator's terminology here is a bit confusing, since these "guides" are in reality lines with a colored stroke and not the guides that can be created using the Views/Make Guides (CTRL/COMMAND+5) menu command or by dragging from the Ruler bars.*

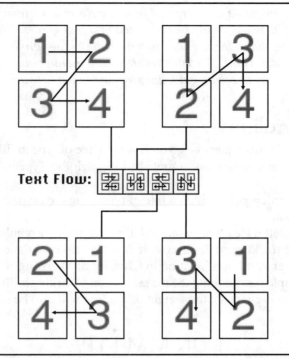

FIGURE 6-9   Text flow among linked containers created using the Rows & Columns command.

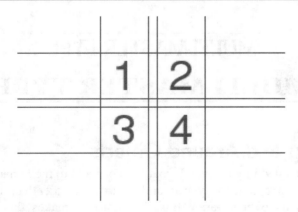

FIGURE 6-10   Horizontal and vertical guides created with the Rows & Columns command.

Tip *Because the guide lines created from the Rows & Columns dialog box are grouped, they can easily be converted into real guides. Click on one of the lines with the Selection tool to select the whole group. Then select the Views/Make Guides (CTRL/COMMAND+5) menu command. This is an excellent way to create guidelines for laying out artwork.*

Fitting Headlines

Occasionally, for stylistic purposes, you'll want a line of type to fill the entire width of its container. This is easily accomplished through the Type|Fit Headline menu command.

Place the insertion point within a line of type in an area type object by clicking with the Type tool.

Select the Type|Fit Headline command. If you are using a regular font, Illustrator 7 will adjust the tracking of the line so it fills the width of the container (see the "Setting Character Attributes" section in **Chapter 5: Working with Type**). If you are using a multiple master font (see the section on "Working with Multiple Master Design" later in this chapter), the weight of the font will also be adjusted.

NON·MM TYPE

N O N - M M   T Y P E

MULTI MASTER TYPE

MULTI MASTER TYPE

Wrapping Text Around Objects

If artwork is included in your type layout, you can add to the dynamic appearance of your design by wrapping the type around the artwork rather than simply including the artwork in its own separate box. Illustrator 7 makes this easy with the Type|Wrap|Make menu command.

Creating a Text Wrap

Create a simple area type object by dragging the Text tool and enter some text.

Now create a drawing object with one of the drawing tools. Position the drawing object so that it partially overlaps the text in the type object you created in the previous step.

Select both objects and then choose the Type|Wrap|Make menu command. The objects will be grouped (see the section on "Grouping and Ungrouping" in **Chapter 8: Selecting and Arranging Objects**) and the text in the type object will now flow around the outline of the drawing object.

Releasing a Text Wrap

Select the entire wrapped group by clicking on one of the objects with the Selection tool and choose the Type|Wrap|Release menu command.

Considerations for Working with Text

The following rules will help you use wrapped text effectively.

- Only text within an area type object can be wrapped.

- An entire area type object (the container and text) must be selected along with another object for the Type|Wrap|Make menu command to be available.

- When working with linked type, the entire linked group must be selected along with another object for the Type|Wrap|Make menu command to be available.

- Type will only flow around objects that are in front of it. If, after choosing the Type|Wrap|Make menu command, your type does not wrap, try bringing the object you're wrapping around to the front of the group by selecting the Object|Arrange|Bring To Front menu command (CTRL/COMMAND+SHIFT+]).

- You can wrap type within the same type object around several separate or grouped objects.

- You can wrap type in one text object around another text object.

■ You can grab the object that type is wrapped around with the Direct Selection tool and move it, and the text wrapping will adjust accordingly.

Working with Multiple Master Design

In Chapter 5, you learned to scale type horizontally and vertically. Unfortunately, when type is scaled, the sometimes subtle harmonies between the shapes making up the typeface can be distorted. To avoid this, several variations such as condensed and extended are often offered within a type face family.

Multiple master fonts offer another solution to this problem. MM fonts are designed with various "axes" such as weight and width. Programs such as Illustrator 7 that support MM technology allow users to adjust these axes along a continuous scale. As the axes are adjusted, MM technology adjusts the letter forms to maintain their balance, as shown here:

HEADLINE

HEADLINE

HEADLINE

Here you see the multiple master typeface Tekton MM compressed horizontally using the horizontal scale setting in the Paragraph palette (top) and using the width adjustment from the MM Design Palette (Type|MM Design menu command). Notice that when the scale command setting is used, the vertical lines of the letter form are thinner than the horizontal ones. Using MM technology, the width of the horizontal and vertical strokes remains balanced.

Changing an MM Font in Illustrator 7

To adjust a font using MM technology in Illustrator 7, select the type to be adjusted and activate the MM Design palette by selecting the Type|MM Design menu option. Sliders and text boxes will be shown for each axes of the MM font, as shown in Figure 6-11.

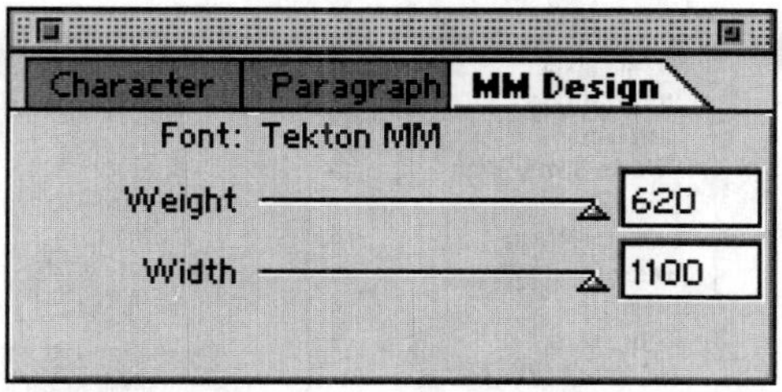

FIGURE 6-11 The MM Design palette

> **Note** *If the font you are trying to adjust is not an MM font, "not MM" will appear in the palette and no slider or text box will be active.*

As you move the slider or type new values into the text boxes, the display of the selected type will change to reflect the new values. The new values will also appear as a style option when you select the MM font from the Character palette or the Type|Font submenu, as Figure 6-12 shows.

Type from Other Sources

Complete text files can be imported into Illustrator 7 with either the File|Open or the File|Place menu command. The file formats that are supported are ASCII text, Rich Text Format (RTF), Microsoft Word, and WordPerfect files. Placed files retain most of their character and paragraph formatting.

Import a text file into a new Illustrator 7 document by selecting the File|Open (CTRL/COMMAND+O) menu command and selecting the text file. A new Illustrator document will be created with the text placed into a single large text box centered on the page.

> **Tip** *When you save your new Illustrator document, be sure to give it a new name to avoid overwriting the original text file.*

To place a text file into an existing Illustrator document, choose the File|Place menu command while an insertion point is active. Locate your file and press the Place button. The text from the file will flow into your Illustrator document beginning at the insertion point.

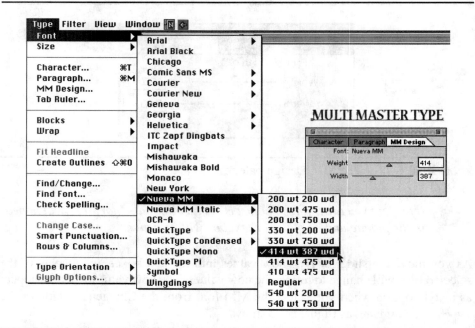

FIGURE 6-12   The MM selections reflected in the Type|Font sub menu

Setting Type Display Options

The type display options affect only the way type appears onscreen; the printed output is unaffected. So why should you care about settings that won't affect your finished product, especially when the default settings work just fine? Because these settings can have a great impact on how quickly and efficiently you can work with Illustrator 7.

The controls for the type display setting are located, for no apparent reason, in the Keyboard Increments dialog box (File|Preferences|Keyboard Increments menu command) as shown in Figure 6-13. They include the Greeking Type Limit, the Anti-alias Type option, and the Type Area Select option.

Greeking Type Limit

Type that is the same size or smaller than the value entered in the Greeking Type Limit text box will be *greeked* on screen. That is, it will appear as gray bars rather

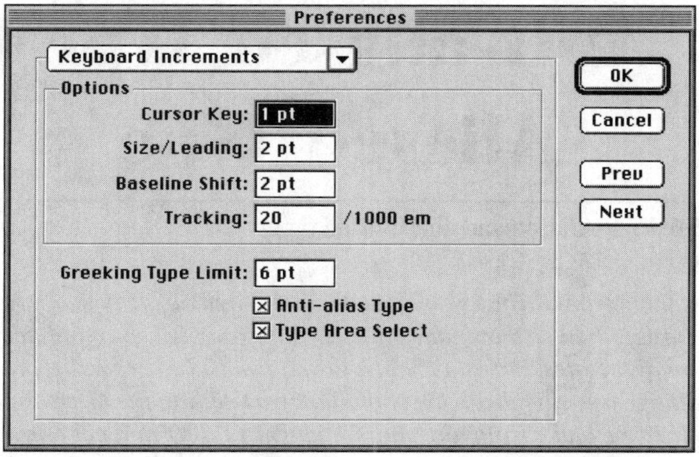

FIGURE 6-13   The Keyboard Increments dialog box

than individual characters, as shown in Figure 6-14. Because it's easier and faster for Illustrator to draw gray bars than letters, greeking improves the display speed of documents containing small text.

Note   *The Greeking Type Limit refers to the onscreen size of the type, not the value specified in the Character palette. For instance, if the limit is set to 6 pt, six-point type will not be greeked if displayed at more than 100 percent and 12-point type will be greeked if viewed at 50 percent or less.*

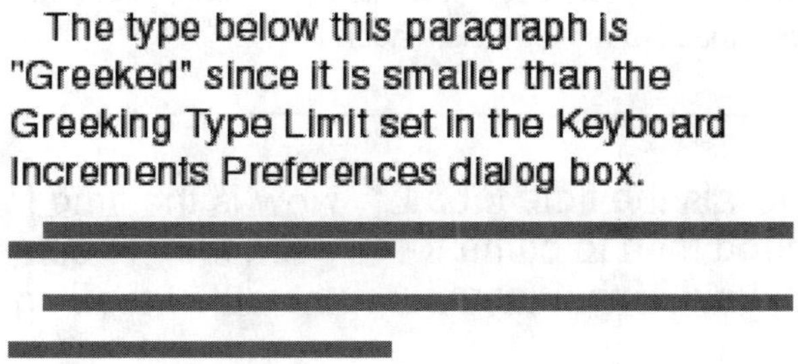

The type below this paragraph is "Greeked" since it is smaller than the Greeking Type Limit set in the Keyboard Increments Preferences dialog box.

FIGURE 6-14   Greeking type at small point sizes increases display speed

Anti-aliased Type
Aliased Type

■ **FIGURE 6-15**   Aliased and anti-aliased type

 Greeking type can be useful in making sure that all the type in your document is larger than a minimum size. If, for example, your publication's style manual dictates that all type in a graphic must be at least 10 points for easy reading, you can check for compliance by setting the Greeking Type Limit to 9.99 pt and displaying the document at 100 percent. Any type which appears as a gray bar does not comply with your style manual.

Anti-alias Type

Anti-aliasing hides the "jaggies" that appear along diagonal lines on a computer monitor by placing lighter pixels along the jagged edges. This tricks the viewer's eye into seeing a smooth line (see Figure 6-15). Checking the Anti-alias Type option causes Illustrator 7 to apply anti-aliasing to all but very large type.

Type Area Select

Selecting the Type Area Select option allows you to select a type object by clicking on the type itself (the method used in the examples in this and the previous chapter). With Type Area Select unchecked, it is necessary to click directly on the baseline of the type to select the type object. Because this can be difficult with certain fonts or if the baseline of the type has been shifted, it is best to leave this option checked unless you have a specific reason to uncheck it.

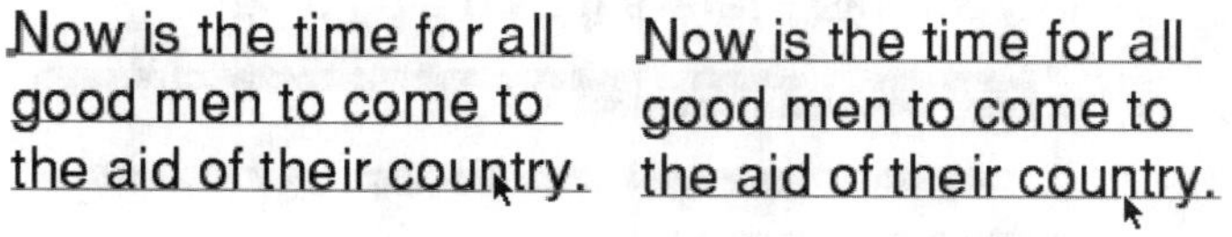

Now is the time for all good men to come to the aid of their country.   Now is the time for all good men to come to the aid of their country.

■ **FIGURE 6-16**   Making a selection with the Select Area Type option checked (left) and unchecked (right)

Setting Tabs in Type

Illustrator 7 supports four styles of tabs: left-justified, centered, right-justified, and decimal-justified. Tabs are set using the Tab Ruler palette (shown in Figure 6-17) and are applied at the paragraph level. Tabs are only applicable to area type and type on a point.

To display the Tab Ruler palette, select the Type|Tab Ruler menu command. The Tab Ruler palette will appear above the selected type object and align with its left edge (for Vertical Type, the Tab Ruler palette will appear to the left of the object and align with its top edge). If no type object is selected, the Tab Ruler palette will appear at the last position it was displayed. When the Tab Ruler palette is displayed you can align it to any type object on the art board. While using the Windows platform version, select the object and click the "-" sign in the upper-right of the palette. While using the Macintosh version of Illustrator, select the object and click the small rectangle in the right corner of the palette's title bar.

Note   *Although it is easier to set tabs visually with the Tab Ruler palette and the selected type object aligned, it is not necessary to align them when setting tabs.*

When the Tab Ruler palette is initially displayed, a series of small *T*s appear above the ruler. These represent Illustrator 7's default tab stops. Default tabs are left-justified and appear at half-inch intervals.

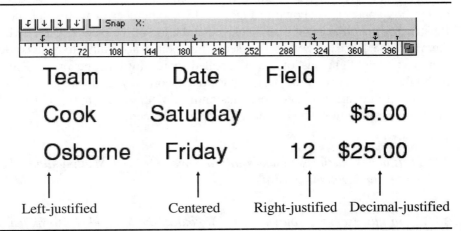

FIGURE 6-17   The Tab Ruler palette and (from left) left-justified, centered, right-justified, and decimal-justified tabs

Note

If a type object is all or partially selected when the tab settings are adjusted, the new settings will apply to all paragraphs which are at least partially selected or to the paragraph with the active insertion point. The new settings will also apply to new type objects. If no type object is selected when the tab settings are modified, existing type objects will be unaffected and the new settings will apply to any new type objects that are created.

To set a new tab, click in the palette on or immediately above the ruler. A left-align tab will appear at the point of the click. All the default tabs to the left of the new tab will disappear. Those to the right will remain.

To move a tab, click and drag it to the new position. The position indicator near the top left of the palette will change to reflect the new location of the tab as it is moved. You can also force the tab to "snap to" the divisions in the ruler by checking the Snap option.

To change the alignment of a tab, click on the tab to select it and then click on the appropriate tab style button in the upper-left corner of the palette. It is also possible to cycle through the various tab alignments by ALT/OPTION clicking on the tab.

Checking Spelling

The Type|Check Spelling menu command is used to check the spelling of all the text in a document. The best way to understand the use of this command is to create a document including the word "Internet" and several intentionally misspelled words.

Select the Type|Check Spelling menu command. When the Check Spelling dialog box appears, as shown in Figure 6-18, the number of words not found in Illustrator 7's dictionary will be displayed at the top of the palette. Directly below them will be listed all words that seem misspelled according to your system's dictionary. Highlight one of the misspelled words by clicking on it. This also highlights the first occurrence of the questioned word in your document so that you can view it in context. In addition, Illustrator 7 offers several possible corrections of the misspelling in the box labeled Suggested Corrections.

Note

It may sometimes be necessary to move the Check Spelling dialog box to see the highlighted word.

Note

In this example, you will jump around in the Misspelled Words list. It is actually more convenient and less confusing to simply work through the words one at a time in the order they are listed.

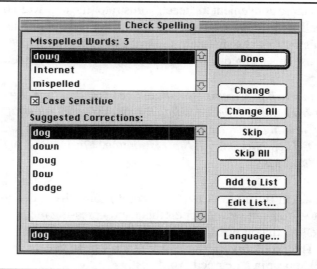

FIGURE 6-18   The Check Spelling dialog box

Below the Suggested Corrections list is the Correction text box. When you click on the Change button the word in this box is substituted for the one highlighted in your document. You can change the word in the Correction box by clicking on a word from the Suggested Corrections list or by typing a new word into the box.

You can also replace the misspelled word in your document by double-clicking on the preferred spelling in the Suggested Corrections list.

If you wish to change all occurrences of the misspelling in your document to the word in the Correction box click on the Change All button instead of the Change button.

Because words you enter into the Correction text box are not spell-checked, it is possible to replace one misspelling with another. Therefore, it's a good idea to check your spelling a second time if you have manually entered new spellings into the Corrections text box.

But what if the so-called misspelled word is actually spelled correctly, like the word *Internet*? One solution is to simply skip over the word by clicking the Skip or Skip All button.

This works well for uncommon words or proper names that are unlikely to appear often in your work, but for words like Internet, which you are likely to encounter frequently, it is more convenient to "teach" Illustrator the new word by highlighting it in the Misspelled Word list and clicking the Add to List button. This adds the word to your system's dictionary so in future works the word will not appear as misspelled. Go ahead and use this technique to teach Illustrator 7 the word Internet.

You can teach Illustrator more than one word at a time. First select all the words from the Misspelled Words list that you want Illustrator to learn. Do this by holding down the CTRL/CMD key while clicking on multiple words in the list. Then click the Add to List button. Illustrator 7 will learn all the selected words.

When you teach Illustrator 7 a new word, it is actually added to a list in your User Dictionary. You can view and edit this list by pressing the Edit List button in the Check Spelling dialog box to display the Learned Words dialog box shown in Figure 6-19. The word *Internet* and any other words you have added to your dictionary will appear in a Learned Words list.

The text entry box at the bottom of the Learned Words dialog box is used to edit existing entries and to add new words to the list. To edit an entry, select the word from the list, type the new spelling into the text box, and click Change.

■ To add a word to the list, type the word into the text box and click on Add.

■ To delete a word from the list, select the word from the list and press DELETE.

■ When you are done editing your list, hit the Done button to return to the Check Spelling dialog box.

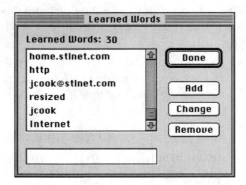

FIGURE 6-19   The Learned Words dialog box

Note   *If you wish to use a foreign language dictionary with your document, the dictionary should be located in the Text Filters folder inside the Plug-ins folder in the Adobe Illustrator folder. To change dictionaries, press the Language button in the Check Spelling dialog box, locate the desired language dictionary and click Open.*

Tip   *Because the user dictionary in many programs such as Microsoft Word is a text file, it is possible to add all the words in an existing user dictionary to Illustrator 7's user dictionary in just a few steps.*

Note   *To prevent accidently saving unwanted changes to your word processor dictionary, you may want to work with a copy of the dictionary file. To make a copy of your dictionary file, follow these steps:*

1. Select the File|Open (CTRL/COMMAND+O) command, locate the user dictionary you wish to import, and click Open. The text from the dictionary will appear in the new document.

2. Choose Check Spelling from the Type menu.

3. When the Check Spelling dialog box appears, select all the words in the Misspelled Words list and click Add to List. The words have now been added to your Illustrator 7 user dictionary.

4. Click Done to close the Check Spelling dialog box.

5. Select Close from the File menu (CTRL/COMMAND+W) to close the document.

Remember   *Do not save changes!!*

Using Find/Change

To search for and, optionally, replace specific words or character strings within an Illustrator 7 document select Find/Change from the Type menu.

When the Find/Change dialog box appears, as shown in Figure 6-20, enter a target string (the word or characters you are searching for) in the Find what text box. To replace the target string with another, enter the replacement string into the Change to text box.

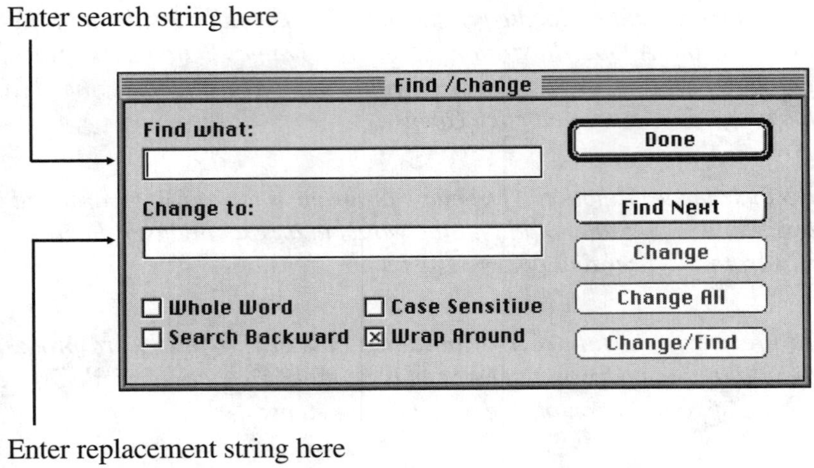

Enter search string here

Enter replacement string here

FIGURE 6-20   The Find/Change dialog box

Choose which of the following options you want to apply to your search.

Whole Word finds only entire words that match the target string ("act" will find "act" but not "fact" or "acts").

Search Backward searches the document in reverse order beginning at the text selection point.

Case Sensitive finds only those character strings that match the case of the characters in the target string ("Bill" will find "Bill" but not "bill").

Wrap Around, which is checked by default, searches the whole document from the text selection point to the end of the document and then continues searching from the beginning of the document back to the text selection point (or the reverse if Search Backward is checked).

When you have made your choices, click Find Next. Illustrator 7 will find and highlight the next occurrence of the target string in your document. You now have six choices for dealing with the found string.

- Click the Find Next button to leave the found string unchanged and find the next occurrence of the target string.

- Click the Change button to change the found string to the replacement string. The replacement text will be highlighted in your document.

- Click the Change All button to change all occurrences of the target string in your document to the replacement string.

Tip *It is usually best to use the Whole Word option when using the Change All command, because allowing Illustrator 7 to replace text within words without first reviewing them can have unexpected results.*

- Click the Change|Find button to change the found text to the replacement string and then highlight the next occurrence of the target string in your document.

- Click the Done button to dismiss the Find/Change dialog box and leave the found string highlighted.

- Enter a new search string into the Find What text box to begin a new search.

Finding Fonts

In addition to searching for character strings, it is also possible to search for and replace occurrences of a font. To search for a font, first select the Type|Find Font menu command.

The Find Font dialog box will appear, as shown in Figure 6-21. The Current Font List will display the names of all the fonts used in your document. The Replacement Font List will display either all the fonts in use in your document or all currently active fonts in your system depending upon which option is selected in the Font List drop-down menu.

Note *You can remove certain types of fonts from the Current and Replacement Font lists by unchecking the associated options at the bottom of the Find Font dialog box.*

To locate a font, select its name from the Current Font list. Illustrator will locate and highlight the next occurrence of that font in your document. Once a font is selected you have several options.

- Click Find Next to highlight the next occurrence of the font in your document.

- Click Change to change the font of the selected text to the font selected in the replacement font list.

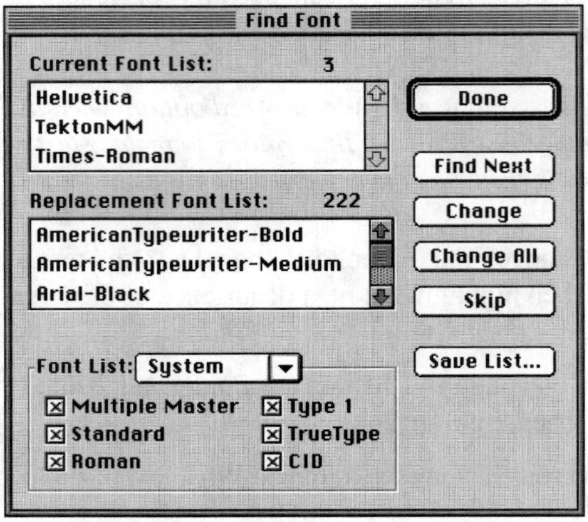

FIGURE 6-21   The Find Font dialog box

- Click Change All to change all occurrences of the font selected in the Current Font List to the font selected in the replacement font list.

- Use Skip, which operates in the same manner as Find Next.

- Save a list of all the fonts in your document to a text file by pressing the Save List button.

- Click on Done to dismiss the Find Font dialog box.

Punctuation Settings

Many people use traditional typewriting characters (straight quotes) and formatting (double spaces after periods) to enter text. Although these conventions were fine for typewritten copy, they lack the typographic sophistication necessary to produce professional-looking typesetting on a computer. The fonts you use with Illustrator offer several special characters (ligatures, curly quotes, ellipses, etc.) that give your type a more polished appearance.

To use these special characters as you enter text, it is necessary to remember several obscure key combinations. Fortunately, the Type|Smart Punctuation menu command allows you to search for and replace traditional typewriter style characters and formatting with more professional-looking typographic characters and formatting. Following is a brief summary of the controls in the Smart Punctuation dialog box, shown in Figure 6-22.

Ligatures

Perhaps the most important typographic detail that computers allow you is ligatures. When characters such as "f" and "i" appear next to each other in a line of type, the overhanging ascender of the "f" and the dot of the "i" make spacing the letters awkward. To solve this problem, typesetters developed ligatures, a single piece of type which combines two or more letters, as shown here:

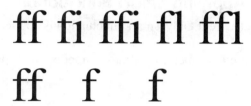

Checking the ff, fi, ffi Ligatures box and/or the ff, fl, and ffl Ligature box replaces these letter combinations with the appropriate ligatures.

Refined Punctuation

Typewritten documents have straight quotes. To curve them for a better looking document use click Smart Quotes.

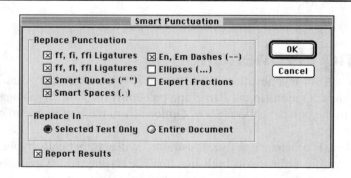

FIGURE 6-22   The Smart Punctuation dialog box

If you click the Smart Spaces option, Illustrator will automatically replace any multiple spaces after a period with a single space.

Click on En, Em dashes (–, —) to replace double dashes (--) with an en dash (–) and triple spaces (---) with an em dash (—).

Click on Ellipses (…) to replace triple periods (...) with the proper spacing and period size for an ellipse (…).

Use Expert Fractions (available only for Adobe Expert fonts) to replace fractions written as separate characters with expert fractions, in which the numerals are set over one another rather than side by side with a slash between them.

Two Ways of Applying Smart Punctuation

If you choose Selected Text Only, smart punctuation is applied only to the selected text.

If you click Entire Document, Illustrator 7 applies smart punctuation to all text in the document.

Report Results

When checked, Report Results lists all substitutions made as a result of the smart substitution command in a dialog box.

Changing Type Case

To change the case of selected type, choose the Change Case command from the Type menu and select the appropriate option, Upper Case (ABC), Lower Case (abc), or Mixed Case (Abc).

Controlling Hyphenation

You Turn on Auto Hyphenation in Illustrator 7 by checking the Auto Hyphenate check box under Options in the Paragraph palette. If the Auto Hyphenate option is not visible in the palette, choose Show Options from the pop-up menu on the right side of the palette.

When Auto Hyphenate is active, Illustrator 7 will automatically hyphenate words within area type according to its built-in rules. The Hyphenation Options dialog box, shown in Figure 6-23, gives you some control over these settings.

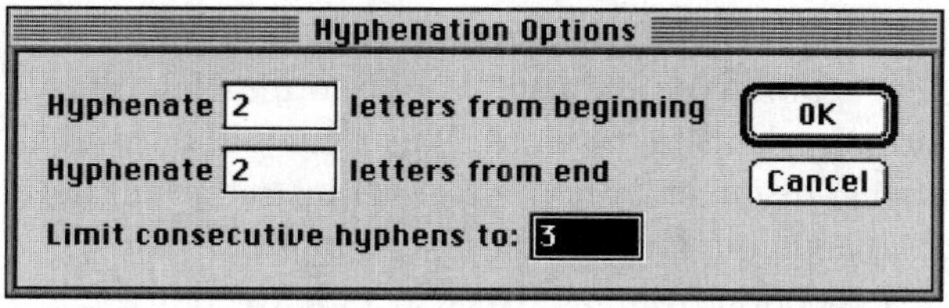

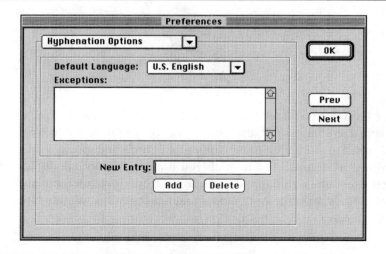

FIGURE 6-23 The Hyphenation Options dialog box

The value you enter into the Hyphenate [blank] letters from beginning text box is the minimum number of letters from the beginning of a word that will be left on a line after hyphenation.

Conversely, the Hyphenate [blank] letters from end value is the minimum number of letters from the end of a word that Illustrator will move to a new line after hyphenating.

The number you enter in the Limit consecutive hyphenations to [blank] represents the maximum number of lines in a row that Illustrator will hyphenate.

You can create exceptions to the way Illustrator auto hyphenates in the Hyphenation Options Preferences dialog box, shown in Figure 6-24. Access this

FIGURE 6-24 The Preferences|Hyphenation Options dialog box

dialog box from the File|Preferences|Hyphenation Options menu item. When the dialog box is displayed, a list of exceptions is shown.

To enter an exception, type the new word into the New Entry text box. If you include one or more hyphens in the word, Illustrator will only break the word at the point of the hyphens. If you enter no hyphens, Illustrator will never hyphenate the word. Click Add to add your entry to the Exceptions list.

To remove an exception from the list, select the word in the Exceptions list and click the Delete button.

You can also choose the default language for Illustrator from the Hyphenation Options Preferences dialog box by selecting your choice from the drop-down menu at the top of the box.

Chapter 6 Tutorial: Type Options and Effects

As a practical exploration of the features and effects discussed in this chapter, follow through in this step-by-step tutorial. As you do so, you may notice that certain of these steps are accompanied by a "Color palette" symbol. This symbol indicates that the step has also been illustrated in full color in the Fundamental Illustrator 7 color insert. The purpose of the color insert is to provide you with a brief overview of the tutorials and act as an overall reference for the practical use of color throughout these tutorials.

Watch for this symbol:

MD's Grill, located downtown on the corner of Sixth and Grand, needs a logo and an appetizers menu. It's just the type of job you're ready to tackle now that you've learned to work with Illustrator's type options and special effects.

As you work through this tutorial, you'll master the techniques introduced in Chapter 6 selections within type objects, transforming type and containers, flowing text into columns, working with multiple master fonts and painting type.

Creating the Logo

Follow these steps in creating your logo:

1. In the Units and Undo Preferences dialog box (select File|Preferences|Units and Undo), set the General Units to inches and the Type Units to points.

2. Because it is easier to locate the outlines of type containers in Artwork mode, switch to that mode by choosing Artwork (CTRL/COMMAND+Y) from the View menu.

3. In the Character palette (CTRL/COMMAND+T) set the font to Helvetica Bold and the size to 14 points.

4. Select the Type tool in the Toolbox palette and click and drag on the artboard to create a rectangular text container about 3 inches wide and 2-1/2 inches high.

5. Duplicate the container by clicking and dragging its outline with the Selection tool while holding the ALT/OPTION and SHIFT keys (the SHIFT key constrains the drag to multiples of 45 degrees). Drag the copy horizontally to the right until its left side aligns with the right side of the original container, as shown in Figure 6-25. When you are satisfied with its location, release the mouse button before releasing the ALT/OPTION and SHIFT keys.

6. Click the Type tool inside the first container to create an insertion point and enter the following text:

   M(return)
   gr(return)
   on the corner of sixth

7. You'll need to change "on the corner of sixth" because it should have been all capital letters. To change it, select the entire line by triple-clicking within it with the Text tool. Choose the Change Case command from the type menu. In the Change Case dialog box, select the Upper Case (ABC) option and click OK.

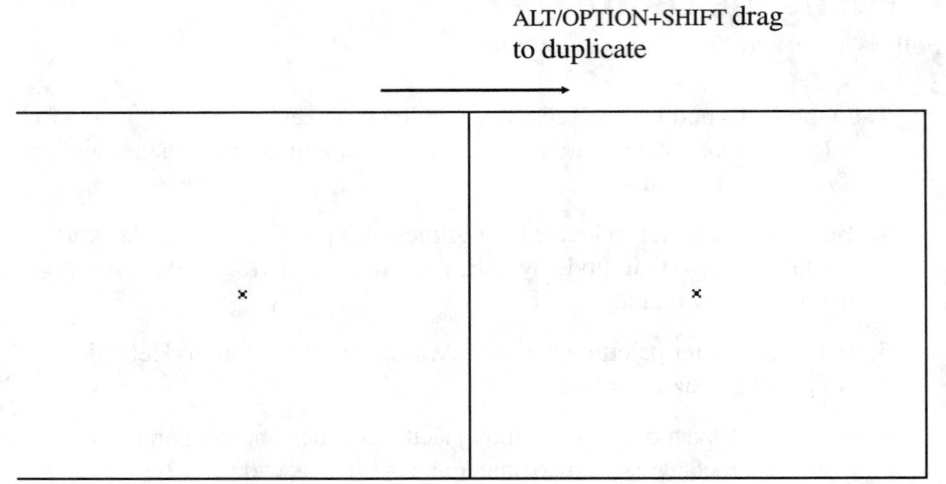

ALT/OPTION+SHIFT drag
to duplicate

FIGURE 6-25   Drag the container while holding the ALT/OPTION and SHIFT keys to duplicate it

8. In the second container enter:

   D's(return)
   ill(return)
   (space)AND GRAND

9. To change the straight apostrophe to a curly one, choose Smart Punctuation from the Type menu. In the Smart Punctuation dialog box, make sure Smart Quotes is checked and Replace In Entire Document is selected. Click OK.

 If the Report Results option was checked in the Smart Punctuation dialog box, a second dialog box will inform you that one quote was changed. Click OK to dismiss the dialog box.

10. Select the type in the first container by clicking on it with the Selection tool. Right-align the type using the CTRL/COMMAND+SHIFT+R keyboard shortcut.

11. Select the Type tool and use triple-clicks to select and format each line of type individually to the specifications shown next.

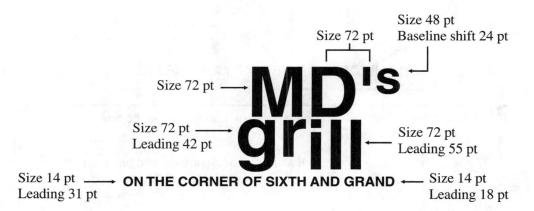

Use triple-clicks to select lines, even lines with only a few letters, because the paragraph return at the end of each line carries leading information just as characters do. If you select the letters but not the paragraph returns, you may not achieve the desired results when you modify the leading.

12. With the Direct Selection tool, click and drag the left side of the first text container until it is about an eighth of an inch from the type. Hold the SHIFT key as you drag to constrain the movement to the horizontal axis.

13. Similarly, click and drag the right side of the right-hand container until it is about an eighth of an inch from the type.

14. With the Direct Selection tool, click and drag the bottom lines of both containers until they are about an eighth of an inch below the bottom line of type. Hold the SHIFT key as you drag to constrain the movement to the vertical axis. The logo should now look like Figure 6-26.

15. Select the first container and its type by clicking on the type with the Selection tool. Shear the type and container by double-clicking on the Shear tool icon in the Tool palette, as shown in Figure 6-27. In the Shear dialog box, enter a shear angle of **-30**, select the Vertical Axis option, and click OK.

16. Repeat the process on the right-hand container and text, this time entering a shear angle of **30**. The logo should now appear as shown on the left side of Figure 6-28.

FIGURE 6-26   Reshape the containers to fit closely around the type

17. With the Selection tool, click and drag the right-hand container and type down until its left edge aligns with the right edge of the other container, as shown on the right side of Figure 6-28. Hold the SHIFT key as you drag to constrain the movement to the vertical axis.

18. Select the type in the right-hand container by clicking on it with the Selection tool. Paint the selected type red by clicking the Fill icon in the tool palette to activate it, then clicking the Color button to display the Color palette, and finally selecting a red color from the Color Spectrum bar in the Color palette.

 Throughout this exercise and the following one, you may want to use the CTRL/COMMAND+Y shortcut to toggle between the Preview and Artwork modes to ensure that color has been applied as expected.

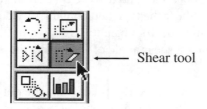   ← Shear tool

FIGURE 6-27   The Shear tool button in the Tool palette

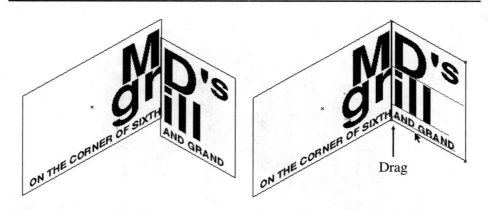

■ **FIGURE 6-28**   The logo after shearing the type and containers (left) and after repositioning the right-hand container (right)

19. In Artwork mode, select the left-hand container, but not its type, by clicking on its outline with the Direct Selection tool. Fill the container with red by selecting the Eyedropper tool (I) and clicking it on the red type in the right-hand container.

20. Select the right-hand container, but not its type, by clicking on its outline with the Direct Selection tool. Fill the container with black by clicking the Fill button in the Toolbox palette to activate it, then clicking the Color button to display the Color palette, and finally clicking on the small black rectangle at the far right side of the Color Spectrum bar.

Tip   *In Preview mode, you cannot use the Eyedropper tool to pick up color from type in a container with a fill. Once a fill is applied to a type container, the Eyedropper (in Preview mode) picks up the fill color of the container rather than the color of the type.*

21. Toggle to Preview mode (CTRL/COMMAND+Y) to view the finished logo, which is shown here:

22. Because you will be using the logo in the next tutorial exercise, save it as a file named MDlogo in a convenient location on your hard drive.

Creating the Menu

Now let's create the menu. Follow these steps:

1. Because you made quite a few changes to the character settings in the previous exercise, reset them in the Character palette (CTRL/COMMAND+T) to those shown in Figure 6-29.

2. Choose Show Rulers (CTRL/COMMAND+R) from the View menu to display the rulers if they are not already visible. Click and drag a vertical guideline from the ruler on the left side of the drawing window. When it is 1/2-inch to the right of the left edge of the page, release the mouse to set the guide. Create a second guideline 1/2-inch to the left of the right edge of the page in the same manner. Similarly, drag two horizontal guidelines from the top ruler and locate them 1/2-inch below the top of the page and 1/2-inch above the bottom of the page.

3. Because it is easier to locate the outlines of type containers in Artwork mode, switch to that mode by choosing Artwork (CTRL/COMMAND+Y) from the View menu.

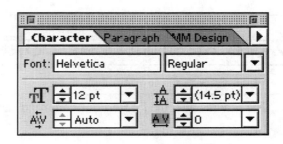

FIGURE 6-29   Before beginning the menu project, reset the character settings as shown here

4. Beginning where the top and left guidelines intersect, drag the Type tool to create a rectangular type container 1/2-inch deep and stretching to the right guide line.

5. Enter the text **ALWAYS AROUND THE CORNER**.

6. With the insertion point active in the container, select all the text using the CTRL/COMMAND+A shortcut.

7. In the Character palette (CTRL/COMMAND+T), set the font to Tekton MM Regular and the size to **24** points.

Note   *Tekton MM is one of the multiple master fonts that comes on the Illustrator 7 Application CD-ROM. If you need help installing fonts into your system, consult your system's user guide.*

8. In the Paragraph palette (CTRL/COMMAND+M), set the paragraph alignment to centered and the left and right indents to **12** points.

9. Choose MM Design from the Type menu. In the MM Design palette, set the Weight to **620** to make the type bold. Don't worry about the Width; this will be automatically adjusted when you fit the headline to its container in the next step.

10. With the type still selected, choose Fit Headline from the Type menu. Your headline should resemble the one shown in Figure 6-30.

ALWAYS AROUND THE CORNER

FIGURE 6-30   The heading after the Fit Headline command has been applied

11. With the Type tool, drag a second type container between the left and right guidelines. Begin 1/4-inch below the first container and make the new container **4** inches deep.

12. In the Character palette, set the font to Times Roman and the size to **18** points.

13. In the Paragraph palette, set the type to left-aligned, the left and right indents to **0**, and the first line indent to **18**.

14. Enter the following text, complete with misspellings, into the container:

   Now is the tyme for all good men to come to the aid of their team. With our beluved Red Birds locked in a tight pennant race, there's no better time than now to show your true colors. So, MD's Grill has declared every Monday night from now until the end of the season, Cardinals Colors Night.

   Taht's right, everyone who wears red to Mad Dogs on Manday will receive a free order of Hot Wings with each Square Value Meal purchased at the regualar price.

15. Select the type you just entered along with its container by clicking on the type with the Selection tool.

16. Choose Rows & Columns from the Type menu. In the Rows & Columns dialog box, set the number of Rows to **1**, the Rows Gutter to **12**, and the number of columns to **3**. Accept the values Illustrator 7 offers for the other settings and click OK.

17. The type would look better if the word *everyone* was hyphenated. Insert a discretionary hyphen by clicking the Type tool between the *y* and *o* to create an insertion point. Then type CTRL/COMMAND+SHIFT+hyphen to create the discretionary hyphen. Choose Open from the File menu, locate the file MDlogo, which you created in the previous exercise, and click Open. Your artwork should now look like Figure 6-31.

18. Select the logo and copy it to the clipboard with the File|Copy (CTRL/COMMAND+C) menu command. Return to the menu document and Paste (choose File|Paste or press CTRL/COMMAND+V) the logo into it.

19. Use the Selection tool to move the logo into the position shown in Figure 6-32.

20. Select the three columns of type by clicking on the type in one of the columns with the Selection tool. Add the left side of the logo to the selection by clicking on it with the Selection tool while holding the SHIFT key. Create a type wrap by choosing the Type|Wrap|Make menu command. The type should now wrap around the left portion of the logo as shown here:

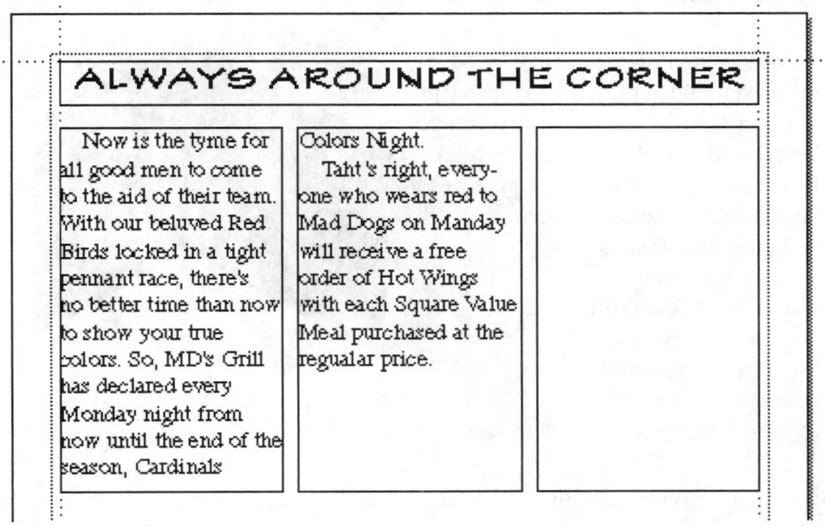

6

ALWAYS AROUND THE CORNER

Now is the tyme for all good men to come to the aid of their team. With our beluved Red Birds locked in a tight pennant race, there's no better time than now to show your true colors. So, MD's Grill has declared every Monday night from now until the end of the season, Cardinals

Colors Night.
Taht's right, every-one who wears red to Mad Dogs on Manday will receive a free order of Hot Wings with each Square Value Meal purchased at the regualar price.

FIGURE 6-31   The type after the Rows & Columns command has been applied

FIGURE 6-32   The logo in position on the menu

ALWAYS AROUND THE CORNER

Now is the tyme for all good men to come to the aid of their team. With our beluved Red Birds locked in a tight pennant race, there's no better time than now to show your true colors. So, MD's Grill has declared every Monday night from now until the end of the season, Cardinals Colors Night.

Taht's right, everyone who wears red to Mad Dogs on Manday will receive a free order

of Wings

21. Don't worry about any of the type that flows behind the right side of the logo, you'll fix that later.

22. Stretch the three linked type containers so that the text does not extend into the third container. First select the bottom line of one of the containers by clicking on it with the Direct Selection tool. Add the bottom lines of the other containers to the selection by holding the SHIFT key as you click on them with the Direct Selection tool. Click and drag one of the selected lines downward to resize all three containers simultaneously (hold the SHIFT key as you drag to constrain the movement to the vertical axis). When the type is totally within the first two columns (as shown in Figure 6-33), release the mouse button.

23. Choose the Group Selection tool from the Toolbox palette, select the container on the right (the one with no type) by clicking on its outline, and cut it from the document using CTRL/COMMAND+X. Then paste it back into the same position using the Paste in Front (CTRL/COMMAND+F) command. This will remove the container from the link sequence without affecting the link between the first two containers.

24. With the Direct Selection tool, click and drag the top of the empty container until it is just below the logo, as shown in Figure 6-34.

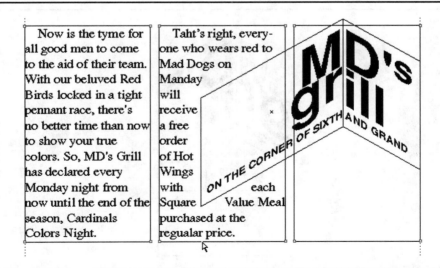

FIGURE 6-33   Resizing the columns of text by dragging the bottoms of the containers with the Direct Selection tool

25. Click theType tool on the outline of the empty container to create an insertion point and enter the following text:

> *WARNING: MD's hot wings may contain spices unfit for small children. Parental discretion is advised.*

26. With the insertion point still active in the container, select all the type in the container using the CTRL/COMMAND+A shortcut. Apply the character and paragraph settings shown in Figure 6-35.

27. Now add color to the headline created in steps 4 through 10. Begin by selecting only the headline container by clicking on its outline with the Group Selection tool.

28. Fill the headline container with red by selecting the Eyedropper tool and clicking it on the left side of the logo. The Eyedropper will pick up the red fill from the logo and apply it to the headline container.

29. Select the headline type and container by clicking on the type with the Selection tool. To apply a white fill to the type, click the Fill button in the Toolbox palette to activate it, then click the Color button to display the

FIGURE 6-34   Resizing the third column by dragging the top of the container with the Direct Selection tool

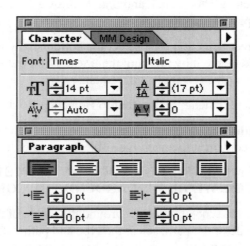

FIGURE 6-35   Character and Paragraph settings for the warning text

Color palette, and finally click on the small white rectangle at the far right side of the Color Spectrum bar.

30. Toggle to the Preview mode to view your work. It should look as shown below. Toggle back to the Artwork mode to continue working.

ALWAYS AROUND THE CORNER

Now is the tyme for all good men to come to the aid of their team. With our beluved Red Birds locked in a tight pennant race, there's no better time than now to show your true colors. So, MD's Grill has declared every Monday night from now until the end of the season, Cardinals Colors Night.

Taht's right, everyone who wears red to Mad Dogs on Manday will receive a free order of Hot Wings with each Square Value Meal purchased at the regualar price.

WARNING: MD's hot wings may contain spices unfit for small children. Parental discretion is advised.

31. With the Rectangle tool, click and drag to draw a rectangle filling the remaining space within the guidelines, as shown in Figure 6-36.

32. With the Direct Selection tool, select the bottom-right anchor point of the rectangle and delete it by pressing the BACKSPACE/DELETE key. The left and top sides of the rectangle will remain.

33. In the Character palette, set the font to Helvetica Bold and the size to 16.

34. Click the Path Type tool on the top line of the remaining portion of the rectangle to convert it to a path type object and enter the following text:

STOP BY MD'S GRILL ON YOUR WAY HOME FOR AN APPETIZER. WE'RE JUST AROUND THE CORNER!

35. As you enter the type, it will flow around the inside of the path. To move it to the outside of the path, select the type and path with the Selection tool and then use the tool to pull the I-beam from one side of the path to the other, as shown in Figure 6-37.

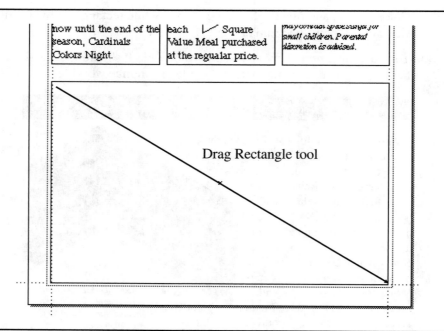

FIGURE 6-36   Dragging the Rectangle tool to create a path for type that will flow around a corner

‫זⱭ‬W Yᗺ ꟼOTƧ̶   →STOP BY MD'S

Drag

FIGURE 6-37   Dragging the I-beam across the path to force the text to wrap around the outside of the corner

36. Drag the I-beam along the path with the Selection tool to position the type so that the corner falls between the words *WAY* and *HOME*.

37. With the type and path still selected, switch to Preview mode (CTRL/ COMMAND+Y) and paint the type red by selecting the Eyedropper tool and clicking it on the left side of the logo. The Eyedropper will pick up the red fill from the logo and apply it to the type.

38. Click and drag the type and path with the Selection tool until the type is within the guidelines, as shown in Figure 6-38.

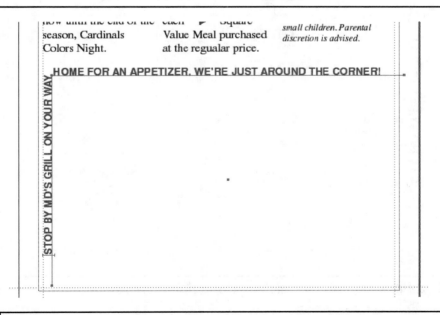

FIGURE 6-38   The menu after the path type has been repositioned

39. Beginning about a 1/4-inch below and to the right of the corner of the path type you created in the previous steps, click and drag the Type tool to create a rectangular type container for the menu text, as shown in Figure 6-39.

40. In the Character palette, set the Font to Helvetica Regular, the size to **18**, and the leading to **21.5** (the Auto setting for 18 point type). In the Paragraph palette, set the space before paragraph to **6** points and all indent settings to **0**.

41. With the insertion point active in the container, choose Tab Ruler from the Type menu.

42. Click at the 2-3/4 inch mark on the ruler in the Tab Ruler palette to create a left-justified tab. Create a second tab at the 6-1/4 inch mark. To change the second tab to decimal-justified, click on it once to select it and then click the Decimal-Justified Tab button in the Tab Ruler palette, as shown in Figure 6-40.

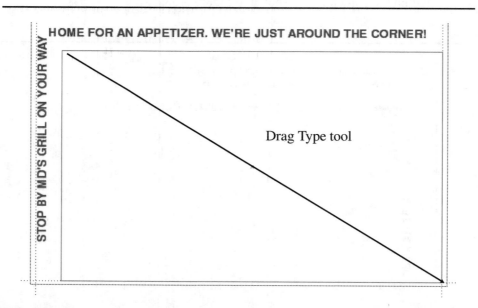

FIGURE 6-39   Dragging the Type tool to create a container for the menu items

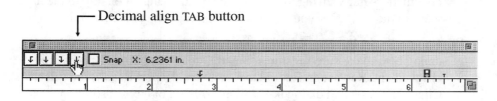

Decimal align TAB button

■ FIGURE 6-40 Changing a selected tab to decimal justified in the Tab Ruler palette. Also shown are the tab settings for the menu items text

43. Enter the following text into the container you have created for the menu text:

> **Appetizers(TAB)Description(ENTER)**
> **Wimpy Wings(TAB)Wings in a mild sauce(TAB) $3.95(ENTER)**
> **Buffalo Wings(TAB)Traditional hot wings(TAB)3.95(ENTER)**
> **MD Wings(TAB)Flamin'(TAB)3.95(ENTER)**
> **Broccoli on a stick(TAB)A specialty of the chef!(TAB)3.50(ENTER)**
> **Square Value Meals(ENTER)**
> **Sandwich, fries, and your choice of a drink(ENTER)**
> **Chicken Sandwich(TAB)Your choice, white or dark(TAB)4.95(ENTER)**
> **Steak Sandwich(ENTER)Rare, medium, or well**
> **done(TAB)5.95(ENTER)**
> **Barbecue Sandwich(TAB)An MD specialty(TAB)4.95**

44. Triple-click in the first line of the menu text to select it. Change the font to Helvetica Bold and the size to **21** points in the Character palette.

45. Triple-click in the line "Square Value Meals" to select it and change the font to Helvetica Bold and the size to **21** points in the Character palette.

46. Triple-click in the line "Sandwich, fries…" to select it and change the font to Helvetica Oblique in the Character palette.

47. Check the spelling in your document by choosing Check Spelling from the Type menu. In the Check Spelling dialog box, the first word in the Misspelled Words list will be selected and also highlighted in your document. After viewing the word in context, change it or skip to the next word in the list. After you have worked through the entire list, click Done.

48. Choose Smart Punctuation from the Type menu. In the Smart Punctuation dialog box, make sure Ligatures, Smart Quotes, and Smart Spaces are checked and Replace In Entire Document and Report Results are selected. Click OK. A second dialog box will inform you of any substitutions that were made. Click OK to dismiss the dialog box.

49. Toggle to the Preview mode to view the finished project, which is shown here:

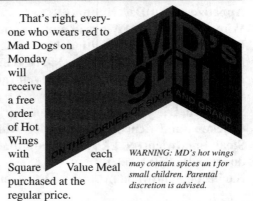

ALWAYS AROUND THE CORNER

Now is the time for all good men to come to the aid of their team. With our beloved Red Birds locked in a tight pennant race, there's no better time than now to show your true colors. So, MD's Grill has declared every Monday night from now until the end of the season, Cardinals Colors Night.

That's right, everyone who wears red to Mad Dogs on Monday will receive a free order of Hot Wings with each Square Value Meal purchased at the regular price.

WARNING: MD's hot wings may contain spices un t for small children. Parental discretion is advised.

HOME FOR AN APPETIZER. WE'RE JUST AROUND THE CORNER!

STOP BY MD'S GRILL ON YOUR WAY

Appetizers	Description	
Wimpy Wings	Wings in a mild sauce	$3.95
Buffalo Wings	Traditional hot wings	3.95
MD Wings	Flamin'	3.95
Broccoli on a stick	A specialty of the chef!	3.50

Square Value Meals

Sandwich, fries and your choice of a drink

Chicken Sandwich	Your choice, white or dark	4.95
Steak Sandwich	Rare, medium or well done	5.95
Barbecue Sandwich	An MD specialty	4.95

50. Save the finished document to your hard drive.

Conclusion

As you've seen, Illustrator 7 offers designers a powerful set of tools for editing, manipulating, and transforming type. This makes it an ideal program for projects such as logos where type is used as a design element, and also for small typesetting projects such as flyers and brochures.

6

Creating and Editing
Drawing Objects

7

S ince its introduction, Adobe Illustrator has been the premiere desktop tool for creating vector images, that is, images made of objects shapes and lines rather than pixels. The advantages of vector images are three-fold:

- They are easy to create and edit.
- They can be resized without loss of detail.
- Vector image files are generally smaller than bit-mapped image files.

This chapter explores the process of creating and editing the basic lines and shapes that will form the core of your Illustrator 7 drawings. In addition, it will introduce the Graph tool, which allows you to quickly create charts and graphs in Illustrator 7.

Creating Paths and Shapes

Although this chapter will discuss drawing objects in terms of paths and shapes, all drawing objects are actually paths made up of two or more anchor points and the line segments linking them. A shape is simply a closed path, that is, a path with its first and last points connected by a line segment.

Working with the Pen Tool

Although the easiest way to create drawing objects in Illustrator 7 is to use one of the drawing tools to create a simple object such as a rectangle or ellipse, you gain a better understanding of drawing objects by beginning with the Pen tool.

Creating Paths

Because a path may be closed, open, straight, and/or curved, you can create and edit one using a variety of tools in Illustrator 7. This section defines closed and open paths in an effort for you to gain an understanding of path behavior and defines other tools in Illustrator 7 used to create these paths.

Drawing Straight-Line Paths

The fill and stroke controls are located in the large box near the bottom of the Toolbox palette, which is shown in Figure 7-1. Click on the small button in the lower-left corner of this box to set the fill and stroke to Illustrator 7's defaults—black stroke and white fill.

Click on the Fill tool to bring it to the front and activate it.

Click on the None button (a white box with a red diagonal slash) to set the fill to none.

 It can be confusing to draw paths filled with a color. Remedy this by working in the Artwork mode (Select View\Artwork or CTRL\COMMAND+Y) or by setting the fill to None and the stroke to Black. You'll learn all about setting fills and strokes in **Chapter 10**, *but for now just follow these instructions.*

To create a path, select the Pen tool (P) from the Toolbox palette as shown in Figure 7-2. Notice that when you move the cursor over the artboard it takes the form of the Pen button with a small "x" to the right side of its base. This indicates you are ready to begin drawing a path.

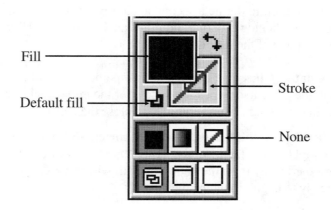

FIGURE 7-1   The fill and stroke controls

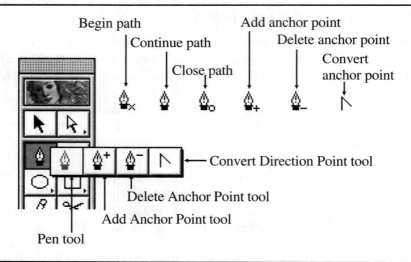

FIGURE 7-2   The Pen tool's pop-out menu in the main Toolbox and the pen cursors

Click and release the cursor on the artboard. Your first anchor point will appear at the site of the click, and the "x" will disappear from the pen cursor to inform you that you are in the process of defining a path.

Click at a new location to define a second anchor point linked to the first by a line segment. Continue clicking to define additional anchor points and line segments. Finish the path in one of the following ways:

- **Close the path**   Click on the initial anchor point (the small circle that appears in the pen cursor when it is held over the initial anchor point indicates that clicking at that location will close the path).

- **Complete the path but leave it open**   Momentarily switch to a Selection tool by holding down the CTRL/COMMAND key and then click on the artboard away from the path. The path will be deselected and you will be ready to begin drawing a new path.

Drawing Curved Paths

The world isn't limited to straight lines and sharp corners and neither is Illustrator 7. Curves in the program are defined by direction lines and points, which are associated with anchor points. If you haven't worked with a drawing program like Illustrator before, this method of drawing may seem awkward at first. Don't be intimidated: with a little practice you'll quickly get used to it. When you do, you'll find you have virtually unlimited control over the paths you create.

Begin a new path with the Pen tool. This time, instead of clicking to create an anchor point, hold the mouse button and drag the cursor a short distance. As you drag, the cursor becomes a solid arrow that pulls a direction line from the anchor point. This direction line actually controls the direction in which the curve will arc from the anchor point you've just created. Don't be too concerned about it right now, you'll learn to adjust it later. Release the mouse button to set the direction point.

Click and drag a second anchor point and direction line. Before you release, move the direction point around the artboard. Notice how its position affects the shape of the curved line segment. When you are satisfied with the shape of the segment, release the mouse button.

Note   *When you click and drag the Pen tool to create an anchor point, you create two direction lines. One affects the path segment preceding the anchor point and the other affects the path segment that follows it. To create only one direction arrow, click and release the Pen tool to create an anchor point. Hold the cursor over that point—it will change to an unfilled arrow—and click and drag to pull a direction line from the point. The new direction line will affect only the next path segment created.*

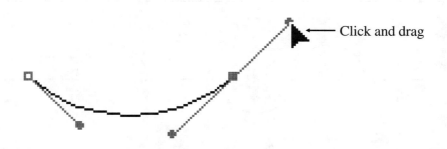

Click and drag

FIGURE 7-3   Clicking and dragging the Pen tool to create an anchor point and direction lines

Continue drawing new line segments. When you are finished with your path, complete it by closing the path or by pressing CTRL/COMMAND and clicking on another part of the artboard as described previously.

Continue to experiment with drawing curved and straight-line segments by attempting to duplicate the path shown in Figure 7-4.

 When drawing a path, hold down the SHIFT key while clicking the Pen tool to create a new anchor point at an angle from the previous anchor point that is a multiple of 45 degrees (or whichever Constrain Angle is currently set in your General Preference dialog box). Holding the SHIFT key while dragging a direction line also constrains the direction line.

Don't be too concerned if your results don't match exactly; the next few exercises will help you remedy the situation.

Reshaping Curved Path Segments

Click the Direct Selection tool on one of the curved path segments you have drawn to select the segment and display the associated direction lines and points.

Reshape the curve by dragging one of the direction points to change the length or angle of the direction line, as shown in Figure 7-5.

Notice that changing the angle of the direction line changes the shape of the path segments on both sides of the anchor point, as Figure 7-6 shows. This occurs because the two direction lines associated with an anchor point are linked locked on the same

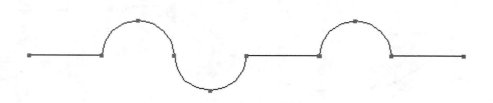

FIGURE 7-4   Practice duplicating this path to develop your skill in combining straight and curved line segments

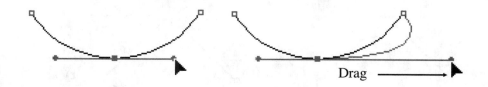

FIGURE 7-5   Dragging a direction point to reshape a curved path segment

axis relative to the anchor point. This linking assures that one curve flows smoothly into the next. You'll learn to break these links later in this section.

Moving and Adding Anchor Points

To move an anchor point, use the Direct Selection tool to click and drag the point to the desired location, as shown in Figure 7-7.

To add an anchor point to a path, click on the path with the Add Anchor Point tool at the location where you want the point to appear, as shown in Figure 7-8. If the point is on a curved segment, direction lines will be created so that the shape of the path is unchanged.

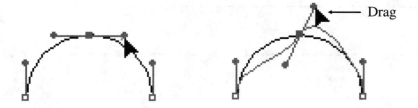

FIGURE 7-6   Changing the angle of linked direction lines changes the curves on both sides of an anchor point

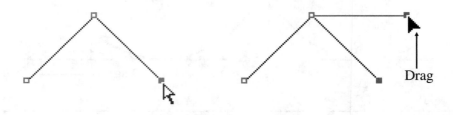

FIGURE 7-7   Moving an anchor point with the Direct Selection tool

Deleting Anchor Points

Delete an anchor point by clicking on it with the Delete Anchor Point tool, shown in Figure 7-9. The anchor point will be removed and the path will be reshaped.

 An anchor point can also be deleted by selecting it and pressing the BACKSPACE/DELETE key. However, deleting a point in this manner breaks the path into two separate paths.

Converting Direction Points

After a path has been created it is possible to add, delete, or unlink direction lines with the Convert Direction Point tool.

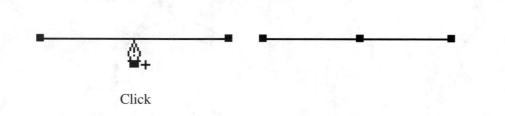

Click

FIGURE 7-8   Adding an anchor point with the Add Anchor Point tool

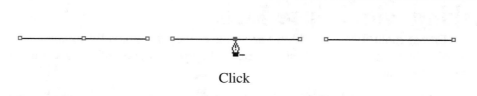

Click

FIGURE 7-9 Deleting an anchor point

To add direction lines to an anchor point, click and drag on the anchor point with the Convert Direction Point tool. As you drag, direction lines will be pulled from the point, as shown in Figure 7-10.

To remove direction lines from an anchor point, click on the anchor point with the Convert Direction Point tool.

To unlink direction lines, click and drag one of the direction points with the Convert Direction Point tool.

To relink direction lines, click and drag on the associated anchor point with the Convert Direction Point tool. New, linked direction lines will be pulled from the point.

Tip   *To momentarily switch to the Convert Direction Point tool from the Pen tool hold down the ALT/OPTION key.*

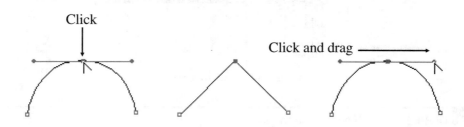

Click

Click and drag

FIGURE 7-10 Using the Convert Direction Point tool to edit a path

Working with Ellipse Tools

The Ellipse tool (N) and its siblings are some of the many tools Illustrator 7 offers to make the drawing of simple shapes easier. Figure 7-11 shows the tools you have at your disposal.

Note   *Now that you'll be working with shapes, it will be easier to work in the Preview mode (select View\Preview or use CTRL/COMMAND+Y to toggle between Preview and Artwork modes).*

*You might also find it useful to set a fill color for the objects you'll be drawing. Click on the Fill button in the main Toolbox (refer back to Figure 7-1) to bring it to the front and activate it (or type X to toggle between Fill and Stroke). Click on the Color button to display the Color palette. Select a fill color by holding the cursor over the Color Bar (it will change to an eyedropper) and clicking on the color of your choice. For more information on setting fills and strokes, see **Chapter 10**.*

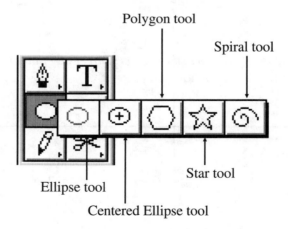

FIGURE 7-11   The Ellipse tools

Creating an Ellipse

To create an ellipse, select the Ellipse tool and do one of the following.

- Click and drag the Ellipse tool on the artboard. As you drag, an ellipse will be displayed. When you are satisfied with the shape, release the mouse button.

 To force Illustrator 7 to draw a circle, hold the SHIFT key while dragging the Ellipse tool.

- Click the Ellipse tool on the artboard to display the Ellipse dialog box, as shown in Figure 7-13. Enter values for the Height and Width and click OK. An ellipse with the specified dimensions will be drawn at the location of the initial click.

Centering an Ellipse

Center an ellipse on a specific point by selecting the Centered Ellipse tool and clicking and dragging from the desired center point.

 Momentarily toggle between the Ellipse tool to the Centered Ellipse tool by holding down the ALT/OPTION key.

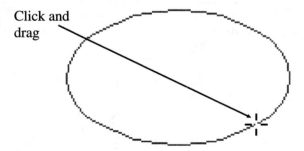

Click and drag

FIGURE 7-12 Dragging the Ellipse tool to create an ellipse

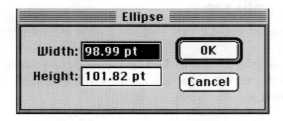

FIGURE 7-13   The Ellipse dialog box

Or click the Ellipse tool on the artboard to open the Ellipse dialog box. Enter Height and Width values and click OK. An ellipse with the specified dimensions will be drawn centered on the location of the initial click.

Drawing a Polygon

To draw a polygon, click and drag the Polygon tool on the artboard. The number of sides drawn will be determined by the most recent setting in the Polygon dialog box. You can add or delete sides as you draw by pressing the UP or DOWN ARROW respectively. To move the polygon as you draw, press the SPACEBAR and drag.

You also can click the Polygon tool on the artboard to display the Polygon dialog box, as shown in Figure 7-15. Enter values for the radius and number of sides and click OK to draw the polygon.

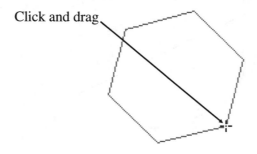

Click and drag

FIGURE 7-14   Dragging the Polygon tool to create a polygon

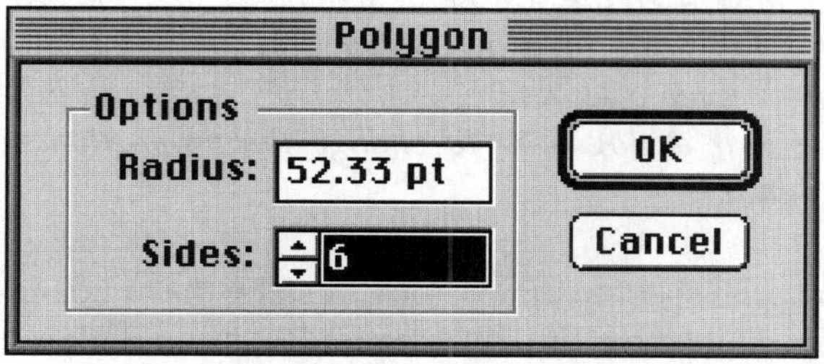

Polygon

┌─ Options ─────────────┐
│ Radius: 52.33 pt   │   OK
│ Sides: ▲▼ 6   │   Cancel
└───────────────────────┘

FIGURE 7-15   The Polygon dialog box

Drawing a Star

Click and drag the Star tool on the artboard to draw a star. The number of points on the star will be determined by the most recent setting in the Star dialog box, as shown in Figure 7-17. To add points as you draw, press the UP ARROW key. To delete points as you draw press the DOWN ARROW key. Press the SPACEBAR while you drag to move the star as you draw it.

You can alter the proportions of a star as you draw it by holding the CTRL/COMMAND key to lock the inner points. When the star reaches the desired proportions, release the CTRL/COMMAND key and drag until the star is the desired size.

7

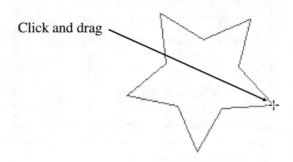

Click and drag

FIGURE 7-16   Dragging the Star tool to create a star

Once you have used the SPACEBAR method to alter the proportions of a star, any additional stars you draw by dragging the Star tool will have the same proportions, even after you have created a star with different proportions using the Star dialog box. To change the proportion, use the SPACEBAR method again.

To draw a star with specific dimensions, click on the artboard with the Star tool to display the Star dialog box. Enter values for Radius 1, Radius 2, and the number of points. The larger radius value is the distance from the star's center to its outer points. The smaller radius is the distance from the center to the inner points. Click OK to draw the star.

Drawing a Spiral

 To better observe spirals, set the fill and stroke to the default values by clicking the Default Fill and Stroke button in the color area of the main Toolbox (refer back to Figure 7-1).

To draw a spiral, click and drag the Spiral tool on the artboard. To increase or decrease the number of winds (360-degree turns) as you draw, press the UP or DOWN ARROW respectively. To move the spiral as you draw, press the SPACEBAR and drag.

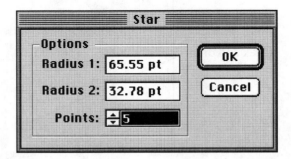

FIGURE 7-17   The Star dialog box

Click and drag

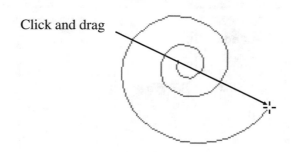

FIGURE 7-18 Dragging the Spiral tool to create a spiral

Optionally, click the Spiral tool on the artboard to display the Spiral dialog box, as shown in Figure 7-19, and enter the following parameters:

■ **Radius**   The radius of the spiral.

■ **Decay**   The amount each wind of spiral decreases (values less than 100 percent) or increases (values greater than 100 percent) from the radius.

■ **Segments**   The number of path segments making up the spiral. Four segments complete one full wind.

Also select a direction for the spiral by clicking one of the Style buttons.

Click OK to draw the spiral.

Working with Rectangle Tools

Drawing a Rectangle

To draw a rectangle, select the Rectangle tool from the main Toolbox, as shown in Figure 7-20, and do one of the following:

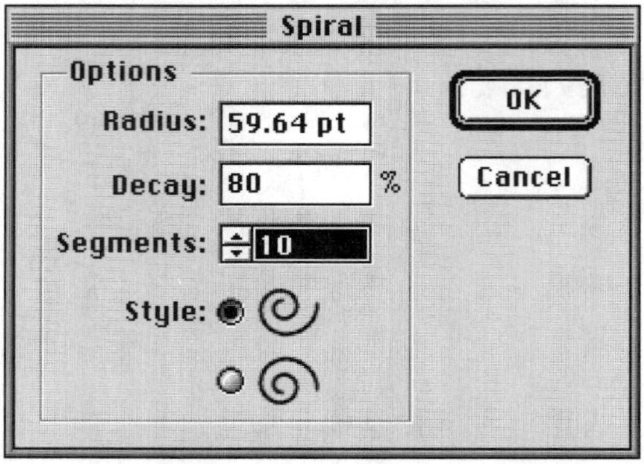

FIGURE 7-19 The Spiral dialog box

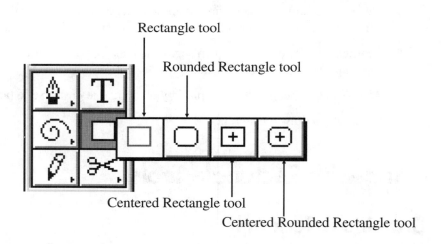

FIGURE 7-20 The Rectangle tools

■ Click and drag the Rectangle tool on the artboard. As you drag, a rectangle will be displayed. When you are satisfied with its dimensions release the mouse button.

Tip *To force Illustrator 7 to draw a square, hold the SHIFT key while dragging the Rectangle tool.*

■ Click the Rectangle tool on the artboard to display the Rectangle dialog box as shown in Figure 7-21. Enter values for the Height and Width (ignore the Corner Radius parameter for now) and click OK. A rectangle of the specified dimensions will be drawn with its upper-left corner at the point of the initial click.

Centering a Rectangle

To center a rectangle on a specific point, click and drag the Centered Rectangle tool from the desired center point.

Tip *To momentarily switch from the Rectangle tool to the Centered Rectangle tool (and vice versa), hold down the ALT/OPTION key.*

Optionally, click the Centered Rectangle tool on the artboard to open the Rectangle dialog box. Enter Height and Width values and click OK. A rectangle with the specified dimensions will be drawn centered on the location of the initial click.

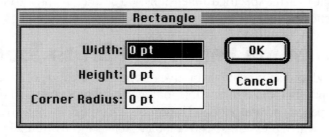

FIGURE 7-21   The Rectangle dialog box

Drawing a Rounded Rectangle

To draw a rectangle with rounded corners, click and drag the rounded Rectangle tool. By default, the corners of the rectangle will have a 12-point radius.

To change the default corner radius or to draw a rounded rectangle to specific dimensions, click either the Rectangle tool or the Rounded Rectangle tool on the artboard to display the Rectangle dialog box. Enter values for Height, Width, and Corner Radius. When you click OK, the new rectangle will be drawn with its upper-left corner at the point of the initial click.

 Rounded and regular rectangles can both be drawn from the Rectangle dialog box no matter which tool was clicked to display it. A Corner Radius value of 0 will draw a regular rectangle and select the Rectangle tool if it was not already selected. Any other Corner Radius value will draw a rounded rectangle and select the Rounded Rectangle tool. The value entered for the Corner Radius will become the new default value for that parameter.

 You can also reset the default Corner Radius from the General Preferences dialog box (select File\Preferences\General or CTRL/COMMAND+K).

Centering a Rounded Rectangle

To center a rounded rectangle on a specific point, click and drag the Centered Rounded Rectangle tool from the desired center point.

Optionally, click the Centered Rounded Rectangle tool on the artboard to open the Rectangle dialog box. Enter Height, Width, and Corner Radius values and click OK. A rectangle with the specified dimensions will be drawn centered on the location of the initial click.

Working with the Pencil and Brush Tools

The tools introduced so far lend themselves well to the creation of precisely drawn paths and shapes, but it is also possible to draw freehand shapes and objects using Illustrator 7's pencil and brush tools. These tools are especially powerful when used in conjunction with a pressure-sensitive tablet such as those offered by WACOM.

The Pencil Tool

To draw a freehand path with the Pencil tool, select it from the main Toolbox, as shown in Figure 7-22, and place the cursor over the point where you want your path to begin.

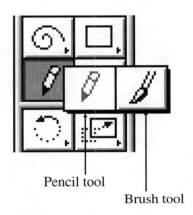

Pencil tool

Brush tool

FIGURE 7-22 The Pencil and Brush tools in the main Toolbox

7

Click and drag to draw the path. As you drag, a dotted line will be drawn on the screen. When you release the mouse, the dotted line will be replaced by a path made of several segments as shown in Figure 7-23.

The Curve Fitting Tolerance setting in the General Preferences dialog box, as shown in Figure 7-24 (select File|Preferences|General or type CTRL/COMMAND+K), determines how closely the new path follows the freehand line you drew onscreen (and consequently how many segments make up the path) as shown in Figure 7-25. The tolerance can be set from 0 (closely conforming, more segments) to 10 (loosely conforming, fewer segments).

You can draw a closed freehand path by simply ending the path with the cursor over its starting point. When a small unfilled circle appears next to the pencil cursor, release the mouse to complete and close the path.

To erase part of a freehand path *while you are drawing it*, hold down the CTRL/COMMAND key (the cursor will change to an eraser) and retrace the path. As you do so, the eraser will delete the dashed line beneath it as shown in Figure 7-26. When you release the CTRL/COMMAND key, the cursor will return to the Pencil and you can continue drawing.

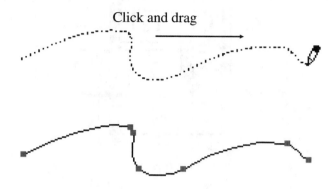

FIGURE 7-23   Drawing a freehand path with the Pencil tool

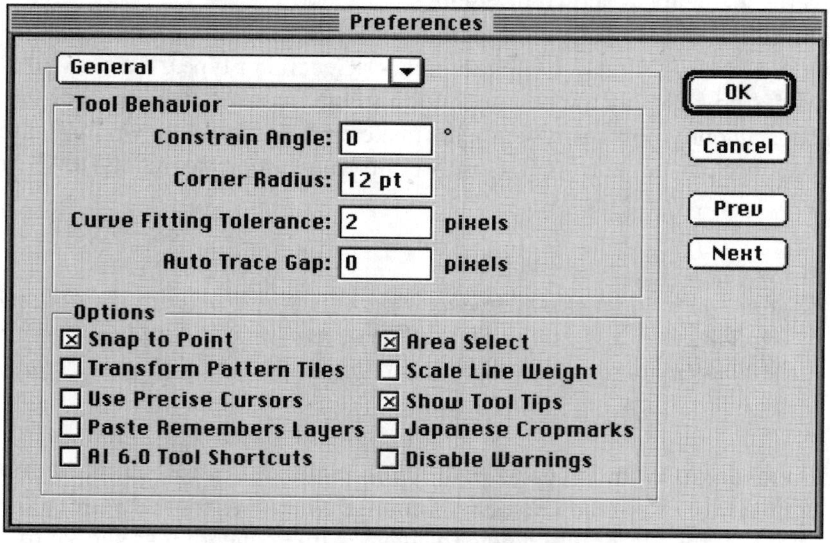

FIGURE 7-24   The General Preferences dialog box

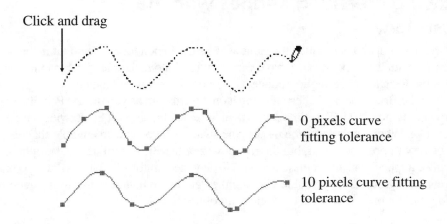

Click and drag

0 pixels curve
fitting tolerance

10 pixels curve fitting
tolerance

FIGURE 7-25   How the Curve Fitting Tolerance affects the final shape of
freehand paths

7

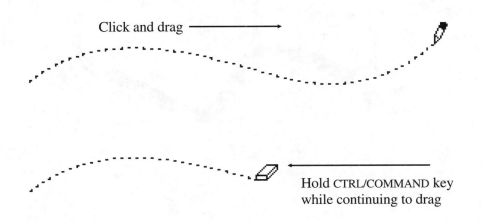

Click and drag

Hold CTRL/COMMAND key
while continuing to drag

FIGURE 7-26   Erasing with the Pencil tool

Drawing Freehand Shapes with the Brush Tool

The Brush tool operates in much the same way as the Pencil tool except that its brush strokes are actually shapes that can have varying widths along their lengths. In that way, they mimic what an artist might produce using a brush or calligraphic pen.

Select the Brush tool and click and drag it on the artboard as you did the Pencil tool, as shown in Figure 7-27. This time rather than a dashed line, you'll be drawing a thick black snake. When you release the mouse, the snake will become an editable shape.

Not very impressive so far, but the real power of the Brush tool lies in the options that can be applied to it. To set these options, display the Paintbrush Options dialog box, as shown in Figure 7-28, by double-clicking the Paintbrush button in the Tool palette.

You will be presented with the following options.

■ **Width**   The value you enter into the text box determines the width of your brushstrokes. If you have a pressure-sensitive tablet attached to your computer, you should also be able to check the Variable option. This will allow you to alter the width of a brushstroke as you draw by varying the pressure you apply.

Click and drag

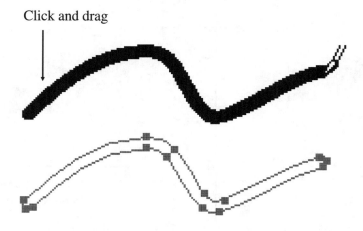

■ **FIGURE 7-27**   Drawing a freehand shape with the Brush tool. The top figure shows the Brush tool being dragged to create the shape shown at bottom.

The Paintbrush Options dialog box showing:

Paintbrush Options

Width
☐ Variable
`18 pt`

OK
Cancel

Style
☐ Calligraphic

Caps   **Joins**

FIGURE 7-28   The Paintbrush Options dialog box

7

- **Calligraphic**   When checked, this option varies the width of the stroke to mimic the use of a calligraphic pen held at an angle. The angle of the pen is set by typing a value into the text box. Strokes along the angle of the setting will be the narrowest. Strokes perpendicular to it will be the widest. This shows you the different results you'll get when you change the calligraphic setting:

- **Caps**   These buttons allow you to choose whether the ends of strokes will be rounded or squared.

■ Illustration **Joins**   These buttons allow you to choose rounded or squared corners where a stroke changes direction.

Editing Paths and Shapes

In order to make the paths you create using the various tools in Illustrator 7 fit your design or illustration, you'll ultimately want to change or alter them in some way. Regardless of the tools used to create your paths, you may edit them freely using a variety of techniques and methods. Some are simple—others are powerful and complex. This section defines Illustrator 7's path-editing tools in an effort to provide you with an understanding of the freedom you have at your fingertips.

Working with Path Commands

The Path commands in the Path submenu of the Objects menu offer several powerful ways to edit existing paths.

Joining Two Paths

To join two paths, select one endpoint from each path. If you wish to select more than one point at a time, click on the first point with the Direct Selection tool (A) and then hold the SHIFT key while clicking additional points to add them to the selection. Choose Object|Path|Join (CTRL/COMMAND+J). A straight-path segment will join the two points and the paths will be merged.

If the selected endpoints of the paths are coincident (located directly on top of each other), the Join dialog box will appear, presenting you with the option of replacing the two points with a single corner or smooth point. Select Corner to create a point with unlinked direction lines. Select Smooth to create a point with linked direction lines as shown in Figure 7-29.

Closing an Open Path

To close an open path, select the entire path with the Selection tool and choose Object|Path|Join (CTRL/COMMAND+J). A straight-path segment will join the endpoints of the path.

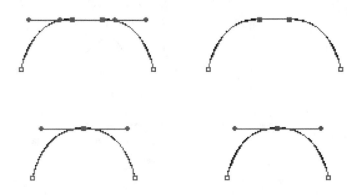

FIGURE 7-29   The effect of the Join command on endpoints of lines with non-coincident and coincident endpoints and on the endpoints of an open path

Averaging

Averaging moves all selected points to a location that is the average of their initial positions. To apply the Average command, select two or more points; choose Object|Path|Average (CTRL/COMMAND+ALT/OPTION+J); select either Horizontal, Vertical, or Both from the Average dialog box; and click OK.

Figure 7-30 shows the results of horizontal and vertical averaging. When Both is selected, all selected points are stacked one on top of the other.

 You can make two selected points coincident by applying horizontal and vertical averaging to them. This is useful when you want to join the endpoints of two paths smoothly rather than with a straight-line segment.

Outlining a Path

The Outline Path command (select Object|Path|Outline Path) replaces a selected stroked line with an object of the same width. Figure 7-31 shows the result of applying the Outline Path command.

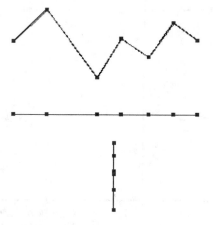

FIGURE 7-30   The results of averaging the points on a path horizontally (above) and vertically (below)

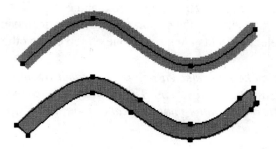

FIGURE 7-31   The Outline Path command converts a stroked line into a shape of the same width

Offsetting a Path

The Offset Path command (select Object|Path|Offset Path) duplicates a path and offsets the individual segments by the amount specified in the Offset Path dialog box, as shown in Figure 7-32. Curved segments are offset and resized. Straight segments are offset but not resized. They are joined in the manner specified in the Offset Path dialog box. Figure 7-33 shows the results of the Offset Path command.

Cleaning Up

Cleanup allows you to remove various invisible objects from your drawing. This will make your drawing easier to work with and more efficient to print.

To apply the Cleanup command it is not necessary to have an active selection. Simply select the Objects|Path|Cleanup menu command and choose from the options displayed in the Cleanup dialog box.

Delete Stray Points removes all points that are not part of a path.

Delete Unpainted Objects removes all drawing objects that are both unstroked and unfilled.

Delete Empty Text Paths removes all type objects (points, paths, and containers) that do not have type associated with them.

Slicing

The Slice command allows you to use a path to cut one or more other paths into pieces in a manner similar to using a cookie cutter.

To slice an object or objects, place the cookie cutter object in front of the target object(s). Select the cookie cutter and choose the Object|Path|Slice menu command.

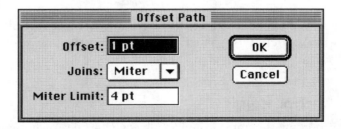

FIGURE 7-32   The Offset Path dialog box

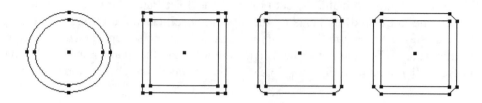

FIGURE 7-33   The results of the Offset Path command

The cookie cutter will be deleted and the target objects will be cut along its outline, as shown here:

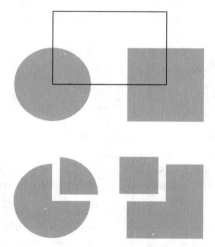

Above you see the cookie cutter and target objects before the Slice command is applied (left), after it is applied (center), and with the resulting objects separated for clarity (below).

Adding Anchor Points

The Add Anchor points command (select Object|Path|Add Anchor Points) adds an anchor point at the midway point of each segment in a path. The shape of the path is unchanged.

Splitting Paths

To split a path, you can simply select and delete an interior anchor point or segment of the path or you can use Illustrator 7's Scissors or Knife tools, as shown in Figure 7-34.

The Scissors Tool

To break a path, select the Scissors tool and click on the path. An open path will be split into two paths at the point of the click. The endpoints of the two paths will be coincident. A closed path will be converted into an open path with its endpoints coincident at the point of the click (see Figure 7-35).

The Knife Tool

The Knife tool is used to cut drawing objects just as you would use a real knife to cut a real object. To use the Knife tool, select it from the Toolbox palette and click and drag it onto the drawing board. As you drag, a line will trail the cursor. When you release the mouse, the line will cut through all objects beneath it, as shown in Figure 7-36.

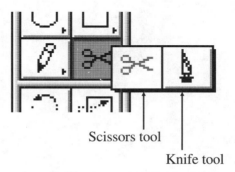

Scissors tool

Knife tool

FIGURE 7-34   The Scissors and Knife tools in the main Toolbox

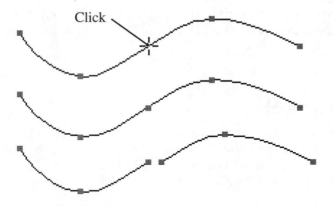

Click

FIGURE 7-35   Splitting a path with the Scissors tool. At the bottom, the paths are separated to show the results.

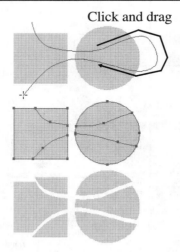

Click and drag

FIGURE 7-36   Objects being split using the Knife tool. At the bottom the split objects are separated to show the results.

The Knife tool is best used on closed paths or on open paths with a fill. Using the Knife tool on unfilled open paths may have unexpected results, for example, there may be no change or your path may be deleted.

The Reshape Tool

The Reshape tool allows you to distort selected points and line segments while maintaining their overall relationships. To use the Reshape tool, select the anchor points to be reshaped with the Direct Selection tool. Choose the Reshape toolbox from the Toolbox palette, as shown in Figure 7-37.

With the Reshape tool, select the anchor point(s) from the original selection that will be used to pull the selection. To select more than one point with the Reshape tool, hold the SHIFT key while clicking on the second and additional points. A hollow rectangle will appear around each anchor point selected with the Reshape tool.

Click and drag on one of the points you have selected with the Reshape tool. The points selected with the Reshape tool will be dragged as a unit. The other points in the original selection will be pulled and distorted as you drag. Points that were not part of the original selection will remain in their original locations. Figure 7-38 shows how the original selection and the selections made with the Reshape tool can alter the effects of the tool on a path.

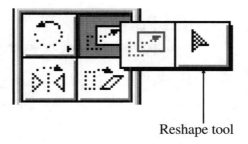

Reshape tool

FIGURE 7-37   The Reshape tool is grouped with the Scale tool in the main Toolbox

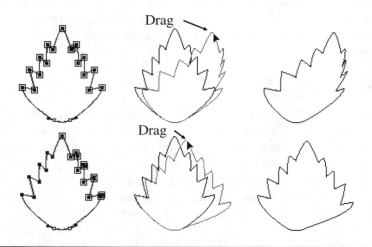

Drag

Drag

FIGURE 7-38   Distorting paths with the Reshape tool

Compound Paths

Compound paths are two or more overlapping paths that have been combined using the Objects|Compound Paths|Make menu command (CTRL/COMMAND+8). Where the paths overlap, holes are punched through the object and the background appears through these holes.

Creating Compound Paths

In this exercise, you will draw two donuts to illustrate the concept of compound paths.

1. First, draw a gray tablecloth by dragging the Rectangle tool.

2. For the first donut, draw two circles, a large black-filled circle with a smaller white-filled circle inside it.

3. For the second donut, draw two black-filled circles similarly arranged. Select the two circles and choose the Objects|Compound Paths|Make menu command (CTRL/COMMAND+8).

Move both donuts partially over the tablecloth as shown here:

There's obviously a problem with the hole in the first donut. However the compound path donut on the right looks great because the background shows through its hole.

 Although the holes in compound paths are transparent, you cannot click through them to select the paths underneath while in Preview mode. To select a path behind a compound object, switch briefly to Artwork mode (select View\Artwork or CTRL/COMMAND+Y) and click on the outline of the path.

Releasing Compound Paths

To remove the transparency and convert a compound path into a regular path, select the compound path and choose the Objects|Compound Paths|Release menu command (CTRL/COMMAND+ALT/OPTION+8).

Blends

The Blend tool, shown in Figure 7-39, allows you to transform one shape into another in a series of steps.

To demonstrate the Blend tool, create a white-filled circle on one side of the artboard and a black-filled square on the other side. Now blend the two objects as follows:

1. Select both objects with the Selection tool.

2. Choose the Blend Tool from the Tool palette (B) and click on the top anchor point of the circle and the top left anchor point of the square. If the Autotrace tool is currently selected, press B to toggle to your tool selection to the Blend tools.

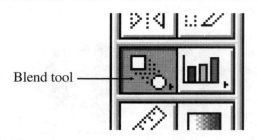

Blend tool

FIGURE 7-39   The Blend tool in the main Toolbox

3. In the Blend dialog box (see Figure 7-40), type **10** for the number of Steps in the transition. Notice the values in the First and Last text boxes change to conform to the new setting. Accept Illustrator 7's recommendation for these values and click OK.

Settings for First and Last determine where the first and last steps in the blend will appear and how much of the transformation of the shapes will have occurred. You can enter values from -100 to 200. Values less than 0 cause the blending to begin before the first object. Values greater than 100 cause the blending to end after the second object (see Figure 7-41).

 You cannot blend between more than two paths at the same time, between an open path and a closed path, a group of objects, or compound paths.

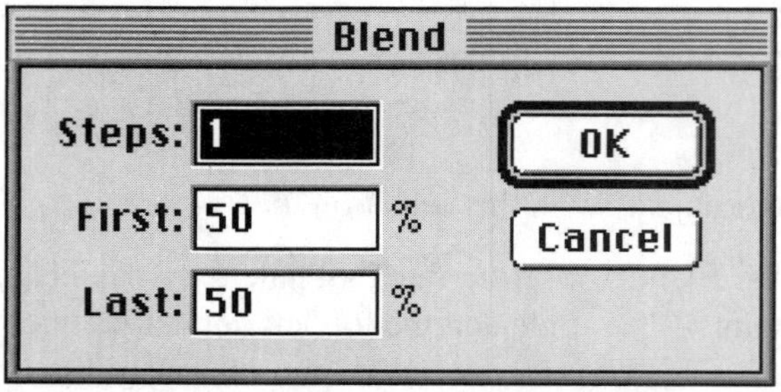

Blend

Steps: 1

First: 50   %

Last: 50   %

OK

Cancel

FIGURE 7-40   The Blend dialog box

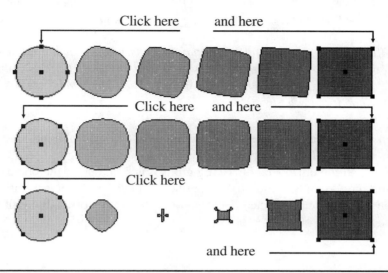

FIGURE 7-41   Blends between the same two objects can yield vastly different results depending upon the orientation of the objects, the points clicked with the Blend tool, and the settings in the Blend dialog box

Masks

Masks are objects that act as windows, allowing only the parts of other objects that are within the boundaries of the masking object to be seen.

Creating a Mask

Follow these instructions to create a mask:

1. Draw several objects.

2. Draw the object that will serve as the mask in front of and partially overlapping the other objects.

3. Select the objects and choose the Object|Masks|Make menu command (CTRL/COMMAND+7).

The front object will become a mask, showing the parts of the other objects that are within its outline and hiding the rest.

To use two or more nonoverlapping objects in one mask, first select the objects and convert them to a compound path (select Objects\Compound Paths\Make or type CTRL/COMMMAND+8). They can then be used as a mask with multiple windows.

When a mask is created, the selected objects become part of a masking group. The mask applies only to the objects in this group.

To select all the objects in a masking group, click on one of the objects in the group with the Group Selection tool. Continue to click on the object until all the objects in the group are selected. Here you see the results of applying the Mask command to a group of selected objects:

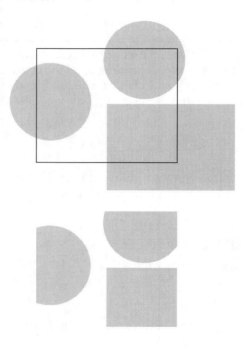

To add an object to a masking group, place the object in the position you want it to appear, cut it (CTRL/COMMAND+X), and paste it in front (CTRL/COMMAND+F) or in back (CTRL/COMMMAND+B) of one of the objects in the masking group.

Releasing a Mask

To stop using an object as a mask, select the masking object and choose the Object|Masks|Release menu command (CTRL/COMMMAND+ALT/OPTION+7). The masking object will revert to a normal Illustrator drawing object with no stroke or fill.

Because masks have no stroke or fill, it is often easier to select them by toggling to Artwork mode (CTRL/COMMMAND+Y). Alternatively, you can select all the masks in a document with the Edit\Select\Masks menu command.

Cropmarks

Although cropmarks are used for different purposes by different industries, in print, they identify the edges in which an image or document should be physically trimmed to the printing vendor. When created, crop marks appear on the film for the image you have created in your Illustrator document and end up printed outside of your image area. A trimming knife is then aligned with these markings to remove the excess printing material from the final product.

Creating Cropmarks

The most common way to create cropmarks in Illustrator 7 is to have the program add default crop and printer's marks to your printed document by choosing the Use Default Marks option in the Separations Setup (choose File|Separations Setup or press CTRL/COMMAND+ALT/OPTION+P). The other option is to define the cropmarks yourself using the Make Cropmarks command.

To define your own cropmarks, draw a rectangle defining the boundaries of your finished piece. Select the rectangle and choose the Object|Cropmarks|Make menu command. The rectangle will be replaced by cropmarks defining its boundaries, as shown here (Japanese-style cropmarks are shown on the right):

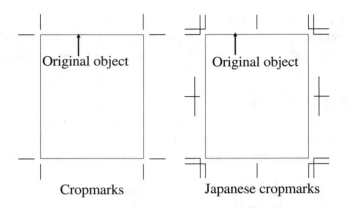

Cropmarks   Japanese cropmarks

 If the Single Full Page option is selected in the Document Setup dialog box (select File\Document Setup or type CTRL/COMMAND+SHIFT+P), you can set cropmarks for the page size specified in the Page Setup dialog box (click the Page Setup button in the Document Setup dialog box) by selecting Object\Cropmarks\Make with no objects selected.

To have Illustrator 7 create Japanese-style cropmarks when the Make Cropmarks command is chosen, select the Japanese Cropmarks option in the General Preferences dialog box (CTRL/COMMAND+K).

Note *You can have only one set of cropmarks in a document.*

Releasing Cropmarks

To release the cropmarks in a document, select the Object\Cropmarks\Release menu command. The cropmarks will be replaced by an unstroked and unfilled rectangle defining the same boundaries.

Graph Tools

Illustrator 7's Graph tools allow you to create various types of graphs complete with axes and labels from data that you enter or import. This section will familiarize you with the basics of graphing in Illustrator by guiding you through the creation and editing of a simple column chart. You will also be introduced to the various graph types that the program can create, as shown in Figure 7-42.

Creating a Simple Column Graph

To create a simple column graph, follow these steps:

1. Select the Column Graph tool from the main Toolbox.

Note   *You could just as easily choose one of the other graph tools. The basic concepts discussed here apply to all graphs created in Illustrator.*

2. Click and drag the Column Graph tool on the artboard to define the area you want the graph to occupy. Or click the Graph tool once on the drawing board, enter Width and Height values into the Graph dialog box, and click OK.

3. The beginnings of your chart will appear on the artboard and the Graph Data dialog box will appear. The most important parts of the dialog box are the Entry Line in the upper-left corner which is used to enter data and the Spreadsheet where the data is displayed.

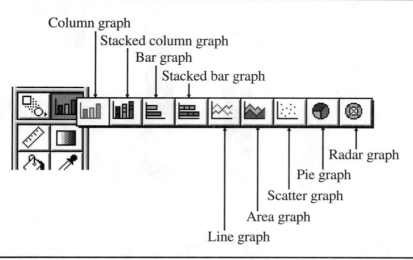

FIGURE 7-42   The Graph tools in the main Toolbox

When you type data into the Entry Line, it is placed into the highlighted cell in the spreadsheet. To highlight a cell, place the cursor inside it and click. You can also navigate the spreadsheet with the following keyboard navigation shortcuts:

- The arrow keys move the selection one cell in the direction of the arrow.

- TAB enters the Entry Line data into the selected cell and moves the selection one cell to the right.

- ENTER enters the Entry Line data into the selected cell and moves the selection one cell down.

Select multiple cells by clicking and dragging across the cells or by holding the SHIFT key while using the keyboard navigation shortcuts.

When multiple cells are selected, the interior of the top left cell is white and data entered in the Entry Line is placed in that cell. Other cells in the selection will appear solid black.

4. Delete the default 1 that appears in the first cell. Leaving the first cell empty, enter legends for your data (**profits** and **taxes**) in the top row and categories (**1998**, **1999**, and **2000**) in the left-hand column, as shown in Figure 7-43.

Here you see the graph of the data presented in Figure 7-43:

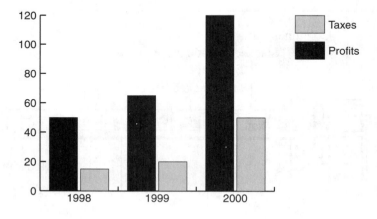

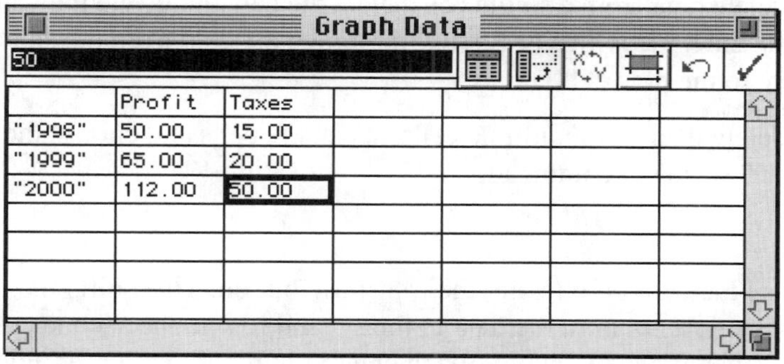

	Profit	Taxes				
"1998"	50.00	15.00				
"1999"	65.00	20.00				
"2000"	112.00	50.00				

FIGURE 7-43   The Graph Data dialog box

Note   *To create a label (legend or category) composed only of numerals (such as 1998), enclose the number in quotes to let Illustrator know it is not to graph the entry. To create a multiline label, use the VERTICAL BAR key to separate the lines Total\Taxes.*

5. Enter the values to be graphed into the relevant data cells.

6. Click the checkmark button in the top right of the dialog box to apply the data to the graph.

Editing Graph Data

To edit a graph's data, select the graph and choose the Object|Graph|Data menu command. The Graph Data dialog box will appear. You can edit the data in the following ways:

■   To edit a single cell, select the cell and type the new value into the Entry Line. Press TAB or ENTER to enter the data into the cell and move to the next cell.

■ To delete data from a single cell, select the cell and delete the value in the Entry Line. Press TAB or ENTER to remove the data from the cell and move to the next cell.

■ To delete data from multiple cells, select the cells and choose the Edit|Clear menu command.

Transpose the data by clicking the transpose button. This shifts the data in the first row to the first column, the data in the second row to the second column, and so on. This is handy when data has been entered in the wrong order. For example, when the legends were entered in columns and the categories in rows.

If you have not yet clicked the Apply button to apply your data changes to the graph, you can undo your changes by clicking the Revert button. The Revert button returns data to the values it held the last time that it was applied to the graph. When you are satisfied with your changes, apply them to the graph by clicking the Apply button.

Data from Other Sources

You can import data from spreadsheet programs by cutting and pasting it into the Graph Data spreadsheet. The text will be pasted in with its top-left cell at the location of the currently selected cell.

You can also import entire tab-delimited text files into the Graph Data spreadsheet by clicking the Import button in the Graph Data dialog box and opening the file. The file will be imported with its top-left cell at the location of the currently selected cell.

Working with Graph Types

You can change a selected graph from one type to another in the Graph Type dialog box, which is displayed by selecting the Object|Graph|Type menu command. The graph types available are described in Table 7-1.

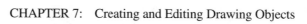

Graph Type	Description	Useful For
Column	The data is represented by vertical rectangles with lengths proportional to the data values	Comparing values
Stacked Column	A column graph with the rectangles for each category stacked rather than side by side	Comparing data sets and the individual values within them
Bar	Similar to a column graph but using horizontal rather than vertical rectangles to represent the data	Comparing values
Stacked Bar	A bar graph with the rectangles for each category placed end to end rather than one above the other	Comparing data sets and the individual values within them
Line	The data is represent as a series of connected points	Showing trends
Area	Similar to a line graph, but the area beneath the line is filled	Showing changes in values
Scatter	Plots data as a series of unconnected points	Identifying patterns in data
Pie	Each data value is represented as a proportionally sized wedge of a circle	Comparing individual values and their contribution to the sum of the data set
Radar	Data is displayed in a circular format	Comparing values in particular categories or at a particular time

TABLE 7-1   Illustrator 7's Supported Graph Types

Graph Type Dialog Box

A variety of other options that affect the layout of the graph are set within the Graph Type dialog box, as shown in Figure 7-44. In addition, certain Graph Types have additional settings available from the drop-down menu at the top of the box. This section will explore the settings for column graphs to introduce you to the concepts involved. You can use what you've learned here to experiment with the settings for other graph types.

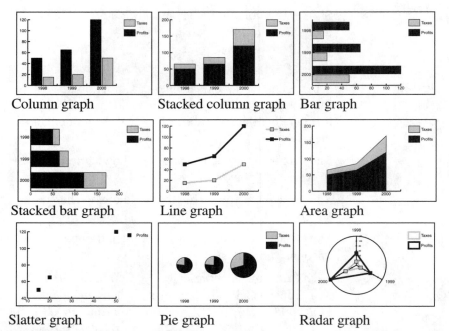

Column graph   Stacked column graph   Bar graph

Stacked bar graph   Line graph   Area graph

Slatter graph   Pie graph   Radar graph

GRAPH OPTIONS PULL-DOWN MENU   This drop-down menu at the top of the Graph Options dialog box offers you access to the Value Axis and Category Axis options. These settings are used to set the minimum and maximum values for the axes, set the number of divisions along the axes, set the number of tickmarks in each division, and add prefixes or suffixes to the labels on the axes.

- **Value Axis**   Determines where the axis appears relative to the graph. The value axis location is set from a drop-down menu

- **Add Drop Shadow**   When checked, adds a drop shadow to the data elements in the graph.

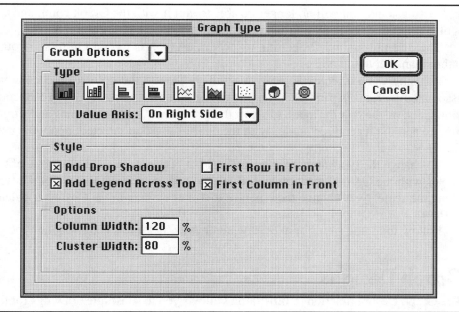

FIGURE 7-44 The Graph Type dialog box showing the Graph Options

- **First Row in Front and First Column in Front** Controls the stacking order of overlapping data elements in column, bar, line, and similar charts.

- **Column Width** Sets the width of each column within a cluster (a *cluster* is all the data elements related to one category, for example, the two columns associated with 1998 in our example). If the value is greater than 100 percent, the columns within each cluster will overlap.

- **Cluster Width** Sets the overall width of each cluster If the value is greater than 100 percent, the clusters will overlap.

Editing Graph Objects

Graphs in Illustrator are sets of grouped and subgrouped objects. As long as the objects remained grouped, the graph is related to the data and settings used to create it. If the objects in the graph are ungrouped, the graph is no longer related to the data and settings, and you will no longer be able to edit it with the Graph commands. It is also important never to ungroup or regroup subgroups within a graph.

The general method for editing objects in a graph is to edit entire subgroups rather than individual objects.

If, using the earlier example, you wish to change the color of the columns associated with taxes, first click on one of the columns with the Group Selection tool. Click on the column again to select the rest of the "Taxes" columns and a third time to add the legend rectangle. With the entire subgroup selected, apply the new fill color.

To change the type along the vertical scale to Times Roman, click on one of the values with the Group Selection tool. Click on it again to select the rest of the type along the scale. Now change the typeface to Times Roman in the Character palette (CTRL/COMMAND+T).

Follow the same steps for axes, division marks, tick marks, and legend type.

Graph Designs

The Graph Design function in Illustrator 7 allows you to substitute drawings for the columns, bars, and markers used to represent data in graphs. Anything you can draw in Illustrator, from a simple button to a complex logo or piece of artwork, can be used as a graph design.

Here you see the various ways graph designs can be used to represent data in graphs. From left, the designs are vertically scaled, horizontally scaled, repeating, and sliding.

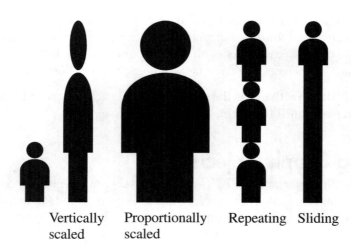

Vertically scaled Proportionally scaled Repeating Sliding

Creating, Accessing, and Editing Graph Designs

You can bring graph designs into your document in two ways: create them yourself or import them from another document.

CREATING GRAPH DESIGNS   The most direct way to bring a graph design into your work is to create it yourself as follows:

1. Create your design as you would any other illustration in Illustrator 7.

2. When your design is complete, use the Rectangle tool to draw a bounding box with no fill and no stroke around the design.

3. Send the bounding box to the back (CTRL/COMMAND+]).

4. If the design will be used as a sliding design, use the Pen tool to draw a horizontal line, the slide line at the point where the design will be stretched or compressed.

5. Select the design, bounding box, and slide line and group them (CTRL/COMMAND+G).

6. Convert the slide line into a guide by selecting it with the Direct Selection tool and pressing CTRL/COMMAND+5.

7. Select the entire group with the Selection tool and choose the Object|Graphs|Design menu command.

8. In the Graph Design dialog box (see Figure 7-45), click the New Design button. Your design will be named New Design followed by a number. Its name will be selected in the list of graph designs in your document and will appear in the preview box.

9. Click the Rename button, enter a more descriptive name into the Rename dialog box, and click OK.

10. Click OK to dismiss the Graph Design dialog box.

IMPORTING GRAPH DESIGNS FROM OTHER DOCUMENTS   You can import graph designs from other Illustrator 7 documents in two ways. Because Illustrator allows you to access graph designs from any open Illustrator document, the simplest way

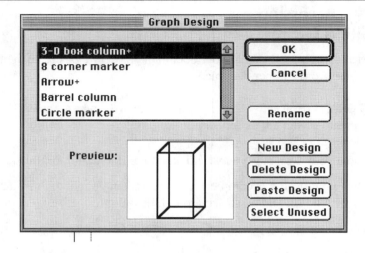

FIGURE 7-45   The Graph Design dialog box

to import a design is to open the document containing it. Once you use the design in one of your graphs, it will be included in your document.

You can also import all the designs in another document by choosing the Window|Swatch|Other Libraries command and selecting the Illustrator document containing the designs you wish to import.

Note   *Illustrator ships with files containing a variety of graph designs. They are located in the Sample Files|Graphs & Graph Designs directory/folder.*

DELETING GRAPH DESIGNS   Delete graph designs from your document by selecting them from the list in the Graph Design dialog box and clicking the Delete Design button. To delete all the unused designs in a document, click the Select Unused button to select them and then the Delete Design button to delete them.

PASTING GRAPH DESIGNS   If you wish to create a new graph design based upon an existing one, click the Paste Design button in the Graph Design dialog box. The artwork for the design will be pasted into your document.

Using Graph Designs

Graphs designs are applied to data objects, such as columns in a column graph or point markers in a line graph, when you select the objects and choose either the Objects|Graphs|Column menu command for column and bar graphs or the Objects|Graphs|Marker menu command for line and scatter graphs.

 You can apply one graph design to all the data objects in a graph by selecting the whole graph with the Selection tool.

In the dialog box that appears, select a graph design from the list of available designs by clicking on its name. It will be displayed in the Preview box so that you can be sure of your choice before applying it.

In the Graph Column dialog box (see Figure 7-46), you will also need to choose how the design will be applied—either vertically scaled, horizontally scaled, uniformly scaled, repeating, or sliding—and whether it will be rotated.

When you are satisfied with your selections, click OK to apply them to the graph and dismiss the dialog box.

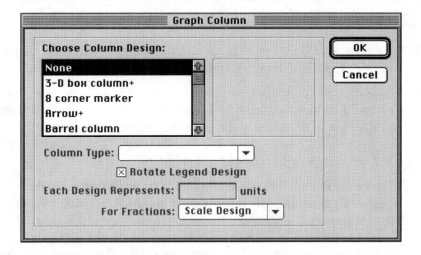

FIGURE 7-46   The Graph Column dialog box

Chapter 7 Tutorial 1:
Special Effects with Simple Objects

As a practical exploration of the features and effects discussed in this chapter, follow through in these step-by-step tutorials. As you do so, you may notice that some of these steps are accompanied by a "Color palette" symbol. This symbol indicates that the step has also been illustrated in full color in the Fundamental Illustrator 7 color insert. The purpose of the color insert is to provide you with a brief overview of the tutorials and act as an overall reference for the practical use of color throughout these tutorials.

Watch for this symbol:

You've been approached by Black Hole Software to design their logo. They also need an illustration of what the logo will look like on a 3.5-inch floppy disk so they can show it to their new CEO.

And, oh yes, we almost forgot to mention it: she arrives in town this afternoon.

Fortunately, you've already learned the basics of building illustrations in Illustrator 7 using simple shapes and paths. So you agree to take the job.

First create the disk and logo by following these steps:

1. Set the General Units option in the Units and Undo Preferences dialog box (select File|Preferences|Units and Undo) to points.

2. Create the basic disk shape by drawing a rounded rectangle. Select the Centered Rounded Rectangle tool from the main Toolbox and click once in the middle of the artboard. Enter the following dimensions in the Rectangle dialog box: Width = **255**, Height = **266**, Corner Radius = **10**. Click OK after you've entered the dimensions.

3. Click on the Default Fill & Stroke button in the main Toolbox (refer to Figure 7-47) to set the fill to white and the stroke to black. Click the Fill button to activate it. Click the Color button to show the Color palette. Place the cursor over the Color Spectrum ramp at the bottom of the Color palette and click on a light blue color to select it for the fill. If necessary, click on the

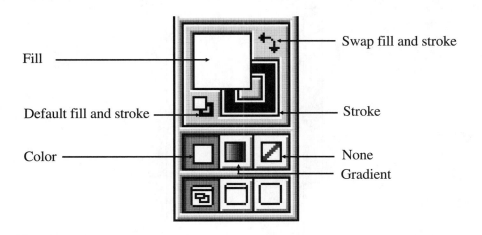

Fill

Default fill and stroke

Color

Swap fill and stroke

Stroke

None

Gradient

FIGURE 7-47   The Fill, Stroke, and Color controls in the main Toolbox

7

Stroke tab in the palette to bring the Stroke palette to the front. Set the stroke width to 1. (See **Chapter 10: Setting Fills and Strokes.**)

4. Draw a second rounded rectangle for the label, with the dimensions Width = **200**, Height = **180**, Corner Radius = **10**. Use the Selection tool to click and drag it to the position shown in the next illustration.

5. While the label is selected, click on the Default Fill & Stroke button in the main Toolbox to set the fill to white and the stroke to black.

6. To create the disk door guide, duplicate the label by clicking and dragging it straight downward with the Selection tool while holding the CTRL/COMMAND and SHIFT keys. When it is in position, release the mouse button before releasing the CTRL/COMMAND and SHIFT keys.

7. Using the Scissors tool (C), cut the label and door guide where they intersect the disk.

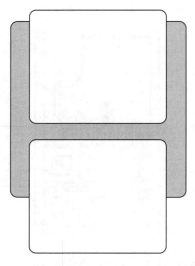

8. Click with the Selection tool on the portions of the label and door guide that are outside the boundaries of the first rectangle to select them and then delete them by pressing the BACKSPACE/DELETE key. After you've used the Scissors tool to cut the rectangles and delete the unnecessary portions, your illustration should look this:

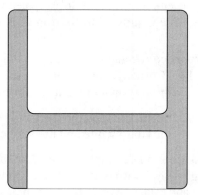

9. With the Selection tool, select the label and join its endpoints by pressing CTRL/COMMAND+J.

10. With the Direct Selection tool, select the three anchor points defining the left side of the door guide (hold the SHIFT key while clicking on the second and third anchor points to add them to the selection). Click and drag these points to the right while continuing to hold the SHIFT key. This is how your work will look after you've reshaped the door guide by dragging selected anchor points:

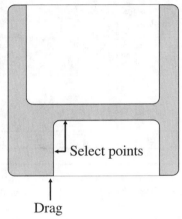

11. Clone the door guide to create the door by selecting the entire guide with the Selection tool, copying it (CTRL/COMMAND+C) and pasting the clone directly in front of the original (CTRL/COMMAND+F).

12. Select and move the three anchor points on the right side of the door to the left using the technique described in step 10.

13. Close the path of the clone by selecting it with the Selection tool and joining the endpoints (CTRL/COMMAND+J).

14. Select the door guide and change the fill to None (/).

15. Choose the Rectangle tool from the main Toolbox and create the access hole in the door by dragging a new rectangle on top of the door.

16. Select the door and the access hole and convert them to a compound path (CTRL/COMMAND+8).

17. While the door is still selected, fill it with a metallic gradient by activating the Fill button and choosing Show Swatches from the Windows menu. You'll see the window shown in Figure 7-48. Click the metallic gray gradient that is offered as one of Illustrator 7's defaults. To learn more about gradients, see **Chapter 4: What's New in Illustrator 7**?

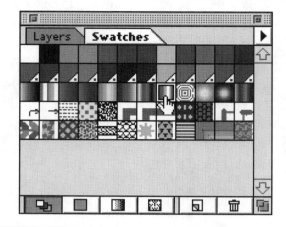

FIGURE 7-48   Illustrator offers several default gradients that can be chosen from the Swatches palette (Windows|Show Swatches)

18. If the Gradient palette is not showing, choose Show Gradient from the Windows menu and enter **30** into the angle text box. The clone is now the disk door.

19. Create the disk lock indicator by dragging a small rectangle that you'll see in the upper-right corner of the disk and filling it with black.

20. Draw a 45-degree path on the artboard by clicking the Pen tool once and then holding the SHIFT key while clicking down and to the right of the first point.

21. Use the Selection tool to click and drag the path into position over the lower-left corner of the disk, as shown in Figure 7-49.

22. With the path still selected, choose the Object|Path|Slice command. The path will slice the disk in two and the disk will jump to the front of the drawing. Select the small piece of the disk with the Selection tool and delete it (press BACKSPACE/DELETE). Return the disk to the back of the drawing by selecting it and pressing CTRL/COMMAND+SHIFT+[. This is what you'll see after you've applied Slice (here the pieces have been separated for clarity):

23. Create a duplicate disk shape at a 45-degree angle from the original by dragging it down and to the right with the Selection tool while holding the ALT/OPTION and SHIFT keys. Send the duplicate to the back with the CTRL/COMMAND+SHIFT+[command. This will become the shadow.

24. Select the entire drawing by pressing CTRL/COMMAND+A. Remove the shadow from the selection by clicking on it with the Selection tool while

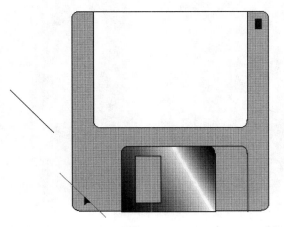

FIGURE 7-49   Positioning the path for use in slicing the disk shape below it

7

holding the SHIFT key. Group the remaining selection by choosing the Object|Group (CTRL/COMMAND+G) menu command.

25. Hide the group by selecting Object|Hide Selection (CTRL/COMMAND+U) while it is selected.

26. Create a scaled duplicate of the shadow shape by selecting it with the Selection tool and double-clicking on the Scale button in the main Toolbox. In the Scale dialog box, select Uniform and enter **90** percent. Click Copy to create the duplicate.

27. Set the fill on the smaller shadow shape to **40** percent black and the stroke to None. Set the fill to white and the stroke to None on the larger shadow shape.

28. Blend the two shapes to form a shadow by selecting both and clicking on equivalent points on each path with the Blend tool. Enter **9** into the Steps text box in the Blend dialog box, accept Illustrator's offerings for the First and Last percentage values, and click OK. Figure 7-50 shows the results.

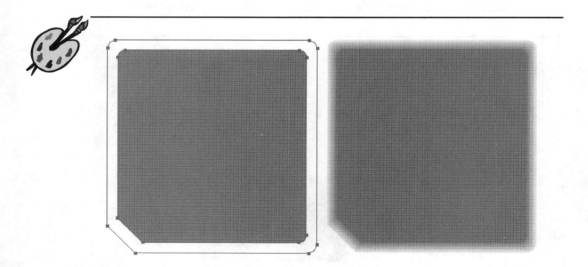

FIGURE 7-50   Blending between two objects to create the shadow

29. Show the disk by choosing the Objects|Show All (CTRL/COMMAND+ SHIFT+U) menu command.

30. Create the Black Hole logo by clicking with the Star tool (from the Ellipse pull-out menu in the main Toolbox) in the middle of the disk label. Enter **60** for Radius 1, **20** for Radius 2, and **20** for Points in the Star dialog box and click OK.

31. While the star is still selected, transform it into a black hole by dragging the Twirl tool (in the pop-out menu of the Rotate tool) around it approximately **120** degrees counterclockwise (see Figure 7-51). Alternatively, press ALT/OPTION, click the Twirl tool in the center of the star, and enter **120** in the Twirl dialog box.

32. While the black hole is still selected, apply the same metallic gradient to it that you used in step 17. Then, if the Gradient palette is not showing, choose Show Gradient from the Windows menu and select Radial in the Type drop-down menu in the Gradient palette. Set the stroke to None.

Click and drag

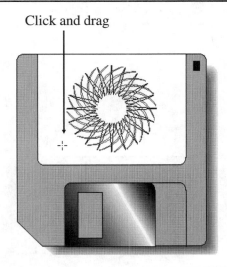

FIGURE 7-51 Transforming the star into a black hole using the Twirl tool

33. Set the type style to Helvetica Bold and the size to 18 points in the Character palette (CTRL/COMMAND+T). Click the Type tool outside the disk and type the words **BLACK HOLE**.

34. Convert the words "Black Hole" to outlines by selecting the text with the Selection tool and choosing the Type|Create Outlines (CTRL/COMMAND+SHIFT+O) menu command.

35. With all the type still selected, group it using the Objects|Group (CTRL/COMMAND+G) menu command.

36. Twirl the type as you did in step 31. Be careful not to distort the type too much or it will become unreadable.

37. Select the grouped type with the Selection tool and drag it into position over the label.

38. With the Rotate tool, rotate the type slightly so that it appears to be falling down the black hole.

39. When the illustration is complete, as shown here, select Save (CTRL/COMMAND+S) from the File menu, name your file Exercise 7.1, and save it to a convenient location on your disk.

Chapter 7 Tutorial 2:
Graphing with Illustrator 7

The folks at Black Hole Software loved your work so much they're hoping you can do a sales projections graphic for a presentation to their venture capitalist. Could you overnight it to them for the meeting tomorrow?

Once again it's Illustrator 7 to the rescue. Follow these steps:

1. To convert the disk in the previous exercise to a Graph Design, choose Open (CTRL/COMMAND+O) from the File menu, locate the file named Exercise 7.1, and click the Open button.

2. Because you grouped the artwork for the disk when you created it, you can select it (and not the logo or shadow) by clicking on one of the objects in the group with the Selection tool. When you have selected the group, copy it (CTRL/COMMAND+C) and close the file (CTRL/COMMAND+W).

3. Create a new document by choosing New (CTRL/COMMAND+N) from the File menu.

4. Paste (CTRL/COMMAND+V) the disk artwork into the new file.

5. Because the disk will be used as a Graphs Design in a bar chart, it should be rotated 90 degrees clockwise for best appearance. Select the disk with the Selection tool and double-click on the Rotate tool button in the main Toolbox. Enter **-90** in the Angle text box of the Rotate dialog box and click OK.

6. With the Rectangle tool, draw a bounding box. The bounding rectangle defines the boundaries of the graph design. (It should have no stroke or fill but is shown with a black stroke here for clarity.) Because the disk will be used as a repeating design, leave a little room between the disk and bounding rectangle so the disks will not touch when they are repeated in the graph.

7

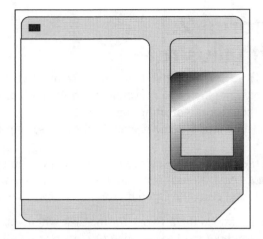

7. Send the bounding box to the back (CTRL/COMMAND+SHIFT+[).

8. Select the bounding box and the disk and group (CTRL/COMMAND+G) them.

9. Select the group and choose the Object|Graph|Design menu command.

10. In the Graph Design dialog box, click New. The disk should appear in the Preview box. Click rename and name the design "Blue Disk". Click OK to dismiss the dialog box.

11. With the disk and bounding box still selected, delete the artwork by pressing the BACKSPACE/DELETE key.

12. To create the graph, select the Bar Graph tool (J) from the pop-out Graph Tools menu in the main Toolbox. Click in the upper-left corner of your page and enter **360** for Width and **432** for Height. These sizes assume that the General Units options in the Units and Undo Preferences dialog box is still set to points. If not, change it to points as described in step 1 of Chapter 7, Tutorial 1.

13. Enter the data for the graph into the Graph Data dialog box as shown in Figure 7-52 (the complete headings are "Games", "Utilities", and "Business"), and apply it to the graph by clicking the checkmark icon in the upper-right corner of the dialog box. Your graph should look like this:

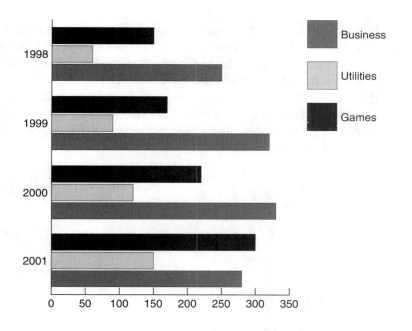

7

14. To apply the disk graph design to the graph, select the entire graph by clicking on it with the Selection tool and choose the Object|Graphs| Column menu command. In the Column Design dialog box, select Blue Disk from the list of available designs, select Repeating for the Column Type, make sure Rotate Legend Design is checked, enter **25** units for Each Design Represents, and select Chop Design for Fractions. After you have made your choices, click OK to apply them to the graph. Your graph will look like this:

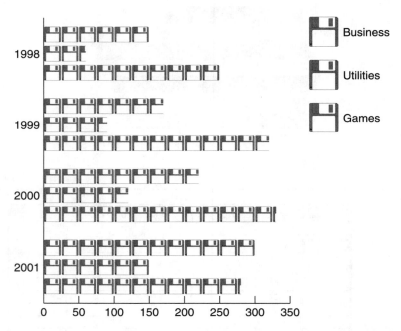

As you can see, it's pretty confusing having the graph designs for Games, Utilities, and Business all the same color. Remedy this problem by creating red and yellow disk Graphs Designs.

15. Choose Graphs|Design from the Object menu. In the dialog box, select Blue Disk and click Paste Design to paste the artwork for the disk into your document. Click OK to dismiss the dialog box. The disk artwork will be pasted into your drawing. If it is pasted over part of your graph, click and drag the disk artwork to an open area of the artboard.

16. Select the blue part of the disk by clicking directly on it with the Group Selection tool.

17. Change the fill to yellow by clicking the fill button in the main Toolbox, clicking the Color button to display the Color palette, and selecting a yellow color from the Color Spectrum ramp.

18. Select the disk artwork and bounding box with the Selection tool and choose the Object|Graphs|Design menu command.

19. In the Graph Design dialog box click New. The yellow disk should appear in the Preview box. Click rename and name the design "Yellow Disk". Click OK to dismiss the dialog box.

20. Use the techniques in steps 17-20 above to create a Red Disk graph design.

21. With the disk and bounding box still selected, delete it by pressing the BACKSPACE/DELETE key.

22. Apply the Yellow Disk design to the Utilities bars in your chart by clicking with the Group Selection tool on the disk labeled Utilities in the legend. Continue to click on the disk until all parts of it are selected. Click on it once more to select the disks representing Utilities sales in the chart.

Note   *If you click once too often, all the disks in the graph will be selected. If that happens, deselect everything by clicking on an open part of the artboard and start over.*

23. With the disks in the Utilities legend and bars selected, choose the Object|Graphs|Columns menu command. In the Column Design dialog box, select Yellow Disk from the list of available designs, select Repeating for the Column Type, make sure Rotate Legend Design is checked, enter **25** units for Each Design Represents, and select Chop Design for Fractions. After you have made your choices, click OK to apply them to the graph.

24. Repeat the process for the Games columns and legend, this time choosing Red Disk for the graph design. You graph should now look like this:

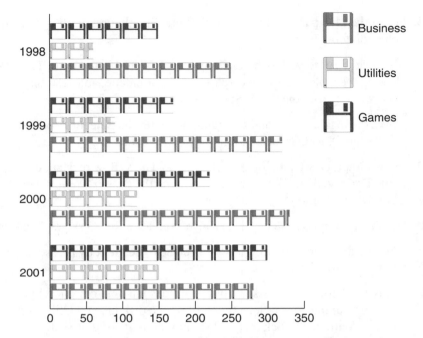

25. With the graph selected, modify the horizontal (values) axis by selecting the Object|Graphs|Type menu command and then selecting Value Axis from the pop-up menu at the top of the Graph Type dialog box. Click the Override Calculated Values check box so the check disappears: this allows you to enter Tick Values. To have the scale go from **0** to **400** in increments of 50 enter **0** for Min, **400** for Max, and **8** for divisions. Click OK to apply the changes.

26. Again, select the Object|Graphs|Type menu command and select Graph Options. This time, place the values axis across the top of the graph and increase the cluster width to 90 percent to allow a little more space between bars in a cluster. Click OK to apply your changes.

27. Format the type in the values axis by clicking on one of the numbers with the Group Selection tool to select it and then clicking on it again to select the remaining numbers. In the Characters palette (CTRL/COMMAND+T), set the type style to Helvetica Regular and type size to 12.

28. Format the labels in the category axis by clicking on one of the labels with the Group Selection tool to select it and then clicking on it once again to select the remaining category labels. In the Characters palette (CTRL/COMMAND+T), set the type style to Helvetica Bold and the type size to 14.

29. Format the legend type by clicking on one of the legend labels with the Group Selection tool to select it and then clicking on it once again to select the remaining legends. In the Characters palette (CTRL/COMMAND+T), set the type style to Times Roman and the size to 18.

30. Add a headline to the graph by clicking above it with the Type tool (T) and typing **Computer Applications Sales (in thousands of units).** Use the Type tool to select the first three words in the headline by clicking and dragging across them. In the Characters palette (CTRL/COMMAND+T), set the type style to Times Bold and type size to 24.

31. Reopen the file with the illustration of the disk. Select the Black Hole logo and type and copy (CTRL/COMMAND+C) it.

32. Return to your graph, paste (CTRL/COMMAND+V) the logo and type onto the page, and drag it into position at the bottom right of the graph. If it overlaps part of the graph, send it to the back (CTRL/COMMAND+SHIFT+[).

The Graph is complete as shown here. Select Save(CTRL/COMMAND+S) from the File menu, name your file "Exercise 7.2," and save it to a convenient location on your system.

7

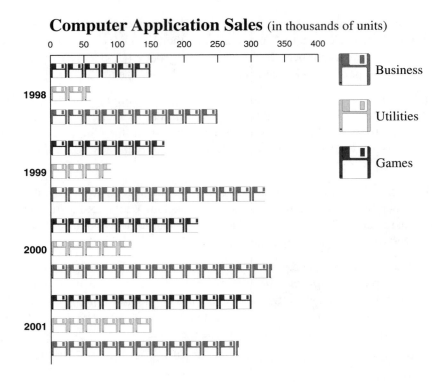

Computer Application Sales (in thousands of units)

Conclusion

This chapter has introduced the basic processes used to create designs and illustrations in Adobe Illustrator 7. Future chapters will build on these processes, introducing several methods that will make it easier and faster to create highly complex documents. But there's really no need to wait—just the tools and functions you've seen so far offer greater functionality than the original Illustrator program offered when it was introduced. So, work through the tutorials and then take a little time to experiment and test your new skills before moving on.

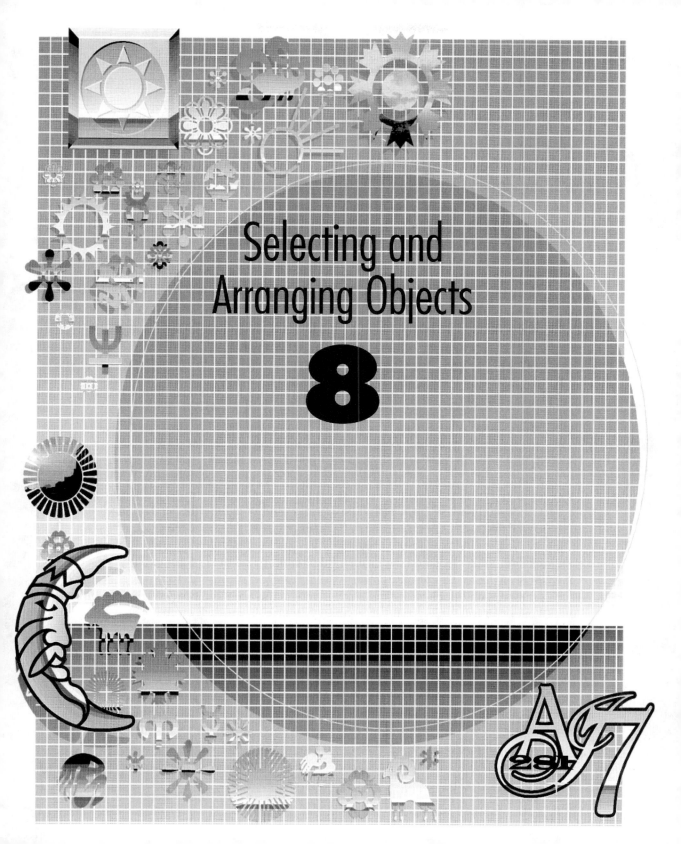

Selecting and Arranging Objects

8

By now you are becoming familiar with drawing techniques and gaining a sense of how the tools in the main Toolbox are used. Objects are filling the page and now it is time to learn how to bring order out of chaos. This chapter answers questions like: "How do I select and move certain objects without selecting and moving others?" and "How do I place objects so they are evenly distributed or along the same horizontal plane?" You will learn how to select the objects according to their attributes to control which objects you will modify. You will also learn how to arrange selected objects in a composition, in a group, and within layers.

Object Selection Methods

Before you make any changes to your objects, you must first select them. Illustrator uses anchor points (square dots) and connecting lines to create objects. As you work with the Pencil tool, each time you click an anchor point is placed and a straight line is drawn from the last anchor point. If you click and drag the anchor point, a curve is created between the new anchor point and the previous anchor point.

An object can be an *open path*, such as a single anchor point similar to a pencil dot on a page or a line segment, or a *closed path*, such as a circle or square. If you were to add color to an open path, Illustrator would complete the straight line between the first anchor point and the last anchor point and fill inside the space with color. As you create new objects, Illustrator assigns them a color. By default, the outline or stroke is black and the inside of the object or fill area is white, but you may apply any color you want.

To select an object, click on the Selection tool in the main Toolbox with the left mouse button or use the keyboard shortcut by typing **V**. Then click on an object (or within two pixels of the object) you wish to select. If you wish to select two or more objects, hold down the SHIFT key and click on the other object(s) you want to select. This process is called *random selection*. You may also drag your Selection tool across the path of any object to select it.

When you select an object, its outline and anchor points change to the default color for the layer it is on. (Layers are discussed later in this chapter.) On the initial layer of the composition, selected objects appear with a light blue outline by default. Selected anchor points are designated as light blue filled squares. If only some of an object's anchor points are selected and you move them, unselected anchor points will stay in place, distorting the shape of the object. You may use this method of editing in some applications to produce special effects.

Once the object is selected, you may shape, fill, scale, transform, and so on to mold the objects into the design and create the desired effect. You select objects so Illustrator applies transformation and coloring only to those objects selected. If you change stroke and fill settings without first selecting an object, Illustrator will apply the new settings only to new objects.

In addition to selecting objects with a click of a mouse button, you can select all objects at once, select an individual object, or select a group of objects according to attributes you determine. These selection methods are *attribute sensitive*. That is, Illustrator looks for objects that have the same attribute values, such as Fill Color or Stroke Color, and groups them by the attribute you determine. Objects matching those values are selected. Object attributes are discussed later in this chapter.

Using the Select All Command

This option selects all objects in the current application in all layers (except those objects that have been locked or hidden). You may select all through Edit|Select All or the keyboard shortcut CTRL/COMMAND+A. Select All gives you the power to group all of the objects so they will be modified or transformed as a unit. Underlined letters in the Edit menu, shown in Figure 8-1, indicate which options may be accessed from the keyboard by pressing ALT/OPTION while typing the underlined letter.

You may select all objects with the mouse by using the Select tool (V), shown here:

or the Direct Selection Tool (A), shown here:

or the Group Selection tool (A), shown here:

8

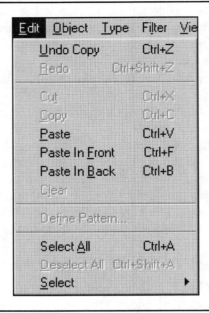

FIGURE 8-1   The Edit menu holds the options for Select All, Deselect All, and the Select flyout menu.

Regardless of which of these three tools you use, you can draw a marquee around the entire object(s) being selected. Drag the Selection tool from upper left to lower right to draw a marquee selection around or through portions of all the objects in your composition, as shown here:

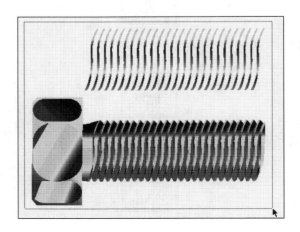

Remember, only those objects that have not been locked or hidden may be selected with the Selection tools.

 When selecting objects using the draw marquee method, all objects or portions of objects within the marquee selection window on all layers will be selected.

 When all objects are selected, the next transformation will affect all objects. For example, if you add color fill, all objects will be filled with the same color.

 When you select objects with menu commands, you may limit the selection for a particular layer by locking all the other layers. For further information, see the section on "Layers" later in this chapter.

Using the Deselect All Command

You may want to continue editing individual objects when you have completed your work on the whole group. Once you have selected all objects, individual objects cannot be selected. You must first deselect all objects before selecting individual objects.

To deselect all objects, choose Deselect All from the Edit menu or use the keyboard shortcut CTRL/COMMAND+SHIFT+A. (See the Edit menu shown in Figure 8-1.) This can also be accomplished by clicking or dragging the mouse away from objects by at least two pixels while in one of the three select modes.

Selecting the Same Paint Style

When you're working with many objects and various fills, it may be tedious to select specific objects one by one using the Select tool (V) and SHIFT while clicking. The Select feature of the Edit menu contains a flyout menu, shown in Figure 8-2, that offers seven different methods you can use to select objects.

Paint styles range from simple solid fills to complex pattern fills. A solid fill has the same color value from border to border inside the object. A gradient fill has a gradual change from one color value to another. Illustrator calculates the gradual mixing of two or more colors designated for an object. Illustrator comes with a Swatch Library. A *swatch* is a square of color including solid fill and ranging to predefined patterns. These are edited and selected from Illustrator's Color Fill palette, Gradient Fill palette, and Swatches palette.

Same <u>P</u>aint Style

Same <u>F</u>ill Color

Same Stroke <u>C</u>olor

Same Stroke <u>W</u>eight

<u>M</u>asks

<u>S</u>tray Points

<u>I</u>nverse

FIGURE 8-2   The Select flyout menu holds the options for selecting by Same Paint Style, Same Fill Color, Same Stroke Color, Same Stroke Weight, Masks, Stray Points, and Inverse selections

 The simplest way to select objects containing the same Paint Style is to click on an object that has the Paint Style you would like to edit and choose Edit\Select\Same Paint Style, as shown in Figure 8-2.

Selecting the Same Fill Color

You may easily select all objects with similar fill color by using Illustrator's Select Same Fill Color feature. To use this feature, follow these steps:

1. Select an object with the fill color you want to use. Click on the Fill Color box in the Color palette, the Gradient Fill Box in the Gradient palette, or a Swatch in the Swatches palette to activate the color you want to select. You may also click on the Swap Fill/Stroke and Default Fill/Stroke button shown here. Click on the Color, Fill or None button.

2. Choose Edit|Select|Same Fill Color, as shown in Figure 8-2, to select all the objects with the same fill.

Selecting the Same Stroke Color

The outline of an object is considered a *path*. Assigning color, style, and/or thickness to a path is called *stroking the path*. An object can have a solid filled stroke or no stroke visible. The width of a stroke is referred to as its weight. Singling out individual objects by their stroke color can be a difficult task if you have to select each object one at a time from hundreds of objects. To select the objects with the same stroke color, as here, follow these steps:

1. Select an object with the stroke color of those objects you want to select. (You could also click on the Swap Fill Stroke area to switch to Stroke Color.) Then, select the Stroke Color box in the Color palette in order to activate which color you want selected. Enter exact values for your stroke color in the color model text boxes.

2. Choose Edit|Select|Same Stroke Color, as shown in Figure 8-2.

Selecting the Same Stroke Weight

Objects may have the same stroke color and yet have a different stroke weight. You use the Same Stroke Weight selection to identify objects having a specific weight you specify. Remember, objects are made up of open and closed paths. Individual line segments have stroke weight just like closed path objects. Suppose you use an effect for shading or highlighting an object with line segments and you need to change their color or weight. You determine which lines are selected from many lines by designating the stroke weight by either selecting an object of the same stroke weight or through the Stroke palette.

The Same Stroke Weight selection option allows you to take advantage of selecting objects of the same stroke weight.

1. First select the object that has the desired stroke weight. You may also indicate the stroke weight from the Stroke palette by selecting Window|Show Stroke|Weight #.

2. Choose Edit|Select|Same Stroke Weight, as shown in Figure 8-2.

> **Note** *Selecting the same stroke weight does not mean that Illustrator will select the same stroke color. An easy way to select the same stroke color once you have selected the same stroke weight is to use the Inverse selection, found on the Select flyout menu. First, use the Same Stroke Weight command designating the specific weight you wish selected. Then choose the Inverse command. Lock these objects temporarily by Object\Lock or CTRL/COMMAND+L, and then select the Same Stroke Color to select all objects of the same weight and color. After modifying the objects with the same stroke color and weight, unlock the locked objects by Objects\Unlock All or CTRL/COMMAND+SHIFT+L.*

Illustrator 7 assumes you know which objects you need to select when using these options to select specific objects. Sometimes digital artists use a blend technique between objects for shading or highlighting. This may generate objects that have the same color and weight value of your defined object selection. If you end up selecting these unwanted objects during your selection procedure, you may deselect them by holding down the SHIFT key while clicking on the unwanted objects with the Selection tool one at a time.

Selecting Masks

Creating a mask in Illustrator is similar to a cutting a hole out of a piece of paper and placing it over an image or object. You can only see the objects directly beneath the hole. If you move the piece of paper, the view through the paper's hole changes. With masks you can select all the mask objects on all active layers.

The Select Masks option enables you to modify, move, or transform objects you have designated as masks. See **Chapter 13: Working with Masks** for more information on masks. When you choose Edit|Select|Masks, any object currently selected that isn't a mask will be deselected. To select a mask, choose Edit|Select|Masks, as shown in the flyout menu in Figure 8-2. Once you have selected a mask, you may modify it as you would any other object.

Selecting Stray Points

When you've been working in Illustrator on a piece of art for a while, stray points can often accumulate. Selecting and deleting them manually can be a tedious and time-consuming operation. A *stray point* is a lone anchor point without any other anchors connected by a path. Stray points may be created when deleting anchor points connected with a path or when the Pen tool (P is the keyboard shortcut for this tool) is inadvertently clicked once in the work space. The Select Stray Points command allows you to locate all stray points quickly.

To select individual stray points, choose Edit|Select|Stray Points, as shown in Figure 8-2. Once you have selected a stray point(s), you may move, transform, or delete them all at the same time. You may also use the Cleanup command, found under Object|Path|Cleanup, to transform or delete those stray points

Selecting Inverse

Inverse may be used as a secondary step to selecting objects that have attributes that don't match. For instance, if you have all red objects selected, you may quickly select all objects that are not red using the Inverse command, as shown in Figure 8-2. Once you have finished editing objects of a similar attribute, you may want to modify the remaining objects using a different effect. After resizing an object, other objects may need to be moved or resized to balance your composition. You may easily switch object selections from one group to all objects that weren't previously selected using the Inverse command.

When you use Edit|Select|Inverse, the objects that were selected are now deselected. The objects that were not selected are now selected.

Arranging Objects

The Arrange commands in Illustrator work on just the active layer of objects. If you send an object to the back or bring it to the front, it is in relationship to the other objects on that particular layer of objects. See the section on "Layers" later in this chapter for more information.

To change the order of an object in your composition, first choose the Object menu, shown in Figure 8-3. This contains the Arrange command's flyout menu, which lets you change the order of objects in a document.

FIGURE 8-3   The Object menu contains the Arrange flyout menu

The Arrange flyout menu, shown in Figure 8-4, lists Illustrator 7's four options for arranging objects along with their keyboard shortcuts. Use the Bring To Front command to bring your selected objects to the very top of the stack. Bring Forward brings the selected objects forward one step at a time. The Send Backward command sends objects backward one at a time, and the Send To Back command sends selected objects to the very bottom of the stack.

Sending Objects to the Back

With Arrange options, you can hide portions of objects. Ragged edges, straight lines, and other aspects of objects that you don't want the viewer to see may easily be hidden by sending the object to the back of the pile. With the object selected, choose Object|Arrange|Send To Back. Once you've selected the object, you may also send it to the back using the keyboard shortcut CTRL/COMMAND+SHIFT+[.

Bringing Objects to the Front

New objects are assigned to the front position as you create them. When your new objects block the view of other objects, you may want to bring some other object to the front to view it.

Certain commands under Illustrator's Pathfinder menu use the object in front to modify the object that is in back. For example, the Trim command uses two or more selected objects. The object in front trims the object beneath like a cookie cutter. You may use objects in front to shape objects to the back.

■ If you want to use the object that is in back to modify the object in front, you may have to bring it to the front first by selecting the object with the Selection tool (V) and choosing Object|Arrange|Bring To Front or CTRL/COMMAND+SHIFT+].

Sending an Object Backward One Increment at a Time

If the object you want to work on is back just one level (rather than all the way at the back), move that object to the back one increment at a time rather than through the whole stack at once. To send an object back one object at a time, choose Object|Arrange|Send Backward or CTRL/COMMAND+[.

```
Bring To Front    Ctrl+Shift+]
Bring Forward           Ctrl+]
Send Backward           Ctrl+[
Send To Back     Ctrl+Shift+[
```

FIGURE 8-4   Options on the Arrange flyout menu

Bringing an Object Forward One Increment at a Time

To bring an object forward one step at a time, select the object and choose Objects|Arrange|Bring Forward or use the keyboard shortcut CTRL/COMMAND+].

Copying or Moving Objects to a Specific Position in the Stack

The Arrange commands provide convenience for moving objects backward and forward if you only have a few objects and you are working on one layer. But when you have a large number of objects and are working with multiple layers, the task of placing an object in a specific order on a specific layer may be difficult. However, Illustrator can accommodate even the most complex layering situations with the Paste commands in the Edit menu, as demonstrated in the following steps:

1. Select the object you want to place with the Selection tool (V) and cut it using Edit|Cut or CTRL/COMMAND+X.

2. Select an object to either paste in front of or behind.

3. Choose the Edit|Paste in Front (CTRL/COMMAND+F) or Edit|Paste in Back (CTRL/COMMAND+B).

When Illustrator pastes objects, they are pasted back into your drawing at the same original horizontal and vertical position as the original, only their ordering in the stack has changed.

Aside from cutting and pasting, you may also copy and paste using the Edit|Copy or CTRL/COMMAND+C to copy the object and then the preferred Paste commands. See the Edit menu in Figure 8-1.

When you paste in front of or behind an object, the result may not at first be obvious to you. That's because an object will maintain its x and y axis location on the page when pasted. The difference is that the stacking order is changed according to the layering of the object you selected to paste in front of or behind.

Use these commands for placing more than one object. Select several objects or groups of objects by using the Selection tools and pressing SHIFT while clicking on each object.

Grouping and Ungrouping

When working with several objects at one time, it may be necessary to group them together in order to modify or perform any number of actions on related objects. A group of objects that you select and group together maintains its position relative to the other objects in the group. Perhaps you will draw a car. You create each object—a tire, tread, hub caps—separately. After you complete the "tire" objects and group them, you may move them into place with the rest of the composition.

When transforming the group, Illustrator 7 changes and acts upon the group as a unit. You may also have groups within groups. Lug nuts may be created and grouped as a part of the hub assembly and then grouped with the complete tire composition. You could then move this lug nut–hub-tire group as a unit. To separate these kinds of groups you would ungroup them to edit groups or objects within groups.

Using the Group Command

Using the Selection tools within the main Toolbox, select two or more objects or groups. Choose Object|Group or CTRL/COMMAND+G. See the Object menu, shown in Figure 8-3, for the Grouping menu options. Once two or more objects are grouped, they take on the characteristic of a single unit. If the group is selected, any modifications will be applied to all the objects of the group. Next time you want to select this group, click on any object in the group and the whole group will be selected.

When grouping objects, keep in mind that objects pulled into groups from a variety of layers will all be moved to the same layer and the group will become the top object in that layer.

At some point, you may need to change a particular group within a group. To do this, choose the Group Selection tool from the main Toolbox. To select an individual object within a group, click on it with the Group Selection tool and click a second time to select this object's group. Even though an object is selected individually out of the group by the Group Selection tool, it will remain a part of that group.

Using the Ungroup Command

Once objects are grouped together, they may subsequently be ungrouped using the Ungroup command. Ungrouping essentially undoes what the group comand does—nothing more than that. To ungroup a set of grouped objects, they must first be selected using one of the many selection methods available in Illustrator 7. Once a group is selected, you may choose Object|Ungroup to free the objects for whatever purpose you choose (see Figure 8-3). When a group of objects has been Ungrouped, each object takes on independent characteristics once again. You may modify a single object without affecting the whole group of objects.

Aligning Objects

In the military, soldiers line up and march on command. Illustrator 7 gives you the capabilities of doing the same with your drawing objects in creating rows or columns of objects. The techniques for achieving this are accomplished through the Aligning and Distributing commands found in a series of buttons in the Align palette. To access the Align palette, select Window|Show Align. Aligning and distributing objects involves changing the position of the objects in relation to their horizontal or vertical placement.

Alignment requires at least two selected objects in order to become available, while distribution commands require a minimum of three selected objects. Objects and groups of objects act the same way in alignment and distribution. In other words, Illustrator 7 treats groups of objects as if they were a single unit.

The Align Palette

Aligning objects takes place along a horizontal axis or a vertical axis. There are three positions to choose from for each axis: objects are aligned horizontally left, centered, or to the right of the vertical axis. Similarly, objects are aligned vertically along the top, centered, or vertically along the bottom of the horizontal axis. Objects aligned right, left, top, or bottom become flush on their corresponding sides. Centered objects are aligned along their center points.

Illustrator measures the vertical axis for horizontally aligned objects in three ways: left vertical axis, center vertical axis, and right vertical axis. When objects are horizontally aligned left, the object furthest to the left becomes the reference object

Horizontal Align Center   Horizontal Align Right   Vertical Align Top   Vertical Align Center

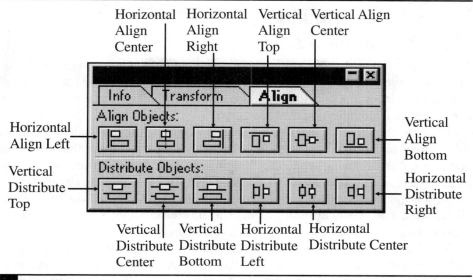

Horizontal Align Left

Vertical Distribute Top

Vertical Align Bottom

Horizontal Distribute Right

Vertical Distribute Center   Vertical Distribute Bottom   Horizontal Distribute Left   Horizontal Distribute Center

FIGURE 8-5   The Align palette is accessed by selecting Show Align from the Window menu

and its leftmost outer path at the anchor point becomes the vertical axis. Illustrator aligns all other selected objects off of this vertical axis.

When objects are horizontally aligned right, the rightmost object becomes the reference object, and its rightmost anchor point becomes the vertical axis to which all other objects are aligned. Think of a column of objects when you use the horizontal options on the Align palette. Objects must be moved right, left, or centered in order to create a perfect column.

Similarly, Illustrator measures the horizontal axis for vertically aligned objects three ways: top horizontal axis, center horizontal axis, and right horizontal axis and uses objects' anchor points to establish these axes.

Objects don't have to be on the same layer for you to align them. Objects may be aligned on multiple layers without affecting their order in the document. Some applications call for aligning objects on a single layer. To align objects on the same layer without affecting objects on other layers, lock out the layers that you don't want to affect and then select objects to be aligned. To use this option, select Window|Show Layers. From the Layers palette, click on the Show/Hide button for each of the layers containing objects that you don't want aligned.

8

Using the Distributing Objects Command

The ability to automatically distribute collections of objects across a given area or space can save you the time and effort of manually moving objects around your screen. But the concept of distributing objects is a difficult one for many new users to comprehend without a practical comparison.

Imagine a bolt that has threads on a shaft at evenly distributed intervals. Once a single thread has been created, it may then be copied for the remaining threads saving hours of tedious drawing work. But keeping the new threads in precise, evenly distributed rows may not always be a simple task. This is where the automation of the Align palette's Distribute commands come into play. Once the new threads are aligned, you may evenly distribute them using this feature. Illustrator's distribution feature places even spaces between all selected objects.

The distance between objects is calculated either on a horizontal or vertical axis, each having three options to choose. On the horizontal axis, objects are distributed according to their left anchor points, right anchor points, or center line. On the vertical axis, objects are distributed according to their top anchor points, bottom anchor points, or center line.

Creating Rows

To create rows with objects, first use Align and then Distribute when aligning objects along a straight symmetrical path. For instance, if you want your objects in a neat and evenly distributed horizontal row follow these steps, referring back to Figure 8-5 for location of the Align and Distribute commands:

1. Create five small objects of any shape anywhere on the page. You may draw them with the Pen tool (P), Rectangle tool (M), or the Ellipse tool (N), all of which can be found in the main Toolbox. Select all the objects using keyboard shortcut CTRL/COMMAND+A.

2. Choose Window|Show Align to access the Align palette. Select the Vertical Align Bottom button. This option aligns all the objects across the same horizontal line with the lowest object as the reference and its lowest anchor point as the horizontal axis. Notice all objects are still unevenly distributed.

3. Select the Horizontal Distribute Center button in the Align palette. Objects are now aligned and distributed evenly in a row.

Creating Columns

To create a column of objects with Align and Distribute, follow these steps:

1. Create several small objects anywhere on the page. Select all the objects for your column using CTRL/COMMAND+A.

2. Select the Horizontal Align Left button in the Align palette. This moves objects left to be aligned along a vertical axis using the left-most object as a reference object and the left-most anchor point as the vertical axis position.

3. Select the Vertical Distribute Center option in the Align palette. Objects are now aligned and distributed evenly in a left-aligned column.

Centering an Object

You might need to center art on a document page. To center an object or grouped objects in the document, follow these steps:

1. For a demonstration of this process, create an object using the Pen tool (P), Rectangle tool (M), or the Ellipse tool (N). Select the Pen tool found in the main Toolbox and click on the upper-left corner of the page to make a second object. This is the smallest object you can create—a single anchor point. Click the Select tool on the main Toolbox to let Illustrator know you are finished with this particular object. Select the Pen tool and click on the lower-right corner of the page to set another anchor point. Click the Selection tool again.

   Now you have all the elements in place to center an object on the document page. As mentioned earlier, Illustrator 7 requires at least three objects be selected to perform a Distribute command.

2. Next, select all the objects you have created using CTRL/COMMAND+A.

3. In the Align palette, click the Horizontal Distribute Center button and then the Vertical Distribute Center button. Your object is now centered on the page.

Working in Layers

Working with layers in Illustrator gives the digital artist the ability to organize artwork into similar groupings. You may put all background work such as bitmaps on one layer, text and notes in another layer, and artwork on still another layer. The wonderful advantage of working with layers is that they may be rearranged to the front or back or made visible or invisible with the click of a mouse button. And working in layers enables you to lock certain layers to prevent them from being edited. To open the Layers palette shown in Figure 8-6, choose Window|Show Layers.

The Layers Palette

To select the Layers palette, choose Window|Show Layers. The active layer is automatically highlighted when the Layers palette appears (see Figure 8-6). A square symbol to the right of each layer name indicates the outline color of objects on the layer, the default of is which is blue.

The Show/Hide option (see Figure 8-6) sets whether a layer is visible or not. Hiding and showing layers is a quick method to display artwork during screen-draw intensive operations such as when tracing and creating artwork from bitmap images.

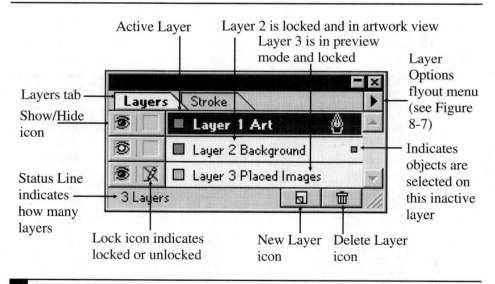

FIGURE 8-6 The Layers palette

Showing or hiding layers may also be used to isolate a specific area of your drawing while viewing a drawing object.

Layers may also be locked and unlocked to allow or restrict editing of them. Locked or unlocked layers are indicated by the square symbol next to the Show/Hide button being stroked out with the symbol of a pencil, as seen in Figure 8-6. Layers which feature this pencil symbol may not be edited unless they are first unlocked.

Adding a New Layer

In Illustrator 7, there are two ways to add a new layer to your drawing. First, you may click on the Add Layer button. Clicking this button quickly adds a new layer to the palette (and your drawing) and applies the generic name New Layer. The second way to add a new layer is through access to the Layers flyout menu by choosing the New Layer command.

Using this command, Illustrator automatically displays options to name the new layer with a name of your choosing and sets other options for the layer as you wish. The dialog which is displayed may be manually accessed for any selected layer by double-clicking on the layer or by choosing Layer Options from the flyout menu, as shown in Figure 8-7. So, while the new layer button quickly adds a new layer and leaves you to manually name the new layer later on, it's the quicker method.

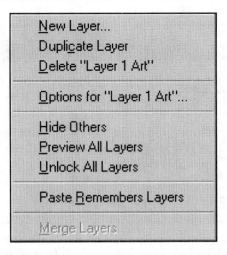

■ FIGURE 8-7   The Layers palette flyout menu

The Layer Options Dialog Box

When you select the New Layer option from the Layers palette flyout menu, you'll see the Layer Options dialog box, as shown in Figure 8-8 . To access Layer Options quickly, double-click on a layer in the Layers palette. Once the Layer Options dialog box is open, you can take advantage of several options.

Naming the Layer

The Layer Options dialog box enables you to name a layer for identification. Using logical names to identify your layers can help a great deal when organizing large documents containing multiple layers.

Using the Layers Color Option

Object outlines and anchor points take on a different default color when selected. This helps the artist determine which objects are selected. Illustrator 7 also gives different outline colors to each layer so artists can easily recognize which layer an object is on.

Here you may quickly set up your new layer's outline color. The outline colors in the Color Selection flyout menu, shown in Figure 8-9, are standard predefined colors that come preset with the Illustrator setup. To create a custom color to use for

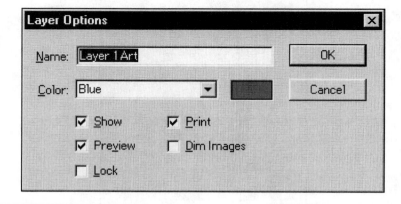

FIGURE 8-8   The Layer Options dialog box allows you to change the working attributes of objects on this layer

FIGURE 8-9   Layers Color Options offers a wide selection of colors for selection outlines and includes the Other option at the bottom

outlines, choose Other at the bottom of the list, which opens the Layers Color palette shown in Figure 8-10.

Using Layers Show Option

As mentioned earlier, the Show option enables you to set a layer to either display or not display. Note that objects on layers that have been set not to show are essentially invisible and cannot be selected or edited.

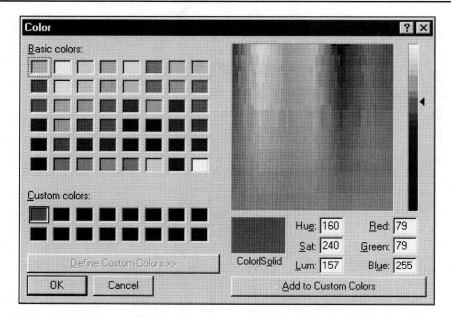

FIGURE 8-10   The Layers Color palette gives you the option of choosing any color you want and storing custom colors for selection outlines for a particular layer

Layers Preview Option

Selecting the Preview option enables you to see a layer in full color. When left unselected, you see the layer only in Artwork view. Select Preview in order to see all the images in color on a layer.

 If you leave the Preview box empty, all your objects and images will be visible only in outline form. This greatly reduces the time that it takes to redraw the screen each time you make an editing change. If you need to look at your artwork as it is being created and edited, consider choosing View|Preview Selection.

Layers Lock Option

Selecting the Lock option locks a layer so that it cannot be edited. If you choose to Lock a layer, none of the objects on the layer may be selected or edited. This locking feature is an important tool in preventing layers from being edited either accidentally or inadvertently. Later, if you need to edit the objects on the locked layer, you may unlock it by deselecting the Lock option in the Layers option dialog.

Layers Print Option

The Print option enables you to be picky about which layers print and which don't. With the Print option selected for a certain layer, the layer will print normally. When unselected, none of the objects on the layer will print. Printing only specific layers is another powerful yet simple feature which sets the Layers functionality apart from other features. For example, if you were an engineer working on a structural drawing and you needed to make a print of only the foundation layout of a floor plan, you could select only *that* layer to print. Or, if you were a layout artist preparing an illustration or diagram containing photographs, you could choose to print only the type objects for proofing, instead of waiting for memory intensive objects such as digital photographs to print.

Layers Dim Images Option

The Dim Images option gives bitmap images a water mark appearance, making identification of vector versus bitmap images simpler. Images and objects are dimmed to roughly 50 to 60 percent.

Layers Palette Flyout Menu

In addition to the New Layer option, the Layers palette flyout menu, shown in Figure 8-7, has seven other options associated with layers.

Deleting a Layer

To delete a layer, choose Window|Show Layers and select the layer from the Layers palette by clicking once on the layer. Open the Layers palette flyout menu by hitting the right arrow in the upper-right corner of the Layers palette. Then choose Delete the "Layer #". Another way to delete a layer is to select the layer to be deleted and click the Delete Layer button (see Figure 8-6). If you have artwork on that layer, a warning dialog box will appear asking if you are sure you want to delete the layer. Choose yes, no, or cancel. One last way to delete a layer is to click and drag the layer to the garbage can.

Duplicating Layers

There are many applications you may use the duplication of layers for, such as when creating a drop shadow behind an object. To quickly duplicate an entire layer of objects using the Layers palette, click the layer you wish to duplicate, open the Layers palette flyout as shown in Figure 8-7, and select Duplicate Layer. The Layers palette names the new layer generically as "Layer # Copy" and it becomes the active layer. To create a quick shadow, select all objects and assign them a dark color such as gray or black. Then click the duplicate layer and drag it down one level in the layer order in your Layers palette.

Using the Hide Others Feature

To hide all layers other than the active layer, click on the Hide Others option in the Layers palette flyout menu, as shown in Figure 8-7. Now the only layer visible is the active layer. You may also accomplish this by holding ALT/OPTION+SHIFT while clicking on the active layer's Show/Hide button.

Using the Preview All/Artwork Mode

Artwork is displayed two ways in Illustrator. It can be displayed in Artwork view or Preview mode. Using Artwork view lets you see all objects not hidden on all layers at the same time in Outline mode. This saves time, since Illustrator redraws objects and recalculates color values each time they are edited in Preview mode. Artwork mode should be used when editing the shape of objects. You may toggle between Preview All and Artwork mode from the Layers palette flyout menu.

Viewing objects in Preview mode lets you see your artwork with all the fill and stroke colors applied. This helps when applying new color schemes to fill and stroke areas in your composition. Preview mode should be used when editing color.

If you ever wish to, it is possible to view one layer in Artwork view and another layer in Preview mode. When you want to reveal all the artwork and layers not hidden in Preview mode, activate this option by selecting the selecting the Preview All Layers option in the Layers palette flyout menu, as shown in Figure 8-7.

Displaying in Artwork View

When working with many gradient fills, Illustrator 7 must take time to redraw each fill as you add new objects and make changes. To save time, switch to Artwork View. All artwork not hidden will be displayed as an outline. All objects not hidden will be superimposed on top of one another. Color can be added to an object in Artwork view, but you won't see it until you view the objects in Preview mode.

Using the Lock Others Feature

When working with multiple layers there is always a chance of inadvertently modifying objects on layers other than the active layer. To limit selections and editing to only the active layer, choose the Lock/Unlock All Layers option in the Layers palette flyout menu (see Figure 8-8). You have three options: Unlock All Layers or Lock Others with multiple layers compositions and Lock All Layers for a single-layer drawing.

Using the Paste Remembers Feature

When active, the Paste Remembers Layers option found on the Layers palette flyout menu has the effect of enabling Illustrator to retain layering information when copying an object and subsequently repasting it. The real advantage to using this feature is that it prevents objects from being copied from one layer and accidentally pasted onto another—unless that is your intention. The object in the *clipboard* (a temporary storage in memory for items that have been copied or cut) will be pasted only to the layer from which it originated. If the Paste Remembers option is not active, the Paste function will add the clipboard object to the active layer.

 With this option selected, you cannot paste objects from this layer to any other layer. You must first deselect the Paste Remembers option before Illustrator will allow you to paste to another layer from this layer.

Merging Multiple Layers

Two or more layers can be merged onto a single layer by selecting them while holding the SHIFT key and choosing Merge Layers from the Layers palette flyout menu. Layers are then merged together into one layer and the name of the lowest numbered layer is maintained. Merging layers is useful when all elements of a composition are completed and no further editing is anticipated.

If you find yourself working with Illustrator 7's layering options frequently and you are creating drawings that feature groups and masks, you may want to take a cautious approach. Groups and masks don't always behave the way in which you might expect them to.

When grouping objects which exist on different layers, keep in mind that the resulting group will automatically end up on the same layer as that of the frontmost layered object in the group. Plus, the newly created group will now be the frontmost object on that layer. This automated layering may not be your intention—but it will nevertheless be the result.

If you would like to group copies of objects while leaving behind the original objects on their respective layers, then do the following: Select the objects you want to group. Drag this selection anywhere on the document page while holding down the ALT/OPTION key, release the mouse button, and then ALT/OPTION. A copy of the objects selected will be created. If you release the ALT/OPTION key first, a copy will not be created. Group the objects by selecting them and pressing CTRL/COMMAND+G. The originals remain in their respective layers while their copies are moved to the frontmost layer of the frontmost object.

If you group masks from different layers, they lose their relationship to the objects they were masking on the other layers. To group the mask along with the objects relating to the mask, be sure to select the objects as well as the mask. If an object selected in the group is located on a different layer closer to the top of the stack than the mask is, the mask and the objects on other layers will be moved from their original layer and placed on the frontmost layer.

Setting Object Attributes

All objects in your drawing have attributes or properties. While the Info palette provides various information concerning the physical size and location of objects on your page, the Attributes palette deals with the images as they will appear on the printed page as well as those images created for a Web page.

The Attributes Palette

To access the Attributes palette, choose Window|Show Attributes (Figure 8-11). The Attributes palette displays the settings and options for whichever object you have currently selected. The Attributes palette enables you to set certain variables for individual or groups of objects, including Overprint Fill, Overprint Stroke, Show/Hide Center, Reverse Path Direction, Output Resolution, and assign a URL (uniform resource locator) address.

Window/Show Attributes   Overprint Stroke option
Overprint Fill option

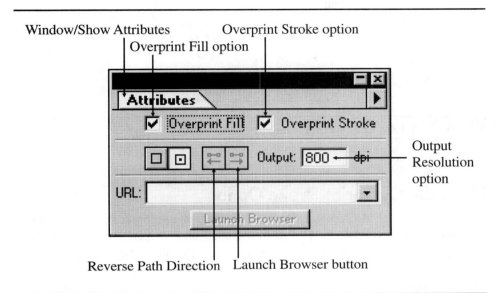

Output
Resolution
option

Reverse Path Direction   Launch Browser button

FIGURE 8-11   The Attributes palette

Options for the Attributes palette display conditions are found on the Attributes palette flyout menu shown in Figure 8-11 and with options shown in Figure 8-12. The Attributes palette is capable of two modes of display: Show Overprint Only and Show/Hide Note. Choosing Show/Hide note sets the Attribute palette to show URL options. The flyout also gives access to the Attributes Palette Options dialog box shown in Figure 8-13, enabling you to set how many URL listings to display in the URL drop-down list, which may be set to display a maximum of 30 URLs at any one time.

Understanding the Overprint Fill Option

When objects overlap, their colors appear opaque in Illustrator. In other words, when printed, the top color eliminates the color of the objects below, causing the object to appear opaque. To eliminate this and simulate transparency in color separation printing, select the object and apply the Overprint Fill option (see Figure 8-11). Illustrator will create an overprint in color separation so the top object appears partially transparent. Although overprint fill is applied to objects, they will still appear the same on screen. This option only applies to printing hard copies of artwork using color separation and not composite printing or onscreen display.

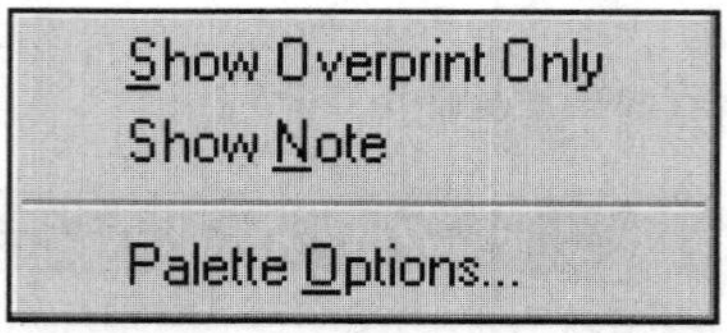

Show Overprint Only
Show Note

Palette Options...

FIGURE 8-12   The Attributes palette flyout menu

Using the Overprint Stroke Option

As with Overprint Fill, Overprint Stroke deals with color separation printing. Choose Overprint Stroke (Figure 8-11) and the stroke colors will overprint each other, causing the strokes to appear transparent in color separation printing.

Center Display

The Show/Hide Center display option of the Attributes palette enables you to set whether the center reference point of objects is displayed or not. For some users who haven't the need to see the center reference of objects, this enables them to further streamline the amount of information they see on their screen at any one time (see Figure 8-11). Leaving the options active enables Illustrator to display an x at the physical center point of an object. This can be convenient visual information when drawing highly specific subject matter such as in drafting or architecture for such

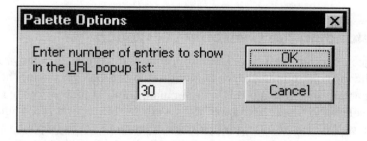

FIGURE 8-13   The Palette Options dialog box

operations as finding radii or any measurement from center using the Measure tool (U) in the main Toolbox. The Measure tool is shown here:

Center Display also provides you with visual reference as to the object's default Point of Origin. When initiating commands that modify and edit objects, the point of origin is first located at the object's physical center. If a group of objects is selected, the physical center of the group before the default Point of Origin is calculated.

Reverse Path Direction

The Reverse Path Direction enables you to make certain areas in compound paths that are invisible once again visible (see Figure 8-11). Objects created in Illustrator are classified as simple by default. A compound path is created when the Compound Path command is applied to two or more objects. The area of overlap between objects becomes transparent to objects behind the complex path.

Output Resolution

If printing is too slow or there are difficulties, set the Output Resolution option (see Figure 8-11) to a lower number. The range for Output Resolution is 100-9600, which is printer dependent. Printer dependent means that, depending on the kind of printer you have, you can obtain up to the 9600 dpi resolution in printed output. Lowering the resolution output to between 100-800 may be your only option if you own a printer of lesser quality. Setting object resolution beyond 800 dpi will only be of benefit when printing on higher resolution printers.

URL Options

The URL option imbeds a URL (uniform resouce locator) address within the objects you have selected so you may associate them to an Internet Web site. This is a powerful feature that can literally make your drawing come alive with information. Either text or shape objects may be associated with Web site addresses in an effect that will enable those viewing your drawing to refer to current information or simply make your drawing interactive via the Web.

Once an object associated with a URL is selected, the associated URL information may be used in a number of different ways. The Launch Browser button may be pressed to view the associated Web site and/or verify the address (see Figure 8-11). Or the information associated with objects may be used in the production of image mapping for use in creating interactive Web site images. URL locations are revealed from previously designated sites to which you can attach the object. You can designate how many sites to display in the Palette Options dialog box as shown in Figure 8-13. Enter the number to be displayed and click OK.

Chapter 8 Tutorial:
Creating Effects with Layers and Layering

As a practical exploration of the features and effects discussed in this chapter, follow through in this step-by-step tutorial. As you do so, you'll may notice that certain of these steps are accompanied by a "Color palette" symbol. This symbol indicates that the step has also been illustrated in full color in the Fundamental Illustrator 7 color insert. The purpose of the color insert is to provide you with a brief overview of the tutorial and illustrate an overall reference for the practical use of color throughout these tutorials.

Watch for this symbol:

Layering effects are used in situations that require many objects to produce shading effects and perhaps machined surfaces. In this tutorial you will create a realistic-looking bolt from a series of replicated threads which you'll modify to add proper curvature. To finish the composition, a shadow will be created from the outline of the bolt.

Using Layering to Draw a Bolt

You will first create two horizontal rectangles to guide your work in creating the threads for your bolt. You will need to zoom in on your work from time to time, so familiarize yourself with the Zoom tool. Let's get started.

1. Choose the Rectangle tool (M) from the main Toolbox. Click in the artboard for the Rectangle dialog box. Enter **2.25** for Width, and press TAB. Enter **.75** for Height, and press ENTER. Click on the Swap Fill/Stroke button and select Fill. Click on the No Fill button. Click on the Stroke button and select black for the Stroke color. Activate the Stroke palette by choosing Window|Show Stroke. Double-click in the Stroke Width text box and enter **.1**. Press ENTER.

2. Choose the Transform palette by Window|Show Transform. Double-click the Width text box and enter **2**. Hold down the ALT/OPTION key and press ENTER. This creates a transformed duplicate. Double-click the Height text box in the Transform palette and enter **.38**. Press ENTER.

3. Open the Layers palette by choosing Window|Show Layers. Double-click Layer 1 and type the name **Layer 1 Guidelines**.

   Now you will create three vertical rectangles to serve as thread guidelines on Layer 2. These vertical rectangles will help you form the first thread for your bolt object. You will use these guides to help determine how much to adjust the threads on the shaft so you're happy with the results.

4. Click on the Create New Layer button in the Layers palette. Double-click Layer 2 and name it **Layer 2 Threads**.

5. Choose the Selection tool from the main Toolbox. Click on the original rectangle and copy it to the clipboard using CTRL/COMMAND+C. Click the Lock/Unlock button for Layer 1 Guidelines.

6. Click on Layer 2 Threads in the Layers palette. Paste the copy of the rectangle using CTRL/COMMAND+V. Double-click the Width text box in the Transform palette and enter **.03**. This is the first vertical rectangle in Figure 8-14.

7. Hold down the ALT/OPTION key and drag a new rectangle a little to the right. Drag another copy. (Release the mouse button before releasing the ALT/OPTION key.) These are the second and third vertical rectangles in Figure 8-14.

8. Zoom in on the three new vertical rectangles using the Zoom tool and, using the Selection tool, position the other two so they align as shown in Figure 8-14.

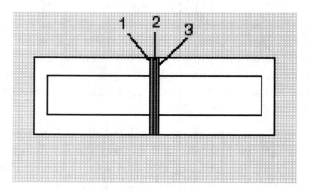

FIGURE 8-14   Creating the rectangular guides

Now you will modify one of the vertical rectangles to create the first thread for your bolt. You will use several of the Pen tools to add anchor points and convert these anchor points to curves and work to achieve a slight *S* curve to the rectangle.

1. Using the Selection tool, move the first vertical rectangle over the other two vertical rectangles, as shown in Figure 8-15. Bring this rectangle to the front (CTRL/COMMAND+SHIFT+]). Select all three rectangles and choose the Align palette (Window|Show Align). Click the Horizontal Distribute Center. Click away from the objects to deselect them.

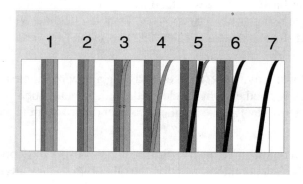

FIGURE 8-15   Creating the first thread

2. Click on the center vertical rectangle. Choose the Scale tool (S). Hold down the ALT/OPTION key and click on the crosshairs that appear at the rectangle's center. A dialog box will appear. Choose the Non-uniform scale, enter **50** for horizontal and **100** for vertical and click OK. See Figure 8-15 for the results.

3. Add anchor points to this center vertical rectangle using the Add Anchor Point tool using the Pen tool (P). Click once at each intersection of the center vertical rectangle and center horizontal rectangle. The vertical rectangle now has four new anchor points. Convert these anchor points to corners using the Convert Direction Point tool (A). Drag each of these four new anchor points to show the direction points. Then drag the direction point again to create a corner anchor point at each of these four new anchor points.

4. Choose the Direct Selection tool (A). Click on the top two anchor points on the center vertical rectangle while holding down the SHIFT key. Drag these points to the upper-right corner of the right vertical rectangle. Click on one of the new center nodes and adjust the direction point to create a smooth curve as shown at 3 in Figure 8-15. Repeat this for the other anchor points, creating a symmetrical curve.

5. Choose the Rotate tool (R). Hold down the ALT/OPTION key and click on the approximate center of the modified rectangle. Enter **-7.5** in the dialog box which appears and click OK. This adds an angle to the thread. Use the Direct Selection tool to select and move each of the top two nodes to match the original horizontal rectangle's upper side. See 4 in Figure 8-15.

6. Choose the Selection tool (V). Click away from the objects to deselect them and select the thread object. Access the Transform palette by choosing Window|Show Transform. Double-click the Angle text box. Enter **180** degrees and press ENTER while holding down the ALT/OPTION key. This creates a rotated copy as you'll see in 5 in Figure 8-15.

7. Drag the new thread over the original thread so the body is flush and aligned with the bottom side of the horizontal rectangle. Using the Direct Selection tool (A), adjust the direction points to match the curve of the original thread. This will ensure that the thread is symmetrical at both ends. See 6 in Figure 8-15.

8. Delete the vertical rectangles that previously served as guidelines. Delete the original thread and the basic outside surface of the thread for your bolt remains, as shown in 7 in Figure 8-15.

You have a single thread placed about in the middle of the horizontal rectangles. You will move the thread to the left end of the center horizontal rectangle and drag a copy to the opposite end of that rectangle. Then you will apply a blend to create the rest of the threads for the bolt. You will also create the left and right inside objects to finish the shape of the bolts shaft.

9. With the Selection tool, drag the thread you just created to the left end of the center rectangle so that the center point rests on the left side of the rectangle. Hold down the ALT/OPTION key and drag a copy to the opposite end of the center rectangle. Be sure the center point of the thread rests on the right side of the center rectangle. Unlock Layer 1 to modify the horizontal rectangles. Select all the objects using the marquee selection with the Selection tool and click on Vertical Align Center. Lock Layer 1 to prevent moving or selecting the horizontal rectangles.

Select both thread objects and choose the Blend tool (B). Click on an anchor point on the first thread. Click on the corresponding anchor point on the second thread. A dialog box will appear. Enter **22** in the Steps option and click OK. As you can see in Figure 8-16, Illustrator evenly adds 24 threads across two inches. Choose the Selection tool (V), select all the threads, and group them together (CTRL/COMMAND+G).

Now you will create the left and right inside portion of the thread. You will accomplish this by freehand drawing using the Pen tool (P). Then you will trim the shape using the Pathways Divide command. You will resize the original horizontal rectangle to become the inside diameter of the thread.

10. Unlock Layer 1 and click on the original horizontal rectangle. Double-click on the Height text box in the Transform palette. Enter **.65** and click OK. Lock Layer 1 again.

11. Zoom in on the two left-most threads in your new line of threads. Choose the Pen tool (P) and click the upper-right corner of the left-most thread. Move down to the top of the horizontal guide and to the right. Click so that the second anchor point falls approximately two thirds the distance between the two threads. Move down and to the left to the bottom side of the original horizontal rectangle. Click a third time just to the right of the last thread and to the left about a third of the distance between the two threads. Click a fourth time at the lower-right anchor point of the left-most thread. Click a fifth time down and to the left approximately the width of the thread. Finally, click a sixth time up and to the right just above and to the left of the upper-left anchor point of the left-most thread. Close the object by clicking on the original anchor point. This gives you an idea of the object you are creating:

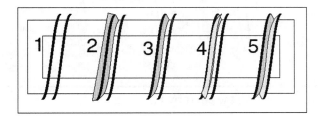

12. Convert anchor points to curves at the intersection of the freehand lines and horizontal rectangle. With the Convert Direction Point tool, drag the anchor points to reveal the direction points. Release the Convert tool and then select the points and drag them again to create a corner.

13. With the Direct Selection tool, edit the line between the threads to approximate the *S* curve, as shown above. Choose the Selection tool and select the thread and the new freehand object you created. Choose Object|Pathfinder|Divide. Ungroup the objects and select and delete the extra object to the left.

14. Select the left-inside thread object with the Selection tool. Double-click on the Angle text box in the Transform palette. Enter **180** degrees, press ALT/OPTION, and ENTER. Move this object to the right to match it with the thread on the right as shown above. Adjust the curves using the Direct Selection tool so they match exactly. Drag copies to the right end of the threads as shown in Figure 8-16.

    What you have accomplished so far is to create all the objects that will become the threads of the bolt shaft you will create. The shapes set the ground work for the composition. Now you will blend the inside objects of the bolt to complete the threads.

15. Select the left inside thread at both ends of the bolt. Bring them to the front using CTRL/COMMAND+SHIFT+].

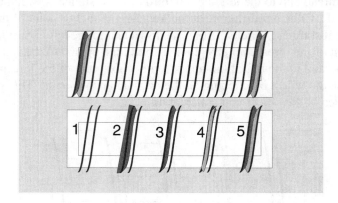

FIGURE 8-16   Creating the shaft by blending

16. Choose the Blend tool (B). Click on corresponding anchor points on both selected left inside threads. Enter **21** for the number of steps and click OK. Choose the Selection tool. While holding down the SHIFT key, click on two objects you just blended. Group the objects (CTRL/COMMAND+G).

17. Select the right inside thread at the left and right ends of the shaft you are creating. Choose the Blend tool and click on corresponding anchor points on the inside-right threads, preferably the top-most anchor point for each object. A dialog box will appear. Enter **21** for the number of steps and click OK. Choose the Selection tool (V) and, while holding down the SHIFT key, click on the original objects that you just blended and group them (CTRL/COMMAND+G).

> *If you have problems with the Blend tool, make sure that you click on the same anchor point for the thread object and its duplicate. Use the Zoom tool to zoom in enough to select the same anchor point for the objects you want to blend. Selecting anchor points in different places of the objects will create a distorted blend between the two thread objects.*

You have created a major portion of the shaft with the three parts of a thread: the left and right inside surfaces and the outside surface. All that you have on your artboard now is the outline of the bolt threads. In the following portion of the tutorial you will create the end of the bolt threads and a bolt outline. You will also fill the bolt with linear gradient color to simulate reflected light off of a clean cylindrical metal surface. First, you will finish off the bolt shaft threads.

18. Choose the Direct Selection tool (A). Click on one right inside thread object. Press ALT/OPTION and drag a copy to the end of the threads and align the object so that it matches the outside thread object at the right end of the shaft.

19. Click on the left inside thread object. Press ALT/OPTION and drag a copy to the end of the new object and align it flush with the right edge so they match.

20. Click on an outside thread object. Press ALT/OPTION and drag a copy to the right end as you did in step 2.

21. Click on a left inside thread object. Press ALT/OPTION and drag a copy to the right end as you did in step 2.

You have added another complete thread to the shaft. This last thread must be trimmed using the Pathfinder|Divide command.

22. Draw a rectangle a little more than the height of the bolt shaft and wide enough to encompass the end of the bolt to the first recess of the thread, as shown here:

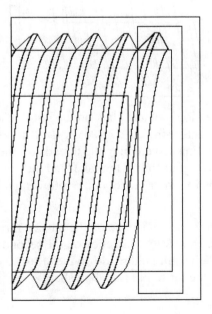

23. Choose the Direct Selection tool from the main Toolbox. While holding down the SHIFT key, click on the rectangle and the three objects that make the complete thread at the right end of the bolt. Choose Object|Pathfinder|Divide.

24. Ungroup these objects using CTRL/COMMAND+SHIFT+G. Using the Direct Selection tool (A), click on each object inside the rectangle, and press the DELETE key twice. Repeat this process until you have a clean edge, as shown here:

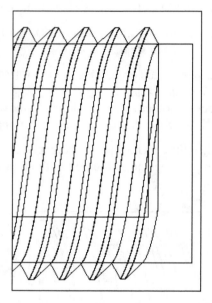

25. Choose the Selection tool and click on the last thread object to the right. Ungroup the objects using CTRL/COMMAND+SHIFT+G.

You are now finished creating the threads for the bolt. Now you will apply a linear gradient fill to make the bolt appear three-dimensional. We used the CMYK color model in the following tables. All values are percentages.

26. With the Selection tool (V), click on the outside thread object at the far left of the shaft. Hold SHIFT and click on the second outside thread object from the left. While still holding down the SHIFT key, click the outside thread object at the far right of the bolt shaft.

27. Open the Color palette (F6) and Gradient palette (F9). Click on the color stop at the far right in the Gradient palette. Enter the values of the following table in the Color palette creating another color stop for each row of values.

Color Values	C	M	Y	K	Position
Color 1	48	0	7.5	0	0
Color 2	0	0	0	100	32
Color 3	14	2	5	0	50
Color 4	80	30	0	0	66
Color 5	100	80	40	10	75
Color 6	15	5	2	0	100

28. Enter **-90** in the Angle text box and press ENTER.

29. Using the Selection tool (V), click on the left inside thread object at the far left. While holding down the SHIFT key, click on the left inside thread object second from the left. Click on the left inside thread object at the far right of the bolt shaft.

30. Click on the color stops in the Gradient palette. Drag the color stops off the gradient spectrum until only two remain. Click on the left color stop and drag it to the far left to position 0. Enter C=**0**, M=**0**, Y=**0**, K=**100** in the CMYK color model. Drag the color stop on the right to the far right in the Gradient palette. Enter C=**60**, M=**2**, Y=**3**, K=**20** at position 100.

31. Enter **-90** in the angle text box and press ENTER.

32. Click on the right inside thread object to the far left. Press and hold the SHIFT key while clicking on the right inside thread object second from the left. While still holding the SHIFT key down, click on the right inside thread object at the far right of the bolt shaft.

33. Choose Window|Show Swatch to access the Swatches palette. Click the flyout menu and select Name. Click on the Chrome preset swatch. In the Gradient palette, remove the white color stop by dragging it down off the gradient spectrum. Click on the color stop farthest to the right and select black in the Color palette. Click and drag the dark brown color stop to the right to about position **80**. Choose the Gradient tool (G), and position your cursor at the top of the threads. Drag from the top straight down to the bottom of the threads and release the mouse button. This applies a uniform fill to all the right-inside thread objects, as you can see in Figure 8-17, as well as in this book's color insert.

The threads are complete with gradient fill representing the lighting and reflection common to metal surfaces. The next section will guide you through creating the outline for the bolt to finish the head and create a shadow to make the bolt appear to pop off the page.

34. Choose the Rectangle tool (M) and click on your artboard. Enter **.5** for the width. Hit TAB and enter **1** for the height. Click OK.

35. Center the rectangle with the threads. Using the Selection tool (V), select all the bolt threads and group them (CTRL/COMMAND+G). Drag the rectangle until it is flush with the left edge of the rectangle guide. Hold down the SHIFT key and click on the thread objects. Open the Align palette by choosing Window|Show Align and click Vertical Align Center option.

36. Now create the outline of the bolt by tracing the shape of the threads and rectangle using the Pen tool. Begin the trace by clicking the Pen tool (P) once on the upper-right corner of the new rectangle. Continue clicking on high and low spots all around the bolt shape, as shown in Figure 8-17. The outline in Figure 8-17 is offset slightly to give you an idea of what the shape will look like when you are done. When you come back around to the original anchor point, click on the beginning to close the object.

37. Send this object to the back (CTRL/COMMAND+SHIFT+[). Fill this new outline with a gray color of **40** percent black. Click on the bolt outline and, while holding down the ALT/OPTION key, drag a copy to just beneath the objects. You will use this object to create the shadow for the bolt later. See the finished outline with threads in Figure 8-17.

You are ready to complete the shaft and begin working on the bolt head. In this next set of steps you will create the three facets of the hex head of the bolt and add a linear gradient to the shapes. This will complete the bolt.

38. Using the Selection tool (V), click on the .5 x 1-inch rectangle you created earlier. Drag this away from the bolt head.

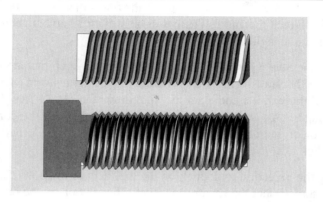

FIGURE 8-17   Create the bolt outline and fill

39. Choose the Pen tool (P) and create an outline of the bolt head starting at the left end of the threads and working counterclockwise. Complete the object by clicking at the starting point. Convert the anchor points that meet the threads into corners. Edit the line that runs parallel with the outside thread with the Direct Selection tool (A) so that its curve is flush with the thread.

40. Choose the Eyedropper tool (I) and click on a right inside thread object that has the modified chrome gradient fill. The Eyedropper tool will apply the modified chrome fill to the new object. Choose the Gradient tool (G) and drag from the upper-inside corner of the new object and drag to the lower-inside corner. Release the mouse button to enable Illustrator to update the chrome gradient.

Next you will create the facets for the bolt head. You will use the Rectangle tool (M) to create each of the sides of the bolt head that are showing.

41. Choose the Rectangle tool (M). Click in the artboard and the Rectangle dialog box will appear. Enter **.50** for width and **.25** for height. Enter **.13** for the corner radius. Click on OK to accept the values. Drag this new rounded rectangle to the .5 x 1-inch rectangle and align it with the top portion of the rectangle.

42. Holding ALT/OPTION, drag a copy of the new object to the bottom of the .5 x 1-inch rectangle. There will be a .5-inch gap between the two rounded rectangles.

43. Using the Selection tool (V), click on the .5 x 1-inch rectangle and activate the Transform palette (Window|Show Transform). Double-click the Height text box and enter **.5**. Hold down the ALT/OPTION key while pressing ENTER and a copy will be transformed. Make the corners of the new object rounded by choosing Filter|Stylize|Round Corners. Enter **.13** and click OK.

44. Using the Selection tool, click on the top facet of the bolt (.50 x .25 rectangle). Select the Eyedropper tool (I) and click on the outer thread object to apply the gradient fill. Repeat the process with the other two round rectangles. Use the Gradient tool found in the main Toolbox to adjust the direction of the gradient pattern on all three objects.

45. Using the Selection tool, click on the .5 x 1-inch rectangle. Choose the Eyedropper tool (I) and click on one of the facets to apply the same fill. Use the Gradient tool to change the direction of the gradient pattern to contrast the facets.

46. Using the Selection tool, select all the bolt head components and group them (CTRL/COMMAND+G). Drag this group of objects into position over the left end of the shaft at the bolt head area. Select this group of objects using marquee selection with the Selection tool and group them. Check your progress against Figure 8-18.

   With the bolt threads and head complete, it is time to create the shadow object to add to the composition. You will use the bolt outline you created earlier.

47. Using the Selection tool, click on the gray bolt outline. Using the Transform palette tools (Window|Show Transform) double-click the Height text box and enter **.5**. Press the ENTER key.

48. Double-click the Height text box in the Transform palette again. Enter **.25** and hold down the ALT/OPTION key while pressing ENTER.

49. Click on the end of the grayscale spectrum in the black area in the Color palette. Select both objects using the marquee selection. Click on the Stroke button and choose the No Stroke button.

FIGURE 8-18   Creating the bolt head

50. Choose the Blend tool (B). Click on the upper-left corner anchor of the gray bolt outline and then click on the upper-left corner anchor of the black bolt outline. Enter **15** for the number of steps to blend. Your bolt's shadow should look like Figure 8-19.

With the shadow complete, all you have to do is add an angle to the bolt to make it appear as though it is lying on a flat surface and then place it over the shadow.

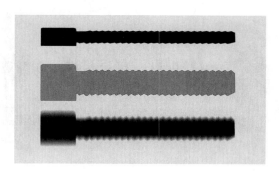

FIGURE 8-19   Creating the shadow

51. Using the Selection tool, click on the bolt group and choose the Rotate tool (R). While holding down the ALT/OPTION key, click on the crosshair point of origin. Enter **-5** for the rotate angle. Click OK.

52. Choose the Selection tool again and drag the bolt into place over the shadow. Check your results against the finished bolt shown in Figure 8-20. A color depiction of the gradients is shown in this book's color insert.

Creating a 3D Coffee Mug

Illustrator 7 has a great capacity to simulate three-dimensional objects in two dimensions using gradients. The following tutorial is designed to help build your three-dimensional visual effects skills and show you how to create professional-looking three dimensional objects.

In this exercise you will build a three-dimensional image of a coffee mug using Illustrator's tools to create objects and fills. Follow the steps closely, and you'll amaze yourself with the kind of artwork you will produce. First, create a new document page if you are working on another project by choosing File|New.

Begin creating the mug by first establishing the shape. The first shape is a simple ellipse to depict the lip or rim of the mug. You will use this ellipse as a guide to create the shape of the mug body. You will continue by creating a handle for the mug and,

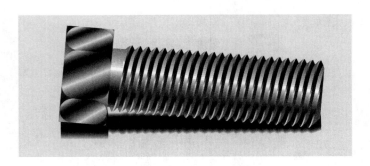

FIGURE 8-20   The finished bolt complete with shadow

lastly create the shadow to add to the illusion of depth. Along the way, you will learn about gradient fills for cylindrical objects.

1. Create an ellipse in the approximate center of the page using the Ellipse tool (N) found on the main Toolbox matching the shape in Figure 8-21.

2. Using the Selection tool (V), click on the ellipse to select it. Press ALT/OPTION while dragging a copy of the ellipse down slightly, releasing the mouse button before you release the ALT/OPTION key. This will ensure that a copy is being created rather than moving the original to the new location.

3. Select the Scale tool (S). While pressing the ALT/OPTION key, click on the crosshair in the center of the ellipse to view the Scale dialog box. Select the Uniform scale option and enter **96** percent, then click OK.

4. Next, select both ellipses by dragging the Selection tool across the paths of both ellipses. Open the Align palette (Window|Show Align). Click on the Vertical Align Center in the Align palette and then click Horizontal Align Center in the Align palette. Choose Object|Pathfinder|Trim. You now have the rim that will become the lip of the mug.

5. Choose Object|Ungroup or CTRL/COMMAND+SHIFT+G. To deselect the objects, click at least 2 points away from the objects. If the ungrouped objects are not deselected, the next action of editing will be applied to both the inside ellipse and the trimmed ellipse. Select the center ellipse and cut it using CTRL/COMMAND+X. You will paste this ellipse later in the tutorial.

6. Open the Color palette and the Gradient palette by choosing Window|Show Color and then Window|Show Gradient. Each of the color sets in the following table relates to the gradient scale arrows. Select the rim you've created and fill it with a gradient fill with the following values from the CMYK table:

Color Values	C	M	Y	K	Position
Color 1	17	50	94	0	0
Color 2	4	21	87	0	43.5
Color 3	18	41	93	0	66
Color 4	2	3	7	0	100

See the elliptical rim in Figure 8-21. Choose Window|Show Layer. Click on the Lock/Unlock button to lock this layer.

Next you will create the body of the mug. You will trace around the bottom portion of the rim you just created to get the shape for the top of the mug. You will take advantage of the layers feature to build the mug on multiple layers.

7. Choose the Layers palette (F7) and double-click layer one. In the Layers Options dialog box, name layer one **Mug Lip**. Click on the Lock/Unlock button in the Layers palette. Click on the New Layer button on the Layers palette and name this layer **Mug Body**.

8. Next, select the Pen tool (P). Begin drawing a shape that approximates the body of the mug, as shown in Figure 8-22. This may be accomplished with as few as eight anchor points. Make sure you close the path by clicking the beginning point when the Pen tool indicates you may close the path by showing a hollow circle.

9. The mug body consists of two curved sides and two straight sides. Using the Convert Anchor tool (P), change the anchors to curves by clicking on the anchor points. Once the anchor point shows two direction points, click and drag the direction points to create corner points. Use the rim as a guide for tracing the curve for the top and bottom of the mug. Use the Direct Selection tool (A) to move and shape the anchors and direction points to match the shape of the ellipse for the top and bottom of the mug body.

The Convert Anchor Points tool (P) can create smooth curves (when you click and drag the anchor point), corner points with curves (when you

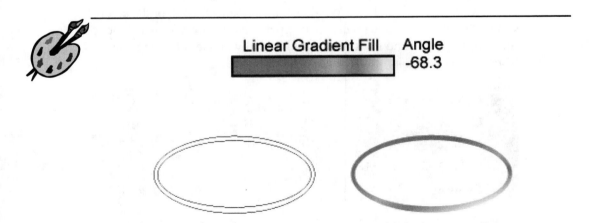

Linear Gradient Fill   Angle
-68.3

FIGURE 8-21   Creating the lip of the mug

click and drag the direction point), or corner points with straight lines
(when you use one click per anchor point).

9. Once you have created the outline as shown in Figure 8-22, work on the
gradient fill by choosing the Gradient (F9) and Color palettes (F6) and
using the color values in the following chart. Click on the arrow to the left
in the Gradient palette. Enter the values for this position of **0** degrees as
shown in the table below. Click on the gradient scale between the two
arrows and enter the next color, and repeat the process until all color
values have been entered. Once all the color values are entered, set the
angle to **0** degrees. Click OK.

Color Values	C	M	Y	K	Position
Color 1	0	0	0	100	0
Color 2	4	21	87	0	45
Color 3	2	3	15	0	71
Color 4	10	30	90	0	100

10. Position the body of the mug flush with the rim of the mug so they match.
Adjust the anchor points of the mug body with the Direct Selection tool
(A). Once you have completed the adjustments, click on the Lock/Unlock
button in the Layers palette for Mug Body Layer to lock this layer.

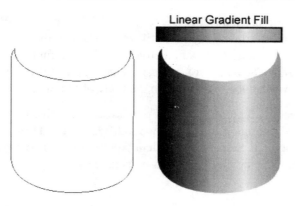

Linear Gradient Fill

FIGURE 8-22   Create the body of the mug using linear gradient fill

You have created the body of the mug by creating the outline and filling it with colors that portray a gold metallic surface. Now you will create the inside of the mug wall and contents of the mug.

11. Click the New Layer button in the Layers palette. Select Edit|Paste or CTRL/COMMAND+V. This will paste an ellipse the same size as the inside of the rim of the mug. You will now begin working on creating the inside wall of the mug and making it appear as though the mug is filled with either hot chocolate or coffee.

12. Create a copy of the ellipse you just pasted by choosing the Selection tool (A) and clicking on the new ellipse to select it. Make a copy by pressing ALT/OPTION and dragging down a little and releasing the mouse button first before releasing the ALT/OPTION key. Move the new ellipse three-fifths of the height of the original ellipse down from the top of the original ellipse so they overlap by two-fifths. Fill the original ellipse and its copy with solid fills, giving each object a different color in preparation for the next step.

13. You will use a Pathfinder command to divide the original ellipse and its copy into three objects. Select the original ellipse and its copy. Choose Object|Pathfinder|Hard. Select the Object menu again, and Ungroup (CTRL/COMMAND+SHIFT+G) so that the three objects created by the Pathfinder command may be edited. Using the Selection tool on the main Toolbox, click away from the selected objects to deselect them. Choose the bottom-most portion of the three new objects and delete it by pressing the DELETE key. You now have two objects left that will become the inside of the mug.

14. Select the top portion of the new object, which is now the inside wall of the mug and fill it with the same fill as the body of the mug by clicking on the Gradient palette to make it active. In the Gradient palette, change the angle to **180**. The angle you've just selected gives the inside of the mug a concave appearance in contrast to the body of the mug.

15. Now select the bottom portion of the new object, which is now the contents of the mug. You will now modify this object to simulate coffee or hot chocolate. Select the Gradient palette (F9) and begin filling with the following values which represent percentages:

Color Values	C	M	Y	K	Position
Color 1	0	0	0	100	0
Color 2	57	81	97	16	47
Color 3	30	48	96	1	85
Color 4	2	8	24	0	100

16. Using the Gradient tool (G), approximate the center of the ellipse so the center is dark and the edge is light. Once you have finished filling the coffee-colored gradient, position both the inner wall and contents in the center of the rim created in the first steps so that the edges of the contents are flush with the edges of the rim. Click on the Lock/Unlock button in the Layers palette to lock this layer. Figure 8-23 shows the outline and completed mug contents.

Now that you have completed the inside wall and contents, the mug should begin to appear three-dimensional. You could stop here if you were only creating a cylinder. To further enhance the composition, let's go on to create a handle for the mug and add a shadow to give the illusion of depth. The handle is made up of four

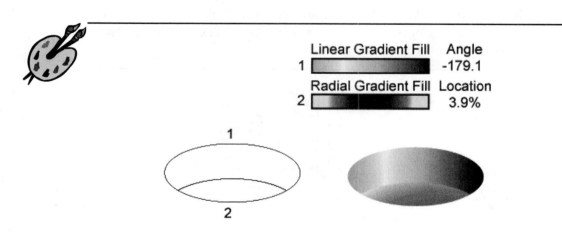

FIGURE 8-23 Creating the concave effect for the inside of the mug using gradients

elements: the depiction of the handle's shading/reflection on the mug body, the inside of the handle that is visible, the handle, and the outside surface of the handle. The handle objects are created freehand, that is, they are approximate shapes that have no exact description other than to draw your attention to the handle object outlines shown in Figure 8-24. The coloring of the handle objects, on the other hand, may be duplicated exactly, and CMYK tables are included for your information.

Click on the New Layer button and type in the name **Mug Handle**. Approximate the shapes shown in Figure 8-24 in proportion to the size of your mug so that the handle is at least $\frac{3}{4}$ the size of the height of your mug. The handle will jut out toward the light source, so you will create a combination shadow/mirror image, indicated in Figure 8-24 with a 1. Because the handle could not be created with one object, you will use several objects, taking advantage of linear gradient fills.

17. Create the handle object first. (See 3 in Figure 8-24). The basic shape is similar to a backwards *C*. Begin drawing with the Pen tool (P) within one-eighth of the height of the mug from the top of the mug body. Draw the outline of the handle and close the object by clicking on the path starting point when the Pen tool shows an empty circle. Convert the anchor points that need to be rounded using the Convert Anchor Point tool (P) and edit the handle with the Direct Selection tool (A).

Create the handle shadow/reflection next, as shown in 1 in Figure 8-24. Choose the Pen tool and draw the outline like the one shown in the figure. Use the Convert Anchor Point tool to convert anchors to curves. Choose the Direct Selection tool to edit the shape.

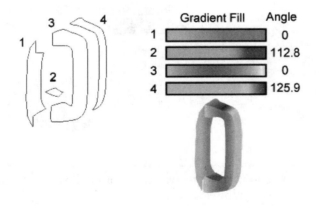

	Gradient Fill	Angle
1		0
2		112.8
3		0
4		125.9

FIGURE 8-24 Creating the handle for the mug using several objects and linear gradients fills

17. Next, create the inside of the handle. Choose the Pen tool and draw this by tracing the lower part of the handle. Convert anchor points using the Convert Anchor tool. Use the Direct Selection tool to edit the inside of the handle to match the shape of outline 2 in Figure 8-24.

18. The last object to create is the outside surface of the mug handle. Choose the Pen tool and trace the top of the handle object following the right edge of the handle to the bottom curve. Continue the line up the center of the object and close the object by clicking on the beginning of the path. Once again, use the Convert Anchor Points tool to create curves and the Direct Selection tool to edit the curves to match object 4 in Figure 8-24.

Now that the handle outline and its parts have been created, fill them one at a time using the color values from the following table:

Color Values	C	M	Y	K	Position
Object #1: Handle Shadow/Reflection: Angle = 0°					
Color 1	0	10	65	7	8
Color 2	9	36	91	5	59
Object #2: Inside of Handle: Angle = 112.8°					
Color 1	1	23	83	0	0
Color 2	9	36	91	37	27
Color 3	1	15	55	0	97
Object #3: The Handle: Angle = 0°					
Color 1	1	13	65	0	1
Color 2	9	36	91	14	44
Color 3	1	1	15	0	95
Color 4	1	11	51	0	100
Object #4: Outside Surface of the Handle: Angle = 126°					
Color 1	1	15	84	0	0
Color 2	1	11	51	0	14
Color 3	9	36	91	37	39
Color 4	5	23	83	0	88

Now that the handle is completed, make sure that the objects are in place on the right half of the mug body. If the Layers palette is not visible, choose Window|Show Layers. Click the Lock/Unlock button for the Mug Handle. Next you will create the shadow for the mug. Once the shadow is completed, it needs to be placed behind the mug body. Click the layer for the mug body in the Layers palette. Click the Lock/Unlock button in the Layers palette for the mug body layer. The shadow is a simple object filled with a radial gradient to depict a fading shadow.

21. Create an object to depict the shadow of the mug which approximates the shape shown in Figure 8-25 using the base of the mug body as a tracing guide for part of the shadow. Extend the shape to the upper left. Add a rounded path to the shadow to approximate the shadow of the top of the mug and bring the line to the left edge of the mug body. Close the object by clicking on the path starting point. Use a gray scale radial fill to represent a fading shadow.

23. Apply the following table of color values through the Color palette (F6) and the Gradient palette (F9):

Color Values	C	M	Y	K	Position
Color 1	0	0	0	100	0
Color 2	0	0	0	57	43
Color 3	0	0	0	35	70
Color 4	0	0	0	29	100

26. Adjust this fill in the mug shadow by choosing the Gradient tool (G).

27. Place the center of the radial fill near the center of the bottom of the mug by clicking and dragging the Gradient tool from the center of the mug toward the upper-left edge of the shadow, then release the mouse button and the fill is applied. This makes the shadow look realistic by fading to the edge of the shadow.

28. Send the object to the back (CTRL/COMMANDSHIFT+[).

Working in Artwork mode allows an artist to see all objects at the same time. It's like looking at an x-ray of the object to reveal outlines that may be hidden in the Preview mode. Artwork mode is important for editing minute details between

Radial Gradient Fill

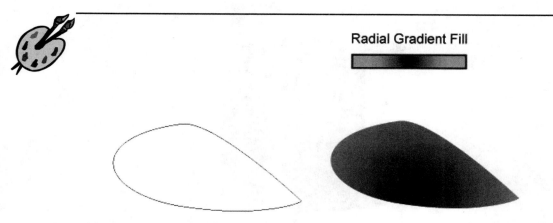

FIGURE 8-25 Creating the shadow of the mug to give the illusions of depth

objects and layers. Use this feature often to aid in perfecting art in your compositions. See the outlines in Figure 8-26.

Preview mode gives the artist the best view possible with all colors present. This also helps the artist consider other changes that may need to be made such as color and shading adjustments. Figure 8-27 shows the finished mug.

You will see the same artwork shown in color in this book's color insert.

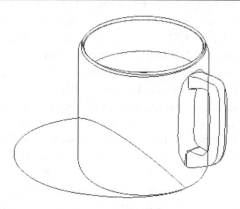

FIGURE 8-26 The mug drawing in Artwork mode

■ **FIGURE 8-27** The finished mug in Preview mode

Tracing a Digital Image to Create a Vector Drawing

The following tutorial was created using a bitmap from Corel's Professional Photo CD People Series 23000. This particular photo is #230031, entitled "Young Woman on Horse." Studying the bitmap gives insight to particular areas of interest. A complete rendering of the woman and the horse could have been made, but for simplicity's sake the horse's head was chosen for this tutorial.

You will trace over the outline and form of the image on the bitmap in preparation for adding fills to depict coloring in the bitmap. This process may be used on just about any subject once the general concepts of tracing and filing are understood. Most people will not have the CD used in this illustration, but the concepts may be used on almost any bitmap following the same procedures found in the following pages. Select a bitmap of a person or a horse to use and follow the steps in the tutorial.

Illustrator can deal with bitmaps in two ways: Illustrator opens a bitmap as a file or links the bitmap as a placed image. A placed image takes less memory so is your best bet if you need small files because of limited storage space. Illustrator links the bitmap and looks for the bitmap file each time it is opened. The disadvantage is if the bitmap file is moved or deleted, the link is lost, and Illustrator will display a message that the linked file could not be found. This is not good if you need to access the linked file in more than one editing session. Illustrator 7 gives you the option of saving the placed image. The alternative is to open the file through Illustrator's dialog box and then save it as an Illustrator native file. This can create large drawing files since bitmap images no longer undergo compression. This alternative was used for the next tutorial.

1. Open the bitmap as a file rather than a placed image. See Figure 8-28. Choose the Layers palette (F7). Double-click the active menu for the Layer Options dialog box. Type in the name **Bitmap** for this layer. Click the Dim Images box and the Lock/Unlock box. Click OK. See the dimmed bitmap with the outline in Figure 8-29.

2. Click on the New Layer button and name the new layer **Outline**. Before drawing, zoom in on the edge of the bitmap subject you have selected to trace by clicking on the Zoom tool (Z). Magnify by clicking on the area to be traced to 1600. Select the Swap Fill button and click the No Fill button in preparation for drawing outlines only. Using the Pen tool (P), begin tracing the outline of the object you wish to render. Figure 8-29 shows the complete outline as a closed path. You can see in the figure that no fill was applied. If a fill were applied it would completely cover the image of the woman and the horse.

FIGURE 8-28   Opening a bitmap as a file rather than a placed image

FIGURE 8-29   Completed tracing of the outline of both horse and rider

3. The outline was simplified by using the Knife tool (C). Your composition may not need to be simplified this way. Click the Lock/Unlock button on the Layers palette to lock this layer. Click the New Layer button and type in the name **Features** for this layer. The features were then traced for the horse's mane, including the shading. This process may be used on any hair image.

4. Next, the features of the neck, ears, and mane between the ears were traced, including highlighted areas and paying particular attention to the shape of light and dark regions, which are to be filled later.

5. The features of the horse's face were traced including the eye, the brow, and the shading of the snout all the way to the nose and mouth.

6. Last, the bridle was traced. Each traced outline is a closed object. The tracing is shown completed in Figure 8-30.

   As you look at the bitmap image tracing, you may need to convert some of the straight lines to smooth curves or corner points or edit anchor points by moving them one way or another. Go back to any section or object completed to edit the outline by converting anchor points to curves by using the Convert Anchor Point tool. (P is the keyboard shortcut for

FIGURE 8-30   The tracing of features of the bitmap is completed

8

the Convert Anchor Point tool, which you'll toggle three times.) You'll also find it in the Pen tool flyout menu in the main Toolbox. Click on any anchor point you need to edit, then activate the Direct Selection tool (A) found on the main Toolbox and edit the direction points for each curve.

7. The Bitmap layer is selected and unlocked. The Show/Hide button for this layer is selected to hide the bitmap allowing you to get a clear outline and tracing of features. This layer is Locked again by clicking on the Lock/Unlock button. You may view the bitmap anytime by unlocking the layer and clicking on the Show/Hide button. Figure 8-31 shows what the final composition will look like.

8. The Outline layer is selected and unlocked. The outline of the hind quarters and rider is selected and deleted. It is prudent to make sure you save work in several files in case you change your mind and wish to keep part of the composition. This has been done and there is no need to redo a tracing that is still intact in another file. The main outline of the horse's head is selected and given a linear gradient fill of warm colors from dark (left) to light (right) to match the coloring of the original bitmap. See Figure 8-32 for the color vales.

■ **FIGURE 8-31**   The bitmap has been hidden and all that shows is the outline and feature tracing

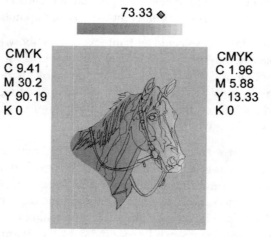

73.33 ◈

CMYK
C 9.41
M 30.2
Y 90.19
K 0

CMYK
C 1.96
M 5.88
Y 13.33
K 0

■ **FIGURE 8-32**   The horse's head remains and the outline of the head and neck is assigned a gradient fill

9. The next step is to fill the mane with brighter colors to give a good contrast to the shading in the horse's neck. The shading will be more subtle in the mane of the horse than on the neck. See Figure 8-33. If you are using a human image, consider filling the hair in a similar fashion using gradients, choosing colors that match your bitmap.

10. The next area to work on is creating some deeper shading in the neck and ears of the horse using linear gradients, staying with warmer hues of yellow and magenta. See Figure 8-34.

If you notice the shape of shaded areas it will help you define the composition quickly and build a realistic-looking picture. Notice the contrast between shading and highlights when creating gradient fills. It will help you match starting and ending points for color gradients. See Figure 8-35.

At this point, the background and hair of your subject is filled with gradient fills. You are working from the back and moving forward. If your object appears to be out of order with other fills, use the arrange feature to bring it forward (CTRL/COMMAND+]) or send it backward (CTRL/COMMAND+[) for proper placement.

Moving on to the facial features of the horse, fill the eye, ears, and nose holes with radial gradients. For convex surfaces, light is concentrated in the center, and

Add fill to the mane and the
mane shading

FIGURE 8-33   Work on creating realism through subtle gradient shading and defining shapes

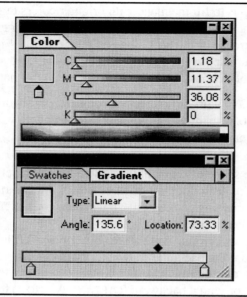

FIGURE 8-34   Gradient settings for filled outlines

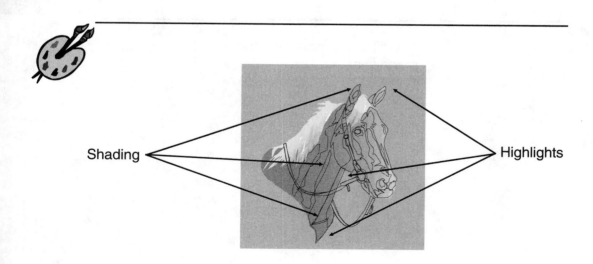

FIGURE 8-35   Adding gradient fills to the neck and ears

for concave surfaces, shading is concentrated in the center of the fill. Notice the difference between linear and radial fills and the effects they have for highlighting and shading in Figure 8-36.

Pay particular attention to the eye of the horse. It is dark in color except for a spot of light that gives it a rounded look. The shiny spot is part of a radial pattern created easily in the Gradient Fill dialog box shown in Figure 8-37.

The horse's head is nearly completed. All that is left is the bridle which is made up of strips of leather easily depicted by linear gradient fills using the Gradient palette and Color palette to set color values. A strip of leather has a much lighter top side. The underside may be depicted with dark browns. Figure 8-38 shows the finished composition.

Drawing a Pencil with Layer and Blends Effects

Mastering Illustrator's features to give a sense of depth to rendered objects should be the goal of every graphics illustrator. There are enough two-dimensional images around. Using the layered features in Illustrator will expand your ability to simulate depth and dimension in your artwork. Where gradient fills leave off, Illustrator's

Add gradient fills to the features of the horse's face

Linear Gradient for the snout

Use Radial Gradients for concave and convex surfaces

FIGURE 8-36   All features are filled and the face is nearly complete except for the bridle

FIGURE 8-37   The settings for the radial fill of the eye

Complete the composition
by filling the reins and bridal
with linear fills

FIGURE 8-38   The completed composition with the black background
for contrast

Blend feature picks up. For instance, you cannot create a conical gradient in Illustrator. But Illustrator can create the effect of a conical gradient by way of its Blend tool.

Let's draw a common object that almost every person has around their home or office—a pencil. You will draw the pencil in stages. First will be the pencil lead using triangles blended together. Then you will create the wood that is visible just behind the pencil lead using triangular shaped objects.

1. Create a triangle that will represent the outline of a tip of a lead pencil using the Pen tool (P). Fill it with a 100 percent black solid fill using the Color palette.

2. Next, create another triangle that is the same height but much narrower and place it inside the first triangle more to the right side. Fill this second triangle with a solid light gray/blue color using the Color palette (F6). Make sure the top points of both triangles match.

3. Next, select both objects with the Selection tool and then click on the Blend tool (B). Choose an anchor point on the narrow triangle and then select a corresponding point on the wider triangle. A Blend dialog box will appear requesting how many steps to take to blend the objects. Enter the number **10** and click on OK. Illustrator will blend objects using intermediate colors and shapes.

4. Select the objects using the Selection tool in the main Toolbox while holding down the ALT/OPTION key. Group the objects (CTRL/COMMAND+G). In Figure 8-39, the blended objects were dispersed to show the gradual shift in color and size of objects created with the Blend tool (B). Using the Rotate tool on the main Toolbox, rotate the object **90** degrees in preparation for building the pencil. Choose the Layers palette (F7) and click the Lock/Unlock button to lock the layer.

    Next, you will draw the portion of the sharpened wood of a pencil. The pencil wood continues the line of the triangles created in the pencil lead and may be represented as a conical object just like the lead. You create a blend between three objects to achieve a conical illusion.

5. In the Layers palette, click the New Layer button and type in the name **Wood Cone**. Using the Pen tool found in the main Toolbox, draw three trapezoids in preparation for creating the blends to represent the conical wood. Click on the lower-right corner of the pencil lead. Click the upper-right corner of the pencil lead. Then extend the line of the pencil lead by clicking about 3/8 of an inch up and to the right of the last anchor point.

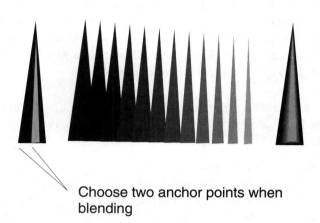

Choose two anchor points when
blending

FIGURE 8-39 Create the pencil lead using two objects and the Blend tool
from the main Toolbox

6. Now click about a quarter of an inch straight down, and then close the
object by clicking on the starting point. Fill the first trapezoid with a solid
dark brown color. If the wood object needs to be adjusted to fit the angle
of the pencil lead, use the Direct Selection tool (A) to adjust the anchor
points. When you are done editing, choose the Selection tool (V) and
click on an empty space in the work area to deselect the wood trapezoid.

7. Now you will create a copy of the first trapezoid. Click on the wood
trapezoid with the Selection tool. Click and drag a copy of the trapezoid
slightly to the right while pressing the ALT/OPTION key. Release the mouse
key before releasing the ALT/OPTION key. Resize the copy of the trapezoid
by choosing the Scale tool (S). Click on the crosshair while pressing the
ALT/OPTION key. From the dialog box that appears, choose Non-Uniform
scale and enter **100** percent for horizontal and **60** percent for vertical. Fill
the copy with a light tan solid fill that you select from the Color palette.

8. Create a copy of this copy by using the Selection tool (V). Drag while
pressing the ALT/OPTION key. Resize this second copy using the Scale tool
(S) and clicking on the crosshair in the center of the second copy while
pressing the ALT/OPTION key. In the dialog box that appears, enter **100**

percent for horizontal and **50** percent for vertical. Fill the object with a light yellow solid fill from the Color palette (F6).

Move the first copy of the trapezoid using the Selection tool by dragging it to the center of the original trapezoid and lining up the left edge of the copy with the left edge of the original. Select and drag the second copy using the Selection tool so that the second copy is centered over the first copy. Line up the left edge of the second copy with the left edge of the original trapezoid.

5. Add the blends by clicking on the original trapezoid with the Selection tool. Click on the copy of the trapezoid while pressing the SHIFT key. Choose the Blend tool (B), click on a corner of the copy of the trapezoid, and then click on the corresponding corner of the original trapezoid. A dialog box will appear. Enter **10** steps for the blend and click OK.

6. Using the Selection tool (V), select the first and second copies of the trapezoid . Repeat the process of the blend by choosing the Blend tool (B). Click on a corner on the copy of the trapezoid and then click on a corresponding corner in the second copy of the trapezoid. Again, enter **10** steps. Select the wood cone blends and group them (CTRL/COMMAND+G). Click on the Lock/Unlock button in the Layers palette. Your wood cone will look like Figure 8-40.

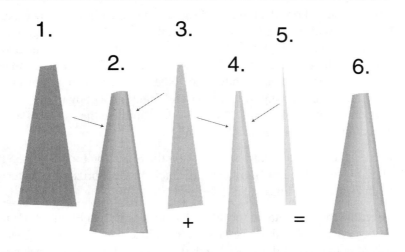

FIGURE 8-40   Creating the cone that represents the sharpened pencil tip

You have just completed one end of the pencil and now you will begin the other end. In the steps that follow you will create a metallic object to represent the crimped metal band that holds the eraser on a pencil. You will create simple objects and fill them with gray scale gradients to represent a metal surface. You will use rectangles and lines to represent crimp marks in the metal band.

12. From the Layers palette (F7), create a new layer by clicking on the New Layer button. Name the new layer **Metal Band**. Create the metal band of the pencil by drawing a rectangle using the Pen tool (P). Modify the outline as shown in Figure 8-41, using the Direct Selection tool (A) to move anchor points. If you need more anchor points, use the Add Anchor Point tool (P). Click on the top side and bottom side to add enough anchor points to create the outline for the silver band. Edit the outline using the Direct Selection, tool to adjust the anchor points. Add a gray scale gradient using the Gradient palette (F9), as shown.

13. Next, create six objects that represent the rings that encircle the pencil. These are thin rectangles filled with a darker gradient than the silver band to depict a recessed crimp mark across the silver band. Use the Rectangle tool (M) to create the rectangles. Apply a darker gradient to these rectangles that represent the rings to add contrast and give the illusion of depth.

14. Next, create a short black line and short white line close together that are **4** points in width using the Pen tool. Set the stroke width through the Stroke palette. See Figure 8-41. Select the Stroke Color from the Swap Fill/Stroke button in the main Toolbox. Select the Color palette and apply the black to one path and white to the other path. Select both objects and duplicate them pressing ALT/OPTION and dragging a copy to the new location below the original. This is used to simulate the marks of a mechanical crimper on the silver band.

15. Select the black and white strokes using the Selection tool and open the Align palette (Window|Show Align). Click on the Horizontal Center Align button. The lines are aligned.

16. Assemble the elements of the silver band according to Figure 8-41, using the Selection tool to drag the objects into place. Place the rectangles toward both ends of the silver band, three per end. Drag the black and white lines to the center of the silver band. Lock this layer by clicking on the Lock/Unlock button in the Layers palette.

You will now create the eraser using a blend between two objects that approximate the shape of an eraser. The object on top will be a lighter shade of pink than the object below.

17. In the Layers palette (F7), click on the New Layer button to create another layer and name it **Eraser**. To create the first object, select the Pen tool (P). Begin drawing an object to the left of the Metal Band that is square on one end and rounded on the other, as shown in Figure 8-42. Close the object by clicking on the path starting point. Click on the Selection tool and click in a blank space in the work area to deselect the eraser.

18. Click on the eraser object and create a copy by pressing ALT/OPTION and dragging a copy to the right. Resize this copy by choosing the Scale tool (S) and click on the crosshair in the center of the object while pressing the ALT/OPTION key. The Scale dialog box will appear. Select Non-Uniform and enter **75** percent horizontal and **50** percent vertical and click OK.

Gradient Fills

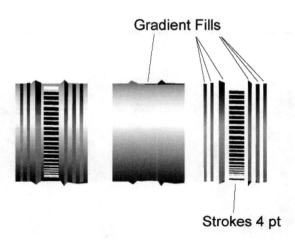

Strokes 4 pt

FIGURE 8-41 Create the metal band using linear gradients to simulate crimped metal

19. You will now fill the objects. Fill the copy and the original eraser using the Color palette (F6). Fill the copy with a light pink solid color value. Fill the original with a dark pink color value.

20. Select both objects and choose the Blend tool (B). Click on the lower-left corner of the original object and click on a corresponding corner in the Copy. Enter **10** in the Blend dialog box and click OK.

21. In the Layers palette, click on the Lock/Unlock button for this layer to lock it.

All the elements are in place except for the main body of the pencil. You are about to create the three visible sides of the pencil through blending objects and adding text.

22. In the Layers palette, click on the New Layer button and name this new layer **Body**. Create the first facet of the pencil body by creating a long rectangle with the Rectangle tool (M). Select the Add Anchor tool (P) and add another anchor point at the left end along the vertical line of the rectangle. Using the Direct Selection tool, pull this new anchor point left about half the distance of the height of the rectangle.

23. Use the Convert Anchor tool to convert this edited anchor point to a smooth curve. Using the Selection tool, press ALT/OPTION and drag a copy

Blend

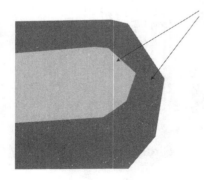

■ FIGURE 8-42   Create the eraser of the pencil by blending light and dark shades of pink

just below the original. Drag a second copy to just below the first copy. Using the Selection tool, select the first copy and resize it using the Scale tool found in the main Toolbox. Click on the crosshair in the center of the first copy while pressing the ALT/OPTION key. Choose Non-Uniform in the dialog box. Enter **100** percent for horizontal and **110** percent for vertical.

24. Let's add color to the pencil facets. Using the Color palette, fill the top rectangle with a strong yellow solid color. Fill the copy with a darker yellow solid color. Fill the second copy with a dark orange solid color.

25. You will use blends on two of the facets to create a highlight. Select the original rectangle with the Selection tool (V). Create a copy by pressing ALT/OPTION and dragging it slightly to the right. Assign a darker shade of yellow solid fill to this copy using the Color palette (F6). Resize this object by choosing the Scale tool (S). Press ALT/OPTION and click on the crosshair in the center of the copy. Choose Uniform and enter **80** percent, and then click OK. Select both objects and Align using the Align palette. Click on Vertical Center Align and then Horizontal Align Right.

26. Use the Blend tool (B) and click on the lower-right corner of the original object then click on the corresponding corner on the copy. Enter **8** steps in the Blend dialog box and click OK. Select the blend and the two objects will be blended. Group them (CTRL/COMMAND+G). Repeat this copying and blending operation for the center facet. No blend is necessary for the third facet. Position the three facets to represent the body of the pencil, as shown in Figure 8-43.

Use ten steps to blend sides

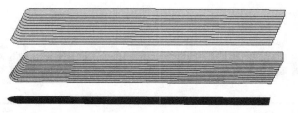

FIGURE 8-43   Creating the main facets of the pencil body

To create a visual effect similar to pencils found in a drawer, add text and lead value to the body of the pencil. Match the text height with the height of one facet to keep it in proportion to the rest of the composition, as shown in Figure 8-44. Place the text in position on the body of the pencil over the second facet group. Click on the Lock/Unlock button for the Body layer.

The pencil elements are complete except for the shadow. Create a shadow for the pencil by first tracing an outline of the finished pencil composition and creating a copy. Solid fill will be added so objects may be blended. You will blend between black and light gray to create a gray scale shadow. Click on the Lock/Unlock button in the Layers palette for the Body layer.

27. Select the New Layer button in the Layers palette and name this layer the **Shadow** layer. Create the shadow using black and light gray as the two solid colors to blend. Create an outline of the pencil using the Pen tool (P). Next, use the Selection tool (V) and press ALT/OPTION while dragging a copy up slightly.

Type 2, rotate and resize horizontally
for lead #2.

Illustrator 7 Graphics

FIGURE 8-44   Creating text to make the pencil look more realistic

28. Using the Scale tool (S), click the crosshair in the middle of the original outline. In the Scale dialog box, select Non-Uniform and enter **100** percent horizontal and **30** percent vertical to simulate perspective. Scale the copy outline to horizontal **80** percent and vertical **10** percent. Center the copy over the original object. Select the copy and the original and blend them together using the Blend tool. Click on any anchor point in the original outline and click on the corresponding anchor point on the copy. In the Blend dialog box, enter **10** for the number of steps. See Figure 8-45.

29. Group the shadow and arrange this layer to the back in the Layers palette by dragging it down the Layer palette list.

30. To assemble the elements, unlock each layer to scale and move the parts into place to fit the pencil body. If a layer is out of place, use the Layers palette to rearrange layers by selecting and dragging the layer up or down in the Layers palette to the new order. See the complete and assembled elements of the pencil in Figure 8-46.

   The composition is amazingly realistic for a computer-generated image. Using simple blends may go a long way to create the illusion of three dimensions, as Figure 8-47 shows.

Blend using ten steps

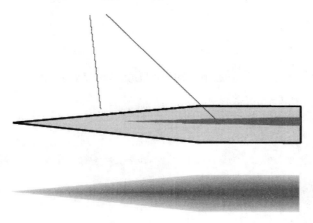

FIGURE 8-45   The completed shadow using gray scale blends

Order groups of blends using
arrange front or back as needed

FIGURE 8-46   Assemble and adjust by scaling the elements of the pencil

The completed Illustrator 7 pencil

FIGURE 8-47   The completed pencil

Conclusion

Take your time learning the lessons in this chapter. If you make the techniques taught here second nature, you can reap many benefits from using layers and layering effects. This chapter has taken you on a journey through Illustrator 7's tools for selecting and arranging objects. You have learned all of the critical ways in which Illustrator 7 enables you to physically select and manage the often thousands of drawing objects your files are or will be composed of. Grouping, layering, aligning, and distributing the objects on your page are all critical to working with core vector and bitmap objects.

Now that you have an understanding of how to manage your drawing objects there's much more to explore in the following chapter.

8

Creating Effects with
Object Transform Tools

9

Illustrator 7 has a number of transformation tools that make editing objects easier for the computer artist. You can transform an object in one of three ways. You may transform an object by using the Object|Transform menu, the various transformation tools from the main Toolbox, or the Transform palette. In addition, you'll learn to use the Info palette to monitor an object's transformation. The illustration on the next page is a simple example of one of the many transformations available in Illustrator. Here the Scale tool was used to enlarge an object.

Also covered in this chapter is the Pathfinder with its 14 commands found in the Object menu. In addition to modifying an object directly with transformation commands, you can use Pathfinder commands, which modify existing objects with other existing objects. Learning to use Transformation tools and Pathfinder commands gives the computer artist the advantage of speed and power in shaping and modifying objects.

Understanding Illustrator's Point of Origin Concept

Illustrator 7 automatically determines the point of origin for each object as you create it. The default point of origin is the physical center of a selected object or group of objects. This is the reference point from which Illustrator calculates the transformations.

You may change the point of origin by selecting a Transformation command and then clicking once in the work area. That first click without dragging sets the new point of origin from which all transformation will now takes place. Calculating the transformation begins when you click and drag from the second location. You gain accuracy in control of the transformation by clicking farther away from the object than nearer.

The second click and drag initiates the transformation by recording the movement of the mouse in distance and direction on the x (horizontal) and y (vertical) axes. When the mouse stops moving and you release the mouse button, Illustrator applies the transformation.

To get an idea of how the Transformation tools work in conjunction with an object's point of origin, here is a simple exercise with the Rotate tool (R is the keyboard shortcut for the Rotate tool), shown here:

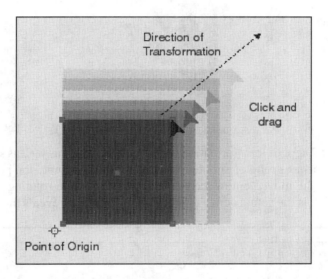

Illustrator rotates an object around its point of origin. If the point of origin is also the center of the object, the object will spin the number of degrees specified in the Rotate dialog box. You activate the Rotate dialog box by pressing the ALT/OPTION key and clicking on the point of origin. Be sure the mouse cursor is a crosshair before clicking; otherwise, you will rotate a copy of an object instead of the original.

When you press the ALT/OPTION key, an ellipsis will appear next to your mouse cursor. If your mouse cursor is an arrowhead, click on the point of origin and the crosshairs will reappear. The object will also rotate around its center when you select the Rotate tool and drag the mouse instead of pressing ALT/OPTION and clicking.

Note   *If you use the Transform tools and specify a preview of the transformation, show preview will remain active. Next time you open the dialog box during the same session, Illustrator will automatically show you a preview of the transformation according to the last settings you entered.*

If you set the point of origin somewhere other than the center of an object, then the object will rotate around the point of origin, as shown below.

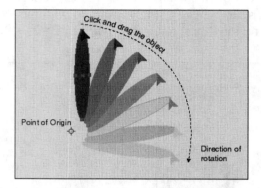

Illustrator 7 applies transformation commands to groups as well as single objects. Figure 9-1 shows a group of simple art objects rotating around the point of origin. We simulated the movement of the duck by copying while rotating. Only the last duck in the line is the actual active object. The Info palette reveals the movement in

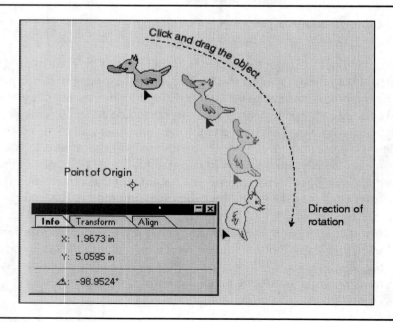

FIGURE 9-1 Rotation around the point of origin

x, y coordinates and in degrees of rotation. The angle of rotation is -98.9824 degrees from its original location.

Using the Info Palette

As you create and modify art objects, Illustrator 7 records the data according to size, location, and direction of the object's transformation. You may view information about an object or the location of the mouse cursor through the Info palette. To activate the Info palette, choose Window|Show Info. The Info palette appears and immediately displays information about a selected object. If you didn't select any objects then the Info palette will display information about the mouse cursor location.

With a transformed object selected, the Info palette will display the information about the object most recently transformed. If no objects are selected prior to opening the Info palette, Illustrator simply displays information about the mouse cursor location on the *x* and *y* axes. When you switch between Transform tools, the Info palette will display information for each tool's previous action.

If you select an object while the Info palette is open, Illustrator will return the *x* and *y* coordinates along with Width and Height information. The Info palette does not display information about the angle or distance because you have not transformed the new selection. Figure 9-2 shows a newly selected object and its information.

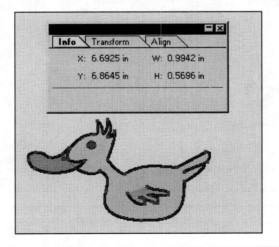

FIGURE 9-2   The Info palette with a selected object

The Info palette displays the distance of a move on the *x* and *y* axes. The Info palette will also show the distance you move an object and direction in degrees. Figure 9-3 shows how distance and angle of movement is displayed.

A valuable tool that you may use with transformation and the Info palette is the Measure tool (U), shown here:

In the main Toolbox, the Measure tool looks like a small ruler. Select the Measure tool with the mouse cursor from the main Toolbox or by typing **U** on the keyboard. When you select the Measure tool, the mouse cursor appears as a crosshair. If the Info palette is not visible, the next click of the mouse cursor will activate the Info palette and set the first location from which to measure distance and angle.

Think of the Measure tool as a combination tape measure and protractor. It works in tandem with the Info palette. As you roll the Measure tool across the screen,

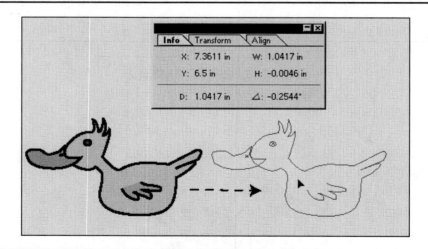

FIGURE 9-3   The Info palette reflecting a straight movement

Illustrator tracks the changes in distance and angle and displays the information in the Info palette. When you release the mouse cursor, Illustrator records the final location of the mouse cursor and displays the measurement.

You may also use the Measure tool (U) in combination with the Transform|Move command. You may move an object using measurements from the Measure tool. To do this, click and drag the Measure tool in the direction and distance you want to move an object. Select an object you want to move. Choose Object|Transform|Move. The Move dialog box appears and displays measurements taken by the Measure tool. To accept the measurements, click OK and Illustrator applies the measurements taken. This is helpful when you need to take measurements from one portion of the artboard and apply it to an object in another section. You may use this feature for precision object placement and duplication.

The Anatomy and Use of the Transform Palette

In addition to the options available in the Object menu and the tools in the main Toolbox, you can apply transformations using the Transform palette, which is accessed by choosing Window|Show Transform.

Figure 9-4 shows the anatomy of the Transform palette, which looks very similar to the Info palette. It shows information about a selected object such as its location on the artboard, width, and height. By entering new information on the palette you may change the position and shape of an object:

- The Transform tab tells you the Transform palette is active when it's white; click on it to select.

- The X axis text box represents an object's absolute horizontal position on the artboard. You change an object's position left or right by entering a positive or negative numeric value in this box and pressing either TAB or ENTER.

- The Object reference point options are similar to the point of origin. Illustrator calculates movement and changes in shape according to the reference point on the object you select. You change reference points to

X axis text box   Transform tab

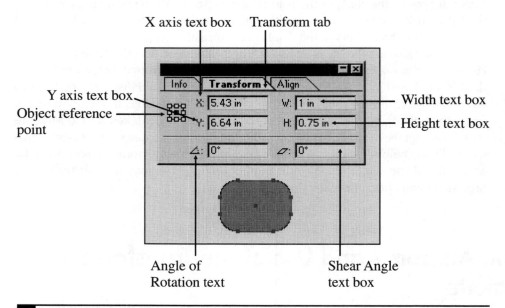

Y axis text box
Object reference
point

Width text box

Height text box

Angle of
Rotation text

Shear Angle
text box

FIGURE 9-4   The Transform palette options

control rotation, shaping, and movement of your selected object by clicking here.

- The *Y* axis text box represents an object's absolute vertical position on the artboard. You change an object's position up or down by entering a positive or negative number.

- Rotate an object by entering a positive or negative numeric value in the Angle of Rotation text box.

- In the Shear Angle text box, you modify the shape of an object by entering a positive or negative number to represent the shear angle.

- The Height text box displays the height of a selected object. Enter a positive number between 0 and 117.5 in. in this box to change the height of an object.

- The Width text box displays the width of a selected object. To change the width of an object, enter a positive number here between 0 and 117.5 in.

Changing the width without changing the height in the Transform palette will cause your object or group to be out of proportion. That is, the height to width ratio will change. This may be exactly what you want. To make proportional changes maintaining a strict height to width ratio, use the Scale tool, choose Uniform, and enter a percentage increase or decrease.

Transform Menu Options

To view the Transform flyout menu as shown in Figure 9-5, choose Object| Transform. The options available are Transform Again, Move, Scale, Rotate, Reflect, Shear, and Transform Each.

Using the Transform Again Command

The Transform Again or CTRL/COMMAND+D has no dialog box. This command duplicates the last Transform action of Illustrator. It applies the same movement, rotation, or modification to an object you have selected.

You would use this command to copy objects in a uniform row or column or in a uniform circle. You could also use this command on individual selected objects or on whole groups of selected objects.

9

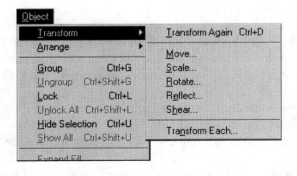

FIGURE 9-5   The Transform flyout menu options

Caution *When using Transform commands on groups of objects, Illustrator 7 no longer modifies individual objects according to their own point of origin but according to the selected group's point of origin. See the group of rotated squares shown here:*

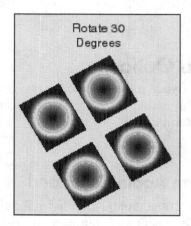

Using the Transform Each Command

Illustrator enables you to apply Transform commands to many objects at one time. Some applications may require the point of origin to remain the same for each object. You may use this command on individually selected objects, but it is primarily used on multiple selected objects.

The options for Transform Each are Scale, Move, and Rotate, as shown in Figure 9-6. You may slide the percentage indicator with the mouse or enter the numeric value in the text box for horizontal and vertical scaling or movement. You may enter angle of rotation in degrees in the Rotate dialog box or move the angle indicator to the desired rotation. To apply the transformations to a copy, click the Copy button. To apply random values to Scale, Move, or Rotate, click on the Random box to select it. To see a preview of transformed objects, click on the Preview box to select it. When you have finished entering information, click OK to apply the transformations.

Because you will use the Transform Each command primarily to modify groups of objects, it is important to notice a difference in application about this Transform feature and other Transform features. The Transform Each command applies transformation to objects using each object's default point of origin. Other Transform commands apply changes in position, rotation, and modification as if selected groups were a single object. The Transform Each command applies changes

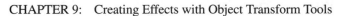

FIGURE 9-6   The Transform Each dialog box

in position, rotation, and modification in relationship to each individual object's position and point of origin as shown here:

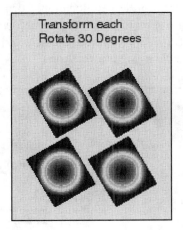

Moving, Scaling, and Rotating Objects

The Move, Scale, and Rotate options in the Transform flyout menu have similar dialog boxes. This will aid you in quickly learning what information to enter and how to apply changes immediately.

The Move command changes the location of an object to anywhere on your artboard, the Scale command resizes objects, and the Rotate command spins an object on its center axis or moves an object in an orbit.

Illustrator can apply all of these Transform commands to a copy of a selected object. This gives the artist a powerful drawing advantage, as you will see in the tutorial section of this chapter.

Using the Move Command

You may use the Move command to relocate objects with great precision or to place a copy of a selected object anywhere on your artboard. To view the Move dialog box as shown in Figure 9-7, choose Object|Transform|Move. You may change the object's position by entering numeric values in the Horizontal or Vertical text boxes or by setting the Distance from present location and Angle up or down. You also have the option of either moving the object or its pattern. See the "Using Pattern Fills" section in **Chapter 10: Setting Fills and Strokes**.

As you enter information, you may preview changes before you accept them by clicking Preview. Once you have the desired move information entered, apply it to the original object by clicking OK or apply it to a new copy by clicking Copy.

You may also move objects quickly by selecting them with the Selection tool found in the main Toolbox or by typing **V** on the keyboard. Click on the object's fill color or on its path and drag to the new location. For more accurate judgment of how far and in which direction to move the object, activate the Info palette by choosing Window|Show Info. As you move your selected object across the artboard, Illustrator will display the changing information.

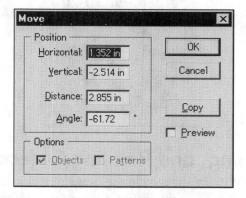

FIGURE 9-7   The Move dialog box

Using the Scale Command

To view the Scale dialog box, choose Object|Transform|Scale. The Scale command in Illustrator changes the size of a selected object or group in two ways. If you choose uniform scale, the dialog box shows one option for percentage of scale for both height and width. You will also see the option to select scale line weight. The weight of the line increases or decreases according to the percentage you use to scale your object when you select scale line weight.

If you select the Non-Uniform Scale option, a different dialog box appears, as shown in Figure 9-8. You may enter a percentage for horizontal scale and a percentage for vertical scale. The Scale Line Weight feature is not an option when changing the size of an object in the Non-Uniform Scale dialog box.

As with the Move dialog box, you may scale objects or patterns. You may apply Scale settings to a copy or to the original object, and you may preview your Scale settings before you apply them. You may also scale selected objects by using the Scale tool found on the main Toolbox or by typing **S** on the keyboard. The Scale tool is shown here:

You may change the size of an object by clicking and dragging any part of the selected object or group. If you click once on any position, you have set the point of origin. This tells Illustrator that you want to reference the next click and drag information to this point of origin location.

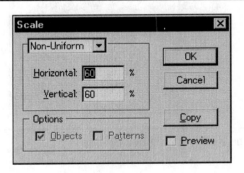

FIGURE 9-8   The Scale dialog box with Non-Uniform scale selected

To bring up the Scale dialog box through the Scale tool, press and hold the ALT/OPTION key and click on the point of origin indicated with a crosshair. The Scale dialog box will appear. Now you may enter numeric information to scale objects through the Scale dialog box.

 When you press the ALT/OPTION key, an ellipsis (...) will appear attached to your mouse cursor indicating that a dialog box will appear on your next click.

 It is difficult to achieve an exact proportional height and width scale by hand on an object when using the Scale tool unless you use the constrain feature by holding down the SHIFT key. To achieve exact proportional scaling, be sure to use the Scale dialog box.

Using the Rotate Command

Illustrator uses the point of origin as the rotation center for the Rotate command. The Rotate dialog box, as shown in Figure 9-9, has one numeric value for degree of rotation, which is entered in the Angle text box.

As in the Move and Scale dialog boxes, you may rotate objects or their patterns. You may also rotate a copy rather than the original. Illustrator arranges a rotated copy in front of the original. See the "Arranging Objects" section in **Chapter 8: Selecting and Arranging Objects**. Illustrator lets you preview the rotation before you apply it by choosing the Preview option. After entering and selecting all the options, you may click OK to apply the rotation.

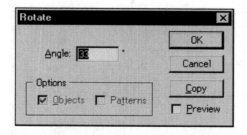

FIGURE 9-9   The Rotate dialog box

You may use Transform options in alternating sequence to produce special effects. For instance, you may use Move with Copy and Scale in an alternating fashion to demonstrate an object shrinking or growing. You may use Rotate with Copy and Scale in alternating fashion to create spiral objects, as shown here:

In the illustration above, the point of origin was set at the small end of the object. With the ALT/OPTION key pressed, the object was rotated with the Rotate tool. Then the object was reduced by 98 percent. This procedure was repeated manually to rotate with Copy and Scale over and over again. This may be a tedious process, but the results are worth the effort.

Using Reflect and Shear

Reflect and Shear are also Transform commands and have dialog boxes similar to the dialog boxes of Move, Scale, and Rotate. The Reflect command mirrors an object or a copy of an object, and the Shear command distorts objects.

Using the Reflect Command

To view the Reflect dialog box as shown in Figure 9-10, choose Object| Transform|Reflect. It offers options for reflecting an object on the horizontal axis, on the vertical axis, or on an angle you specify. In addition to reflecting objects or their patterns, you may also reflect a copy of an object, which would produce a mirrored effect. As with other Transform dialog boxes, you may preview the Reflect command before you apply it to your artwork.

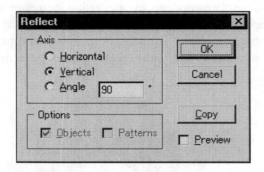

FIGURE 9-10   The Reflect dialog box

In the illustration shown here, a copy of text was reflected to make it appear to be sitting on top of a mirrored surface.

In this illustration, the text was converted into an outline and filled with a gradient fill. A copy was reflected on the horizontal axis and then rasterized before being given a texture.

You may reflect objects with the Reflect tool, shown here,

by locating it on the main Toolbox or by typing **O** on the keyboard. After selecting the image, click on the Reflect tool. The point of origin appears at an object's center by default. If you click and drag, the reflected object will rotate around the point of origin. Release the mouse cursor when you have the reflected object in place. If you want a copy of the reflected object, press the ALT/OPTION key while you are moving the reflected image.

To bring up the Reflect dialog box, choose the Reflect tool from the main Toolbox. Press the ALT/OPTION key and then click on where you want to place the point of origin. The Reflect dialog box will appear, allowing you to create a reflected image.

Using the Shear Command

The Shear command gives an object a slanted effect, distorting an object to create special effects such as shadows. To do this, use the Shear command with Copy and then arrange the copy behind the original with CTRL/COMMAND+SHIFT+[. Last, apply a dark fill to finish the shadow.

Other uses include distorting an object to simulate looking at it from an angle. To view the Shear dialog box as shown in Figure 9-11, choose Object| Transform|Shear. The Shear angle represents the angle of the shear in degrees. The Axis option lets you select Horizontal or Vertical for the orientation of modifying the object or enter a numeric value in the Angle text box. You also have the option of shearing selected objects or their patterns. As with other Transform dialog boxes, you have the option of shearing the original object or a copy and previewing the shear results by choosing the Preview option.

You may also shear an object by using the Shear tool, shown here:

Select the Shear tool with the Select tool or type **W**. The point of origin crosshair will appear in the center of the object or selected group. When you click and drag the Shear tool, the object will change shape. When you release the mouse button,

9

Illustrator applies the shear to the object. To create a copy while shearing, press the ALT/OPTION key after you start dragging the Shear tool. To open the Shear dialog box, press the ALT/OPTION key before you click and set the point of origin.

To activate the Shear dialog box through the Shear tool, select the Shear tool on the main Toolbox, press the ALT/OPTION key, and click in the artboard where you want to place the point of origin. When you release the mouse button, the Shear dialog box will appear. Then you may enter your information for your shear modification.

Using the Twirl Tool

Late in the evolution of Illustrator 7, the software developers added the Twirl tool, shown here,

and placed it in the Rotate tool flyout menu on the main Toolbox. Even though you will not find Twirl under the Transform menu options, there is really no other way to describe it. It affects objects as if Illustrator is applying shear and rotate at the same time. To apply the Twirl option, first select an object and then choose the Twirl

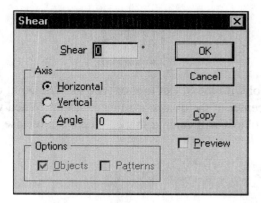

FIGURE 9-11   The Shear dialog box

tool. Click and drag anywhere on the artboard and watch as Illustrator spins the object. The best way to master this tool is to experiment, paying close attention to how the point of origin and dragging the Twirl tool work together to transform an object.

To access the Twirl tool dialog box using the Twirl tool from the Rotate flyout menu on the main Toolbox, press the ALT/OPTION key and click on the artboard where you want to locate the point of origin. The Twirl dialog box will appear, enabling you to enter the angle of rotation.

> **Note**   *Unlike other Transform tools, pressing ALT/OPTION after you start to drag the mouse cursor will not apply the effect to a copy of the object.*

Working with Pathfinder

Illustrator 7 applies Transform commands directly to selected objects using a point of origin. In contrast, the Pathfinder commands utilize existing objects to modify other existing objects. It is like having special cutting tools to snip and shape at objects to create the desired effect. The tutorial section found later in this chapter explores several ways to use the Pathfinder options to shape and trim for visual effects.

To use the Pathfinder commands, you must first select two or more objects that overlap by choosing the Selection tool found in the main Toolbox or through the keyboard by typing **V** and then holding down the SHIFT key while clicking on each object. Then choose Object|Pathfinder to open the list of 14 commands and an option for Pathfinder settings, as shown in Figure 9-12.

Using the Unite Command

Applying the Unite command to two or more overlapping objects results in one object with one outline. Illustrator uses the fill color and paint style of the front object of the selected group and applies it to the new object.

The Unite command is useful for creating objects to serve as shadows in a composition. In order to create a united object for creating a shadow, you must create copies of the multiple objects you will unite.

Using the Intersect Command

The Intersect command creates a new object out of the overlapping section of two objects. Illustrator deletes everything outside the intersection and applies the fill color and paint style from the front-most object. Use the Intersect command to create

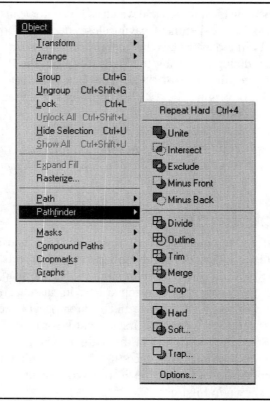

FIGURE 9-12   The Pathfinder menu options flyout

shapes that may be difficult to produce using the Pen or Pencil tools. To view possible shapes that you may create, choose View|Artwork. Outlines are clearly visible in Artwork view.

Using the Exclude Command

The Exclude command creates very interesting contrast studies. You may use Exclude with many objects at one time. Illustrator will use the fill color and paint style of the object on top of the stack to fill the resulting object that the Exclude command creates. Exclude will "knock out" or leave holes where there is an even number of overlapping objects. Exclude will fill spaces where there is an odd number of overlapping objects.

Using the Minus Front and Minus Back Commands

The Minus Front and Minus Back commands are very similar. The Minus Back command uses all the front-most objects to "trim" the object behind. Illustrator leaves only the back-most object's portion that had no overlap. The Minus Front command uses all the objects in back to trim the front-most object's overlap portion and leaves behind only that portion of the front object that had no overlap.

You might use the Minus Front command to create a skyline. You might use the Minus Back command to create a lake's edge. Perhaps you will use the Minus Front command to create a window to view a background through another object.

Using the Divide Command

With the Divide command, Illustrator uses the outlines of all the shapes you select to apply a dividing line to all the visible parts of the objects, just as a cookie cutter cuts smaller shapes out of bigger shapes. Illustrator deletes every object part covered by another object. After applying the Divide command, your objects will not look different until you ungroup the objects. Each piece of an object maintains the color of the original object.

Using the Outline Command

The Outline command creates outlines according to the shapes of the objects you select. The outlines become individual line segments, and Illustrator applies the fill color to the outline. Overlapping objects color the outlines below. Illustrator divides each line segment at the intersection of outlines from other objects. You may ungroup and manipulate these line segments individually.

The Outline command is useful for creating traps for printing. A *trap* is an overprint of an object's color to ensure coverage of ink in the event of a misregistration.

Using the Trim Command

The Pathfinder Trim command uses the top object in the stack to trim the overlap of the bottom object in the stack. The topmost object remains intact while Illustrator trims the objects underneath.

This tool can be used to shape your artwork with preset shapes that you create. Over time, you may accumulate shapes to use as "trimmers." You may make this set of trimmer tools as diverse as your artwork demands.

Using the Merge Command

The Merge command combines objects of the same fill color and trims objects of different color or objects filled with a gradient. If objects are all different colors, then the Merge command will act like the Trim command. If there are two or more adjacent objects with the same fill color, Merge creates one new object out of the same filled objects and deletes any hidden portion of the objects. If all the objects you select are the same fill color, then the Merge command behaves similar to the Unite command, creating one object out of all the overlapping objects. You may create special effects by using the Merge command in conjunction with Select Same Fill Color.

Using the Crop Command

When you apply the Crop command, Illustrator 7 deletes everything outside the top object's shape and leaves nothing except the trimmed bottom objects. The object at the top of the stack actually becomes a frame for the bottom objects. You may see bottom objects in the stack within the framework of the top object. You can use the Crop command to eliminate portions of your artwork that you no longer need.

Using the Hard and Soft Commands

The Hard and Soft commands combine solid filled objects to create a semitransparent look. The Hard command produces a straight mix of colors to create a gel overlay effect. When you apply the Hard command, Illustrator mixes the color without further input from the artist. Illustrator uses the highest value on the CMYK scale for mixing the colors between objects. For instance, if the top object was filled with a solid color of 34 percent cyan, 41 percent magenta, 15 percent yellow, and 10 percent black, and the bottom object was filled with a solid color of 10 percent cyan, 54 percent magenta, 30 percent yellow, and 15 percent black, the resulting color would be 34 percent cyan, 54 percent magenta, 30 percent yellow, and 15 percent black.

The Soft command, on the other hand, has a dialog box as shown in Figure 9-13. Illustrator allows you to set the level of transparency or color mix of the bottom fill colors with the top object's fill. The lower the percentage, the less transparent the mix will be.

You may only use Hard and Soft commands on objects with solid fills. Illustrator trims gradient and pattern fills rather than applying the Hard or Soft command. Where objects overlap, the Hard and Soft commands divide the objects.

Using the Trap Command

The Trap command creates a filled area that overlaps adjacent objects. You create this overlap to prevent a blank area in print known as a *misregistration*. The Trap dialog box, as shown in Figure 9-14, lets you set the Trap thickness, height, width, tint reduction, and other options. For more information see the section called "Traps" in **Chapter 17: Printing from Illustrator 7**.

Using the Repeat Pathfinder Command

When you use a Pathfinder command, Illustrator records the settings and command information in memory. When you select objects and choose Object| Pathfinder|Repeat, Illustrator will apply the last command you used to the new group of selected objects. The keyboard shortcut for this command is CTRL/COMMAND+4.

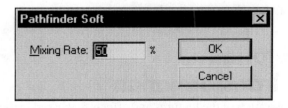

FIGURE 9-13   The Pathfinder Soft dialog box

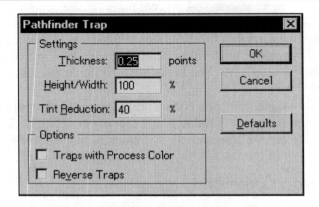

FIGURE 9-14   The Pathfinder Trap dialog box

Setting Pathfinder Options

The last item in the list of the Pathfinder flyout menu is the Pathfinder Options Settings, which opens the dialog box shown in Figure 9-15. This is where you set the precision for Illustrator's calculating accuracy, the default setting of which is 0.028 points. You may also choose the Remove Redundant Points option and the Divide & Outline command to extract unpainted artwork.

The Redundant Points option removes anchor points in overlapping objects that have no visible effect on the shape of the path they control. The Divide & Outline command will occasionally create unpainted artwork. You may have both these commands extract unpainted artwork automatically if you choose this option. You may also click on the Defaults option to set the Pathfinder options back to the defaults that the Software manufacturers set. To accept the changes of the dialog box, click OK. If you do not want the changes, click Cancel.

Chapter 9 Tutorial:
Effects with Transformation

As a practical exploration of the features and effects discussed in this chapter, follow through in this step-by-step tutorial. As you do so, you may notice that some of these

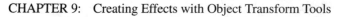

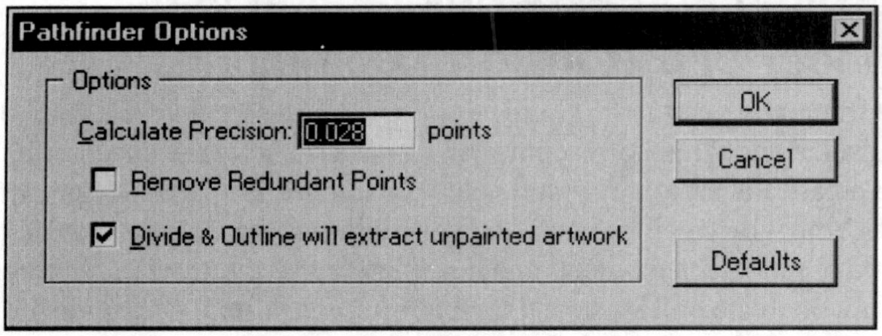

FIGURE 9-15   The Pathfinder Options dialog box

steps are accompanied by a "Color palette" symbol. This symbol indicates that the step has also been illustrated in full color in the Fundamental Illustrator 7 color insert. The purpose of the color insert is to provide you with a brief overview of the tutorial and act as an overall reference for the practical use of color throughout these tutorials. Watch for this symbol:

9

The first part of this tutorial has been designed to help you learn Pathfinder and Transform commands through experimentation. You will become familiar with every command if you follow along through each exercise. You will also create a chart for your visual reference on how each command works.

The point of the second section of this tutorial is to get you involved in the practical application of many of the commands of this chapter. You will use Transform and Pathfinder commands to create a barn scene, which has been the domain of pencil, pen, and water color artists. Now you will learn how to create the same kind of effects in the digital world using Transform and Pathfinder.

The third part of the tutorial will lead you through producing a clock with mechanical precision by using the dialog boxes in Transform to enter precise information to create the effects you want. Do not feel you have to stick with the color schemes presented in this tutorial. Experiment and apply those colors that suit your artistic eye.

 Fundamental Illustrator 7

Exploration and Experimentation with Pathfinder and Transform Commands

The first thing you need to do is create a few art objects on your artboard to apply the Pathfinder and Transform commands. We used several different shapes and colors to create a chart to guide and help yourself see at a glance which commands do what. You will create objects on your artboard to help you understand the interaction of the selected objects and how they change with the various commands. First, you will create an ellipse and then a rectangle, a star and then an octagon.

 You will need to set the preferences to inches in the Units and Undo Dialog Box to follow along with these tutorials. Choose File\Preferences\Units and Undo. Click on the General Options down arrow and select inches. Click OK.

1. Choose the Ellipse tool (**N**).

2. Click once near the top of the artboard. An Ellipse dialog box will appear. Enter **0.38** for both height and width of the ellipse. Click OK.

3. Move the ellipse you just created by using the Transform palette. Choose Window\Show Transform. Click on the center square of the Reference Point option. Enter **1.43** in the *x* axis text box. Enter **8.62** in the *y* axis text box.

4. Fill the circle with a solid color fill using the Color palette (F6). If the CMYK Color model is not showing, click on the Color Model flyout menu and choose the CMYK model. Double-click in the cyan text box and type **57**. In the yellow text box enter **100**. Press ENTER to apply the color to the circle. Magenta and black values should be **0** percent.

Now you will create and place a rectangle behind the circle you just created. Remember, you must have overlapping objects to apply the Pathfinder commands.

5. Choose the Rectangle tool (**M**) and click in the artboard anywhere near the circle. In the Rectangle dialog box, enter **0.63** for Width and **0.38** for Height. Press ENTER or click OK to accept the values.

6. Move the new rectangle using the Transform palette. Double-click the *x* axis text box and enter **1.41**. Press TAB and enter **8.93** in the *y* axis text box.

7. Now, send the rectangle to the back (CTRL/COMMAND+SHIFT+[).

8. Add color to the rectangle by entering **2** for cyan box, **30** for magenta, **98** for yellow, and **0** for black text Color palette.

   Now, add two polygons to the group. The first will be a five-pointed star and the second will be an octagon.

9. Choose the Star tool (**N**) from the Ellipse tool (**N**). Click once near the other two objects on the artboard. In the Star tool dialog box, double-click on the Radius 1 text box and enter **0.15**. Double-click in the Radius 2 text box and enter **0.30**. Set the number of points to 5. Click on OK to create the star.

10. To become familiar with the Transform Rotate option, rotate the star by double-clicking in the Transform palette's Angle text box and typing **33.69**. Move the star into position by entering **1.64** for the *x* axis and **8.97** for the *y* axis. Press ENTER to accept the changes.

11. Next, position the star behind the circle by pressing CTRL/COMMAND+[. The star is now tucked in between the rectangle and the circle.

12. Add color to the star by double-clicking in the cyan=**96**, magenta=**45**, **yellow=0**, and black=**0** in the Color palette text boxes. Press the ENTER key to accept the color.

   Now, create the octagon and apply a red fill.

13. Choose the Polygon tool from the Ellipse tool (**N**). Click once near the other objects on the artboard and the Polygon dialog box appears. Enter **0.28** and set the sides to **8** and click OK.

14. Move the octagon by **1.28** for the *x* axis and **9.01** for the *y* axis in the Transform palette text boxes. Click OK.

15. Position the octagon behind the circle (CTRL/COMMAND+[). This places the octagon between the circle and the star.

16. Now add color to the octagon. Enter cyan=**0**, magenta=**100**, yellow=**100** and black =**0**, and press ENTER to apply the color.

You have just created the standard "set" of objects you will experiment on while teaching yourself the Transform and Pathfinder commands. We have created this set to copy from and look back at to see how objects looked before changes were applied. Do not apply Transform commands directly to this set, but rather create copies to which you'll apply the Transform and Pathfinder commands. Your group will be arranged to look similar to Figure 9-16.

While you were creating these objects, you used the Transform commands Move and Rotate and you set the point of origin for objects by clicking on the artboard. Using these commands will become second nature the more you use them to modify and transform your objects.

Pathfinder | Unite

Now let's create the first copy of the set of objects to which we'll apply the Pathfinder|Unite command.

1. Select all the objects you have created using the Selection tool (V). Marquee-select all the objects.

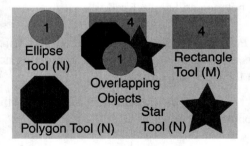

FIGURE 9-16   The Standard Object Set used for applying Transform and Pathfinder commands

2. Create a copy by choosing Object|Transform|Move. Enter **1.85** in the Horizontal text box and click on the Copy button. Now you have your second group to which to apply the first Pathfinder command.

3. Choose Object|Pathfinder|Unite.

The Unite command combines all the objects and creates a new object using the outline of all the objects and the fill of the top object in the group's stack. Figure 9-17 shows the new object. Your object will look the same but will have a green fill.

If you chose only two of the four objects, the result would be similar. You would have a new outline of the overlapping objects with the top object's color. To experiment, press CTRL/COMMAND+Z to Undo the last command. This reverses Unite so that you may modify the objects again. Select different combinations of objects to which to apply the Unite command. When you finish experimenting, select the Type tool from the main Toolbox or by typing **T** and type **Unite** above the new group of united objects.

Pathfinder | Intersect

Now you will apply the Pathfinder|Intersect command to another copy of the standard set.

1. Select the standard set of objects. Move a copy by choosing Object|Transform|Move. In the Move dialog box, enter **3.70** and click on the Copy button. A copy of the standard set appears.

2. Choose Object|Pathfinder|Intersect.

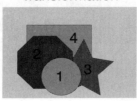

FIGURE 9-17   Pathfinder|Unite before and after

The new object is what the Intersect command leaves behind. It is not much. It is the shape created where all the objects you selected intersect. See the application of Intersect in Figure 9-18. It looks different because we added the outlines to show where the objects use to be. Notice where they intersect. This is the shape left behind on your artboard. To undo the last command, press CTRL/COMMAND+Z. Now you may select any of these two objects to experiment with Pathfinder|Intersect. Once you have completed your Intersect experiments, choose the Type tool from the main Toolbox or type **T** and type **Intersect** above this application.

Pathfinder | Exclude

The next Pathfinder command to explore is Pathfinder|Exclude. Elementary art classes have spent hours drawing outlines by hand and filling in odd overlaps. The digital artist may accomplish this in seconds.

1. Select the standard set of objects. Move a copy by choosing Object|Transform|Move. In the Move dialog box, enter **5.55** in the horizontal text box and click on the Copy button. A copy of the standard set appears.

2. Apply the Exclude command by choosing Object|Pathfinder|Exclude.

The results will look similar to the arrangement in Figure 9-19. When you apply the Exclude command to overlapping objects, Illustrator 7 uses the outlines to divide

Before
Transformation

After
Pathfinder > Intersect

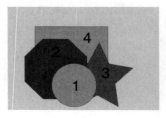
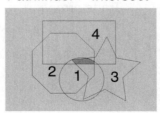

FIGURE 9-18   Pathfinder|Intersect Before and After

Figure 5-1

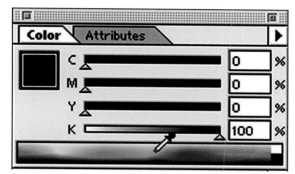

Figure 5-2

Catch The Wave

Figure 5-1: A color fill is applied to the headline by clicking the Fill button to activate it, then clicking the Color button to display the Color palette, and finally choosing a color from the Color Spectrum bar (Figure 5-2) in the Color palette

Figure 5-2: Fill the headline with a bright blue color by placing the cursor within the Color Spectrum bar in the Color palette (it will change to an eyedropper) and clicking in the blue area as shown here. Your selection will be indicated in the Fill button in the Tool palette as shown in Figure 5-1

Figure 5-3a: The headline before kerning

Figure 5-3b: The headline after kerning

Figure 5-3c: The headline after painting

Figure 5-3a

Figure 5-3b

Figure 5-3c

Figure 5-4: The text of the letter after formatting and coloring the type

Figure 5-5: The completed coupon

Figure 5-6: The completed flyer

Dear Wet Head,

We know you've been waiting all year for summer to return so you could hit the beaches at the Water Works. Well, the wait is almost over because we reopen June 1.

This year promises to be our biggest, best and most exciting ever because **THE BIG KAHUNA** has just arrived. That's right, the world's first surfing simulator is here and it offers the best waves this side of Hawaii.

So come on in and join the the fun! Bring in the coupon below and hang ten on the house.

Hey, come to think of it, why not bring the whole family and hang 40!

The Water Works staff

P.S. Don't forget to sign up for the first ever Kansas State Surfing Championships coming in August.

Figure 5-4

Figure 5-5

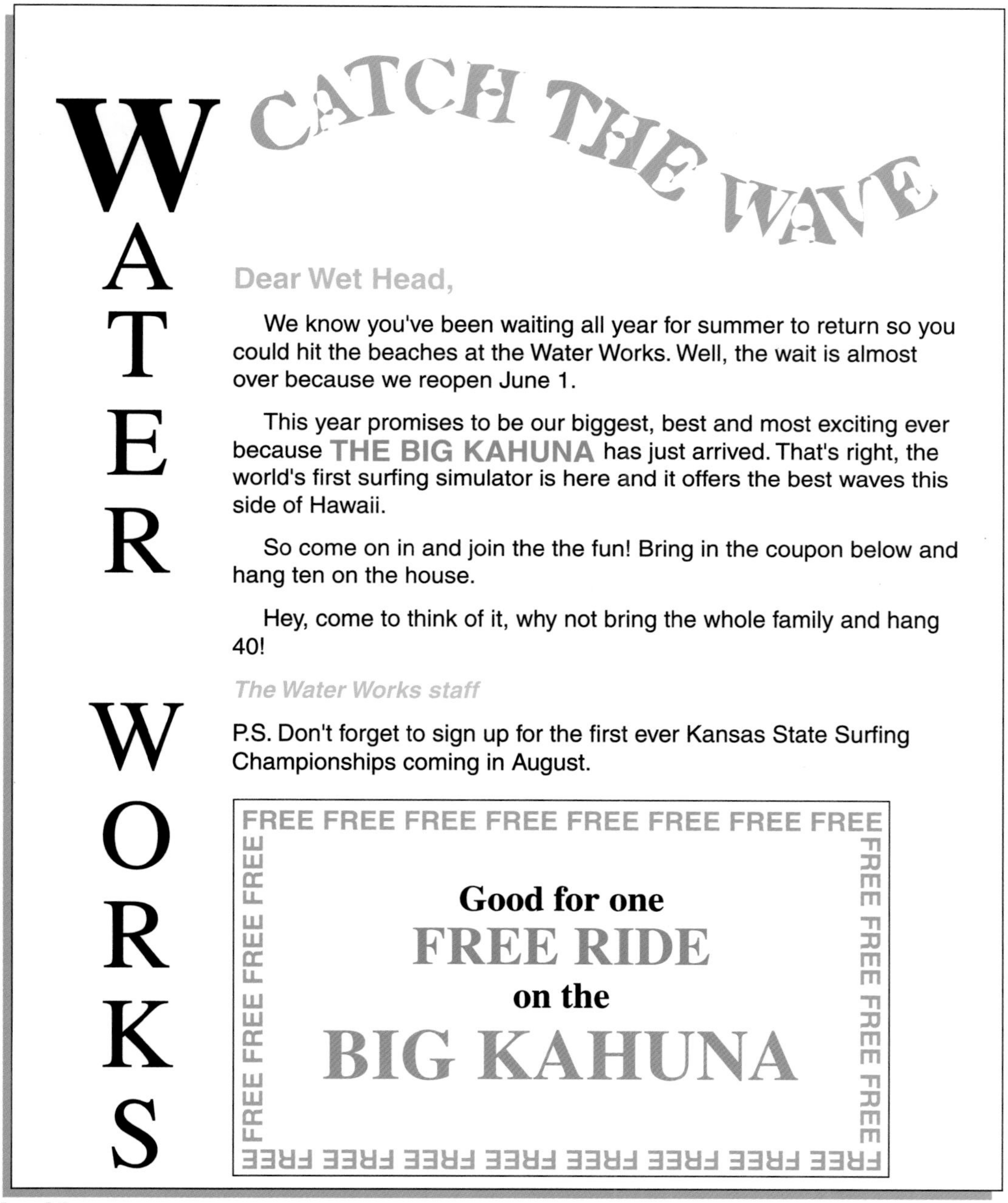

WATER WORKS

CATCH THE WAVE

Dear Wet Head,

We know you've been waiting all year for summer to return so you could hit the beaches at the Water Works. Well, the wait is almost over because we reopen June 1.

This year promises to be our biggest, best and most exciting ever because **THE BIG KAHUNA** has just arrived. That's right, the world's first surfing simulator is here and it offers the best waves this side of Hawaii.

So come on in and join the the fun! Bring in the coupon below and hang ten on the house.

Hey, come to think of it, why not bring the whole family and hang 40!

The Water Works staff

P.S. Don't forget to sign up for the first ever Kansas State Surfing Championships coming in August.

FREE FREE FREE FREE FREE FREE FREE FREE

Good for one

FREE RIDE

on the

BIG KAHUNA

FREE FREE FREE FREE FREE FREE FREE FREE

Figure 5-6

Around The Corner

Figure 6-1: The completed logo

Figure 6-2: The columns of type after they have been wrapped around left side of the logo

Figure 6-3: The menu after the text has been formatted and wrapped around the logo and color has been applied to the headline and its container

Figure 6-4: The finished menu. Illustrator's spell checker caught (and corrected) several typos so the diners can focus on the entrees and not the errors

Figure 6-1

ALWAYS AROUND THE CORNER

Now is the tyme for all good men to come to the aid of their team. With our beluved Red Birds locked in a tight pennant race, there's no better time than now to show your true colors. So, MD's Grill has declared every Monday night from now until the end of the season, Cardinals Colors Night.

Taht's right, everyone who wears red to Mad Dogs on

Manday will receive a free

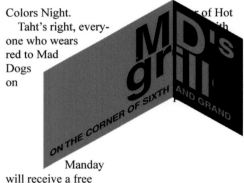

Figure 6-2

ALWAYS AROUND THE CORNER

Now is the tyme for all good men to come to the aid of their team. With our beluved Red Birds locked in a tight pennant race, there's no better time than now to show your true colors. So, MD's Grill has declared every Monday night from now until the end of the season, Cardinals Colors Night.

Taht's right, everyone who wears red to Mad Dogs on Manday will receive a free order of Hot Wings with Square

each Value Meal purchased at the regu/al price.

WARNING: MD's hot wings may contain spices unfit for small children. Parental discretion is advised.

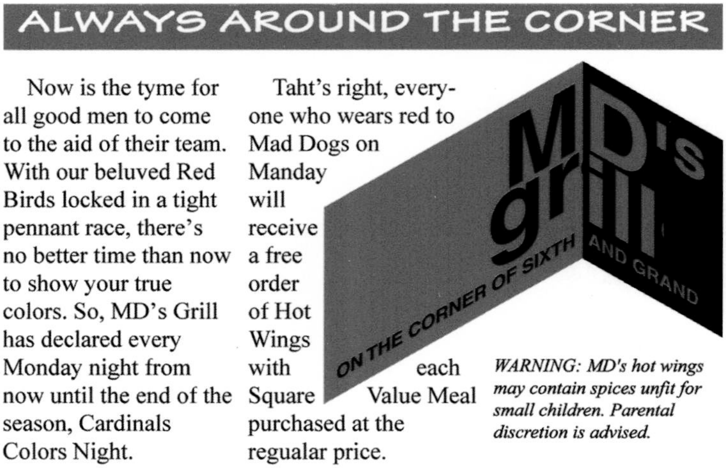

Figure 6-3

ALWAYS AROUND THE CORNER

Now is the time for all good men to come to the aid of their team. With our beloved Red Birds locked in a tight pennant race, there's no better time than now to show your true colors. So, MD's Grill has declared every Monday night from now until the end of the season, Cardinals Colors Night.

That's right, everyone who wears red to Mad Dogs on Monday will receive a free order of Hot Wings with each Square Value Meal purchased at the regular price.

MD's grill

ON THE CORNER OF SIXTH AND GRAND

WARNING: MD's hot wings may contain spices un t for small children. Parental discretion is advised.

HOME FOR AN APPETIZER. WE'RE JUST AROUND THE CORNER!

STOP BY MD'S GRILL ON YOUR WAY

Appetizers	Description	
Wimpy Wings	Wings in a mild sauce	$3.95
Buffalo Wings	Traditional hot wings	3.95
MD Wings	Flamin'	3.95
Broccoli on a stick	A specialty of the chef!	3.50

Square Value Meals

Sandwich, fries and your choice of a drink

Chicken Sandwich	Your choice, white or dark	4.95
Steak Sandwich	Rare, medium or well done	5.95
Barbecue Sandwich	An MD specialty	4.95

Figure 6-4

Charting the Black Hole

Figure 7-1: Building the disk illustration by working with simple shapes

Figure 7-2: Illustrator offers several default gradients which can be chosen from the Swatches palette (Windows/Show Swatches). To learn more about gradients, see Chapter 7

Figure 7-3: Blending between two objects to create the shadow

Figure 7-4: The finished disk illustration

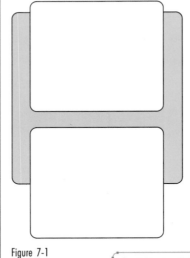

Figure 7-1

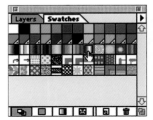

Figure 7-2

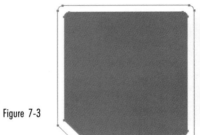

Figure 7-3

Figure 7-4

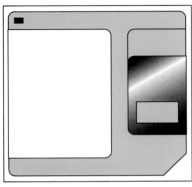

Figure 7-5

Figure 7-5: The bounding box defines the boundaries of the Graphs Design

Figure 7-6: The graph after the disk Graphs Design has been applied

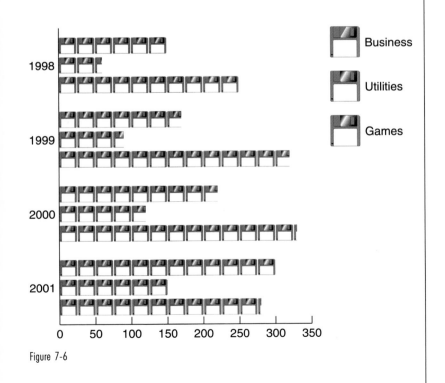

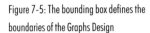

Figure 7-6

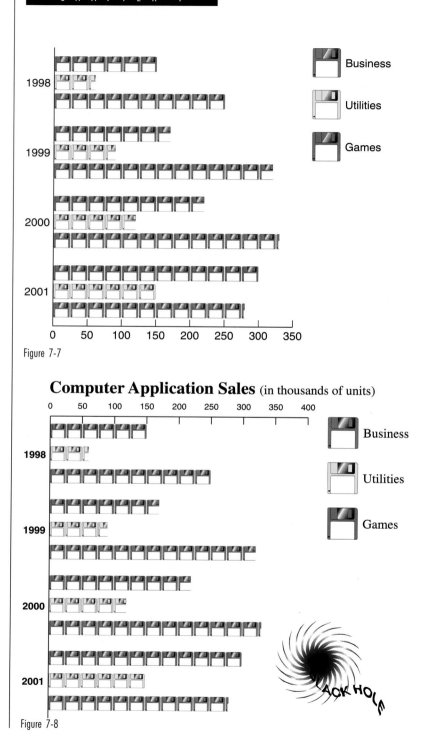

Figure 7-7: The graph with different color
Graphs Designs applied to each category

Figure 7-8: The finished graph

Figure 7-7

Computer Application Sales (in thousands of units)

Figure 7-8

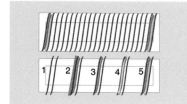

Figure 8-1

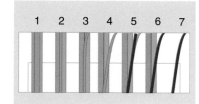

Figure 8-2

Nuts and Bolts

Figure 8-1: Create the first thread

Figure 8-2: Copy the thread

Figure 8-3: Align and distribute threads

Figure 8-4: Trace bolt outline around threads

Figure 8-5: Create bolt head outlines and fills

Figure 8-6: Assembled objects

Figure 8-7: Finished bolt complete with shadow

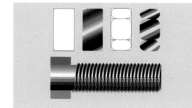

Figure 8-3

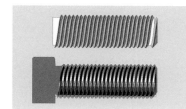

Figure 8-4

Figure 8-5

Figure 8-6

Figure 8-7

Good to the Last Drop

Figure 8-8: Create the lip of the mug

Figure 8-9: Create the body of the mug

Figure 8-10: Create the inside of the mug

Figure 8-11: Create the mug handle

Figure 8-12: Create the shadow of the mug

Figure 8-13: Assemble the objects to create a mug

Figure 8-14: The finished mug complete with shadow

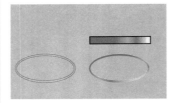

Figure 8-8

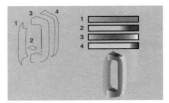

Figure 8-11

Figure 8-9

Figure 8-12

Figure 8-10

Figure 8-13

Figure 8-14

Figure 8-15

Figure 8-16

Figure 8-17

Figure 8-18

Figure 8-19

Figure 8-20

Figure 8-21

Figure 8-22

Figure 8-23

Horse Sense

Figure 8-15: Select a bitmap

Figure 8-16: Trace an outline

Figure 8-17: Trace a detailed outline of features

Figure 8-18: Planning fills carefully

Figure 8-19: Filled outline of the head

Figure 8-20: Filled mane adds depth

Figure 8-21: Fill neck and ears

Figure 8-22: Filled features

Figure 8-23: Completed horse

Illustrator 7 Tutorial Images

Right to the Point

Figure 8-24: Create the pencil lead

Figure 8-25: Blending objects to create the cone-shaped wood

Figure 8-26: Create the metal band using gradients and lines

Figure 8-27: Create the eraser using the blend tool

Figure 8-28: Create the body of the pencil using the blend tool

Figure 8-29: Use the text tool to create wording and number

Figure 8-30: Use gray scale blends to create a shadow

Figure 8-31: Assemble the elements of the pencil

Figure 8-32: Full view of the completed pencil

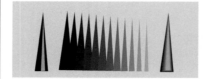

Figure 8-24

Figure 8-25

Figure 8-26

Figure 8-27

Figure 8-28

Figure 8-29

Figure 8-30

Figure 8-31

Figure 8-32

Figure 9-1: Standard Objects

Figure 9-2: Unite

Figure 9-3: Intersect

Figure 9-4: Exclude

Figure 9-5: Minus Front

Figure 9-6: Minus Back

Figure 9-7: Divide

Figure 9-8: Outline

Figure 9-9: Trim

Figure 9-10: Merge

Figure 9-11: Merge Same Color

Figure 9-12: Crop

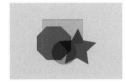

Figure 9-13: Hard

Figure 9-14: Soft at 20%

Figure 9-15: Soft at 50%

Figure 9-16: Soft at 75%

Figure 9-17: Soft at 100%

Figure 9-18: Trap

Figure 9-19: Move

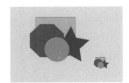

Figure 9-20: Scale 25%

Figure 9-21: Rotate 90°

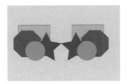

Figure 9-22: Reflect-Vertical

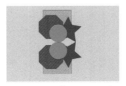

Figure 9-23: Reflect-Horizontal

Figure 9-24: Shear

Barn Raising

Figure 9-25: Create a tree line using Unite

Figure 9-26: Trim the background with the tree line

Figure 9-27: Create the elements of the barn

Figure 9-28: Create details for the barn using the pen & pencil tools

Figure 9-29: Use Duplicate, Reflect and Scale to finish the tree line

Figure 9-30: Understanding how the details overlay the barn

Figure 9-31: The Barn Scene with grass and fence added

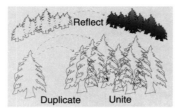

Figure 9-25

Figure 9-26

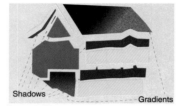

Figure 9-27

Figure 9-28

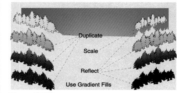

Figure 9-29

Figure 9-30

Figure 9-31

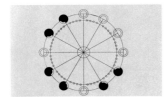

Figure 9-32

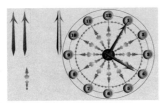

Figure 9-33

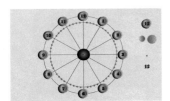

Figure 9-34

Figure 9-35

Figure 9-36

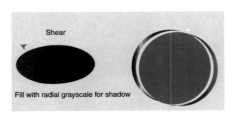

Shear

Fill with radial grayscale for shadow

Figure 9-37

Decorative Clock

Figure 9-32: Create the circles for the clock face

Figure 9-33: Complete the clock dial using Rotate & Copy

Figure 9-34: Add fill and numbers to the hour and minute indicators

Figure 9-35: Create clock hands and decorations

Figure 9-36: Add fill and decorations to the clock face

Figure 9-37: Create a shadow and gold rim

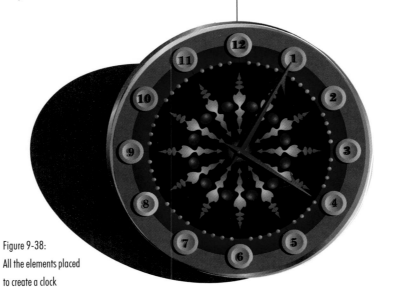

Figure 9-38:
All the elements placed
to create a clock

Illustrator 7 Tutorial Images

Type B Behavior

Figure 10-1: The high-contrast red fill was applied to the letter B and, to make the stroke more interesting, a 12 point dashed line was added. Diagonal stripes were applied to another B using Illustrator's Color palette features

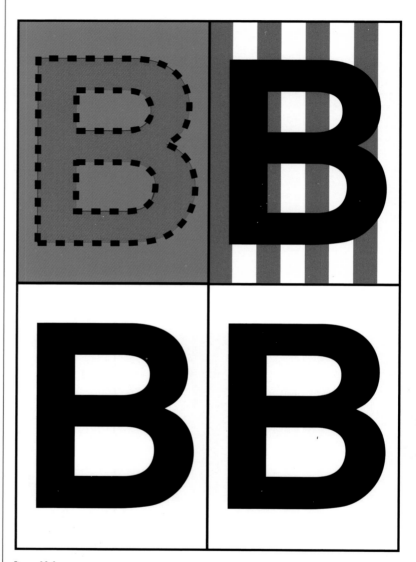

Figure 10-1

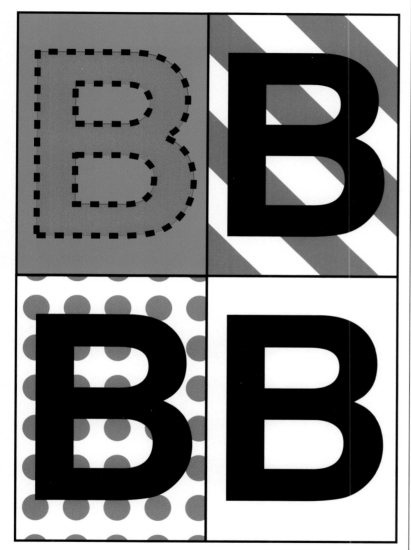

Figure 10-2

Figure 10-2: A new swatch, consisting of a transparent box with an open circle filled with red, was created and then the swatch was applied to the background of the B's box

Figure 10-3: A simple gradient fill from Illustrator's Swatch palette was applied to the last B's box to get this light-to-dark effect

Figure 10-3

Figure 10-4: A Radial gradient fill was applied for a slightly different effect, and the stitch-like stroke was added to complete the piece

Figure 10-4

Color Models

Figure 11-1: A full color and grayscale image. Grayscale images represent a tonal range of values from 0 (black) to 255 (white). Grayscale images contain no color information. Note that the yellow flower is almost white in grayscale

Figure 11-2: RGB Color is the color model used by scanners, computer monitors, and television screens to display color. Each tiny pixel is comprised of one red, green and blue light emitting phosphors, each which has a range of 256 settings from 0 (black) to 255 (full intensity). Combinations of the three colors (RGB) produce 16.7 million combinations. This is also referred to as 24-bit color depth. RGB color is sometimes called additive color because adding the three primary colors of red, green and blue light together produces pure white. Red and green produces yellow, green and blue produces cyan, blue and red produces magenta

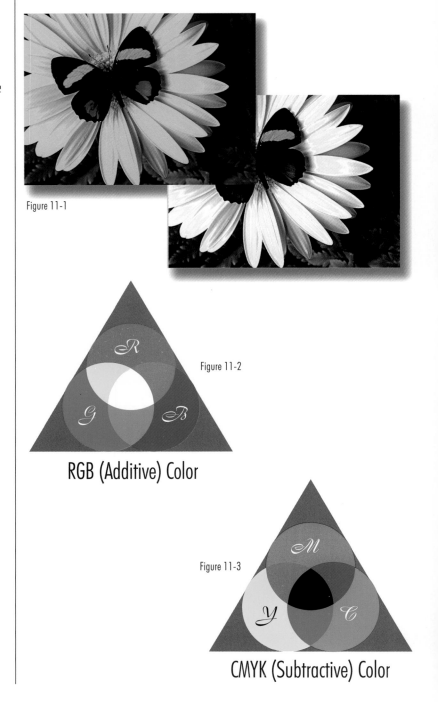

Figure 11-1

Figure 11-2

RGB (Additive) Color

Figure 11-3

CMYK (Subtractive) Color

Illustrator 7 *Tutorial Images*

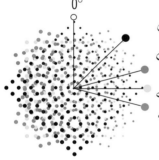

Figure 11-4

0°

Black 45°
Magenta 75°
Yellow 90°
Cyan 105°

Figure 11-7

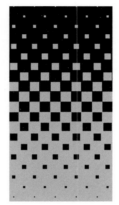

Figure 11-5

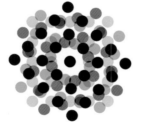

Figure 11-6

Figure 11-8

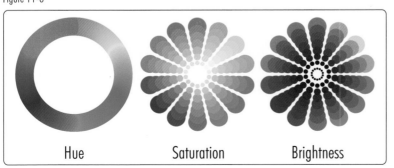

Hue   Saturation   Brightness

yellow. A fourth separation, (black) is produced containing the grayscale information, and adds depth to the colors

Figure 11-4: Commercially printed images are made up tiny dots of CMYK ink. The dots are printed on top of each other producing the illusion of full color

Figure 11-5: A screen is used to translate the continuous tonal range of an image into a series of dots. The size of the dot determines the lightness or darkness of each CMYK color

Figure 11-6: The four process color inks (CMYK) are transparent

Figure 11-7: To avoid distracting moiré patterns, the screens for the CMYK colors are rotated. When the screens are properly angled, tiny "rosette" patterns occur

Figure 11-8: The HSB (hue saturation and brightness) color model is used to specify RGB and CMYK color. There are 360 hues (colors) arranged in a circle. Each of the 360 hues can be modified in terms of saturation, (the amount of white in the color), brightness, (the amount of black), and combinations of all three

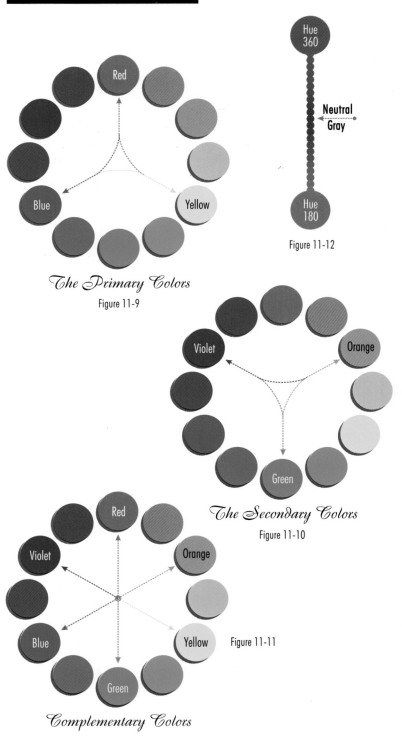

Color Theory

Figure 11-9: A simple color wheel with the three "primary" colors, red, yellow and blue noted. In theory red, yellow and blue cannot be matched by mixing any other colors, however the primary colors can be mixed to create any color

Figure 11-10: The secondary colors are comprised of equal amounts of primary colors. For example, green is a mixture of 100% blue and 100% yellow

Figure 11-11: Colors that are at opposite ends of the color wheel are called complementary colors

Figure 11-12: Complementary colors when mixed in equal amounts produce neutral gray. In this instance using the HSB color model, hue #360 red was blended with its complementary hue #180

The Primary Colors
Figure 11-9

Figure 11-12

The Secondary Colors
Figure 11-10

Figure 11-11

Complementary Colors

Illustrator 7 Tutorial Images

*Rollin Fishman
CPA & Free Spirit*

Figure 11-14

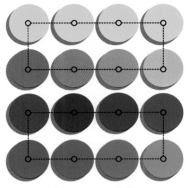

Analogous Colors

Figure 11-13

Figure 11-13: Colors that are in near proximity to one another on the color wheel are called analogous colors

Figure 11-14: A palette of secondary colors, is used for this logo

Figure 11-15: The Qwerty logo uses an analogous palette of orange and yellow orange

Figure 11-16: The three primary colors plus black create a forceful image

Figure 11-17: The colors associated with Christmas (red and green) are an example of a complementary color scheme

Figure 11-18: A pattern fill employing pastel analogous colors is applied as a Path Pattern to a spiral

Figure 11-15

Figure 11-16

MERRY CHRISTMAS

Figure 11-17

The Nautilus Chamber Music Society and Orchestra Foundation

Figure 11-18

Tutorial

Figures 11-19, 20 & 21 are from the tutorial in Chapter 11

Figure 11-19: The small window pane is filled with a custom gradient fill. The small inset to the left shows the actual fill. The Gradient Tool is dragged using the same starting and ending path used for the sphere causing the two fills to align exactly

Figure 11-20: The windowpane highlight is selected and the colors lightened

Figure 11-21: The window pane highlight appears transparent

Figure 11-22: This technique can be used with pattern fills. A darker version of the checker fill was created and applied to the shadow

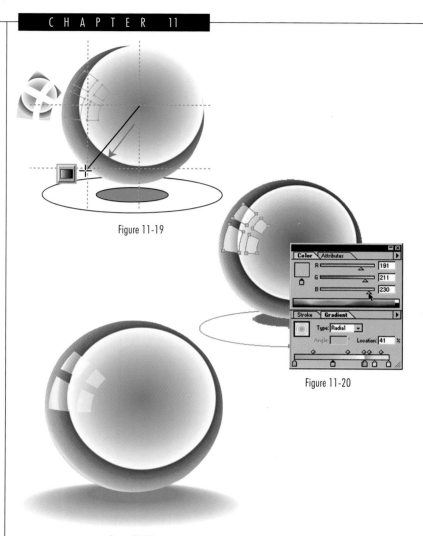

Figure 11-19

Figure 11-20

Figure 11-21

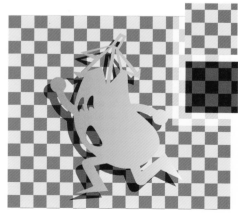

Figure 11-22

Illustrator 7 Tutorial Images

Figure 12-1

Figure 12-2

Figure 12-3

Figure 12-4

Figure 12-5

Figure 12-6

Figure 12-7

Figure 12-8

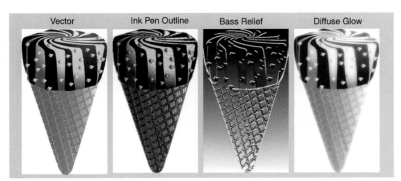

Figure 12-9

Ice Cream Cone Deluxe

Figure 12-1: Create the cone

Figure 12-2: Create Trim Pattern

Figure 12-3: Create the Waffle Design

Figure 12-4: Trim the Waffle Pattern

Figure 12-5: Create the Ice Cream

Figure 12-6: Create the Swirl top

Figure 12-7: Apply Swirl & Nuts

Figure 12-8: Assemble the parts

Figure 12-9: Bitmap filters applied for special effects

Packaged to Go

Figure 12-10: Creating and filling the spheres with radial gradients in preparation for rasterizing

Figure 12-11: Create the package objects and type effects

Figure 12-12: Completing the composition with Ink Pen Filter Effects

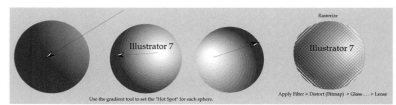

Figure 12-10

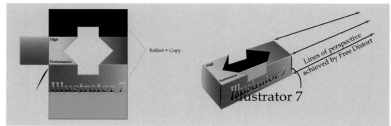

Figure 12-11

Figure 12-12

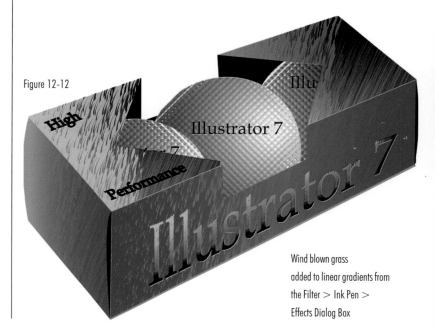

Wind blown grass added to linear gradients from the Filter > Ink Pen > Effects Dialog Box

Figure 12-13

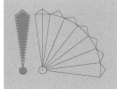

Figure 12-14

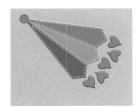

Figure 12-15

Colorful Effects

Figure 12-13: Create a heart shape. Apply a Zig-Zag filter 2/40

Figure 12-14: Create Necktie Shapes. Rotate > Copy every -7.5°

Figure 12-15: Complete the color wheel. Rotate > Copy every -15°

Figure 12-16: Add red border and apply the Zig-Zag filter 12/30. Rasterize and apply the Craquelure filter

Figure 12-17: Artwork > Sponge Applied

Figure 12-18: Roughen Filter Applied

Figure 12-19: Distort > Twirl Applied

Figure 12-16

Figure 12-17

Figure 12-18

Figure 12-19

Bitmap Filters

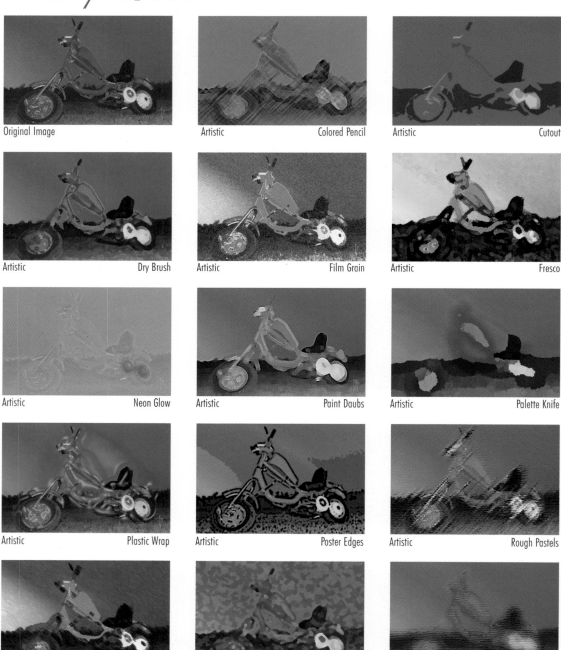

Original Image

Artistic   Colored Pencil

Artistic   Cutout

Artistic   Dry Brush

Artistic   Film Grain

Artistic   Fresco

Artistic   Neon Glow

Artistic   Paint Daubs

Artistic   Palette Knife

Artistic   Plastic Wrap

Artistic   Poster Edges

Artistic   Rough Pastels

Artistic   Smudge Stick

Artistic   Sponge

Artistic   Underpainting on Canvas

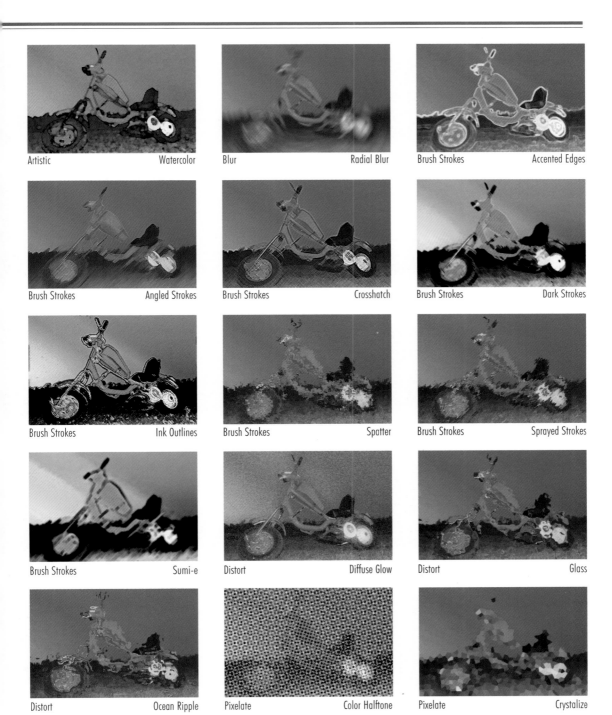

Artistic — Watercolor	Blur — Radial Blur	Brush Strokes — Accented Edges
Brush Strokes — Angled Strokes	Brush Strokes — Crosshatch	Brush Strokes — Dark Strokes
Brush Strokes — Ink Outlines	Brush Strokes — Spatter	Brush Strokes — Sprayed Strokes
Brush Strokes — Sumi-e	Distort — Diffuse Glow	Distort — Glass
Distort — Ocean Ripple	Pixelate — Color Halftone	Pixelate — Crystalize

More Bitmap Filters

Pixelate	Mezzotint
Pixelate	Pointilize
Sketch	Water Paper
Stylize	Glowing Edges
Texture	Craquelure
Texture	Grain
Texture	Mosaic Tiles
Texture	Patchwork
Texture	Stained Glass
Texture	Texturizer—Brick
Texture	Texturizer—Burlap
Texture	Texturizer—Sandstone

Original Image

Sketch   Bas Relief

Sketch   Chalk & Charcoal

Sketch   Charcoal

Sketch   Chrome

Sketch   Conté Crayon

Sketch   Graphic Pen

Sketch   Halftone Pattern

Sketch   Note Paper

Sketch   Photocopy

Sketch   Plaster

Sketch   Reticulation

Sketch   Stamp

Sketch   Torn Edges

Sketch   Water Paper

CHAPTER 13

A Love Affair

Figure 13-1: The screen capture of Illustrator 7's credit screen with the 200-point heart-shaped mask pasted in from the Windows Character Map, or the Apple Key Caps menu

Figure 13-2: The heart-shaped mask is used to crop the image of Venus

Figure 13-3: The end result: a fitting tribute to Adobe Illustrator, with a border around the heart, text added and drop shadows applied

Figure 10-1

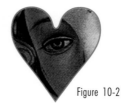

Figure 10-2

I ♥ Illustrator

Figure 10-3

the objects into smaller objects. Where there is an odd overlap or a single object, Illustrator fills the shape with the fill from the top object in the group's stack.

Use the Undo feature to return to the four objects. Experiment with using two or three shapes. When you are finished experimenting, select the Enter tool from the main Toolbox or by typing **T** and type **Exclude** above this group.

Pathfinder | Minus Front and Back

The Minus Front and Minus Back commands work the same way. You will apply them to two sets of the standard set of objects to see how they work.

1. Select the standard set of objects. Move a copy by choosing Object|Transform|Move. In the Move dialog box, double-click the vertical text box and enter **-1.50**. Click on the Copy button and a copy of the standard set appears. Choose Object|Transform|Move. In the Move dialog box, double-click the horizontal text box and enter **1.85**. Click on the Copy button and another copy of the standard set appears.

2. Select the first copy of the standard set of objects to which to apply the Minus Front command. Choose Object|Transform|Minus Front. Your results will look like Figure 9-20. The only portion that Illustrator leaves behind is a trimmed portion of the rectangle or object number 4. Remember that you arranged the rectangle toward the back, so Illustrator removed everything in front including that overlapping back portion that was below the front objects.

Before Transformation	After Pathfinder > Exclude

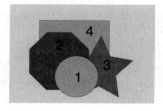 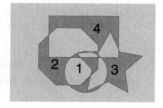

FIGURE 9-19   With the Pathfinder|Exclude command, odd numbered objects are filled and even numbered overlaps are open

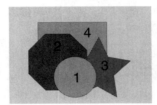
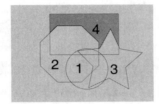

FIGURE 9-20   With the Pathfinder|Minus Front command, only the bottom object in the stack has any portion left

3. Select the second copy of the standard set of objects.

4. Apply the Minus Back command by choosing Object|Pathfinder|Minus Back.

You may check your results against Figure 9-21. Notice the difference in results of Minus Front and Minus Back. Minus Front used the front objects to trim the object to the back. Minus Back used the objects to the back to trim the front object. To undo the commands, press CTRL/COMMAND+Z until you undo both Minus Back and Minus Front. Experiment, using different combinations of overlapping objects and applying Minus Front and Minus Back. When finished experimenting, select the Type tool from the main Toolbox or by typing **T** and type **Minus Front** over the first copy and **Minus Back** over the last copy.

Pathfinder | Divide

Prepare your artboard for the next Pathfinder command. Make another copy of the standard set of objects. You will apply the Divide command to this next set.

1. Select the standard set of objects. Move a copy by choosing Object|Transform|Move. In the Move dialog box, double-click in the Distance text box and enter **4**. Double-click in the Angle text box and enter **-21.372**. Click on the Copy button and a copy of the standard set appears.

2. Choose Object|Pathfinder|Divide.

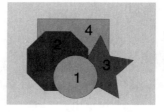

Before
Transformation

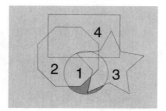

After Pathfinder >
Minus Back

FIGURE 9-21   When you use the Pathfinder|Minus Back command, only
the top object in the stack has any portion left

At first, you may not notice the results. To explore what has happened, Ungroup
(CTRL/COMMAND+SHIFT+G) the objects. Deselect all objects (CTRL/COMMAND+SHIFT+A).
Now, drag any of the objects away from the others. You'll discover Illustrator used
the outlines of each object to "cut up" the other objects involved. See the exploded
view of the objects in Figure 9-22 that we separated to show the results of the Divide
command. Choose the Type tool (**T**) and type **Divide** above this application group.

Pathfinder | Outline

Let's create another copy for the Outline command. By now you are gaining a sense
of how the Transform|Move dialog box works. This helps you manage object
placement with great precision.

1. Select the standard set of objects. Move a copy by choosing
   Object|Transform|Move. In the Move dialog box, click on the word
   Distance in the dialog box and enter **5.8125**. Click on the word Angle and
   enter **-13.753**. Click the Copy button and a copy of the standard set of
   objects appears.

2. Apply the Outline command by choosing Object|Pathfinder|Outline.

Illustrator 7 divides the objects into individual line segments without fill and
applies the fill color of the visible part of each object to the line segments that cross
over or under an object's fill. Although you can't see the color of line segments in

Before
Transformation

After
Pathfinder > Divide

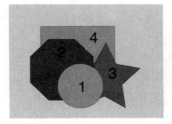
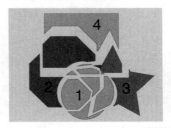

FIGURE 9-22　The Divide command breaks objects into shapes according to the outline of other shapes

Figure 9-23, you may notice the different shades of gray. Ungroup the outlines (CTRL/COMMAND+SHIFT+G) and drag them to see how the command has affected the objects. Choose the Type tool from the main Toolbox or by typing **T** and type **Outline** above this group of outlines.

Pathfinder | Trim

The Trim command uses one object's shape to remove the portions of another, essentially behaving as if the first object were a hole punch—only the hole isn't

Before
Transformation

After
Pathfinder > Outline

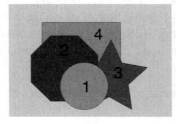
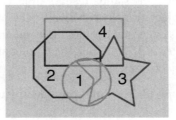

FIGURE 9-23　The Pathfinder|Outline command converts objects into colored outlines that correspond to the colors that overlap and split lines into segments

necessarily round. Objects in the foreground of your selection act as the punch shape while objects behind act as the victims of the punch. Prepare for this next Pathfinder command by making a copy of the standard set of objects.

1. Select the standard set of objects. Move a copy by choosing Object|Transform|Move. In the Move dialog box, click on the word Vertical and enter **-2.9375**. Click on the Copy button and a copy of the standard set appears.

2. Apply the Trim command by choosing Object|Pathfinder|Trim.

3. Choose the Type tool (**T**) and type **Trim** over this group.

Ungroup (CTRL/COMMAND+SHIFT+G) and deselect all objects (CTRL/COMMAND+SHIFT+A). Click on an object in the group and drag it away from the group a short distance. Notice how each object on top trimmed the objects below. You separated the objects in Figure 9-24 to show the effects of the Trim command. The circle object remained intact while Illustrator trimmed all the other objects.

Pathfinder | Merge

In preparation for this command you will copy two sets of the standard set of objects. We will show how Merge works with different colored objects and objects with the same fill color. You will apply this option to two sets of the standard group of objects.

Before Transformation	After Pathfinder > Trim

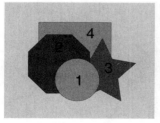 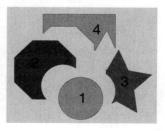

FIGURE 9-24　The Pathfinder|Trim command divides objects into new shapes much like a cookie cutter forms a cookie

After applying the Merge command to the first group in a straightforward fashion, you will modify the second group by moving objects and changing color to see how the Merge command acts with objects of the same color.

1. Select the standard set of objects. Move a copy by choosing Object|Transform|Move. In the Move dialog box, click on the word Distance and enter **3.45**. Click on the word Angle and enter **-57.077**. Click on the Copy button and a copy of the standard set appears. Choose Object|Transform|Move again. In the Move dialog box, enter **1.85** and click on the Copy button.

2. Select the first group of objects and apply the Merge command by choosing Object|Pathfinder|Merge. Ungroup (CTRL/COMMAND+SHIFT+G) and drag your objects apart to view how Illustrator applied the Merge command. Compare your results against Figure 9-25. Select the Type tool (T) and type **Merge Different Color** over this arrangement.

3. In the second group of objects, move both the octagon and the star slightly to overlap the rectangle and circle. The rectangle and circle should be adjacent to each other.

4. Select the circle and click on the Fill Color Box in the Color palette. Click in the Green Fill Color Box and drag to the rectangle until a dotted square and plus sign appear. Release the mouse button and the rectangle will change color to match the circle. Select all four objects in this second group. You are ready to apply the Merge command on this group.

Before Transformation	After Pathfinder > Merge
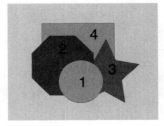	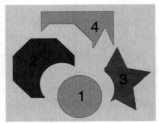

FIGURE 9-25   The Pathfinder|Merge command divides different colored objects into new shapes

5. Apply the Merge command by choosing Object|Pathfinder|Merge.

Ungroup the objects (CTRL/COMMAND+SHIFT+G), and drag the rectangle away from the other objects. Compare your results to Figure 9-26. You will discover Illustrator has merged the circle and the rectangle. Choose the Text tool (T) and enter the words **Merge Same Color**. Merge Same Color acts like two tools in one. Depending on placement and color of objects, applying Merge Same Color to a group of objects can produce trimmed and united objects in one command.

Pathfinder | Crop

Now you will create another copy of the standard set of objects in preparation for using the Crop command.

1. Select the standard set of objects. Move a copy by choosing Object|Transform|Move. In the Move dialog box, enter **6.30** at the word Distance and **-27.5821** as the Angle. Click on the Copy button and a copy of the standard set appears.

2. Apply the Crop command by choosing Object|Pathfinder|Crop.

The Crop command is sort of like looking through a glass-bottom boat. The top object acts like a window to view the objects underneath. Illustrator deletes

Before
Transformation

After
Pathfinder > Crop

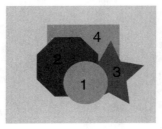
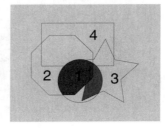

FIGURE 9-26 The Pathfinder|Merge command combines objects of the same color into one object

everything outside the shape of the top object in the stack and keeps the objects created underneath the shape of the top object. The shapes maintain their individual colors. Choose the Enter tool from the main Toolbox or by typing **T** and type **Crop** above this application.

Pathfinder|Hard

The next Pathfinder command creates interesting effects similar to transparency gels overlaying each other. The Hard command takes the highest values for the CMYK model of each color between objects and applies it to the overlapping sections. When Illustrator applies the Hard command, the overlapping sections become individual objects. Apply the Pathfinder|Hard command to a copy of the standard set of objects.

1. Select the standard set of objects. Move a copy by choosing Object|Transform|Move. In the Move dialog box, enter **-4.375** for the Vertical measure and click on the Copy button.

2. Apply the Hard command by choosing Object|Pathfinder|Hard.

Check your results with Figure 9-27. You will see an effect similar to semitransparent colors overlapping. If you ungroup the group, you will find Illustrator has cut the objects into smaller shapes where objects overlap. You may undo the Pathfinder|Hard command and experiment with different colored objects. Choose the Type tool (**T**)and enter the word **Hard** above this group of objects.

Before
Transformation

After
Pathfinder > Hard

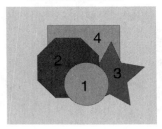 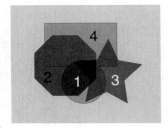

FIGURE 9-27   The Pathfinder|Hard command combines colors with a straight mix, giving a semitransparent look

Pathfinder | Soft

The Pathfinder Soft command is similar to the Hard command in that it also creates a semitransparent effect on overlapping objects. The difference between the Hard and Soft commands is the control the artist has over the level of transparency. The Soft command has a dialog box to aid in setting the amount of color to show through the layers of objects.

1. Select the standard set of objects. Move a copy by choosing Object|Transform|Move. In the Move dialog box, click on the word Distance and enter **4.80**. Click on the word Angle and enter **-65.8852**. Click on the Copy button and a copy of the standard set appears.

2. To apply the Soft command you must first enter information into the Soft command option box. Choose Object|Pathfinder|Soft. The default setting is 50 percent. The higher the number, the more transparent the objects appear. The lower the number, the more opaque the objects appear. Choose a setting and click OK. Choose the Type tool (**T**) and enter the word **Soft** along with your percentage value above this application group.

See the various settings for the Soft command in Figure 9-28. Illustrator can only apply the Soft and Hard commands to solid-filled objects. You may not make gradient-filled and pattern-filled objects look transparent in Illustrator. There is a way to simulate gradient transparency by creating a gradient appearing object through the Blend command, applying Trim to the objects, and then applying Hard or Soft commands to the remaining objects.

 With too many objects selected while using the Hard or Soft commands, you may encounter a memory caution instead of Illustrator applying any filter effects.

Pathfinder | Trap

The Trap command in Illustrator creates a thin color fill area at the edges of where objects and their fills overlap each other. The trap is actually an object that Illustrator creates. You may manipulate it like any other object once you apply the Trap command. In printing colors, a trap aids registration by assuring proper color coverage. Occasionally, during printing, a sheet of paper is not placed in the right spot to receive the ink. This is called a misregistration. Illustrator allows an area of fill overprint overlapping the edges of bordering objects to prevent "unprinted" areas

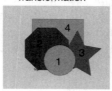

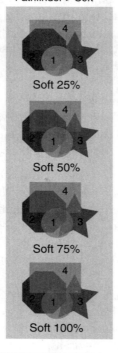

FIGURE 9-28   The Pathfinder|Soft command combines object colors with percentages of the top object's color, giving a semitransparent look

between objects in the event of a misregistration. Prepare the artboard to create a trap by creating another copy of the standard set of objects.

1. Select the standard set of objects. Move a copy by choosing Object|Transform|Move. In the Move dialog box, click on the word Distance and enter **5.75**. Click on the word Angle and enter **-49.1134**. Click on the Copy button and a copy of the standard set appears.

2. Apply the Trap command by choosing Object|Pathfinder|Trap. The Trap dialog box appears. If you clicked OK with the present default settings, a trap would only appear between the rectangle and the star objects. Change the trap's Thickness to **6** points, leave the Height/Width at 100 percent, and change the Tint Reduction to **60** percent. Now click OK.

Illustrator applies the trap to the blue star. We greatly exaggerated the trap's thickness to make it plainly visible. Before you changed the thickness the amount was .25 points, which is the default setting. See the Trap results in Figure 9-29. Choose the Enter tool from the main Toolbox or by typing **T** and type **Trap** above this application group. To see the trap up close, use the Zoom tool found on the main Toolbox and click on the area to enlarge.

Transform | Move

Now you will finish your reference chart with the Transform commands. Prepare your artboard by creating another copy of the standard set of objects.

1. Select the standard set of objects. Move a copy by choosing Object|Transform|Move. In the Move dialog box, click on the word Distance and enter **6.6.** Click on the word Angle and enter **-38.6782.** Click on the Copy button and a copy of the standard set appears.

2. Apply the Move command again by choosing Object|Transform|Move. In the Move dialog box, enter a word Distance of **.90** and a word Angle of **-28.2806.** Click on the Copy button and Illustrator moves a copy of your application group. Choose the Type tool (**T**) and type the word **Move** over this application group.

9

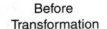

Before
Transformation

After
Pathfinder > Trap

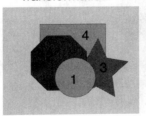

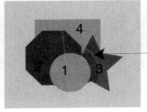

Notice trap
area in white

FIGURE 9-29   The Pathfinder|Trap command creates an overprint of an object's color to prevent white space between objects on a printed page due to a misregistration problem

You used this same command many times to place objects on your artboard. Check your results with Figure 9-30. Now you will use more of the Transform commands to help you gain a familiarity with these commands as well.

Transform | Scale

Create another copy of the standard set of objects to prepare for the Transform| Scale command.

1. Select the standard set of objects. Move a copy by choosing Object|Transform|Move. In the Move dialog box, click on the word Distance and enter **-5.60**. Enter a word Angle of **-93.5495**. Click on the Copy button and a copy of the standard set appears.

2. Apply the Scale command by choosing Object|Transform|Scale. Notice the word Uniform in the Scale dialog box. If you wanted to scale an object other than proportionally you would choose Non-Uniform. You will scale height and width in proportion. Enter **25** and click on the Copy button. A scaled copy will appear over the top of your original set of objects.

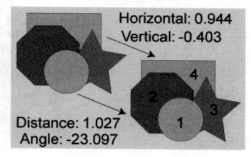

Before Transformation	After Transform > Move

Horizontal: 0.944
Vertical: -0.403

Distance: 1.027
Angle: -23.097

FIGURE 9-30   The Move command places an object with great precision through the Move dialog box. Place an object by entering Horizontal and Vertical distances or by entering the distance and angle

3. Drag this scaled copy down and to the right so that it no longer overlaps the full-size copy. Choose the Type tool (T) and enter the words **Scale 25 percent** above this group of objects.

You may use the Scale command to proportion objects to fit into a composition. Scale is also useful for creating scaled copies for special effects, to simulate movement away, or for shrinking objects. Check your results with Figure 9-31.

Transform | Rotate

Prepare your artboard by creating another copy of the standard set of objects. You will rotate the group of objects **90** degrees, using the default point of origin. The default point of origin is the group's center point. Rotate with Copy is an easy way to produce the effect of motion in your artwork. You may also create decorative designs through Rotate and Copy.

1. Select the standard set of objects. Move a copy by choosing Object|Transform|Move. In the Move dialog box, click on the word Distance and enter **6**. Enter a word Angle of **-71.8984**. Click on the Copy button and a copy of the standard set appears.

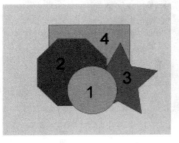
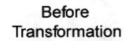
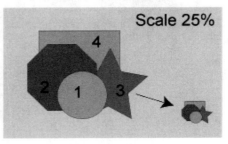

Before Transformation

After Transform > Scale

Scale 25%

FIGURE 9-31   The Scale command increases or decreases size according to the Scale dialog box information. You can also scale a copy

2. Apply the Rotate command by choosing Object|Transform|Rotate. Enter **-90** and click OK. Illustrator rotates the objects clockwise by 90 degrees.

Check your results with the rotated object in Figure 9-32. Choose the Type tool (T) and then type **Rotate -90 percent** above this application group. Rotating on center and rotating around the point of origin 2 inches from center create quite different results. You will use this command in the last tutorial in this chapter to produce a clock face.

Transform | Reflect

Prepare your artboard again by placing a new copy of the standard set of objects in the location indicated. You will scale this copy before creating a reflection to make room for the reflected copy. You may use the Reflect command to create the effect of reflections and shadows.

1. Select the standard set of objects. Move a copy by choosing Object|Transform|Move. In the Move dialog box, click on the word Distance and enter **6.65**. Click on the word Angle and enter **-60**. Click on the Copy button and a copy of the standard set appears.

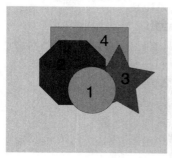
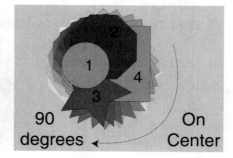

FIGURE 9-32   The Rotate command spins an object around the point of origin, which happens to be the center point for the group of objects shown

2. Now you will resize the new copy. Choose Object|Transform|Scale. Enter **75** percent and click OK.

3. You are ready to use the Reflect command. To place the copy to the right of the application group, you will use the Reflect tool (**O**). To set the point of origin, press the ALT/OPTION key while you click once just to the right of the application group. The Reflect dialog box appears. The default reflect setting is vertical and that is what you want. Click the Copy button and a reflected copy of the application group appears.

Check your results with the reflected copy in Figure 9-33. Choose the Type tool (T) and then enter the words **Reflect Vertical** above this group of objects.

Transform | Shear

Prepare the last copy of the standard set of objects for the Shear command. You may use this command to create shadows and special effects.

1. Select the standard set of objects. Move a copy by choosing Object|Transform|Move. In the Move dialog box, click on the word Distance and enter **7.7**. Click on the word Angle and enter **-48**. Click on the Copy button and a copy of the standard set appears.

Before
Transformation

After
Transform > Reflect

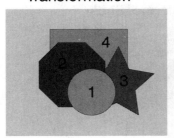

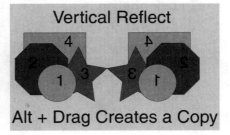

Vertical Reflect

Alt + Drag Creates a Copy

FIGURE 9-33 The Reflect command can reflect an object vertically (shown) or horizontally

2. Resize the group of objects by choosing Object|Transform|Scale. If you are still working after the Scale session, the Scale dialog will show 75 percent in the Scale text box. If not, enter **75** and click OK.

3. Apply the Shear command by choosing Object|Transform|Shear. Enter **60** and click the Copy button. Drag the new copy to the right of the original group of objects. Choose the Type tool (T) and enter the words **Shear 60 degrees** above the group of objects.

Check your results against the object sheared in Figure 9-34. You created the sheared object in the example using the Shear tool. You placed the point of origin in the lower-left corner of the object group before applying the Shear tool.

These exercises in Pathfinder and Transform have given you a well-rounded working knowledge of the various commands. You are ready to move on to the next tutorial and apply these new skills to application artwork.

Save your work (CTRL/COMMAND+S) and print a copy for your reference (CTRL/COMMAND+P). Close the file (CTRL/COMMAND+W).

Creating a Barn Scene Using Transform and Pathfinder Commands

You will create much of the work in the following tutorial freehand. You have minimized the amount of freehand work required by using Pathfinder and Transform commands to create the shapes from freehand shapes you draw.

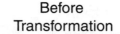

Before Transformation	After Transform > Shear

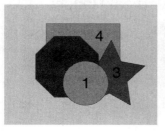
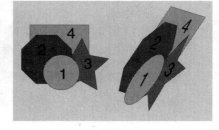

FIGURE 9-34 The Shear command stretches and reshapes objects, slanting them so they appear to lean

Take this tutorial one step at a time. Patience is a requirement in order to complete an artistic masterpiece—regardless of your medium. When you reduce the total work into simple steps, you'll be amazed at what you accomplish.

You will create the tiny elements that make up the whole composition and step by step apply what you have learned. Let's begin.

Create the Treeline

The first object to create is an evergreen tree outline. Look at Figure 9-35 to gain a sense of the shape of the evergreen tree. Using the Pen tool, you will create this tree with all straight lines. You will not add much detail, since you will scale and reduce this object for the final composition. You will complete the first tree outline, make several copies, and unite them as shown. You will produce several copies of the final shape while reflecting vertically. You will place all these elements in your composition later. You are creating your "tools" and "cookie cutters" at this point.

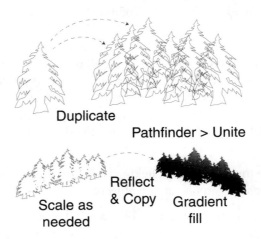

FIGURE 9-35 Creating an evergreen tree line from a single outline

You will create the outline of an evergreen tree using either the Pen tool or the Pencil tool, depending on which tool you prefer to work with. Follow these steps:

1. Create the outline of an evergreen tree as shown in Figure 9-35 by choosing either the Pen tool (P) or Pencil tool (Y). Begin drawing the outline by clicking on the artboard with the Pen tool or clicking and dragging the Pencil tool.

2. Click on the Swap Fill/Stroke button to choose the Fill option. Click the No Fill option (square with a red slash through it). Click on the Swap Fill/Stroke button to choose the Stroke option. Click on the Stroke Color button. Select black from the Color palette to make the path color black.

3. Continue creating the outline. You don't need to be precise here because you can always go back later with the Direct Selection tool (A) to edit the shape by moving anchor points. When your outline is nearly complete, click on the starting position when your Pen or Pencil Tool shows a hollow circle to close the object. If your object needs to be adjusted, choose the Direct Selection tool and move anchor points to modify the outline.

Now you will copy the evergreen tree outline to create the treeline you will use in the barn scene.

1. Choose the Select tool (V) and deselect all the anchor points. Click on the tree object to select it. Drag the tree and press the ALT/OPTION key. Release the mouse button first and then the ALT/OPTION key, and you have created a copy of the tree outline. Create at least seven copies this way. Make sure the tree branches overlap by selecting and dragging each copy into place.

2. Select all the tree outlines by clicking and dragging the Selection tool and drawing a marquee around all the objects.

3. You are ready to apply the Unite command. Choose Object|Pathfinder|Unite. Illustrator will unite the tree outlines into one object. Illustrator may also give you a message saying complex paths have been created. Don't worry about this now.

4. Illustrator may also create little pieces of objects that you do not want as a part of this treeline. Ungroup the new object (CTRL/COMMAND+SHIFT+G) and select the outline. Move the outline away from this area by dragging it to a new location on the artboard. You will see little objects left behind. Select and eliminate them with the DELETE key.

Now that you have created the forest outline, you are ready to resize it and reflect a copy.

1. Select the treeline and scale it proportionally to approximately one inch in width. Double-click the Width text box in the Transform palette. Enter **1**, press and hold the CTRL/COMMAND key, and press ENTER. Use this method to precisely scale the object: Open the Info palette (Window|Show Info). Check the width of the treeline object. Divide the number into one inch. The result will be the percentage to scale your object to one inch.

2. Choose Object|Transform|Scale, choose Uniform, and enter the percentage of the proportional scale to make your treeline one inch wide. Click OK.

Now you are ready to apply the Reflect command while creating a copy of the treeline. You are creating a reflection of the original treeline to add to the background of the barn scene.

1. Choose the Reflect tool (**O**). Press the ALT/OPTION key and click an inch or so to the right of your treeline.

2. The default reflect is vertical, which is what you want. Click the Copy button and a reflected copy of the treeline appears.

3. Next, fill the reflected copy of the treeline with green gradient fill. Open the Gradient palette (F9). If the Gradient palette is showing a grayscale, click the flyout menu in the Color palette and choose the CMYK model (or SHIFT-click in the color box).

4. Click on the color stop on the left side of the color scale in the Gradient palette. Click in the yellow-green area of the CMYK spectrum in the Color palette. Click on the color stop in the Gradient palette. Click on the dark green section of the CMYK spectrum in the Color palette. This sets the gradient for your treeline.

5. Set the angle of the gradient so the lighter color is in the tree tops and the darker color is in the bottom of the trees. Click in the Angle text box and enter **-90**. Press the ENTER key to apply the gradient to the treeline.

You have completed the first part of your barn scene by coloring the treeline with gradient fill. Copy this tree line several more times, filling each with lighter fill gradients to depict distance and perhaps a haze.

Create the Sky

Now you will create a background of sky for the barn scene. Use the Rectangle tool (M) to create a large rectangle and trim the bottom edge using the treeline you created. See Figure 9-36 to gain perspective of how the work will progress. Figure 9-36 was modified with a larger version of the treeline than the 1-inch model you created. Scale the treeline as necessary to achieve the desired look for your composition.

1. Create a rectangle 6 inches by 3 inches. Choose the Rectangle tool (M) and click on the artboard. The Rectangle dialog box appears. Enter **6** in the Width text box. Enter **3** as the Height and enter a decimal fraction of an inch if you desire rounded corners on your rectangle. Click OK. The rectangle will be filled with the last gradient or solid fill you were working with before you created it. You may change the fill color or gradient through the Color palette or Gradient palette.

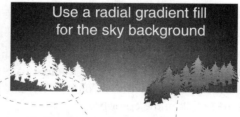

Use a radial gradient fill for the sky background

Select and delete this area

Use treeline to trim the background With Pathfinder > Trim

FIGURE 9-36   Create a skyline using Pathfinder|Trim

2. Send this new rectangle to the back of the stack (CTRL/COMMAND+SHIFT+[).

3. Now apply the Trim command to the rectangle. Move the treeline by selecting and dragging it to the lower-left corner of the rectangle to trim the corner. Use the Selection tool (V) to select both the rectangle and treeline. Choose Object|Pathfinder|Trim. Once the Trim is complete, ungroup the treeline and rectangle.

4. Repeat the steps until you have trimmed along the entire bottom of the rectangle. You can repeat this action quickly using CTRL/COMMAND+4. Ungroup the skyline and click away from the artwork. Select the skyline again and move it to another location up on the artboard. You will see little pieces left behind. Select and delete these by pressing the DELETE key.

5. Select the skyline and fill with a radial Gradient fill from light blue to dark blue. Use the Gradient tool (G) to set the center of your gradient an inch or two below the rectangle. For help on using these tools, see the section in Chapter 10 on using and applying gradient fills.

To keep your work organized begin working on a different layer. Open the Layers palette (F7). Double-click the selected layer. Name this layer **Skyline** and click OK. Click the new Layer button, and click the Show/Hide button for Layer 1 Skyline. You will return to this layer later. Double-click on Layer 2 and add **Barn** to the Layer 2 title. Click OK.

The Barn Walls and Roof

Now you are ready to create the barn walls and roof. This portion of the barn scene is the most straightforward to create. It is simply a matter of using the Pen tool to make straight lines for the outline of walls and roof. We created the structure with walls and roof overlapping and placed together to match height and widths of adjacent structures. We pulled the barn walls and roof apart so you could see their shape in Figure 9-37. Refer to this figure often to gain a sense of object shape and outline.

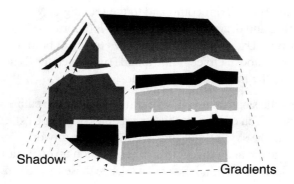

Shadows   Gradients

FIGURE 9-37   Creating barn walls and roof using simple shapes

We borrowed the concept for the barn scene from a pencil sketching book. The original art was published in *Pencil Drawing Techniques* by Watson-Guptill Publications, 1515 Broadway, NY 10036.

1. Create the left wall using the Pen tool (P) to outline the three shapes that make up the left wall. The first object to create is the "loft" wall shaped like a triangle. To close the outline, click on the starting point. Remember, straight lines are created by clicking and curves are created by dragging when using the Pen tool. This wall will be the backdrop for lines that will represent barn boards.

2. Fill the loft wall with a dark brown solid fill.

3. Create the main floor barn wall by clicking along the bottom of the loft shape. Follow the line created by the triangle and extend it out a little farther and click. Click straight below that point to the "corner" of the barn. Now bring the line across the bottom of the wall. Notice the little jog in wall shape in Figure 9-37. Complete the outline of the wall and close the object by clicking on the starting point. Make adjustments to the shape using the Direct Selection tool to move anchor points.

4. Fill the main floor wall with a tint darker than the loft wall.

5. Create the "basement" wall by following the bottom line of the "main floor" wall. Drop short of the right edge of the wall and angle up to complete the shape. This basement wall will become the backdrop for adding stone outlines later. Make adjustments to the shape using the Direct Selection tool to move anchor points.

6. Fill this basement wall with a brown gradient fill.

Let's move on to create the barn roof with the Pen tool. Studying the barn roof will help you see its basic shape. You can see the upper side of the roof to the right and the underside of the eves to the left. The right side is a near typical parallelogram leaning to the left. The upper-left corner of the roof is projected out a little from the peak of the loft wall. This will be our starting point for the first anchor location.

1. Using the angle of the right edge of your loft wall to judge the slope, create the left edge of the parallelogram by starting at the top and sloping down to the right. Then click to the right to draw the bottom edge of the roof. Angle up and to the left to create the right edge of the parallelogram and finish the shape by clicking on the starting point. If necessary, make adjustments to the shape using the Direct Selection tool to move anchor points.

2. Fill the roof shape with a black and gray linear gradient.

3. Now create the "front" walls with shadow sections. The barn has two walls visible. The wall to the left is in the shade. The wall to the right is in the sun; we will call that wall our front wall.

4. Create the first shadow section by following the bottom edge of the barn roof using the Pen tool. Stop short of the right edge and drop down a short distance before returning to complete a rectangular shape. Complete the shading of the object by clicking on the starting point. Make adjustments to the shape using the Direct Selection tool to move anchor points.

5. Fill this section with a dark brown solid fill.

6. Create the next section of the wall by making your first pen click in the lower-left corner of the shaded section you just created. Follow the bottom edge of the shaded rectangle to the right using the Pen tool. Click

at the right edge to match with the corner line and drop straight down to draw the right corner. As you click along the bottom edge of this wall section, create "square" indentations to represent short and long boards. Many older barns are patched up with uneven board lines. Complete the outline by clicking on the starting point.

7. Fill this wall section with tan or even a yellow solid fill.

8. Create the next shade area below the wall overhang using the Pen tool (P). Create a rectangle the same width as the previous two sections and high enough to overlap all the indentations you created along the bottom of the last section. Arrange this new rectangle to the back. Move the rectangle to the left to give an impression of an overhang. Press SHIFT and click on the previous section you created. Trim the new rectangle using Object|Pathfinder|Trim. Ungroup the objects (CTRL/COMMAND+SHIFT+G).

9. Fill this basement wall front with the same values of solid color fill as the main floor wall front. Do this by clicking on the trimmed object. Choose the Eyedropper tool (I) and click on the other shaded section. The new fill will be applied to the trimmed section.

10. You have one last wall section to create. Choose the Selection tool (V). Drag a copy of the trimmed section down while pressing the ALT/OPTION key.

11. Choose the Eyedropper Tool (I) and click on the light tan section of the front wall to apply the fill.

12. Move the new section so the upper edge of this new object overlaps the bottom edge of the original object. Choose the Direct Selection tool and adjust the bottom anchor points to match the bottom of the left basement wall.

13. Now you may finish the main barn structure by creating the visible eaves on the left edge of the barn slope. Start at the top and match the upper-left corner of the barn roof with your first click of the Pen tool. Follow the slope of the loft wall down and to the left. Continue the slope of the main floor wall and past the left corner a little bit. Click out to the left to show the roof extension and follow the angle up and to the right. Complete the object by clicking on the starting point. Make adjustments to the shape using the Direct Selection tool to move anchor points.

14. Fill this section with a very dark brown solid fill.

Detailing the Walls and Roof of the Barn

Your barn outline is complete. Now you will create barn boards, stone wall, windows, and roof patterns. You will use the Pen tool for the barn boards, Pencil tool for the stone wall, and the Centered Rectangle tool for the windows. Let's create the windows first.

1. Choose the Centered Rectangle tool from the Rectangle tool (**M**). Create the first window about one-third the distance from the left edge of the main floor front wall. Click and drag in the middle of the wall just below the shadow. Release the mouse button when the rectangle is about half the height of the wall.

2. Add a solid fill close to the color of the yellow wall, but slightly more dark.

3. Create a copy by dragging while pressing the ALT/OPTION key. (Release the mouse button before the ALT/OPTION key.)

4. Select both the windows and the shadow object and choose Object|Pathfinder|Soft. Enter a value of **60** percent and click OK.

5. Choose the Centered Rectangle tool (M). Create a new rectangle inside one of the original rectangles you just created. Fill this with 100 percent black by selecting the black fill of the CMYK spectrum in the Color palette.

6. Hold ALT/OPTION while dragging to create a copy of the new rectangle and place the copy over the other window frame, centering it over the larger rectangle.

   Now that you have created the windows on the main floor front wall, you will need to create the illusion of depth in the windows. Create a beam to fit across the black space of the window and apply the Soft command. Then you will create thin strips of white to simulate light cracks in the far wall.

7. Using the Pen tool (P), begin drawing a path, setting the first anchor point on the left window in the center of the left edge of the black rectangle. Set the next anchor point on the right edge of the black rectangle, only a little higher than center. Set the next anchor below the midpoint on the same edge. Cross over the black rectangle to the left edge and set an anchor point so the bottom line's angle matches the top line. Click on the starting point to close the path.

8. Fill this new object with dark brown solid fill.

9. Drag a copy to the window on the right while pressing the ALT/OPTION key. Place the copy over the black rectangle higher in this window.

10. Press the SHIFT key and click on the black rectangle of the right window. Apply the Pathfinder|Soft command by pressing CTRL/COMMAND+4.

11. Do the same with the other window and wooden beam you just created and copied. Select the beam and the black rectangle in the window to the left. Apply the Pathfinder|Soft command by pressing CTRL/COMMAND+4. Deselect all objects (CTRL/COMMAND+SHIFT+A).

   Now you will add the white strips to the windows to create the illusion of light filtering through the back wall.

12. Click on the Swap Fill Stroke button on the main Toolbox to choose the Fill. Click on Color palette in the white of the CMYK spectrum.

13. Choose the Pen tool (P) and set an anchor point on the bottom edge of the black rectangle in the left window. Set the second anchor point straight up and on the edge of the beam. Set another anchor point back down on the bottom edge very close to the starting point. Close the object by clicking the last click on the starting point. You have created the first white strip to represent the light peeking through the far wall. Make several more on the bottom side of the beam and one or two white strips above the beam in this window. Create the same kind of effect in the window to the right.

   You have now completed the windows on the main floor of the barn. There are several more windows to create on the basement level of the barn.

14. Choose the Rectangle tool (M). You will need to toggle to the regular Rectangle tool instead of the Centered Rectangle tool. Create a small square to represent one of the small twin basement windows located between the two main floor windows and along the upper edge of the overhang shadow.

15. Click and drag while pressing the ALT/OPTION key a copy of the square you created to the left to leave just a small gap between the original and the copy.

16. Create another window with the Rectangle tool (M). Begin drawing another window below the main floor window to the left. Drag a rectangle the height of the overhang shadow and the width of the main floor window to the left.

17. Create another window on the basement wall to the left. Create a window a little larger than one of the twin windows on the front basement wall.

18. Fill all of these windows with 100 percent black solid fill. You have completed the windows of the barn. Now we will create the open doorway on the far right of the front basement wall.

19. Choose the Pen tool (P). Set your first anchor point at the top edge of the overhang shadow just under the main floor right window. Set the next anchor point just short of the right edge of the overhang shadow. Bring the line straight down and set the next anchor point at the bottom edge of the front basement wall. Set the next anchor point to the left and immediately under the starting point. Click the starting point to close the path.

20. Fill this new doorway with 100 percent black fill from the Color palette (F6).

21. Create the white strips over the top of the doorway, just as you did for the main floor windows, to simulate light peeking through the inside far wall of the barn. Don't make them very wide. The thinner they are, the better the illusion. Another way to make these white strips is to create various widths of white strokes and place them in position.

Now you are ready to create the barn boards, rock wall, and roof slats to finish the barn details. See the details in Figure 9-38. The barn boards are nothing more than thin lines created by setting one anchor point at the top of the wall and two at the bottom and then coloring them with black fill using the Color palette (F6).

We created the rock wall by drawing simple rounded objects with the Pencil tool and filling each with a brown radial gradient from the Gradient palette. Later, we selected each rock object as a group, copied and arranged them behind the original stone objects, and filled in with black to create a shadow.

We created the barn roof slats with a rectangle at each end of the roof and blended the two objects across to let Illustrator create the in-between objects. They were then ungrouped and filled with linear gradient fills on an approximate 38-degree angle.

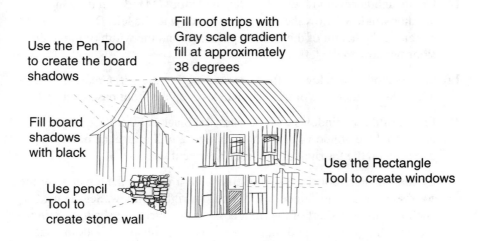

Use the Pen Tool to create the board shadows

Fill roof strips with Gray scale gradient fill at approximately 38 degrees

Fill board shadows with black

Use pencil Tool to create stone wall

Use the Rectangle Tool to create windows

FIGURE 9-38   Detailing the walls and roof of the barn

Preparing the Final Backdrop for the Barn Scene

You have already created the major elements of the barn scene. All that remains is to create more copies of the tree line. To accomplish this, you must open the Layers palette once more (F7). Click the Show/Hide button for the Layer 1. Click the Show/Hide button for Layer 2. You will come back to Layer 2 to complete the final composition. Your barn will vanish for the time being until you are ready to apply the finishing touches.

Create four levels of shades and sizes of treeline sections. To depict trees that are close to the barn, copy and resize a treeline and fill with a very dark green gradient. To depict trees that are farther away, fill them with a very light gradient and scale copies by reducing them to **75** or **60** percent of their current size. Place darker trees lower in your composition and light trees higher on the artboard and arranged behind the darker trees.

Although Figure 9-39 shows treeline segments with black outlines, select all treeline segments and remove the outline by clicking on the No Outline button in the main Toolbox.

Practice placement of the treeline objects until you feel comfortable with the arrangement. Make more copies of the treeline objects if you have open gaps. When

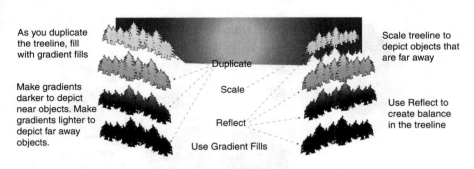

As you duplicate the treeline, fill with gradient fills

Make gradients darker to depict near objects. Make gradients lighter to depict far away objects.

Duplicate

Scale

Reflect

Use Gradient Fills

Scale treeline to depict objects that are far away

Use Reflect to create balance in the treeline

FIGURE 9-39 Completing the background scenery in preparation for the final composition

you are done with the treeline, click in the Layers palette on the Lock/Unlock button for Layer 1.

Checking Details of the Barn

Check out the details in Figure 9-40 and compare them with your composition. Click in the Layers palette on Layer 2's Show/Hide button to view the barn. If you need to make adjustments or add details you missed earlier, then apply those adjustments now.

You may need to select the whole barn and move it up or down or resize to fit your background scenery. Make appropriate adjustments through the Scale Command or through the Move command.

Completing the Barn Scene

Complete your barn scene by creating an object to represent a dark grass patch that also serves as a shadow on the left side of the barn. Fill it with a dark green linear gradient fill from the Gradient palette. See Figure 9-41 for final details of the barn scene and to gain a sense of the fence.

Create the fence posts using four vertical rectangular objects filled with brown linear gradient fills using the Gradient palette to represent tall cylinders. Make the boards for the fence using horizontal rectangles with solid dark brown fills. Create the cross boards for the fence using rectangles on an angle and an almost black solid fill from the Color palette.

9

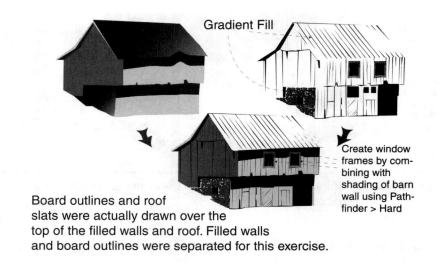

Gradient Fill

Create window frames by combining with shading of barn wall using Pathfinder > Hard

Board outlines and roof slats were actually drawn over the top of the filled walls and roof. Filled walls and board outlines were separated for this exercise.

FIGURE 9-40   The barn outline and details brought together

Creating a Clock Using Pathfinder and Transform Commands

In this tutorial, you will use Transform commands to create a clock through precision placement. You will use most of the Transform commands: Move, Scale, Rotate, Reflect, Shear, Transform Again. You will also use some of the Pathfinder commands to modify objects, such as Trim.

Creating the Basic Elements for the Clock Face

Most clock faces are round. Even if the face is unusually shaped, the hands still rotate in a circular motion from the center of the clock face. You will use the Rotate

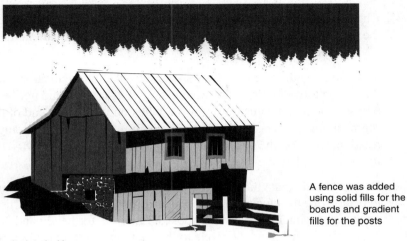

A fence was added using solid fills for the boards and gradient fills for the posts

Grass is depicted with a gradient fill and serves as the shadow for the barn

FIGURE 9-41 The completed barn scene

command to create many of the elements of the clock. In this first part of the tutorial, you will set the size and angles in preparation for creating the whole clock.

1. To help guide you in creating objects, first apply a grid to the artboard. Set up the grid by choosing File|Preferences|Guides & Grid. Set the frequency of gridlines option to one per inch, and subdivisions options to 8. Check the Grids in Back option. Choose OK to accept the changes. Choose View|Show Grid, and then choose View|Snap to Grid. This will help you create precisely measured objects.

2. Create a vertical line segment ¾ inch tall by choosing the Pen tool (P) from the main Toolbox. Click once at a grid line intersection. Count up 6 divisions and click a second time at the intersection.

9

3. Set the stroke weight to **0.1** point in the Stroke palette (F10).

4. Choose the Color palette (F6) and click on the Swap Fill/Stroke button on the main Toolbox to select Stroke. Click on the black square in the CMYK spectrum.

5. You will copy the line to create "spokes" for the hour indicator. Choose the Rotate tool (**R**). Press and hold the ALT/OPTION key and notice an ellipse now accompanies your cursor. Click on the bottom end of the line segment you created. In the Rotate dialog box enter **-30** for the angle of rotation. Click on the Copy button. Duplicate (CTRL/COMMAND+D) this 11 times to complete the spokes of the clock face.

6. Now you will create the outside circle where you will place the hour indicators for the clock. Choose the Centered Ellipse tool (**N**). Click once on the center intersection of the spokes. Enter **1.5** for height and **1.5** for width. Click OK. Send the circle to the back (CTRL/COMMAND+SHIFT+[).

7. You will create an inside circle where you will place the minute indicators for the clock. Choose the Scale tool (**S**). Hold the ALT/OPTION key and click on the center of the circle. Choose Uniform Scale and enter **85** for the percentage of reduction. Click on the Copy button.

8. Choose the Centered Ellipse tool (N). Click once at the top of the circle at 12 o'clock. In the Centered Ellipse dialog box, enter **0.17** in Width and the same **0.17** in Height. Click OK to accept the values.

9. Click on the Swap Fill/Stroke button in the main Toolbox to select fill. Click on the No Fill button on the main Toolbox. You did this to see objects below this set of circles.

10. Choose the Centered Ellipse tool (N) once again. Click on the 12 o'clock position again. Enter **.12** in Width and Height and click OK.

11. Click on the 12 o'clock position for the minute indicator circle. This is the inner circle. Enter **0.02** for both Width and Height. Check your work against Figure 9-42.

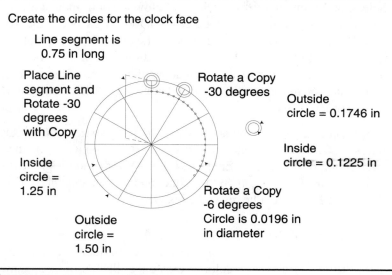

Create the circles for the clock face

Line segment is 0.75 in long

Place Line segment and Rotate -30 degrees with Copy

Rotate a Copy -30 degrees

Outside circle = 0.1746 in

Inside circle = 0.1225 in

Inside circle = 1.25 in

Rotate a Copy -6 degrees Circle is 0.0196 in in diameter

Outside circle = 1.50 in

FIGURE 9-42   Initial elements of the clock face

Completing the Clock Face

Now all your elements that make up the clock face are in place except for the hands which we will create later. Complete the clock face using Rotate with Copy.

1. Choose the Selection tool (V) and click on the small inside and outside circles you created at the 12 o'clock position. Open the Stroke palette (F10) and enter a value of **1** for the stroke thickness of the minute indicator. Press ENTER to apply the stroke weight. We will use this to select all the minute indicators later for applying the radial gradient.

2. Choose the Rotate tool from the main Toolbox. Press the ALT/OPTION key and click at the intersection of the spokes at the very center of the Clock Face. Enter **-30** in the Angle of rotation. Click on the Copy button. Duplicate this (CTRL/COMMAND+D) ten times to complete the hour face indicator placement.

3. Select the Minute indicator circle just below the hour indicator at the 12:00 o'clock position using the Selection tool (V). Choose the Rotate tool (R), press ALT/OPTION, and click on the clock face center at the spoke intersection. Enter **-6** in the Angle of Rotation option. Click on the Copy button. Create four copies and then delete the original. Select these four copies and rotate a copy -30 degrees. Duplicate (CTRL/COMMAND+D) this operation ten times.

4. Create another circle at the heart of the clock face where the spokes intersect. Choose the Centered Ellipse tool (N) again. Click on the intersection of the spokes. Enter **0.24** in the Width and Height text boxes and click OK. Click again on the spoke intersection and enter **.03** in the Width and Height text boxes and click OK.

You have completed the clock face with all the initial elements. You will add decorative objects to the clock later using the same technique with Rotate and Copy. Now you will fill the circles with color to create the illusion of three-dimensional objects. Check your progress with Figure 9-43.

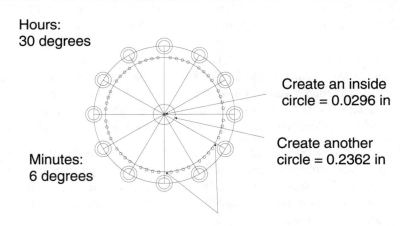

Hours:
30 degrees

Create an inside
circle = 0.0296 in

Create another
circle = 0.2362 in

Minutes:
6 degrees

Remove minute indicators
from the hour locations

FIGURE 9-43   Completing the clock dial

Adding Color Gradient Fills to the Clock Face

In these exercises, you will begin to bring depth to the face of the clock using a few tricks of color in application. You will create shadows for the hour "buttons" by using Move with Copy. Use the Zoom tool to zoom in on small objects to see what you are working on. Zoom in by 1200 or 1600 percent. This will let you see the details necessary to apply all the changes in the following exercises.

1. Select the center circle at the hour location for 12 o'clock using the Selection tool (V).

2. Open the Gradient palette (F9) and the Color palette (F6) so you may choose colors for the gradients.

3. Click on the left color stop on the gradient bar in the Gradient palette. In the CMYK Model text boxes enter the following values: cyan =**0**, magenta=**20**, yellow=**60**, and black=**0** percent. Click on the right color stop on the gradient bar. Enter cyan=**30**, magenta=**35**, yellow=**100**, and black=**15** percent. Make sure the linear gradient options is selected in the Color palette.

4. Apply this same gradient values to all the center circles on the hour locations. Select the inner circle at the 12 o'clock hour position. Click in the gradient display box to apply the gradient. Apply this gradient fill to all the other inner circles by clicking in the gradient box in the Gradient palette and dragging to each center circle in the hour positions.

5. Select the Outside circle at the hour location 12 o'clock. Click in the Color gradient box of the Gradient palette. This will apply the yellow gradient to the outside circle. Double-click the angle text box and enter **180**. Press ENTER to apply to the selected circle.

6. Click on the gradient box in the Gradient palette and drag the new gradient to each outside circle at each hour location.

   Now you will create the outside circle located at the hour positions by using the Selection tool. Clicking on each circle will create a shadow for each outside circle.

7. Select each while pressing and holding the SHIFT key.

8. Choose Object|Transform|Move. Enter a word Distance of **0.02** and a word Angle of **-165**. Click on the Copy button.

9

9. Send this new group of circles to the back (CTRL/COMMAND+SHIFT+[) and bring the group forward one step (CTRL/COMMAND+]).

10. Add a solid black fill by clicking on the black square in the CMYK spectrum of the Color palette.

   You filled all the hour buttons and created the shadow for each location. Now fill the minute indicators with a gradient fill. You created the minute indicators without a gradient fill so they could be filled with the same angle of radial gradient. When you rotate and copy, the gradient rotates as well.

11. Click on the outer circle of any hour indicator to add the fill to the Gradient palette (F9). Deselect the hour indicator (CTRL/COMMAND+SHIFT+A). Select the radial gradient option and click on a minute indicator. Select all the other minute indicators using Edit|Select|Same Stroke Weight. Click on the gradient box to apply the new gradient to all the minute indicators at once.

12. Remove the stroke from around all the minute indicators by clicking on Stroke from the Swap Fill/Stroke button. Click the No Color button (square with red slash) in the main Toolbox.

   Working your way toward the center of the dial, fill the two small circles in the center of the clock face in the spoke intersection with the following procedure. Deselect all objects (CTRL/COMMAND+SHIFT+A).

13. Click on the left color stop on the gradient scale in the gradient palette. Enter the following values in the CMYK model text boxes: cyan=**95**, magenta=**5**, yellow=**0**, and black=**0**. Click on the right color stop and set cyan=**95**, magenta=**90**, yellow=**35**, and black=**30** percent.

14. Select the larger of the two center circles. Click in the gradient display box to apply the gradient. Deselect all objects (CTRL/COMMAND+SHIFT+A).

15. Click on the left color stop on the gradient scale in the Gradient palette. In the Color palette, enter cyan=**0**, magenta=**80**, yellow=**80**, and black **0**. Click on the right color stop and enter cyan=**30**, magenta=**80**, yellow=**80**, and black=**25** percent.

16. Click and drag from the gradient box in the Gradient palette to the tiny center circle and apply the gradient as before.

   Now that you have added color to the details of the clock, create the hour numbers for the clock face.

17. Choose the Type tool (T) and choose Type|Font, and select a type face you want to use. We chose Century Schoolbook at **6** points.

18. Deselect Snap to Grid by View|Snap to Grid. Position the I-beam cursor near the 12 o'clock position. Be sure the I-beam is a dotted square rather than a dotted greater than/less than sign. Anything other than a dotted square will transform the circle into a guideline and the gradient fill will be lost. Enter **12**. Choose the Selection tool from the main Toolbox. Drag a copy by pressing and holding the ALT/OPTION key while dragging. Fill the original "12" with solid color by setting the color values cyan=**20**, magenta=**30**, yellow=**95**, black=**30**. Select the copy "12" and fill with solid black.

19. Arrange the copy over the original to create a shadow effect similar to the angle of the hour indicator shadows.

20. Select both 12s and place them over the 12 o'clock position.

21. Continue in the same way to create and place the rest of the hour numbers in the hour locations. Check your work against Figure 9-44.

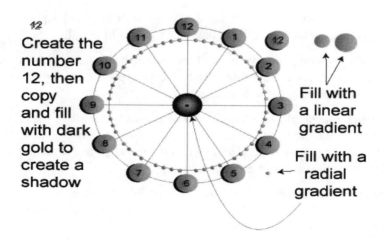

FIGURE 9-44   Adding fill and numbers to the clock face

Create Clock Hands and Decorative Shapes to Add to the Clock Face

Shapes for the clock minute hand and hour hand are a matter of preference. We chose to create a stylized arrow pointer with curved sections in the arrowhead while the other lines are straight. Choose a shape and draw, whether from this illustration or some other, to form the minute hand.

We will first walk you through creating the decorative trim for the clock. The shape is not important. We created a decorative object with several anchor points that matched right and left to give a symmetrical look. We converted the anchor points into corners using the Convert Direction Point tool on the Pen tool flyout menu. Then we pulled the direction lines to create symmetrical curves left and right using the Direct Selection tool to edit the anchor points.

Create a decorative object on your own, making it **0.60** inches in length. Place it in the 12 o'clock position.

1. Activate the Snap to Grid option by choosing View|Snap to Grid. Select the decorative object you created. Choose the Rotate tool (R). Press the ALT/OPTION key and click on the spoke intersection. Enter **-30** and click the Copy button.

2. Duplicate the object (CTRL/COMMAND+D) for each hour.
   Now that you have added decorations to the clock you are ready to create the minute and hour hands.

3. When you draw the minute hand, create it as if the hand is pointing to 12 o'clock. Make the minute hand **0.85** inches in length.

4. When you complete the shape of the minute hand, fill it with the same gradient values as the center circle, except apply a linear gradient and change the angle to **90** degrees.

5. Create a rectangle **1** inch high by **0.25** inches wide. Move the rectangle over the minute hand you created. Line up the rectangle so that the left half of the minute hand is visible and the left edge of the rectangle is in line with the center of the minute hand.

6. Select both the minute hand and the rectangle. Choose Object|Pathfinder|Trim. Ungroup (CTRL/COMMAND+SHIFT+G) the selection and delete the rectangle.

7. Select the left portion of the minute hand that remains with the Selection tool on the main Toolbox and Reflect with Copy. Choose the Reflect tool (**O**) and press the ALT/OPTION key and click on the right edge and in the center of the minute hand. Choose Vertical and click on the Copy button.

8. Change the gradient fill of the reflected copy by switching the color stops below the gradient scale from left to right and right to left.

9. Add color to the path of the minute hand by selecting both sides of the minute hand and select Stroke from the Swap Fill/Stroke button. Click on the gold section between red and yellow in the CMYK spectrum. Group (CTRL/COMMAND+G) the two halves of the minute hand. Using the Stroke palette, set the stroke width to **.25**.

10. Make a copy of the minute hand by pressing the ALT/OPTION key while dragging the minute hand to a new location using the Selection tool.

11. Choose the Direct Selection tool (A). Draw a marquee selection box around the anchor points at the bottom of the minute hand. Press the ARROW UP key several times to shorten the minute hand and transform it into the hour hand.

12. Select the tiny circle in the center of the spoke intersection and bring it to the front (CTRL/COMMAND+SHIFT+]).

13. Move the minute and hour hands into place by selecting both with the Selection tool (V) and dragging them to the 12 o'clock position. Deselect all objects (CTRL/COMMAND+SHIFT+A) and then select the minute hand. Click on the Rotate tool (R), press the ALT/OPTION key, and click on the intersection of the spokes. Enter **-30** and click OK. Select the hour hand and then the Rotate tool. Press the ALT/OPTION key and click on the spoke intersection again. Enter **-123** and click OK.

Check your work against Figure 9-45. Your clock and the clock face in the figure should look very similar.

Adding Fill and Final Decorations to the Clock Face

To finish the clock face, add another outside circle and fill this and other circles using solid fills.

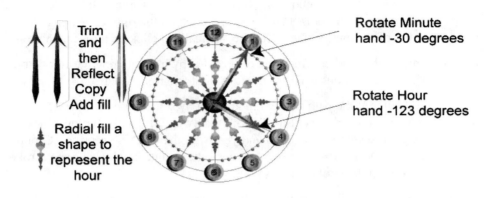

■ FIGURE 9-45   Creating the clock hands and decorative shapes

14. Select the circle that the hour buttons are resting on with the Selection tool. Choose the Scale tool from the main Toolbox. Press ALT/OPTION and click on the spoke intersection. Enter **115** percent and click on the Copy button. Send this circle to the back (CTRL/COMMAND+SHIFT+[).

15. Fill this circle with a solid olive color from the CMYK spectrum in the Color Palette (F6).

16. Select the next circle in, on which the hour buttons rest. Fill this circle with the same fill values for the red button in the center using a radial gradient. Adjust the diamond above the gradient bar to make the gradient visible in the circle.

17. Select the next circle in, on which the minute indicator circles rest. Fill this circle with solid black fill.

We created one more decoration to add to the clock. We created an ellipse and filled it with the same radial gradient fill as the tiny circle at the spoke intersection. We placed it between the other decorative shapes and Rotate/Copied -30. Check your results with Figure 9-46.

Radial fill
ellipse and
Rotate Copy
-30 degrees

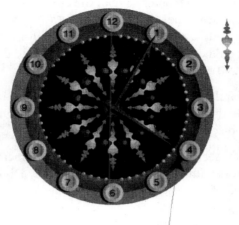

Rotate Copy
stylized hour
indicator -30
degrees.

Fill Clock
face with solid
green, red
gradient and
solid black

Create a shadow for the hour indicators by
selecting outside circles and Copy while
Moving. Add black fill and arrange
behind hour indicators.

FIGURE 9-46   Completing the clock face with solid and gradient fills

Creating a Shadow and Gold Trim

Creating a shadow is straightforward. Click on the outer circle of the clock face.
Choose the Shear tool (W). Press the ALT/OPTION key and click at the bottom edge
of the clock face. Enter **-30** and click on the Copy button. Send it to the back
(CTRL/COMMAND+SHIFT+[). Fill the new circle with a radial black and gray gradient
fill and the shadow is created. The center is black fading to gray on the outside edges.

Now let's create the gold rim around the clock. We will use the Pathfinder divide
command for this.

1. Select the outside edge of the clock face using the Selection tool. Press
   ALT/OPTION while dragging a copy to another empty spot on the artboard.
   Create another copy the same way except overlap the two copies with the
   back copy showing a thin portion of its left edge. You will use
   Pathfinder|Divide on these two circles to create an outer edge left and
   right from the overlap.

2. Select both copies of the outer edge of the clock face using the Selection tool. Choose the Scale tool (S). Press the ALT/OPTION key and click in the center point of both selected circles. Choose Uniform Scale and enter **107** percent. Click on the Copy button. Send this copy to the back (CTRL/COMMAND+SHIFT+[).

3. Select all the circle copies you have been working on using the Selection tool (V). Apply the Divide command by Object|Pathfinder|Divide. Ungroup the objects (CTRL/COMMAND+SHIFT+G).

4. Select the center section and delete it. Add a gold linear gradient alternating colors with adjacent objects created by Divide. See Figure 9-47 for an idea of how the gradient will look.

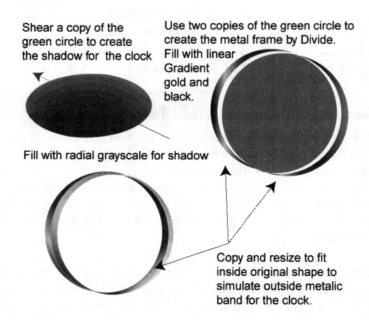

Shear a copy of the green circle to create the shadow for the clock

Use two copies of the green circle to create the metal frame by Divide. Fill with linear Gradient gold and black.

Fill with radial grayscale for shadow

Copy and resize to fit inside original shape to simulate outside metalic band for the clock.

FIGURE 9-47 Create a shadow and gold rim for the clock

5. Group the objects (CTRL/COMMAND+G) and send them to the back (CTRL/COMMAND+SHIFT+[).

6. Drag the group to the clock face and place it behind the green outer circle. Arrange the group forward one level (CTRL/COMMAND+]). The shadow will drop behind this new group of objects. Check your final work against Figure 9-48.

Conclusion

As you continue learning more of the uses of the Transform commands, their powers for illustration will be apparent. Pathfinder commands are an invaluable asset to Illustrator 7. Your familiarity with these tools will give you the ability to draw anything. Your imagination is the only limit to what you may create through these tools and commands.

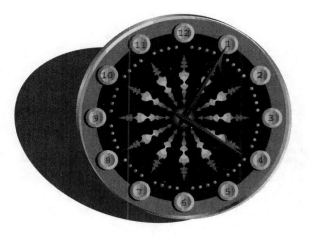

FIGURE 9-48   All the elements of the clock in place

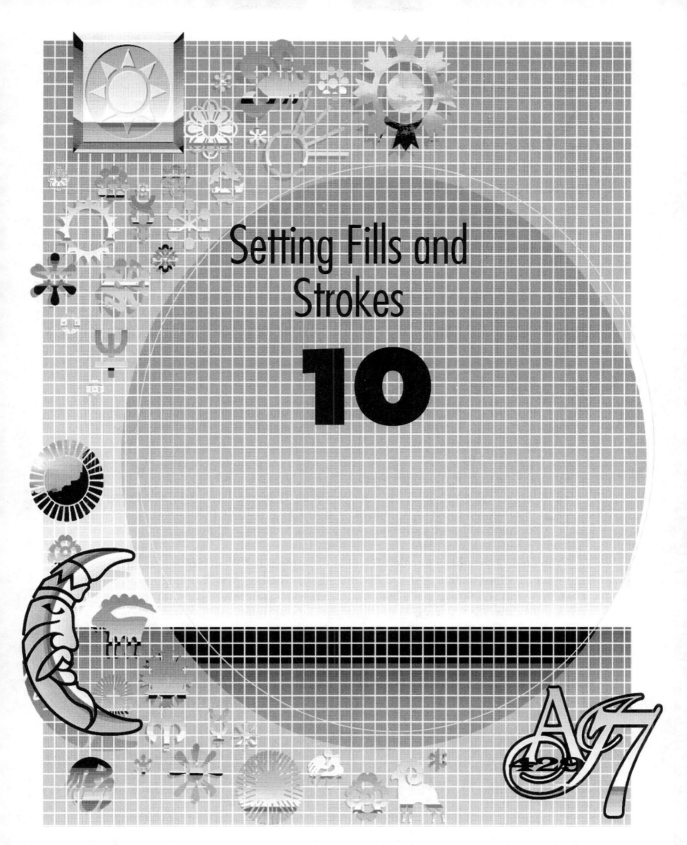

Setting Fills and
Strokes

10

Selecting fill and stroke properties and assigning them to your objects breathes existence into them where before there was none. Objects which haven't been assigned either a fill or stroke property are all but nonexistent. In other words, besides the fact that they are freeloading in your Illustrator 7 document, without a fill and stroke property assigned to them, they're simply not visible.

When you launch Illustrator 7 for the first time, its defaults give your objects a white fill and a black stroke. Although this may be fine for drawing the simplest of graphic objects, what most users will eventually progress to using is rich, glorious color.

In this chapter, you'll explore how to add color to the objects that you create, how to store those colors for future use, how to create color gradients, and how to set options for the width, shape, and style of strokes.

Setting Fill and Stroke Modes

To Illustrator, all objects are made up of two basic parts: a fill and an outline (which in Illustrator is called a *stroke*). An object's fill is the area defined by the inside shape created by an open or closed path, while the stroke could be considered the path itself. These two object parts may be colored and controlled independent of each other while still defining a single object.

Users of previous versions of Illustrator will likely notice the absence of a Paint Style palette. For these users, the implementation of keyboard shortcuts for selecting fill, stroke, color, and none tools will no doubt take some getting used to, but in the end will greatly improve their efficiency in working with these tools.

You control the characteristic fill and stroke properties of each object through the main Toolbox palette. At the bottom of the Toolbox you'll notice an area containing Fill and Stroke mode buttons. Each mode button sets Illustrator 7's color controls to either the Fill mode or the Stroke mode; you simply click one or the other button to make it active. Here you can see how these buttons overlap:

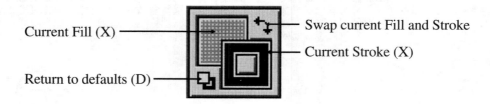

Current Fill (X) ——— ——— Swap current Fill and Stroke

——— Current Stroke (X)

Return to defaults (D) ———

The currently selected mode is the one that appears to be in the foreground of these two buttons. Typing **X** toggles the mode between the two.

While in Stroke mode, all color changes made to an object will affect the stroke of currently selected object. Similarly, while in Fill mode, all color changes made to an object will affect the fill of your currently selected object. Changes to fills and strokes must be made separately.

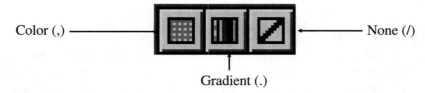

Note

Object color assignments are normally applied independently for fill and stroke colors unless you're using specialized tools such as the Paintbucket tool (which is discussed later in this chapter).

To swap the active fill color with the active stroke color, click on the Swap Fill and Stroke symbol to the upper-right of the Fill and Stroke buttons in the main Toolbox. If an object is selected, clicking the Swap Fill and Stroke arrow will swap the object's fill color with its stroke color. A gradient fill will prevent the Swap Fill and Stroke arrow from doing anything. If the fill is a pattern, clicking the Swap Fill and Stroke symbol will swap the properties, but objects will be assigned a gray stroke rather than the selected pattern.

To return Illustrator 7 to the default fill and stroke colors—a white fill color with a black stroke color—click on the black-and-white symbol to the lower-left of the Fill and Stroke buttons in the main Toolbox or type **D** on your keyboard.

Just below the Fill and Stroke buttons on the main Toolbox are three more buttons: Color, Gradient, and None, as shown here:

Color (,) ──────────────   ──────────── None (/)

Gradient (.)

Clicking on the Color button or typing **,** (a comma) will open the Color palette. Clicking on the Gradient button or typing **.** (period key) will open the Gradient palette. Clicking on the None button or typing **/** will assign a fill or stroke of None to your object, depending on whether you are currently in Fill or Stroke mode. In other words, if Stroke mode is currently active, clicking the None button will remove your object's stroke, setting its color to None. If the Fill mode is active, clicking the None button will remove your object's fill color, making it transparent.

Tip   *When Illustrator 7 was first released, its Quick Reference Card and documentation specified that shortcuts to the Color and Gradient buttons on
the main Toolbar were quickly accessed by pressing the < and > keys
respectively. This is incorrect, due to the fact that to access these keystrokes
you need to hold the SHIFT key. Instead, as shown here, use the , (comma)
and . (period) keys to quickly access these buttons.*

Working with Swatches

For a moment, imagine yourself using traditional artist tools such as a classic
painters' palette. You're holding in your hand a piece of wood with small amounts
of paint in basic primary colors. In the center of this wooden palette is an empty
space used for mixing paint colors together in order to create secondary and tertiary
colors. And if you're an experienced painter, you may even have a few premixed
colors at hand. To achieve certain special hues and tints of colors you may have a
list of mixing portions to follow in order to remember how your favorite colors are
created. Illustrator 7 works in a similar way.

All the colors you can assign to an object in Illustrator 7 are controlled from
three palettes: the Swatches, Color, and Gradients palettes. The Color and the
Gradients palettes can be thought of as the space where you mix your colors together.
The Swatches palette works just like your own digital paint supply—the key
difference being that Illustrator 7 enables you to paint with not just solid colors, but
also with mixtures and gradients of color, as well as color patterns.

Using the Swatches Palette

When you open Illustrator 7 for the first time, you're presented with 60 colors found
in the Swatches palette. There are three general types of color that may be stored
on the Swatches palette: uniform colors, gradients, and patterns. Illustrator 7's
default Swatches palette features 12 process colors, 12 spot colors, 12 gradients,
and 24 patterns.

Here you see an overview of the features and options contained in the Swatches
palette in Swatch view:

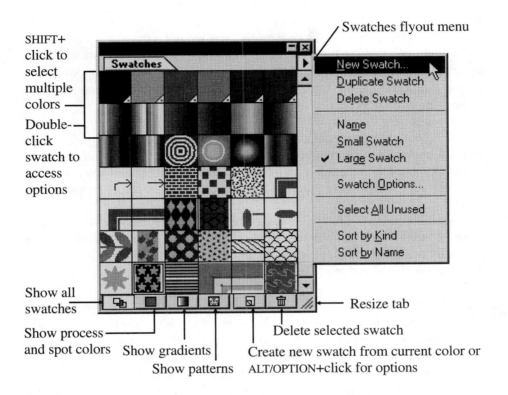

SHIFT+ click to select multiple colors

Double-click swatch to access options

Swatches flyout menu

Show all swatches

Show process and spot colors

Show gradients

Show patterns

Resize tab

Delete selected swatch

Create new swatch from current color or ALT/OPTION+click for options

Note *Although the 60 Swatches palette colors are defaults, you may add or remove colors in this collection by editing your Illustrator Startup (Macintosh) or Startup.ai (Windows) file. For information on creating a custom startup file turn to the section on "Creating a Custom Startup File" in **Chapter 2: Managing Illustrator 7 Files**.*

To change an object's colors, select the object and click on a swatch. If the Stroke mode is active, clicking on a swatch will paint the object's stroke with the color of the swatch. Conversely, if the Fill mode is active, clicking on a swatch will paint the object's fill with the color of the swatch.

You may also paint an object by dragging a swatch from the Swatches palette onto the object, regardless of whether the object is selected. Again, if the Stroke mode is active, the drag will affect the object's stroke, and if the Fill mode is active, the drag will affect the object's fill. But, if you hold down your SHIFT key when dragging, the inverse holds true. If the Stroke mode is active, pressing SHIFT and dragging will affect the object's fill, and if the Fill mode is active, pressing SHIFT and dragging will affect the object's stroke.

In the upper-right corner of the Swatches palette is a small triangle; clicking it reveals a flyout menu that enables you to select view options for the palette. You will learn about these shortly, but for now select the Name option to view the Swatches by name. Notice each item listed includes a small preview icon to the left of the name seen in the center. Additional icons indicate if the colors are patterns or gradients and whether the swatch is based on a spot or process color.

Along the bottom of the Swatches palette are six more buttons. The first four buttons set which type of swatches are displayed in the palette. The first button displays all available colors, followed by buttons for displaying process and spot colors, gradients, and patterns.

Tip   *Don't be alarmed when switching views if the palette unexpectedly changes from Name to Swatch view or vice versa. The reason for this is that when switching between color, gradient, and pattern options, the palette remembers and displays the last selected view for each category of color, such as viewing options for Name, Small Swatch, or Large Swatch. When selecting the all available option, the palette will display with the selected view assigned to the previous option.*

Following these first four buttons, the next two buttons on the bottom enable you to create new or deleting existing swatch colors. When you click on the new Swatch button, it adds a new swatch color to the Swatches palette based on the currently selected color (or gradient) in the Toolbox and/or in your document. Pressing ALT/OPTION while clicking on this button will display a dialog box that asks you to name the swatch, and in the case of colors, to determine whether the color is a spot or process color. Clicking on the Delete Swatch button permanently deletes the currently selected swatch color from the palette. You may also delete several swatch colors by holding the SHIFT key to select them before pressing the Delete button.

Note   *Use care when deleting swatches, for there is no warning dialog box to help prevent you from accidentally deleting them. However, you may Undo (CTRL/COMMAND+Z) a deletion.*

Resizable Swatches Palette

The Swatches palette may be resized to show more and fewer swatches by dragging on the resize handle in the lower-right corner of the Swatches palette. You can stretch the Swatches palette as large as you wish.

In Name view, stretching the palette horizontally will just increase the line length (and white space) of each swatch. In Small Swatch or Large Swatch mode, stretching the palette horizontally will cause the display of swatches to fill up the available space starting from the upper left. But even if you get the Swatches palette stretched out so far that all of the icons are on one row, the palette still has a minimum height of four names, four rows of small icons, or two rows of large icons, depending on the palette's view mode.

If you have more swatches in your palette than the current size of your palette will show, scroll bars will appear on the right side of the palette enabling you to move up and down to find the swatch you desire.

Types of Swatches

There are two kinds color swatches: process colors and spot colors. A *process color* is any color that can be separated during printing into percentage values of cyan, magenta, yellow, and black—the four inks that are used in four-color process printing. A *spot color* is any ink that requires, at printing, separation onto its own color plate. Spot colors may include special inks by PANTONE and TOYO, as well as all metallic and fluorescent inks. In Illustrator you may define any color, spot, or process by using one of four color models: RGB, HSB, CYMK, or Grayscale.

When viewing the Swatches palette in Name view, you will see from left to right: swatch samples representing the color, the color's name, an icon representing the color's model, and an icon representing whether the color is spot or process. Colors defined by the RGB and HSB models will have an icon with three stripes, one each of red, green, and blue. CMYK colors will have an icon with four triangles, one each of cyan, magenta, yellow, and black. Grayscale colors will have an icon filled with

10

a gradient from black to white. The far-right icons will be a gray square for process colors and a square with a gray circle inside for spot colors.

The Small Swatch and Large Swatch views do away with the name and color model icon. All you see are squares filled with the color, and in the cases of spot colors, a small white triangle in the lower-right corner.

 *Both spot and process colors will be printed normally to a composite color printer. The distinction between spot and process becomes important when preparing a file that will be used for creating film on an imagesetter or plates on a platesetter. See **Chapter 17: Printing from Illustrator.***

Gradients are smooth color transitions between colors. They can be a simple movement from one color to another, such as the Black, White gradient that comes preset in Illustrator. Or they can be a complex movement through multiple colors, such as the Rainbow gradient preset. There are two type of gradients: linear and radial. A *linear* gradient transitions from left to right, whereas a *radial* gradient expands outward in a circular fashion. No differentiation is made on the Swatches palette between linear and radial gradients; however, the difference should be obvious from the Preview icons.

 Gradients may not be applied to the stroke of a path.

Patterns are shapes that are designed to repeat over and over, sometimes inside a path, such as the Bricks preset, sometimes as a path pattern along a path. Although certain patterns were designed for one purpose or the other, in practice both kinds can be used interchangeably. The Swatches palette makes no differentiation between path and fill patterns, because both are interchangeable, but the names of path patterns usually end with ".side", ".outer", or ".inner".

 Patterns may be applied to an object's fill just like any color or gradient. However, patterns may only be applied to an object's stroke using the Filter\Stylize\Path Pattern filter.

Displaying Swatches

As you have seen previously, you can view the Swatches palette in one of three modes: Name, Small Swatch, and Large Swatch. These modes can be changed by selecting the mode from the options menu and, as noted, will sometimes change when you click on one of the view option buttons at the bottom of the palette.

In Name view, as seen in the illustration below, from left to right, you'll notice a color box previewing the color, the color's name, and symbols representing the color's model and type.

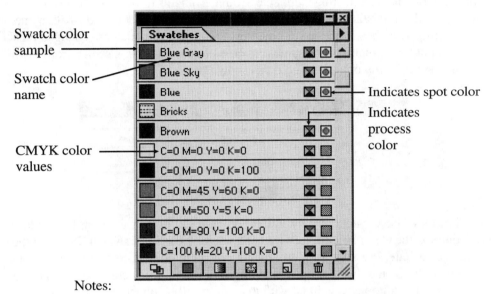

Swatch color sample

Swatch color name

CMYK color values

Indicates spot color

Indicates process color

Notes:
    ALT/OPTION+click swatch color to select current gradient-stop if gradient is selected, CTRL/COMMAND+ALT/OPTION+click in list then press letter keys to select swatch by name

Both the Small Swatch and Large Swatch view show only color box previews of colors (and a white triangle for spot colors). Small Swatch shows a Preview icon that is 15 pixels high. The Large Swatch icon is 31 pixels high.

 When trying to see certain detailed patterns and gradients, the Large Swatch is the most helpful view.

Adding and Deleting Swatches

Adding a swatch color is as straightforward as clicking on the New Swatch button at the bottom of the Swatches palette. Clicking this button creates a new swatch

based on the currently selected color (or gradient) in the main Toolbox. Holding
ALT/OPTION while clicking on the New Swatch button will automatically display the
Swatch Options dialog box, enabling you to assign a name to your new swatch color.
In certain cases, you may also specify whether you wish the new color to be a spot
or process color.

The same dialog box appears when you select New Swatch from the Swatches
palette flyout menu. Selecting Duplicate Swatch from this flyout will create an exact
duplicate of an existing swatch, adding the word "copy" to the end of its name.
Duplicating swatches is useful for creating new swatches which are changed only
slightly, but retain many of the same properties as the original. Use the drop-down
menu to specify spot or process color, as shown here.

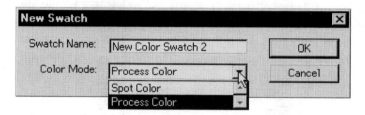

You may also create a new swatch by dragging a color or gradient from either
the toolbox, the Color palette, the Gradient palette, or another swatch library to the
Swatches palette. Pressing ALT/OPTION and dragging the new color will replace an
existing color on the Swatches palette with the new one. If the color being replaced
is a spot color, all objects painted with that color will be updated to the new color.
If the color being replaced is a process color, only the currently selected objects will
be updated.

Note   *Be aware that replacing a swatch will globally change the artwork in your
current document, changing the color of every object that was originally
painted with that swatch color.*

Dragging an object to the Swatches palette will create a new pattern swatch based
upon the shape of the object. This is the same as choosing Edit|Pattern.

Clicking on the Delete Swatch Color button deletes any currently selected
swatches. The same result occurs from selecting the Delete Swatch command from
the Swatches palette flyout menu. Press SHIFT and click on additional swatch colors
to delete multiples. You may also reduce the number of colors in your Swatches
palette *en masse* by selecting Select All Unused from the Swatches palette flyout

menu and clicking the Delete Swatch Color button (or by choosing Delete Swatch from the flyout menu). Choosing the Select All Unused command from the flyout menu selects all of the swatches in the Swatches palette that are not currently being used in your Illustrator 7 document. Deleting unused swatches from your document may significantly reduce your document's file size.

 It's best to delete unused swatches once you are relatively certain your work in the file is complete and you won't require access to the remaining unused swatches you are preparing to eliminate. Deleting them using the Delete button or the Delete Swatch command deletes the selected swatches forever.

Working with Swatch Options

The Swatch Options dialog can be accessed by double-clicking on a swatch or by selecting Swatch Options from the Swatches palette flyout menu, shown below. The Swatch Options dialog box enables you to rename a swatch for the purposes of reorganizing or editing colors. This feature also enables you to convert a spot color to process and vice versa. The dialog box generated by choosing this command is the same as that for creating a new Swatches palette color.

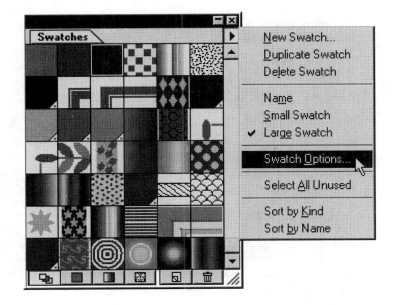

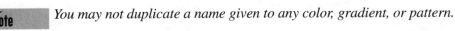 *You may not duplicate a name given to any color, gradient, or pattern.*

Sorting Swatches

You may sort the Swatches palette in one of two methods. The default method, Sort by Kind, groups all process colors, then all spot colors, then gradients, then patterns. It alphabetizes the swatches within each group.

By choosing Sort by Name from the Swatches palette flyout menu, you may switch the ordering so that all swatches are alphabetized, regardless of what each swatch is. The ability to sort through swatches is useful when locating certain swatches in very large swatch collections or when attempting to create a new collection of swatches based on an existing swatch.

Swatch Libraries

As you work with your drawings, you'll begin to choose certain colors more often, and eventually you'll end up with a selection of professional or personal preferences. Plus, if you work in engineering, illustration, or design fields, you may have a selected group of colors you need to access only for certain types of work. This is where Illustrator 7's library feature proves useful. Using the Libraries feature you may access existing swatch libraries as shown here, or create new libraries of swatch colors for importing into your new documents depending on your current color needs:

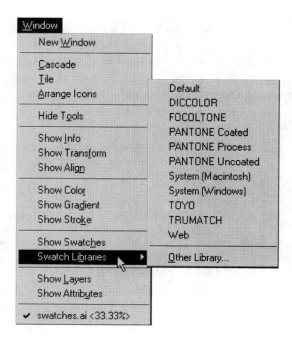

Although the new colors, gradients, or patterns that you create and store in the Swatches palette are available only to the document they were created in, you may use the Library feature to transfer swatches between documents. You may also save frequently used colors by placing them in the Swatches palette of your Adobe Illustrator Startup (Macintosh) or Startup.ai (Windows) file. For more information on adding Swatch colors to your Illustrator 7 Startup file, see "Customizing your Startup File" in **Chapter 15: Getting the Most Out of Illustrator**.

You may also use the Swatch Libraries command (Window|Swatch Libraries) to import colors, gradients, or patterns from another document or color library. Illustrator ships with a number of color libraries. These include spot and process colors for printing, such as the PANTONE Process Color System, the "Netscape-safe" World Wide Web palette, and the system palettes for both Windows and Macintosh.

Using Swatch Libraries

To open a new swatch library, select Swatch Libraries from the Window menu and select the library that you wish to open. You may open the new swatch library as a secondary Swatches palette or you can add individual colors to the main Swatches palette of your current document. To add colors to the Swatches palette, select the color swatch you wish to add and drag them from the new swatch library to the Swatches palette, or choose Add to Swatches from the Swatch Libraries flyout menu.

To see how this works, create a new document and open the PANTONE Coated Library (Window|Swatch Libraries|PANTONE Coated). Drag PANTONE 104 CVC (a yellowish hue) from the PANTONE Coated palette to the Swatches palette. Draw a rectangle and fill it with PANTONE 104 CVC.

To replace one color with another, follow these steps:

1. Hold ALT/OPTION while dragging the new color from a swatch library onto an existing color in the Swatches palette.

2. Replace the PANTONE 104 CVC you just created with PANTONE 274 CVC (a bluish hue).

3. Hold ALT/OPTION and drag the PANTONE 274 CVC from the PANTONE Coated Library onto the PANTONE 104 CVC in your Swatches palette. This changes the color of the PANTONE 104 CVC swatch from yellow to blue. Notice that the rectangle has also changed colors from yellow to blue, but the name of the swatch is still PANTONE 104 CVC.

4. Double-click the swatch or select Swatch Options from the Swatches palette flyout menu and change the name to PANTONE 274 CVC.

Note *Although ALT/OPTION dragging will replace a color, it will not replace the name of that color.*

Colors in a swatch library are not editable. However, swatch libraries may be edited after they are added to the main Swatches palette of your current document.

Note *If you drag the same color twice to the Swatches palette Illustrator will append the word "copy" to the end of the duplicate color's name.*

If you have created a custom Adobe Illustrator Startup (Macintosh) or Startup.ai (Windows) file from which you've deleted Illustrator 7's default swatches, you can restore those colors by choosing the Default Library. For more information on customizing your Startup file, refer to the section "Customizing Your Startup File" in **Chapter 15: Getting the Most Out of Illustrator 7**.

Importing Swatches from Other Documents

You can import color swatches from any other Illustrator 7 document. Importing swatches from another file is similar to importing swatches from a library. To import a color swatch into your current document, choose Window|Show Libraries|Other Library. A dialog box will appear allowing you to choose the document that you wish to import the colors from, as shown here:

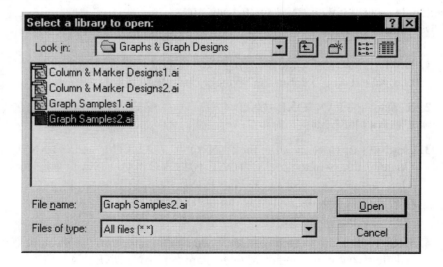

When you import swatches from another file, a new palette will appear, as shown here:

Indicates name of original Illustrator 7 document

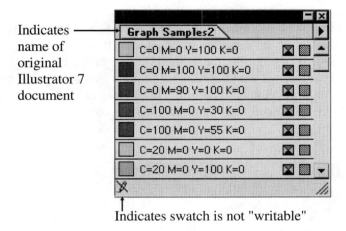

Indicates swatch is not "writable"

The Palette tab will contain the name of the file that you imported the colors from, and will display just like any other color library. You may add colors from this "library" to your Swatches palette the same way you would add a color from another library.

 Each time you import an additional new swatch from another document using the Other Library command, Illustrator 7 groups the swatches into the newly opened Swatch palette.

Problems with Duplicate Colors

Because you have the ability to name and create your own colors in Illustrator 7, you also are faced with the possibility that you may at some point name two colors with identical names. Because Illustrator 7 cares little about the names of colors the names you assign to colors are not for the benefit of the software but for your own benefit—you have to keep track of your color names and remember that duplicating them could cause problems during printing.

Ending up with two different colors with identical names can be done accidentally or by way of importing colors from other documents. If the other document has a color with the same name as a color currently in your Swatches palette, Illustrator posts no warnings; it simply adds the color. So, you could end up with two very different colors named Blue, for example. When Illustrator 7's print command encounters an object that has been assigned a certain named color, it places that name on the actual film separation during the printing process. If two colors have the same name, it can—and likely will—cause some confusion during subsequent processes.

When adding a duplicate color from a standard library, Illustrator will append the word "copy" to the end of the duplicate color's name. If you try to rename a swatch with a name already in use using the Swatch Options dialog box, Illustrator 7 will warn you to choose another name. It does not provide either safeguard when adding a duplicate name from another document. Having two or more colors with the same name in your documents can cause unwelcome color shifts or excess separations when printing.

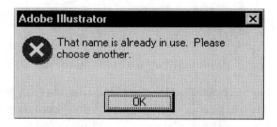

 Take care when adding colors from other documents; you could end up with duplicate names in your Swatches palette, thus causing problems when printing.

The Merge Spot Colors filter is designed to correct duplicate color problems in Illustrator 7. Its purpose is to search for multiple occurrences of spot colors with the same name and/or same color values and merge them together into a single color.

To see how the Merge Spot Colors filter works, follow this example:

1. Create two rectangles and fill them with a spot color and a tint of that spot color. For this exercise, choose Aqua.

2. Using Swatch Options, change Aqua to a CMYK process color.

3. Fill another new object with the altered process swatch color. Although this new object appears similar, during the printing process it will reproduce in standard process colors; the original objects are still spot color.

4. Next, change Aqua back to a spot color. Color another object with the spot Aqua. The last object is also colored Aqua, but will separate on a different plate, even though there is only one color called Aqua.

5. To confirm this, open the Separation Setup dialog box (File|Separation Setup). Turn off Convert to Process Colors. Notice now that two colors are named Aqua—both with the same composition—but they will now print on separate plates. The Merge Spot Colors filter will merge the two Aquas into one color.

 The Merge Spot Colors command only works on spot colors that were inadvertently created; it will not merge duplicates on the Swatches palette.

For more information on printing in process color, see "Printing Color Separations" in **Chapter 17: Printing from Illustrator 7**.

Working with Uniform Fill Colors

As mentioned previously, there are two kinds of color swatches: process colors and spot colors. Colors are mixed in the Color palette. Specifying whether they are spot or process color is done using the Swatch Options dialog box.

You may also paint an object by dragging a color from the color fill box in the Color palette onto the object, regardless of whether the object is selected. You can also select the object, then click on a color in the color spectrum ramp. You do not need to add the color to the Swatches palette first. By default, a color dragged from the Color palette is automatically defined as a process color. The action of dragging colors from the Color palette works the same as dragging from the Swatches palette.

In Stroke mode, dragging the color to your object will change its Stroke color, and while in Fill mode the dragging operation will affect its fill. Holding the SHIFT key while dragging causes the reverse to occur. In other words, if Stroke mode is active, pressing SHIFT while dragging a new color will change the object's fill, and if Fill mode is active, pressing SHIFT and dragging a new color will change the object's stroke to the new color.

Using the Color Palette

The Color palette can be viewed minimized or fully or partially expanded. These views are selected by selecting Hide/Show Options from the Color palette flyout menu, or by double-clicking on the Color palette tab. The Color palette features some useful options and shortcuts for assigning color to the fills and strokes your objects, as shown next.

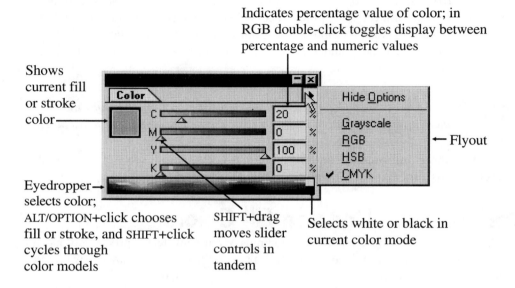

Indicates percentage value of color; in RGB double-click toggles display between percentage and numeric values

Shows current fill or stroke color

Hide Options

Grayscale
RGB
HSB
✓ CMYK

← Flyout

Eyedropper selects color; ALT/OPTION+click chooses fill or stroke, and SHIFT+click cycles through color models

SHIFT+drag moves slider controls in tandem

Selects white or black in current color mode

With the Color palette fully extended, four options are visible: a color sample showing the currently selected color, three or four color sliders, numeric or percentage value boxes, and a color spectrum ramp. With a partially extended Color palette, only the color spectrum ramp is visible, enabling you to sample and apply colors to objects. The available color options and controls change slightly depending on which color model you have selected and whether the Color palette is expanded or minimized.

While viewing spot color or while in Grayscale mode, a single slider exists; Grayscale mode will display the letter K to the left of the slider representing a black value. While viewing a spot color, simply the color's name is shown below the slider. In CMYK mode, four sliders exist, each controlling values for cyan, magenta, yellow, and black inks. In RGB or HSB modes, there will be three sliders corresponding to the color channels for those models.

The slider and numeric or percentage value boxes mimic one another. To set specific values of colors or adjust the currently selected colors, you may use the slider controls or enter exact values. In other words, you have the choice of using whichever method suits the task at hand.

Each slider is composed of a mini color spectrum ramp, enabling you to quickly choose and identify a color. As a practical way of experiencing how this feature operates, follow these steps:

1. Create a new rectangle object.

2. Fill it with a process color. For the sake of this example, set the color values to C=0 M=45 Y=60 K=0.

3. Observe the position changes on the color spectrum ramp on the magenta slider. Notice that if you manually move this slider to the left (toward 0 percent) that the orange begins to turn yellow. The reverse occurs if you move the slider to the right towards 100 percent—the orange will become more red. Notice also that the color possibilities in each slider change dynamically as you move any of the other sliders.

The color spectrum ramp enables you to quickly create colors and tints by picking up a color from a tint gradient (spot color and Grayscale modes) or a spectrum of colors (RGB, HSB, and CMYK). To use the color spectrum, move the cursor over the desired hue or tint and watch it change to an Eyedropper tool. Click in the color spectrum ramp and choose a random color. Notice the preview icon fills with the color you chose.

The modes Grayscale, RGB, HSB, and CMYK may be selected from the Color palette flyout menu or by dragging a color of the appropriate model from the Swatches palette. Spot color mode may only be selected by dragging a spot color from the Swatches palette.

Grayscale Mode

In Grayscale mode, the color you choose is a tint of the process color black. You may adjust the tint of color from a 0 percent tint (white) to 100 percent (black). Grayscale colors are the same as CMYK colors, with 0 percent tints assigned for cyan, magenta, and yellow.

Spot Color Mode

In spot color mode, the color you choose will be a tint of the spot color that you dragged onto the Color palette from the Swatches palette. The color tint of the spot color may be assigned a value within a range from 0 percent tint (white) to 100

percent. You may also drag tints directly from the Color palette to the Swatches palette. Color tints retain all color properties including their original name, but, because they are tints, they will separate and print as percentages of the original spot color.

 You may only select spot color mode by dragging a spot color from the Swatches palette to the Color palette.

RGB (Red, Green, Blue)

New to Illustrator 7 is the RGB (red, green, blue) color model used mostly for creating images for screen, multimedia, broadcast, or online images. Digital artists using Adobe After Effects, Adobe Premiere, Macromedia Director or any similar application can now create illustrations in a native color space. The RGB color model is the same system used by your monitor and television to display images. If you look closely at any white pixel, you will see that it is actually comprised of three pixel components, one each of red, green, and blue.

 By default, Illustrator will display the colors of each channel on an 8-bit scale, from 0 to 255. To enter a percentage instead, double-click to the right of the sliders.

HSB (Hue, Saturation, Brightness)

The HSB (hue, saturation, brightness) color mode is based on the standard color wheel. Standard color wheels are based on color values assigned to correspond to the 360 degrees in a circle. Hues are described in degrees relative to red at the top of the wheel, ranging from 0 degrees (red) to 120 degrees (green) to 270 degrees (violet). Saturation is described as a percentage from 0 percent being a neutral gray, to 100 percent being vivid, full-strength color. The brightness component is also described as a percentage, ranging from 0 percent (black) to 100 percent (bright, full-strength color). White is any color with a saturation of 0 percent and a brightness of 100 percent.

CMYK (Cyan, Magenta, Yellow, Black)

Illustrator 7's CMYK (cyan, magenta, yellow, black) color model is used when assigning colors to drawing objects that are mostly destined for traditional four-color process printing. The Color palette describes all four components of a CMYK color as a percentage from 0 percent to 100 percent.

Using the Eyedropper and Paintbucket

The Eyedropper and Paintbucket tools enable you to sample the fill colors of one object and transfer them to another. The advantages of using the Eyedropper (I) tool over other tools, such as the Selection tool, is that it enables you to sample both the fill and stoke colors of an object with a single click. Samples are displayed in both the Fill or Stroke buttons on the main Toolbox palette and on either the Color or Gradient palette, depending on the fill or stroke properties. Sampling object colors and adding them to your Swatches palette is a quick way of building new collections of colors based on existing objects.

After sampling an object with the Eyedropper tool, the color you sample automatically becomes the active color in both the Toolbox as well as the Color palette. To assign the sampled color to another object, drag the color from the palette to the new object.

Note   *On the Macintosh platform version of Illustrator 7, you aren't limited to sampling colors from objects within Illustrator 7. By dragging the Eyedropper pointer to anywhere on your monitor, you can pick up a color from another open window, a palette within Illustrator 7, or your desktop. As you drag your mouse around the screen, watch the Toolbox: the color of each pixel that you drag over will flash into the active color icon in the toolbox and Color palette. When you release the mouse button, the color you selected is then copied to both locations. This feature does not apply to Windows 95 or Windows NT platform versions.*

The Paintbucket tool works in the opposite way. Instead of *sampling* fill and stroke colors and registering them in Illustrator 7's respective palettes, it enables you to quickly *apply* currently selected fill and stroke colors. The advantage of using the Paintbucket tool is that it enables you to quickly apply current fill and stroke properties to selected objects only.

To use the Paintbucket tool, choose it from the main Toolbox (or type **K**) and click on an object to apply the current Fill and Stroke properties simultaneously. The object you apply the new fill and stroke to need not be selected to apply the new properties.

10

 *You can temporarily toggle your cursor between the Eyedropper and Paintbucket tools by holding down the ALT/OPTION key.*

Using preference options built into the Eyedropper and Paintbucket tools, you can set either one of these tools to respectively sample or apply fill or stroke properties individually as you require as shown here:

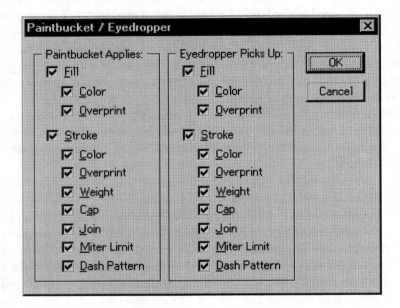

To access these preferences, double-click on either of the tools in the main Toolbox to display the Paintbucket/Eyedropper Options dialog box. Options in this dialog box enable you to set not only whether the Eyedropper or Paintbucket affect either the stroke, the fill, or both, but also which fill and stroke options are sampled by Illustrator 7.

Applying Gradient Fills

To the user, gradient colors appear as a complex progression of one color into another. Yet to Illustrator 7, a gradient is just another color that can be stored in the Swatches palette and dragged into an object.

But there are certain complications to working with gradients that set them apart from working with other colors. As with any color, gradients may be stored in the Swatches palette. And gradients also may be assigned to objects by dragging and dropping them from the Gradient palette onto an object or sampled by the Eyedropper—but there the similarity ends.

A gradient may be a straightforward blend between two colors. But a gradient may also be a complex movement through multiple colors and tints. Gradient colors are capable of supporting spot colors, tints of spot colors, and process colors in RGB, CMYK, or HSB mode—all in the same configuration. That's the good news. The bad news is that although you may create gradients to contain all colors from any of Illustrator 7's color models, mixing all those colors together may not be a wise strategy.

First, complex and mixed mode gradients take considerably longer to print. Plus, unless the drawing you are creating specifically requires graduating colors between mixed spot and process colors, it may be better to stick with either one color model or the other.

Tip *You can create a gradient that blends two different spot colors. However, in order to print this on the proper spot color separation, you must deselect the Convert to Process option in the Separation Setup dialog box.*

Note *Selecting a gradient by clicking on the Swatches, Toolbox, or Gradient palettes will automatically switch Illustrator from Stroke to Fill mode. This is because gradients may only be applied to the fill of an object.*

Working with the Gradient Palette

The Gradient palette (F9) is made up of five interface elements, as shown next: the preview window, the gradient bar, the flyout menu containing further options, the Angle box, and the Location box. The flyout menu in the upper-right corner enables you to view either full options or partial options showing only the gradient bar via the Show/Hide Options command. The preview window provides a quick preview of the gradient of any currently selected object.

Shows preview of current gradient,   Select linear   Current angle in degrees,
ALT/OPTION+click resets gradient to   or radial   current location in percentage
black-to-white   values (0 at left, 100 at right)

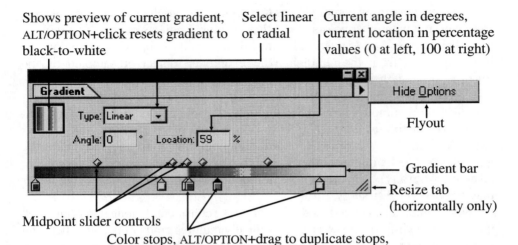

Flyout

Gradient bar

Resize tab
(horizontally only)

Midpoint slider controls

Color stops, ALT/OPTION+drag to duplicate stops,
ALT/OPTION+drag one stop over another to swap stop colors

With a partial Gradient palette, only the gradient bar is visible. As with other palettes, you may also cycle through a collapsed palette, a partial palette, and a full palette by double-clicking on the Gradient palette name tag.

The Gradient palette drop-down menu features options for specifying your gradient as either a linear or a radial style. A straightforward linear gradient moves uniformly from one color to another in a single direction, while a radial gradient graduates color concentrically from the center of the object. The angle value shown on the palette indicates an angle relative to the orientation of your page. Because a radial cannot be angled, the angle box is grayed out and unavailable while Radial is selected from the drop-down menu.

The gradient bar is the most significant feature of the Gradient palette. The bar itself displays a preview of the currently selected gradient colors including all color stops and their midpoints. These color stops represent the colors in your gradient, while the diamond-shaped midpoints enable you to set the halfway point between each gradient color. This halfway point is also referred to as the gradient "step" and indicates the point at which equal values of the two colors being gradated are measured. The location box indicates the position of the color stop or the midpoint currently selected. These values are indicated in percentages, 0 being at the far left of the gradient bar and 100 percent at the far right.

Although color stop locations are measured in percentages across the entire length of the gradient bar, the midpoint positions are measured in percentages based on a position between the two corresponding stops.

Creating and Editing Gradients

Illustrator 7 features enable you to edit gradients by adding or removing beginning, ending, or intermediate colors of currently selected gradients.

To explore this gradient-editing procedure, follow these steps:

1. Create a new rectangle object.

2. Apply any of the currently existing gradients found in the Swatches palette by dragging one of them onto your new rectangle.

3. With the Gradients palette (F9) displayed and maximized, drag one of the midpoints of your chosen gradient away from its original position and observe the results in your rectangle. This action changes the "step" or midpoint position of the gradient between two color stops.

4. Add a new color to your gradient by displaying the Color palette (F6), choosing a color, and dragging it into the slider bar in the Gradients palette. You may also define a new color by clicking below the slider bar on the Gradients palette. The color currently selected on your Color palette is added to the gradient.

5. Customize the gradient by adding additional colors or changing the midpoints of the gradients. Each time you make a change to the gradient, it is reflected in the selected object in your drawing and in the gradient bar in the Gradient palette.

6. To add your newly edited gradient to the Swatches palette, drag the rectangle to your Swatches palette. If you wish to name the new gradient, double-click it in the Swatches palette and enter a name in the dialog box that appears.

You can continue this process to create new gradients based on existing ones by editing, applying, and sampling existing gradients in a never-ending process if you wish. In theory, a gradient fill may have an unlimited number of color stops assigned to it. But there is a practical limit of 100 stops—one stop for each percentage of color.

New gradients are created by editing existing ones. To redefine a color on the gradient, click the appropriate color stop and then press ALT/OPTION and click a color swatch; create a new color by using the sliders or the color spectrum ramp in the Color palette; or drag a color from the Swatches palette. To add a new color to the gradient, click just below the gradient bar or drag a color from the Swatches palette to the Gradient palette. The gradient may be adjusted by dragging the appropriate color stop. The midpoint between any two colors may be adjusted by dragging the appropriate midpoint diamond.

Saving a Gradient

Saving a gradient is just like saving a color: drag the completed gradient from the Gradient palette to the Swatches palette. You may also drag the gradient from the main Toolbox Fill box to the Swatches palette or click the New Swatch button in the Swatches palette.

Versions of Illustrator prior to version 4.0 do not support color gradients. If you attempt to save your Illustrator 7 document in a format earlier than version 4.0, any gradients assigned to objects will be lost and objects will subsequently be assigned the first color found in the gradient.

Remember that gradients are only saved with your current document, although you may import a gradient from another document by using libraries (Window\Show Libraries\Other Library).

Resizing Option

Unlike other resizable palettes, the Gradient palette may only be resized horizontally. The ability to resize in a horizontal direction enables you to see more detail of gradients and accurately position your color stops. If you wish, you can stretch the palette so that it completely stretches to the width of your screen; resizing the Gradient palette helps you see detail when viewing highly complex gradients as you can see next:

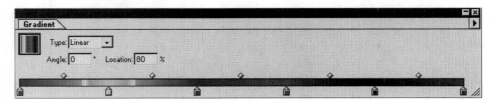

If the Gradient palette is docked with other palettes, such as the Color palette, you'll need to ungroup it before it may be resized.

Using the Gradient Tool

The Gradient tool (G) adjusts the beginning and ending points of gradients within objects. It enables you to visually change the angle of linear gradients and move the center of a radial gradient. It enables you to set new beginning and endpoints for a gradient. With the Gradient tool you can set a gradient across multiple objects.

Step by Step

The most efficient way to learn the use of the Gradient tool is to practice using it. To this end, roll up your sleeves and follow these steps:

1. Draw a rectangle and fill it with a gradient, such as the Pink, Yellow, Green linear-style gradient using the Gradients palette (F9).

2. Select the Gradient tool (G). Position the pointer in the center of the rectangle. This is where your gradient will begin. Drag diagonally up and to the right across the object and release the mouse just inside the upper-right corner.

3. Notice how the lower-left corner of the rectangle is filled with pink as the starting point of the gradient is now in the middle of the rectangle, and that the rest of the gradient has been compressed into the upper-right quadrant.

4. To continue your exploration of this feature, create a five-point star and fill it with a gradient. For the sake of this example, use a yellow-to-orange gradient applied using a radial-style gradient selected from the drop-down menu in the Gradient palette.

10

5. Select the Gradient tool and position the pointer in the upper spike of the star, where the center of the gradient will be.

6. Click and drag straight down, and release the mouse near the bottom of the star object. Notice how the gradient you just applied appears to radiate from the top of the star.

Note *Holding down the SHIFT key will constrain the Gradient tool assignments to 45-degree angles.*

A second use for the Gradient tool is in applying gradients across more than one object. As a practical exercise in learning this procedure, follow these steps:

1. Create a new rectangle object.

2. As a shortcut to creating multiple objects, use the Rows & Columns command (Type|Rows & Columns) to break your rectangle into four separate objects by choosing two columns by two rows.

3. Fill each object with the Yellow & Orange radial gradient stored in the Gradient palette, the Swatches palette, or the Paintbucket tool.

4. Select the objects and choose the Gradient tool (G).

5. Click in the center of the four rectangles, and drag to the upper-right corner. The gradient is now centered between the four objects and spans them as if they were one object.

6. To review using the Gradient tool, select the object filled with the gradient color.

7. Position the pointer at your desired beginning point of the gradient, and drag across the objects in any direction and release the mouse button to define the endpoint of the gradient.

Using Patterns

Patterns are vector objects that have been defined into pattern tiles. When patterns are applied as fills, the pattern repeats as many times as necessary in order to completely fill an object. Patterns work in a similar way to gradients and colors in that you may fill objects with patterns by dragging and dropping them onto objects in your drawing from the Swatches palette.

Note   *Patterns may be applied to either the stroke of an object or path, but you must attach them using the Path Patterns filter. If you apply a pattern to the stroke of a path using the Swatches palette, the path will be stroked with gray instead.*

Illustrator 7 ships with a number of path patterns found in the default Swatches palette as shown here:

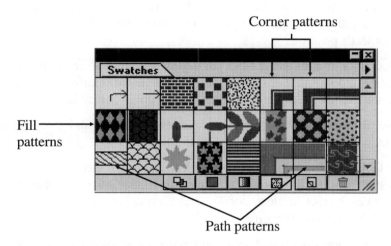

Both fill patterns and stroke patterns are interchangeable and may be applied to either strokes or paths, but applying a fill pattern to a stroke or a path pattern to a fill can lead to unpredictable or undesirable results.

Note   *Although almost any vector object can be made into a pattern, you cannot use an object comprising a mask or containing a gradient as a pattern.*

10

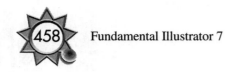

Creating Fill Patterns

Creating a pattern can be as straightforward as creating the artwork that you wish to use as a pattern tile and dragging it to the Swatches palette. Instead of dragging, you may also use the Define Pattern command (Edit|Define Pattern) to add your pattern to the Swatches palette.

In an effort to quickly learn how to sample a pattern, follow these steps:

1. Create a new rectangle (a sqaure in this case) by holding the SHIFT key and dragging with the rectangle tool to create a square approximately one-quarter to one-half inch in size.

2. To create a copy of the square aligned horizontally with the first, hold ALT/OPTION+SHIFT while dragging the new square to the right. Release the mouse once the copy is beside the original. Position the copy so that the sides of the squares are touching. Be careful not to leave a gap. If necessary, use the Transform palette (Window|Show Transform) to verify the object's position.

3. Select both squares and use the same copy procedure to create two more squares underneath these. As before, be sure that all four squares are aligned exactly touching each other. Alignment is critical here.

4. Color the top-left and bottom-right squares with black, and group them together (CTRL/COMMAND+G).

5. Fill the remaining two squares with white and group them also (CTRL/COMMAND+G). Grouping squares of similar color will place them next to each other in Illustrator 7's stacking order and increase the pattern's screen redraw time.

6. Select all four squares and drag them to the Swatches palette. A new swatch named New Pattern will appear. Double-click the new pattern or use the Swatch options menu to assign the new name B&W Checkerboard.

Not all patterns you create will be this straightforward. Investigating the patterns that appear in the default Swatches palette or the additional sample patterns found on your Illustrator 7 program disc will provide more ideas of the creative freedom that Illustrator 7's pattern-creation feature gives you.

Note
A fill pattern tile should be roughly 0.5 to 1 inch square. Patterns created to render a higher degree of detail by using smaller objects cause slower screen redraw time and printing time. Conversely, pattern tiles created using objects that are too large may require large areas in order to completely tile out.

Viewing Patterns

All fill patterns tile parallel to the page orientation, beginning from the top-left and continuing to tile in a left-to-right direction from top to bottom, until the object is filled. Unlike gradients, whose origin may be changed by using the Gradient tool, in order to adjust where a pattern begins tiling, you must change your document's ruler origin. Moving the ruler origin will affect all objects you subsequently assign patterns.

Under default preference settings, patterns display when in Preview view. To reduce screen draw time of fill patterns, you may change to Artwork mode (CTRL/COMMAND+Y or View|Artwork) or turn off the Print & Preview Patterns option in the Document Setup (File|Document Setup or CTRL/COMMAND+SHIFT+P) dialog box.

For more information on controlling views, see "Customizing Windows and Display" in **Chapter 3: Making Illustrator 7 Easy to Use**. For more information on setting Document Setup options, also see the section called "Setting Document Options" in **Chapter 3**.

Tip
To speed viewing and printing of patterns, remove unnecessary detail from your pattern objects and group objects that are painted with the same color so that they are adjacent in the stacking order.

Transforming Objects Filled with Patterns

By default when you transform an object containing a pattern, the pattern will not change. Select the Transform Pattern Tiles option in the General Preferences dialog to specify whether a pattern within an object will change when you apply a transformation command such as shearing, rotating, or scaling. You may also decide on a case-by-case basis to transform tiles by selecting the Transform Patterns option in each transform dialog box.

If you have transformed an object containing a pattern, any subsequent objects that you create using that pattern will have the same transformation applied to the

Fundamental Illustrator 7

pattern. To make the pattern fill normally, select another fill type—such as solid color or gradient—and then reapply your desired pattern.

Although it's possible to successfully create a blend between two patterned objects, both objects must be filled with the identical pattern. To learn more about using the Blend tool see "Creating Blends" in **Chapter 7: Creating and Editing Drawing Objects**.

In order to edit a fill pattern as individual objects, you must first use the Expand Fill command (Edit|Expand Fill). The Expand Fill command converts patterns into a set of masked objects. Running the Expand Fill command can be helpful if you are having difficulty printing objects filled with patterns. This has the effect of reducing the complexity of objects.

Adding Path Patterns

The action of applying a pattern to a path is quite different from that of applying a fill pattern. Path patterns, as they are referred to, are not applied from the Swatches palette, nor do you need to be in Stroke mode to add a path pattern. Instead, path patterns are applied using the Path Patterns filter (Filter|Stylize|Path Pattern), as shown next:

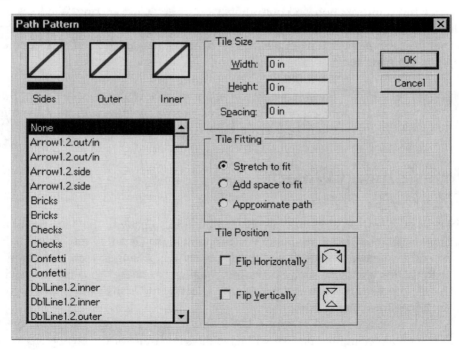

When a pattern is applied to a path, the pattern immediately becomes an editable path. To edit a fill pattern as individual objects, you must first use the Expand Fill command (Edit|Expand Fill). Path Patterns are typically used to create frames, borders, and ornamental effects.

For learning purposes, follow these practical steps to apply a sample path pattern:

1. Using the Pen tool (P) draw an "S" shape.

2. Give the line you just created a fill and stroke value of None (/). Changing to artwork mode (CTRL/COMMAND+Y) may help you see the path.

3. Choose the Path Patterns filter (Filter|Stylize|Path Pattern).

4. Click the Sides box in the upper-left of the Path Pattern dialog box.

5. From the list in the Path Pattern dialog box, click the Rope.side pattern. By default, this pattern will be applied to the side of the path. Because the S-curve you created has no corners, leave the other two entries as None.

6. Click OK.

You've just assigned a Rope pattern to a path using the Path Patterns filter effect. What was previously a path is now a complex series of grouped outlines in the shape of a rope sitting atop a deselected path as shown here:

10

Note   *Ensure that the path you apply the Path Pattern filter effect to has a fill and stroke of None. The Path Pattern filter does not delete the original path, so any fill and stroke assigned to the path may be visible after applying this effect.*

For a practical exercise in how the effects of applying corner tiles to paths behave, follow these steps:

1. Use the Rectangle tool (M) to create two long and overlapping rectangles that resemble a cross. Create one vertically oriented, the other horizontally oriented and center them on each other. Thicker cross beams will yield better results.

2. SHIFT+click to multiple-select both rectangles and unite them using the Objects|Pathfinder|Unite command.

3. Select the Path Pattern filter (Filter|Stylize|Path Pattern). With the Sides box selected, choose the Laurel.side pattern.

4. With the Outer box selected, select the Laurel.outer pattern.

5. Finally, click on the Inner box, and choose the Laurel.inner pattern.

6. Leave all other options as they are and click OK. Notice how the two corner patterns have added a smooth join at both the cross' interior and exterior joints, as shown next:

The Path Pattern filter also features a number of options for fitting the pattern to the path. The Stretch to Fit option will lengthen or shorten the pattern tile in order to fit the object. The problem with using Stretch to Fit is that it can result in uneven tiling. The Add Space to Fit option adds blank space between each pattern tile. This will create an even application of the tiles, but may cause undesirable gaps between them. The space between each tile is added proportionately to the selected object. You have a choice of allowing Illustrator to determine the amount of space between the tiles automatically, or you may specify an amount in the Tile Size Spacing text box.

The Approximate Path option works best when the Path Pattern is applied to a rectangle and you wish the pattern to tile evenly. Where normally Path Patterns are applied at the exact center on a path, the Approximate Path command will apply the pattern either slightly inside or outside the path to maintain even tiling. The Tile Position option can be used to flip the pattern horizontally, vertically, or both. This is useful, for example, when trying to cause the smaller line of the DblLine1.2.side pattern to appear on the outside of an object.

When you select a pattern to apply to a path, the actual size of a tile appears in the Tile Size section. You may scale the pattern by entering a new width or height for the pattern tile. Illustrator will only scale the tiles proportionately; you can't enter anamorphic height and width values. To create a donut effect when applying a pattern to a circle, use a width smaller than one-half of the circle's radius. Depending on the pattern, a tile width of somewhere between the circle's radius and half that will create a solid effect. Larger tiles can create some very unpredictable results when applied to a circle.

 If you need to know the actual size of a fill pattern's tile, you can use the Path Patterns dialog to get that measurement.

Creating Path Patterns

A path pattern is created using procedures similar to creating fill patterns. To create a path pattern, create your tile effect using objects and drag the new pattern to the Swatches palette.

 When creating new path pattern tiles for applying to corners or sides, it may help somewhat to differentiate the tiles from each other using a creative naming scheme.

In order to speed screen redraw time and minimize printing complexities, side tiles for path patterns should be no larger than between 0.5 and one inch in height and one to two inches in width. It's also essential that corner tiles be the same height as the side tiles, and that their shape remain square.

Modifying Patterns

Modifying a pattern is a straightforward procedure. Edit the pattern artwork and press ALT/OPTION while dragging it to the Swatches palette. All objects painted with the modified pattern will be automatically updated with the new design.

To select a tile to modify, deselect all objects in your document (CTRL/COMMAND+SHIFT+A). Drag the pattern you wish to modify from the Swatches palette into your document. For this example, drag the bricks swatch to your document. Color the brick's fill Aqua. Hold ALT/OPTION while dragging the bricks back to the Swatches palette directly on top of the existing swatch and the Bricks pattern will be updated with the new color.

Selecting Stroke Mode

As demonstrated earlier in this chapter, selecting Stroke mode can be as straightforward as clicking on the Stroke button in the main Toolbox or typing **X** to toggle from the Fill mode. Setting the mode to stroke is only important when you want to affect a path's stroke color. Otherwise, you can add a path pattern or you can make adjustments using the Stroke palette while an object is still in Fill mode.

Assigning Stroke Colors

Assigning a color to an object's stroke is accomplished exactly as with assigning a color to its fill. Select Stroke mode, and drag or press ALT/OPTION or click a color from the Swatches palette to your object. Only solid colors may be assigned to path strokes. Gradients may not be assigned to a stroke, and patterns must be applied using the Path Patterns filter.

Using the Stroke Palette

The Stroke palette (F10) is used to select all stroke properties of paths and lines, including the line weight or thickness, the stroke cap and join, and the style of stroke's dash as shown next:

Enter line weight or thickness value

Sets size limit for changing from miter to beveled joint

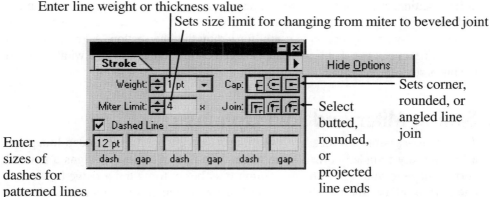

Sets corner, rounded, or angled line join

Select butted, rounded, or projected line ends

Enter sizes of dashes for patterned lines

Like other palettes, the Stroke palette may be viewed fully, partially, or minimized. Partial view shows only the line weight values, while the fully displayed palette includes options to control a line's cap, join, and dash characteristics.

Setting Weight Options

The line weight sets the width of the stroke, in points. You may type a value using any measurement system. Whether you use inches (in), picas (p), millimeters (mm), or centimeters (cm), Illustrator will automatically convert your entry to an equal value in points. Illustrator centers the stroke on the path, with half of the stroke inside the path, half outside.

To remove the stroke from a path, you must use the None icon (/) in the main toolbox. Entering a weight of 0 will cause Illustrator to display and print a 1 pixel-wide line. On your screen, 1 pixel is equal to roughly 1/72 of an inch, while on a laser printer 1 pixel is equal to 1/600 of an inch. At high-resolution output from hardware such as an imagesetter, one pixel can be so thin that it is irreproducible—it can be as narrow as 1/3600 of an inch. The reason for this is that Illustrator 7 rounds out the line weight to the nearest pixel size, so a value of zero gets rounded to the smallest single pixel size. In general, avoid assigning a line thickness less than 0.25 points (hairlines) because of their limited visibility in final higher-resolution printing.

Setting Line Cap Options

The cap option determines what the end of an open path will look like. A Butt Cap ends a line with squared ends that extend no further than the endpoint. This is the default setting. A Round Cap gives a line an end cap that is a circle centered on the endpoint with a width equal to the line's stroke. When you create lines that meet at angles, the Round Cap option is useful for hiding the intersection. A Projecting Cap gives a line an end cap that is a square centered on the endpoint with a width equal to the line's stroke.

Setting Miter and Join Options

The Join icons control what a line looks like at a corner point. A Rounded Join gives a line slightly rounded corners. The Miter Join line cap option assigns a pointed corner shape to your line. The miter limit may be set to within a range between 1 and 500. It adjusts the threshold where Illustrator switches from a miter join to a bevel join. The miter limit default is 4.

This means that when the length of the point, the distance between the tip of the miter and the endpoint, reaches four times the stroke weight, the program switches from a miter join to a bevel join. Thus a thicker line is more likely to result in a miter join. A miter limit of 1 causes a bevel join to be used. A Bevel Join creates a square corner. You may specify only one type of join per line; however, due to the miter limit, a line may contain both mitered and beveled corners.

Setting Dashed Line Options

The Dash option determines whether a line is solid or dashed. Click the Dash option to produce a dashed or stylized line. You use the Dash Pattern text boxes to delineate a dash sequence by entering the span of each dash and the gaps between them. You need not fill in every box. For example, the default dash has a width of 12 points while leaving the other boxes empty. Because the dash and gap widths that you type are repeated in sequence, once you have determined the pattern, you don't need to continue filling in the boxes. Dash patterns are specified in points, but you may enter your dash spans in any measurement unit and Illustrator will perform an automatic conversion.

Working with Ink Pen Effects

The Ink Pen filter enables you to convert your paths into textured drawings that simulate ink pen drawings. Ink Pen enables you to simulate cross hatching and variable patterns such as wood grains.

Unlike other similar filters, Ink Pen works only on vector art, and produces vector art. It works by converting the selected object into a mask and then drawing the pattern behind it. The pattern can be quite detailed and take up a huge amount of memory. Running the Ink Pen filter should be one of the last steps in creating an illustration, as you may find Illustrator running out of memory from the instant you apply an Ink Pen effect.

The basic texture element behind the Ink Pen filter is the hatch. You may apply a hatch from either the Effects or Hatches dialog boxes. The Effects dialog box gives you more control over the final output. The Hatches dialog gives you minimal output options, but enables you to create and modify your hatch settings.

The Ink Pen filter literally enables you to create millions of different textures. Experimentation is the key to mastering the Ink Pen filter. You should play around with different settings before actually applying Ink Pen effects.

Using Ink Effects

The Ink Pen Effects dialog box, shown next, is the main control center for applying ink pen effects.

Ink Pen Effects

Stipple medium

Hatch: Dots   New ...
Color: Match Object   Delete
Background: Hatch Only   Update
Fade: To White   Reset
Fade Angle: 0

Density
100

OK
Cancel

Import...
Save As ...

☑ Preview

10

When you first enter the dialog box, you'll notice a drop-down menu in the upper-left corner that provides access to various effects styles. It contains a number of predefined styles. For example, if you select the Stipple Medium setting, you will be given a hatch setting of Dots, a color of Original, a background of Hatch Only, no fade, and maximum density. The Fiberglass light setting brings a worm hatch and a 22 percent density to the picture. These previously defined options are a good place to start experimenting with Ink Pen effects.

Hatch Options

Traditional art hatching is defined as the marking of a surface with fine, closely spaced, parallel or criss-crossed lines that represent shading. The Hatch Effect dialog box is the cornerstone of the Ink Pen filter. It is meant to replicate the shading found in common drawings.

The Hatch Effects drop-down menu enables you to select from one of Illustrator's 7 default textures. You may also create your own textures or import new ones from your Adobe Illustrator program disc. To import other hatch settings, click the Import button, find the settings you desire, and click Open.

 You can speed up Illustrator by turning off the Hatch Preview option at the lower-right of the Ink Pen Effects dialog box.

Color Options

Illustrator 7 also provides two options for assigning color to hatching patterns. You may select Original to retain the color the hatch was originally created with: all of Illustrator's default hatches are black. You may also save new hatches with any color you wish. The Match Object To matches the hatch's fill to the currently selected object's fill.

 When using the Match Object To option, avoid using target objects that feature pattern fills. Using pattern fills in this way can overload system memory and possibly cause further memory problems.

Background Options

The Background drop-down menu gives you the option of keeping the fill of the original object when you create the hatch. The Retain Fill option will apply the hatch in its original color on top of the object's fill color. The Hatch Only option will remove the fill from the object.

 If your original object is filled with black, selecting Retain Fill will cause black hatches to be created on top of a black background, thus rendering the hatches invisible.

Fade and Fade Angle Options

Rather than just creating uniform hatching across an object, Illustrator 7 provides four options for fading your hatching. A fade of None will have no effect. The To White option will fade the hatch to white, while conversely the To Black option will fill the hatch to solid black. If your original object is filled with a gradient, the Use Gradient option will enable you to base the fade's direction and colors upon the gradient. If you choose either the To White or To Black options, enter an angle for the hatch's fade in the Fade Angle text box.

Hatch Concentration

The Concentration drop-down menu enables you to designate whether to apply the hatch uniformly, in a pattern, or not to apply the option. You may alter the hatch's Density, Dispersion, Thickness, Rotation, and/or Scale. The Density slider adjusts the number of hatch elements applied to the selection. To alter the density, drag the handle or enter values in the text box.

Dispersion controls the gap between hatch elements. Thickness determines the line weight of the hatch elements. The Thickness option is unavailable (and grayed out) if the selection has no stroke thickness or color assigned. Rotation sets the angle at which the hatch elements are applied. Scale establishes the size of the hatch elements. The Update button enables you to save any changes that you've made to the setting you started with.

The Dispersion, Thickness, Rotation, and Scale options will bring up a second menu, which determines how the effect is applied. The None option deselects the current adjustment. The Constant option applies the effect evenly, while the Linear option will increase the effect progressively and give you access to range sliders that affect the minimum and maximum amount of the effect. The Reflect option alters the effect outward from the center of the object. The Symmetric varies the effect proportionately and evenly, for example, if applying hatches to round or cylindrical shapes. Use the Random option in order to apply the effect irregularly.

Creating Your Own Hatches

Illustrator 7 enables you to create and save your own hatches or modify existing hatches and save them for reuse. Use the Ink Pen Hatches dialog box, shown next, to save your hatches.

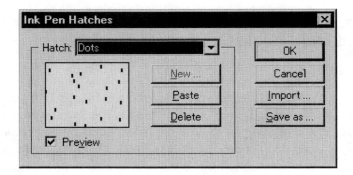

To create a hatch, draw the objects you wish to convert to a hatch design for the ink pen effect. In this case, draw several wavy lines with the freehand tool, leaving the fill set to None, and a black stroke with a thickness of 0.5 points. Select the lines and run the Hatch filter (Filter|Ink Pen|Hatches). Click the New button, type a name for your new hatch (Squiggle Hatch, for example) and click OK. To save your new hatch, click OK again. Use the Save As button to save the hatch for reuse with other documents.

Deleting Hatches and Hatch Settings

To delete saved hatches and hatch settings, follow this quick example:

1. Choose the Ink Pen Effects filter (Filter|Ink Pen|Effects).

2. Select the hatch setting you wish to delete and click the Delete button.

3. Repeat this process for every setting you wish to disable.

4. Click OK to save your changes.

 Unless you make these deletions in a customized Adobe Illustrator Startup (Macintosh) or Startup.ai (Windows) file, they will affect only the current document.

To delete a hatch, run the Hatches filter (Filter|Ink Pen|Hatches) and select the hatch you wish to delete. Repeat this process for every hatch you wish to disable. Then click OK to save your changes.

Customizing Hatches

To learn how to customize a hatch, follow this practical exercise:

1. Begin by making sure you have no objects currently selected.

2. Choose the Hatches filter (Filter|Ink Pen|Hatches). For this exercise, choose the Crosshatch1 style from the Hatch drop-down menu.

3. Click the Paste button. The cross hatch will now have been pasted into the document.

4. Click OK.

5. Edit the hatch. In this case, rotate it by 15 degrees using the Transform palette (Window|Show Transform) and entering **15** in the Angle box and pressing ENTER.

6. With the rotated cross still selected, choose the Hatches filter again.

7. Click the New button and name the new hatch in the New Hatch dialog box as shown next.

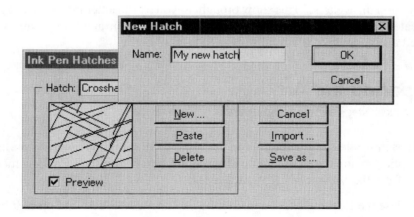

8. Click OK and the new hatch is added to your Hatch list.

Note *Illustrator will not let you overwrite an existing hatch. If you wish to replace an existing hatch, you must delete the original hatch first*

Chapter 10 Tutorial: Effects with Fills and Strokes

As a practical exploration of the features and effects discussed in this chapter, follow through in this step-by-step tutorial. As you do so, you may notice that some of these steps are accompanied by a Color palette symbol. This symbol indicates that the step has also been illustrated in full color in the Fundamental Illustrator 7 color insert. The pupose of the color insert is to provide you with a brief overview of the tutorial and act as an overall reference for the practical use of color throughout these tutorials.

Watch for this symbol:

Gradient Tutorial

The local graphics arts league, Brushstrokes, is once again having its charity competition and auction. Somewhat to promote themselves, the theme of the competition this year is, "This show brought to you by the letter *B*." So, we're going to create an Andy Warhol-like piece for the competition and apply what we've learned about patterns, fills, and strokes to this project.

Preparing the Art

Follow these steps to prepare your art:

1. Being able to view the fills and strokes we're creating is more important than seeing their onscreen paths, so switch to Illustrator's Preview mode from the View menu (CTRL/COMMAND+Y).

2. Use the Rectangle tool and create a box about 3.5" x 5" and place it in the upper-left corner of your page, as shown in Figure 10-1.

FIGURE 10-1   The first step in creating the piece for the competition

3. We'll be making more interesting fills and strokes later on in the tutorial, but for now give the box a transparent fill and a 3-point stroke. After making the box active with the Selection tool, click on the Stroke swatch in the Tools palette. In the Color palette, select black (if it isn't already the default color). Then type **3** into the Weight text box (found under the Stroke tab). Click on the Fill swatch in the Tools palette and select the None button below it.

4. Now, we want to create a letter *B* that we'll then copy and apply various fills to. So, in the Character palette (CTRL/COMMAND+T) choose Helvetica (Bold) at 350 points. Click on the Text tool and type the letter **B**. Use the Selection tool to line up the *B* so it sits within the 3-point box as shown in Figure 10-2.

10

FIGURE 10-2 The 350-point letter B

5. Next, we change the type from fonts to paths so that we have more available options for stroking and filling our letter B. Make sure the *B* is selected, and choose Create Outlines from the Type menu (CTRL/COMMAND+SHIFT+O). The character now changes into a series of anchors and curves.

6. Use the Select All command (CTRL/COMMAND+A) from Illustrator's File menu to highlight both the box and the *B*. In Warhol fashion, we'll repeat the *B* motif three more times. But there is no reason to repeat all of the steps; instead, we can simply copy what we've created to date.

 If you first press CTRL/COMMAND+SHIFT_" *to enable the snap to ruler, it's easier to align all four* B *boxes.*

7. Under the Object menu, select Group (CTRL/COMMAND+G). Both objects can now be selected at once. Click Edit|Copy (CTRL/COMMAND+C) and then Edit|Paste (CTRL/COMMAND+V). A second "*B*-in-a-box" will appear. Use the Selection tool to move this new boxed *B* to the upper-right corner of your screen.

8. We need two more boxed *B*s, but you don't have to copy the original again since it still resides on the computer's clipboard. Simply press Edit|Paste (CTRL/COMMAND+V) to create one more *B* and, using the Selection tool, move the new box to the lower-left corner. Repeat the process and paste in a fourth *B* and use the Selection tool to position it in the lower-right corner.

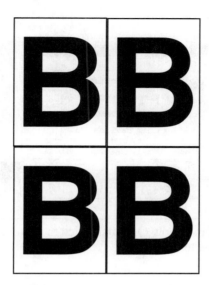

9. Now that all four boxes are positioned where we want them, we can ungroup them and apply fills to the letters and their boxes independently. If we don't ungroup them and apply a fill to a box, the fill will also apply to the letter within it. Press Edit|Select All (CTRL/COMMAND+A)—all the objects on the screen become highlighted. Now, choose Object|Ungroup (CTRL/COMMAND+SHIFT+G). Deselect all objects by clicking the Selection tool on a blank portion of the artboard, so we can work with the letters and their boxes independently.

Strokes and Fills

1. Let's begin our work on the *B* in the upper-left corner. First, highlight it with the Selection tool and then go to the Color palette and click on the right-pointing arrow shown at the right of the words "Stroke" and "Gradient" at the top of the Color palette dialog box. Select Show Options, as shown in Figure 10-3.

2. Now, we want to give the *B* a red fill. First, select the stroke from the Tool palette, and click on the red square in the Swatch palette to indicate that red fill. Add an 8-point stroke by typing **8** into the Weight text field in the Color palette. To make the stroke more interesting, click on the Dashed Line radio button in the Color palette. For this option, the Illustrator default is 12-point dashes with 12-point spaces.

10

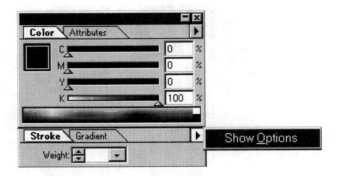

FIGURE 10-3   Use the Show Options choice to change the outline features of the letter *B*

3. Click on the upper-left box, and choose a green color from the Swatch palette and you'll see a red fill with a green background—a somewhat Christmas-like look with good high-contrast colors.

We're sure to catch the judge's eyes with this!

4. Now, we'll add some details to the upper-right *B* box. First, select this *B* and then locate the swatch in the Swatch palette that looks like a bull's-eye and click on it. Now the interior of this *B*'s box has alternating red and white concentric circles. Although this is a good effect, diagonal stripes are eye-catching too, so let's use that instead. Click on the Gradient tab in the Color palette. Now, click on the arrow to the right and choose Show Options. Move to the drop-down Type box, as shown in Figure 10-4, and change Radial to Linear.

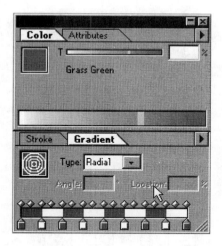

FIGURE 10-4 Changing the gradient style from Radial to Linear makes the stripe pattern in the box change to vertical stripes from concentric circles

5. If you want to make the stripes in the box diagonal, click on the Angle text box in the Gradient palette, under Show Options and type in **45.** The stripes will now slope down and to the right, as shown below.

10

6. If you want to keep this new candy-stripe fill pattern, click on the New Swatch button in Illustrator's Swatches palette and the fill will automatically be stored in the current swatch library, which is shown in Figure 10-5.

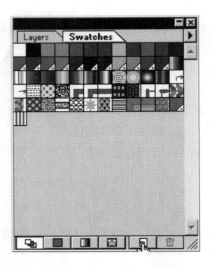

FIGURE 10-5   Swatch libraries make it easy to apply patterns to your creations

7. Now, let's add some polka-dots to another *B* box to add additional contrast to the candy-stripes. Using the Rectangle tool, create a box roughly ¾"x ¾" somewhere off to the side of the artboard. Give this box a transparent fill by first clicking on the Fill swatch in the Toolbox palette and clicking on the None (/) button below it. Click on the Stroke swatch in the Toolbox palette and give the box a transparent stroke by doing the same.

8. Switch to Artwork mode from the View menu (CTRL/COMMAND+Y). In the middle of the new box you just created, place a circle using the Ellipse tool and hold down the SHIFT key to constrain its proportions, as shown in Figure 10-6. Use the Selection tool to make sure the circle is lined up in the middle of the box. The cursor keys are good for making fine movements like this, as is the Align palette.

9. Now, select the circle and switch back to Preview mode from the View menu (CTRL/COMMAND+Y). We want to give the circle a red fill, either by selecting a red swatch in the Swatches palette or by using the color picker in the Color palette. Make sure that the circle's stroke is transparent.

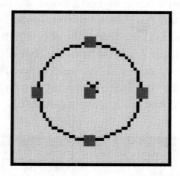

FIGURE 10-6 Creating the beginnings of a polka dot

10. Now highlight both the red circle and the transparent square using the Selection tool and dragging across the square's area. Once both are selected, click on the circle/box combination, drag it to the Swatches palette, and release the mouse button. You have just created a new swatch that appears in the palette.

11. Because our pattern is now stored in the Swatch library, we can delete the original box and circle from onscreen. Select the two objects and press the DELETE key. If, for any reason, you want to see the original artwork that went into making the pattern, just drag the swatch from the Swatch palette onto the artboard.

12. Select the lower-left *B* box, and make sure the fill swatch is active in the Toolbox palette. Click on the new polka-dot swatch in the Swatches palette and you'll fill the background of this box with the new polka dots.

13. High-contrast color, stripes, and polka dots are an eyeful on the same page, so for the last *B* box, we'll build our own gradient fill for some simple but effective variety. Select the *B* box in the lower-right corner, and fill it with a simple gradient from the Swatches palette, perhaps an attractive two-color gradient. Then, select the Gradient tab in the Color palette. You'll notice two little swatches beneath the gradient slider that signify the start and end colors, as shown here.

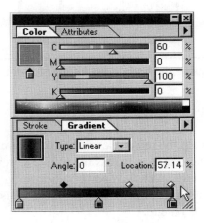

Click on the start swatch and choose green from the color picker right above. Immediately, you'll see the colors change in the B box on your screen, as shown next:

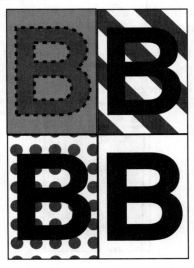

14. The gradient just created shows a variation in colors from light to dark. To create a different type of gradient and to see some variation from what you've just created, click right below the middle of the gradient slider. When the new color swatch appears, choose blue for this swatch.

15. Click on the end color swatch (the one always to the right) and choose green from the color picker. You can use the diamonds above the gradient slider to choose the midpoints of the color blends to create a gradient that fades in color from two sides, as shown on your screen.

16. There are still more gradient types to explore; to see an additional choice choose Radial instead of Linear on the Gradient tab in the Color palette.

17. One last step. Let's make that last *B* a bit more interesting. Using the Selection tool, highlight the remaining unchanged *B*. The letter still has a solid black fill, which we'll keep, but we'll can give it a stitch-like stroke to impress the competition judges. Click on the Stroke swatch in the Toolbox palette. Choose a yellow from the color picker and type **5** pt into the Weight text box. Click on the Dashed Line radio button, and type **5** pt into the first text box and **7** pt into the second. Finally, choose the middle "Round Cap" icon from the row labeled "Cap." The finished entry into the competion is shown below.

10

Conclusion

In this chapter, you have explored a wide range of tools for specifying color and stylizing objects. Illustrator 7's ability to re-create and enhance artistic effects as well as the program's speed and ease of use should please artists trained in traditional methods as well as computer artists.

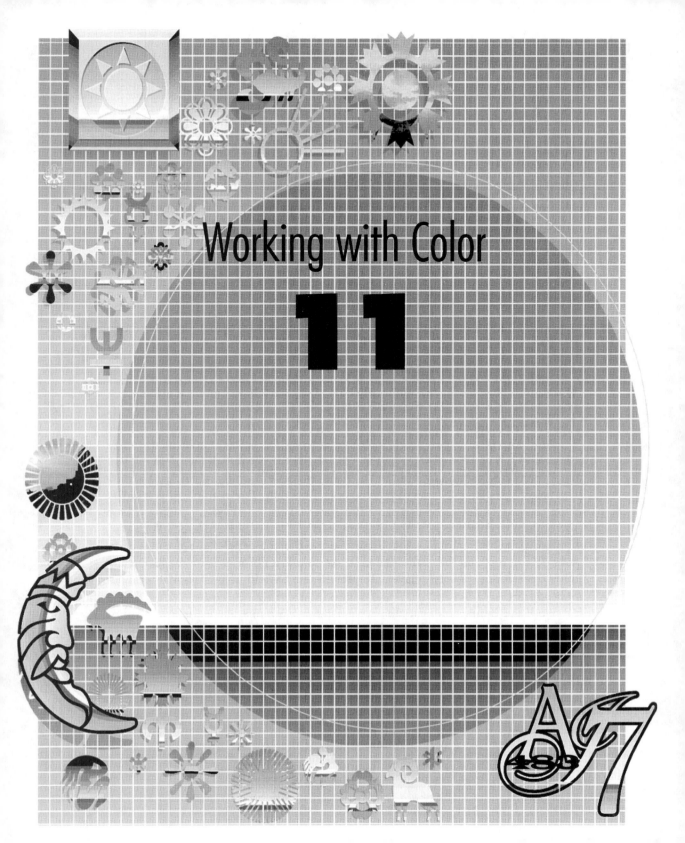

Working with Color

11

W e live in a colorful world. Creating colorful images in Adobe Illustrator is relatively straightforward, but sometimes getting these images to output (print) as colorfully as they were created is not. The secret to printing great color successfully lies in understanding how the different color models work and knowing what their capabilities and limitations are. In this chapter we'll visit the different color models, see where they live, explain how they work, and determine how and when to use each model.

Adobe Illustrator offers a variety of color models to work with: Grayscale, RGB, CMYK, and HSB. In this chapter we'll see what these abbreviations stand for. We'll look at the difference between spot and process colors as well as other standards for defining color: Pantone, TRUMATCH, TOYO, FOCOLTONE, and more. Because World Wide Web graphics are becoming increasingly important, we'll also look at Illustrator's Web palette of 216 non-dithering colors and compare the merits of JPEG and GIF image file formats.

We'll also discuss how to create a Startup color file so that you can customize Illustrator 7 to your work style preferences. A Startup file tells Illustrator how you want your workspace configured and then makes the new settings the default so they will be set automatically every time you open Illustrator. For example, if you create a ton of Web graphics, you can make Illustrator's Web palette your opening palette so you'll have easy access to the files you need. If you do a lot of spot color work, you can make the Pantone swatch library your default color palette. You can specify your default font and font size, fill and stroke colors, units of measurement, and any other preferences you might have. **Chapter 15** also has additional information about Startup files.

We'll also define color gamuts, explain gamut warnings, and learn how to adjust out-of-gamut colors. We'll learn how to use Illustrator's Color Management System to optimize color consistency in display, input, and output devices. And finally, we'll snoop around in Illustrator's Color and Swatch palettes, see what's what, learn how they relate to your illustrations, and learn how you can modify and customize the palettes to fit the way you work.

Understanding Color Models

Color models are different systems used by computers and input and output devices to define color. Here are the four different color models used by Illustrator 7 (and most design and image editing software). For color model reference, see pages 20-23 in the color insert.

Grayscale

Grayscale refers to the range of shades in between white and black. A black-and-white photograph is an example of a grayscale image. Illustrator uses an 8-bit grayscale model consisting of 256 shades of gray with 0 representing white (no value) and 255 representing solid black. Illustrator can also convert a color bitmap image to grayscale by rasterizing it. Individual spot colors and CMYK colors can be selected and converted to their grayscale equivalents. When Illustrator rasterizes a color image to grayscale—that is, it converts the vector image to a bitmap image—it discards all of the color information, retaining only the range of values between black and white.

The success you have in converting a color image to grayscale will depend upon the amount of light and dark definition between the colors. Colors that are close in value—those colors with a similar amount of light or dark in them, such as pale yellow or salmon pink—may appear very different to the eye but, when converted to grayscale, may be virtually indistinguishable. When converted to grayscale, bright red translates in value to almost solid black, while yellow when translated to grayscale becomes almost white. So, some experimenting is not a bad idea before converting to grayscale.

RGB Color

Computer monitors, color scanners, and television screens use a color model called RGB color (which stands for Red, Green, and Blue). Images are comprised of tiny luminescent dots, or pixels of color comprised of these three primary colors. Look at your computer monitor or television screen with a strong magnifying glass and you'll see these tiny red, green, and blue pixels. The RGB model works by assigning each pixel one of 256 values for each color with 0 representing no color and 255 representing the color's full intensity.

Each pixel is actually comprised of three separate pixels, a red pixel, a green pixel and a blue pixel. The combination of the three colored pixels produces an incredible combination of 16.7 million colors or 24-bit color. The RGB color model is also referred to as additive color because adding 100 percent red, green, and blue light produces white. RGB colors are also known as screen colors because we see these colors on the computer monitor or television screen. On computer monitors and television screens, each pixel is actually made up of a red, green, and blue pixel. The intensity of each pixel determines the actual color.

When you're working in the RGB color space and producing images in Illustrator that will be viewed on the World Wide Web, deselect or uncheck the Simulate Print Colors on Display option in the Color Settings section of the File menu. This will cause Illustrator's screen display to show colors as they will appear on Web browsers such as Netscape Navigator, or Microsoft's Internet Explorer. See the section below on Web palettes for more on this subject.

CMYK Color

The acronym CMYK represents the names of the four ink colors used in commercial four-color printing: cyan, magenta, yellow, and black. (The letter K is used to represent black to avoid being confused with B for blue.) CMYK color is known as *subtractive color* because you have to subtract all four colors to get white. In theory, adding the three subtractive primary colors, cyan, magenta, and yellow, produces black. In reality, the color is closer to a muddy brown, so black is added to increase the color depth and add detail.

In the CMYK model, full-color images are broken into the three primary colors of cyan, magenta, and yellow producing color separations—film that is used by the printer to produce printing plates. A fourth separation containing black is created to add detail, density, and depth to the image. As the negative film used to produce color separations can only display black or white (actually black or clear), the image on each piece of film is translated into tiny dots. The size of each dot controls the amount of ink that will be printed on the paper. A series of very thin yellow dots for example, produces pale yellow, while a series of heavy yellow dots produces solid yellow. Process inks are transparent, so printing solid yellow over solid cyan produces green. Magenta printed over yellow produces red, and so forth.

If the final output for your image is a four-color printed document, then make sure that Simulate Print Colors on Display is checked in the Color Settings section of the File menu. The colors on your screen will appear darker, but in reality they more accurately represent the final printed colors.

HSB Color

Another model for specifying color is HSB, which stands for hue, saturation, and brightness. This model can be used to specify either RGB or CMYK colors. In this model, colors are divided into 360 hues (full-intensity colors) which can be visualized as 360 colors arranged around a color wheel, beginning and ending with red. Each of the 360 hues can be further modified in terms of saturation and brightness. *Saturation* is the strength or purity of the color (the density or intensity), whereas *brightness* is the relative lightness and darkness.

A bright red (hue 0) is at full strength when the Saturation and Brightness settings are at 100 percent. When Brightness is 100 percent but Saturation is very low, let's say 10 percent, the result is very pale pink. When Saturation is set to 100 and Brightness is set to 50 percent, the result is a deep red.

Spot Color and Process Color

There are two very different color systems used in commercial printing, spot color and process color. *Spot colors* are those solid colors created by mixing printing inks to a specific formula—kind of like following a recipe when you bake a cake. *Process color*, also known as CMYK color (cyan, magenta, yellow, and black), uses four transparent, colored printing inks to create full-color images like the ones in the color insert of this book. Spot colors are commonly used when only two or three solid colors (or tints of these colors) are needed. The important thing to note is that even though Illustrator enables you to pick spot colors and use them in your image, only about half of the spot colors can be accurately reproduced using process colors. We'll explain this in greater detail when we discuss color gamut later in this chapter.

Spot Color

CMYK produces a universe of colors by printing a combination of cyan, magenta, yellow, and black dots. Spot colors are solid single colors made of custom printing inks or pigments. The most widely known source of spot colors is the Pantone Matching System (PMS). Other providers of spot color matching systems follow a strict formula for mixing printing inks and identifying individual colors by number, so that ten printers in ten different locations using ten different types of printing press can print the same exact color. Spot colors are commonly used for one-, two-, and three-color printing projects, where a specific and accurate color scheme is desired. It is not uncommon for designers to create projects using a combination of spot and process colors, CMYK for the photographs and one or more extra spot colors (or tints of these colors made by screening the solid color) for accents, or special colors for matching precise corporate identity requirements.

Illustrator lets you use spot color in two ways. You can design with all spot colors, in which case Illustrator will output a separate piece of film for each image. Or you can specify Pantone or other spot color matching systems and let Illustrator convert the spot colors to process for four-color (CMYK) printing.

Be aware that only slightly better than half of the Pantone spot colors can be accurately matched in four-color printing due to the limitations of the four-color printing process. Six-color Hexachrome printing, which adds a special green and orange, can exactly match closer to 80 percent of Pantone's spot colors. In either case there are going to be some spot colors that will never match exactly when reproduced in four-color process printing.

Using Special Swatch Libraries

In addition to the Pantone Matching System mentioned above, Illustrator 7 has Swatch Libraries for several other custom color specifying systems. These libraries are collections of specially numbered or coded colors that can be used to reproduce specific colors. There are swatch libraries for both spot color and process color.

The Swatch Libraries are found under the Windows pull-down menu in the Swatch Libraries flyout menu. These libraries include DICCOLOR, FOCOLTONE, PANTONE C (Coated) and U (Uncoated), PANTONE PROCESS, System (Mac), System (Windows), TOYO, TRUMATCH, and Web.

Be aware that color prints differently on coated and uncoated paper. Colors printed on uncoated stock lack the intensity of colors printed on coated stock, hence the need for the coated and uncoated specifications. Many color matching systems offer a swatch book of coated and uncoated colors. Choose your colors from the appropriate swatch book for best results.

To work effectively with these color matching systems (except System and Web), it is wise to have a special swatch book from which to specify colors. The color samples in these swatch books are printed in the actual ink colors to ensure their accuracy when printed. Swatch books can usually be purchased from art supply stores or from the specific companies directly. Of the palettes in the Swatch Library, the most commonly used are: FOCOLTONE, a system of 763 CMYK colors, PANTONE, spot (in coated and uncoated colors for printing on coated or uncoated paper) and Process, (PANTONE's four-color approximation of their spot colors), and TOYO, a collection of a thousand spot colors based on the most common printing inks in Japan.

Another popular color matching system is TRUMATCH, a library of two thousand CMYK colors based on 40 tints and shades of 50 hues. The TRUMATCH system is shown in Figure 11-1. Because this system is based upon digitally generated colors, TRUMATCH is a very reliable method for specifying process colors. TRUMATCH ColorFinder Swatching Systems are available in coated and uncoated editions. The Show Swatches option, which should not be confused with Swatch Libraries, toggles the Swatches palette on and off the screen.

 The printed color samples in swatch books are very light sensitive. Avoid leaving your swatch book in bright sunlight or keep them in a dark place when not in use. Invest in a new swatch book every year or two as the colors can fade over time even if you have exercised proper caution.

Pantone offers a variety of products to help you specify spot color including fan books of colors and books with tear-out color chips, which are helpful in planning color schemes or showing clients or printers the exact color, or colors, you wish to use. Pantone offers separate color matching material for pastel colors, metallic colors, tints—all on coated and uncoated paper. Pantone also offers guides specific to four-color (process) and six-color (Hexachrome) color.

All of these color matching systems assign a unique number or code to each color which corresponds to the naming of colors in each particular swatch library. For example, if you decide to print a logo in TRUMATCH 18-a5 (dark green), you open the Swatch Libraries menu under the Window pull-down menu and select TRUMATCH. The TRUMATCH custom swatch library appears on your page and you select your colors from that.

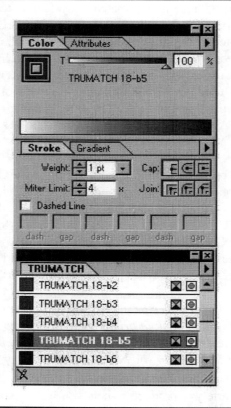

FIGURE 11-1   The TRUMATCH palette is one of ten custom Swatch
Libraries found in the Window menu in the Swatch
Library flyout menu

    *If you work with a Swatch Library often and want to have that library
available, you can drag the title bar from the library to the title bar of the
Swatches menu, as shown in Figure 11-2. You don't have to drag the swatch
library to just the Swatches menu. You can drag it to any appropriate menu
and it will reside there whenever you work with that document. To make the
arrangement permanent see the section "Customizing Your Startup File"
in **Chapter 15: Getting the Most Out of Illustrator**.*

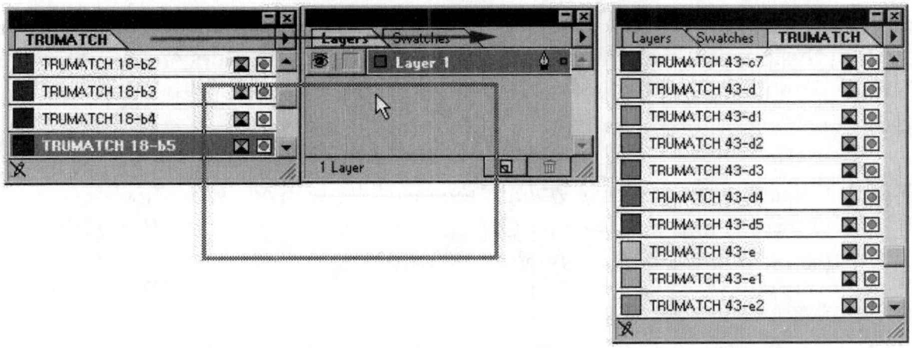

FIGURE 11-2   Swatch Libraries can be easily added to other menus—just drag over the title bar of the menu you wish to add it to the new menu's title bar

Caution   *Because different monitors display color differently and room lighting and surrounding colors can affect your perception of color, to ensure accurate color reproduction use the appropriate swatching library when specifying colors. If possible, use a color-corrected light to view the swatch book.*

The remaining three palettes in the Swatch Library are System (Mac and Windows) and Web. It should come as no surprise that the standard 256 System colors on the Macintosh are not the same standard 256 System colors on Windows computers, which explains the need for two different System Swatch Libraries.

If you're creating 256-color bitmap images that will be viewed exclusively on one platform or the other, use the appropriate library to ensure pure, non-dithering colors. *Dithered* colors use a system of colored patterns placed over solid colors to create the appearance of additional colors beyond the 256-color palette. The result is often distracting and unattractive when viewed on monitors limited to 256 colors.

The Web Swatch Library contains 216 non-dithering colors that are common to both Macintosh and Windows computers and are best used for Web graphics exported in the GIF file format. This is important when you are creating images with

large areas of solid color because these colors will appear solid. If you use colors not in the Web palette, when people view your site on a 256-color monitor the image colors may be badly dithered and can result in ugly, unanticipated results.

Both System and Web palettes are comprised of RGB colors and are best used with the Simulate Print Colors on Display option unchecked in Illustrator's Color Settings section of the File menu.

 When creating Web graphics that will be viewed on multiple-computer platforms and exported as GIF files, pick colors from the Web palette for the most consistent cross-platform results.

Creating a Custom Color Startup File

Creating a custom Startup file allows you to tailor Illustrator 7 to your style of working. This is a great time-saver, because once you have created your custom Startup file, Illustrator will remember to configure your work space to your personal preferences every time you open the program. You can add custom Swatch Libraries so they will be available at all times. You can decide which palettes you want to be available, specify default units of measurement, change your default type font, size, and style, and make any other changes that seem appropriate. Any modifications or additions to this file will appear every time you open Illustrator so you don't have to reinvent the wheel every time you fire up the program. Follow these steps to create your custom Startup file.

The first step is to copy your current default Startup file. On the Macintosh, the Startup file is named Adobe Illustrator Startup and is found in the Plug-ins folder. In Windows, the Startup file is named Startup.ai and resides in the Plug-ins folder.

 In Windows, highlight the filename in the Explorer, click on the right mouse button, and choose Copy. Then right mouse button click in the directory and select Paste. Windows appends "copy of" to the filename. You do not have to exit Illustrator to do this.

Open the copy of your Startup file, which is the copy of Adobe Illustrator Startup in the Mac or the copy of Startup.ai in Windows. This will serve as a template for the new Startup file. On the screen you'll see labeled squares filled with all the default colors, patterns, and gradients currently available in the default Swatches palette.

1. **Edit the Swatches palette.** Add, modify, or delete any unwanted colors, patterns, and gradients. Delete any colors, patterns, or gradients both from their respective palettes as well as from the artwork in the Startup file, otherwise these items will reappear next time you start Illustrator.

2. **Customize the rest of your work environment.** Modify any options you want as default settings in the Page Setup and Document Setup dialog boxes. For example, specify units of measurement, which palettes you want open on Startup, and so forth.

3. **Save your new template file.** Save your file as Adobe Illustrator Startup (Macintosh) or Startup.ai (Windows). Be sure to save it in the Plug-ins folder. Next time you open Illustrator, your workspace will reflect your changes. If you need to alter your setup, simply repeat this process.

Converting Between Color Models

Grayscale, RGB, CMYK, spot color, or HSB, Illustrator lets you work in any or all of these color spaces at the same time. You might have a RGB bitmap image, several Pantone spot color-filled graphics, a few gradient and pattern fills. Ultimately, you'll want to have all your color ducks in a row depending on how the image is going to be used. If you're creating Web graphics, you'll want your colors to be specified in RGB because this is the color space in which the image will be viewed. If your final output is to paper, and you plan to print in two colors, you will want to use grayscale and/or spot colors. If you plan to output to four colors for printing on a four-color press, you will need to specify CMYK.

Illustrator makes switching between and among the color models easy. Make sure that the Color palette is open (FG or Windows|Show Color). Select each color and click on the small triangle in the right side of the palette to open the Color model flyout menu and change the properties to the desired color model, as shown in Figure 11-3.

Bitmap images can be converted by selecting the bitmap and then opening the Filters drop-down menu and selecting the desired color model. Unfortunately, gradient fills and pattern fills need to be changed manually. With gradient fills it's possible to have a combination of grayscale, RGB, and CMYK colors, so you need to click on each color indicator slider and change each color individually if need be. Pattern fills need to be opened, edited, and then redefined in the Edit menu.

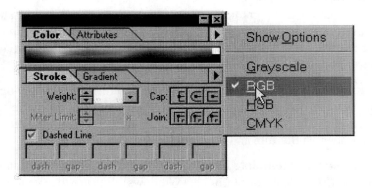

FIGURE 11-3   Clicking on the triangle on the top right of the Color palette produces a flyout menu with color model options

You can also drag and drop the revised pattern fill back into the Swatches palette to replace the current swatch. Your changes will be applied globally to all objects using the revised fill. Drag the revised pattern file directly over the pattern you're replacing and then click on the ALT key (Windows) or the OPTION key (Mac) and drop the swatch.

Remember   *When converting Pantone spot colors to CMYK, keep in mind that only about 50 percent of these spot colors can be matched exactly. About 20 percent additional colors come close. The rest may vary greatly from the actual Pantone color swatch found in the Pantone swatch book. To be sure of exact color matching, refer to a CMYK swatchbook, such as Pantone's Solid to Process guide or the TRUMATCH ColorFinder fan book. When exporting files to bitmap, the TIFF file format gives you the option of saving either RGB or CMYK information. If you plan to edit your image in Photoshop, use the RGB format. If you plan to output your file directly to color separations, use CMYK. If you have Photoshop 4.0, Illustrator can export to Photoshop's native PSD file format in grayscale, RGB, or CMYK.*

Web Image File Formats: GIF or JPEG?

There are two primary file formats used for creating images for the World Wide Web, GIF (Compuserve's graphic image format) and JPEG (Joint Photographer's Experts Group). The burning question is not simply which file format to use but how to pronounce GIF. Some folks prefer the *G* to be pronounced like a *J* or *Jif*, others prefer *Gif* to be pronounced as in *Gift*, minus the *t*.

However you pronounce it, both file formats have built-in compression schemes that greatly reduce the file size—an important consideration when creating bandwidth-friendly images for posting on the Web. GIF images can contain up to 256 colors. JPEG images can contain up to 16.7 million colors. GIF 89a images support a transparent background color, which allows images to be displayed in shapes other than rectangular.

The GIF file format is best for graphics such as logos, text, and buttons. The JPEG file format is best for photographic images because it contains 24-bit color information and produces a cleaner, smoother image. JPEG files support a range of compression so file size can be kept relatively small without sacrificing quality. GIF files can display photographic images by dithering colors—a process of overlaying various color patterns to create the appearance of more colors, as you can see shown in Figure 11-4. GIF files are safer if your images are being viewed on monitors that can only display 256 or fewer colors. JPEG images band (smooth blends are reduced to broad bands of a single color) and lose most of their definition on 16-color monitors.

When you export an image to the GIF file format, you are presented with several confusing color options which include: Exact, System (Mac or Windows), Web, and Adaptive. Use Exact if your image uses only a few non-dithering colors and you want to keep the size of your file small. Use System (Mac or Windows) when you're creating images specifically for one platform or the other that need to be confined to 256 colors.

The Web option saves your image in a "safe" palette of 216 colors that display the same on Mac or Windows computers. These 216 non-dithering colors display solid (non-dithered) on any computer platform, as shown in Figure 11-5. Each RGB color has a value of either 0, 51, 102, 153, 204, or 255. Bright yellow, for example, is composed of Red=255, Green=255, Blue=0. Black is composed of Red=0, Blue=0, Green=0. The Adaptive option saves your image in the best possible 256 colors and will display best on monitors that can display 256 colors or more.

The Adaptive palette generally produces a superior GIF image—compared to the Web or System palettes—that often ranks with a JPEG image, because it selects the best 256 colors from a 24-bit palette to display the image. The downside is that

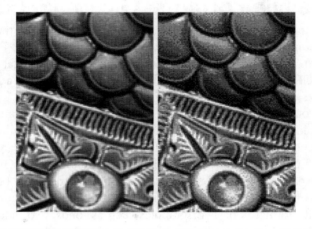

FIGURE 11-4   The same image shown in JPEG and GIF format. The JPEG image has 16.7 million colors to select from, whereas the GIF image contains only 216 dithered colors. Both images are shown at 300 percent actual size.

Adaptive palette GIF files may not display properly on 256-color monitors that are limited to specific system colors. When in doubt, your safest bet is the Web palette.

Gamut Colors

We touched briefly on gamut when we discussed the limitations in trying to match specific spot colors in CMYK four-color process printing. *Gamut* refers to the number of colors that can be viewed or printed. The human eye is capable of seeing close to a billion colors, give or take a few million. Computer monitors are capable of displaying up to 16.7 million colors, not quite as many as the human eye but a heap of colors nonetheless. Commercial printing has a more restricted color gamut. Many vibrant colors that can be viewed on a computer monitor are out of CMYK gamut and will not reproduce with the same intensity when printed on paper.

Furthermore, color viewed on your computer monitor is brighter because it is generated by millions of tiny colored lights. This is similar to looking at two versions of the same photograph, one in a transparency viewed on a light box and the other

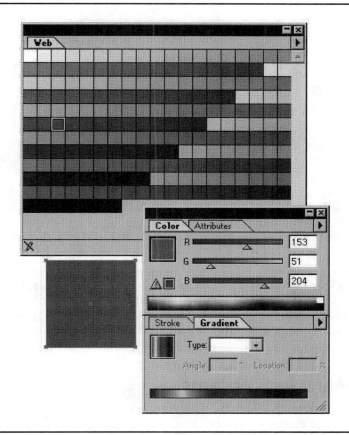

FIGURE 11-5   The Web palette contains 216 non-dithering colors which will display solid on browsers (Netscape Navigator, Microsoft Internet Explorer) on Macintosh and Windows computers

11

in a photograph viewed as a paper print. The image that is backed with light appears brighter and more vibrant that the same image viewed as a paper print.

When you're working in RGB or HSB mode and a selected color is beyond the CMYK color gamut, a small square containing the color appears on the Color palette accompanied by a small triangle with an exclamation mark. (You'll see this right above the hand pointer in Figure 11-6.) Clicking on the small colored square brings the color back into the CMYK gamut. The result is a color that may not be as intense but will print as displayed.

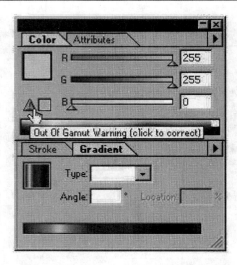

FIGURE 11-6 Colors that are out of the CMYK printing range (gamut) are flagged with a small box and a triangle with exclamation point. Clicking on the small colored box brings the color back into gamut.

Color Matching Systems

While your scanner sees color one way, your monitor displays it another way, and your color output device interprets color in yet another. This makes it difficult to ensure predictable color throughout the design process. The goal of Illustrator's Color Matching System (CMS) is to get your scanner, monitor, and printer all defining color in the same terms by a process known as *calibration*. Simply put, CMS is a process of getting your components to speak a common language so that the red seen by your scanner sees is the same red that Illustrator 7 sees which is the same red that a printing press prints. The whole idea is to keep the red on the page and not on your face.

Illustrator's Color Matching System is based upon the International Color Consortium (ICC) standards and ensures that your colors are not only hardware consistent—scanner, monitor, printer—but software consistent as well, so that your image will appear the same in other ICC-Compliant software programs such as Adobe Photoshop and Adobe PageMaker. The beauty of the CMS is that it manages color in all of Illustrator's color models, RBG, HSB, and CMYK, for consistent input, output, and display.

Illustrator automatically installs a Color Matching System in the System folder (Macintosh) or the Windows/System subdirectory (Windows) when you first install the program. The color-conversion plug-in filter must also be installed in the Plug-ins folder. Illustrator uses two different Color Matching Systems, ColorSync for Macintosh and Kodak Digital Science Color Management for Windows. Each CMS is optimized specifically for each platform.

For best results, set your CMS settings before you begin to create images. Open the Color Settings menu (File|Color Settings), as shown in Figure 11-7. From the Monitor drop-down menu (Windows only) select a setting for your monitor.

If you do not see a profile for your monitor, check the documentation that came with your monitor to determine a compatible Gamma setting. If you are unable to find this information, contact your monitor manufacturer's technical support for their recommendation. Next, make sure the profile is listed for your output device in the Printer drop-down menu. If you plan to optimize for your desktop color printer,

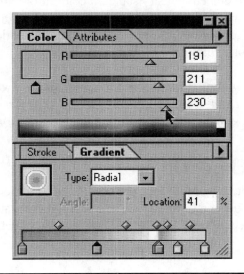

FIGURE 11-7   The Color Settings menu, found in the File menu, calibrates input and output devices and ensures color consistency between applications using the same settings

then make sure that device is listed. If you plan to output to a Linotronic imagesetter, then make sure this is the device that is specified. In order to specify an output device, you need to have printer driver(s) installed for your target output device(s). Refer to your system documentation for additional information about installing printer drivers.

Note *Monitor settings for Macintosh systems can only be changed in the ColorSync color management application. See the documentation that comes with your Macintosh ColorSync CMS application for more details.*

Finally, select from the contents of the Intent drop-down menu to determine your primary purpose. The Image option works best with scanned or photographic images and represents a realistic approximation of the printed output. The Graphics option enhances colors for optimum brightness for business graphics—charts, slides, and such—at the expense of color accuracy. The Colormetric option produces an accurate RGB screen image, but some colors may be out of the printing gamut. If you're producing images for the Web or multimedia projects, use the Colormetric option.

Checking the Use ICC (International Color Consortium) Profiles with TIFF option enables you to embed industry standard color information when you export a TIFF (Tagged Image File Format) bitmap image and ensures consistent reproduction across a variety of output devices. Selecting this option lets you use ICC profiles to color manage imported TIFF image files as well.

Remember *Check the Simulate Print Colors on Display option if you're creating images for printed output. If you're creating images to be viewed in the RGB color model—Web graphics or onscreen presentations—leave this option unchecked.*

Profiles for Other Devices

If you can't find a device profile for your scanner, monitor, or printer, contact the manufacturer and request a device specific profile. Many manufacturers maintain Web sites where these profiles can often be downloaded directly for free.

Colorful Ways to Apply Color in Illustrator 7

Illustrator has two complementary color palettes, the Color palette and the Swatches palette, as shown in Figure 11-8. The Swatches palette displays solid colors, gradient fills, and pattern fills. The Color palette edits colors, line weights, and fills.

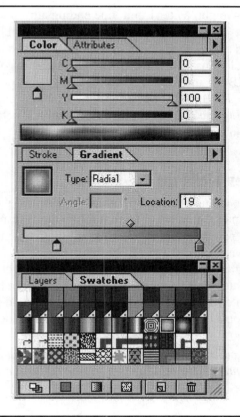

FIGURE 11-8   The Color palette and Swatches palette. Solid, gradient, and pattern fills are picked in the Swatches palette and modified in the Color palette

Illustrator's Color Palette

The Color palette is subdivided into four tabbed sections, Color, Attributes, Stroke, and Gradient. To move between these sections, click on the appropriate tab. These menus can be toggled on and off by clicking Show or Hide in the Window pull-down menu. You'll see additional controls on the bottom of the main Toolbox.

Use the Color palette to specify and/or edit colors, fills, patterns, and outline attributes. The square under the Color tab on the Color palette represents the fill state—fill or outline. A solid square indicates the fill state and displays the current fill which remains as is until altered. The heavy outline indicates outline attributes including color, line weight, Miter Limit, line ending attributes, Cap and Join, and solid or dashed line. The Color palette is context sensitive. The editing options change depending on the selected object. If a spot color-filled object is selected, the percentage of the color may be modified. If an object is currently filled with a CMYK, RGB, or HSB fill, the edit controls change to these specific modes. You can convert color modes, RGB to CMYK for instance, in the Color palette by clicking on the small triangle to the right of the Attributes tab and selecting a color model from the fly-out menu. (Refer back to Figure 11-3.)

The Swatches Palette

The Swatches palette contains solid fills, gradient fills, and patterns. There are six buttons on the bottom of the palette. The first four buttons display: 1. All solid fills, gradient fills, and all pattern fills, 2. Solid fills only, 3. Gradient fills only, 4. Pattern fills only, 5. New Swatch, and 6. Delete Swatch.

To apply solid, gradient, and pattern fills, select the object to be filled and then click on the appropriate fill. If you modify an existing color or fill or create a custom color or fill, you can click on the New Swatch button to add it to the palette. You can also drag and drop a color, gradient, or pattern directly into the palette.

 You can add custom colors and fills to the Swatch palette only in the current document—unless you make the effort to modify your Startup file.

Solid Colors

There are two sets of solid colors in the default Swatches palette. The first set of colors can be CMYK, Grayscale, HSB, or RGB. The second set of colors, distinguished by the small triangle in the lower-right corner, are spot colors, as shown in Figure 11-9. The top row are CMYK, RGB, or HSB colors, the bottom row are spot colors and are differentiated by the triangle on the lower-right corner. The color mixing portion of the menu is "context sensitive" and changes to reflect the options available for the current selection. Spot colors can only be modified by tint ranging from 100 percent (solid) to 0 percent (no color). Spot colors can be converted to mixed color status by clicking on the flyout button in the Color palette and selecting the desired color model from the menu.

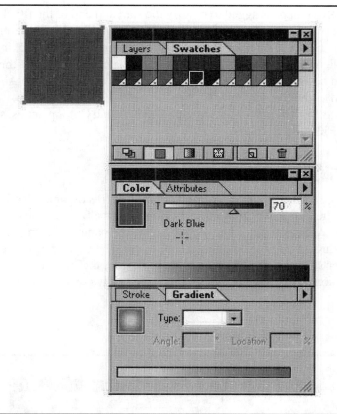

FIGURE 11-9 The solid colors in the Swatch palette

Gradient Colors

11

Gradient colors can be linear or radial. You can toggle between the two using the drop-down menu under the Gradient tab on the Color palette. Colors can be edited in regard to beginning and ending color, halfway point, and additional colors, as shown in Figure 11-10. Colors may be added by clicking under the gradient display and dragged to any position. The diamond slider above the gradient display determines the halfway point between the colors. The two colored boxes under the gradient fill area can be dragged to modify the start and end of the fill. The diamond object just above the gradient fill area, can be dragged in either direction to move the center of the fill. Colors may be added to gradient fills by clicking under the colored gradient area and then using the appropriate sliders to edit the new color. New fills can be dragged into the palette or added by clicking on the Add fill button at the bottom of the Swatch palette.

For more information on working with Gradient and Color palettes, see **Chapter 10: Setting Fills and Strokes**.

Pattern Fills

Pattern fills are applied the same as solid or gradient fills by first selecting the object to be filled, then clicking on the desired pattern in the Swatch palette, as shown in Figure 11-11. Patterns can be altered by dragging the pattern swatch onto the page or artboard, editing the fill, and dragging it back to the palette. Holding down the ALT key (Windows) or OPTION key (Macintosh) and dragging the modified swatch over the previous version replaces the old version with the newly created or modified one.

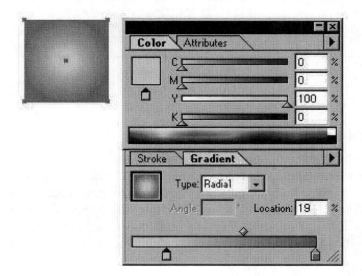

FIGURE 11-10   The Gradient edit options in the Color palette

FIGURE 11-11   The Pattern Fill section of the Swatches palette contains a series of two-color fills that produce a seamless repeating pattern. A white background will be transparent.

Note *Adding, deleting, and modifying colors and fills only applies to the currently opened document unless you create a new Startup file as detailed earlier in this chapter.*

The Main Toolbox Palette

The Main Toolbox palette offers additional controls for determining color and stroke attributes, as shown in Figure 11-12. The large solid square and square outline at the bottom of the main Toolbox palette toggles between fill and stroke (outline) when the appropriate button is clicked. The square in front represents the current mode, for example, when the solid square is in front, Illustrator is in Fill mode; when the outline is in front, Illustrator is in Outline mode. Clicking on a color, gradient, or pattern in the Swatch palette or mixing a custom color in the Color palette makes this the current fill. If the fill and stroke colors are solid, clicking on the arrows to the top right of the fill and stroke squares reverses the fill color and stroke color. The three small boxes under the fill and stroke squares represent the current default solid color, gradient fill, and no color. Clicking on the no-color square (with the red diagonal line) sets the fill or stroke color to none, depending upon which is currently selected.

There are three more color controls on the main Toolbox palette, the Eyedropper tool (I), the Paintbucket tool (K), and the Gradient tool (G). Clicking on an object with the Eyedropper tool (I) copies the color attributes to the currently selected

11

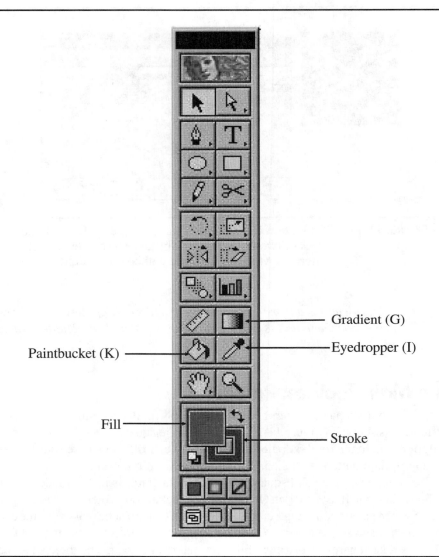

Gradient (G)

Eyedropper (I)

Paintbucket (K)

Fill

Stroke

FIGURE 11-12   The main Toolbox palette toggles between fill and stroke, fill and no fill, and stroke and no stroke. The Paintbucket tool (K) fills any object with the default color and stroke. The Eyedropper tool (I) fills the selected object with the attributes of any object it clicks upon. The Gradient tool (G) determines the direction and length of any selected gradient fill

object. This is a very efficient way to copy attributes from another object. The Paintbucket tool fills any object you click on with the current fill and stroke. The object does not need to be selected. The Gradient tool lets you edit the center and fill direction of any gradient fill. Click inside the shape to be modified and drag in the direction you want the fill to travel.

> **Caution** *Type can only be filled with solid colors, or tints of solid colors, unless you have selected the Create Outlines option in the Type menu. Creating outlines eliminates the ability to edit the text attributes, so only use the Create Outlines option when you have finished editing your type.*

Chapter 11 Tutorial:
Creating a Transparent Highlight

As a practical exploration of the features and effects discussed in this chapter, follow through in this step-by-step tutorial. As you do so, you may notice that some of these steps are accompanied by a "Color palette" symbol. This symbol indicates that the step has also been illustrated in full color in the Fundamental Illustrator 7 color insert. The purpose of the color insert is to provide you with a brief overview of the tutorial and act as an overall reference for the practical use of color throughout these tutorials.

Although Illustrator cannot create an actual transparency, here's a cool technique you can use to create a transparent effect on a metallic sphere. The Fundamental Illustrator 7 color insert shows the final illustration plus several key steps from this tutorial in full color. Walk this way as we step through the process.

1. Draw a circle and an two ellipses, as shown in Figure 11-13.

2. Open the Swatch palette as shown here. Select the gradients (the third button on the bottom). Select the circle and click on the second gradient fill, as shown in Figure 11-14.

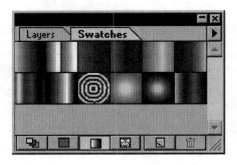

Illustrator 7 IN ACTION

The three-dimensional moon shown here was created entirely in Illustrator using a combination of old and new features. The moon shape is actually the letter *C* from Adobe's Mythos font, an alphabet comprised of medieval-type designs. The letter is converted to outlines, filled with a radial fill, and then rasterized, and bitmap effects are applied, as shown next. A star pattern fill is created, duplicated, and modified to create the illusion of a transparent drop shadow.

Notice how the white highlight falls roughly in the middle of the moon adding a three-dimensional effect. Illustrator's Gradient tool (G) was used to offset the center of the fill to acheive this effect.

The letter *C* is set in Adobe Mythos to a cap height of 300 points. The type is first converted to outlines (Type|Create Outlines) to allow a gradient fill to be applied. A default linear gradient fill was applied, then changed to a radial gradient fill, and the Gradient tool (G) was used to offset the beginning and ending path of the fill. The moon was Rasterized (converted to a bitmap) at 266 dpi, Grayscale, and the Anti-Alias (smoothing) and Create Mask options were selected. Using the Create Mask option, a clipping path around the bitmap makes the background invisible. A texture filter (Filter|Texture-Craquelure) was added to give the surface an antique-like appearance, as shown next. The following settings were used to get this texture: Crack Spacing 20, Crack Depth 8, Crack Brightness 10.

Illustrator 7 IN ACTION

A rectangle was placed behind the moon. A star pattern fill, from the Pattern Fill section of the Swatch palette is modified making the stars larger and altering the star and background colors. The process for doing this is quite simple. The existing star pattern swatch is dragged from the palette onto the page. The Scale tool (S) is used to increase the size of the fill 200 percent. The elements are ungrouped and the colors changed creating what we'll refer to as a normal star pattern. The fill elements are selected and the swatch is dragged into the Pattern Fill palette so that the fill can be applied directly from the Swatch palette. A duplicate of the normal star pattern fill is created by dragging the fill from the palette back onto the page, where the colors are darkened, and the new swatch dragged back into the palette.

The rectangle is filled with the normal star pattern. A duplicate of the moon is placed over the star-patterned background and the darker version of the fill applied. Because the dark pattern is a variation of the normal star pattern, the elements align perfectly adding the effect of transparency to the shadow. The moon figure is positioned on top of the shadow.

The background rectangle is selected and a Roughen distortion applied (Filter|Distort-Roughen) with these settings: Size 5 percent, Detail 20 /in, Points-Smooth, giving the rectangle the look of torn paper.

Note   *If you move a pattern-filled object, the pattern will no longer align. However, if you apply a solid fill to the object, then reapply the pattern fill, the patterns will once again align.*

11

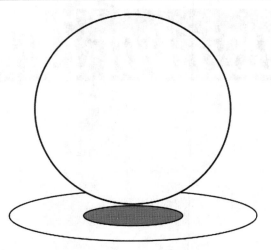

FIGURE 11-13   Draw a circle and two ellipses. Fill the smaller ellipse with 40 percent black

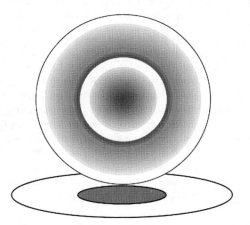

FIGURE 11-14   Select the circle and apply a gradient fill

3. Open the Color palette (Window|Show Colors). Click on the Gradient tab. From the drop-down menu, select Radial.

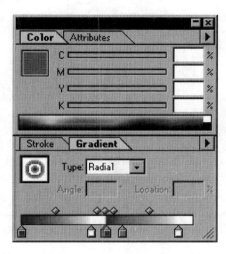

The Linear fill now becomes a Radial, fill as shown in Figure 11-15.

4. Click on the Gradient tool (G) on the main Toolbox palette. With the circle still selected, click right and above center and drag down on a 45-degree angle to the edge of the circle and release. Drag guidelines from the rulers so they cross at the begin and end point of the gradient, as shown in Figure 11-16. If the Rulers are not displayed, select Show Rulers from the View menu.

Note *Every time you drag the Gradient tool (G), the fill changes its orientation. So if you drag the Gradient tool and are not happy with the results and you drag again, the orientation of the fill changes. If you fill the circle with a solid color, then reapply the radial fill, the orientation resets to the default position.*

Note *If you drag the Gradient tool (G) and are unhappy with the results, select Undo (CTRL/COMMAND+Z) from the Edit menu. Keep using Undo until you're happy with the fill. Illustrator resets the orientation of the fill each time you use the Gradient tool and, for this exercise, it is important that the orientation for the circle and the highlight be the same.*

11

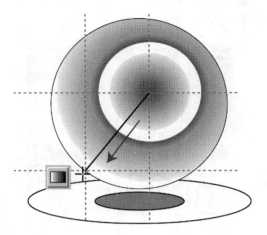

FIGURE 11-15 Change the Gradient fill type to Radial

FIGURE 11-16 Drag guidelines from the Rulers to mark the start and end of the gradient fill path. Drag the Gradient tool (G) from slightly right and top of center, downward to the edge of the circle.

5. Edit the colors and position, as shown in Figure 11-17.

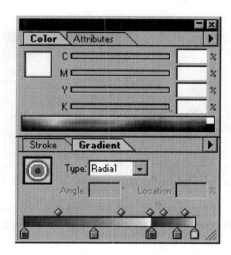

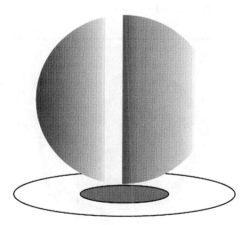

FIGURE 11-17 Here's what the fill looks like when you have edited the colors

6. Click on the New Swatch button on the bottom of the Swatch palette to add the fill.

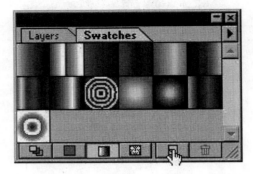

7. Draw a window pane highlight. Make sure that the four sections are a Compound Path (Objects|Compound Path). Position it over the circle (see Figure 11-18.)

8. Select the window pane highlight and click on the new radial fill that you just created in the swatch palette. Select the Gradient tool (G) from the Main Toolbox palette and use the guidelines to drag the exact same gradient path as in Step 4. The new fill will match the sphere and appear to be invisible, as shown in Figure 11-19.

FIGURE 11-18   Draw a window pane highlight and position it over the circle

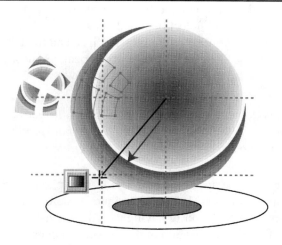

FIGURE 11-19   Select the window pane highlight and apply the lighter version of the radial fill. Drag the Gradient tool along the same path as for the circle

9. Edit the colors using the HSB model (available via the flyout menu). Make each of the colors lighter by increasing Brightness and decreasing Saturation.

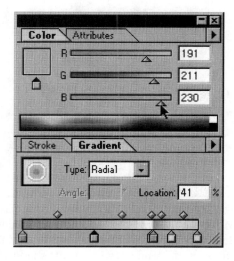

11

10. Move the smaller ellipse under the circle and fill it 40 percent black. Fill the large ellipse white. Select both and click on the Blend tool (B). Click on the bottom center node of the larger ellipse and then the same node on the smaller ellipse. The Blend menu will appear, as shown in Figure 11-20. Click OK to produce a soft drop shadow.

This soft shadow technique works on colored surfaces too—just make the larger shadow object the same color as the background and the smaller shadow object a darker version of the background color.

The final image has the appearance of a semi-transparent highlight on a shiny sphere, as shown in Figure 11-21. This technique is useful for creating a range of realistic transparent effects. If you're having a hard time visualizing how this looks in color, you'll find a color illustration of this project on page 24 in the color insert.

This technique can be used to create a variety of realistic transparency effects. For example, by matching a normal, light, and dark fill you can achieve a realistic embossed look or create the appearance of a transparent glass sign. You can use this

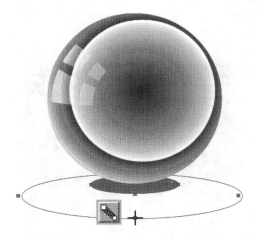

FIGURE 11-20   The lighter gradient should match the circle's gradient fill. Move the 40 percent black-filled ellipse under the circle. Select the larger white-filled ellipse and the small gray ellipse and Blend to create a soft shadow.

FIGURE 11-21   In the final image the window pane highlight appears transparent, giving the sphere a highly polished look

technique to create a circular glass vase displaying a realistic highlight and flower stem. Building on this technique, you can create the illusion of a transparent drop shadow under text or an object by matching the gradient fill of the shadow to the gradient fill of the background and then altering the colors of the shadow gradient fill to make them uniformly darker. You can see an example of this on page 24 of the color insert. Illustrator 7's powerful color editing and creation tools integrate well with Illustrator's feature set giving you the power to create professional quality images for electronic and traditional media.

Conclusion

In this chapter we learned the color models that Illustrator uses, what they are, and how and when to use them. We learned about spot color, process (CMYK) color, and custom Swatch Libraries as methods for working with and applying color. We discovered the limited range of RGB and CMYK color called gamut and how to correct out of gamut colors.

11

We learned how to train Illustrator to cater to our desires by creating a custom Startup file. We got thoroughly confused talking about the different export options for saving GIF files, and how GIF files compare to JPEG files. Finally, we had some show and tell examples of creating a three-dimensional type object in the Illustrator In Action section and a step-by-step method for creating matching gradient fills. You can apply the knowledge and these techniques just learned when you create illustrations for print or multimedia projects.

PART
III

Beyond Basic Tools

Mastering Filter Effects

12

Illustrator 7 offers a plug-in architecture that provides you many capabilities. These plug-ins and filters enable you to perform all sorts of automated tasks including adjusting object colors, simulating textures, and performing other special effects on objects. And, while some filters are designed to perform minor production-related tasks, most filters are capable of dramatically altering your artwork, often completely changing the design, mood, or appearance of vector or bitmap images in your drawing.

Illustrator 7 ships with over 90 plug-in filters. A *plug-in* is a software module that can add functionality to a program such as Illustrator 7. A *filter* is a plug-in that adds functionality specifically to the Filter menu. While the majority of plug-ins add functionality and extra features under the Filter menu, they may also come in the form of new tools such as those found in the main Toolbox, palettes, or menu commands.

Some of Illustrator 7's filters are designed to work only on paths, whereas others operate solely on bitmap images. And a select few filters apply to both types of objects. Because Illustrator 7's plug-in architecture is open to development by third parties, other additional filters can be obtained which create effects not normally available in Illustrator. Some demonstration third-party filters may be found on your Adobe Illustrator 7 program disc.

How Filters Work

As you browse the command menus, you'll likely notice Illustrator 7's filters have been organized into categories under various submenus in the Filters menu. These have broadly been divided into three separate sections, delineated by menu separators. The top section includes the reapply commands—commands that have already been performed and filters that have recently been used. The object and program filters are located in the middle section, and the bottom section contains filters specific to bitmap effects and raster image plug-ins. Filters that have similar features are grouped together in submenus, as shown in Figure 12-1.

Reapply commands enable you to apply filters repeatedly to the same object or to multiple objects and are accompanied by keyboard shortcuts. The Apply Last Filter (CTRL/COMMAND+E) command applies the most recently-used filter to the selected artwork including any settings or options that were last selected in the filter's dialog box controls. The Last Filter (CTRL/COMMAND+ALT/OPTION+E)

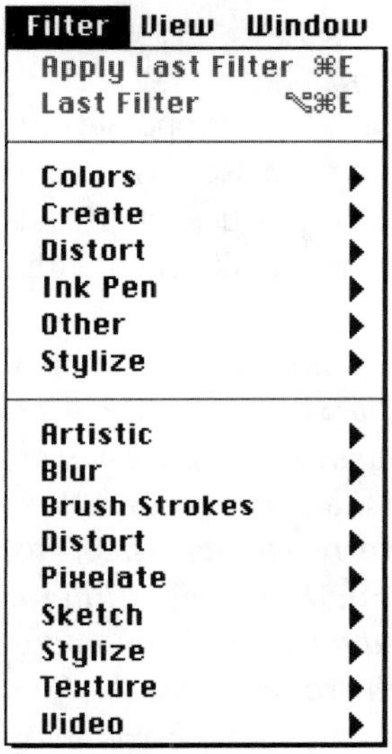

```
┌────────────────────────────────┐
│ Filter  View  Window            │
├────────────────────────────────┤
│ Apply Last Filter  ⌘E           │
│ Last Filter        ⌥⌘E          │
├────────────────────────────────┤
│ Colors                 ▶        │
│ Create                 ▶        │
│ Distort                ▶        │
│ Ink Pen                ▶        │
│ Other                  ▶        │
│ Stylize                ▶        │
├────────────────────────────────┤
│ Artistic               ▶        │
│ Blur                   ▶        │
│ Brush Strokes          ▶        │
│ Distort                ▶        │
│ Pixelate               ▶        │
│ Sketch                 ▶        │
│ Stylize                ▶        │
│ Texture                ▶        │
│ Video                  ▶        │
└────────────────────────────────┘
```

FIGURE 12-1   The Filter menu

command opens the options dialog box for the last filter used. This enables you to reapply the previous filter, but with different settings.

Note   *In regard to the reapply filter commands, Illustrator 7 differs slightly from previous versions. You won't see the Apply Last Filter or Last Filter commands in your Filter menu. Instead the commands to apply the last filter have been replaced by the actual name of the last filter you used. For example, if you last applied the Apply Drop Shadow filter, the actual command listed in the reapply filters area will appear as Apply Drop Shadow.*

The object filters have been designed to modify paths of objects created or imported into your Illustrator 7 drawing document. For example, the Add Arrowheads filter attaches arrowheads to the ends of open lines. Program filters, such as Make Riders, affect the entire document regardless of which objects are currently selected.

12

Note   *If a filter is grayed out and unavailable in the Filter menu, most likely the filter cannot be used on the selected object.*

The bitmap and raster image plug-ins operate only on placed images and objects that have been rasterized using the Rasterize (Object|Rasterize) command. For example, the Colored Pencil filter applies an effect to bitmap objects which makes the result appear as if the bitmap was sketched with colored pencils.

Note   *If you discover that certain filters are missing from Illustrator 7's Filter menu, it may be that they have been moved or certain program preferences have been altered. Illustrator enables you to select which folder your filters are stored in through the Preferences command (CTRL/COMMAND+K).*

To verify that the correct folder is being used, use the plug-in Preferences dialog box options (File\Preferences\Plug-ins & Scratch Disks) to ensure that you have selected the folder containing the plug-in modules you wish to use. By default, Illustrator 7 uses the Plug-ins folder within your Adobe Illustrator program folder, though you may change it to be any folder on your hard drive.

*Also, place all plug-ins in a single folder. Although you can nest plug-ins in folders within folders, Illustrator 7 enables you to select only one plug-in folder at a time. See the section "Setting Preferences" in **Chapter 3: Making Illustrator 7 Easy to Use** for information on setting your plug-in preferences.*

Working with Object Filters

Object filters are used to alter an object's shape and direction. Some filters alter an object's color. For the most part, object filters are designed to work only on vector paths. The colors filters—with the exception of the Blend and Overprint filters—apply to both bitmap images *and* vector objects. Some filters, such as the Object Mosaic filter, create paths based on the contents of a bitmap object.

In the section to follow, you'll explore the capabilities and uses of each filter. In most cases, you'll discover these filters are capable of creating an enormous variety of visual effects. The description of many of these filters is brief, leaving the most productive exploration of the effects that are possible up to you. Don't hesitate to experiment, changing settings until you achieve a desirable effect.

Before you begin though, be aware that when you use certain filters, you make your Illustrator 7 document more complex. In some cases, filter effects may become so complex that the required memory exceeds that of your computer. Save often, and when possible monitor your system resources in an effort to avoid exceeding available memory.

Using the Color Filters

The Color filters enable you to alter your object's color mix and are capable of converting the color model on which the object is based. The Adjusting, Convert, Invert, and Saturate filters also work on bitmap images. The Color filters submenu is shown in Figure 12-2.

In order to affect objects that have pattern or gradient fills, you need to expand the object's fill (Object|Expand Fill) so that the object is converted into editable parts. If you attempt to adjust the color of an object that contains a gradient or pattern, you will be given this alert:

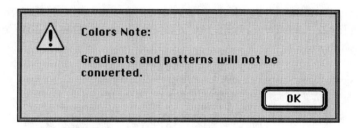

Colors Note:

Gradients and patterns will not be converted.

OK

Note   *Color filters do not affect objects that have been assigned gradient or pattern fills.*

The Adjust Colors Filter

12

The Adjust Colors filter enables you to add or subtract color values from the overall Grayscale, RGB, or CMYK values in selected objects. Adjust Colors causes a linear

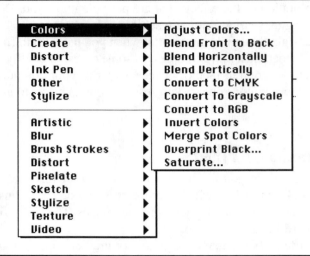

FIGURE 12-2   The Colors submenu

color transformation to be applied to your object, meaning that it performs the same transformation to each vector object or pixel in a bitmap. The Adjust Colors dialog box is shown here:

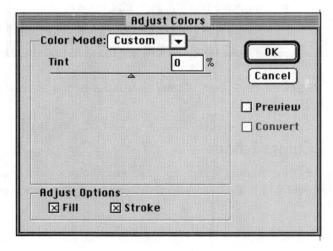

Follow these steps to experiment with the Adjust Colors filter:

1. In a new document, create a new rectangle object.

2. Fill it with a color of your own choosing. For the purposes of this exercise, choose a process color orange with the corresponding values of C=0 M=45 Y=60 K=0.

3. Choose Filter|Colors|Adjust Colors.

4. Click on the Preview option to interactively see the changes as you make them.

5. Move the magenta slider to **+55** and notice the rectangle is now a bright red.

6. Experiment with the effects and operation of this filter by moving the other sliders in a random fashion, observing the colors as they change.

 Filter preview options enable you to see your changes interactively. If you have a large or complex selection to adjust, leaving Preview unselected will speed up this filter's operation. The Adjust options also enable you to affect an object's Fill or Stroke independently or at the same time.

The Convert option enables you to convert the color space—or "model"—of an object between process color (CMYK), RGB, and Grayscale, the primary models in Illustrator 7. If an object has a CMYK fill, you cannot make RGB adjustments unless the Convert option is checked, indicating your object's format uses the RGB color. If you have multiple objects selected in different color models, you may choose to alter the colors in any one color model. Or, by selecting the Convert button, you can alter colors of all selected objects. The Custom color model option also enables you to adjust the tint of spot colors.

The Blend Filter

The Blend filter is designed to create a progression of color within a group of three or more filled objects. The effects achieved by using the Blend filter should not be confused with the term *gradient*. Blending is a term often used to describe the smooth transition between two colors contained within a single object, which is also referred to in some applications (such as CorelDraw) as a fountain fill. In this case, blending refers to the action of altering object colors to form a smooth color transition between three or more objects.

12

The Blend filter has no dialog box — it simply applies the effect directly to the selected objects. The color blend effect applies to the first and last object of your selection, based on your object's layering and stacking order and/or its vertical and horizontal orientation. The filters do not affect your object's stroke properties, nor will they have any effect on unpainted objects. The results of applying the Blend filter can be seen in Figure 12-3.

The Convert Filter

The Convert filter enables you to convert the color model of any object or bitmap to CMYK, RGB, or Grayscale. The color model is the color principle on which an object is based.

 You may not convert objects with gradient or pattern fills or Encapsulated PostScript bitmaps.

The Invert Colors Filter

The Invert Colors filter has the effect of changing your object to appear as a negative of its original color state. For example, an object assigned a black stroke and white fill changes to an object with a white stroke and black fill when this filter is applied. For objects in the CMYK and RGB color spaces, the Invert Colors filter creates a color negative. Figure 12-4 depicts the results of applying the Invert Colors filter.

Before   After Blend

FIGURE 12-3   The Blend filter in action

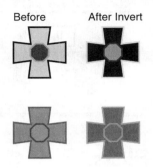

Before   After Invert

FIGURE 12-4   The effects of applying the Invert Colors filter. Left column
is for B&W pages and right for color, at designer's discretion

The Overprint Black Filter

The Overprint Black filter enables you to globally set black objects to overprint other
objects assigned colors other than black. The Overprint Black dialog box options
(shown below) enable you to set or remove overprint attributes from black fills or
black strokes.

```
┌═════════════════ Overprint Black ═════════════════┐
│                                                    │
│  ┌─────────────────────┐                           │
│  │  Add Black      ▼   │         ┌──────────────┐  │
│  └─────────────────────┘         │      OK      │  │
│  Percentage: │100│  %            └──────────────┘  │
│  Apply To: ⊠ Fill   ⊠ Stroke     ┌──────────────┐  │
│                                  │    Cancel    │  │
│ ┌─Options ──────────────────┐    └──────────────┘  │
│ │  ☐ Include Blacks with CMY │                     │
│ │  ☐ Include Custom Blacks   │                     │
│ └────────────────────────────┘                     │
│                                                    │
└────────────────────────────────────────────────────┘
```

The Saturate Filter

The Saturate filter makes a color richer by increasing or decreasing the saturation of a
color. Increasing saturation usually has the effect of making the image darker. For objects
filled with spot colors, the Saturate filter adjusts the relevant tints of spot color.

12

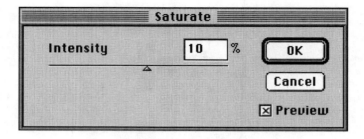

Using the Create Filters

The Create filters add new paths to your document. Three different filters reside under the Create category including Fill & Stroke for Mask, Object Mosaic, and Trim Marks, as shown in Figure 12-5.

The Fill & Stroke for Mask Filter

The Create Fill & Stroke for Mask filter is another filter that features no dialog box options but simply applies an effect. This filter creates two paths identical to the mask applied to an object. One has a black stroke and no fill in front of the Mask. The other has a gray fill and no stroke in the back of the Mask. You may then fill and stroke these two objects individually. The stroke is the most important because it creates a visible border for your object. Most of the time the gray fill that is created by Fill & Stroke for Mask is invisible, and you'll never know that it is there, especially if the masked object completely fills the mask's area.

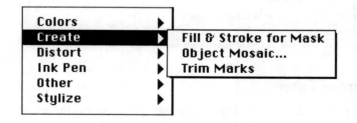

FIGURE 12-5   The Create filters submenu

Note *You can apply fills and strokes to the Mask, but Illustrator will promptly forget the application. For years this was a big frustration, until the Fill & Stroke for Mask plug-in came along, but even this plug-in is not an ideal solution.*

The Object Mosaic Filter

The Object Mosaic filter creates a checkerboard effect using your selected object for reference. Based upon the underlying bitmap, Object Mosaic creates a series of tiles that are vector paths resembling the underlying image. The Object Mosaic dialog box (shown below) enables you to control the size of each tile, the spacing between tiles, and the total number of tiles. The more tiles you add, the more closely the mosaic effect will resemble the original bitmap.

```
┌─────────────────────── Object Mosaic ───────────────────────┐
│                                                              │
│  ┌─ Current Size ─┐  ┌─ New Size ──────┐    ┌──────────────┐ │
│  │                │  │                 │    │      OK      │ │
│  │ Width: 219 pt  │  │ Width: [219 pt] │    └──────────────┘ │
│  │                │  │                 │    ┌──────────────┐ │
│  │ Height: 164 pt │  │ Height: [164 pt]│    │    Cancel    │ │
│  └────────────────┘  └─────────────────┘    └──────────────┘ │
│                                                              │
│  ┌─ Tile Spacing ─┐  ┌─ Number of Tiles ┐   ┌──────────────┐ │
│  │                │  │                  │   │   Use Ratio  │ │
│  │ Width: [0 pt]  │  │ Width: [10]      │   └──────────────┘ │
│  │                │  │                  │                    │
│  │ Height: [0 pt] │  │ Height: [10]     │                    │
│  └────────────────┘  └──────────────────┘                    │
│                                                              │
│  ┌─ Options ─────────────────────────────────────┐          │
│  │ Constrain Ratio: ● Width  ○ Height             │          │
│  │                                                │          │
│  │         Result: ● Color  ○ Gray                │          │
│  │                                                │          │
│  │      ☐ Resize using Percentages                │          │
│  │      ☐ Delete Raster                           │          │
│  └────────────────────────────────────────────────┘          │
└──────────────────────────────────────────────────────────────┘
```

12

Note *Adding more tiles to your Illustrator 7 document also requires more objects be created in turn, which results in your document requiring more memory. Subsequently, when using the Object Mosaic filter, be sure to monitor your system's resources in an effort to avoid overloading available memory.*

The Object Mosaic filter works with any type of bitmap image format Illustrator can place (except Encapsulated PostScript bitmaps), as well as with bitmap images you created with the Rasterize command. When the Object Mosaic filter acts on a bitmap image, it creates a tiled copy, leaving the original bitmap image intact. Selecting the Delete Raster option also enables you to delete the original image.

The following options in the Object Mosaic dialog box give you control over the filter's output. New Size enables you to resize the mosaic. Clicking on Resize Using Percentages enables you to express the mosaic size as a percentage of the bitmap, rather than as an absolute value. Tile Spacing determines the distance between each tile in the mosaic. The Number of Tiles options enables you to enter values to determine the number of tiles horizontally and vertically in the Object Mosaic result. The Constrain Ratio option enables you to lock either the height dimensions or the width dimensions of the mosaic to equal those of the original bitmap image. The Use Ratio button figures an appropriate number of tiles based on the Size and Constrain options you've selected. The Result radio buttons enable the mosaic to appear as a color or grayscale image.

Figure 12-6 shows an example of the effects of the Object Mosaic filter.

The Trim Marks Filter

The Trim Marks filter is used to create multiple corner marks around an object and features no dialog box for additional options. Similar to cropmarks, trim marks may be used to indicate where an image should be trimmed. However, whereas you may not create more than one set of cropmarks on a document, using the Trim Marks filter you may place as many trim marks in your file as you wish.

Unlike cropmarks, trim marks are not special objects to Illustrator 7. They are simply indication lines created automatically using this filter. Trim marks are useful, therefore, when you need to have cropmarks around several objects on a page, such as the sheet of business cards shown in Figure 12-7. Trim marks are not used in lieu of cropmarks created with the Make Cropmarks command or in the Color Separation Setup dialog box.

The position of the trim marks are determined by an imaginary rectangular bounding box represented by the vertical and horizontal measures of an object.

Using the Distort Filters

The Distort filters alter a path's shape and direction. In some cases the Distort filters make some radical and highly stylized changes to paths. The Distort filters collection

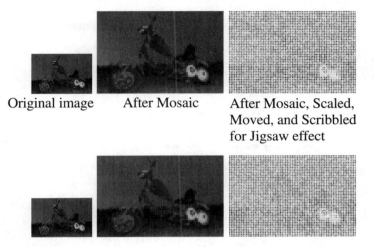

Original image   After Mosaic   After Mosaic, Scaled,
                                               Moved, and Scribbled
                                               for Jigsaw effect

FIGURE 12-6   The effects of applying the Object Mosaic filter

includes Free Distort, Punk & Bloat, Roughen, Scribble and Tweak, Twirl, and Zig Zag, as shown in Figure 12-8.

The Free Distort Filter

The Free Distort filter enables you to skew, scale, and add perspective to a vector object. You may vary the shape of your selection by dragging the control points of the sample object in the Distort dialog box. This sample box represents the four corners of an imaginary rectangle surrounding your selection. As you drag on the box's corners, the object's shape will be altered accordingly.

The Punk & Bloat Filter

The Punk & Bloat filter gets its name from the fact that its distortions can make an object look alternately like a punk rocker with a mohawk-style haircut or a metabolically-challenged individual bloated with fat. *Punking* curves the object inward from its anchor points and moves the anchor points outward. *Bloating* curves

12

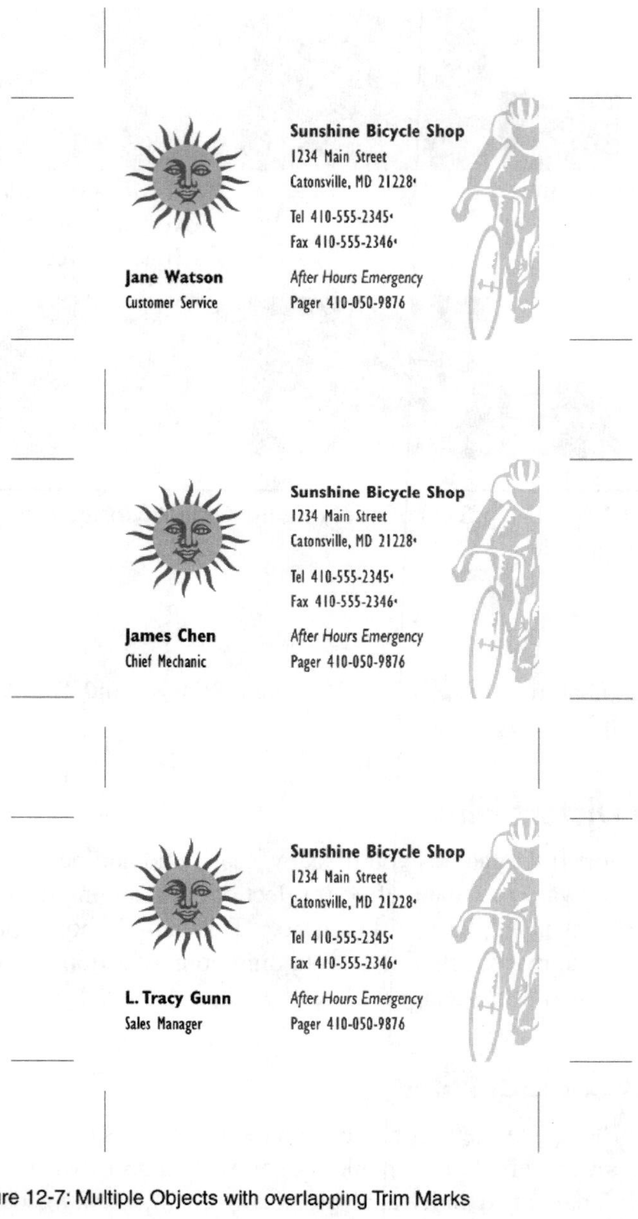

Sunshine Bicycle Shop
1234 Main Street
Catonsville, MD 21228‹

Tel 410-555-2345‹
Fax 410-555-2346‹

Jane Watson
Customer Service

After Hours Emergency
Pager 410-050-9876

Sunshine Bicycle Shop
1234 Main Street
Catonsville, MD 21228‹

Tel 410-555-2345‹
Fax 410-555-2346‹

James Chen
Chief Mechanic

After Hours Emergency
Pager 410-050-9876

Sunshine Bicycle Shop
1234 Main Street
Catonsville, MD 21228‹

Tel 410-555-2345‹
Fax 410-555-2346‹

L. Tracy Gunn
Sales Manager

After Hours Emergency
Pager 410-050-9876

Figure 12-7: Multiple Objects with overlapping Trim Marks

FIGURE 12-7   Multiple objects with trim marks

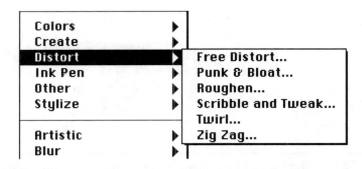

FIGURE 12-8   The Distort filters submenu

the object outward from its anchor points, and moves the anchor points inward. The Punk & Bloat filter dialog box is shown here:

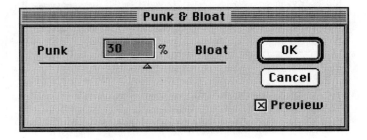

Figure 12-9 depicts the results of applying a Punk & Bloat filter effect to an eight-sided object.

The Roughen Filter

The Roughen filter adds anchor points and moves them in a jagged fashion from the original object, creating a rough edge. The Roughen dialog box is shown next. The Size slider controls how far from the original path the new anchors are placed. The

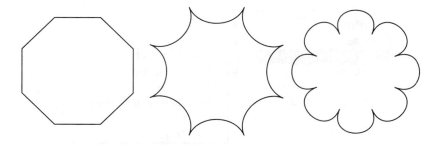

FIGURE 12-9   Applying a Punk filter effect of -20 percent and a Bloat filter effect of 30 percent

Detail slider affects the number of anchors that are added. The Points radio buttons give you a choice of Smooth, for smooth turns, or Corner, for sharp edges.

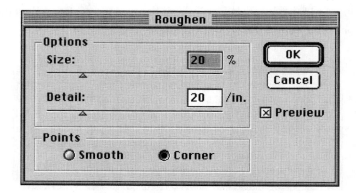

Figure 12-10 depicts the results of applying the Roughen filter to an eight-sided object. In the left example, options are set at Smooth, 5 percent for Size and 10 per inch for Detail; in the right example, options are set at Corner, 20 percent for Size and 20 per inch for Detail.

The Scribble and Tweak Filter

The Scribble and Tweak filter makes random changes to an object based on the parameters that you specify. The Scribble option randomly moves anchor points away from the original object. The Tweak option randomly moves anchor points on

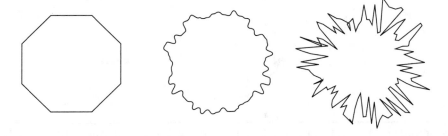

FIGURE 12-10   Results of applying the Roughen filter effect

the selected object within your parameters. The Scribble and Tweak filter dialog box is shown here:

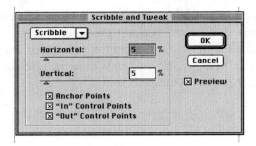

Figure 12-11 depicts the results of applying the the Scribble & Tweak filter. Here, an eight-sided object has Scribble options of 5 percent vertical and 5 percent horizontal applied and Tweak options of 10 percent vertical and 10 percent horizontal applied.

Both options make random, irreproducible changes. As a practical exercise in the effects of this filter, follow these steps:

1. Create a rectangle.

2. Choose the Scribble and Tweak (Filter|Distort|Scribble and Tweak) filter. The filter's dialog box appears.

3. Position both the horizontal and vertical sliders to **20** percent. Note the new shape of your object.

4. Move one of the sliders to **21** percent and observe the degree of change in the object's shape. Return the slider to **20** percent and notice that the new shape bears little resemblance to the previous shape.

12

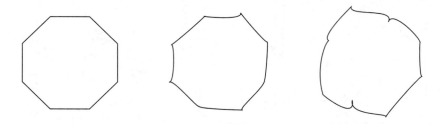

FIGURE 12-11   The effects of applying the Scribble and Tweak filter

Scribble and Tweak physically operates by moving the anchor and control points of selected objects. It does not add any anchor points. The horizontal and vertical sliders control how far from its original position the filter may move an anchor point in each direction. The options control whether Scribble and Tweak moves the anchor points. Anchor Points enables the filter to move anchor points. The option "In" Control Points enables the filter to move control points that lead into anchor points on the path whereas the "Out" Control Points enables the filter to move control points that lead out of anchor points on the path.

The Twirl Filter

The Twirl filter mimics the results of the Twirl tool, which you used by holding ALT/OPTION and clicking an object. This filter essentially rotates a selection in a spiral manner. The Twirl effect also adds additional anchor points to the selected object when applied. The Twirl dialog box features a single angle option, as seen here:

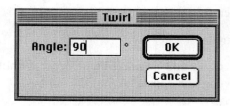

Figure 12-12 depicts the results of applying the Twirl filter to an eight-sided object using a single twirl angle of 90 degrees and an angle of 315 degrees applied twice in succession.

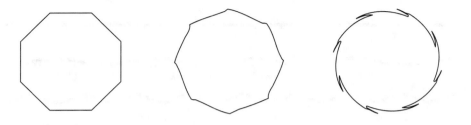

FIGURE 12-12 Applying the Twirl filter effect to an object

The Zig Zag Filter

The Zig Zag filter adds anchor points to an existing line and then moves them away from the line in alternating directions. The Zig Zag filter dialog box features slider controls to adjust both the Amount and Ridges of a path, as shown here:

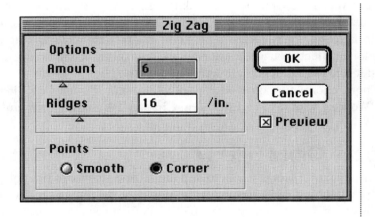

A value entered in the Amount slider sets the distance that the new anchors are moved away from the original line. The Ridges slider sets the number of ridges created per inch. The Smooth option creates smooth points, resulting in a sine wave. The Corner option creates corner points, resulting in a classic zigzag pattern.

Figure 12-13 depicts the results of applying the Zig Zag filter to a straight line using values of Amount=8, Ridges=16 and Amount=6, and Ridges=16.

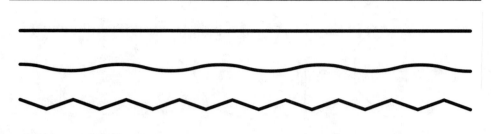

FIGURE 12-13   Applying the Zig Zag filter to a straight line

Using the Ink Pen Filter

The Ink Pen filter creates textured gradations and enables you to convert your paths into textured drawings that simulate ink pen sketches. The Ink Pen filter enables you to simulate cross hatching and variable patterns such as wood grains. Unlike other similar filters, Ink Pen works only on vector art, resulting in the creation of objects that are also vector art. Options in the Ink Pen Effects dialog box, shown in Figure 12-14, illustrate how extensive this single effect is, involving options for Hatch, Color, Background, Fade, Fade Angle, and Density and including commands for saving Ink Pen effects you create yourself and managing the styles contained in the styles list located in the upper-left corner of the dialog box.

For more information on working with Illustrator 7's Ink Pen filter, see the section "Working with Ink Pen Effects" in **Chapter 10: Setting Fills and Strokes**.

Using the Other Filters

The Other group of filters is meant to be a miscellaneous mix of filter plug-ins that don't fit precisely into any other category. However, the only filter that ships with Adobe Illustrator 7 in this category is the Riders filter seen in the submenu shown in Figure 12-15. If you don't see the Riders filter under the Other menu, it may be because this filter doesn't install by default, but instead must be physically copied from the Illustrator 7 program disk and placed into your Illustrator 7 plug-ins folder. If you don't have anything that belongs in the Other filters menu installed, the Other option simply doesn't appear in the Filter menu.

The Make Riders filter is located in the Riders folder inside the Utilities (Macintosh) or Utility (Windows) folder. To install it, exit Illustrator (CTRL/

Ink Pen Effects

Angled lines gradation ▼

Hatch: Vertical lines ▼   New...

Color: Original ▼   Delete

Background: Hatch Only ▼   Update

Fade: None ▼   Reset

Fade Angle: [   ] °

OK

Cancel

Import...

Save As...

Density ▼

75.25

☒ Preview

FIGURE 12-14   The Ink Pen dialog box

COMMAND+Q), drag the Riders folder to the Plug-ins folder, and relaunch Illustrator 7.

Note   *If you haven't moved the Riders plug-in from the Utilities (Macintosh) or Utility (Windows) folder to the Plug-ins folder, the Other category does not appear in the Filter menu.*

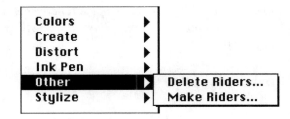

Colors ▶
Create ▶
Distort ▶
Ink Pen ▶
Other ▶   Delete Riders...
Stylize ▶   Make Riders...

FIGURE 12-15   The Other submenu

The Make Riders Filter

The Make Riders filter creates a file containing PostScript page description information that overrides the method normally used to print a document. It can be used to change a halftone pattern or screen frequency, or you may use it to change halftone dots from circles to diamonds or ellipses or even lines. When you select the Make Riders filter, the Make Riders dialog box appears, as shown here:

```
┌────────────────────────────────────────────────┐
│ ══════════════════ Make Riders ═══════════════  │
│                                                  │
│   ┌──────────────────────────────────────────┐  │
│   │  Screen Frequency:      Flatness:         │  │
│   │  ┌────────────┬───┐     ┌────────────┬───┐│  │
│   │  │ 30 lpi     │ ▼ │     │ None       │ ▼ ││  │
│   │  └────────────┴───┘     └────────────┴───┘│  │
│   │  Screen Angle:          Annotation:       │  │
│   │  ┌────────────┬───┐     ┌────────────┬───┐│  │
│   │  │ 90°        │ ▼ │     │ None       │ ▼ ││  │
│   │  └────────────┴───┘     └────────────┴───┘│  │
│   │  Spot Function:             Error Handler:│  │
│   │  ┌──────────────────┬───┐   ┌──────────┬─┐│  │
│   │  │ Diamond          │ ▼ │   │ Include  │▼││  │
│   │  └──────────────────┴───┘   └──────────┴─┘│  │
│   └──────────────────────────────────────────┘  │
│                              ┌────────┐┌───────┐ │
│                              │ Cancel ││ Make  │ │
│                              └────────┘└───────┘ │
└────────────────────────────────────────────────┘
```

This dialog box enables you to save a file called Adobe Illustrator EPSF Riders. Save this file in your Plug-ins folder. Only one file, named Adobe Illustrator EPSF Riders, is created when you choose the Make Riders filter. You cannot create multiple Riders files, and you must not change the name of the Adobe Illustrator EPSF Riders file. To activate the Riders file, you must quit and restart Adobe Illustrator. To embed the Riders information in a document, you will need to resave it after the Rider has been activated.

Note   *After creating the Riders file, do not attempt to rename the Adobe Illustrator EPSF Riders. If you change the name, Illustrator 7 will not be able to use information in the file.*

The Make Riders dialog box offers the following choices:

- **Screen Frequency**   The Screen Frequency drop-down menu enables you to designate a line screen. The screen frequency value may be set within a range between 1 and 999.

- **Screen Angle**   The Screen Angle drop-down menu asks you to specify a screen angle for the halftone dots.

- **The Spot Function**   drop-down menu determines the halftone dot's shape.

- **Flatness**   The Flatness drop-down menu is used to simplify complex paths. The Riders Flatness setting must be between 0.2 and 200 and is applied to all curves in an Illustrator document.

- **Annotation**   The Annotation drop-down menu enables you to enter an annotation of up to 254 characters. The annotation prints at the bottom-left corner of the page.

- **Error Handler**   Choose the Error Handler option to print error information on the page if a PostScript error occurs. It is recommended that you use the use the Error Handler built into the latest version of Adobe's PostScript printer driver.

Tip *To temporarily disable the Adobe Illustrator EPSF Riders file, move it out of the Plug-ins folder. If Adobe Illustrator is open, you must quit and restart it. You can move it anywhere, but moving it into the Illustrator folder or directory will make it easier to find later on.*

Note *The Adobe Illustrator EPSF Riders file is in PostScript language code. If you don't understand the PostScript language or have no instructions to use Make Riders in order to solve a specific printer problem, avoid using this filter.*

The Delete Riders Filter

The Delete Riders filter removes the Adobe Illustrator EPSF Riders file from your system. When running this filter, you will be presented with a standard open dialog box asking you to locate the Adobe Illustrator EPSF Riders file to delete.

Using the Stylize Filter

The Stylize filters offer a number of effects which, for the most part, modify paths or alter them in order to make them more visible. Stylize effects include Add Arrowheads, Calligraphy, Drop Shadow, Path Pattern, and Round Corners, as seen in the submenu shown in Figure 12-16.

The Add Arrowheads Filter

The Add Arrowheads filter applies various styles of arrowheads or tails to any selected open path. The resulting arrows are paths that can be edited like any other object. The Add Arrowheads dialog box looks like this:

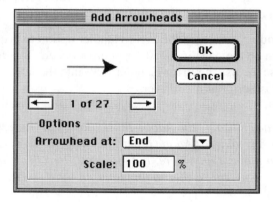

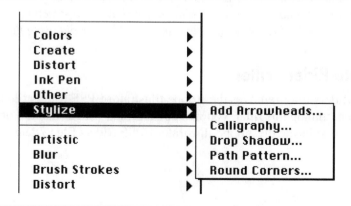

FIGURE 12-16 The Stylize submenu

The Add Arrowheads dialog box presents you with 27 various arrowhead styles. You may browse through the available selection by clicking the forward and backward buttons below the Preview Arrow window. You may also rescale the size of an arrowhead by entering the percentage you want in the Scale text box. The arrowheads are scaled relative to the width of the line. The Start or End option places the arrowhead at either the beginning of the line, the end of the line, or both. But if you wish to place differing arrowhead and tail designs on each end of the path, you must apply the Add Arrowheads filter twice, once for each arrow style. Figure 12-17 depicts several examples of Illustrator 7's arrowhead styles.

The Calligraphy Filter

The Calligraphy filter gives a path the appearance of being drawn with a calligraphic pen. This filter works best when applied to a path comprised of smooth curves. The Calligraphy filter dialog box contains the options shown here:

Calligraphy	
Pen Width: 0p4.5	OK
Pen Angle: 120 °	Cancel

Note   *The Calligraphy filter work only with paths, not with type.*

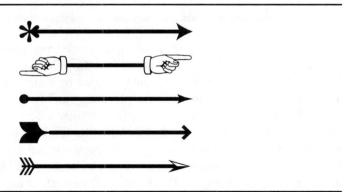

FIGURE 12-17   Various arrowheads available using the Add Arrowheads
filter effect

The Pen Width option affects how wide the widest part of the stroke will be. The Pen Angle option enables you to set how wide the stroke will be at its widest point. When the angle of the curve is tangent to the selected angle, the path will be at its widest. When the angle of the curve is perpendicular to the selected angle, the sides of the path will cross and the width becomes zero.

The Drop Shadow Filter

The Drop Shadow filter creates a hard shadow. This shadow object is simply a copy of the selected object filled with a percentage of black ranging from 0 to 100 percent and based on the CMYK color model.

As shown in the dialog box below, options associated with using this filter include X Offset and Y Offset measures, Intensity, and a Group Shadows option that allows you to group the shadow object with the original. Adding drop shadows is one of the most common effects applied to type for all sorts of illustration and design needs, making this filter effect one of the more popular in use.

Drop Shadow

Options
H Offset: 0p3
Y Offset: 0p3
Intensity: 50   %
☐ Group Shadows

OK
Cancel

You can offset the drop shadow any distance from your object along the x or y axis, and you may adjust the darkness of the drop shadow. The Drop Shadow dialog box enables you to control the amount of space by which the shadow copy is offset. The Intensity text box controls what percentage of black ink is added to the copy.

If the original to which you apply this filter effect contains spot colors, the shadows will be created using the CMYK color model. The Group Shadows option will place the shadow immediately behind each original in the stacking order. When the Group Shadows option is unselected, all shadows will be placed at the bottom of the stacking order. Figure 12-18 depicts the effects of applying the Drop Shadow filter to an object.

FIGURE 12-18   Using the Drop Shadow filter, from left: the original, with shadow ungrouped, and with shadow grouped

The Path Pattern Filter

The Path Pattern filter lets you automatically outline objects with patterns in order to create simple borders, frames, or decorative effects. Path pattern options enable you to individually control the assigned pattern to the sides and inner and outer shapes of an object using options in the Path Pattern dialog box, shown here:

12

For more information on working with path patterns, see **Chapter 10: Setting Fills and Strokes.**

The Round Corners Filter

The Round Corners filter converts the corner points of your selection to smooth curves. The Round Corners option is capable of applying round corners to rectangles (or other objects) with assigned radius of between 0.001 inches and 55.555 inches, which you enter in the Round Corners dialog box, shown here:

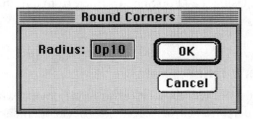

Figure 12-19 depicts the results of applying rounded corners in 4-point and 9-point radius.

Working with Bitmap Filters

Illustrator 7 enables you to use plug-ins designed for Adobe Photoshop, version 3.0 or later. Because of this, bitmap or raster image plug-ins are commonly known as Photoshop plug-ins. Illustrator comes with over 60 Photoshop plug-ins. If you have

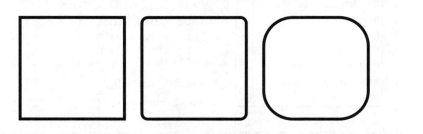

FIGURE 12-19   The Round Corners filter effect applied with 4-point and 9-point radius

other Photoshop-compatible plug-ins, either from Adobe or a third-party, that you wish to use with Illustrator, just copy them to your Plug-ins folder. For a color reference of the effects that may be achieved using Illustrator's bitmap filters, see pages 28-31 in the color insert.

Note   *To avoid wasting available hard drive space by having duplicate copies of your Photoshop filters, make an alias (Macintosh) or shortcut (Windows) of your Photoshop plug-in filters inside of your Illustrator plug-ins folder. Photoshop filters can take considerable space, and using an alias or shortcut can greatly reduce the amount of memory space required.*

Photoshop plug-ins may be used on any bitmap object in your document. The exception to this rule is that you may not run filters on placed Encapsulated PostScript bitmaps. Some filters will require you to change the color mode of the image—you may use the Convert filters to do this. For example, if you try to apply the Colored Pencil filter to a bitmap that is assigned colors you receive an error message like the one shown here:

To avoid this error message, apply the Convert to RGB filter (Filter|Colors| Convert to RGB) to your bitmap object before applying the Colored Pencil filter.

Most of the Photoshop plug-ins that ship with Illustrator 7 present you with a dialog box that provides certain levels of control over their applied effect. The majority of filters also contain a Preview window that provides an accurate representation of the final results based on the options and variables you select.

A few words of advice though: Make your bitmaps small. Applying Photoshop plug-in filters can be very memory intensive on systems using the minimum program requirements. On any platform, when available system memory is exceeded, you'll get Illustrator 7's out-of-memory alert, shown next:

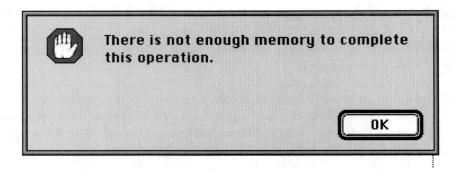

Most of the Photoshop plug-ins that ship with Illustrator 7 will give the best results when used on images that feature image resolution within a range between 133 and 175 dpi (dots per inch).

 Illustrator may run out of memory when filtering overly-large bitmaps.

Using the Artistic Filters

The Artistic set of filters apply a painterly look to bitmap objects. They're designed to mimic the appearance of various natural media in order to make your illustrations appear less digital or computer-generated. These filters work best when applied to color images.

There are 15 Artistic filters in total, including Colored Pencil, Cutout, Dry Brush, Film Grain, Fresco, Neon Glow, Paint Daubs, Palette Knife, Plastic Wrap, Poster Edges, Rough Pastels, Smudge Stick, Sponge, Underglow, Underpainting, and Watercolor, as seen in the submenu shown in Figure 12-20.

For the most part, the results of applying the Artistic filter effects are reflected in their name. The dialog box commands are straightforward to use, and the previews—although often slow to display—are quite accurate. To see examples of the results of applying Artistic filter effects on bitmap objects, see the Fundamental Illustrator 7 color insert.

FIGURE 12-20   The Artistic submenu

Results of applying these filter effects are summarized by the following descriptions:

- The Colored Pencil filter effect simulates a colored pencil drawing.

- The Cutout filter gives the effect of a construction paper collage.

- The Dry Brush filter mimics a painting produced with a minimal amount of paint.

- The Film Grain filter recreates the grain and spotting inherent in old or bad film.

- The Fresco filter approximates a fresco painting.

- The Neon Glow filter creates the effect of a night shot lit by neon lighting.

12

- The Paint Daubs filter simulates a painting made with an overlarge brush.

- The Palette Knife filter is a sloppy effect, making your image appear as if it were painted with a knife.

- The Plastic Wrap filter gives your image the appearance of being covered with common household plastic wrap.

- The Poster Edges filter posterizes an image and enhances its edge contrast. Posterizing an image has the effect of enhancing some colors while subduing others in an effort to create an interesting visual effect.

- The Rough Pastels filter imitates the use of pastel chalks on a rough surface.

- The Smudge Stick filter imitates the use of pastel chalks on a smooth surface.

- The Sponge filter simulates a painting made with a sponge.

- The Underpainting filter creates a painterly effect and adds texture to an image.

- The Watercolor filter imitates a watercolor painting.

Using the Blur Filters

The Blur filters are used to smooth sharp edges and reduce contrast. They smooth transitions by averaging adjacent pixels of bitmap images. Radial Blur is the only Blur filter that ships with Illustrator 7; its submenu is shown in Figure 12-21.

The Radial Blur Filter

The Radial Blur filter can spin an image around its center or make it appear that the image is radiating from its center. To see examples of the results of applying Radial Blur filter effects on bitmap objects, consult the color insert.

The Radial Blur dialog box, shown next, gives you a number of choices for controlling the effect. With the Spin blur method, the blur is created in concentric circles. The Zoom method makes your image appear that it is rapidly disappearing

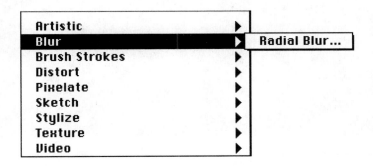

FIGURE 12-21   The Blur submenu

down a rectangular tunnel. The Amount slider controls the intensity of the blur. The Quality radio buttons enable you to balance rendering speed versus image quality.

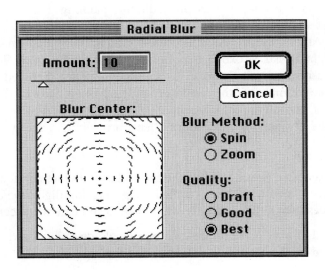

Figure 12-22 depicts the effects of applying the Radial Blur filter effect to a bitmap image using the Zoom and Spin options.

FIGURE 12-22   The effects of the Radial Blur filter using Zoom and
Spin options

Using the Brush Strokes Filters

The Brush Strokes filters simulate color painting and drawing media. Whereas the
Artistic filters simulate various artistic media, the Brush Strokes filters re-create
various styles and techniques used in traditional painting. Figure 12-23 lists the
Brush Strokes styles available in Illustrator 7.

Like the Artistic filters, the Brush Strokes filters work best on color images.
There are eight Brush Strokes filters in all, including Accented Edges, Angled
Strokes, Crosshatch, Dark Strokes, Ink Outlines, Spatter, Sprayed Strokes, and
Sumi-e. To see examples of the results of applying Brush Strokes filter effects on
bitmap objects, consult the color insert.

The results of applying these filter effects are summarized by the following
descriptions:

■ The Accented Edges and Ink Outlines filters both increase the edge
contrast of an image, but Accented Edges then highlights the edges,
whereas Ink Outlines adds a dark outline to simulate ink accenting.

■ Angled Strokes and Crosshatch create single-directional and
crossed-stroke hatches.

■ Spatter and Sprayed Strokes simulate spray can and airbrush paintings.

■ The Dark Strokes and Sumi-e filters accentuate an image's shadows.

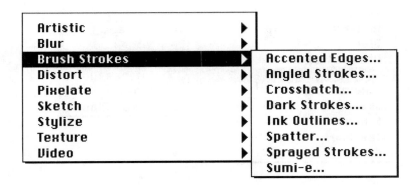

FIGURE 12-23   The Brush Strokes submenu

Using the Distort Filters

The Distort filters geometrically warp bitmap images to simulate the distortion caused by lenses or liquids. There are three Distort filter effects: Diffuse Glow, Glass, and Ocean Ripple, as shown in Figure 12-24. To see examples of the results of applying Distort filter effects on bitmap objects, consult the color insert.

The results of applying these filter effects are summarized by the following descriptions:

■ The Diffuse Glow filter diffuses an image's highlights in order to create a glowing effect.

■ The Glass filter gives an image the appearance that it is being viewed through various types of glass.

■ The Ocean Ripple filter makes your image appear as if it is sitting beneath rippling water.

Using the Pixelate Filters

The Pixelate filters impose patterns upon your image. They reduce its sharpness by grouping together pixels of similar color values into cells. The Pixelate filter has

12

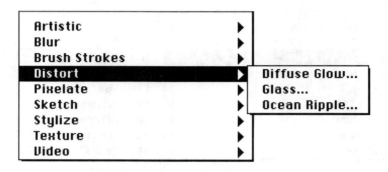

FIGURE 12-24 The Distort submenu

four styles, including Color Halftone, Crystallize, Mezzotint, and Pointellize, as shown in Figure 12-25.

The Color Halftone Filter

The Color Halftone filter can give your image a newspaper or comic book feel. It creates an enlarged halftone screen for each channel of the bitmap. The Color Halftone dialog box includes options for setting the Maximum Radius and screen angles for four channels with values in degrees, as shown here:

The Color Halftone filter works by drawing squares around groups of pixels. The Max. Radius option controls the size of each square. The filter then fills each

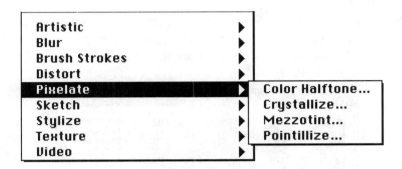

FIGURE 12-25 The Pixelate submenu

square with one circle of color for each channel used. Grayscale images only use channel 1; channels 2 through 4 are unused. For RGB mode images, channels 1, 2, and 3 correspond to the red, green, and blue channels, and channel 4 is unused. For CMYK images, the four channels correspond to the cyan, magenta, yellow, and black channels, respectively. You must specify a screen angle for each channel in use.

The Crystallize Filter

The Crystallize filter makes your image appear as if it were painted onto a crystal formation. It imposes a polygonal pixel grid upon similarly colored pixels. Options for the Crystallize filter are shown here:

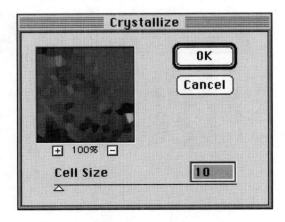

12

The Mezzotint Filter

The Mezzotint filter can cause your image appear as if it were engraved on a roughened piece of metal. It will redraw your image using dots, lines, or strokes. Options for the Mezzotint filter dialog box are shown here:

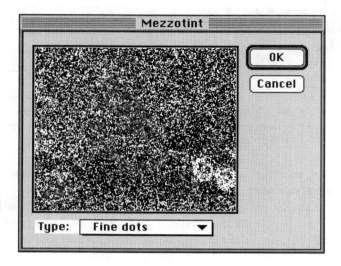

Pointillize

Georges Seurat fans can rejoice at the Pointillize filter. It makes your image appear as if were a pointillist painting. Pointillize breaks an image down into random dots of various colors and sizes. Options included in the Pointillize dialog box are shown here:

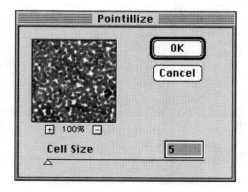

Using the Sketch Filters

The Sketch filters replicate drawing media. They can give any bitmap image the appearance of being hand drawn. With the exception of the Water Paper filter, the Sketch filters remove the color from your images. There are 14 Sketch filters in total, including Bas Relief, Chalk & Charcoal, Charcoal, Chrome, Conté Crayon, Graphic Pen, Halftone Pattern, Note Paper, Photocopy, Plaster, Reticulation, Stamp, Torn Edges, and Water Paper, as shown in Figure 12-26.

The results of applying these filter effects are summarized by the following descriptions:

- The Bas Relief, Note Paper, and Plaster filters create variations on embossed effects.

- The Charcoal and Chalk & Charcoal filters simulate a drawing made with charcoals and chalk.

- The Chrome filter makes your image appear as if it were painted with liquid mercury.

- The Conté Crayon filter mimics a drawing using a black conté crayon; it gives texturizing options, but offers no control over crayon color.

- The Graphic Pen filter emulates a rapidograph (professional-style ink pen) drawing.

- The Halftone Pattern filter prescreens an image to simulate the scan of an already printed image. Beware of unwanted moiré when using the Halftone Pattern filter.

- The Photocopy filter mimics a poorly generated copier image.

- The Reticulation filter can make your image appear as if it were a sand painting.

- The Stamp filter thresholds an image to give the appearance of being placed with a rubber stamp.

- The Torn Edges filter replicates a ripped paper cutout.

- The Water Paper filter simulates a painting made on wet paper.

Figure 12-27 depicts examples of these filters applied to a bitmap image.

12

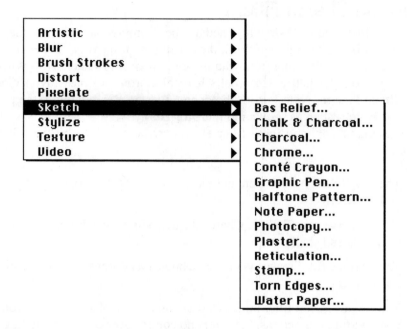

FIGURE 12-26   The Sketch submenu

Using the Stylize Filter

The only filter on the Stylize submenu is the Glowing Edges filter, as shown in Figure 12-28, which makes your image appear as if has been constructed out of neon glass tubing. To see examples of the results of applying the Glowing Edges filter to bitmap objects, consult the color insert.

Using the Texture Filters

The Texture filters can take a seemingly flat bitmap and make it seem that it was painted on a rough surface. The six Texture filters include Craquelure, Grain, Mosaic Tiles, Patchwork, Stained Glass, and Texturizer, as shown in Figure 12-29. To see examples of the results of applying Texture filter effects on bitmap objects, consult the color insert.

FIGURE 12-27 The results of applying the Sketch filters to a bitmap image

12

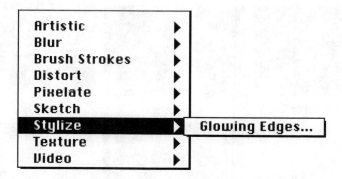

FIGURE 12-28   The Stylize submenu

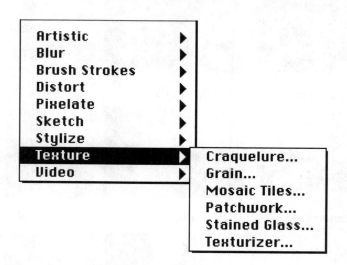

FIGURE 12-29   The Texture submenu

The results of applying these filter effects are summarized by the following descriptions:

- The Craquelure filter makes your image appear as if it was painted on a stucco surface.

- The Grain filter texturizes your image by applying a variety of grain patterns such as clumps, speckles, or stipples.

- The Mosaic Tiles filter makes your image appear as if it was created with hand-cut tiles.

- The Patchwork filter makes your image appear as if it was sewn together.

- The Stained Glass filter should actually be called the honeycomb filter, as it gives your image the appearance that it has been painted inside the cells of a honeycomb.

- The Texturizer filter enables you to apply a brick, burlap, canvas, or sandstone texture to an image. These options can make a bitmap image appear as though it was painted onto one of these surfaces. Texturizer also enables you to load a grayscale bitmap in Photoshop format as a texture.

- Four other filters included with Illustrator 7 have texturizing options—the Glass, Rough Pastels, Grain, and Fresco filters—that are based on the Texturizer filter.

Using the Video Filters

The Video filters include the De-Interlace filter and the NTSC Colors (National Television Standards Committee) filters, as shown in Figure 12-30.

The De-Interlace Filter

The De-Interlace filter smoothes images captured from video such as still shots from a videotape. It operates by removing either the odd or even interlaced lines in a video image. De-Interlace enables the option of replacing the discarded scan lines by

12

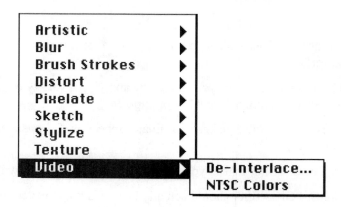

FIGURE 12-30   The Video filter submenu

duplicating the line above or interpolating the lines above and below the removed line. You see the De-Interlace dialog box shown here:

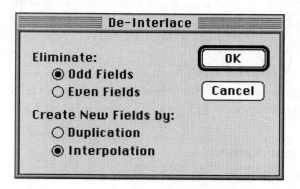

The NTSC Colors Filter

The NTSC Colors filter will mute the color gamut in a bitmap, so that only colors acceptable for television reproduction remain in the image. This prevents oversaturated colors from bleeding across television scan lines. The NTSC Colors filter makes the most obvious changes in saturated yellows and reds.

Third-Party Plug-ins

Rather than trying to cram every imaginable feature into Illustrator and thus creating an unstable, crash-prone program, Adobe has prized stability over overload. This is not to say that Illustrator is featureless, as you've likely discovered by now. Instead, Adobe has created an open architecture for both Illustrator and Photoshop that has enabled a wide variety of vendors to fill gaps and niches that you probably never imagined existing.

Some plug-ins, such as Extensis' *VectorTools 2.0,* are general suites of tools that are designed to help everyone be productive. Other plug-ins, such as Avenza's *MAPublisher,* are geared towards the niche market of GIS and mapping.

To install a third-party plug-in, drag it to your Plug-ins folder.

Macintosh Plug-ins

Although Adobe Illustrator for the Macintosh can use filters written for Adobe Photoshop for the Macintosh, it cannot use filters written for either program on Windows. Many vendors provide plug-ins for both platforms, some only support one. Please keep this in mind when exploring the plug-in market.

The Adobe Illustrator CD for Macintosh contains a variety of demonstration third-party plug-ins. All are feature-disabled versions of each plug-in designed to give you a taste of what the full version is like. These plug-ins can be found in the Third-Party Products folder. Some of these plug-ins have installers that will place them in the proper location, whereas for others you will need to drag the file with the associated Adobe Illustrator Plug-in icon, shown here, to your Plug-ins folder.

 Both Illustrator and Photoshop plug-ins have similar icons, but Illustrator plug-ins are yellow, whereas Photoshop plug-ins are red.

12

If you like what the demo version of a particular plug-in does, information provided along with each demo plug-in explains where you can purchase the full version and how much it will cost.

Macintosh Plug-ins		
Illustrator Plug-ins		
Avenza	*MAPublisher*	*MAPublisher* is a plug-in that enables you to attach GIS and database information to your illustrations. It also enables you to import/export mapping data in a variety of formats.
Extensis	*VectorTools 2.0*	VectorTools 2.0 is a collection of nine productivity tools. VectorTools includes: VectorBars, customizable toolbars; VectorNavigator, which enables you to quickly navigate a document; VectorTips, Illustrator Tips and Tricks in a searchable palette; VectorShape, which easily creates 3-D effects; VectorLibrary; VectorColor; VectorObjectStyles; VectorMagicWand; and VectorFrame.
Hot Door	*CADtools*	CADtools features 33 drafting and dimensioning tools including Line, Rectangle, Chamfer, Horizontal Dimension (by Line), Horizontal Dimension (by Points), Diameter Dimension and Triangle Label.
Illom	*Magnet Tool*	When using the *Magnet Tool*, a tool on the Tools palette, all selected points/handles will be moved towards the cursor position. The movement is done while you are holding down the mouse button. The longer you hold it down, the longer the points will move. You can also move the mouse while holding down the mouse button and the points will move towards the current position of the cursor.

	Select Handles	The *Select Handles* plug-in adds a menu command in the Edit menu called Select Handles. This command will cause all bezier handles to be selected so that you can then easily modify the handles.
Letraset	*Envelopes*	Envelopes enables you to quickly distort objects with a series of predefined shapes and distortion envelopes.
Kara	*KF-HeadSetter 1.0*	KF-*HeadSetter* is a separate application designed to set three-dimensional headline type.
Vertigo	*3DWords*	3DWords renders text on the fly in three dimensions.

Photoshop Plug-ins

Andromeda	*Series 2 3-D Demo*	Series 2 3-D filters enable you to wrap images onto a variety of three-dimensional surfaces.
	Series 3 Screens Demo	Using *Series 3 Screens*, you can select a special effect screen such as a mezzotint, mezzogram, or a mezzoblend and create a richly textured image your gray scale bitmap.
	Series 4 Techtures Demo	The *Techtures* filters contain a collection of hand-rendered textures, each of which may be used to texturize your image or as a background.
	Velociraptor	Velociraptor is a plug-in that provides a variety of motion trails for bitmaps.
Extensis	*Intellihance*	*Intellihance* provides automatic color correction for your scanned photographs or PhotoCD images.
MMM	*HoloDozo*	HoloDozo is a set of 28 plug-ins enabling users to create three-dimensional effects without using complicated modeling software.

12

Vertigo	*Dizzy*	Dizzy lets you import models, change their position and size, add lights, adjust your camera view, choose from a number of rendering styles—all with a few simple clicks.
WildRiver	*SSK*	The *SSK* filter suite consists of seven filters: DekoBoko, which creates 3-D style frames; Chameleon remaps a user-defined range of color to a newly defined range; MagicMask is a set of 24 effects; MagicCurtain creates gradational fills based on selected waves; MagicFrame creates straight gradational color frames; TileMaker generates mosaic tiles; TV Snow adds beam distortion to a selected area.
XAOS	*Paint Alchemy*	Paint Alchemy enables you to transform your images and photographs into stunning "paintings" by applying a variety of paint and organic effects.
	Terrazzo	Terrazzo enables you to create regular patterns and tiles.

Windows Plug-ins

The Adobe Illustrator CD for Windows contains a slightly different variety of demonstration third-party plug-ins than does the Mac CD. As with the Macintosh, these plug-ins are feature-disabled versions designed to give you a taste of what the full version is like. These plug-ins can be found in the Third Party directory. Some of these plug-ins have installers that will place them in the proper location, while for others you will need to copy the .AIP (Illustrator plug-in) or .8BF (Photoshop plug-in) file to your Plug-ins directory.

Although Adobe Illustrator for Windows can use filters written for Adobe Photoshop for Windows, it cannot use filters written for either program on the Macintosh. Many plug-in vendors are now writing versions of their plug-ins for both platforms. But keep in mind that the plug-in market for Macintosh Illustrator has had a two-year head start and is thus more established than the Windows Illustrator plug-in market.

	Windows Plug-ins	
	Illustrator Plug-ins	
Avenza	*MAPublisher*	Same as Mac version.
Hot Door	*CADtools*	Same as Mac version.
Illom	*Magnet Tool*	Same as Mac version.
	Select Handles	Same as Mac version.
Vertigo	*3DWords*	Same as Mac version.
Photoshop Plug-ins		
Andromeda	*Series 1 cMulti Demo*	The *Series 1* filters are a package of nine filters designed to replicate darkroom effects including: cMulti, Rainbow, Star, Designs, Velocity, sMulti, Diffract, Prism, and Reflection. Only the cMulti Demo, a filter that arranges multiple copies of a selection in circular manner, ships on the Illustrator CD.
	Series 2 3-D Demo	Same as Mac version.
	Series 4 Techtures Demo	Same as Mac version.
	Velociraptor	Same as Mac version.
Auto F/X	*Typo/Graphic Edges*	*Typo/Graphic Edges* is a Photoshop plug-in that enables you to add edge effects to bitmap images.
Extensis	*Intellihance*	Same as Mac version.

Creating Your Own Filters

If you have a few programming abilities and a specific need that must be met, you can write your own plug-ins. Adobe has created a standardized API (Application Programming Interface) that enables would-be programmers to create their own plug-ins. The open architecture of the Illustrator and Photoshop APIs enables

third-party developers to create features that are accessible from anywhere within the program.

If you want to write Illustrator- or Photoshop-compatible plug-in modules, visit the Adobe Web site, **http://www.adobe.com**. You can also contact the Adobe Developers Association (ADA) by telephone. In the United States, call 408-536-9000; in Europe, call +31-20-6511 275. You can reach the ADA by e-mail at devsup-person@adobe.com.

Exploring Filter Effects

As a practical exploration of the features and effects discussed in this chapter, follow through in these step-by-step tutorials. As you do so, you may notice that some of the steps are accompanied by a "Color palette" symbol. This symbol indicates that the step has also been illustrated in full color in the Fundamental Illustrator 7 color insert. The purpose of the color insert is to provide you with a brief overview of the tutorial and act as an overall reference for the practical use of color throughout these tutorials.

Watch for this symbol:

We designed the tutorials of this chapter to help you understand filters and their possible applications in illustration work. Many of the filters in Illustrator work the same and apply similar effects to objects. You will benefit greatly by experimenting with different settings for both Vector and Bitmap filters.

The first tutorial walks you through creating an ice cream cone. You will take advantage of gradients, duplication, distort filters, and bitmap filters. We included many tools from other chapters to help you fix them in your memory. If you need information on commands from other chapters, please refer to those sections for precise instruction.

The second tutorial of this chapter will guide you through creating a box of golf balls using Vector and Bitmap filters to produce effects on simple objects. These objects include a rectangle, an edited rectangle, and a circle, which you'll manipulate using the Type tool, Free Distort filter, and Glass filter on a rastered image.

The last tutorial introduces several Vector distort filters such as ZigZag, Roughen, and Twirl. You will also apply a Bitmap filter to create the Craquelure texture on your image.

Chapter 12 Tutorial 1: Using Filter Effects to Create a Three-Dimensional Image of an Ice Cream Cone

You will use several of the filter effects to create an image that looks like an ice cream cone in this first tutorial. Along the way, you will learn how to use several of the Object filters and a few of the Bitmap filters.

First, let's create the cone outline.

1. Select the Pen tool (P) from the main Toolbox.

2. Click anywhere near the center of the artboard for your first anchor point. Now place another anchor down and to the right of the first anchor. You have created the first line segment of the cone.

3. Click another anchor point just to the right of the last anchor point. Click another anchor up and to the right of the last anchor, placing it even with the first anchor point.

4. Click on the starting point to close the object.

5. To make the bottom part of the cone rounded, select the Convert Anchor tool found in the Pen tool flyout. Click and drag the lower-left anchor point, release, and then adjust the direction line using the same tool to make this a corner anchor. Do the same with the lower-right anchor point.

6. If you need to fine-tune the shape of the curve, use the Direct Selection tool (A) to edit the anchor points, as shown in Figure 12-31. You've just completed the main shape for the cone.

   Now create an overlap as you might see in a waffle cone. Choose the Selection tool (V). Click on the object and drag while pressing the SHIFT and ALT/OPTION keys to drag a copy to the right. Match the top edge of both objects leaving an offset to the right, as seen in Figure 12-31.

7. Select both objects by pressing the SHIFT key while selecting both.

8. Choose Object|Pathfinder|Divide. Ungroup these objects by CTRL/COMMAND+SHIFT+G. Deselect the group by clicking anywhere on the artboard away from the objects.

12

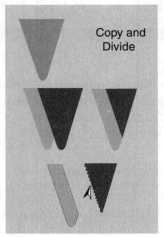

Copy and
Divide

Add anchors and edit
to create an uneven edge

FIGURE 12-31   Creating the base for the ice cream cone

Click on the new object farthest to the right and delete it by pressing the DELETE key.

Now you have two objects that make up the base of the ice cream cone. The work is not yet complete. You need to add a ridge to one of the objects to simulate an edge of a waffle cone.

10. Using the Selection tool, select and drag the new triangle object on the right away from the object on the left.

11. Choose the Add Anchor Point tool from the Pen tool flyout. Click along the left edge of this inverted triangle to add many anchors.

You will need to create a Cookie Cutter object to trim the waffle design you will create later. Using the Rectangle tool, you will create a square larger than both objects of the cone. You will then apply the Pathfinder Trim command to create a cookie cutter.

12. Choose the Rectangle tool from the main Toolbox.

13. Drag a square around the two objects until they are completely covered by the square. Release the mouse button. Fill the square with a different solid fill than the cone base objects by choosing a color from the Color palette. Activate the Color Palette by Window|Show Color.

14. Arrange the new square to the back using CTRL/COMMAND+SHIFT+[.

15. Select all the objects by Edit|Select All or by using CTRL/COMMAND+A.

16. Trim the square by choosing Object|Pathfinder|Trim. Ungroup the objects by CTRL/COMMAND+SHIFT+G. See the cookie cutter shown in Figure 12-32.

    Now we are ready to create the waffle pattern we will apply to the cone. We will create a diamond-shaped object using the Pen tool and apply the Stylize|Round filter to it to create rounded corners. Then we will duplicate this simple object to create the waffle grid.

Create a square solid filled
object and trim with the cone
parts in preparation for trimming
the waffle design later.

FIGURE 12-32   Creating the trim pattern

17. Using the Rectangle tool (M) while holding down the SHIFT key, draw a small square. Rotate it **45** degrees with the Rotate tool (R) and then using the Shear tool (W), drag it to make a trapezoid.

18. Choose Filter|Stylize|Round Corners. Enter a number commensurate with the size of your trapezoid. For example, if your trapezoid is **1** inch long, then apply eighth-inch rounded corners.
    Now you are ready to duplicate the trapezoid and create the waffle grid. Use the Selection tool to drag a copy and then duplicate the process using CTRL/COMMAND+D.

19. Choose the Selection tool from the main Toolbox. Select the trapezoid you created and drag it while pressing the ALT/OPTION key.

20. Repeat the process until you have a waffle grid larger than the square cookie cutter. See the waffle grid in Figure 12-33.
    With the waffle pattern complete, you are ready to apply the cookie cutter to trim a cone outline.

21. Select the cookie cutter object and arrange it to the front by using CTRL/COMMAND+SHIFT+].

22. Place the Cookie Cutter over the waffle pattern so that the cone objects cover the waffle pattern. Select the waffle pattern and the cookie cutter.

23. Choose Object|Pathfinder|Trim. Ungroup the objects by using CTRL/COMMAND+SHIFT+G.

24. Select and delete the cookie cutter and the stray waffle pattern pieces.

25. You have just trimmed the waffle pattern into two bunches matching the shapes of the cone outlines. Select each bunch of waffle patterns and group them.

26. Apply a linear gradient fill from dark brown to a light tan using the Gradient tool found in the main Toolbox. Now you will create the inside of the waffle design.

27. Select one group and apply Object|Transform Each|Scale 75 percent horizontal and vertical and select copy.
    Fill these new objects with a darker gradient to offset them from the first objects and group them with the original waffle object. Repeat this

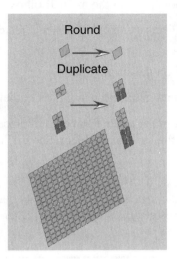

We created the arrows in this example by Filter > Stylize > Add Arrowheads

Create a single waffle trapezoid. Use the Filter > Stylize > Round to make the corners rounded. Copy the trapezoid to create the waffle pattern shown.

FIGURE 12-33   Creating the waffle pattern

process with the other waffle group applying the same gradient values. See the trimmed waffle pattern in Figure 12-34.

28. Select the original cone outlines and apply a dark brown to tan gradient using the Gradient palette.

29. Select each waffle pattern group and place it over the corresponding cone outline. Bring these two sections together to complete the cone portion of your composition.

Now that the cone is complete, you will create the ice cream portion. You will use the Pen tool to "rough out" an approximate shape to represent ice cream on top of a cone. Use a shape that is similar to the one in Figure 12-35.

12

30. Choose the Pen or Pencil tool found in the main Toolbox.

31. Using the top of the cone objects as a guide for size, create an object to represent the ice cream.

32. Close the object by clicking on the starting point.

33. Fill the ice cream object with a radial fill using the Gradient palette.

34. Choose the Gradient tool from the main Toolbox and place the "hot spot" in the upper-right corner of the ice cream object. See the Ice Cream object in Figure 12-35.

35. Move the object to the back with CTRL+SHIFT+[.

    Many kinds of ice cream cones have a swirl of chocolate in the top portion. You can duplicate this effect using the Twirl filter. You will create

After trimming the waffle pattern we added a linear gradient fill and Transformed Each by Scaling a copy by 75%. We then added a different linear gradient fill to the inside of the waffle pattern.

FIGURE 12-34   Trimming the waffle pattern

We created a shape for the
Ice Cream Top using the Pen
Tool and filled it with a radial
gradient.

FIGURE 12-35   Creating the ice cream top

an elongated triangle and use the Rotate and Copy commands to produce
the object that you will use as the chocolate swirl.

36. Choose the Pen tool from the main Toolbox.

37. Create an elongated triangle and close the object by clicking on the
starting point.

38. Fill the object with a dark brown to lighter brown radial gradient fill using
the Gradient palette.

39. Rotate a copy by clicking at the point of the triangle. Rotate while
pressing the ALT/OPTION key to produce a copy. Release the mouse key
before the ALT/OPTION key. And then after you begin to drag the next

12

copy press the ALT/OPTION key again. Repeat this process until you have created a chocolate-spoked wheel.

40. Select all the chocolate objects by dragging a marquee selection box around them, and then group the objects. Choose Filter|Distort|Twirl. Type **180** degrees and then click OK.

41. Choose Filter|Distort|Free Distort. You'll see the Free Distort edit box, as shown here:

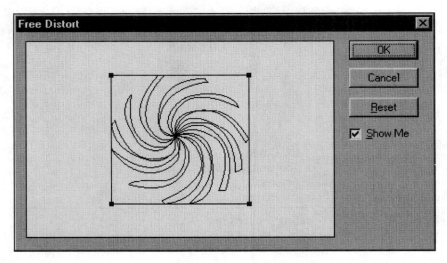

42. Drag the top corner nodes down and a little toward the center of the edit box. Here you see the end result of the Free Distort filter:

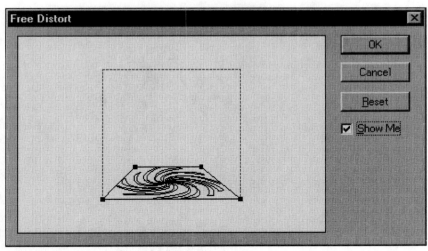

43. Click OK to accept the changes.

Now that you have created the chocolate swirl for the ice cream, you can edit these objects to complete the ice cream. See the finished result of the swirled top in Figure 12-36. You will use the Add Anchor tool and Direct Selection tool to pull several of the chocolate "spokes" down over the ice cream object.

44. Choose the Selection tool from the main Toolbox. Select the chocolate swirl.

45. Drag the chocolate swirl until it is over the ice cream object. Position the swirl toward the top of the ice cream.

If you created a larger ice cream object than the swirl, adjust by scaling the swirl using the Scale tool in the main Toolbox. You can also scale the swirl smaller using the Scale tool to fit the ice cream object's size.

12

FIGURE 12-36   The Chocolate Swirl was created using a simple elongated triangle by Rotating and Copying over and over. Then, Twirl and Free Distort was applied to give the object perspective.

46. Choose the Add Anchor tool from the main Toolbox. Add four extra nodes to the end of each chocolate spoke.

47. Choose the Direct Selection tool and edit the objects, as shown in Figure 12-37.

48. Choose the Convert Anchor tool to create curves in the spokes where needed.

You are now ready to complete the composition using simple objects to represent chopped nuts. These objects consist of two triangles placed back to back. One triangle is light tan solid fill while the other is dark brown solid fill. See the completed ice cream top in Figure 12-37.

49. Assemble the pieces of the cone portion with the ice cream top. Select and group the objects using CTRL/COMMAND+G. Apply a raster to the object to use the bitmap filters. Choose Object|Rasterize. Select a low setting of **72** dpi for lower resolution and a small file, or select a high

Place Swirl on Top

Add Anchors
and Edit

We gave the objects
that make up the Swirl
a dark brown radial
gradient fill.

Create Nuts
& add to top

FIGURE 12-37   To apply the Swirl and Nuts, anchors were added to the
Swirl and the shapes were edited with the Direct Selection
Tool. Then triangular objects were added to represent
chopped nuts.

setting of **300** dpi for higher resolution and a large file. Figure 12-38
shows the finished ice cream cone.

Once your composition is complete, it is only a matter of choosing
a filter to change the look of your artwork. There are many filters to
choose from. We chose a variety of filter groups to show the effects on a
rastered image.

Giving Your Image an Ink Pen Outline

When you apply the Ink Pen Outline, Illustrator creates lines in the composition that
follow the contours of gradients and shapes of objects you create. This effect is similar

12

FIGURE 12-38   The finished ice cream cone with all the
components assembled

to drawing and shading with an ink pen and later applying a color on top of the
artwork. You can find the Ink Pen Outline filter under the Brush Strokes filter group.

Applying the Bas Relief Filter

When you apply the Bas Relief filter, Illustrator creates an image that emulates
a three-dimensional carving, using contrasting black and white areas to depict
shading and shape of the object. You can find the Bas Relief filter under the Sketch
group of filters.

Softening an Image with Diffuse Glow

We applied the Diffuse Glow filter to soften lines and produce a soft lens effect. This
filter gives a realistic depth to the ice cream cone, removing the "computer" look of
Vector-rendered images. You can find Diffuse Glow under the Bitmap Distort group
of filters. Figure 12-39 shows the filter applications.

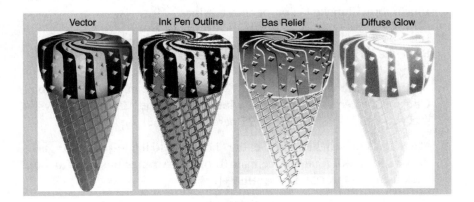

FIGURE 12-39 Once the Vector image was converted into a rastered image, several Bitmap Filters were applied, found in the Brush Strokes, Distort and Sketch Filter options

Chapter 12 Tutorial 2: Using Filter Effects to Create Realistic Golf Balls

This next tutorial incorporates both Vector Filters and Bitmap filters in a drawing of a package of golf balls.

1. Create the shape and fill for a golf ball.

   A golf ball is simple to create. It is basically a perfect sphere with imperfections on the surface. We will use the Ellipse tool to create a circle and fill it with a radial gradient. We will make the sphere look like a golf ball by applying a Glass filter in the Distort Filter group.

2. Choose the Ellipse tool (N) from the main Toolbox.

3. Press the SHIFT key to constrain the ellipse to a circle while dragging. Release when your circle is the approximate size of a golf ball which is 1-$^9/_{16}$" in diameter. We used 1.65 inches for our golf ball drawing. Or you can also click once on the artboard and enter 1.65 inches for width

and height. (Units do not need to be set to inches, just type **1.65** in and Illustrator will make the proper conversions.)

4. Fill with a black and white radial gradient using the Gradient palette. Place the hot spot using the Gradient tool in the upper-right corner of the golf ball.

    Create a second sphere by the Scale tool found in the main Toolbox. Click on the center of the object while pressing the ALT/OPTION key. Set scale type to "Uniform." Type **95** percent and click on Copy.

5. Move this copy to the right. Set the "hot spot" to the left of center using the Gradient tool found in the main Toolbox. Arrange this copy to the back using CTRL/COMMAND+SHIFT+[.

6. Create the last sphere by selecting the original sphere and scaling a copy to 105 percent. Move this copy to the left and move the hot spot off to the far upper-right using the Gradient tool.

7. Rasterize each object separately by choosing Object|Rasterize. Choose the resolution setting of **300** dpi, create mask, and click on OK for each sphere.

8. Choose Filter|Disort (Bitmap group)|Glass; a 10/6 ratio works well. Select the Tiny Lens texture and increase scaling to approximately **170**. Click OK. See the spheres in Figure 12-40.

    Next we will use a rectangle to create the box for the golf ball package. There are five sides visible in the golf package composition. There is the top, right side, left end, left inside, and bottom. (The bottom is not actually visible but rather created for reference.)

    We used the Free Distort filter to create the basic angles for perspective and later adjusted the corners of objects using the Direct Selection tool so they matched. A little bit of technical fudging is required now and then to match corners and make lines appear straight.

9. Set the grid pattern in preparation for creating the objects for the golf ball package. Choose File|Preferences|Guides and Grid and set Grids at every inch with eight subdivisions. Click OK to accept the changes. Choose View|Show Grid. Choose View|Snap to Grid.

10. Create the first rectangle, which will be your front right side. Choose the Rectangle tool from the main Toolbox. Click near the center of the artboard where you will draw the rectangle, preferably at the intersection

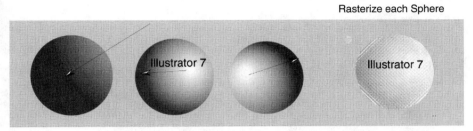

Rasterize each Sphere

Use the gradient tool to set the "Hot Spot" for each sphere.   Apply Filter > Distort (Bitmap) > Glass ...>Dense

FIGURE 12-40   Creating spheres and applying radial gradient fills, Rasterize, and Glass filters

of two gridlines. A rectangle dialog box will appear. Type in values that reflect a 1 to 3 height to width ratio. The height should be the same as the diameter of your largest golf ball. Click OK to apply a rectangle.

11. Create a copy of the rectangle by choosing the Selection tool and drag this rectangle up while pressing and holding SHIFT and ALT/OPTION. Release the mouse button when the bottom of the new rectangle is even with the top of the original rectangle.

12. Choose the Add Anchor tool and add four new anchors to the top line of the new rectangle copy by clicking along the line four times.

13. Choose the Direct Selection tool from the main Toolbox and edit the new anchor points. Drag the middle two anchor points down and then drag each point out. Hold down the SHIFT key as you drag to constrain the movement straight down and then sideways. You will create a rectangular indentation in the center of the rectangle a little less than half the height of the rectangle for its depth and width, as shown in Figure 12-41.

14. Create the top of the golf ball package by choosing the Pen tool. Click on the modified rectangle's upper-left corner to set the first anchor point. Move the mouse cursor the distance of the height of the rectangle straight up and click the next anchor point. Move the mouse cursor to the right the distance even with the left edge of the indentation and click the third anchor. Now visualize a diagonal line between this anchor and the first anchor. Click in the center of that imaginary line for the fourth anchor point. Now click the last anchor point at the upper-left corner of the

12

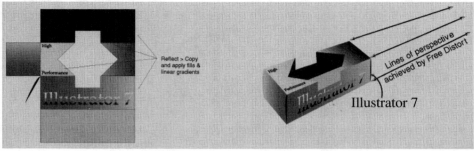

FIGURE 12-41   Using filter effects on converted type and objects to add perspective

indentation. Click on the starting point to close the object. See the object with the words High Performance in Figure 12-41.

15. Choose the Rectangle tool again and create a square (using the SHIFT key to constrain it to a square) out to the left of the objects you have been working on. Make it the same height as the rectangle. Choose the Selection tool and move the new square so it is flush with the left end of the package top.

16. To complete the top, create a copy of the "High Performance" object you created earlier. Choose the Selection tool from the main Toolbox and select the object. Choose the Reflect tool from the main Toolbox. Press the ALT/OPTION key while you click in to the right of the new object and in the center of the rectangle. Click Copy to create a vertical reflected copy. Use the Selection tool to move the object to make it flush with the modified rectangle.

17. Create the last object to be used in the package composition. Select the modified rectangle with the Selection tool. Make a copy of the selected rectangle by pressing ALT/OPTION and dragging.

Now all the objects are in place except for the text that you will add next. You will use the Type menu to covert the type to graphic objects by the Create Outlines option.

18. Select the Type tool from the main Toolbox and click at the top-left corner of the object that will become the top of the package. Type **High.** Click on the Selection tool to let Illustrator know you are done typing.

19. Select the Type tool again and click at the bottom-left corner of the package top. Type **Performance.** Click the Selection tool again.

20. You may need to adjust the size of the type to fit snugly in this section of the object. Once you have the size you want, convert the type to outlines by selecting both type objects. Choose Type|Create outlines. Group the new objects using CTRL/COMMAND+G. Apply a black fill to the type using the Color palette.

21. Choose the Type tool again. Click on the right side of the package and type **Illustrator 7** or text of your choosing. Resize the type to fit under the indentation and make sure it is long enough to spread across the length of the modified rectangle. Convert this to outlines using Type|Create Outline. Group the new objects using CTRL/COMMAND+G. Apply a linear gradient to the text using yellow to black with the Gradient palette and setting the gradient angle with the Gradient tool. Group the Type to the right side and to the top of the package so it will be modified as the rectangles are modified.

Now all the elements are in place. You have created the layout of the package for the golf balls. If you were to print this and cut it out, you could form the rectangular solid that would hold the golf balls.

The next step is to distort the objects you just created using the Free Distort filter. This takes some experimentation to master since there are no exact settings to enter. It is helpful to create lines of perspective for the desired result of the distortion. If you need to adjust the distortion, simply undo the last command using CTRL/COMMAND+Z. You will need to reflect the left side of the package horizontally before you apply the Free Distort filter to it. Once you have reflected the left side, arrange it to the back using CTRL/COMMAND+SHIFT+[. Its not necessary to apply the Free Distort filter to the bottom rectangle since it will not be visible in the final composition. Apply the Free Distort filter to each object until you have achieved the desired effect, as shown in Figure 12-41. If you find you need to fine-tune the distorted objects, use the Direct Selection tool until you achieve the desired effect.

Once you have achieved the desired effect with the Free Distort filter, you are ready to place the golf ball objects in the midst of the package. If you will be adding

12

text to the golf balls, add it before you move the objects. Group the text with the golf balls so it will move with the golf balls.

Select the golf balls and place them as shown in Figure 12-42. Arrange them to the back using CTRL/COMMAND+SHIFT+[. Then bring the golf balls forward using CTRL/COMMAND+]. Once everything is in place you can apply the vector Ink Pen|Effects filter.

Use the following process to apply the Ink Pen|Effects filter to the object:

1. Select the object with the Selection tool.

2. Choose Filter|Ink Pen|Effects.

You have a huge number of choices and settings to work with in creating effects with the Ink Pen filter. For your golf ball package, choose the Wind Blown Grass Hatch from the Hatch pop-up menu at the upper left of the dialog box.

In the Color dialog box choose Original. Choose Retain Fill in the Background dialog box. Choose Use Gradient in the Fade dialog box. Select the density by typing in a percentage value or clicking on the gradient at the bottom left. Click OK to apply the values to your selected object.

 Using the Ink Pen tool creates a large number of line segments and will slow down program performance. It is a good idea to wait until you're almost finished creating your composition before applying this filter.

We applied the Wind Blown Grass to the top, right side, left end, and to the Illustrator 7 type outline. Figure 12-42 shows the finished composition.

Chapter 12 Tutorial 3: Creating a Quilted Image Using the Texture Filter

You will learn how to create a quilted image using the Craquelure Texture filter in this tutorial. We included special application filters such as Zig Zag, Roughen, and Twirl. You apply texture filters to rastered objects and imported bitmaps.

You will rasterize the objects you create in order to apply the filters later. The objects used in this tutorial are not difficult to create. They involve freehand editing, which will help improve your shaping skills. Once the basic shapes are created, Illustrator will do the rest. The four basic shapes we will create are a heart, a necktie,

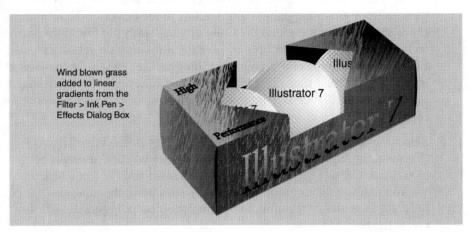

Wind blown grass
added to linear
gradients from the
Filter > Ink Pen >
Effects Dialog Box

High

Illus

Illustrator 7

Performance

FIGURE 12-42   Completing the composition with the Ink Pen Effects filter

an ellipse, and a square. We will use Illustrator's tools and filters to modify the shapes
and filters to create the desired effects and apply the desired colors.

Create a Heart

1. Choose the Pen tool from the main Toolbox. Click once in the artboard
   and drag a short distance. Click a second time up and to the left and drag
   to begin shaping the heart. Continue clicking and dragging to complete
   the outline for the heart. Do not worry if the shape is not exact. You can
   go back and edit the shape later with the Direct Select tool.

2. Choose the Color palette by Window|Show Color. Fill the object with **100**
   percent Magenta and **100** percent Yellow solid fill, leaving Cyan and
   Black at **0** percent.

3. Choose the Stroke color on the main Toolbox and apply a **100** percent
   black stroke color. Choose the Stroke palette by Window|Show Stroke
   and type **.1** for the point size of the line.

12

4. Create a copy of the original heart using the Scale and Copy tools. Choose Scale from the main Toolbox. Click in the center of the heart. Enter **85** percent and click on the Copy option. Apply No Fill to the copy and select the Stroke Color option. Give the Stroke a pale yellow color. Choose the Stroke palette by Window|Show Stroke. Type **1** for the Weight in points, **4** for the Miter Limit. Select Dashed Line and type **.75** points for the dash and **3** (points) for the space. Select a rounded cap. Press ENTER to apply the changes.

5. Select the original heart with the Selection tool. Choose Filter|Distort (Vector)| Zig Zag. Enter **2** for amount and **40** for number of ridges per inch. Click OK to apply. Group the original heart and the stitch heart.

   You will use this heart by scaling copies and rotating copies in different locations of the quilt. See the heart object in Figure 12-43. Now create the necktie shape.

6. Choose View|Show Grid. Choose View|Snap to Grid.

7. Create a circle using the Ellipse tool on the main Toolbox. Click in the artboard to view the Ellipse dialog box. Type **2.75** for the width and height. Click OK to accept the values.

8. Create a second circle using the Ellipse tool on the main Toolbox. Click on the center line for the previous circle. Type **2.5** for the width and height. Click OK to accept the values.

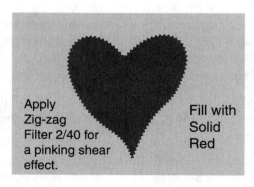

FIGURE 12-43   Create the heart object with zigzag edges

9. Create a third circle using the Ellipse tool on the main Toolbox. Click on the center line for the previous circle. Enter **.0625** for the width and height. Click OK to accept the values.

10. Choose the Pen tool from the main Toolbox and click on the center line of the circles to place the first anchor. Move the mouse cursor to the top of the largest circle and click a second time. Choose the Selection tool to let Illustrator know you are done drawing lines.

11. Choose Edit|Deselect All. Click on the new line you created. Rotate a copy of the line by choosing the Rotate tool from the main Toolbox. Click on the center line of the circles while pressing the ALT key. Enter **-7.5** for the angle of rotation and click on the Copy option. Select the original line again and apply the Rotate tool to it once more. This time enter **7.5** for the angle of rotation and click on the Copy option. Choose these three lines you just created and lock them by Object|Lock.

12. Create the necktie outline by choosing the Pen tool from the main Toolbox. Click at the top of the original line. Place the next anchor point by clicking at the intersection of the second line to the right and the 2.5 inch circle. Place the third anchor point by clicking at the intersection of the .0625 circle and the line to the right. Place the fourth anchor point by clicking at the intersection of the line to the left and the .0625 circle. Place the fifth anchor at the intersection of the line to the left and the 2.5 inch circle. Click at the starting point.

13. Use the Zoom tool in the main Toolbox to zoom in on the center line. Adjust the anchors using the Direct Selection tool in the main Toolbox to match the intersection points exactly. Do the same with all the anchor points so they match each corresponding intersection. Choose Edit|Deselect All.

14. Choose the Selection tool and select the new necktie object. Choose the Rotate tool from the main Toolbox and click on the center line while pressing the ALT/OPTION key. Type **-15** degrees and click on the Copy option. Duplicate the process by CTRL/COMMAND+D until you have completed the wheel. Fill each necktie object with a different color to represent a rainbow, starting with red and going to orange and yellow around the wheel to finish with blue, purple, and back to red.

You have created the necktie object and created the basic pattern to be used in the quilt tutorial. The necktie object is shown in Figure 12-44. Now we will apply a stitching to the necktie pattern.

15. Select the original necktie object. Choose the Scale tool and click on the point of origin crosshair while pressing the ALT/OPTION key. Enter **95** percent and click on the Copy option. Apply No Fill to the copy and select the Stroke Color option. Give the Stroke a pale yellow color. Choose the Stroke palette by Window|Show Stroke. Enter **1** for the Weight in points, **4** for the Miter Limit. Select Dashed Line and type **.75** points for the dash and **3** points for the space. Select a rounded cap. Press ENTER to apply the changes.

16. Choose the Rotate tool once again. Click on the center line while pressing the ALT/OPTION key. Type **-15** degrees and click the Copy option. Duplicate the process by CTRL/COMMAND+D until all the necktie objects have stitches.

17. Next we will add hearts to the composition. You will resize your heart to rotate two circular rows of heart copies around the outside of the necktie pattern.

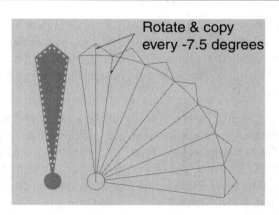

FIGURE 12-44   Creating the necktie object

18. Choose the Selection tool from the main Toolbox. Select the heart group and drag while pressing the ALT/OPTION key to produce a copy. You may need to resize your heart object to correspond to proportion of the necktie pattern. Use the Scale tool to make the heart bigger or smaller and choose the Scale Line Width option before clicking OK. Place the heart just above the original necktie object.

19. Reflect the heart group horizontally by choosing the Reflect tool from the main Toolbox. Choose the Rotate tool and click on the center line of the necktie pattern while pressing the ALT/OPTION key. Enter **-15** degrees and click the Copy option. Duplicate the process all around the outside of the necktie pattern.

20. Select the heart on top of the necktie pattern. Drag a copy to the right slightly so that it is between two other hearts. Rotate the heart until its point is aiming toward the center line. Rotate a copy by clicking on the center line of the necktie pattern while pressing the ALT key. Enter **-15** degrees and click the Copy option. Duplicate this process by CTRL/COMMAND+D until you have placed the second row of hearts around the necktie pattern. See the two rows of hearts in Figure 12-45.

    Now you are ready to create a square border around the composition. We will use the Center Rectangle tool to create the border.

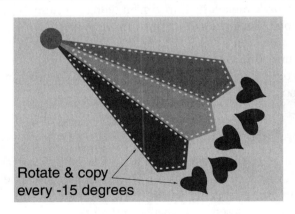

Rotate & copy every -15 degrees

FIGURE 12-45   Creating the two circular rows of hearts that surround the necktie pattern

12

20. Choose the Center Rectangle tool from the Rectangle tool flyout. Click the center line of the necktie pattern and type **3.25** inches for the width and height. Click OK to accept the values. Send this square to the back by CTRL/COMMAND+SHIFT+[. Fill this square with white and select No Stroke Color.

21. Create a second square using the same method except enter **3.75** inches for the width and the height. Send this to the back and fill with the same red values as the heart.

22. With this square still selected, choose the Filter|Distort (Vector)|Zig Zag. Type **12** for the Amount and **40** for the Ridges per inch.

23. Select the original heart object and move it to the center line of the necktie pattern. Arrange this heart to the front using CTRL/COMMAND+SHIFT+]. You now have all the elements in place to create the quilt.

24. Select all the objects using CTRL/COMMAND+A. Rasterize the objects by Object|Rasterize. Set the resolution to **72** dpi for low resolution or **300** dpi for very high resolution (but be forewarned that this will take a long time to complete at high resolution). Make sure the Create Mask option is not selected.

25. Apply the Craquelure filter to the rastered image by Filter|Texture|Craquelure. Experiment with the settings to achieve the desired look. Then click OK to apply your values.

Your quilt composition is complete. You can use this process to create virtual quilt designs before you make the first cut in cloth. See the finished quilt composition in Figure 12-46 and the color insert section of the book.

Using Other Filters

There are several other filters that we did not cover in this tutorial. Many of them are only slightly different from each other. Each filter has its unique appearance that you can utilize to create amazing works of art. Explore the different filters using different settings to gain a sense of what each filter does.

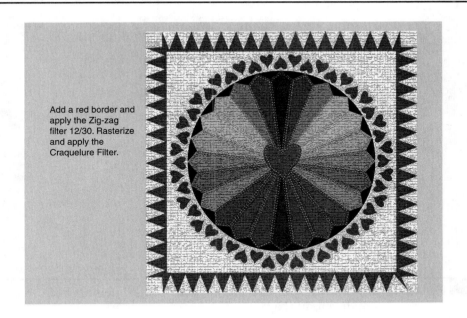

Add a red border and
apply the Zig-zag
filter 12/30. Rasterize
and apply the
Craquelure Filter.

FIGURE 12-46   The elements come together to create a quilted effect

You can use filters in combination and in different stages in the development of your artwork. For instance, Figure 12-47 shows a heart to which we applied the Zig Zag filter before we rasterized it. After we rasterized it, we applied the Artistic|Sponge filter.

You can create various distortions with vector images using the Distort filters. One such filter we have already used is the Zig Zag filter. Another filter is the Roughen filter, the effects of which are shown in Figure 12-48. We applied this filter to an ellipse using the smooth setting to create rounded corners.

Last in our tutorial on filter effects we chose the Twirl filter. Figure 12-49 shows the Twirl filter applied to a square object at 180 degrees rotation. You can use all of these Distort filters to change the basic outline of any vector image you create. These filters save time.

12

Fundamental Illustrator 7

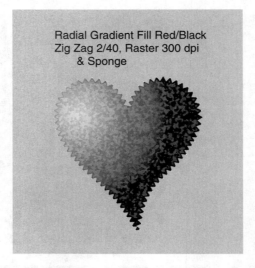

FIGURE 12-47　The Zig Zag filter and Artistic|Sponge filters applied to a heart shape

FIGURE 12-48　The Roughen filter applied to an ellipse

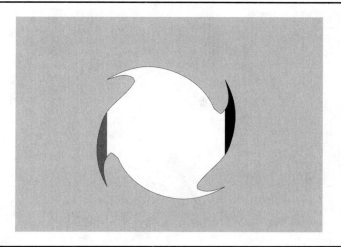

FIGURE 12-49   The Twirl filter applied to a square at 180 degrees rotation

Conclusion

The power of filters gives you unlimited range in changing the appearance of your images. Add in a slew of third-party filters, and you have the ability to create an infinite variety of effects and new styles of illustration. However, don't overdo the filter effects. As with all design, simpler is almost always better; avoid the temptation of using filters to create unnecessarily complex documents.

12

Working with Masks

13

In Chapter 12 you learned how to use Illustrator 7's filters to create sophisticated artwork and apply special effects. These can be used quite effectively to give artistic and painterly effects to your images. But one of the reasons that you're using Illustrator 7 is to help you break away from the limitations of traditional art. Who wants to be limited to a rectangular canvas? With the variety of masks that Illustrator 7 offers you, you don't have to be.

Understanding Illustrator 7's Mask Concept

A *mask* is an Illustrator 7 path that forms a cutout shape, cropping out the area beyond the path's boundary. That shape could be a freehand drawing, a star, or even type converted to paths. The ability to mask frees you from the limitations of a rectangular canvas, as you can see in Figure 13-1.

 Photoshop users will recognize that what Illustrator 7 refers to as masks, *Photoshop refers to as* clipping paths. *Each drawing program has its own distinct name for this function.*

FIGURE 13-1   Masks can be used to knock out a complex shape, add a new background, or replace a rectangular canvas with a fun shape

Creating a Mask

Creating a mask is as easy as drawing or importing a background, drawing a cutout, and applying the Object|Masks|Make command. As a practical exercise in creating a mask, follow these steps:

1. Begin by selecting the Rectangle tool (M) and drawing a rectangle.

2. Using the Swatches palette (F9), fill the rectangle with the Bricks pattern by dragging the Brick pattern onto your rectangle.

3. Select the Star tool (N) and draw a star directly on top of the rectangle.

4. Using the Selection tool (V), select both the star and the rectangle.

5. Use the Objects|Masks|Make command (CTRL/COMMAND+7), and the bricks will be masked inside the star.

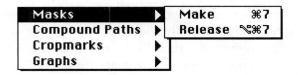

6. Save and name the file for use in steps to follow later in this chapter.

In this example, the star is serving as the mask for the brick-filled rectangle. The mask is the object that defines which area of the background is cropped. The ordering or layering of the object you create determines which object is used for the mask. In this example, if we were to bring the bricks to the front or place them on a higher layer, the rectangle that contained them would become the mask.

In order to create a mask, more than one object must be selected. The top object must be a path that is not grouped or joined in any way to any other object. In other words, a bitmap image cannot become a mask. A path that is part of a group cannot be used as a mask. However, after the mask is created it may be grouped freely.

The bricks are what we call the background. An unlimited number of objects, either bitmap or vector, on one or more layers, may be in the background. As you can see in Figure 13-2, the background may remain the same while the mask changes, giving your work very different appearances.

13

FIGURE 13-2   Not only are masks easy to make, but they also make it easy to make changes, such as this skewed brickwork

Working with Masks

Using masks saves you time and work. Traditionally, masks are used with raster images, but you can also work easily with masks in vector art as well. By leaving the underlying objects intact, the Mask function enables you to crop an object and then go back and edit either or both the mask and the masked object.

Compare that with using Illustrator 7's Pathfinder functions. Pathfinder can crop one path inside another, but what happens if you need to move the interior path? You will end up redrawing that path because Pathfinder destroyed the extraneous data. Because Mask leaves the underlying data intact, moving the path is painless. So, although you can create identical effects using Pathfinder and Mask, the Mask function gives you editing capabilities the Pathfinder lacks.

Filling and Stroking Masks

When you turn a path into a mask, any fill and stroke attributes that were attached to the original path are lost. Obviously this is not an ideal situation. Fortunately, Adobe has provided the Fill & Stroke for Mask plug-in so that you can re-create those lost attributes. To work the filter, use the Selection tool (V) to select the mask, then use Filter|Create|Fill & Stroke for Mask.

This filter creates two paths identical to the mask. One has a black stroke and no fill in front of the mask. The other has a gray fill and no stroke in the back of the mask. You may then fill and stroke these two objects individually. The stroke is obviously the most important as it will give your object a visible border (see Figure 13-3). Most of the time the gray fill that is created by Fill & Stroke for Mask is invisible, and you'll never know that it is there, especially if the masked object(s) fill 100 percent of the mask's area.

> **Tip** *If you only need the stroke and not the fill, it's a good idea to delete the fill object to conserve memory.*

> **Note** *You can apply fills and strokes to the mask, but Illustrator 7 will promptly forget the application. For years this was very frustrating, until the Fill & Stroke for Mask plug-in came along, but even this plug-in is not what we would call an ideal solution.*

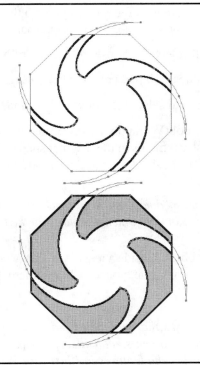

FIGURE 13-3 For the top object the spiral seems to be missing a border, while the bottom spiral features both a border and background

13

Editing a Mask

A mask is a path that you can edit just as you would any other path in Illustrator 7. Even after you have created the mask, you can change its shape, add or delete points, or apply a filter to the mask. As previously mentioned, the beauty of masks is that they leave the underlying data intact. By the same token, a background can be moved, sheared, rotated, or be otherwise transformed without affecting the mask.

To see how this works, follow these steps:

1. Open the brick-and-star mask you created previously.

2. Using the Direct Selection tool (A), drag a point or line segment on the star.

3. Notice that while parts of the star are moving, the bricks remain motionless. If you dragged far enough you would discover that you can quickly move beyond the edge of the background.

4. With the star still selected, choose Filter|Distort|Punk & Bloat.

5. Enter a Bloat value of **10** percent and click OK.

6. Deselect the star, and select the brick background.

7. Using the Shear tool (W), apply a skew transformation to the bricks. Notice that the star remains in the original shape. Figure 13-4 shows how editing the mask or the background doesn't affect either entity.

Note   *If using the Shear tool doesn't move the bricks, ALT/OPTION-click the Shear tool to access this tool's options and make sure that the Patterns option is selected.*

If you have multiple objects inside a mask, you can arrange the objects as if they weren't masked. This means that you can bring them forward and send them backward as necessary.

Tip   *When creating masks that may be edited later on and when working with highly complex documents, consider placing your mask objects on a separate layer using the features in Illustrator 7's Layers palette (F7). For more information on using the Layers feature, see the "Working in Layers" section in **Chapter 8: Selecting and Arranging Objects**.*

FIGURE 13-4 Masking allows you to edit the mask separately from the background without the changes to one affecting the other

Undoing a Mask

Illustrator 7 offers you two ways to clear a mask. The easiest way is to simply select the mask and delete it. Although attractive in its simplicity, this method of removing a mask is extremely destructive and may result in deleting objects you worked hard to create.

The preferred method of removing a mask is to select the mask and choose Object|Masks|Release (CTRL/COMMAND+ALT/OPTION+7). This command has the effect of separating the mask from the background. The former mask is now a path with no fill and no stroke in front of the background.

Note *The Release Mask command will only release the mask itself. In other words, simply clicking a background object and using the Release Mask command may not achieve your desired results.*

Caution *Be careful not to inadvertently misplace the former mask object following the Release Mask command. Because objects used as masks often have no fill or stroke it will be difficult to find if deselected. Releasing a mask will have no effect on objects created with Fill & Stroke for Mask. They will still exist in their former positions.*

13

Adding and Removing Objects from Masks

After creating a mask, you'll often discover you need to add additional objects to the group of objects you have masked. The logical but tedious way to add objects is to release the mask and then remake the mask with appropriate objects.

But there's an easier way. You may also add an object to the mask by clicking the mask background object and using the Edit|Paste in Front (CTRL/COMMAND+F) or Edit|Paste in Back (CTRL/COMMAND+B) commands to paste an object currently on your clipboard. Depending on which is appropriate, the pasted object will end up either immediately above or below the selected object in the stacking order. To add an object to a mask, create an object, cut it to the clipboard, select an object in the mask, and apply the Paste in Front command (see Figure 13-5).

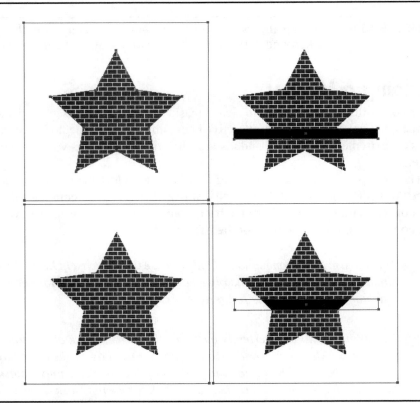

FIGURE 13-5   Adding an object to a mask

The easiest way to remove an object from a mask is to select it, then delete it using either the Edit|Clear command or pressing your DELETE key. Releasing the mask will also remove any masked objects from the mask. You may also cut an object to remove it from the mask.

Note   *Be sure that the mask and any objects it contains are deselected before using the Edit|Clear command; otherwise you'll end up pasting the object right back into the mask.*

Advanced Masking

The true power of masks is limited more by your imagination than by program limitations. One of the best features of masks is that they enable you to create special illustration effects. Although there are countless creative uses for masking, the following section will depict basic examples in an effort to provide you with a clear understanding of a few advanced techniques.

Moving Gradients

When you fill an object with a radial gradient, the gradient will always emanate from the object's center. By using masks with radial gradients you gain control over them. For example, consider the star example that you created at the beginning of this chapter. As a practical exercise, follow these steps:

1. Open the star file you created earlier or create a new file using the steps described earlier in this chapter. You should have two objects in front of you, the star mask and the brick background.

2. Delete any extraneous objects that you may have created during the editing masks example.

3. Duplicate the star mask using the Copy (CTRL/COMMAND+C) and Paste (CTRL/COMMAND+V) commands, and move the copy off to the side.

4. Select both the new star and the brick background.

5. Fill both with the Yellow & Orange Radial gradient stored in the Swatches palette (F5).

13

6. Deselect the star and position the background so that the center of the gradient is at the top tip of the star. You may need to stretch the background to fill the mask, but now the gradient is centered in a useful location.

 When moving the background, move the entire *background. Moving points to stretch the box will leave the gradient in place.*

Complex Mask Shapes

Illustrator 7 does not limit you to creating masks with simple shapes. Compound paths also make excellent masks. You may not use type as a mask unless the type is first converted to outlines. As a practical exercise in applying type as a mask, follow these steps:

1. Reopen the star mask example created earlier.

2. Release the mask using the Release Mask command and delete the star.

3. Using the Type tool (T), type the word **MASK** over the background.

4. Adjust the font and size of your type to approximate the same size of the background.

5. Choose the Type|Create Outlines (CTRL/COMMAND+SHIFT+O) command to convert the type to a paths only. This will convert the text into four paths with each character a single compound path.

6. Choose the Object|Compound Paths|Release command to split each compound path character object into two separate paths.

7. With all of the text outlines still selected, choose the Object|Compound Paths|Make command; this will combine all of the text outlines into a single compound path.

8. SHIFT-click to add the background to your current selection of objects, and choose the Object|Masks|Make command.

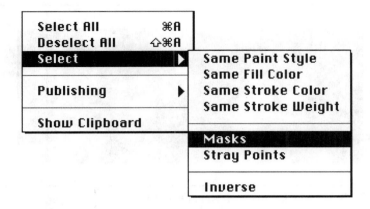

You have completed making your type a mask, as shown next:

Note *In order to use a compound path as a mask you must select the entire path. Selecting just one subpath of a compound path and trying to create a mask with that subpath will result in an error.*

If you don't release and remake the type as a compound path the mask creation process will create a mask from just the last letter of the word. In the previous example, that would be the letter K.

You can place masks inside other masks(see Figure 13-6). Each new mask treats the previous mask as if it were just one object. You create a mask inside a mask just as you would any other object.

Troubleshooting Masks

Beware of overusing masks. They are very memory intensive. Many designers have had to re-create artwork when their complex drawings overtaxed their output device.

13

FIGURE 13-6   Masks inside masks. One mask partially covers each moon, being moved over the sequence to gradually reveal more of the moons. The other mask hides each moon behind the horizon.

When using complex shapes as a mask, try to minimize the number of points on the mask path. A simpler shape (fewer anchor points and line segments) will greatly enhance the chances for problem-free output.

Mask paths that are created by using a freehand tool such as the Pencil tool (Y), a tracing tool such as the Autotrace tool (B), or Adobe Streamline can be extremely complex. Mask paths that have been altered by filters, such as Punk & Bloat, can have many unnecessary points added to them. Successful printing may require that you remove points or split the paths.

Removing points is easy—use the Delete Anchor Point tool (P), and click each of the points you want to remove.

But what happens when your mask is an organic shape, such as a coastline, that won't simplify easily? In **Chapter 3: Making Illustrator 7 Easy to Use**, you learned about the option in the Document Setup dialog box to split long paths. Unfortunately, with masks splitting long paths could end up producing a piece that only shows a fraction of the background. In this case you must manually split the mask. As a practical exercise, follow these steps:

1. Select the mask and choose Object|Masks|Release (CTRL/COMMAND+ ALT/OPTION+7) to release it.

2. Use the Scissors tool (C) to break the mask into smaller pieces, and choose Object|Path|Join (CTRL/COMMAND+J) to make each piece a closed path.

3. Define each piece individually as a mask. This will require you to make duplicates of the background object.

Sometimes keeping track of the masks in your document can be very difficult. If you can't remember where your masks are, just choose Edit|Select|Masks. This will select all masks and related background objects in your document. If any other objects are selected when you run this command, they will be deselected.

Chapter 13 Tutorial: Exploring Mask Commands

As a practical exploration of the features and effects discussed in this chapter, follow through in this step-by-step tutorial. As you do so, you may notice that some of these steps are accompanied by a "Color palette" symbol. This symbol indicates that the step has also been illustrated in full color in the Fundamental Illustrator 7 color insert. The purpose of the color insert is to provide you with a brief overview of the tutorial and act as an overall reference for the practical use of color throughout these tutorials.

Watch for this symbol:

By now you're well aware of the power of Illustrator 7.0. So, to show our appreciation for the engineers at Adobe Systems, we're going to design a tribute to our favorite drawing application. Of course, we'll also be applying the techniques you learned in this chapter for creating and manipulating masks.

We'll also direct you around stickier ways Illustrator handles these features and take advantage of Illustrator's ability to combine different file formats—in this case, a vector drawing and screen-shot bitmap.

13

Preparing the Image to Be Masked

1. Start with a new document (CTRL/COMMAND+N). Illustrator creates new documents in portrait orientation with the page taller than it is wide. For this tutorial, we'll want to work with our page in landscape orientation (which means the page is wider than tall). Select File|Document Setup and click on the Print Setup button for Windows or the Page Setup button for Macintosh.

2. Select File|Document (CTRL/COMMAND+SHIFT+P), select Print Setup, and click on Landscape in the Orientation section of the Print Setup dialog box. Then click on "use print setup," and click OK, as shown in Figure 13-7.

Now, your document will be oriented as shown in Figure 13-8.

Illustrator 7's Preview mode is best for working with masks, so select it from the View menu (CTRL/COMMAND+Y).

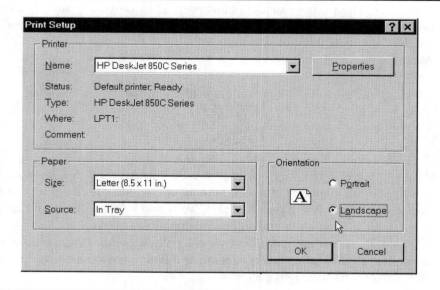

FIGURE 13-7   Changing your working space to Landscape orientation

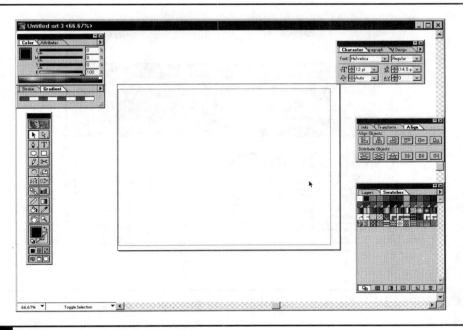

FIGURE 13-8 The correctly oriented workspace

3. Next, we're going to use the image of Botticelli's Venus that Adobe flashes for you each time you launch Illustrator. Click on the about Illustrator button in the main Toolbox, and Adobe's credit screen will be shown, as in Figure 13-9.

We're going to take a snapshot of the image of Venus's face. First, make sure that your cursor is not actually touching her face. If you are a Windows user, press the Print Screen button and you'll copy the contents of your screen to the clipboard.

To save your screen image, launch any basic image editor program such as PC Paintbrush (Windows) or Macpaint (Macintosh), open a new document, and select Edit|Paste to paste the image as a new document, as shown in Figure 13-10. Save the image with a file name that makes sense to you. Quit your image editor and return to Illustrator 7.

If you own a Macintosh, the process of capturing Venus's image may require fewer steps. Press COMMAND-SHIFT-3, and you'll hear your Mac make a camera

13

FIGURE 13-9   The Venus in Adobe's Illustrator credit screen

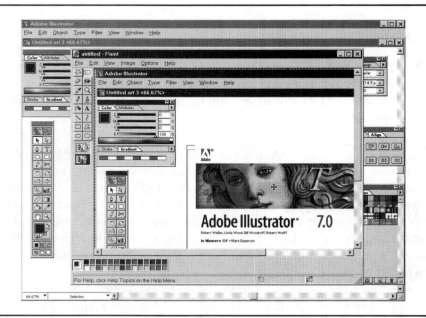

FIGURE 13-10   Displaying Illustrator's credits screen in Paint

motor-drive sound, and a PICT image called "Picture 1" will appear in your system folder, as shown in Figure 13-11.

To ensure that the screen capture was a success, choose Finder from the menu on the upper-left corner of your screen, and click on the icon for your startup hard drive. Clicking on this drive's icon will launch SimpleText or another associated image-editing application and you'll be able to view your screen capture image. You can then drag this file to another location, or just leave it in your root directory.

No matter which platform you're working on, remember where it is that you've stashed the file of the lovely Venus because we'll be coming back to this file shortly.

Note *By the way, these screen-shot techniques don't only work with Illustrator 7.0 — they are part of your computer's operating system. They're system-level commands that can grab a screen from almost any Windows or Mac application (some games won't work, nor will programs that intentionally block screen captures).*

	Name	Size	Kind	Label	Last Modified	Version
	Macintosh HD					
	14 items		413.4 MB in disk			99.8 MB available
	Picture 1	536K	SimpleText docum...	–	Tue, Aug 5, 1997, 2:00 PM	–
▷	Adobe Photoshop 3.0	–	folder	–	Wed, Mar 6, 1996, 4:24 PM	–
▷	Adobe Premiere™ 4.2.1 ƒ	–	folder	–	Wed, Nov 27, 1996, 1:29 AM	–
▷	Adobe Type Utilities	–	folder	–	Sun, Nov 24, 1996, 6:39 PM	–
▷	dan's	–	folder	–	Sun, Jun 29, 1997, 8:16 AM	–
▷	dan's Apple Extras	–	folder	–	Mon, Jan 15, 1996, 11:59 AM	–
▷	debab	–	folder	–	Sun, Dec 1, 1996, 6:28 AM	–
▷	DeBabelizer® 1.6.5 Folder	–	folder	–	Wed, Jan 8, 1997, 8:00 PM	–
▷	Delmar7/16	–	folder	–	Thu, Aug 1, 1996, 9:02 AM	–
▷	Jaru Syquest	–	folder	–	Sun, Aug 11, 1996, 12:04 PM	–
▷	Live Picture 2.5.1	–	folder	–	Sun, Jun 29, 1997, 8:22 AM	–
▷	Netscape Navigator™ 2....	–	folder	–	Mon, Jun 17, 1996, 10:41 PM	–
▷	System Folder	–	folder	–	Wed, Jul 30, 1997, 2:09 PM	–
▷	Utils	–	folder	–	Fri, Jul 19, 1996, 8:08 PM	–

FIGURE 13-11 The Macintosh file of Illustrator's credits screen

13

Preparing the Mask

Now that we have selected the image we want to use, we need to build a heart-shaped mask in order to frame our Venus. We could use the Pen tool (P) to create curved paths in the shape of a heart, but why bother? Our computers already provide us with a heart in the Symbol Character Map .

To view the entire Symbol font, Windows users can use the Character Map application from the Accessories entry in Windows 95/NT4.0's Start|Programs menu. Once you have selected Character Map, select Symbol from the Font pull-down menu in the upper left corner. You'll see a heart, as well as the other card suits, about halfway down the window. Double-click on the heart and it will appear in the text box on the right side of the window, as shown in Figure 13-12. Press the Copy button on the far right and then the Close button.

Note   *If you know the keyboard shortcuts, you can dispense with navigating to the Character Map and just use the shortcuts. On a Windows machine, the shortcut for the heart character (which is the "©" copyright character in most fonts) is ALT-0169. If you want to create the heart image in this way, be sure to use the numeric keypad—the number keys on the top of the QWERTY keyboard won't work.*

Macintosh users can use Apple's corollary Key Caps application which is found in the Apple menu. Double-click the icon to launch Key Caps and select Symbol

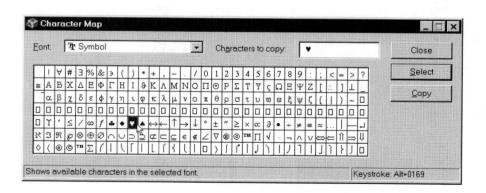

FIGURE 13-12   The Windows Character Map

from the Key Caps menu. The onscreen keyboard will now show you the Greek characters of the Symbol font, but no heart. That's because the onscreen keyboard will only show those characters that appear on the screen if they were typed without using the SHIFT or OPTION keys. So, press the OPTION key, and the onscreen keyboard changes. You'll notice that a heart is now where the G key usually is. Type **G** while you hold down the OPTION key, and a heart will appear in the text box on the top of the Key Caps menu, as shown in Figure 13-13. Next, highlight the heart with your mouse and select Edit|Cut (CTRL/COMMAND+X).

On both platforms, our heart character is now on the clipboard, so we can return to Illustrator and move on. Select Symbol from the drop-down menu on Illustrator's Character palette (CTRL/COMMAND+T). Let's try a 200-point heart:type **200** into the Point Size text box on the upper right of the Character palatte. Select the Type tool (T) from the main Toolbox palette and click on the artboard. Now, select Edit|Paste (CTRL/COMMAND+V), and a 200-point heart appears for our use, as shown in Figure 13-14.

Note   *If you know the keyboard shortcuts, you can dispense with the Character Map/Key Caps detours and use them instead. For the Mac, the keyboard shortcut is OPTION+G.*

4. Now, let's bring in our screen shot of Venus. Select Place from Illustrator's File menu and go to the directory where you stored the screenshot to select it.

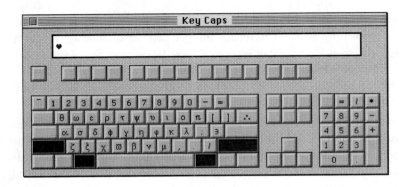

FIGURE 13-13   The Macintosh Key Caps feature

13

FIGURE 13-14   The heart shape that will house the Venus

Note   *You'll see that you are not able to import Adobe Illustrator files in this dialog box. If you wish to bring in more Illustrator art, you must open it as a separate document and use the Copy command (CTRL/COMMAND+C) from the Edit menu.*

Now switch back to your work document by using the Window menu (other open documents will appear at the bottom of the menu), and use the Paste command (CTRL/COMMAND+V) to bring the items from the clipboard to your screen.

The Link checkbox, shown in Figure 13-15, on the bottom left of the Place dialog box is very important. When selected, Illustrator doesn't import the art into your work file; it just remembers where the art file is located on your hard drive and reads in the data when required. When the checkbox is empty, the application actually copies the art into your Illustrator document. The advantage of using linked files is a considerable saving of disk space—especially when using multiple-megabyte files associated with print work. The disadvantages can be infuriating: if you move the art file to a different directory or change it, you'll have problems the next time you open the Illustrator file that references it.

For right now, just make sure the link checkbox is selected, and press OK.

5. Because the mask must go in front of the image for proper alignment, just as you'd put a matte in front of a picture you are framing, make sure the image of Venus is sitting behind the heart image you have selected and enlarged. Using the Selection tool (V), make sure the art is selected, and choose Arrange|Send to Back (CTRL/COMMAND+SHIFT+[) from the Object menu, as shown in Figure 13-16.

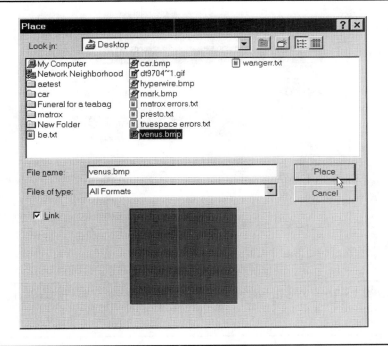

FIGURE 13-15 Inserting the Venus bitmap file into our workspace

6. Now, use Illustrator's Scale tool (S) to size the picture of Venus so that the heart corresponds to the size of Venus's face, as shown in Figure 13-17. Be sure to hold down the SHIFT key to make any scaling uniform since significantly changing the aspect ratio of a raster image can create bizarre effects. Don't be too concerned if the positioning isn't perfect; we can tweak it later.

Creating the Mask

Follow these steps to create the mask:

7. Use Illustrator's Select All command in the Edit menu (CTRL/COMMAND+A) to select both the background art (that's Venus) and the heart. Remember from the earlier discussion in this chapter that both the mask *and* the object to be masked must be selected when creating a mask. Now click on Masks|Make (CTRL/COMMAND+7) in the Object menu. Wait—nothing happens! That's because Illustrator can't make a mask out of type, and our heart is really a piece of type that we're treating as a shape.

13

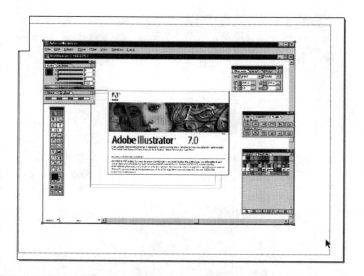

FIGURE 13-16　The image of Venus shown in front of the heart image

FIGURE 13-17　The heart shape cutout is just about the same size
as Venus' face

We can easily remedy this problem. Select Create Outlines from the Type menu (CTRL/COMMAND+SHIFT+O) and the heart is now converted into a closed curve.

Now, position the correctly-sized heart over the portion of Venus' face that we want to create a mask for, as shown in Figure 13-18.

In addition to letting you make masks out of type, Illustrator's Create Outlines command is very helpful when you know you'll be transporting files from machine to machine (for example, from your work computer to the local service bureau). As long as your fonts are all outlines, you don't have to worry about lugging around all the printer fonts included in the file. On the other hand, outlines are much more difficult to edit than straight type.

Now, let's try making a mask again. Follow these steps:

8. Make sure all our objects are selected by using the Select All command in the Edit menu (CTRL/COMMAND+A) to select both the background art and the heart.

FIGURE 13-18   Indicating the size and shape of the mask

9. Click on Masks|Make (CTRL/COMMAND+7) in the Object menu. The heart turns into a transparent mask, with the background art peeking though, as shown below.

10. Deselect all the objects, click on the background art with the Selection tool (V), and click and drag to position the art correctly behind the mask. Cursor keys are a quick way to make fine adjustments. You may have to use the Scale tool again, also, to adjust the size of the mask.

The mask is created, but our heart still doesn't look right. Let's make an outline around the mask to more clearly define the outline of the heart. Select the heart, and try adding a stroke to it using the Color palette (F6). Again, nothing happens. Illustrator forces us to make one more step.

With the heart selected, click on Create|Fill & Stroke for Mask in the Filter menu. This creates another object in front of the mask. Now you can use the tools in the main Toolbox and Color palette (F6) to place a three-point stroke around the mask.

If nothing happens when you try changing the stroke weight, you probably still have the mask selected and not the Fill & Stroke for Mask object the filter created. Click on Lock under the Object menu. That will lock the mask down, making the stroke-able object easier to select.

Finishing the Design

The mask doesn't have to be the top object. We can now add some more type with the Type tool (T). Select Times (Roman) in the Character palette (CTRL/ COMMAND+T) at 170 pt, place the Type tool to the left of the heart, click, and type **I** as shown in Figure 13-19.

11. Click the Type tool (T) on the right side of the heart, and type in the word **Illustrator**. Zoom out using the Zoom tool (Z) to see your finished artwork as shown in Figure 13-20.

12. Now all we have to do is make sure this image and the text we've just added fits on the page. Pick the Scale tool (S) to select all, hold down the SHIFT key and grab a corner of the selected objects. Drag to scale the selected objects until they fit on your page.

FIGURE 13-19   Adding text to our Adobe appreciation creation

I ♥ Illustrator

FIGURE 13-20   Creating the text for our bumper sticker

13. Use the Selection tool (V) to center the art on the page, and the tutorial is complete. The finished image is shown here:

Conclusion

This chapter has covered basic applications of applying masks to objects, while providing a brief exploration of real life techniques. Illustrator 7's Mask features may appear confusing at first, but once you have mastered the concept you'll likely find yourself using it frequently. Masking either vector or bitmap objects is the most efficient way of cleaning up or packaging your drawing elements. Plus, the creative doors that open for you in using the Mask feature are virtually unlimited.

Working with Bitmap Tools

14

One tired, old saying maintains that "A picture is worth a thousand words." In the world of digital publishing though, a "bitmap" can be worth a thousand words, and very possibly hundreds of thousands of "bytes," and even more "pixels."

Adobe Illustrator 7 is capable of working quite comfortably with bitmap images, but the tools and techniques for working with these types of objects differ slightly from those of other vector drawing programs and dedicated image editing programs such as Adobe's Photoshop. But, because Illustrator 7 now includes Photoshop plug-ins (little scripts in the form of filters used to enact special effects on bitmap images), you now have much of the digital artistic freedom and power available to this premier image editor.

For new users to Illustrator and digital publishing, this chapter describes the characteristics of bitmap images and provides information for you to be able to identify bitmap formats and implement them into your drawings. Expert users will discover some tips for working with bitmap tools in Illustrator 7 and considerations for fine-tuning them for specific purposes such as offset printing and the World Wide Web.

What's a Bitmap?

Although this may seem like a simple question, it can easily generate a long-winded, complex, and confusing answer. But, simply put, the term *bitmap* is used to describe a digital photographic-type image that can feature color, quality, size, and detail properties. The term "bit" refers to a binary digit, which is the smallest unit of information capable of being measured by a computer. Bits are the very essence of data we all know as "ones" and "zeros" or "on" and "off " states. While on, a bit may also represent a color state, depending on how it's been set.

Building on this concept of ones and zeros slightly, a bitmap is a class of file format that contains digital dot patterns measured in resolution values. Bitmaps may feature various states of color depth such as 1-bit, 2-bit, 4-bit, 8-bit, 24-bit, and 32-bit, depending on which color model they have been mapped to. Most commonly, you'll be working with 1-bit, 8-bit, 24-bit, and 32-bit formats. In the digital world, each of these bitmap "hybrids" has their own purpose. For example, 8-bit and 24-bit formats can best be used for Web images, whereas 32-bit formats are commonly used for four-color process printing.

The following guide to bitmap image color depth gives more precise information:

Color depth	Bit level
Black and white	1-bit
16-level true gray	4-bit
256-level true gray	8-bit
16 color	4-bit
256 color	8-bit
16.7 million colors	24-bit

A bitmap image is quite a different animal from a vector object. Where vector objects feature editable anchor points to edit their shape, a freshly placed bitmap just sort of sits there on your screen. But, even if there are a few things you can't do with it, there's also plenty you *can* do. You can use virtually any of the transformation tools in Illustrator 7 on an imported bitmap object including scaling, rotation, shear, and reflection. Plus, Illustrator offers masking tools and filter effects that open up a universe of creative applications.

Working with Bitmap Formats

When choosing a bitmap format, you need to consider a number of factors including the image's physical size, resolution, color depth, and memory size. In many cases, you may even be the one preparing the image for use in your drawing. Preparation considerations such as resolution and size are critical when implementing bitmaps into Illustrator 7. In most instances, you'll want to do as much of the refining work in a dedicated bitmap editor such as Photoshop. Preparation procedures can include scanning, adjusting colors and color depth, cropping, and any other manipulations you wish to apply.

 When using Illustrator 7, set memory-intensive properties of your imported bitmap such as size and resolution before attempting to place the image into your drawing.

There are any number of sources for obtaining bitmap images for use in your drawing. In recent years, technology has advanced and hardware prices have become affordable for almost anyone. The following lists a few of the more commonly used methods of acquiring images using hardware and software:

14

- Low-end hand scanners
- Common flatbed scanners
- High-end drum scanners
- Video capture
- Kodak Photo CD
- Texture generation software
- Other vector graphic programs
- Image-editing programs
- 3D rendering software
- Animation software
- Screen-capture software

Bitmap images come in all varieties, shapes, colors, and sizes. Illustrator 7 is fully compatible with a wide range of these including the following formats:

- Adobe Photoshop 4 PSD
- Adobe Photoshop Filmstrip
- Amiga IFF
- BMP
- CGM (computer graphics metafile)
- GIF 89A (graphical interchange format version)
- JPEG (Joint Photographers Expert Group)
- Kodak Photo CD
- Macintosh PICT
- MacPaint
- PCX (PC Paintbrush)
- Pixar
- PixelPaint

- PNG (portable network graphic)

- TIFF (tagged image file format)

- TGA (Targa)

- WMF (Windows Metafile)

For more information on Illustrator 7's import file formats, see the section "Importing with the Place Command" in **Chapter 16: Importing and Exporting from Illustrator 7**.

Bitmap Properties

The properties associated with your images will determine its physical characteristics such as level of detail, size, and color. Depending on your specific use (i.e., color proofing, print or Web design), some of these properties will likely need attention or adjustment. Many of these adjustments can be accomplished through the use of filter effect commands.

Resolution

Image resolution is one of the most confusing properties surrounding the use of bitmap images. Perhaps the reason for this is because the resolution of a bitmap image can be measured in a number of different ways including screen resolution, inherent resolution, and output resolution. Each of these resolution values are measured in different ways—depending on the medium reproducing the image, it could be measured either in parts (or bits) per inch (PPI), dots per inch (DPI), or lines per inch (LPI).

Note   *Although Illustrator 7 does not include direct commands to alter the resolution of imported bitmap images, you may "re-rasterize" objects using the Object\Rasterize command, which features options to increase or decrease the amount of inherent resolution.*

When a bitmap image is created, whether the creation process is via image-recording hardware (such as a scanner) or the filter of a software program, the image is divided in a checkerboard or grid pattern whereby each checkerboard square is assigned a color or shade. When your computer "sees" one of these checkerboards, it projects the corresponding color to your computer screen or printer. Resolution is a property of this checkerboard pattern.

Screen resolution is what you see when you view your bitmap image onscreen. Although drawing programs can simulate the inherent resolution of your image, what you see onscreen is simply a representation based on the data in the bitmap. This screen representation never exceeds a value ranging from 72 to 96 dots per inch (DPI), depending on the platform being used.

Just to add to the confusion, another "screen" resolution measure comes into play when working in the offset printing industry. Screens in offset printing have nothing whatsoever to do with computer screens. Printing screen resolutions measure the number of rows of dots that make up the detail of a printed *halftone*. A halftone is an image prepared with various-sized dots arranged in rows to simulate a continuous tone, photographic, or graphic image when printed. Halftones are traditionally produced by photographing a continuous-tone original onto graphic arts negative film contacted with a specialized halftone screen. Some screens are coarse while others are quite fine; a screen's value depends on the inherent capabilities of the printing press reproducing the image. Printing screen resolutions are measured in lines per inch (LPI), which is in essence the physical number of rows of dots in a linear inch.

The "inherent" screen resolution of a bitmap image is the number of squares of the checkerboard that are measured horizontally or vertically in an inch. It may be measured either in pixels (which are measured in parts per inch) or in DPI. The higher the resolution of a bitmap image, the more detail it will render to your computer screen or printer.

Illustrator does not include any internal tools for adjusting the inherent resolution of an imported image; this must be set before the image is placed in your Illustrator 7 document. If your bitmap images include too much information, you may be wasting valuable resources working with the extra resolution. If your images don't feature enough resolution, the final image quality might be unacceptable.

If your drawing is destined for a printing press, your images need to feature a resolution that is twice that of the final printing screen resolution. If the printing screen resolution is 150 LPI, then your bitmap image will need to feature roughly 300 DPI. Images destined for use in Web page designs only need to include enough resolution to render to a computer screen, that is, 72 DPI. Any excess resolution will waste resources.

Knowing correct resolution is one of the strategies discussed in **Chapter 15: Getting the Most Out of Illustrator 7**. For more information on improving performance or increasing productivity habits, review Chapter 15.

Color Depth and Color Models

Color depth measures the capabilities of a digital image to render color, shade, and tone, while color models determine a set of characteristics of the colors being measured. The color depth of an image is usually associated with its bit value, as in 1-bit, 2-bit, 8-bit, and so on. Color models are associated with image color type such as RGB (red, green, blue) CMYK (cyan, magenta, yellow, black), HSB (hue, saturation, brightness), and Grayscale. But, while Illustrator 7 supports these four main standard color models, the HSB model is used only to represent color values in palettes and dialog boxes.

For more information on working with color models, see the section "Understanding Color Models" in **Chapter 11: Working in Color**.

The color model you assign to your digital image will depend on how you are accustomed to working with and measuring color and will ultimately match the image's eventual purpose. Color models in Illustrator are defined as follows:

- **RGB**   Stands for red, green, blue; measures color based on individual values ranging from 0 to 255. For example, colors may be identified solely by their values as in "0,255,0" indicates a very bright green and "255,0,0" indicates a bright red. Illustrator 7 is also capable of measuring and displaying RGB color values in percentages. The RGB color model features a depth of 24 bits per pixel (24-bit).

- **CMYK**   Stands for the four standard process colored inks used in offset printing: cyan (C), magenta (M), yellow (Y), and black (K). CMYK values are measured percentages usually denoted where "C60,M100,Y100,K0" indicates a pure red color and "C0,M50,Y100,K0" denotes a pure orange color. The CMYK color model features a depth of 32 bits per pixel (32-bit).

To check out the details of your imported bitmap image, click on the bitmap and choose Selection Info from the File menu. The Info dialog box reveals bitmap information including size, color model, channels, memory size, and resolution.

- **HSB** Stands for hue, saturation, brightness; while Illustrator supports this color model for use in the display of color in the Color palette and certain dialog boxes, it cannot convert bitmap images to this color model.

- **Grayscale** The Grayscale color model supports 256 shades of gray ranging in value from 0 to 255. And, as you might have guessed, the grayscale color model only supports a color depth of 8 bits per pixel (8-bit).

You may convert bitmap images using various filters under the Color command located in the Filter menu. During the conversion process from one color model to another, Illustrator 7 performs the function automatically and transparently. In other words, if you select to convert a CMYK (32-bit) image to RGB (24-bit), Illustrator 7 assumes you are aware of the increase or decrease in your image's color characteristics and proceeds with the conversion.

About Image Headers

Another characteristic that may or may not apply to the bitmap images you work with is something called an image or preview header. A *header* is a collection of image data integrated into the bitmap file, which can be read by the host program—in this case, Illustrator 7.

Header images are representations of the image data and not the actual data the image file contains. Often the header is more crude in appearance than the original itself. When working with bitmap images which are "linked" (rather than embedded) to your Illustrator 7 drawing, it's important to understand that what you are looking at onscreen is simply a preview built by Illustrator instead of the actual image data. Although previews of linked images can be transformed or altered, the data they represent remains unchanged.

Note *After applying a filter effect to a linked imported bitmap image, Illustrator automatically embeds the resulting image in your drawing file, adding the required data to your Illustrator 7 document. To take advantage of the linking capabilities when working with very large images, apply the desired bitmap effects using a dedicated bitmap editor such as Photoshop before placing the file in your Illustrator drawing.*

For example, when you link a bitmap image to your Illustrator 7 drawing and subsequently perform transformations to it, the changes are visually reflected on your screen using the preview image, while the original stays the same. Preview images often occupy less space than the data they represent, and so working with linked images enables you to keep your Illustrator 7 drawing file size relatively small. Previews are created for the various zoom views used to view your drawing and the necessary information is cached to the scratch disk providing Illustrator 7 with the ability to quickly display bitmap previews.

Note *When you import a bitmap file into Illustrator 7 using the Place command, a preview is automatically created based on the characteristics inherent in the original bitmap image including color, resolution, size, and so on. When exporting an image from Illustrator, you may set the preview header to certain color depth specifications. Header images add to the exported image's file size, though, and the more detailed you make the header, the larger the size of the resulting file. For more information on exporting bitmap images, see the "Bitmap Filters" section in **Chapter 16: Importing and Exporting from Illustrator 7**.*

If you choose at some point to embed the image into your Illustrator 7 drawing file, you're essentially transposing all the data that represents that image into your file, which usually causes the physical drawing file size to increase dramatically.

Converting Vectors to Bitmaps

Illustrator 7 enables you to take objects you have created in your drawing and convert them into bitmap images just as they appear, including any applied fill and stroke assignments. To convert objects, first select them and then choose Rasterize from the Objects menu. Illustrator prompts you with a dialog box asking how you'd like to convert the object:

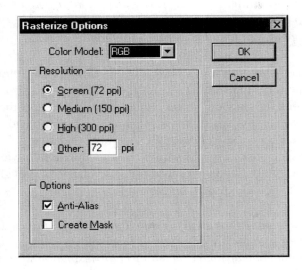

From here, your decisions will be based on how you intend to reproduce your drawing elements. Your choices for rasterizing vector objects into bitmaps include color model, resolution, anti-aliasing, and transparency mask options.

■ **Color Model**   When performing your conversion with Illustrator 7, you have the luxury of being able to specify whether the eventual bitmap will use RGB, CMYK, Grayscale, or Bitmap. The Bitmap option is slightly confusing in that you actually will create a bitmap no matter which model you choose. In this case though, Illustrator gives you the option to convert your color objects to a color depth of 1-bit. Images that feature a 1-bit color depth are monochrome—or strictly black and white. Monochrome can be black and white or simply a single color.

■ **Resolution**   The resolution choices available offer standard Screen (72), Medium (150), or High (300) DPI resolution values, or you may specify an exact resolution by choosing the Other option and entering your own value. The Other option is capable of setting resolution between a range of 1 to 2,400 DPI.

■ **Anti-Alias**   Choosing the Anti-Alias option enables the Rasterize command to "blend" or soften the edges of objects of different colors. *Anti-aliasing* reduces the effects of jagged edges associated with non-anti-aliased images. The Anti-Alias option may be used in combination with all color models except the Bitmap option.

Avoid using anti-aliasing effects if your bitmap image is to be masked and placed on a colored background. Illustrator's anti-aliasing effects cause white halos to appear around an object placed against a colored background

■ **Create Mask**   Choose the Create Mask option when creating bitmap conversions of unevenly shaped objects. This has the effect of interpreting the sum of all paths in your object and uses the Make Mask command to create and apply a new object based on their combined shapes. When the Create Mask option is left unselected, a rectangular bounding box is created around the resulting bitmap object regardless of whether it is rectangular-shaped or not.

When using the Create Mask option, Illustrator literally creates a mask object and groups it to the newly created bitmap object. If, for whatever reason, you wish to eliminate the mask object, click on the mask object and choose Object, Mask, Release (CTRL/COMMAND+ALT/OPTION+7).

When Illustrator 7's Rasterize command is applied to selected objects, the original objects are not preserved in any way. So, if you're planning to edit the objects later on as actual objects, be sure to make a copy first. If you used Rasterize before making a copy, use the Undo command (CTRL/ COMMAND+Z) to reverse your actions.

After selecting your preferred options for converting objects to bitmaps, click the OK button. Illustrator 7 embeds all bitmaps created with the Rasterize command directly into your drawing.

If converting large sections of your drawing to bitmaps at high resolution using the Rasterize command, export the objects directly to a bitmap format (such as TIFF) using the File\Export command instead. By exporting the objects to a bitmap format and then re-importing it with the Place command, you have the option of creating a link to the external file which reduces the file size of your actual Illustrator 7 drawing. Illustrator 7's Export command also gives you the benefit of file compression to make bitmap files even smaller:

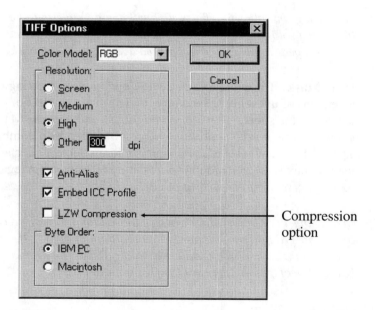

Compression option

Sampling Bitmap Colors

You may obtain a quick color sample of any part of a bitmap image through use of the Eyedropper tool and the Color palette. These two tools work in combination with each other to quickly identify the exact color of any given point of a bitmap image according to the color model the bitmap was prepared in. To identify a bitmap color, follow these steps:

1. With Illustrator 7 running and your drawing file open, locate the bitmap you wish to sample. You need not actually select the bitmap in order to sample its color.

2. Select the Eyedropper tool (press I) from the main Toolbox palette

3. To display the Color Palette (F6), click the Color palette shortcut button near the bottom of the main Toolbox palette or press the comma key.

4. Click the point on the bitmap you wish to sample. The results appear in the Color palette. The exact color and color model type is indicated.

To further clarify the Color palette's action, when you sample your bitmap using the Eyedropper tool, the Color palette automatically measures the sample in the color model inherent in the sampled bitmap. If you wish, you may also get more detailed information about equivalent colors values in other color models. To do this, select a different color model from the flyout menu on the Color palette. The palette immediately displays the current color in whichever color model you select as shown in Figure 14-1. Once another color is sampled, the Color palette returns the display to the bitmap's original color model.

Applying Bitmap Effects

Now that Illustrator 7 ships with a large assortment of Photoshop plug-ins, you can apply a wide array of effects to any bitmap images that exist in your drawing, regardless of their source. Applying a bitmap effect is a relatively basic operation, but the options involved in some filters can be confusing and nonintuitive for new users.

 Certain filter effects in Illustrator 7 can be applied only to vector objects, while others can be applied only to bitmap (raster) objects. Vector filters include Distort (vector), Ink Pen, and Stylize filters; bitmap filters include Artistic, Blur, Brush Stroke, Distort (bitmap), Pixelate, Stylize, Sketch, Texture, and Video filters.

To use any of Illustrator 7's bitmap effects, select the bitmap you wish to apply the effect to and choose a filter style from the Filter menu. Bitmap filters are grouped together below the separator line under the Filter menu. Each filter, and there are

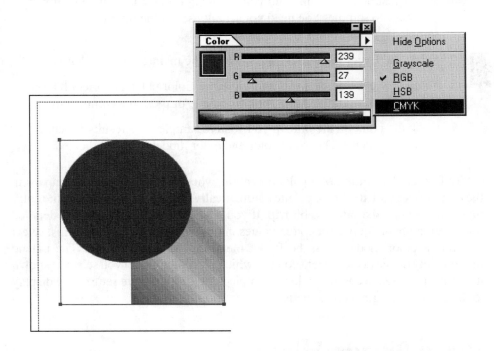

FIGURE 14-1   You may cross-reference colors between color models using the Color palette display

54, has been categorized under Artistic, Blur, Brush Strokes, Distort, Pixelate, Sketch, Stylize, Texture, or Video.

Exploring each of these filters to familiarize yourself with the effects they achieve is time-consuming, to put it mildly. But, thankfully, most of the exploration has been done for you in the section called "Working with Bitmap Filters" in **Chapter 12: Mastering Filter Effects**.

If none of the filters appear available— if they are "grayed out" on the menus—it may indicate that the object you are attempting to apply the effect to is not a bitmap object. If a certain filter effect is not available, it may be because the filter you are attempting to apply works only with certain color models such as RGB or CMYK. For more information about the object you are attempting to apply the effect to, select the object by clicking on it and choose Selection Info from the File menu.

Tracing Bitmap Images

Not so long ago, it was common practice for illustrators to use bits and pieces of traced images when composing hand-drawn diagrams and illustrations. Tracing images meant time saved, and long hours were usually spent using pen, ink, and vellum over something called a light table. These days, this method has gone largely digital through the use of scanned images and drawing programs such as Illustrator 7. But, as you're about to discover, the thrust of the procedure is largely unchanged.

With many illustrators trying to achieve photographic results using vector object tools, the ability to trace over a bitmap image is by far one of the more useful skills to master. Illustrator has long been the drawing tool of choice for tracing images, whether they are pencil traces or photographic images. The beauty of working with vector illustrations over bitmaps is that they can be resized smaller or larger to nearly limitless dimensions without a loss in quality. Plus, when printing vector objects, the detail is set by the quality of the printer being used as opposed to the inherent properties of the object itself. This way, regardless of the size of your vector illustration, the output may be as refined as you wish.

Many illustrators swear by the quality of vector illustration style over that created using strictly bitmap-editing programs such as Adobe Photoshop. If you've ever had to enlarge a bitmap image versus a vector image you might agree that working with strictly bitmaps does have its drawbacks.

When tracing either with the Autotrace tool or manually with the Pen or Pencil tools, it can help a great deal to set the fill of new objects created to None and the Stroke to a color easily seen when placed on top of the bitmap image, such as yellow or red. For example, if when tracing a newly created object your fill is set to a color, as you trace over your bitmap image Illustrator automatically fills the object with the current fill color, obliterating the image beneath it. Setting the fill color to None enables you to see what you are tracing, while setting the stroke to a thin yellow or red color enables you to see the path you are creating.

Bitmaps can be traced manually using the Pen tool or automatically using the Autotrace tool. The manual method may appear laborious, but experts often prefer it. Although the Autotrace tool is fast, it lacks the control required to closely adhere to a bitmap's contours or ignore detail if necessary.

14

*Whether manually or automatically tracing bitmap images in Illustrator 7, you may find it useful to use dimming options in the Layers palette. To dim an image in the Layers palette, press F7 to show the palette and double-click on the name of the layer where the bitmap resides. Then, select the Dim Images option and click OK as shown below. Your images will be dimmed by roughly 50 percent of their original intensity and may be traced in the usual way. For more information on using options in the Layers palette see the "Working in Layers" section in **Chapter 8: Selecting and Arranging Objects**.*

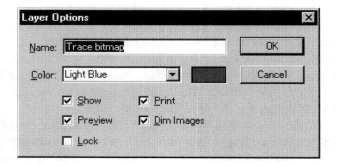

Using the Autotrace Tool

The Autotrace tool is nestled in the main Toolbox palette with the Blend tool, which at first may seem like an unusual spot to find it. But, because the Blend tool is often used for blending colors sampled from bitmaps, and bitmaps are used as sources for tracing, it stands to reason that these tools be near each other.

The Autotrace tool may be used to trace lines or fill areas of a bitmap image. Its purpose is to quickly create open or closed objects of existing areas. To use this tool, simply select it from the main Toolbox palette and click the area of a bitmap image you wish to trace. Current fill and stroke settings are automatically assigned to the newly created object resulting from the trace operation.

Controlling Autotrace Behavior

Illustrators either love or hate the Autotrace feature. For some, it works beautifully, while others claim it creates more work for them than manually tracing images.

Much of the operation of this feature depends on how you set its parameters and the type of images you are tracing. Loving or hating the results also depends on how picky you are about details. Autotrace is controlled by behavioral options set in the Preferences, General dialog box through the Autotrace Gap and Curve Fitting Tolerance settings as shown here. The default Curve Fitting value is 2 pixels.

Autotrace Gap

Bitmaps often contain *gaps*—pixels that contain no apparent assigned color. Under certain conditions, the Autotrace tool may sometimes stop tracing once it detects one of these gaps, which usually defeats the purpose of the tool. The Autotrace Gap setting determines the distance between pixels the Autotrace tool may skip over when performing a trace operation.

For example, setting the gap distance to a value of 2 enables the trace operation to jump two pixels that contain no detectable color when tracing a bitmap. Autotrace Gap may be set to either 0, 1, or 2. Default for the Autotrace Gap setting is 0.

Curve Fitting Tolerance

Although it is mostly used to set behavior of curves created with the Pen and Pencil tools, the Curve Fitting Tolerance setting also determines how closely the Autotrace tool fits the contours of shapes in your bitmap image. Curve tolerance, which is

14

measured in pixels, may be set between 0 and 10. The lower the curve tolerance value, the more closely the curve will match the contours of a shape.

 There are drawbacks to constantly using lower curve tolerance settings when tracing large areas. Lower curve tolerance values often result in longer trace times and highly complex objects, which ultimately require simplification and can complicate the printing of your drawing.

Linking Bitmaps

As mentioned in previous chapters, Illustrator 7 gives you the option to create links to externally stored bitmap images. Linking images enables you to store the majority of data representing the bitmap image separately from your Illustrator drawing file. When Illustrator 7 creates a link between a bitmap and your file, it builds a visual representation of the image into your drawing so that you may position and manipulate it without changing the original bitmap condition.

The link between your bitmap image file and your Illustrator 7 drawing is created during the import function using the Place command. Whenever a bitmap image is imported into Illustrator, options to link the file are always available. The default condition for this linking option is on for every image until deselected, as shown here:

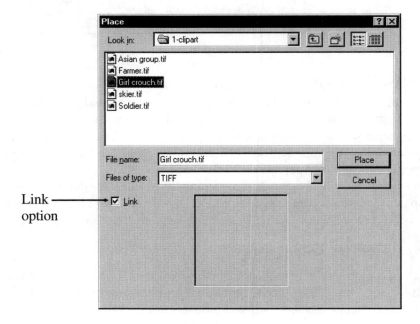

When you deselect the Link option, a copy of the bitmap image you are importing is stored within your drawing file, often adding significant size to the file. The down side to this is that the larger your Illustrator file, the longer file operations such as Saving and Closing take.

To obtain a quick summary of all the files linked to your Illustrator 7 drawing file, deselect all objects in your drawing (CTRL/COMMAND+SHIFT+A), select Document Info from the File menu, and choose Linked Images from the drop-down menu as shown here:

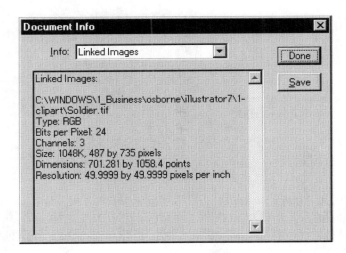

A linked image behaves just as any other imported image, except when transporting your drawing files from one location to another for operations such as film output for offset printing. If you leave your files in the link condition without embedding them into your Illustrator 7 drawing file, you must transport your linked bitmap images along with the drawing file.

Embedding Linked Bitmaps

Embedded files are essentially the opposite of linked files. When a bitmap image is embedded into your drawing, all the data needed to describe and reproduce the image is stored in the Illustrator 7 file. Most embedded images are imported using the Place command with the Link option in the dialog box left unselected. Bitmaps created through the Rasterize command are also automatically embedded in your drawing.

14

While working in your drawing file, it's much more efficient to work with externally linked images. But, at some point you may find it necessary to combine all the files into your Illustrator drawing. The quick method of doing this is with the Save As command (CTRL/COMMAND+SHIFT+S). When you use the Save As command, Illustrator offers you the options of creating a new file with a different name and embedding all linked files as shown here:

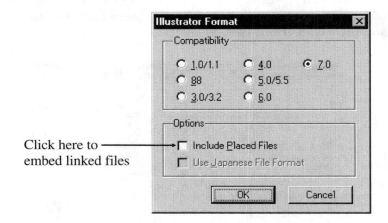

Click here to embed linked files

Tip

To get a quick summary of all the files embedded in your Illustrator 7 drawing file, deselect all objects in your drawing (CTRL/COMMAND+SHIFT+A), select Document Info from the File menu, and choose Embedded Images from the drop-down menu as shown here:

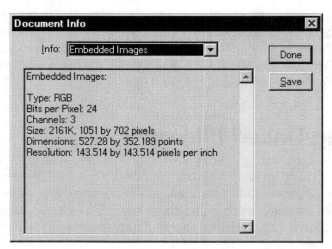

Conclusion

If you're a seasoned digital artist working with digital images, you're probably already aware of the value they can bring to the quality of your drawing and as source references. As with other general function tool types, bitmap tools in Illustrator 7 have been spread throughout the program in various toolboxes, palettes, and dialog boxes. This chapter has summarized many of the issues dealing with working with bitmap images and has identified the location of bitmap-specific tools.

The tools for working with bitmaps in Illustrator 7 have been considerably improved since version 6 on the Macintosh, while the most significant change in this current release of the program is the inclusion of the enormous number of Photoshop plug-ins. If it hasn't been on your reading list yet, make **Chapter 12: Mastering Filter Effects**, your next stop.

Getting the Most Out of Illustrator

15

O nce you've invested time and effort to learn how to do something, it's inevitable that someone will eventually look over your shoulder while you're working and tell you there's a better way to do what you're doing. "Why are you doing it *that* way?" you will hear. "Didn't you know you could do it faster (or easier, cheaper, better) another way?" Don't worry—there is no clear answer to a question like this.

This is the chapter you'll need to read from start to finish to avoid those situations. You'll explore productivity tips, which you would usually discover after months or even years of learning the program on your own. And you'll learn some not-so-obvious troubleshooting tips that have been engineered into Illustrator 7.

Although a few of these performance issues are discussed in other chapters of *Fundamental Illustrator 7*, many are not. This chapter collects all of these issues together in an effort to centralize the information for you, assuming you have thumbed here for information on how to fine-tune your system, your work habits, or both. You could equate learning these tips with the strategies of competitive swimmers, who shave their heads in order to reduce drag and erase a fraction of a second from their race times. In the same vein, these tips could be likened to runners who change their sneaker brands in order to finish a few seconds earlier in a marathon. The only difference is, to gain the advantage of the information provided by this chapter, you don't need to shave your head.

Working Smarter in Illustrator 7

In order to make your drawing experience in Illustrator 7 more productive, you should address three main issues. The first area deals directly with you, the user. You can start by fine-tuning your physical work environment to reduce distractions, improving your posture at the computer, reducing monitor glare, convincing the boss to raise your pay, and so on. However, these are issues that you'll need to deal with on your own terms. And good luck with the boss.

Regarding your own performance, you can also start by adopting a good set of work habits: for example, taking advantage of some of the features in Illustrator 7 most new users ignore. This includes features such as reducing screen draw time, using shortcuts, and a few other things that can help you work smarter rather than harder.

Saving and Making Backups

Topping the list of productivity tips must always be save and backup issues. If you've ever had the misfortune of losing more than a few minutes worth of work on your computer, you'll probably agree that adopting the habit of regularly saving (CTRL/COMMAND+S) and backing up your files is the smartest thing you can do.

Saving Files

Because of their typically memory-intensive sizes, saving your drawing files too often can be an irritation and inconvenience for many users. Some experts claim that files should be saved only as often as the time you are willing to lose by not performing the save. For example, if you can stand to lose ten minutes of drawing work, then back up your file every ten minutes. If your limit is half an hour, then so be it.

Other users save their work whenever it's convenient for them. They make a habit of hitting the Save command whenever they glance away from their screen for more than a minute or so, or when they leave the room for a few moments. Ultimately, saving your files should also be done prior to performing any file imports, exports or other memory intensive functions—even in other programs.

Making Backups

If you've ever had that sinking feeling that results from reaching to turn on your computer and finding that nothing happens, you know that making backups of your files is also one of the keys to becoming a successful computer user. Although some computer applications enable you to make backups of your working files automatically, Illustrator does not. So, in the area of backing up your Illustrator 7 files, you're essentially on your own.

You can back up files any number of ways, depending on the sophistication of your computer setup. If you happen to be connected to a network in a large company with lots of memory space and technical people to maintain it for you, then placing your backup files onto the network is likely the most ideal way of saving them. If you use an external third-party storage medium like magnetic or magneto-optical drives, this is also an excellent way of storing and archiving files. If you happen to have the luxury of owning a CD-ROM disc burner, you may also choose to archive your files using this medium. Finally, there's the disk method, whereby files are placed and stored onto floppy diskettes.

The important thing to note here is that you should never use the background available space on your system's hard drive for storing or archiving your work. Even the best hard drives don't last forever and have been known to fail. Plus, the larger a hard drive and the more data it contains, the slower it performs. Hard drives can become fragmented with overuse and poor system maintenance. This happens when your computer is forced to store a single data file across several tiny available memory blocks and should periodically be defragmented in order to maintain proper performance.

Some experts say that when you are down to using the last ten percent of a hard drive's available space, you're taking an unnecessary risk by entering the "danger" zone. For example, if you had a 1 gigabyte hard drive, the danger zone starts when you begin using the last 100 megabytes of free disk space.

If you have an Internet connection, you have one of the simplest and cheapest ways of backing up your files—at least on a temporary basis. If you're desperate for a place to store your files, try e-mailing them to yourself. When you're ready to collect them, simply log back onto the Internet and receive the files again. This method is generally not recommended unless you are in dire straits.

Previewing Selectively

One of the most counter-productive situations faced by anyone using drawing software is the wait time involved whenever your screen redraws the objects and images you have created. Screen redraw occurs each time you change views, windows, or artwork/preview modes. While many new users simply endure these pauses in productivity, Illustrator 7 does feature some nifty methods of controlling this unfortunate phenomenon.

One of the simplest ways to limit redraw occurrences is to restrict most of your working time to Artwork (toggle on and off with CTRL/COMMAND+Y) view and to use Preview (again, toggle on and off with CTRL/COMMAND+Y) only when necessary. Only in Preview does Illustrator 7 take the extra time to screen-draw EPS, bitmap, uniform and pattern fills, and strokes. However, when working constantly in Artwork view is counter-productive, you can dramatically increase redraw time through use of the Preview Selection (CTRL/COMMAND+SHIFT+Y) command, as shown in Figure 15-1. With this method, you have the luxury of limiting redraw of the elements on your screen only to those you have currently selected.

Plus, in combination with this Preview state, you can further increase redraw time by choosing to Hide Edges (toggle on/off with CTRL/COMMAND+H), which

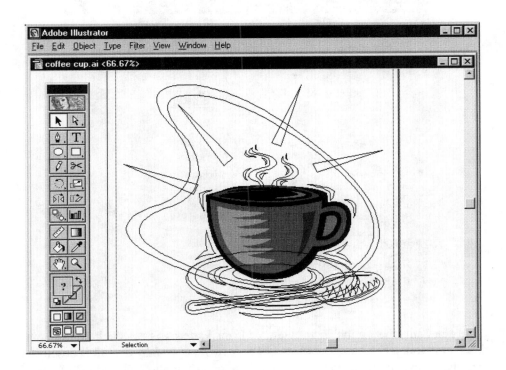

FIGURE 15-1   The coffee cup in this drawing is selected to preview using Preview Selection and Hide Edges commands

essentially limits the view of your object to its current appearance, minus the display of anchor points. Although anchor points help identify the number and location of the points that compose an object, if you're not interested in editing the object's shape you may not need to see them. In order to show anchor points, Illustrator takes just a little longer to draw the object on your screen.

By far, two of the most time-intensive elements to redraw are objects which feature pattern fills and strokes and imported EPS objects.

To reduce the time it takes to redraw these types of objects further, Illustrator 7 enables you to disable previewing of patterns temporarily and control how EPS files are displayed. These two options are document-sensitive and can be found in the Document Setup (CTRL/COMMAND+SHIFT+P) dialog box shown here.

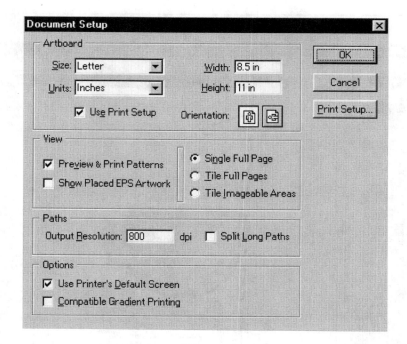

By default, the option to Preview & Print Patterns is selected, so you must deselect it yourself. The Show Placed EPS Artwork option by default is deselected already, so you simply need to confirm this state. When Show Placed EPS Artwork is selected, a 1-bit image of the EPS file is displayed in Artwork view and, when it is deselected, no image is displayed.

 If you choose to disable the preview and printing of patterns, remember to activate it once again when viewing your final drawing and before printing your document to final proof.

Working in Multiple Windows

A feature few people take advantage of in Illustrator 7 is the ability to open more than one window of a given drawing. Opening more than one drawing window of the same document enables you to view, adjust, and compose a drawing in two different windows at the same time—without the need to zoom or change views. Often, new users will find themselves spending extra time navigating through a drawing using Zoom and Hand tools and scroll bars when all they really need to do is open another drawing window.

15

When you open a new window of the same drawing, Illustrator 7 automatically numbers the new window in sequence and places it in the foreground of your program window, making it the current active window. If you prefer, you can leave these windows in this state and switch between them by selecting them to view from the bottom of the Window menu one at a time. If you are using the Windows version of Illustrator 7, another value of this feature comes into play when you choose the Tile command to view both windows at the same time, as shown in Figure 15-2.

Each open window of your drawing is capable of being viewed independently of the others, enabling you to either work simultaneously in Artwork and Preview views, set various magnifications, or a combination of both. Whatever changes are made to one of the views are automatically updated in the other.

For more information on setting views, see the View Commands section in **Chapter 3: Making Illustrator 7 Easy to Use**.

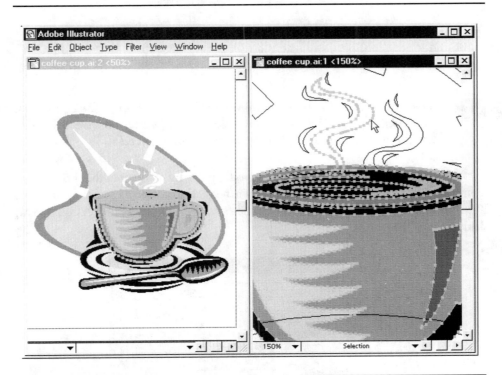

FIGURE 15-2   Use multiple open windows of the same drawing to avoid zooming or changing views

Creating Custom Views

If working in multiple windows doesn't suit the way you work, there's another way to speed viewing your document. Illustrator 7 features the ability to save views of your drawing for quick recall, including location, layers, magnification, and various view features.

The ability to save and recall views enables you to navigate and work on areas of large drawings quickly, without wasting time fiddling with Zoom tools and scroll bars. To save your current view, choose New View from the View menu, identify it by entering a name into the New View as shown next, and click OK to save the view. To recall saved views, choose the name of the view from the bottom of the View menu, or choose the shortcut which Illustrator 7 automatically assigns to that view (CTRL/COMMAND+ALT/OPTION+SHIFT+*the assigned view shortcut number*).

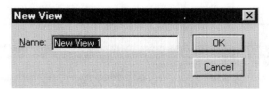

Note   *A new view cannot be saved while you are using the Preview Selection view mode due to the fact that Illustrator 7 cannot save and recall object selections, although specific view settings can be saved.*

You may also rename or delete saved views by choosing the Edit Views command from the View menu, as shown next. For more information on using Illustrator's view feature, see Creating and Saving Views in **Chapter 3: Making Illustrator 7 Easy to Use**.

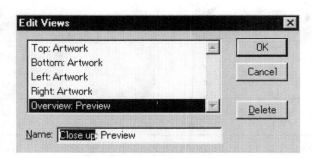

Using Keyboard Shortcuts

Using keyboard shortcuts for commonly used commands enables you to reduce the number of times you reach for your mouse to access menu commands. Each time you use your mouse, it takes an extra few seconds to look for the cursor, reposition it over a menu and point it to the correct menu command. For Mac users and other users accustomed to clicking and holding the mouse button down, the strain on hand and finger muscles can also take its toll. You already have one hand free to access the keyboard—why not use it?

Keyboard shortcuts are often used for accessing program dialog boxes. When it comes to keyboard shortcuts, Illustrator 7 includes those for the most commonly accessed dialog boxes, and they're logically named to make it easier to remember. Getting to know these shortcuts will involve some memory work on your part, but it's ultimately worth the effort.

If you're just beginning to use Illustrator 7, or if you've renewed your acquaintance with it after skipping a program version or changing platforms, one basic strategy is to have the Quick Reference Card close at hand. Although this card may be large and unwieldy to keep open on your desk at all times, you can always make a photocopy and tape the shortcuts you use most often to the side of your monitor or the wall next to you, so long as it's positioned so that you can view the shortcuts while you work.

The Quick Reference Card has been logically organized into these categories: Selecting & Moving, Path Editing, Painting & Transforming, Shapes, Viewing, and Type keyboard shortcuts. The Quick Reference Card also features Toolbox and palette shortcuts.

For a comprehensive list of shortcuts included on the Quick Reference Card—and several that aren't—see **Appendix B: Summary of Keyboard, Toolbox, and Palette Shortcuts**.

Linking Large Images

The larger the file, the longer core file operations such as opening, screen drawing, and saving will take. While large drawing file sizes are usually unavoidable, you can do a few things to minimize their size through linking. There's little you can do if your drawing files become large simply because they contain large numbers of vector objects, but usually the worst-case situations which create the largest file sizes occur when you're working with large bitmap files in your Illustrator 7 drawing.

Whenever you import a bitmap file such as TIFF, BMP, PCX, PICT, JPEG, GIF89A, Kodak PhotoCD, CGM or PNG, the Place dialog box always features a

Link option. Without using the Link option, Illustrator takes full ownership of a bitmap image. In other words, the Illustrator file into which you place the image contains all the data needed to describe and print the file and any other data that may tag along with it. This procedure can grossly swell the size of your Illustrator drawing file and cause grief whenever you need to open, save, or move the file.

Using the Link option, which is selected by default, enables Illustrator 7 to contain representative reference to the original image, as shown below. When you link an image to your Illustrator 7 file, Illustrator remembers the linked file name and its drive and folder location. If your drawing features a number of linked images, you can readily obtain a summary of all link information using the Document Info command, as shown here.

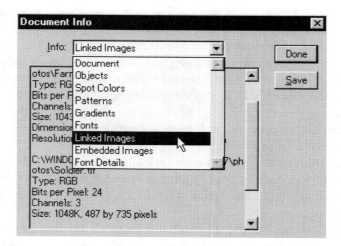

The Document Info command found under the File menu enables Illustrator 7 to summarize many types of document statistical information, such as linked images. By choosing Document Info and selecting Linked Images from the drop-down menu, Illustrator displays linked image information in the following example format:

```
Linked Images:
Drive Letter:\folder\folder\Filename.tif
Type: RGB
Bits per Pixel: 24
Channels: 3
Size: 1043K, 730 by 488 pixels
Dimensions: 1051.2 by 702.721 points
Resolution: 49.9999 by 49.9999 pixels per inch
```

Tip   *When importing images into your drawing file using the Place command, Illustrator 7 features a hidden option to replace current images with newly imported ones. The new image is positioned in the same location as the current one, saving you the extra steps involved with having to position it manually once it is imported. To perform this automatic replacement, select the image you would like to replace and proceed with your Place command to import the new one. On importing the new image, Illustrator 7 displays options to replace the selected image.*

Tip   *When you are using the Link option to place bitmap images into your drawing file, there may come a time when you want to include all the linked images into your file quickly for transport to a service bureau. If so, there's a fast procedure you can follow. Use the Save As command to save the file under a different new name and click the option to Include Placed Files as shown below before clicking OK.*

For more information on linking images and working with bitmap images see Linking Bitmaps in **Chapter 14: Working with Bitmap Tools**.

Using Correct Image Resolution

Long before your bitmap images ever reach your Illustrator document, they need to be prepared in the proper resolution. For example, if you are preparing your drawing to eventually be reproduced on a conventional printing press using offset printing methods, you will need to prepare your bitmap images with a resolution of roughly double that of the line screen resolution (LPI) of your final printed drawing (actually 1.8 times, to be exact).

In other words, if your final printed drawing is to be reproduced at a screen resolution of 150 lines per inch, then your bitmap image will need to be prepared at roughly 300 dots per inch. Excessive inherent resolution of bitmap images is counter-productive. In other words, preparing your bitmap image with *more* than double the resolution of the final printed drawing will ultimately be a waste of creation time, printing time, and all steps in between—including your own time spent opening, editing, and saving the file.

On the other hand, if the drawing you are preparing features a bitmap that is destined for use on the World Wide Web, it need be only high enough in resolution to be reproduced on a computer screen. Computer screens aren't capable of the level of detail associated with offset printing. The standard bitmap resolution for World Wide Web images is only 72 dots per inch. So, preparing and subsequently working with bitmap images with a higher resolution is also a wasted effort.

Deleting Unused Patterns

Because of their memory intensiveness and slow screen draw time, it may be wise to delete some of the more wild patterns you will probably never use from your Swatches palette. Patterns are stored in two places: your Illustrator 7 Startup file, and your drawing file.

Deleting these patterns will speed the time it takes your Swatches palette to redraw—something it does each time the palette is opened, resized, or a program window is changed. Plus, if during the creation of your drawing you happened to create patterns you no longer need, it may be wise to delete them to reduce the size of the native Illustrator 7 drawing file.

To delete any unused pattern files from your Illustrator 7 drawing file, follow these steps:

1. Open the Swatches palette (F5) and select to show the pattern colors by clicking the Show Pattern Swatches icon located at the bottom-center of the palette.

2. Select All Unused from the flyout menu on the right side of the palette, as shown in the illustration below. Illustrator automatically highlights the unused patterns in the Swatches palette.

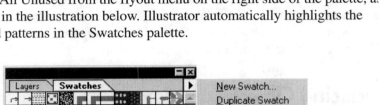

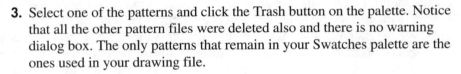

Trash button

3. Select one of the patterns and click the Trash button on the palette. Notice that all the other pattern files were deleted also and there is no warning dialog box. The only patterns that remain in your Swatches palette are the ones used in your drawing file.

4. Save (CTRL/COMMAND+S) and close (CTRL/COMMAND+W) your drawing file.

If you mistakenly delete a pattern file, you can reverse the action through the Undo command (CTRL/COMMAND+Z).

Before deleting any unused patterns in your file, be sure that you have finished your drawing and will never need the deleted patterns again. Otherwise, you may find yourself wasting time reimporting pattern files into your drawing from other files.

Deleting patterns from your Startup file is a tricky exercise, and you'll need to take a few precautions before going too far. For more information on deleting patterns from your Illustrator 7 Startup file, skip ahead to the section called "Customizing Your Startup File" later in this chapter.

Reducing Object Complexity

One of the most effective ways to speed your system's performance and avoid crippling problems when it comes time to print your drawing is to simplify paths. Paths are the series of joined anchor points which make up the contours of each object. When paths contain excessive numbers of points, the single collection of data needed to completely describe them can often become too large for your system to interpret quickly and much too large to print. Other factors contributing to this phenomenon involve strokes applied to complex objects, such as large amounts of text.

Complex paths are usually associated with extremely large and detailed drawings such as cartographic maps, engineering-type drawings, traced bitmap images, and some types of converted clip art. A good indication of complex paths is often demonstrated by long file open or save times or very long screen redraw times. When printing, a sure sign of complex paths comes if you receive PostScript *limitcheck* errors from your printer in the form of "lineto" or "curveto" errors. These types of errors are a dead giveaway that one or more of the paths in your drawing are choking the life out of your printer's memory.

For more information on printing and some troubleshooting strategies, see Troubleshooting Printing covered in **Chapter 17: Printing from Illustrator 7**.

Having identified instances where complex paths occur, Illustrator 7 features a relatively straightforward solution. In the Document Setup (CTRL/ COMMAND+ SHIFT+P) dialog box, the option split long paths may be selected, as shown below, before you save your final drawing or prior to printing it. The Split Long Paths option enables Illustrator 7 to detect complex paths that may have trouble printing and, literally, divides them up into smaller, easily readable objects. Objects that have been split appear the same when previewed or printed, but the evidence can be seen using Artwork view (CTRL/COMMAND+Y). These smaller pieces can then be easily digested by both your system or your printer.

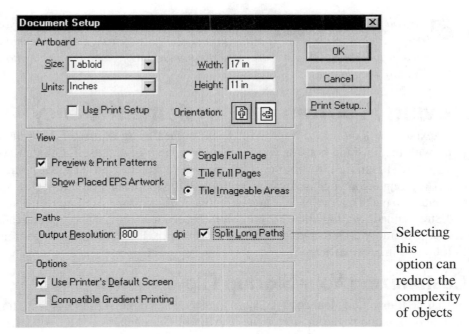

Selecting this option can reduce the complexity of objects

It's not all good news, though—there is a price to pay for using the Split Long Paths command. Because Illustrator literally—and physically—splits large paths into smaller ones, it changes the construction of your objects, often irreparably. For this reason, the Adobe engineers have implemented a dialog box to warn you of the impending changes to your objects and give you a chance to cancel the command and back out, as shown in the illustration below. So, before you choose this option it's wise to make a second backup copy for insurance.

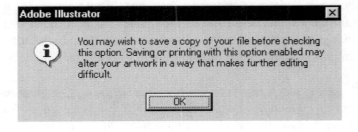

If you inadvertently used the Split Long Paths command on a file that you neglected to make a backup of, you may be able to reverse the command using the Undo (CTRL/COMMAND+Z) command. Or, close the file without saving the changes.

Improving Program and System Efficiency

The next area to look into to improve efficiency when using Illustrator 7 has more to do with the nuts and bolts of your system than the program itself. Granted, we don't all own lightning-fast Pentium 1000s, nor are you likely to have several pounds of RAM mounted on your system's motherboard. But there are a few strategies you can follow to make operation of your computer and Illustrator 7 itself more efficient and streamlined. Startup file customization, program Scratch Disk options, and available memory all affect your drawing performance. Here are some suggestions to follow to improve efficiency.

Customizing Your Startup File

Each time Illustrator is launched it takes a long look at a number of things including fonts and something called a Startup file. The Startup file contains all kinds of default information Illustrator needs to remember, based on the options set when you last used the program.

The Startup file also contains a selection of default patterns created when you first installed Illustrator 7. Patterns can be memory-intensive depending on their complexity. And, if you find that you never use some of these patterns and Illustrator 7 is dragging them along as excess baggage each time it loads, you can eliminate them as you see fit.

On the other hand, you may also have created some nifty patterns which you find you use every day and which often need to be loaded from other existing files to make them available in your current drawing. Custom patterns may be created using the Define Pattern command located under the Edit menu or by dragging directly from your drawing into the Swatches palette (F5). Each time you create a new pattern, it is stored with the drawing file itself rather than in the Startup file.

 To import patterns you created in other drawing files or from any of the pattern collections on the Illustrator 7 program disc, choose Swatch Libraries from the Window menu, select Other Libraries, and locate the Illustrator file or pattern file containing the pattern. The patterns are then loaded into the Swatches palette associated with the drawing file you currently have open.

Constantly loading pattern files from other documents may become tedious and repetitive and ultimately wastes time. By loading patterns into your Startup file, you can make them available in the Swatches palette each time you open a new drawing file. To add or delete patterns from your Startup file, follow these steps:

1. First, locate the Startup file in the Plug-ins folder in the main Adobe Illustrator folder (Macintosh) or the Adobe/Illustrator 7.0/Plug-ins folder (Windows).

2. Back up this file by making a copy and saving it using the same name but in a different location.

3. Then, open your existing Startup file and use it as a template on which to build a new Startup file, as shown in Figure 15-3.

4. With the Startup file as the active document, choose the Swatches palette to display (F5). To delete any unused patterns, locate them in the Swatches palette and drag them to the trash button located at the bottom of the palette. Then, locate the objects on the Artboard of your Startup file which feature the corresponding patterns and delete them also.

5. To add new patterns to your Startup file, click Window|Swatch Library|Other Library and locate one of the files that contains your new patterns, as shown below.

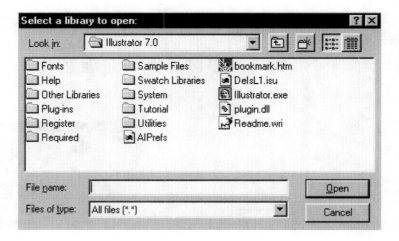

6. While there, you may also select the options you want as default settings whenever a new file is opened, by opening the Page Setup, Document Setup (CTRL/COMMAND+SHIFT+P) dialog boxes and setting your desired options.

7. Once you have completed saving your Startup File preferences and new patterns, click Save (CTRL/COMMAND+S) and close (CTRL/COMMAND+W).

Streamlining Your Font Use

A second strategy for speeding the launch of Illustrator 7 involves uninstalling unused fonts on your system. Having excessive numbers of fonts loaded on your system can drain valuable resources which theoretically should be made available to applications. To uninstall fonts from your system, follow the procedures appropriate to your system.

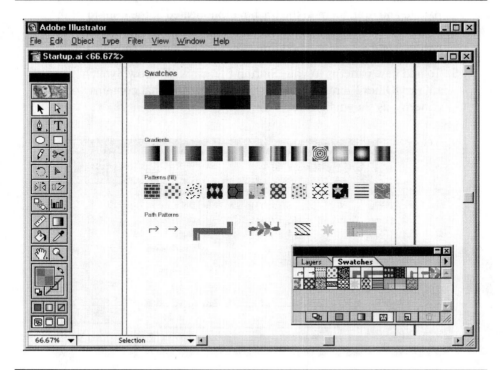

FIGURE 15-3   The Startup file contains all default settings, including pattern files

Uninstalling fonts which may be needed for certain files to open can be a hazardous task for other applications on your system. Some applications give no warning about missing fonts when they are opening files, and so undesirable font substitutions can often occur. Fortunately, Illustrator 7 warns you when it is opening files which feature fonts not currently installed on your system, offering you the opportunity of backing out and reinstalling the fonts or choosing an appropriate replacement.

Using a minimum font collection to work with can greatly streamline your system resources, but of course you'll need to carefully choose the fonts you wish to uninstall.

Setting Scratch Disk Options

A *scratch disk* is a temporary hard drive location to which Illustrator 7 can write temporary information while you are working on your drawing.

Ideally, your Scratch Disk should be located on your fastest drive —usually a local root drive of your computer where your system and program software are stored. Scratch disks options in Illustrator 7 enable you to set both a primary and secondary location for your Scratch Disk temporary information. If your primary drive is constantly running out of space or another drive—such as a network drive— is available, you may also set it as your secondary drive.

Scratch disk location options are set by selecting Preferences from the File menu (CTRL/COMMAND+K) and choosing Plug-ins & Scratch Disk from the pull-down menu in the Preferences dialog box that appears, as shown here.

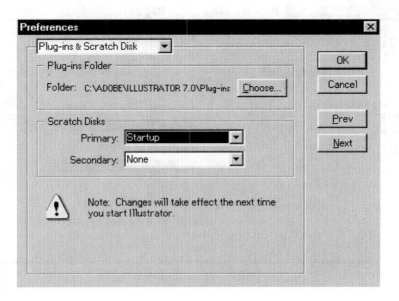

Note   *If you make changes to your Scratch Disk location options, you must restart Illustrator 7 in order for the changes to take effect.*

Increasing Memory Application Size (Mac Only)

When working in Illustrator 7 on the Macintosh or Power Macintosh platforms, you can greatly improve Illustrator's performance by increasing the application memory size allotted to it. On the Macintosh platform, the system and each open program are allotted a maximum amount of RAM (Random Access Memory). In Illustrator 7 (and in previous versions), if this memory limit is reached, Illustrator begins using the Scratch Disk locations to write temporary files, which can slow performance as the program accesses and writes to the specified drive.

To increase Illustrator's share of RAM, you'll need to do a bit of research. With Illustrator running (and any other programs you usually have constantly open while you're working), check out how much memory is currently available. Do this by going to the Finder and choosing About This Macintosh from the Apple menu, as shown below. Note the value beside the words "Largest Unused Block:". Notice that this value is measured in thousands of bytes (K). Make a note of this value.

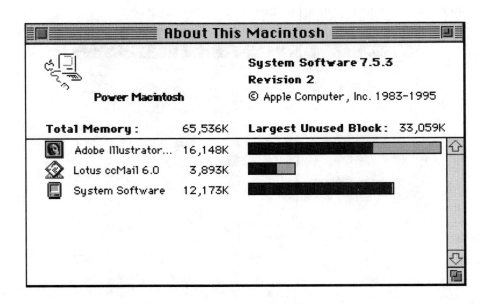

15

Quit Illustrator (COMMAND+Q) and locate the original program icon in the Adobe Illustrator 7 folder (do not choose the program's shortcut icon on the desktop) and click on it to highlight it. Choose Get Info (COMMAND+I) from the File menu. You'll see an Information dialog box, which provides various information about the program, its size, date of creation, and so on, as shown here.

Adobe Illustrator® 7.0 Info

Adobe Illustrator® 7.0

Kind: application program
Size: 7.7 MB on disk (8,116,480 bytes used)
Where: Macintosh HD: Adobe Illustrator® 7.0:

Created: Wed, May 7, 1997, 4:58 AM
Modified: Thu, Aug 28, 1997, 4:42 PM
Version: 7.0, © 1987-1997 Adobe Systems Incorporated.
Comments:

Memory Requirements
Suggested size: 16120 K
Minimum size: 12120 K
☐ **Locked** Preferred size: 16120 K

Note: Memory requirements will decrease by 4,120K if virtual memory is turned on in the Memory control panel.

Enter a value equal to roughly 90 percent of the Largest Unused Block value. For example, if the Largest Unused Block you made a note of was 10 megabytes, set the Preferred Size option to 9 megabytes. The next time you launch the program, this value will take effect.

 To improve memory performance on Macintosh and Power Macintosh platforms, turn off the Use Virtual Memory option in the Memory section of the Control Panel.

Conclusion

Straight out of the box, you'll probably agree that Illustrator 7's performance has been engineered with user productivity in mind. But, if you've read this chapter through from start to finish, you now have some opportunities to improve it even further. This chapter has given you some insight into productivity and performance issues when using Illustrator 7. If you're an expert user, some of these issues may

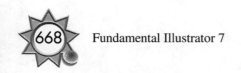

not come as too much of a surprise to you, but most new users to Illustrator 7 wait months or years to discover these things on their own.

This chapter also concludes **Part III: Beyond Basic Tools**. For information on developing your Illustrator 7 drawings past your screen and into the real world, continue on to **Part IV: Creating Print, Web, and File Images** in the next section.

PART
IV

Creating Print, Web,
and File Images

Importing and
Exporting from
Illustrator 7

16

Τhe ability to import and export files through Illustrator 7 opens a whole world of file sharing and transferring opportunities for digital artists working with multiple programs. In the background of Illustrator 7's technical workings, import and export functions are handled by specialized "I/O" (import/export) filters, some of which are created by Adobe and others of which are industry standard filters. These I/O filters work as a type of "revolving door" whereby various file types can be traded or exchanged between applications as a way of sharing information.

For many artists, exchanging files between programs is a common practice. Even though Illustrator is capable of a wide array of tasks, other programs with more specialized purposes are often required (including some of Adobe's own applications). For example, although Illustrator features tools for creating pages containing text, it is not a page layout program, and while Illustrator is capable of handling many bitmap-specific file operations, it is not specifically a bitmap editing program. For these types of tasks, other more specialized programs, such as PageMaker, PageMill, SiteMill, or Photoshop, far exceed the capabilities of Illustrator 7. Using the correct software tool for the matching task is key to producing published documents in all the various mediums of today's diverse communications industry.

As with other operations in Illustrator 7, the tools you'll be using are found in a variety of places. This chapter shows where the commands can be found and covers the ins and outs of using Illustrator 7's import/export filters in an effort to provide you with an understanding of their inherent capabilities—in other words, what they can and can't do. You'll also learn how to accomplish the same task a number of different ways and discover a few not-so-obvious shortcuts for using these tools.

A Primer on Importing and Exporting

For many of its applications, Adobe has adopted the term *Place* as an alternative to using the term import, although that's exactly what occurs when you choose to

"Place" a file into your Illustrator 7 drawing. When you import a specific file type into Illustrator 7, an import filter interprets and deciphers the information in the file, putting it in a format readable by Illustrator 7. For the purposes of clarity in this chapter and other related chapters of *Fundamental Adobe Illustrator 7*, placing files also will be referred to as *importing*.

Exporting is common practice when preparing drawing files for use in other programs. Illustrator 7 features a standard Export command for accomplishing this, but it also includes features in the Save As (CTRL/COMMAND+SHIFT+S) and Save a Copy As (CTRL/COMMAND+ALT/OPTION+S) commands for exporting to EPS or Adobe's portable document format (PDF).

In keeping with the overall high quality and efficiency of Illustrator 7, import and export filters are extremely accurate and up-to-date and capable of interpreting or writing to the most current file formats for various programs. But it's also important to keep in mind that in a few cases some of the inherent properties of objects in the file Illustrator is interpreting or preparing may not exactly match what the filter is capable of reading or producing. So, whereas you may have assumed that certain object colors, sizes, fonts, and so on of your imported or exported file would appear, this may not always be the case.

Having presented that little disclaimer, Illustrator 7 *is* capable of effectively importing and exporting many different file types from and to other programs including Adobe's own native program files and various text, bitmap, vector, and competing graphic file formats such as CorelDRAW. Depending on the type of file, Illustrator may offer options for creating external links to imported files or specific options when preparing other file formats.

Importing with the Place Command

You'll most likely import files into your Illustrator 7 drawing with the File|Place command. The Place command is compatible with 24 file formats described in detail later in this chapter. When using this command, you may choose a specific filter type from the drop-down menu or choose to view All Formats as shown here:

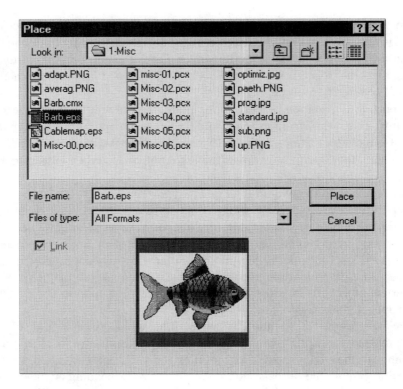

To import a file using the Place command, follow these steps:

1. With your Illustrator 7 drawing file open, choose File|Place. The Place dialog box opens.

2. Choose All Formats from the Files of Type drop-down menu or select the filter that matches the file format you wish to place from the drop-down menu.

3. Locate the file you wish to import, click it in the file window, and click OK. The file is imported. If the file is a bitmap format, you have the option to maintain a link to the file by clicking the Link option. And, if the file features a preview header readable by Illustrator 7's filter (i.e., for Illustrator or EPS files), a brief thumbnail image will appear in the preview window near the center of the Place dialog box.

Unlike other applications, which often display every file contained in the current folder when the All Formats option is chosen, Illustrator 7 shows you only those files that it is capable of placing. Choosing All Formats enables Illustrator 7 to assign a filter specific to the format of the selected file, once it is recognized. Selecting an individual import filter is optional and essentially enables you to narrow your search when placing files in folders that contain many files and/or types of file formats.

 When files are imported into Illustrator 7, they are automatically placed onto the active Layer selected at the time of import with the Place command.

 Although Illustrator 7's EPS file filter is not listed in the Files of Type drop-down menu, you can still import these files with the Place command by choosing the All Formats selection.

Depending on which file format you choose to place, Illustrator 7's filter may present you with an additional dialog box enabling you to make further choices or decisions about how you would like to import the file. Most file formats import through Adobe Illustrator's filters directly though, without additional options.

 When importing files on the Windows platform of Illustrator 7, the three-letter extension applied to the name of the file lets Illustrator know which import filter to use. Incorrect extensions may result in Illustrator 7 using the wrong filter or importing files incorrectly.

If you wish to create a link between imported bitmap files and your Illustrator 7 drawing file, the Place command dialog box features a Link option that, by default, creates a link automatically. Linked files contain merely image preview information and refer to the externally stored original only when more detailed information is required (such as when printing). Disabling the Link option during the import operation "embeds" the image into your drawing file. You may also embed the image using the Save As command.

For more information on using the Save As command, see "Closing and Saving Files" in **Chapter 2: Managing Illustrator 7 Files**.

Exporting Files

Getting drawings from Illustrator 7 into various other file formats presents a slightly different and marginally more complex scenario. The File|Export command handles

all non-Adobe file formats, while Save As (CTRL/COMMAND+SHIFT+S) and Save a Copy As (CTRL/COMMAND+ALT/OPTION+S) commands handle Adobe Illustrator, Adobe EPS, and Adobe PDF file formats.

To Export a file from Illustrator 7, choose the File|Export command as shown here:

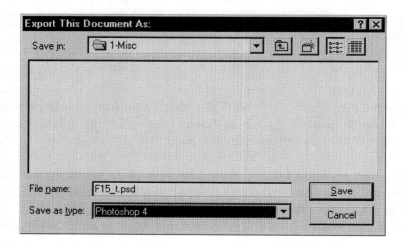

Nearly all types of export filter formats offer additional options and choices when preparing files. Bitmap filters often feature size, color model, and resolution choices, while other file types mostly ask for specific version numbers of the format to which you're exporting.

To export a file using Illustrator 7's Export command, follow these steps:

1. With your Illustrator 7 drawing file open, choose File|Export. The Export dialog box opens.

2. Choose a file type in which to prepare your artwork by choosing it from the drop-down menu. By default, the name of your original file is used. Windows users will see that the file extension is added automatically.

3. Locate the folder you wish to export your file into. By default, Illustrator 7 exports your new file to the same folder in which the original is stored.

4. Click Save to create the export file. Depending on which file format you selected to export to, the filter you chose may present additional options. Choose any additional export options and click OK to continue exporting the file.

16

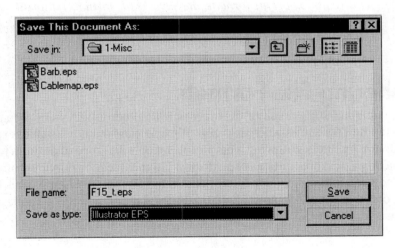

When exporting drawings from Illustrator 7, the entire drawing is exported; you cannot export selected portions of your drawing.

The rest of your task is considered more of a native file creation–type of process than anything else. Under the Save As or Save a Copy As file commands, you have the option of saving to Adobe EPS or Adobe PDF. To save your file in either of these formats, follow these steps:

1. With your Illustrator 7 drawing file open, choose File|Save As(CTRL/COMMAND+SHIFT+S) or File|Save a Copy As (CTRL/COMMAND+ALT/OPTION+S). The Save As or Save a Copy As dialog box opens as shown here:.

2. Choose either EPS or PDF from the drop-down menu.

3. Locate the folder you wish to save the file to and click OK. The file is saved. If you choose EPS as a file format, you will be presented with further options in the EPS Format dialog box as shown here:

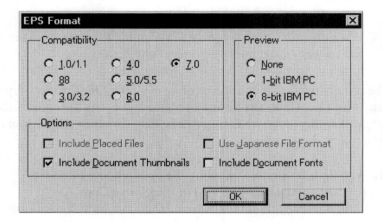

 Unlike the export file formats, the Save As file formats retain all information in an Illustrator file including layers, groups, and text flow. Exporting operations wipe out this information.

Deciphering File Formats

When approaching the use of digital files from other programs or preparing your drawing files for use in other programs, it's important to know what to expect from Illustrator 7's filters. Knowing what you'll end up with is one of the keys to working efficiently across applications or platforms. This next section provides some insights into how Illustrator's various filters behave and prepares you for what is to come.

For reference, the complete list of import and export filters is comprised of these formats, defined as follows:

Adobe Native Formats

Because they all come from the same software family and are geared toward working together efficiently and flawlessly, Adobe's own formats are included as part of the filter arsenal and provide a solid foundation for transferring and exchanging data between Adobe programs. These formats include native Illustrator files, as well as EPS, PDF, Photoshop (PSD), filmstrip files and, for certain uses, print (PRN) files.

Adobe Illustrator

This filter both reads and writes Illustrator native formats. It's compatible with Macintosh, Windows 95, and Windows NT platform versions as well as all previous versions of the program including the original Illustrator 88 version, as well as 1.0 to 6.0 and all versions in between. Adobe has also gone to great lengths to ensure these formats are capable of "porting" beween platforms. In other words, you are able to open any of these formats in any platform version of Adobe's programs. Nearly all features inherent in these file formats are supported by Illustrator.

Note   *Although Illustrator documents may be opened into Illustrator 7 using the File\Open command (CTRL/COMMAND+O), they cannot be directly imported using the File\Place command. Instead, part or all of an Illustrator drawing may be imported using drag-and-drop operations or Clipboard functionality through Copy (CTRL/COMMAND+C) and Paste (CTRL/COMMAND+V) commands.*

For more information on saving files to Illustrator native file formats, see "Closing and Saving Files" in **Chapter 2: Managing Illustrator 7 Files**.

Adobe Illustrator EPS

The EPS file format isn't *really* a native format, although it was originally developed (and continues to be) by Adobe. But over the years, encapsulated PostScript (EPS) has become an industry standard when importing or exporting files. This format is commonly used whenever images are eventually going to be reproduced on PostScript-compatible printers. Adobe Illustrator has its own brand of EPS file, however; although their names and file properties are similar, standard EPS file formats differ from Illustrator EPS file formats.

The distinction often comes as a surprise when importing files into competing programs such as Freehand or CorelDRAW. Where standard EPS import filters may not be capable of distinguishing between the two formats, a specifically prepared Illustrator EPS filter often can.

Encapsulated PostScript files are based on page description language that supports both vector and bitmap file formats. An EPS file can be an individual graphic object or a complete printed page. Printed pages are produced in PostScript format when creating print (PRN) files through use of the Print to File option in Illustrator 7's main Print dialog box (CTRL/COMMAND+P). For more information on creating print files, see the section called "Preparing a Print File" in **Chapter 17: Printing from Illustrator 7**.

Importing an EPS file into your Illustrator 7 drawing occurs directly through the Place command, with no further options offered specifically by the filter. And, when exported, an EPS file may be prepared to feature certain properties such as version, linked files, fonts, and preview headers, which are used to view a representative image of the file when incorporating the file into Illustrator 7 drawings or other programs as shown here. The EPS format is created directly from your Illustrator 7 drawing file through use of the Save As command (CTRL/COMMAND+SHIFT+S).

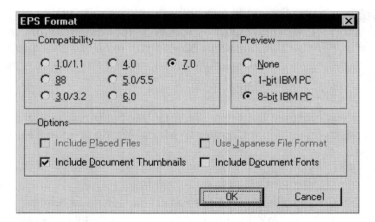

EPS files may be saved to specific version compatibility including all previous versions of Illustrator. You may also set preview header options to either None, 1-bit (monochrome), or 8-bit color. Previews are useful when positioning your EPS image onto a host document page. If you choose to, you may also embed any linked images and/or fonts into your file. Embedding linked files and fonts can help avoid the confusion associated with managing this extra data when exchanging your EPS files between Illustrator drawings or other programs. The Include Document Thumbnails option creates a preview of the file for visual reference in the preview window when placing or opening the EPS file.

Adobe Filmstrip (FLM)

A filmstrip file is a specific type of file created from the digital video editing program named Adobe Premiere. Filmstrip files are files containing single or sequence digital video images produced as hybrid file types from Premiere. Filmstrip files are commonly used for editing individual frames of digital movies. Adobe Photoshop is also capable of opening and editing filmstrip files. Filmstrip files can only be imported into Illustrator 7 and cannot be exported in any way.

When Illustrator 7's filmstrip filter imports a filmstrip file, no import options are offered and the entire "strip" is brought in as a single bitmap image. It retains all of its properties and displays including the time stamps on each of the digital movie sequences. Although this import format may be attractive for incorporating single captured digital movie frames as bitmap images into your Illustrator 7 drawing, the import function lacks options and may be more trouble than it's worth.

Photoshop 4 and Earlier (PSD)

Illustrator 7 is capable of both reading and writing Adobe Photoshop files version 4.0 and earlier from any platform. The Photoshop format imports through the Place command seamlessly and retains all of the properties inherent in the original file, without any secondary dialog box options.

When exporting to the Photoshop native format though, Illustrator 7's PSD export filter offers color model and resolution options standard to bitmap exporting but also includes an extended option to apply an anti-aliasing effect as shown here:

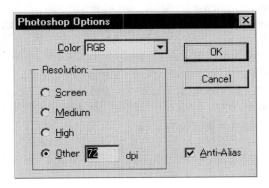

For exported Photoshop formats, the bitmap export dialog offers RGB, CMYK, or Grayscale color model choices, and preset resolution options of Screen (72 DPI), Medium (150 DPI), High (300 DPI), or Other, capable of setting resolution within a range between 72 and 2,400 DPI.

Bitmap Filters

Illustrator 7's filters include all the standard bitmap formats used in most other applications. By far, the most commonly used export format for your Illustrator 7 drawing images will be one of several bitmap file formats available in Illustrator 7. With only a few exceptions—such as Adobe portable document format (PDF), Kodak PhotoCD (PCD), JPEG, and GIF—bitmap formats each follow standard export options comprised of color model and resolution options described next. Illustrator 7 is capable of both reading and writing most bitmap formats.

Adobe Portable Document Format (PDF)

As mentioned earlier, even though you won't find Adobe's portable document format (PDF) in the export Files of Type drop-down menu, it is nevertheless a format to which Illustrator is capable of both reading and writing. Creating a PDF is done via the Save As (CTRL/COMMAND+SHIFT+S) or Save a Copy As (CTRL/COMMAND+ALT/OPTION+S) commands. And, to a limited extent, you may also open PDF files in Illustrator 7 through the File|Open (CTRL/COMMAND+O) command.

The PDF format has become widely used as an efficient way of creating and distributing digital documents from certain applications such as PageMaker. PDF documents have unique abilities to feature hyperlink text whereby large text and image-based documents may be navigated. Many World Wide Web sites offer page display with the PDF browser plug-in, making this format popular on the Internet.

Adobe Reader, the software used for viewing PDF files, is distributed free of charge in virtually all Adobe applications and through the corporate Web site. However, the "Distiller" software used for creating these full-featured portable documents is purchased separately.

*For more information on working with PDF, see the "Using PDF Formats" section in **Chapter 18: Illustrator 7 and the Web**.*

Amiga IFF

The Amiga interchange file format (IFF) is commonly used when working with the Commodore Amiga system, which enjoys most of its popularity in parts of Europe (but is also used in segments of the video and graphics industry in North America).

It is widely supported on many different image-editing applications such as Electronic Arts' DeluxePaint. Illustrator 7 is capable of both reading and writing IFF, which uses standard bitmap export options for resolution as shown here:

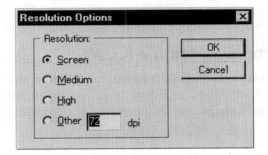

Windows Bitmap (BMP)

This readable and writable bitmap image format is one of the original and more common bitmap formats used on both Macintosh and Windows (but mostly Windows) platforms. When exporting to BMP format, Illustrator 7's filter offers standard resolution options followed by further options to set either Windows or OS/2 formats, as well as options for 1-bit, 4-bit, 8-bit, and 24-bit color depth as shown here. When using either the 4-bit or 8-bit options you may also elect to use run-length encoding compression, which enables you to reduce the file size of the resulting BMP file.

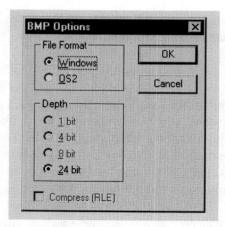

Computer Graphics Metafile (CGM)

Computer graphics metafile (CGM) is another of the older formats widely used on Windows platforms that Illustrator 7 supports in both import and export operations. Both functions operate seamlessly, in that no further options exist when performing either task.

JPEG

This is a bitmap format developed by the Joint Photographers' Expert Group (JPEG) that Illustrator 7 is capable of both importing and exporting. Because of its lossy image compression properties, the JPEG format has been widely adopted for use in the World Wide Web as a means of storing and quickly displaying Web page images. When importing using the JPEG filter, Illustrator 7's filter simply imports the image file directly. When exporting to JPEG format, the filter offers several options through a secondary dialog box as shown here:

16

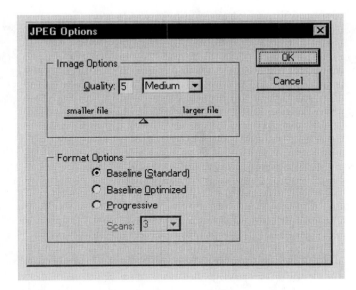

Note   *For more information on using the JPEG file format with the World Wide Web, see "Using JPEG Formats" in **Chapter 18: Illustrator 7 and the Web**.*

GIF89A

The graphical interchange file format (GIF) is used widely on the World Wide Web as a means of storing and displaying image formats. Two main formats have existed up to now: GIF87A and GIF89A, the latter of which is more recent and includes more features. This format supports a number of different options on exporting, including palette type, halftone dithering, color depth, interlace display, and image map options as shown here:

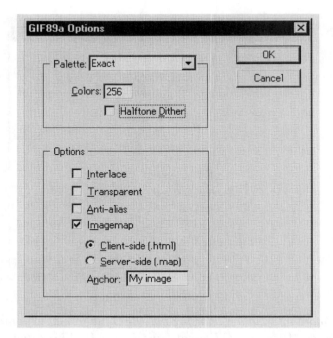

 *For more information on using the GIF89A file format with the World Wide Web, see "Using GIF Formats" in **Chapter 18: Illustrator 7 and the Web.***

Kodak PhotoCD

The Kodak PhotoCD file format is available only when importing images into your Illustrator 7 drawing. This is a proprietary data and image format originally developed and owned by Kodak for viewing images stored on specialized discs. The format was adopted by the digital industry as a high-quality method of scanning, storing, and distributing high-resolution images. Import filters have been adopted for use by most image and graphic software applications.

 Using Kodak PhotoCD is a one-way street; you can import from but not export to PhotoCD using Illustrator 7. In fact, only Kodak's own proprietary scanning software is capable of creating images in the PhotoCD format and only Kodak scanners are capable of writing to PhotoCD discs.

Kodak PhotoCD images are imported into Illustrator 7 through use of the Place command. Illustrator 7's Kodak PhotoCD filter is quite a bit more advanced than when it was originally released by Kodak. PhotoCD gives you these options to choose from, including five image proportions measured in pixels and comprised of (from smallest to largest) 128 x 192, 256 x 384, 512 x 768, 1024 x 1536, and 2048 x 3072:

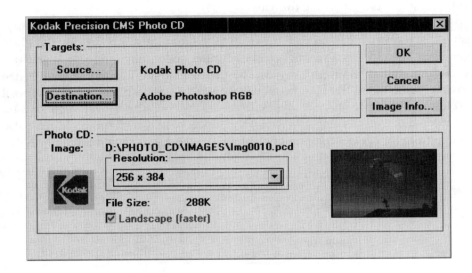

The filter also enables you to obtain information about the source of the image and its eventual destination. Destination options are comprised of Photoshop RGB and Photoshop CIELAB color models. You may also obtain information on the original image format.

Note *When Illustrator 7's PhotoCD filter imports, it enables you to maintain a link to the original image. If your image is small, you may want to embed it by deselecting the Link option. Otherwise, when it's time to print, you may be prompted to supply the disc containing the image, causing more work than it's really worth. For larger images though, it's wise to maintain a link to the original PhotoCD disc. Large images can occupy dozens of megabytes of disc space, making removable media storage an advantage worth using.*

Macintosh PICT (PICT)

Macintosh PICT format originated on the Macintosh platform but has also been adopted for use on Windows platforms. PICT format is prized for its compression capabilities with file formats that incorporate large areas of flat color. Besides encapsulated PostScript, it's one of the few formats that is capable of supporting both vector and bitmap image formats.

Illustrator 7 is capable of importing and exporting (Macintosh platform only) using this format. When a PICT file is imported into Illustrator 7 using the Place command, the process is seamless and no further options are offered. Images may be saved in RGB, CMYK, or Grayscale when using the PICT format options. When exporting with the RGB color model you may choose either a 16-bit or 32-bit pixel resolution. Grayscale image formats enable you to choose from 2-bit, 4-bit, or 8-bit color depth. If you're using a Macintosh equipped with QuickTime, you may also choose from four JPEG compression options for the file as shown here:

```
┌─────────────────────────────────────────────────────────┐
│         ▭ Macintosh HD ▾            ▭ Macintosh HD        │
│  ┌──────────────────────────────┐  ┌──────────────────┐  │
│  │ 📁 Adobe Type Utilities    ⬆ │  │      Eject        │  │
│  │ 📄 AGT Output                │  ├──────────────────┤  │
│  │ 📁 America Online v3.0       │  │     Desktop       │  │
│  │ 📁 Apple Extras              │  ├──────────────────┤  │
│  │ 📁 Apple LaserWriter Software⬇│  │     New 📁        │  │
│  └──────────────────────────────┘  └──────────────────┘  │
│  Save this document as:             ┌──────────────────┐  │
│  ┌──────────────────────────────┐   │     Cancel        │  │
│  │ Picture 1.PCT                │   ├──────────────────┤  │
│  └──────────────────────────────┘   │      Save         │  │
│  Format: [ PICT File        ▾ ]     └──────────────────┘  │
│  ☒ Append File Extension                                  │
└─────────────────────────────────────────────────────────┘

┌─────────────────────────────────────────────────────────┐
│                                                            │
│  Image Quality:  Fair      Good  Excellent   ┌─────────┐  │
│                  ├─┬─┬─┬─△─┬─┬─┬─┬─┤          │  Save   │  │
│  Compression: Excellent  Good      Fair      ├─────────┤  │
│                                              │ Cancel  │  │
│                                              └─────────┘  │
└─────────────────────────────────────────────────────────┘
```

MacPaint

The MacPaint file format is commonly used and one of the most basic bitmap formats native to the Macintosh platform. In fact, MacPaint was one of the first paint programs released by Apple for the Macintosh platform. Although Illustrator 7 is capable of importing MacPaint files from within any version, the export function is available only on Macintosh versions. Even then, the plug-in filter that enables this operation is optional and must be manually installed into the Adobe Illustrator 7 plug-ins folder.

PC PaintBrush (PCX)

The PC PaintBrush (PCX) file format is the equivalent of MacPaint on the Macintosh platform in that it is one of the most basic bitmap formats in use. Illustrator 7 is capable of both reading and writing to PCX format. On placing a file, the operation is seamless. And on exporting to the PCX format, nothing further than standard bitmap resolutions are offered.

Pixar (PXR)

Pixar is a format used specifically by PIXAR computer workstations, which are computers designed specifically for high-end graphics applications and digital animation production. Illustrator 7 is capable of both reading and writing Pixar format files. Importing through the Place command is seamless, and exporting involves only standard bitmap resolution options.

PixelPaint

Another format used solely by Macintosh-based programs, PixelPaint is a file format native to the program of the same name and is supported by versions 1.0 and 2.0. Although Illustrator 7 is capable of both reading and writing to the PixelPaint file format, the filter is an optional plug-in that must be manually placed into the plug-ins folder.

PNG

The PNG (portable network graphic) format is an alternative Web image display format similar to GIF. Illustrator 7 is capable of reading and writing the PNG file format and, while importing through the Place command is seamless, exporting is a two-step process. The first dialog box offers standard resolution options and the second offers display and compression options as shown here:

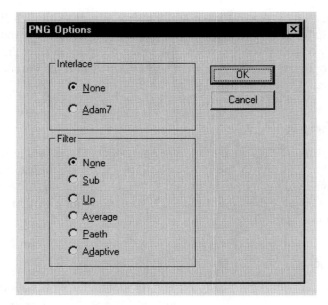

 *For more information on using the PNG file format with the World Wide Web, see "Using PNG Formats" in **Chapter 18: Illustrator 7 and the Web**.*

Windows Metafile

The Microsoft Windows Metafile (WMF) format is supported by many of the more popular Windows applications. This file format can contain both bitmap and vector graphics. Illustrator 7 supports both reading and writing of WMF files containing both vector and bitmap objects and both importing and exporting operations are seamless, involving no additional options to set.

Targa

Targa (TGA) is a specialized bitmap file format developed for use with proprietary video boards made by a company called Truevision. Illustrator is capable of both reading and writing Targa file formats. Importing a TGA file is seamless; exporting involves a two-step process that begins with standard resolution options and ends with color depth resolution options comprised of 16-bit, 24-bit, and 32-bit depths as shown here:

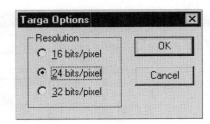

Text Filters

Illustrator 7 also supports four basic text file formats when working with large amounts of type: Microsoft Rich Text Format, Microsoft Word, ASCII Text, and Corel WordPerfect. In terms of text formats, Illustrator 7 reads from and writes to all four of these formats. When importing text files, the process is seamless and involves no import options for any of the four formats. You import text through the Place command, placing it onto the center of the page in a type box equivalent to the width of the original text format, with the exception of text (TXT) files.

Exporting is a different story, however, depending on which format you choose to export to. Illustrator 7 offers the capabilities to convert all text contained in a drawing file into a single text file of your choosing including all type objects, type on paths, and type in containers. Three of the formats Illustrator 7 supports actually retain type properties such as type size, type style, and alignment.

The type within an Illustrator drawing is generally converted based on the position of the type on the Artboard, from top to bottom and left to right. Carriage returns between paragraphs are added wherever they have been entered in the document text and between individual type objects.

Note   *When exporting to any of Illustrator 7's text formats, vertical type, area type, and path type are all successfully converted, but the resulting text is oriented normally.*

When exporting to Microsoft Rich Text Format (RTF), Illustrator 7's filter enables you to save to various versions of the rich text format, comprised of ANSI Character Set, Code Page 850, Macintosh Character Set, Microsoft Word version

6.0 (Macintosh), PC Character Set, or Microsoft Word version 6.0 (Windows), in a secondary dialog box, as shown here:

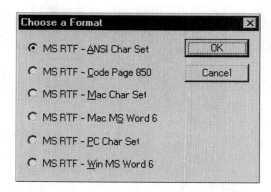

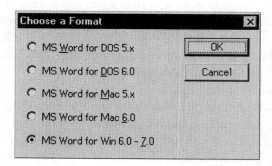 *When exporting to any of Illustrator 7's text formats, the text and URLs assigned to objects using the Attributes palette are ignored and remain unconverted.*

When exporting the text in your drawing to Microsoft Word (DOC) format, Illustrator 7 offers a secondary dialog box that lets you choose a specific version. Choose between MS Word for DOS 5.x, MS Word for DOS 6.0, MS Word for Macintosh 5.x, MS Word for Macintosh 6.0, and MS Word for Windows versions 6.0 to 7.0, as shown here:

Exporting to Corel WordPerfect (WPD) format also offers a secondary dialog box, enabling you to choose from WordPerfect for DOS 6.x, WordPerfect for Windows 6.x, or WordPerfect for Windows 7.0, as shown here:

Choose a Format ×

(•) WP for DOS 6.x   OK

( ) WP for Win 6.x   Cancel

( ) WP for Win 7.0

Importing by Drag-and-Drop

It may not seem like it should come under the heading of importing or exporting, but drag-and-drop functionality does use the same filters as your importing and exporting operations. Only, in the case of drag-and-drop, the action is intentionally made to operate seamlessly and without any secondary dialog box options. Illustrator 7 is capable of employing drag-and-drop functionality for operations such as the following:

■ Copying objects between two open documents within Illustrator 7

■ Copying objects between your Illustrator drawing and the desktop

■ Copying objects between Illustrator 7 and Photoshop 3.5, 4.0, or later versions

■ Copying objects between Adobe's Dimensions, Streamline, PageMaker, PageMill, SiteMill, and After Effects applications

If you're not familiar with the term, *drag-and-drop* stems from the action of clicking on an item, dragging it to a given location on your screen, and releasing your mouse to let the object drop into another location.

When objects are dragged between Illustrator 7 documents, all properties of the object supported by Illustrator 7 are retained. The vehicle used to transport them is actually your system's clipboard, so importing and exporting is essentially the same as copying and pasting the object, only quicker. To perform a drag-and-drop operation, your Illustrator 7 program window or document window(s) will likely need to be adjusted for you to see the destination of your dragged objects.

When moving objects between Illustrator 7 and the desktop, objects you drag are converted to Adobe's EPS format as a picture clipping (Macintosh) or Scrap (Windows) document.

In other words, Macintosh files use the Macintosh PICT export filter, while Windows files use the Windows Metafile (WMF) format, each of which are capable of supporting both bitmap and vector objects.

Each time you drag an object to the desktop, it is automatically named in sequence. Once an object is dragged to the desktop it remains there until deleted—even after Illustrator 7 has been closed. When these objects are eventually dragged from the desktop into an Illustrator 7 file (or other program file), the PICT (Macintosh) or WMF (Windows) import filter is used to recognize and decode the information it contains.

Exporting Using the Clipboard

To a certain extent, the clipboard may be used as a quick method for copying objects between Illustrator 7 documents or other applications. Clipboard commands are comprised of Copy (CTRL/COMMAND+C), Cut (CTRL/COMMAND+X), and Paste (CTRL/COMMAND+V) and use a reserved part of your computer's system memory to temporarily store information. When copying between Illustrator documents, all aspects of your objects are preserved.

However, when working between Illustrator 7 and other applications, clipboard results may vary greatly depending on the type of application you are copying to or from. Because the clipboard essentially uses the same export filters as Illustrator 7's export commands, in general the functionality operates reliably when performing the following operations:

- When copying and pasting *text* objects between Illustrator 7 and most up-to-date word processing or page layout programs while retaining most or all text properties such as type font, size, style, and alignment.

- When copying and pasting *paths* between Illustrator 7 and Photoshop, Adobe Streamline, Adobe Dimensions, and Adobe Premiere. Paths are commonly copied to the clipboard as EPS (PostScript) objects. In most cases, objects retain all their properties depending on the program version being copied to.

- When copying *drawing objects* from Adobe Illustrator to the Clipboard as *bitmap* images. Most up-to-date applications are capable of importing or accepting typical bitmap images in at least RGB color format. To automatically convert drawing objects to bitmap images "on the fly," hold down the OPTION key on the Macintosh when copying the objects or simply copy (CTRL+C) on Windows versions.

Working Between Illustrator 7 and Photoshop

If you work with both Adobe Illustrator 7 and Adobe Photoshop, as many users do, you'll find it convenient to be able to exchange objects between the two applications. Illustrator 7 and Photoshop each support drag-and-drop functionality and often use the same import and export filters when exchanging data. In this regard, you're able to capitalize on much of the sophistication and commonality built into these two programs.

Drag-and-drop is the best and most convenient method of trading both bitmap and vector objects between the two programs. In each case, objects are copied and placed as bitmap images or paths to the active layer of the application. To copy a vector path, hold CTRL/COMMAND when dragging from Illustrator to Photoshop. When the path reaches Photoshop, it becomes a Photoshop path. When copying bitmaps from Photoshop to Illustrator 7, holding the CTRL/COMMAND key automatically converts the selection to a 72 DPI RGB bitmap object.

Note *When working with Photoshop version 3.04 or earlier, you can drag from Photoshop into Illustrator, but you can't drag from Illustrator into Photoshop.*

Conclusion

Knowing how to get information from one program to another intact and with as few surprises as possible is key in becoming an expert at any program. In the worlds of printing, publishing, or technical illustration, nobody works in a bubble anymore. Users often choose—or are forced—to work with a combination of programs. The challenge is to make them work as seamlessly as possible with each other.

This chapter has detailed the entire collection of importing and exporting filters and operations available in Illustrator 7. You've learned detailed information about how these filters operate as well as your options before and during importing and exporting operations.

Printing from
Illustrator 7

17

Printing your Illustrator 7 files can be one of the most enlightening events you'll experience during the course of creating your drawing. At last, you'll be able to actually hold something tangible in your hands, rather than just seeing objects on the screen. For many computer users who come from traditional art backgrounds, a drawing isn't real until you can touch it, hold it, and feel it.

But, as with anything in life, there are good printing experiences and bad ones, often depending on how your drawing was created or how your system is set up. It's been said that if you give three different people the same tools to accomplish the same task, you'll see it done three different ways. In printing, the first person's drawing might print quickly and easily, the second person's drawing might take a long time to print and look only half as good, and the third might not print at all.

With drawing programs, the same holds true. Although many simple drawings print without a hitch, more complex drawings can be plagued with problems. The good news is that Adobe—inventors of the standard PostScript page description language—are the kings of printing. So, you'll seldom find blame for unfortunate printing experiences pointed at Illustrator 7 itself.

Unless the drawings you're creating are used strictly for exploring, used only on the computer screen, or only seen on the Web, at some point you're going to need to use the print features in Adobe Illustrator 7. Getting a hard copy from Illustrator 7 is much easier than it was in previous versions of the program. The Print Engine (as it's referred to) is now quite sophisticated and includes a wide array of options and features.

The topics covered in this chapter might seem tedious at first glance, but if you're curious about Illustrator 7's printing features or you need to reference this chapter to solve a printing problem, you'll likely find it one of the more interesting chapters to visit. At times during your printing process, it may seem as if you're performing dialog box acrobatics, due to the way Adobe has implemented these features. But if you persevere, the reasons behind Adobe's setup will become clear as you proceed through the printing steps and you'll find they follow a logical sequence after all.

This chapter explains much of the mystery that surrounds the printing process, whether printing from your desktop printer or offset printing from a high-volume press. You'll learn what all the options are for and how to use them effectively. You'll also discover some troubleshooting tips for those times when you attempt to print and nothing happens.

Setting Up to Print

Before printing your document, you need to set up a few parameters that are specific to your Illustrator 7 drawing. Illustrator will not allow you access to certain printing functions until you specify exactly what it is you're printing and what type of printer you intend to use. These parameters may be set using a shortcut button from the Document Setup dialog box (CTRL/COMMAND+SHIFT+P) (shown here) to get to the Print Setup dialog options.

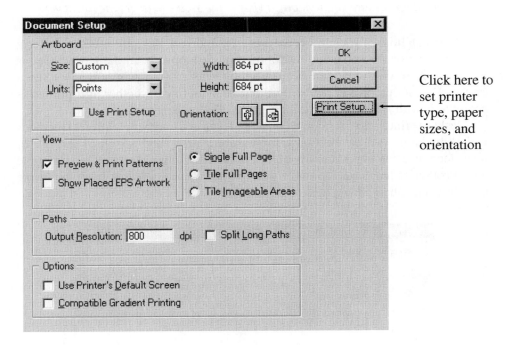

Click here to set printer type, paper sizes, and orientation

 If you wish to automatically set the size and orientation of your Artboard to match options you have set in the Print Setup dialog box, click the Use Print Setup option in the Document Setup dialog box.

The Printer

The printer type you set is perhaps the most critical parameter in all of these dialog boxes. The type of printer you will be printing your Illustrator 7 drawing to will determine whether you can produce output such as composite color, separations, and so on later in the process. Before you can even select a printer, the printer drivers must be installed on your system and operating properly. It helps to have the most up-to-date driver for the printing hardware you are using.

 Most desktop printer manufacturers such as Canon, Hewlett-Packard (HP), Textronix, and so on have a presence on the World Wide Web. In nearly all cases, these companies have made their printer drivers available for downloading. If you are missing a printer driver or seeking to obtain the most up-to-date version, pay a visit to the Web site to get the latest version.

The capabilities of your printer are preset by its driver. Regardless of the platform you are using or the make and model of your desktop printer, the key to options Illustrator 7 presents to you are determined by whether your printer is a PostScript or non-PostScript printer. In simple terms, it defines whether the printer is *compatible* with Adobe's PostScript page description language.

Desktop printer reproduction technology features a number of different methods including laser, ink-jet, bubble-jet, dye sublimation, and so on. The type of reproduction technology is usually a hint as to whether the printer itself is compatible with PostScript language. To make your printer choice, select it from the Name drop-down menu as shown here for Windows:

Print Setup		? ×

Printer

Name:	Linotronic 330 ▼	Properties
Status:	Ready	
Type:	Linotronic 330	
Where:	FILE:	
Comment:		

Paper

Size:	Letter.Extra ▼
Source:	AutoSelect Tray ▼

Orientation

A

○ Portrait

● Landscape

OK   Cancel

To select your printer on the Macintosh, use the Chooser menu in the Apple drop-down menu.

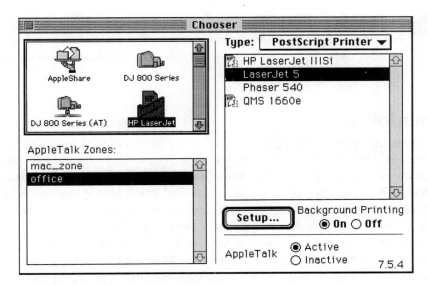

Note that when you choose your printer, the driver informs Illustrator 7 of the hardware's capabilities.

Paper

The second most critical choice you will make is the size of the material you choose to print your drawing onto. Various printer types offer an equally variable range of page sizes, most commonly letter size paper, which is 8.5 by 11 inches. Most printers aren't capable of printing to the very edges of the page though, which is something that is eventually reflected when you view your drawing and is indicated by a dashed rectangle inside the perimeter of your page. Some printers, such as high-resolution imagesetters, are actually capable of printing *beyond* the edges of your Artboard (this is called *bleeding* off the page in printing terms). In cases where the printer is capable of printing beyond your Artboard size, there are no indicator lines.

The ability of a printer to print beyond your Artboard dimensions is key to imaging film for things like color separations to high-resolution film such as a laser imagesetter or direct-to-plate technology. In these cases, printer page sizes usually include size options which include the term *extra*, meaning at least an extra 0.5 inches is added to each side of the page. This extra space can accommodate

things like printers' marks, densitometer scales, and so on without affecting the printed image.

 The term Paper *is one of the most confusing terms in the Print Setup dialog box. Paper actually means "output material" since the material you are printing on could theoretically refer to photographic material, plastic, cloth, nylon, or acetate-based film.*

Orientation

Another of the more confusing terms you'll hear when printing your document is *orientation*. The industry has kicked around various terms to describe orientation over the years and finally settled on these: *portrait* and *landscape*. The thrust of the concept is that unless the material you are printing onto is square, one side is longer than the other. The long side of the printing material you select sets how it is oriented—either horizontally (landscape) or vertically (portrait).

As a simple example, printing a letter-sized, portrait-oriented drawing to a letter-sized, landscape-oriented material will cause your drawing to be printed incorrectly on the page. Because you are trying to print something 11 inches wide to material that is only 8.5 inches wide, your output will be wasted. In essence, you'll be cutting off portions of your drawing.

It's easy to master the concept of printing letter-sized drawings to a letter-sized printer. But it's far more confusing to print to other materials such as a roll of film on an imagesetter take-up cassette or large format plotter. The orientation of the material you are printing to is determined to a large extent by the properties of the printer. Don't worry though, Illustrator will attempt to warn you if it appears you are making an orientation error. Plus, Illustrator features a Preview window to allow you to view how your output will look before you print it.

You can set your printed material size to any of the sizes available in the Size drop-down menu and, in certain cases, set the source of this material. These two options will vary according to the type of printer you are using and the specific hardware options available. Choose the options for portrait or landscape as they match your output material format.

Illustrator 7's Print Command

Once you've chosen your printing device in the Print Setup dialog box, you can proceed with the printing process. Options pertaining to the actual printing of your drawing using the Page Range, Output Format, and Number of Copies can be set using the basic controls shown here. To access Illustrator 7's main Print dialog options, press CTRL/COMMAND+P.

Print   ✕

Printer: Linotronic 330 on FILE:
Status: Ready
Type: Linotronic 330
Where: FILE:
Comment: ☑ Print to File

┌─ Print Range ──────────────┐   ┌─ Copies ──────────────────┐
  ○ All   Number of Copies: |1   ▲▼

  ○ Pages From: | | To: | | ┌─┐ ┌─┐ ┌─┐
                                              1 |1| 2 |2| 3 |3| ☐ Collate
  ◉ Selection   └─┘ └─┘ └─┘

Output: |Composite   ▼| | Separation Setup... |

PostScript®: |Level 2   ▼| Data: |ASCII   ▼|

☐ Force Fonts to Download | OK | | Cancel |

- ■ **Print Range**   The Print Range options enable you to specify exactly which pages of your Illustrator document you wish to print—a moot point, because Illustrator 7 does not support multiple pages. By default this is set to print All pages. If you wish, you may also choose only to print the objects currently selected in your document, which enables you the freedom of printing only desired portions of your drawing.

Note   *Although there are several creative ways of setting up Illustrator 7 documents to contain multiple pages, Illustrator 7 does not include any multiple-page document features. In other words, each document file supports a maximum of one page. When it comes to printing though, Illustrator 7 is capable of producing multiple pages of the same drawing, meaning you can print multiple copies, color separations, or tiled printing of the same drawing.*

- **Copies**   This option enables you to print multiple copies of your drawing. An additional option, to Collate the copies, is also somewhat rhetorical, because Illustrator 7 doesn't support multipage documents. On the bright side, the maximum number of copies you are able to print using this options can be as high as 9,999 copies.

- **Output**   Output options depend on the model of printer you are using. For example, if your printer is capable of printing in color, you can choose to print either a composite color proof of your drawing or separations of the colors. When printing to a PostScript printer, an additional output option becomes available and contains two choices: Level 1 or Level 2. Although the Level 1 option is present, Illustrator always defaults to the Level 2 option.

Note   *According to Adobe, when Illustrator 7 was shipped, an option to use PostScript Level 1 was available in the main Print dialog box. Selecting this option has no effect on the PostScript level used by Illustrator's print engine. Instead, the default Level 2 is always used. Printing from Illustrator 7 is no longer limited to printing to older printers using PostScript Level 1 page description language.*

- **Print to File**   Select this option to create a computer file written in page description language; the file can then be downloaded to a printer remotely. For more information on creating "print files" see "Preparing a Print File" later in this chapter.

- **Separation Setup**   The Separation Setup button is a shortcut to the Separation Setup command (CTRL/COMMAND+ALT/OPTION+P) found under the File menu. This button will only become available if your PostScript-compatible printer is capable of printing color separations.

- **Data**   The Data option becomes available only when using the Print to File option. Using this option, print files may be prepared to either ASCII or Binary format.

Printing Color Separations

For users creating drawings that will be printed using traditional offset reproduction methods, the ability to print color separations is critical. Illustrator 7 is capable of printing color separations to suit the needs of all conventional reproduction methods including both spot and process color printing and combinations thereof. There's a definite knack to getting to know and use these tools though, and an order of sequence to follow, beginning with specifying a PPD (PostScript printer description) file. Unless you set up this mysterious little file, you won't have access to any of the color separation controls available in Illustrator 7.

To access the Separation Setup dialog options shown here, press CTRL/ COMMAND+ALT/OPTION+P, choose Separation Setup from the File menu, or use the Separation Setup shortcut button from within the main Print dialog box (CTRL/COMMAND+P).

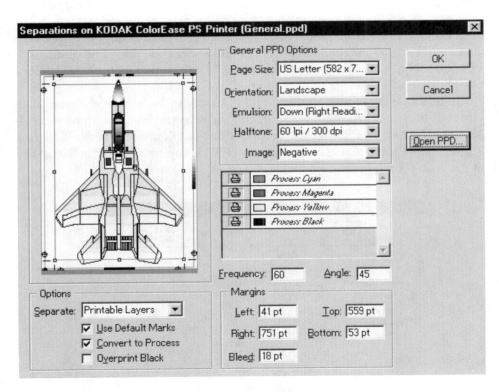

If you have not chosen a printer capable of printing color separations in the Print Options dialog box, you will not have access to the Separations Setup shortcut button through the main Print options (CTRL/COMMAND+P). To access the Print Options dialog box, use the shortcut button available in the Document Setup dialog box (CTRL/COMMAND+SHIFT+P).

Opening a PPD File

Setting your PostScript printer description (PPD) file tells Illustrator 7 about all the properties and capabilities of your printing hardware. A printer description is actually a physical file on your system which defines the properties and capabilities of your chosen printer. For most black-and-white or color desktop printers, the options are fairly straightforward, but for high-resolution film printers such as Agfa or Linotronic imagesetters, the properties and capabilities can be quite involved.

Adobe Illustrator ships with its own "general" printer description as a default PPD, but ultimately you'll want to use your own up-to-date version, which is often supplied by your printer manufacturer. The PPD file for your printer should be stored in your System Extensions folder (Macintosh) or your Win95/System folder (Windows). But if you need to use it, the "general" PPD file that ships with Illustrator 7 is stored in the Adobe/Illustrator 7.0/Utilities/PPD folder. If you are using Windows NT, you may find additional PPD files in the System32\Spool\ Drivers\w32x86 folder.

To select the PPD file, click the Open PPD button in the Separation Setup dialog box and browse to locate the file as shown here (in Windows) and next (in Macintosh). Once the PPD file has been located, click OK to select the file. Illustrator 7's Separation Setup dialog indicates which PPD is currently loaded in the title bar of the dialog box.

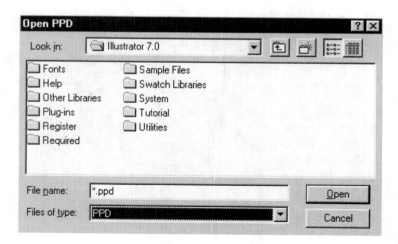

Separations on LaserJet 5 (No PPD File Selected)

General PPD Options

Page Size:

Orientation: Portrait

Emulsion: Down (Right R...

Halftone:

Image: Negative

OK

Cancel

Open PPD...

Frequency: Angle:

Options

Separate: Printable Layers

☒ Use Default Marks
☒ Convert to Process
☐ Overprint Black

Margins

Left: Top:

Right: Bottom:

Bleed:

Note   *The printer or imagesetter you plan to use to print separations must match the PPD file you specified when setting up the separations. If the printing device you have set doesn't match your installed PPD file, you will receive an error message, and the separations may not print.*

Adobe's Web site features downloadable PPD files for many different types of printing hardware for both Macintosh and Windows platforms. For Windows users, you may also download INF hardware printer profiles. Adobe distributes these files as a convenience for users, and the collection is periodically updated. At the time of this writing, the PPD and INF files listed next were available for download.

Note   *Although PPD files can be downloaded from Adobe's Web site, the most current versions available at shipping time are also stored on the Illustrator 7 program disc in the Illustrator 7/Adobe EPS/PPDs (Macintosh) Illustrator 7/Adobe EPS/PPDs folder (Windows). For the most up-to-date version though, your best bet is Adobe's Web site.*

Windows version PPD Files are available from:
http://www.adobe.com/supportservice/custsupport/LIBRARY/pdrvwin.htm.

Manufacturer	File Download Size	Manufacturer	File Download Size
3M	48K	Management Graphics	29K
Adobe	26K	Mannesmann Scangraphic	33K
Agfa	122K	Mitsubishi Electric	50K
Apple	135K	Monotype	52K
AST	22K	Mutoh	31K
Autologic	174K	NEC	81K
Birmy Graphics	32K	NeXT	21K
Bull Italia	23K	Oce Graphics	22K
CalComp	39K	Okidata	139K
Canon	142K	Panasonic	37K
COLORBUS Software	57K	Pix ColorLink	23K
Colossal	41K	PrePRESS Solutions	172K
Compaq PageMarq	43K	QMS	95K
Crosfield Electronics	50K	Qume	22K
Dainippon	150K	Radius	36K
Dainippon Printing Co. Ltd.	24K	Ricoh	43K
Dataproducts	82K	Samsung	196K
Digital	128K	Seiko Epson	68K
DuPont	24K	Seiko Instruments	83K
Eastman Kodak	75K	Shinko	22K
EFI	114K	SofHa GmbH	46K

Manufacturer	File Download Size	Manufacturer	File Download Size
Fargo Electronics	34K	Sony	114K
Fuji Xerox	104K	Schlumberger	22K
Fujitsu	22K	Scitex	72K
GDT Softworks	31K	Sun	24K
Hewlett-Packard	135K	Tektronix	305K
Hitachi	46K	Texas Instruments	130K
IBM	51K	Unisys	31K
IDT	21K	Varityper	214K
Indigo	36K	VerTec Solutions	24K
Laser Graphics	30K	XANTE Corporation	189K
Laser Press	31K	Xerox	
Linotype-Hell	179K		
Windows version INF files:			
3M, Agfa, and Apple	219K	PDFWriter	
Autologic to CalComp	194K	Oki, Panasonic, and Pix	219K
Canon to Crosfield	193K	PrePRESS Solutions	219K
Dainippon and Fuji	219K	QMS to Sun Microsystems	219K
DataProducts to EFI	219K	Tektronix, Texas Instruments, and Unisys	293K
Epson to Indigo	219K	Varityper	208K

17

Manufacturer	File Download Size	Manufacturer	File Download Size
Laser Graphics to Oce Graphics	219K	VerTec Solutions, XANTE, and Xerox	189K

Macintosh version PPD files are available from: http://www.adobe.com/supportservice/custsupport/LIBRARY/pdrvmac.htm.

Manufacturer	File Download Size	Manufacturer	File Download Size
Adobe	5K	Laser Press	18K
Agfa	146K	Management Graphics	26K
Apple LaserWriter	173K	Mannesmann Scangraphic	85K
AST PS-R4081	5K	Mitsubishi Electric	44K
Autologic	219K	Monotype	48K
Birmy Graphics PowerRIP	18K	NEC	87K
Bull Italia PageMaster	13K	NeXT	3K
CalComp	29K	Oce Graphics	5K
Canon	159K	Oki	121K
COLORBUS Software	58K	Panasonic	27K
Colossal	33K	Pix Computer Systems (ColorLink)	6K
Compaq PageMarq	34K	PrePRESS Solutions	222K

17

Manufacturer	File Download Size	Manufacturer	File Download Size
Crosfield Electronics	46K	QMS	107K
Dainippon	191K	Qume QumeScripTEN	5K
Dainippon Printing Co. Ltd. (RIPStick)	7K	Radius	24K
Dataproducts	90K	Ricoh	26K
Digital	147K	Schlumberger	5K
DuPont	7K	Scitex	76K
Eastman Kodak	49K	Seiko Epson	71K
EFI Fiery	138K	Seiko Instruments	72K
Fargo Electronics	21K	Shinko	5K
Fuji Xerox	124K	SofHa GmbH	41K
Fujitsu	5K	Sony	137K
GDT Softworks	34K	Sun Microsystems	7K
Hewlett-Packard	347K	Tektronix	361K
Hitachi	39K	Texas Instruments	157K
IBM	36K	Unisys	17K
IDT	4K	Varityper	275K
Indigo	24K	VerTec Solutions	7K
Laser Graphics	16K	XANTE Corporation	220K
Linotype-Hell	141K	Xerox	233K

Note   *The Adobe Web site also includes foreign language Macintosh PostScript drivers available for download.*

About the Preview Window

Within the Separation Setup dialog box is a Preview window that reflects certain currently selected Separation Setup options such as page size, orientation, emulsion, and margin settings (each will be described shortly). You might say that the Preview window is where all the action happens. It also indicates the existence of printer's (crop) marks, color density scales, and registration marks necessary for aligning film negatives and controlling registration and ink coverage of printed images on a printing press.

Note *Changing the position of your image on the printed page does not affect its position on your Artboard.*

If necessary, you may change the printable page size or the relative position of your drawing on your printing material using your mouse pointer as follows:

■ **Changing printable page size**   The printable page size is available area on your page that will eventually receive your printed image. This area is indicated by a thin, black rectangle surrounding the image and features small black-outlined markings in the corners and sides of this shape. To change the printable page area, click on any of these indicator marks and drag using your mouse pointer as shown here. This area may also be set using the Top, Bottom, Left, and Right Margin settings described next.

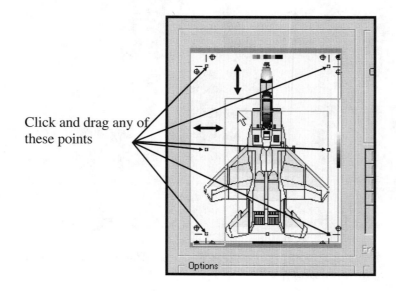

Click and drag any of these points

17

- **Changing image page position**   To change the position of your image on the printed page, click anywhere on the image in the Preview window and drag the image to your desired position as shown here:

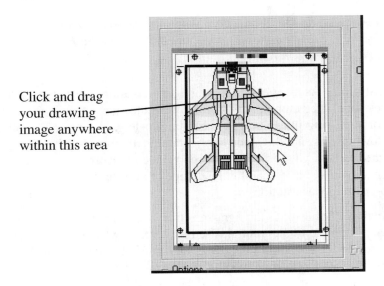

Click and drag your drawing image anywhere within this area

 When printing tiled pages, the Preview window is incapable of displaying more than one page at a time and cannot indicate where the tiles will be divided.

PPD Options

The PPD Options area of the Separation Setup dialog box sets printed image dimensions and orientation as well as how the image will be imprinted onto your printing material. Here's what each option controls:

- **Page size**   The available page sizes you have to choose depend on the particular PPD file you currently have installed, making it critical that you are using the PPD specific to your printing device. In general, page sizes are listed in standard measures such as Letter, Legal, Tabloid, and so on. To set page size, choose it from the Page Size drop-down menu. Printed page sizes are immediately reflected in the Preview window.

Tip *When printing to a roll-fed device such as a large format plotter or a high-resolution imagesetter, you may save output material costs by choosing*

the Transverse page size, depending on the dimensions you have set for your Artboard. Transverse page sizes have the effect of printing your output sideways on the output material.

Note   *Page sizes set in the Separation Setup are determined by the currently loaded PPD file, as opposed to the size selected in the Print Setup/Page Setup dialog box controls.*

- **Orientation**   As mentioned earlier, page orientation is critical to getting successful printed output. An incorrectly oriented page usually results in part or all of your image being cut off. Fortunately, Illustrator 7's Preview window reflects changes made to orientation and immediately shows whether parts of your drawing will be lost due to incorrect orientation. Orientation may be set to either landscape or portrait through this drop-down menu selection.

- **Emulsion**   Emulsion is the light-sensitive side of photographic material. When printing to film output, this setting controls whether the image is mirrored on the emulsion side, essentially causing it to print either normally, or as a reflection reading. The terms *right reading* and *wrong reading* describe whether the text on the printed image can be read as a normal image or whether it appears as a mirror image. The default setting is Emulsion Down (right reading), meaning when the film is viewed with the emulsion side facing away from you, the image is right reading. The Emulsion Up (wrong reading) setting is often used when imaging film for reproduction methods in silk screening. Emulsion options are set through this drop-down menu and results of the selection are reflected in the Preview window.

- **Halftone**   The term *halftone* refers to the screen frequency of your output and is measured in lines per inch (LPI). Halftone settings may also include setting the resolution of the image to be output, which is measured in dots per inch (DPI). If you are using the correct PPD for your printing device, these settings are often set to common defaults. Due to the physical limitations of your computer screen, halftone frequency and resolution settings cannot be reflected in the Preview window.

- **Image**   This setting controls whether your drawing image is printed negative or positive. *Negative* images print clear on a black background, while *positive* images print opposite of this. The term *reverse* is often associated with printing in negative format and is common when producing film output for the offset printing industry, while positive film output is common to silk screen reproduction. Whether you select to print negative or positive, image selection results are *not* reflected in the Preview window.

Choosing Ink Colors to Print

Just below the PPD options in the Separation Setup dialog box is a list box that lists the ink colors your drawing contains. Because printing inks can only be specified in either spot or process colors, you won't see any RGB colors named here. Instead, this list box identifies all existing ink colors that have been applied to objects in your drawing, regardless of the color model used. Any colors that have been specified using RGB (red, green, blue), HSB (hue, saturation, brightness), or Grayscale color models are automatically converted to the four process ink colors CMYK (cyan, magenta, yellow, and black).

Along with the assigned ink colors in your drawing, this list box also displays the name of the color, its current selected printing status (on or off), and a visual color sample representing the onscreen color. If more than six separate inks are present in your drawing, you may use the scroll bar to see further down the list. To choose a specific ink color to print, click the area to the left of the ink name as shown here:

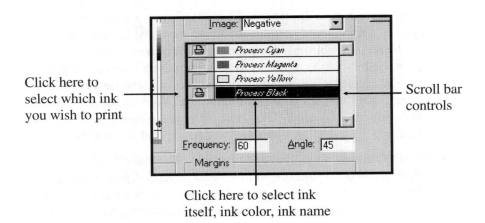

Click here to select which ink you wish to print

Scroll bar controls

Click here to select ink itself, ink color, ink name

Setting Screen Frequency and Angle Options

When a certain ink is selected to print, Illustrator includes options for setting the screen angle and frequency of the printed output. These should be set according to your printer's capabilities and the requirements of your reproduction process. If you are unsure of these values, contact your service bureau or offset printing provider for the exact settings. These settings can often be set globally on the imagesetting device itself; in that case, you don't need to set them here at all.

To set either the screen angle or frequency, first click on the ink name to highlight it. If you are certain of the values you would like to set, enter them in the Frequency and Angle boxes.

Setting Print Options

Illustrator 7's print options control a potpourri of leftover options not defined by any other printing options, yet still essential to the printing process. These options are comprised of separations to print, printers' marks, process color conversion, and black overprinting. By default, Illustrator is set to print printable layers, printers marks, and convert to black. If these terms seem mysterious, they're defined as follows:

- **Separate**   This drop-down menu offers three choices: Printable Layers, Visible Layers, and All [layers]. The first two options are a function of using layers in your drawing. In Illustrator 7, you may set individual layers in a document to certain conditions using the Layers palette. Layers may be set as visible or hidden and printable or nonprinting. The Separate option enables you to plug into the conditions you have set for your assigned layers by selecting to print all layers assigned as Printable Layers, only those which are currently set as Visible Layers, or All layers existing in your document. For more information on using layers, see "Working in Layers" in **Chapter 8: Selecting and Arranging Objects**.

- **Use Default Marks**   This option enables Illustrator 7 to include printers' marks on your output material. The term *default* implies that the Illustrator 7 is using its own markings rather than you fabricating your own marks in your drawing, which some printing experts insist on. Selecting this option positions eight registration marks.

17

> **Tip**
>
> *When choosing to include printers' marks on your printed output, be sure to select a material size that is large enough to accommodate printing these marks. The Preview window indicates page sizes quite accurately and so, if it appear that markings are missing or cut off, it may be that the page size you have selected to print to is too small to accommodate them. Try choosing a larger page size or setting your own using Custom page size (provided your currently selected PPD supports custom page sizes).*

■ **Convert to Process**   This option automatically converts any spot colors assigned to objects in your drawing to adapt to the CMYK color model and then prints them accordingly. For example, a Pantone 185 Red spot color converts to C0,M100,Y100,K0 and so, if you choose to print only the cyan ink of your drawing, you will not see any indication of this object. The Convert to Process option is set to on by default, and, while in this state, spot colors are indicated as converted to process with a symbol in the ink colors list box as shown here:

Click a second time in this box to convert spot colors to process

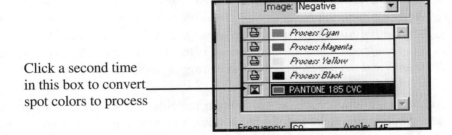

> **Tip**
>
> *You can switch individual spot colors to process colors without choosing the Convert to Process option by clicking twice in the printing state area of the ink colors list box.*

■ **Overprinting black**   The term *overprint* refers to the procedure of printing one ink color on top of another. This option is one of the simpler strategies of trapping color in your drawing and makes manual trapping processes much faster, especially when it comes to type. Type is commonly specified to print using black ink, and so if the type in your drawing is situated over an object acting as a colored background,

choosing this option will allow the black type to print over the background color.

Setting Print Margins

Although it is much more intuitive to set your margins using your mouse pointer, you may set print margins to exact measures by entering numeric values in the Margins boxes. Margin markers are set according to the Left, Top, Right, and Bottom markers using inches to indicate their relative page positions.

The trick to using the Margins option is to recognize where exactly the left, top, right, and bottom margins are, regardless of whether your page has been oriented to portrait or landscape formats. Illustrator 7 operates on the principle that the original corners and sides of your page remain consistent whether the page is being rotated 90 degrees from portrait to landscape or vice versa during printing. When printing, pages that are rotated from one orientation format to another always rotate clockwise.

 Setting the margins values for your page can be tricky if you are attempting to enter the values manually in the Margins options. If you're not comfortable entering these values numerically, try using your mouse pointer to change the corner position of your printed page margins in the Preview window instead. To familiarize yourself with operation of the page margin values, observe the numeric results as they change when dragging these markers.

Although the left, top, right, and bottom margins may be set directly in the Preview window, you cannot set the bleed values the same way. As you saw earlier, *bleed* refers to the amount of overlap of the printed image beyond the edge of the printed page. The amount of bleed may be set within a range between 0 and 1 inch to two decimal points. Having your printed pages bleed the image is often critical to certain types of offset printing where ink coverage extends beyond the limits of the printed page. Setting bleeds can also be useful when printing tiled pages, discussed next.

Printing Tiled Drawings

The printing of tiled documents can be tricky if you're not paying close attention. Illustrator 7 includes features where documents may be tiled if they feature an Artboard size that is larger than the material being printed onto. The general idea is that once tiled pages have been printed, they can be reassembled later using whatever means necessary, be that glue, tape, or string.

The page tiles that are destined to be printed can be viewed directly on your Artboard when using either the Tile Full Pages or Tile Imageable Areas options found in the Document Setup dialog options (CTRL/COMMAND+SHIFT+P). The page to be tiled is indicated on your Artboard by dotted black lines as shown in Figure 17-1. The individual tiles are numbered so you can identify them when it comes time to reassemble them. Numbers are shown in order from left to right, top to bottom.

 The placement of multiple tiled pages is based on the position of the first tile, which is set automatically. The good news is that you may reposition the tiled pages wherever you choose using the Page tool. (The Page tool is found with the Hand tool in the main Toolbox, or by typing **H** and toggling twice.) By repositioning the printed tiles, you can often reduce the total number of tiles to print and manipulate, thereby reducing the complexity of reassembling your drawing.

For example, the drawing depicted in Figure 17-1 is being viewed with the Tile Imageable Areas option in the Document Setup dialog box (CTRL/COMMAND+SHIFT+P) and indicates that a total of 12 pages will print. Some of these pages include only a

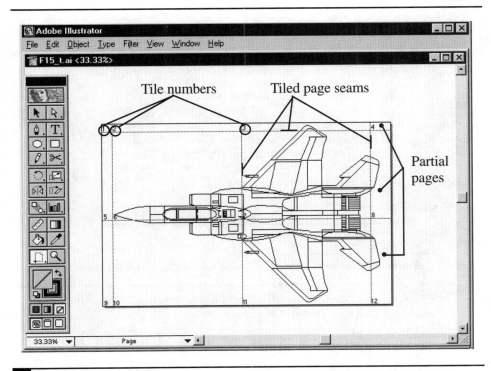

FIGURE 17-1   This drawing is currently destined to print in 12 tiled pages

small part of the Artboard, though. By repositioning tile positions using the Page tool, you can reduce the total number to just nine, using the same printed page size, as shown in Figure 17-2.

The Page tool (H) is grouped together with the Hand tool (H) in the main Toolbox palette. To use the Page tool, select it from the Toolbox and click on your Artboard Page precisely where you would like the first tile of your printed page to be positioned, and the remaining tiles are placed automatically. The Page tool uses the bottom-left corner as reference when placing the tiles. Once the position of the Page tool is clicked on the Artboard, the positioning of the remaining pages is automatically set and numbered.

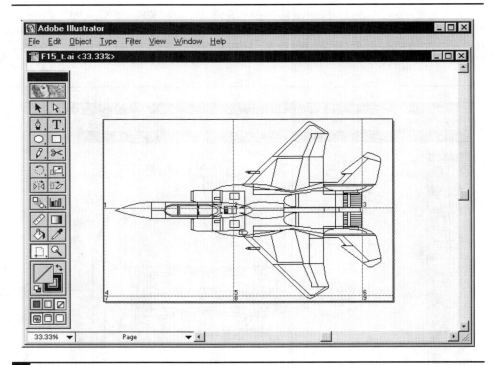

FIGURE 17-2　By repositioning the tiled pages, you may be able to reduce the total number of tiles to print

17

Before Printing

Before you finally print your drawing, there are a number of steps you may take to simplify your file and your drawing objects in an effort to avoid running into printing problems. To begin with, the following can serve as a quick checklist to reference before you proceed to the printing stage:

- **Clean up**   Although only objects on the Artboard are considered printable by Illustrator 7, the printing process still examines all objects in your drawing, including objects that may be placed off the Artboard. Simplify your drawing by deleting any extraneous objects in this area.

- **Reduce object complexity**   If you suspect your file contains highly complex objects with excessive anchor points on compound paths, click the Split Long Paths option in the Document Setup dialog box (CTRL/COMMAND+SHIFT+P).

 Be sure to make a copy of your file before setting this option, as it may permanently alter the physical structure of objects in your drawing.

- **Consider fonts**   If your file uses *only* typical printer-resident PostScript fonts, you can avoid having Illustrator 7 send font information to your printer each time the file is printed. Simply do not select the Force Fonts to Download option in the main Print dialog box (CTRL/COMMAND+P).

- **Embed fonts**   If you are sending your file to a service bureau for output, and your file contains type formatted in your own proprietary fonts, you may avoid having to supply the service bureau with these font files by embedding fonts in your file.

- **Delete empty text paths**   During the course of creating your drawing, you may have inadvertently created empty text paths, which ultimately take up space in your file and can trick your printer into downloading unnecessary font data. Font data takes additional time to download during printing of your drawing. To clean up your file, choose Object|Path|Cleanup and select to delete the Empty Text Paths option as shown here. The Cleanup command

option also enables you to delete any Stray Points and Unpainted Objects using the remaining two options.

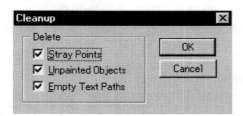

- **Set color trapping through overprinting**   When printing to color film separations, poorly registered printing can result in your drawing reproducing badly on the press. Press registration is ultimately controlled by the press operator, but you can help reduce the likelihood of poor registration by setting certain colored objects—mostly strokes on objects, to "overprint." Overprinting has the effect of enabling one color of ink to print directly over another. The Illustrator 7 Attributes palette (F11) includes options to overprint selected fills and strokes in an effort to create "traps" for specific objects as shown below. For more information on setting overprint options, see the "Setting Object Attributes" section in **Chapter 8: Selecting and Arranging Objects**.

- **Trap using the Trap filter**   Another strategy for trapping object colors in an effort to reduce the likelihood of press misregistration is through use of the Trap filter. The Trap filter is a function of the Object, Pathfinder command and enables you to create color traps for selected objects using Thickness, Height/Width, and Tint Reduction values as shown below. The Trap filter actually creates additional objects in your drawing with fill and stroke overprinting applied. The process is largely automatic and creates the new objects according to the selected options. For more information on using the Trap filter, see the section called "Working with Pathfinder" in **Chapter 9: Object Transform Tools.**

Pathfinder Trap ☒

Settings
Thickness: 0.25 points
Height/Width: 100 %
Tint Reduction: 40 %

OK
Cancel
Defaults

Options
☐ Traps with Process Color
☐ Reverse Traps

17

Creating a Print File

For users who have the luxury of printing directly to a local printer, creating a print file will be of little interest. And if you intend to print your images via a service bureau, you'll ultimately want to leave the printing up to them, once the proper printing instructions have been applied. But, if you do need to create a print file, doing so is a quick process in Illustrator 7.

A print file is a data file that contains all the information necessary to print your image and includes all the parameters you have set in the Separation Setup dialog box. Once this data file has been created, it may be transferred and downloaded to a remote printer (without requiring that the host computer have Illustrator 7 installed). Once a print file has been created, there is little hope of editing or changing it unless you happen to be an expert in interpreting and writing in native PostScript page description language. Therefore, setting your separation options correctly the first time around is paramount to successful printing.

Note   *Some of the technical documentation that accompanies Adobe Illustrator 7 refers to the process of creating a print file using the term "Save Separations." For the purposes of printing, these two phrases refer essentially to the same operation.*

To create a print file in Illustrator 7, carefully follow these steps:

1. Open the file you wish to create a print file from and load the correct PPD file for the printing device you will be printing to, using procedures

detailed in this chapter in the section called "Opening a PPD File." PPD files may be loaded using the Open PPD button from within the Separations Setup dialog box (CTRL/COMMAND+ALT/OPTION+P). *It is critical that the correct PPD file be installed before choosing any further options.*

2. Set all the necessary color separation options in the Separation Setup dialog box (CTRL/COMMAND+ALT/OPTION+P), as detailed in the previous section of this chapter called "Printing Color Separations."

3. Once these options have been set, choose File|Print (CTRL/COMMAND+P).

4. Select any further print options, as detailed previously in Illustrator 7's Print Command.

5. Choose Separate from the Output drop-down menu.

6. Click the PostScript File (Mac) or Print to File (Windows) option in the main Print dialog box, and click Save (Mac) or Print (Windows).

7. When the PostScript File (Mac) or Print to File (Windows) option is chosen, an additional dialog box appears just prior to the file being created, enabling you to give the file a name. Accept the default filename, or enter another name for your print file. If you use the default filename, Illustrator appends the filename with .ps (Mac) or .prn (Windows) to indicate it is a PostScript or print file.

8. Set the file location using the dialog box options as shown next:

9. Click OK to create the file.

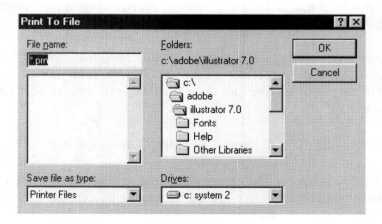

Troubleshooting Printing

One of the keys to isolating a print problem is tracking it to where it goes afoul. When you print from any application, three basic processes occur. Knowing where the process falls apart may help you determine whether the problem lies with you, your system, your printer, or the file you've created.

First, when printing begins, a progress meter appears and begins to grow from zero to 100 percent. At this point Illustrator 7's print engine is analyzing your file for number of objects, pages, colors, and fonts, according to printing options you have selected and the PPD file you have installed. Then it creates a data file for your system to deal with. Once the progress meter reaches 100 percent, Illustrator 7's printing function is complete. If print progresses beyond this point, the problem may be further down the line instead of with your drawing file.

Illustrator 7 then passes the printing information to your system and the data is passed on to the printer itself. If it makes it this far, any printing problems likely aren't with your software or system but with your printer. From here your troubleshooting exercise takes on a back-to-front scenario. This brings us to what should always be the first three items on your troubleshooting checklist:

- Make sure the printer is plugged in, turned on, well stocked, and properly connected.

- Make sure your printer is selected as the default printer in Illustrator 7's Print Setup dialog box.

- Try printing to the same printer from a different program on your system. If successful, the printing problem likely has something to do with either your file, a certain object in your file, or Illustrator 7 itself.

Desperate Strategies

Desperate situations often call for desperate measures. If the process stopped at the system processing stage, it may be that your system has run out of resources (such as RAM) or your printer's memory has become overloaded. It could also be that Illustrator 7 is having difficulty interpreting an object in your file, or the way in which you are trying to print it. At this point, you may want to follow one or all of these strategies:

- Search for any temporary files on your system and delete them. Make sure your hard drive has plenty of available hard drive space—ideally 10 to 20 percent of free hard drive should be available. Exit all programs that are currently running (except Adobe Illustrator 7 itself).

- One by one, reboot your printer, Illustrator 7, or your system, and try printing again after each step.

- If you use a print-spooling utility, try disabling it.

Drawing Files That Don't Print Correctly

Depending on which printing device, PPD, or printer driver you are using, you may run into situations where your onscreen drawing doesn't print correctly. Check to see that you are using the most up-to-date printer driver for your hardware. As a rule, printer manufacturers update their drivers quite often, and using the correct printer driver can make a world of difference to printer operation. When using Illustrator 7, this also means using the correct PPD for your target printer. That consideration aside, the most common reason for non-WYSIWYG printing relates to fonts not printing correctly.

Check Illustrator 7's Preview window to see if your drawing looks as it should. If fonts are appearing in your system default font or one of your drawing objects is printing with an obscure character, you may have a computer-to-printer communication problem. Once again, check that your computer-to-printer connections are secure.

- If you're using a printer switch or network printer, try connecting to the printer directly if possible.

- Check that the cable connecting your printer to your computer isn't damaged in some way.

Simplify Your Drawing

One of the major reasons your printer may quit printing is excessive file complexity. Reducing file complexity doesn't necessarily mean eliminating key parts of your drawing (although sometimes it may). There are two major issues that affect file complexity: graphic objects and printing options.

File complexity can be reduced by examining your file for objects featuring an overabundance of anchor points. Anchor points control the shape of vector objects, which compose most drawing objects. Imported or traced objects are famous for their high degree of anchor point complexity. If you suspect some of your objects have too many anchor points, try breaking the most complex objects—such as compound objects—into smaller parts using the Release Compound Objects command (CTRL/COMMAND+ALT/OPTION+8), or choose the Split Long Paths option in the Document Setup dialog box (CTRL/COMMAND+SHIFT+P).

The next most common complexity is bitmap-related. Avoid masking complex type fonts to objects, especially if the objects being masked are bitmap formats. Certain type fonts feature extensive numbers of inherent anchor points. If your file contains text to which you've applied a stroke color, try printing without the stroke. Type strokes can add excessive complexity to drawings, and rarely does stroked type look appealing when printed. Also, avoid applying strokes to highly complex drawing objects.

Finally, color-separated drawings can create enormous print data files that can overwhelm printer memory. If you're having troubles printing several separations to your printer, try selecting them to print individually.

Using the PostScript Error Handler

Although PostScript errors have little to do with Illustrator 7 itself, they can often provide clues as to why your printer refuses to print your drawing. All Mac and Windows PostScript drivers feature options to activate the PostScript error handler. To activate the error handler for your particular printer, refer to your printer's documentation. The option to activate the error handler is usually located in the Advanced options section of your Print Setup options accessed from your Document Setup dialog box (CTRL/COMMAND+SHIFT+P).

The PostScript Error Handler is designed to print an error message to the selected printer when printing fails. But if you've ever had the experience of seeing one of these errors print out, you likely already know they aren't much help unless you know how to interpret them. Here's a quick run-through of the most common printing errors associated with nonprinting files.

- **Limitcheck. Offending Command=Nametype: EOCLIP**   This error message tells you that your printer is unable to complete rendering of an object due to the complexity of its fill. Try changing the fill of the object to a simple color. If you're printing color separations, try printing them individually.

■ **Limitcheck. Offending Command=Nametype: EOFILL**   This message notifies you of a problem creating an object's fill due to the complexity of the path composing the object. Try reducing the complexity of the object using strategies discussed earlier in this chapter.

■ **Limitcheck. Offending Command=Nametype: LINETO or CURVETO**   This is usually an indication of too many anchor points on a path. Again, try reducing the complexity of the object using strategies discussed earlier in this chapter.

■ **Stack Overflow**   This is often an indication of embedded encapsulated PostScript files or overly complex objects or fill patterns exceeding printer stack limits. Again, try changing the fill of the object to a simple uniform color. If you're printing color separations, try printing them individually instead of in a single printing session.

Invalid font   The last error message anyone using text ever wants to see. This error is often associated with printing a file that is using a font file that has somehow become corrupted. The only option here is to remove the offending font from the host system and reinstall it on the system you are printing your document from.

Conclusion

The printing functions in Illustrator 7 have been significantly enhanced since previous versions, and to new users they may seem intimidating at first glance and confusing to use. But, by taking the process one step at a time, as this chapter has done, the process can be demystified. This chapter has detailed all of Illustrator 7's printing options and functions in an effort to provide you with a solid understanding of the process. With luck, this will make all your printing experiences positive and successful.

Illustrator 7 and the WWW

WWW

18

These days, it seems you can't do anything without hearing about the World Wide Web (WWW). In many respects, this new medium of presentation, communication, and information exchange has taken on a life all its own. Some people view the Web as complex and confusing and for use only by sophisticated computer users. Others see it as an intriguing and exciting opportunity to expand their business horizons and publishing opportunities. Illustrator 7 is no exception to this trend, and although its Web-related capabilities are best suited to the needs of electronic artists creating drawings, it does include some interesting options specifically geared toward Web image creation.

This chapter will be a critical read for anyone using Illustrator 7 to create WWW images as either standalone design elements, comprehensive navigation graphics, or presentation images. To their credit, the Adobe engineers have implemented these tools not as a separate Web utility but directly into the program's tool palettes that you probably use every day. You'll discover where to find the tools and how to maximize your Web image-creation potential. You'll also learn the best way to prepare images for the Web and some insight into the often confusing terminology used in image production for this groundbreaking new medium.

Linking Objects to the Web

To realize the full potential of the Web tools at hand, you'll need to grasp two main concepts. Illustrator 7 enables you to use the Web to its maximum potential by providing the user with the capabilities to accomplish two goals. First, Illustrator enables you to *link* drawing objects to the Web and directly connect to a specified location on the Web through your own *browser* software via assigned *URLs*. The term URL (Uniform Resource Locator) describes a site's actual link address on the Web, while a browser is the name given to a program that enables you to locate and display a prepared Web page published or posted to the Web.

Note *Although Illustrator 7 features an excellent tool set for creating Web page images, it doesn't enable you to create complete Web pages. Instead, Adobe develops and markets separate software specifically for this purpose, including Adobe PageMill, which is geared toward creating individual pages, and SiteMill, which enables users to create and manage larger Web sites. Adobe's recent release of its market-leading PageMaker software also enables users to create multipage Web sites automatically from existing documents.*

The second capability of Illustrator 7's Web tools enables you to assign Web locations to objects in advance of preparing them for use in Web pages through Illustrator's Export command. While all Web page creation software programs enable designers to assign URLs to text and graphic images, most lack the capability to assign multiple URLs to specific areas of an image. This process is called *image mapping*.

For example, if you were creating an image of a map for a Web page design and you needed to assign different URL links to various regions on your map, Illustrator features the tools to do this, where many Web page creation programs can't. The application of this image mapping technology extends well beyond the uses of literally mapping regions on a map graphic. In essence, the ability to assign URL links to objects enables you to make any images in Web page designs clickable and interactive. With a little imagination, the creative applications are nearly limitless.

Before going much further here, it's important for you to grasp the difference between Illustrator 7's two linking strengths. One enables you to link to a Web page through a browser directly from your Illustrator 7 document, while the other enables you to prepare image maps for use in Web page design—with the eventual aim of linking through the Web to specific URL links. It's a slightly fuzzy line that will probably become much clearer to you as you follow along in the remaining sections of this chapter.

The Attributes Palette URL Command

For both linking strategies described in the previous section, the initial controls reside in the Attributes palette, as shown here. The Attributes palette (F11) includes options for assigning links to objects as well as providing you with the ability to verify the link addresses you have assigned to objects through a Launch Browser button.

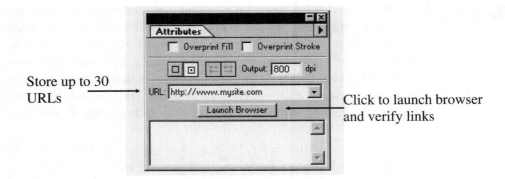

Store up to 30 URLs

Click to launch browser and verify links

The Attributes palette also contains other options specific to printing, transforming, output resolution, and annotating objects in your Illustrator 7 drawing. For more information on using the Attributes palette and these options, see "Setting Object Attributes," **Chapter 8: Selecting and Arranging objects**.

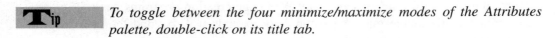

To toggle between the four minimize/maximize modes of the Attributes palette, double-click on its title tab.

To assign a URL to an object you must first select it and then enter the complete address in the URL box on the Attributes palette. Once the URL has been entered, press the ENTER key to complete the command. The new URL you entered is automatically added to the URL drop-down menu. This drop-down menu automatically lists the most recent URLs you have assigned to objects and allows you the convenience of selecting them from the list to assign them to subsequent objects. The drop-down list is capable of showing up to 30 recent addresses.

To increase the number of URLs listed, choose Palette Options from the flyout menu at the right of the palette and enter a value up to 30, as shown next. The URL list is not document-specific and carries with it the most recent URL addresses between documents and program launches.

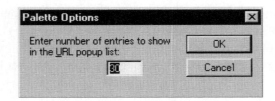

You may also use clipboard functions associated with Cut (CTRL/COMMAND+X), Copy (CTRL/COMMAND+C), Paste (CTRL/COMMAND+V), and Clear when entering URL addresses in the Attributes palette. Windows users may also right mouse button-click to access these commands while Macintosh users may use COMMAND+click to view context-sensitive information.

When entering a URL, it's critical to enter the complete address. Typical Web page addresses feature the prefix "*http://*" before the specific address names, although this may not always be the case. Some addresses may point to other types of Web site addresses indicated by the FTP (File Transfer Protocol) prefix. The colon and forward-slash characters are also critical to the address. The remainder of the URL address will deal specifically with the location of the Web site on the Internet. Although many addresses begin with the three Ws and include periods for separations, many do not, and it wise to check.

Entering a URL is a new concept for many users, and for this reason Adobe has implemented a way for you to double-check and verify that you have the correct one. The Launch Browser button on the Attributes palette enables you to test the link you have entered. To verify this address, you'll need to have browser software installed on your system and a functioning Internet connection. Connections can be made directly through service providers or indirectly via a network or gateway connection. The two most popular browsers are Microsoft Internet Explorer and Netscape Navigator.

 If you select multiple objects which have different URLs assigned to them, the Attributes palette indicates that <multiple URLs> are selected in the URL drop-down menu.

If you have a working Internet connection and browsing software, you may verify an object's URL by following these steps:

With Illustrator 7 running and a new or existing file open, select the object you wish to assign a URL link to and press F11 to access the Attributes palette.

1. If the Attributes palette isn't maximized far enough to show the URL box, double-click on the title of the palette until it is.

2. With the object selected, enter your Web page link address in the URL box and press ENTER. Although nothing seems to happen, you have just assigned a URL to your object.

3. To verify the link you have just assigned, and with the object still selected, click the Launch Browser button. Notice that your browser software is launched and your connection procedure is carried out, including your usual password sequences and so on. If you receive an error message indicating that there is no valid location for the address, check the address to make sure it includes the proper prefixes and format.

4. To return to Illustrator 7, select it from the application icon (Mac) or the Task Bar (Windows).

Once your browser is launched, you may check other objects with URLs assigned in your document using the same procedures by clicking on the object and clicking the Launch Browser button again. Illustrator 7 will automatically make your browser the active application each time the Launch Browser button is pressed.

 You can assign URL addresses to multiple objects by selecting them and entering or selecting a link address in the URL box.

Illustrator 7's Web Page Command

If you have an Internet connection, you probably already know that there's an entire world of information out there on the Web just waiting for you to explore. With this in mind, Adobe has implemented two shortcuts to make it easier for you to access their own Web site and other sites that may be of interest to you, including Image Club, makers of the clip art images included with your Illustrator 7 program.

Both shortcuts are located under the Help menu and launch your browser software automatically to take you to a specific location on each of these Web sites. In the case of the Image Club Web site, certain information about your program, such as the serial number and exact release version of your Illustrator 7 program, is exchanged with the site, and you are presented with a screen similar to the one shown in Figure 18-1.

In the case of the Adobe Illustrator Web site shortcut, you are presented with a screen similar to the one shown in Figure 18-2. For Illustrator 7 users, both sites provide valuable information about new products and resources available and information regarding any current software updates for Illustrator 7, as well as troubleshooting, frequently asked questions (*FAQs*,) and so on.

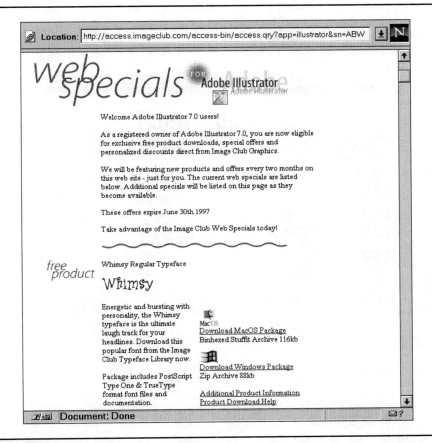

FIGURE 18-1   The Image Club link takes you directly to the Image Club
Web site

For more information on the resources available on the Web at the Osborne
Fundamental Illustrator 7 Web site, see **Appendix C: The WWW.Osborne.com/
Illustrator7 Web Site**.

Preparing Images for the Web

When you are creating drawing elements for the Web, there are a number of
considerations and issues to familiarize yourself with before you proceed too far.

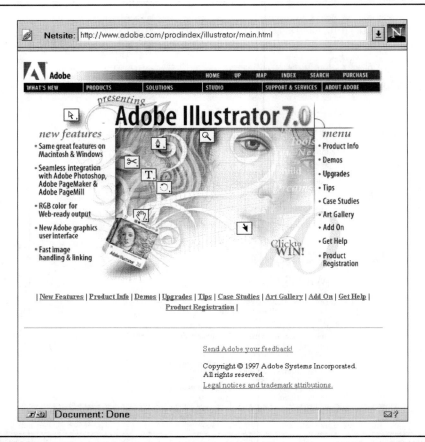

FIGURE 18-2   Adobe's Illustrator 7 Web site offers software updates, news and product information, and technical data

Although producing images for the print world is a fairly straightforward process easily accomplished through Illustrator 7's print engine, preparing images for the Web is another story completely. The Web world has been standardized to a great extent, but several image formats exist. Some involve simple export procedures, while others require specialized steps depending on the condition your drawing images are in.

For example, if your drawing objects are to be used as Web page design elements, the most common formats involved are JPEG (Joint Photographers Expert Group)

and GIF (Graphical Interchange Format) file types. Before preparing to export your drawing elements, you will have a number of questions to answer, such as image color depth, image shape, file compression, display methods, and so on. While JPEG (pronounced "Jay-peg") format offers varying degrees of file compression with the aim of producing files that are as small as possible, the GIF (pronounced "Jiff") compression remains fixed. It's also important to keep in mind that both JPEG and GIF are bitmap file formats.

Regarding color, JPEG offers the widest range of color depth, featuring more than 16 million possible colors. The GIF format offers only an 8-bit color palette up to 256 colors in depth. JPEG is best suited to square or rectangular-shaped photographic images, while GIF can be adapted to suit nonrectangular shaped images by way of color masking options. The GIF file format also offers the potential to create crude animations using special image-assembling software. In recent years, the ability to include these animations has made GIF images the format of choice for many such images.

For display options, these two formats differ also. Standard JPEG images display in a linear fashion while recently "progressive" JPEG formats have made it possible to display these images more quickly. The term *progressive display* refers to the ability of images to begin their display quickly but crudely and become more detailed as the complete file loads onto a Web page.

On the other hand, GIF images have long had the ability to display progressively, in a venetian-blind fashion. And, although their color is limited to a 256-color palette, GIF images can display as nicely as JPEG images, although in some cases the file size may be larger than the JPEG format. So, as you might guess, the issues are sticky ones, and although this section describes how to prepare images in both of the popular and standard image formats, the real decision is up to you once you've answered the following questions for yourself:

- What shape will the final image be: rectangular or odd-shaped?

- How many colors will my final image be: just a few or many?

- Is the image photographic or graphic?

- Is file size a factor?

- How do I want the image to display on the Web page?

- Are there any current restrictions on the type of image format I can use?

If some objects in the drawing you are preparing for the Web contain detailed color such as gradients, the JPEG format may be provide better results than GIF.

Exporting to the Web

Once you've answered these questions for yourself, you can proceed with the preparation of your image. Image preparation is accomplished through use of Illustrator 7's Export command found under the File menu. This section describes the export process to both JPEG and GIF formats as well as the PNG (portable network graphic) format which is on its way to becoming more popular.

Exporting your drawing images to the Web is a highly specific purpose that requires the Export command, but if you aren't familiar with usual exporting procedures you might find the whole process a mystery. Instead of proceeding beyond this point, it may be best to thumb through the section called "Using Export and Save As Commands" in **Chapter 16: Importing and Exporting from Illustrator 7**.

  Once your drawing objects are exported to bitmap, you will no longer be able to edit them as vector objects. Instead, bitmap images may best be edited using a dedicated bitmap editing program such as Adobe Photoshop.

Using JPEG Formats

Before using the JPEG format to export your drawing objects, let's explore a little more of this format's characteristics. First, one of the unique strengths of JPEG is that it offers varying degrees of file compression in a sort of trade-off scheme. JPEG is capable of producing very small file sizes in exchange for compromised image quality. In other words, the smaller the file, the worse it looks, and vice-versa.

This compression technique is referred to by its creators as *lossy* compression. Lossy compression can be set in various settings to sacrifice image quality for file size. For some types of images, a certain degree of your image's quality loss can be tolerated if the resulting smaller file size is a priority.

The JPEG export filter in Illustrator 7 enables you to set these varying degrees of image compression and format options using an interactive slider control with numeric, drop-down menu options as shown below.

JPEG Options ☒

Image Options

Quality: [5] [Medium ▼]

smaller file   larger file
△

Format Options
  ⦿ Baseline (Standard)
  ○ Baseline Optimized
  ○ Progressive
      Scans: [3 ▼]

[OK]

[Cancel]

18

The JPEG filter features two main categories of options for you to select from, comprised of image and format options. While the image options enable you to set the amount of lossy compression, the format options set the display style according to your preferences. Image quality options within the JPEG export dialog box consist of the following:

■ **Quality (numeric entry)**   You may set the quality of the image within a numeric range between zero and ten. Entering a value of zero produces the poorest image quality but the smallest file size, while a value of ten renders the highest quality but the largest possible file size. Values entered in the numeric box are reflected in both the drop-down menu and the slider control. The default value is set to the middle-of-the-road setting of five.

■ **Quality (drop-down menu)**   As a form of convenience and demonstrated explanation, you may choose from one of four preset quality selections: Low (1), Medium (3), High (6), and Maximum (8).

■ **Slider control**   Using the slider control to interactively set the image quality level has the same effect as entering values in the numeric quality box. It's simply a more intuitive way of setting your JPEG image quality level.

Image display options for your resulting JPEG image may be set to one of three formats: Baseline (Standard), Baseline Optimized, and Progressive. These options set your image display qualities as follows:

- **Baseline (Standard)**   Using this setting produces a JPEG image in standard color format readable by all browsers.

- **Baseline Optimized**   This setting produces a JPEG image to an optimized color format also readable by all browsers. The optimized option often takes a little longer to compress an image file but results in smaller file sizes by as much as 30 percent without any noticeable image quality loss. This option may also produce images which decompress faster than the Baseline (Standard) option.

- **Progressive**   The Progressive option creates a slightly different type of display style for your resulting image. Progressive JPEG is a relatively new style of JPEG readable by most recently released browsers. The resulting image is loaded into the Web page browser, beginning with a crude, low-quality representation which continuously improves in steps as the remaining image data is loaded. In effect, progressively displaying images enables the audience of your Web page to get a general idea of what the image is depicting before it finishes loading into the host browser. When the Progressive option is selected, the Scans drop-down menu becomes available, enabling you to set the number of steps in the file loading progression. Scans may be set to either 3, 4, or 5.

Note   *Although Progressive JPEG files load into a browser in a most intriguing way, they require more file memory size and host system RAM (random access memory).*

The resulting file size of your JPEG image will ultimately be determined by the physical dimensions of the drawing objects you are exporting, the level of quality you choose, and other display options you select.

Using GIF Formats

Now, you may not normally get too excited about something as mundane as export file formats, but GIF is a format which has proven more versatile than any other image format to date. The original GIF image was created specifically for Compuserve, one of the first worldwide privately established online networks. GIF comes in two basic flavors: the original GIF 87A (not available in Illustrator 7's export options) and extended GIF89A formats. Without knowing the identity of the original creators of this format, you can't help but consider them incredible visionaries. While GIF images offer only one level of compression, this format can be set to generate a wide variety of display results.

In contrast to the JPEG lossy image format, GIF compression is *lossless,* meaning image quality can't be sacrificed for file size. The GIF image format uses LZW (Lempel-Ziv-Welch) compression, which enables relatively high image quality together with reasonably small file sizes. The wild card in the GIF format is in the number of colors required to reproduce the resulting image.

GIF images carry their own color palette recipe which they need to display properly. This color palette can hold up to 256 colors and can be any of the 16.7 million colors reproducible on a computer monitor. And, as you might have guessed, small color palettes mean smaller file sizes. Hence, GIFs can be fine-tuned to contain the least number of colors in order to reduce their overall file size.

But the greatest strength of GIF images may not be their flexible color palette size so much as the other properties they can feature. The GIF format is capable of supporting the following properties:

- Transparency masks

- Multiple images

- Global color palettes

- Image looping in the form of simple animation

- Nondestructive text blocks, including hidden comments, display text, and application blocks

- Interlace and time-limited delay display

- User input display

- In the case of Illustrator 7, image map support through HTML

Now, while some of these amazing properties are not available through Illustrator 7's GIF export filter, it's important to realize they exist. Granted, many of us use a wide variety of applications to "get the job done" and so consider this an insight into the many potentials of GIF. Once a GIF file has been created, other programs exist to enable you to edit the hidden potentials not available in Illustrator 7's export filter.

Getting back to reality, Illustrator 7's GIF export filter, does contain a number of options for generating these types of images. The are comprised of palette controls and display options as follows:

- **Palette**   The GIF image palette may be set to be created with one of several palette "recipes" depending on where your image is to be used and how it is to be displayed. Palette options are comprised of Exact, System (Macintosh), System (Windows), Web, Adaptive, or Custom. For the purposes of creating images for the Web, it's best to choose the Web palette option. This is best when creating a GIF image which is to be used with other images on the same Web page. The Web palette contains 216 colors common to both Macintosh and Windows browsers and maps colors featured in your GIF image directly to a corresponding color in this palette. The bottom line here is that the Web palette option is probably your best choice.

Note   *Beware when using the Exact or Adaptive GIF image palettes in situations where the image you are creating for the Web is to be used with other GIF images. If the color palettes of each GIF image on the Web page differ greatly, the host browser may not display the images properly due to palette display conflicts. Play it safe by selecting the Web palette.*

- **Colors**   The Colors option becomes available when using the Exact or Adaptive palette options and may be set to map your image as closely as possible to a specified number of palette colors from 1 to a maximum of 256.

- **Dither**   Use the dither option if the drawing objects you are exporting are of a photographic or highly detailed nature, such as those images containing gradient colors. Dithering has the effect of adding a checkerboard pattern to your GIF images in an effort to simulate color and tone and slightly increases file size.

- **Interlace**   The term *interlace* refers to the display style of the GIF image. Selecting this option enables your images to load progressively in a venetian-blind manner and essentially enables the audience of the Web page the advantage of seeing a crude representation of the image before it finishes loading.

■ **Transparent**   Use the transparent option if the image you are preparing for the Web is uneven in shape. In effect, this places a transparency "mask" into your image so that the background of the Web page shows through instead of a white bounding box (the default). Transparency masks are unique to—and one of the strengths of—the GIF image format. Illustrator 7's GIF export filter automatically chooses a color not found in your image and assigns it as transparent.

■ **Anti-alias**   The term *anti-alias* refers to the effect of blending adjacent, or "touching," colors in your image. Anti-aliasing is best suited for exporting graphic images where undesirable jagged color edges would otherwise appear. But, while anti-aliasing improves the image effects when exporting graphic objects, it has little effect on photographic type images except to add an undesirable blending effect around the perimeter of the image.

■ **Image map**   Select the Image Map option if you have assigned URLs to the object(s) you are exporting. Image maps load with the image into the Web page, making the image clickable and interactive in an effort to enable the Web page audience to follow links to other Web pages. Selecting the Image map option creates either a client-side or server-side information file which contains the link information for the image you are exporting.

■ **Client-side/Server-side**   Client-side image maps is the correct selection to make if the image map you are creating is to be used in a Web page creation program such as Adobe's PageMill or SiteMill. An extra file is created to accompany the GIF image and contains coordinates and URL information needed to complete the link. This extra file is created as an HTM (Windows) or HTML (Mac) document and is needed when creating the final Web page layout. Select the Server-side image map option only if you are certain of the parameters of the server on which the image file will reside. The best advice here is to contact the service provider or server administrator for the necessary parameters.

■ **Anchor**   Anchors are information files which are created only when using the client-side option. Anchors are used in situations where more than one image map exists on a Web page and offer a way of uniquely identifying the HTML linking information they contain. By default, the

18

name of the Anchor file matches the name of your exported image file, but it may be any name you wish.

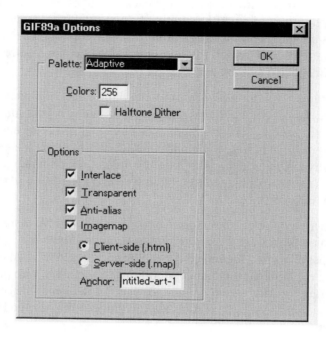

Using PNG Formats

The PNG (portable network graphic) format is essentially an alternative to the GIF format. Although this format isn't as flexible or versatile as GIF, it can serve as a useful second choice. The PNG export dialog options come in the form of a two-step image export process, the first of which involves choosing a resolution of your image, as shown here.

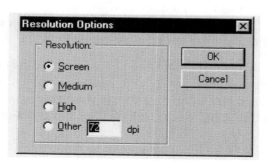

Resolution options are comprised of Screen (72), Medium (150), High (300), and Other. For the Web, though, only Screen and Other apply. Using the Screen option automatically sets your exported PNG file to a resolution of 72 dpi—optimum for most screen viewing. Medium and High options far exceed screen-display capabilities.

PNG files may also feature interlace display and various compression options selected in the second stage of this export process, as shown below. To set interlace display, choose Adam7.

Compression options in the second stage of the PNG export dialog box are comprised of various filtering algorithms such as Sub, Up, Average, Paeth, and Adaptive, all of which generate similar-quality images. The PNG features lossless compression, and file sizes vary slightly depending on the filtering algorithm selected.

To its credit, the PNG format supports 24-bit color, which is higher than that of GIF. Unfortunately, the PNG format does not support transparency masks, so images must always be rectangular-shaped, nor does it feature any of the other advantages of the GIF image format. In rare cases where the GIF file format isn't an option, PNG may serve as a potential substitute.

Preparing Drawings in PDF

Adobe's PDF (portable document file) format has long been touted as one of the leading page composition and display formats for use on the World Wide Web.

However, before you plunge headlong into saving all of your drawings in this format, there's something you need to be aware of.

In order to view a PDF page, your Web audience needs to have the correct plug-ins installed into their Web browser—an extra step the majority of Internet Web site visitors never take. For many new users to the Internet, installing a plug-in is akin to rocket science. In fact, with the growing number of image-specific plug-ins for viewing specialized images on Web pages, the likelihood that someone viewing a "PDF-enabled" Web page will have the PDF plug-in installed is far less likely.

However, having stated that disclaimer, a growing number of applications are continuing to support PDF, and while not everyone may be capable of reading the pages online, it does offer a wide variety of versatility and flexibility and is uniformly portable across UNIX, Macintosh, Windows, and DOS platforms.

The PDF format essentially uses PostScript Level 2 page description language as a basis and is capable of displaying both vector and bitmap images as well as any compatible type font. Documents may also be set to include an electronic table of contents and hyperlinks between various pages and sections. Adobe's Acrobat Reader Version 3.0 software is included on the Adobe Illustrator 7 program disc.

Illustrator 7 features the capability of saving individual drawings readable by Adobe Acrobat Reader but lacks the capability to create multiple pages and hyperlinks between sections. However, PDF files may be opened, edited, and resaved using the current filters in Illustrator 7. But, because Illustrator 7 does not support multiple pages featured in many PDF files, you may only open one page at a time for viewing, editing and saving.

To open a PDF file into Illustrator 7, use the Open (CTRL/COMMAND+O) command and choose PDF as the file type. If the file features only one page, Illustrator opens it directly. If the PDF file contains more than a single page, use the Acrobat PDF Plug-in to specify which page to open, as shown below.

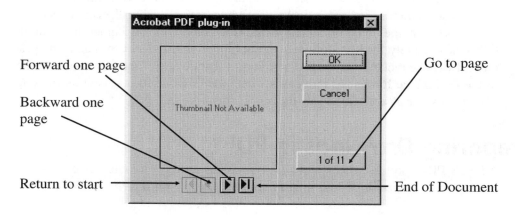

Forward one page

Backward one page

Return to start

Go to page

End of Document

The PDF plug-in filter enables you to open a specific page by clicking on the arrow buttons indicated. If a miniature preview of the page is available, it will appear in the thumbnail window. Once the page has been opened, it can be edited and resaved using Illustrator 7's Save (CTRL/COMMAND+S) or Close (CTRL/COMMAND+W) commands. Pages that are opened from multiple documents are automatically returned in the same page sequence they were opened from.

When Creating Image Maps . . .

As described earlier in this chapter, image maps are created by assigning individual URLs to objects and exporting the collection of objects to the GIF89A file format with the Image Map option selected. An image map is an image which has been prepared specifically for use in a Web page browser whereby certain areas of the image have been designated with a unique URL link. Image maps enable Web page visitors to click on the image they see and interactively follow a link to a page containing information related to where they clicked. In the case of image mapping, a picture can be worth *far more* than a thousand words.

The beauty of being able to create image maps directly in Illustrator 7 is that you needn't waste time and energy tracking down and employing the use of a third-party image map utility. Image map utilities usually involve designating specifically shaped areas of an image to a certain URL link. These third-party utilities often came in the form of shareware or freeware and were greatly limited in their capacity to match mapping shapes to exact image shapes. Illustrator 7's image mapping feature automatically assigns a map area to an object based on its shape.

Tip *Although Illustrator enables you to create an image map quickly and automatically from an existing drawing which contains assigned URL links, it does not feature any method to edit the image map once it's been created. This can present problems if you're not careful. For example, you may encounter problems when assigning URL links to very small drawing objects which may be difficult for your Web page audience to click on. In cases such as these, it may be wise to create an invisible larger object around the smaller object and assign the URL link to it instead. You can make objects seemingly invisible by assigning both the object's Fill and Stroke to None.*

Note *If at all possible, review and test the image map you create before posting it to the Web or integrating it into a Web page design. To do this, use the procedures described in the previous section, "Attributes Palette URL Command," in this chapter.*

Conclusion

Adobe Illustrator 7 includes some very powerful and useful Web-related functions which enable you to link your drawing objects directly to the Web and prepare images specifically for use in Web page design. This chapter has identified and fleshed out these features for you, which are spread throughout various locations in the program. You've also explored some of the issues dealing directly with Web images and their preparation.

Fundamental Illustrator 7 may help you further explore some of the functions related to preparing other types of images, namely through exporting your images. Be sure to thumb through the section called "Using Export and Save As Commands" in **Chapter 16: Importing and Exporting from Illustrator 7**. You may also find information related to resolution and bitmap image properties a useful read in sections at the start of **Chapter 14: Working with Bitmap Tools**.

PART

V

Reference

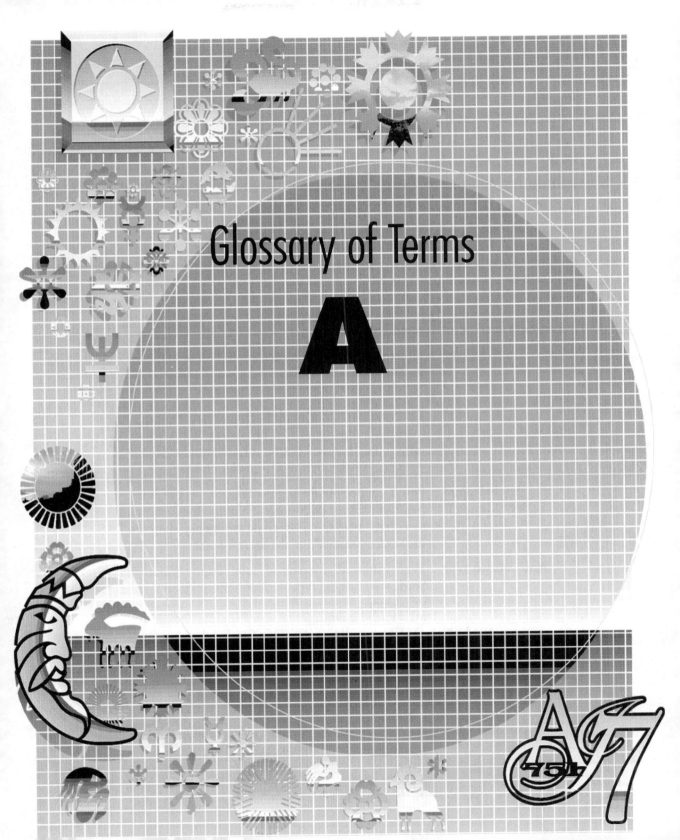

Glossary of Terms

A

Throughout Fundamental Illustrator 7 you may find yourself reading terms specific to certain technical worlds. This book reaches into a number of areas that often detail particular techniques, features, or drawing strategies when using Illustrator 7. These terms may stem from areas such as digital illustration, printing, design, art, or the World Wide Web.

This alphabetical glossary provides you with a comprehensive definition of these terms as they pertain to using the program and the topics they discuss. It is by no means a complete index to all terms used throughout your Illustrator 7 drawing experiences but will likely provide you with ample insight into areas you may not be familiar with. Consult it regularly.

1-bit	This refers to a color format consisting of black (or any RGB color) and white only and usually refers to color schemes associated with line art.
8-bit	This color format features the maximum available for thumbnail viewing of files consisting of 256 colors only and usually refers to color schemes associated with preview headers or GIF image formats.
Anchor point	Points connecting the segments of a path. Anchor points on curved paths have direction lines and points associated with them which determine the shapes of the segments adjoining the anchor points.
Anti-aliased type	Type displayed onscreen with lighter pixels along its borders so that the type outlines appear smooth rather than jagged.
Area type	Type in a container that can be either a closed or open path.
Artwork mode	A method of viewing an Illustrator 7 document that displays the outline of paths but not their fills or strokes.
Autotrace gap	A setting in the Preferences|General dialog box which sets the behavior of the Autotrace tool.

Baseline The imaginary straight line on which all type rests. Baselines usually align with flat-bottomed letters (not including descenders in letters such as *p* or *q*). The bottom edge of rounded letters usually falls below the baseline, creating the illusion that they are aligned with the baseline. Baselines are used in typography to measure the leading of type.

Baseline shift The amount of space a character is offset above or below its baseline.

Brush stroke A brush stroke is simply a shape drawn with the Paint Brush tool. Once created, shapes drawn in this manner have no special characteristics.

Byte The smallest measure of file size, equivalent to 8 bits of digital information.

Calligraphic lines Actually shapes drawn with the Paint Brush tool. The shapes vary in width along an axis specified in the Paint Brush Options dialog box (double-click the Paint Brush icon in the Tool palette), but otherwise have no special characteristics.

Character attributes Formatting options that can be applied at the level of individual characters.

Clip art Third-party vendor artwork sold for commercial use and free of any associated royalties to the artists who created it. Clip art has been in existence for decades in one form or another and can be an extremely useful resource for both commercial artists and nonartistic users alike.

Closed path A path with its first and last anchor points connected.

CMYK Stands for the four basic ink colors used in process color printing, cyan, magenta, yellow, and black.

Color model A model by which color properties of all bitmap (and conventional) colors are measured. Illustrator features four basic color models: CMYK, RGB, Grayscale, and 1-bit models.

Compound paths   Two or more overlapping paths that have been combined using the Objects|Compound Paths|Make menu command (CTRL/COMMAND+8). Where the paths overlap, transparent holes may be seen through the object.

Constrain   In the case of Illustrator 7, constrain is the act of limiting movement, transformation, or rotation of objects or tool actions to 45-degree angles.

Curve fitting tolerance   A setting in the Preferences|General dialog box (CTRL/COMMAND+K) which sets behavior of how tightly or loosely a path conforms to the freehand line used to create it when using the Pen, Pencil, or Autotrace Tools.

Default   A system's software setting when shipped from the software publisher. In most instances, default means that you may change the setting to something other than the default.

Desktop   Refers to the interface part of your computer where you can manage shortcuts and have quick access to major computer components or network drives. If no programs are currently opened on your computer, the desktop is what you will see.

Direction line   A handle extending from an anchor point; the location of the direction point at the end of the direction line determines the shape of the adjoining path segment.

Direction point   A point at the end of a direction line, the location of which determines the shape of the adjoining path segment.

Discretionary hyphen   (CTRL/COMMAND+SHIFT+HYPHEN): A hyphen used to break a word at the end of a line of type if necessary. Discretionary hyphens appear only if a word requires hyphenation due to column spacing limitations.

DPI   Stands for dots per inch and refers to the resolution—or degree of detail—of a digital image.

Drag-and-drop   This term refers to dragging files from a file folder directly to a program icon or program window and is usually associated with object linking and embedding (OLE) commands, file open commands, or importing functions.

Em dash   A dash the width of the small letter *m* in a given font.

Embed   A file or font is said to be embedded if it features no external links to source files and can be transported from one location to another without requiring any additional data files.

En dash   A dash the width of the small letter *n* in a given font.

EPS   Stands for encapsulated PostScript and refers to the self-contained page description language used as a standard in the digital imaging and desktop publishing industry. EPS was invented by Adobe Systems.

File extension   This refers to the two- or three-letter code following most Windows file names.

Fill   The color within the boundaries of an open or closed path of an object or type. The fill may be solid color or a gradient between two or more colors. Fill may also be a pattern.

Font family   All the characters, including letters, numbers, and symbols, of a typeface.

Font size   The height available for the characters of a font family. It includes room for capital letters, ascenders, descenders, and optional space above and below the characters.

Font style   A variation, such as bold or italic on a typeface design.

Font substitution   Font substitution is something you'd like to stay away from if at all possible. Font substitution occurs automatically and usually incorrectly when a file is either opened or imported. If the host system does not have the proper fonts installed, the host program will usually substitute its own font in place of the missing fonts.

Freehand path A freehand path is simply a path drawn by hand with the Pencil tool. Once created, paths drawn in this manner have no special characteristics.

Gradient The continuum between two color selections in a filled object used for shading and coloring objects.

Grayscale This term stems from the early days of film developing. In those days, it represented a standard measure of gray values, which by sheer coincidence was the invention of someone by the name of Gray and has since been adapted to the digital world. Gray values were divided into set values to establish benchmarks for consistent film developing. It's also one of the four color models by which Illustrator 7 measures, creates, or converts color objects or images. The Grayscale color model is based on process color black ink and is measured using percentage values between 0 and 100.

Greeked type Small type that is displayed onscreen as gray bars rather than individual characters.

Greeking When waiting for text to draw on your screen becomes tedious or excessively time-consuming, type can be "greeked." This means that instead of your screen rendering all type details, a gray bar is used instead. Enabling your text to greek through options in the Preferences (CTRL/COMMAND+K) dialog box will greatly increase the speed at which your screen redraws very small type.

Group Two or more objects connected as a unit by the Group Command.

Header A portion of a file that contains information visually describing the file. Headers usually consist of low or medium resolution information in either 1-bit or 8-bit color. Also referred to as a "preview."

HSB Stands for hue, saturation, and brightness and is one of the color models used in the digital world to measure color and brightness values of a digital image.

Insertion point The point at which type will appear when it is entered. Indicated by a flashing vertical line.

Kerning The amount of space between adjacent characters.

Landscape In Illustrator 7, this term refers to the orientation of the page size you are currently drawing on or the orientation of the material you intend to print your drawing onto. Landscape orientation indicates that the page is oriented with the longer measure as the width. The term is actually borrowed from the an art reference to landscape painting formats, where wider frame sizes could accommodate a larger landscape area.

Leading The point measure between baselines of two or more lines of type.

Ligatures A single piece of type which combines two or more letters, such as *fl* or *fi*.

Linked containers Type containers joined using the Type|Blocks|Link menu command so that type flows from one container to the other.

LPI Stands for lines per inch, and is commonly associated with the number of dots counted in a linear inch when measuring screen frequency of film output.

Macro A series of file commands that are carried out automatically as a way of increasing productivity. Macros can be recorded, stored, and played back at the command of the user.

Marquee selection Dragging the mouse while holding down the left mouse button to draw a rectangle around objects to be selected.

Mask In the case of Illustrator 7, a mask essentially represents a clipping path for objects or images and is an object used as a frame for other objects. A mask uses its outline as the frame of all objects that are visible inside the mask's boundaries. When used for rasterized images, the mask serves as the visual boundary for the bitmap image. This term also comes into play when referring to transparency masks, which are automatically assigned to unevenly shaped objects as a method of making the negative space around objects transparent. Transparency masks are often used when creating unevenly shaped graphics for use in Web page design.

MDI Stands for multiple document interface, meaning the ability to open more than one file at a time.

Multiple master fonts Fonts designed with various "axes," such as weight and width, which can be manipulated to create a virtually unlimited number of new stylistic variations of the font.

Native file format The term "native" refers to the exclusive file format created by a host program, such as Adobe Illustrator's "AI" file format.

Object selection All or part of one or more objects chosen with a Selection tool for manipulation or painting.

Object transform tools Tools such as the Scale tool and Shear tool that allow you to manipulate the shape, size, and location of objects and type.

Objects In Illustrator, an object may be a single anchor point, a line segment including two anchor points, or several connected line segments and anchor points that join to form an open or closed path.

Opaque An object through which no light or color may be seen, such as a brick wall. In contrast, a glass window is transparent.

Open path A path with its first and last anchor points unconnected.

Orientation   This term refers to the way in which a page is aligned. Pages may be set to landscape (wide) or portrait (tall) orientation.

Painting   The action of applying a stroke and/or fill to an object or type.

Paragraph attributes   Formatting options that apply to entire paragraphs

Path   A series of anchor points and the segments connecting them.

Path commands   Commands, accessed from the Path submenu of the Objects menu, used to edit existing paths.

Path type   Type that follows the contour of a path.

PICT   A file format commonly used on Macintosh that supports both vector and bitmap.

Pixel   The smallest measure of a bitmap image or screen resolution.

Plug-ins   Adobe includes plug-ins for all sorts of commands, filters, and features. A plug-in is essentially a programming script that carries out a series of commands.

Port   The term used to describe a native program file that is readable between platform versions of a program—for example, opening an Adobe Illustrator 7 Windows version file on a Macintosh or Power Macintosh platform.

Portrait   In Illustrator 7, this term refers to the orientation of the page size you are currently drawing on, or the orientation of the material you intend to print your drawing onto. Portrait orientation indicates that the page is oriented with the longer measure as the tall side. The term is actually borrowed from the an art reference to portrait painting formats, where taller frame sizes better accommodated paintings of people.

A

Preferences   In the software world, this refers to a set of editable global program parameters and settings that enable you to customize operation of a program.

Preview   A portion of a file that contains information visually describing the file. Previews usually consist of low- or medium-resolution information in either 1-bit or 8-bit color. Also referred to as a "header."

Preview mode   A method of viewing an Illustrator 7 document that displays the fills and strokes of paths. Preview mode approximates what the final, printed document will look like.

Printable page   The portion of your artboard indicated by the inner dashed line of two rectangles. Printable page size is determined by the page size set in your Page Setup dialog box options and the physical properties of your selected printer.

Printed page   The portion of your artboard indicated by the outer dashed line of two rectangles. Printed page size is determined by the page size set in your Page Setup dialog box options.

Random selection   The ability to choose any object randomly while other objects remain selected.

Raster   Another term used to describe bitmap. In Illustrator 7, vector objects may be converted to bitmap formats using the Rasterize command found under the Object menu.

Resolution   Describes the inherent detail contained in a digital image such as a bitmap. Resolution may be referred to in dots per inch or parts per inch.

RGB   Stands for red, green, blue and originally referred to the three colored light guns used to project color in hardware such as your television screen, computer monitors, and presentation equipment. RGB is also widely used in the digital industry to measure color values with each color graduated on a scale between 0 and 255.

Scratch disk Illustrator 7 uses scratch disks to store temporary files when working with drawings on systems where not enough RAM is present to serve Illustrator 7's needs. Temporary files can be stored on either a Primary or Secondary scratch disk.

Selection The active object indicated by the visible default color outline and anchor points.

Service bureau An outside vendor used to supply high-resolution digital output or high-quality and/or high-volume color proofing and printing. Some specialize in electronic prepress and/or support services such as scanning and/or computer-to-plate technology.

Shortcut icon An icon may be a representation of a program file or folder. Icons are usually set up on the desktop of your operating system interface and may represent quick access to programs or folders, such as the Trash (Macintosh) or Recycle (Windows) folders. For example, on a Macintosh desktop, you may notice when you first install the Mac version of Adobe Illustrator 7 that a shortcut icon is automatically created on your desktop.

Slope This refers to the difference in position between the x and y coordinates on your Illustrator page.

Smart Quotes Curly quotes rather than the straight ones found on typewriters.

Startup file This file stores all of the information, preferences, and custom information you have created while using Illustrator 7. The startup file may be customized to suit your needs.

Stroke The line segment or outline properties of a shape or type object whether color or weight.

System default font	The font installed on every system that is used by all programs in system interface mapping. On Windows platforms, the system default font is Arial, while on Macintosh platforms the system default font can be Helvetica or Courier.
Text selection	Consists of one or more characters chosen with a Type or Selection tool for editing and/or formatting. A text selection is indicated by highlighting. An object selection consists of all or part of one or more objects chosen with a Selection tool for manipulation or painting.
TIFF	Stands for Tagged Image File Format and is a commonly used bitmap format supporting all color modes and models.
Tiling	Documents set to print to page sizes smaller than their artboard dimensions can be printed in "tiles" and reassembled later. Illustrator offers sophisticated tiling features for viewing and printing tiles.
Tracking	When the spacing between words and letters is evenly spaced. Tracking may be adjusted to varying degrees of "looseness" or "tightness."
Type case	How type is capitalized. The three options offered in Illustrator 7's Change Case dialog box are upper (all capitals), lower (no capitals), and mixed (the first letter of each word is capitalized).
Type container	An open or closed path that contains type within its boundaries.
Type object	A point, path, or shape containing editable text.
Type on a point	Type that appears at, and is formatted relative, to a point.
Vector	This term refers to a mathematical description by which straight or curved paths can be described when joining reference points.

Vector images   Images made of objects and lines rather than pixels. The advantages of vector images are that they are easy to create and edit, they can be resized without loss of detail, and vector files are generally smaller than bit-mapped images files.

Vector object   Vector objects are shapes that are made up of line and curve points which join to form open or closed paths.

Vellum   For traditional illustrators, vellum is a smooth drawing material used with pen and ink in drafting and creative arts.

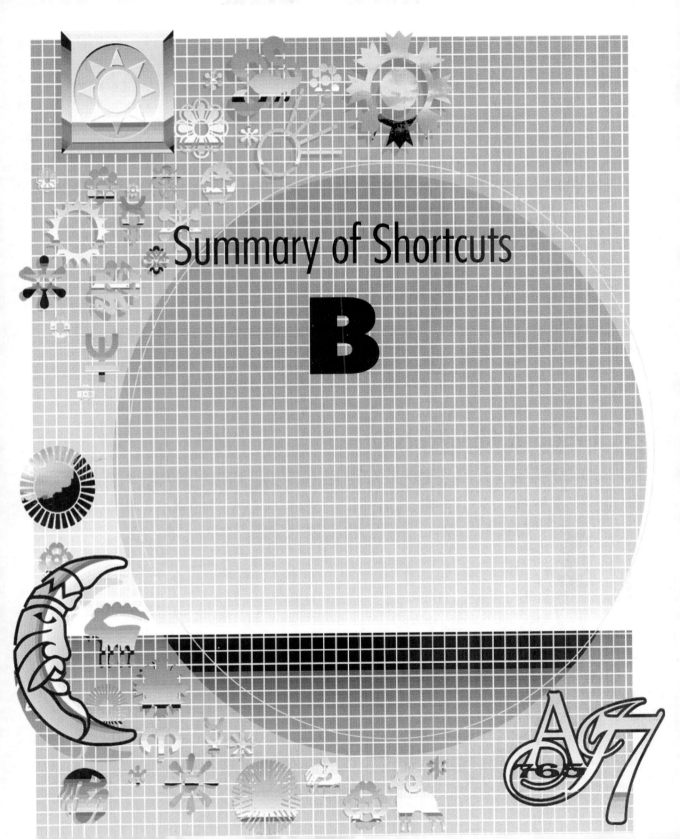

Summary of Shortcuts

B

In the creation and evolution of Illustrator up to version 7, the engineers at Adobe have gone to great lengths to enable program users to increase their productivity by implementing shortcuts. In fact, few other drawing programs even come close to incorporating this level of sophistication. In marrying this enormous collection of mouse and keyboard shortcuts, Adobe has opened the doors for users to learn Illustrator faster and more easily as they become familiar and comfortable with Illustrator 7's commands, effects, and procedures.

In terms of reference, this appendix is perhaps one of the most valuable sources of information in *Fundamental Illustrator 7*. Shortcuts come in all forms including simple keystroke shortcuts, keyboard combinations, and keyboard-and-mouse actions. Some involve reducing time spent accessing command menus, while others assist in reducing object creation, drawing layout, and production time.

Clipboard Shortcuts

Undo	CTRL/COMMAND+Z
Redo	CTRL/COMMAND+SHIFT+Z
Copy	CTRL/COMMAND+C
Paste	CTRL/COMMAND+V
Paste in Front	CTRL/COMMAND+F
Paste in Back	CTRL/COMMAND+B
Cut	CTRL/COMMAND+X

General Menu Commands

New	CTRL/COMMAND+N
Open	CTRL/COMMAND+O
Close	CTRL/COMMAND+W

Save	CTRL/COMMAND+S
Save As	CTRL/COMMAND+SHIFT+S
Save a Copy	CTRL/COMMAND+ALT/OPTION+S
Revert	F12
Separation Setup	CTRL/COMMAND+ALT/OPTION+P
Document Setup	CTRL/COMMAND+SHIFT+P
Print	CTRL/COMMAND+P

Tool and Shape Shortcuts

To display the Options dialog box, which features various settings for the respective tool, double-click on these tool buttons in the Toolbox palette.

B

Move options	Double-click the Selection tool
Paintbrush options	Double-click the Paintbrush tool
Rotate options	Double-click the Rotate tool
Reflect options	Double-click the Reflect tool
Shear options	Double-click the Shear tool
Graph Type options	Double-click the Graph tool
Show Gradient palette	Double-click the Gradient tool
Paintbucket options	Double-click the Paintbucket tool
Eyedropper options	Double-click the Eyedropper tool

Holding certain keyboard combinations while creating shapes such as ellipses, rectangles, stars, polygons, or spirals enables you to interactively manipulate the object's shape and how it is created in the following ways:

Create from center	Hold ALT/OPTION while creating Ellipse or Rectangle
Constrain proportions	Hold SHIFT while creating Ellipse or Rectangle
Set center with dialog box	Mouse click (without dragging) using any shape tool

Reposition shape	Hold the Spacebar during creation of Star, Spiral, or Polygon
Add/Delete sides	Press Up or Down arrow keys while creating Polygon
Add/Delete coils	Press Up or Down arrow keys while creating Spiral
Add/Delete coils relative to size	Alt/Option and drag while creating Spiral
Add/Delete Star points	Press Up or Down arrow keys while creating Star
Reduce inner radius	Ctrl/Command and drag while creating Star

Palette Shortcuts

Character palette	CTRL/COMMAND+T
Color palette	F6
Gradient palette	F9
Info palette	F8
Layers palette	F7
Paragraph palette	CTRL/COMMAND+M
Stroke palette	F10
Swatches palette	F5

General Palette Shortcuts

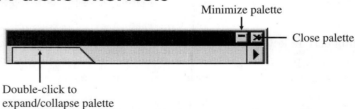

Minimize palette

Close palette

Double-click to expand/collapse palette

Click to delete layer or swatch, ALT/OPTION+click deletes without warning message

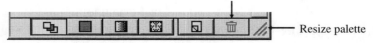

Resize palette

General Notes to Palette Function

SHIFT+TAB to show/hide palettes
TAB to show/hide Toolbox and palettes

When entering palette numeric values:

TAB moves to next field, SHIFT+TAB moves to previous field
SHIFT+ENTER/RETURN applies value and leaves box active
CTRL/COMMAND+~ highlights first value field of most recently
used palette

Toolbox

B

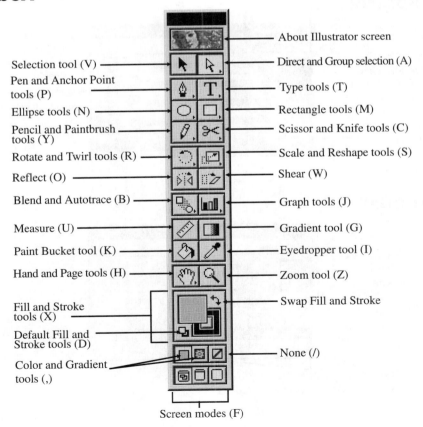

About Illustrator screen

Selection tool (V)
Direct and Group selection (A)

Pen and Anchor Point tools (P)
Type tools (T)

Ellipse tools (N)
Rectangle tools (M)

Pencil and Paintbrush tools (Y)
Scissor and Knife tools (C)

Rotate and Twirl tools (R)
Scale and Reshape tools (S)

Reflect (O)
Shear (W)

Blend and Autotrace (B)
Graph tools (J)

Measure (U)
Gradient tool (G)

Paint Bucket tool (K)
Eyedropper tool (I)

Hand and Page tools (H)
Zoom tool (Z)

Fill and Stroke tools (X)
Swap Fill and Stroke

Default Fill and Stroke tools (D)

Color and Gradient tools (,)
None (/)

Screen modes (F)

Character (CTRL/COMMAND+T)

SHIFT+click to increase/decrease in large increments

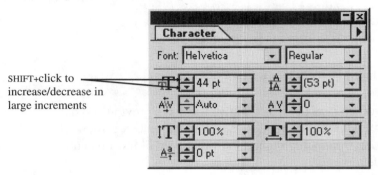

Color (F6)

ALT/OPTION+click chooses fill or stroke, SHIFT+click cycles through HSB, RGB, CMYK, and Grayscale color spaces

In RGB mode, double-click to display percentage/numeric values

SHIFT+drag moves sliders in tandem

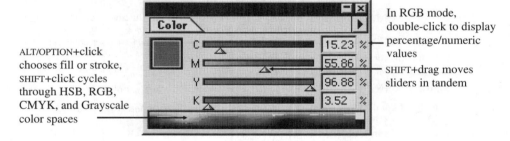

Gradient (F9)

CTRL/COMMAND+click to reset colors to black and white

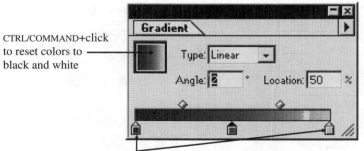

Color Stops: ALT/OPTION+drag to duplicate stops, or ALT/OPTION+drag stop over another stop to swap colors

Layers (F7)

Click to show/hide layer, ALT/OPTION+ click hides/shows all others, drag through eye column to affect multiple layers

Click to lock/unlock layer, ALT/OPTION+click locks/unlocks all other layers

CTRL/COMMAND+click selects Artwork/ Preview view, ALT/ OPTION+click selects view for all other layers

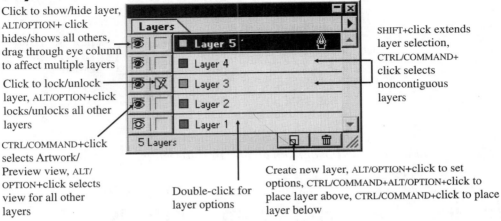

SHIFT+click extends layer selection, CTRL/COMMAND+ click selects noncontiguous layers

Double-click for layer options

Create new layer, ALT/OPTION+click to set options, CTRL/COMMAND+ALT/OPTION+click to place layer above, CTRL/COMMAND+click to place layer below

Swatches (F5)

Double-click to set options, ALT/OPTION+drag to replace colors

SHIFT+click to select range of colors, CTRL/COMMAND+ click to select non-contiguous colors

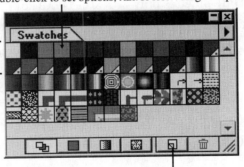

ALT/OPTION+click to display options

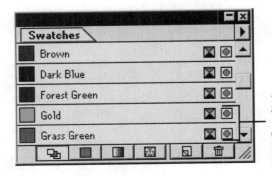

ALT/OPTION+click to choose current gradient stop if gradient is selected

CTRL/COMMAND+ALT/OPTION+click in list, then select first letter of color to select color

Transform

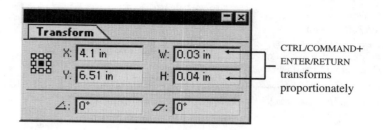

CTRL/COMMAND+
ENTER/RETURN
transforms
proportionately

Note *ALT/OPTION+ENTER/RETURN applies transformation to duplicate*

Viewing, View, and Zoom Shortcuts

Show/Hide Toolbox palettes	TAB key
Show/Hide palettes only	SHIFT+TAB key
Hide Selection	CTRL/COMMAND+U
Show All	CTRL/COMMAND+SHIFT+U
Artwork/Preview	CTRL/COMMAND+Y
Preview Selection	CTRL/COMMAND+SHIFT+Y
Zoom In	CTRL/COMMAND+PLUS key
Zoom Out	CTRL/COMMAND+MINUS key
Fit in Window	CTRL/COMMAND+0
Actual Size	CTRL/COMMAND+1
Hide Edges	CTRL/COMMAND+H
Show/Hide Rulers	CTRL/COMMAND+R
Hide Guides	CTRL/COMMAND+SEMI COLON (;)
Lock Guides	CTRL/COMMAND+ALT/OPTION+SEMI COLON (;)
Make Guides	CTRL/COMMAND+5
Release Guides	CTRL/COMMAND+ALT/OPTION+5
Show/Hide Grid	CTRL/COMMAND+QUOTE (")

Snap to Grid (on, off)	CTRL/COMMAND+QUOTE (")
Show next open document	CTRL+F6 (Windows only)

Note   *In Illustrator 7, CTRL/COMMAND+TAB is used to switch between Selection tools in the first row of the Toolbox, in keeping with Illustrator's long-standing behavior. This means that you cannot use this shortcut to switch between document windows within the application.*

The shortcuts above apply to specific view or zoom commands; the following apply to mouse and keyboard combinations while using tools.

Choose Hand Tool	Hold the SPACEBAR using any tool
Choose Zoom In Tool	Hold CTRL/COMMAND+SPACEBAR using any tool
Choose Zoom Out Tool	Hold CTRL/COMMAND+ALT/OPTION+ SPACEBAR with any tool
Set view to 100 percent	Double-click the Zoom tool in the Toolbox
Fit artwork in window	Double-click the Hand tool in the Toolbox
Reset marquee zoom	Begin marquee drag, then hold SPACEBAR using the Zoom tool and continue dragging to set marquee
Toggle horizontal/vertical guide	Hold ALT/OPTION while dragging guide

Type Shortcuts

Character palette	CTRL/COMMAND+T
Paragraph palette	CTRL/COMMAND+M
Link Block	CTRL/COMMAND+3
Unlink Block	CTRL/COMMAND+ALT/OPTION+3

B

The following keyboard combinations provide you with formatting shortcuts while you are working with normal, Vertical, Area, or Path Type tools:

Flush left type	CTRL/COMMAND+SHIFT+L
Flush right type	CTRL/COMMAND+SHIFT+R
Center type	CTRL/COMMAND+SHIFT+C
Justify type	CTRL/COMMAND+SHIFT+J
Justify last line of type	CTRL/COMMAND+SHIFT+F
Reset horizontal scale	CTRL/COMMAND+SHIFT+X
Increase point size	CTRL/COMMAND+SHIFT+>
Decrease point size	CTRL/COMMAND+SHIFT+<
More leading	ALT/OPTION+UP ARROW key
Less leading	ALT/OPTION+SHIFT+DOWN ARROW key
More kerning/tracking	ALT/OPTION+LEFT ARROW key
Less kerning/tracking	ALT/OPTION+RIGHT ARROW key
More kerning/tracking (x5)	CTRL/COMMAND+ALT/OPTION+LEFT ARROW key
Less kerning/tracking (x5)	CTRL/COMMAND+ALT/OPTION+RIGHT ARROW key
More baseline shift	ALT/OPTION+SHIFT+LEFT ARROW key
Less baseline shift	ALT/OPTION+SHIFT+RIGHT ARROW key
More baseline shift (x5)	CTRL/COMMAND+ALT/OPTION+SHIFT+LEFT ARROW key
Less baseline shift (x5)	CTRL/COMMAND+ALT/OPTION+SHIFT+RIGHT ARROW key
Select single word	Double-click word with any Type tool
Select paragraph	Triple-click word with any Type tool
Move cursor left, right, up, or down	LEFT, RIGHT, UP, or DOWN ARROW keys

Select characters	Hold SHIFT key+LEFT, RIGHT, UP or DOWN ARROW keys
Select words	Hold CTRL/COMMAND+SHIFT key+LEFT, RIGHT, UP or DOWN ARROW keys

Object Selection, Move, and Transform Shortcuts

Select All	CTRL/COMMAND+A
Deselect All	CTRL/COMMAND+SHIFT+A
Select recent Selection tool	Hold CTRL/COMMAND with any tool (except Selection tools)
Toggle selection tool	CTRL/COMMAND+TAB to toggle between Selection and last used Group or Direct Selection tools
Toggle Direct/Group	Hold ALT/OPTION to toggle between Direct and Group Selection tools
Add/subtract selected	Hold SHIFT with Selection, Direct, and Group Selection tools
Duplicate selection	Hold ALT/OPTION while dragging selected objects
Move selected objects	Press UP, DOWN, LEFT, or RIGHT ARROW keys
Lock all unselected	CTRL/COMMAND+ALT/OPTION+L
Transform Again	CTRL/COMMAND+D
Bring to Front	CTRL/COMMAND+SHIFT+]
Bring Forward	CTRL/COMMAND+]
Send to Back	CTRL/COMMAND+SHIFT+[
Send Backward	CTRL/COMMAND+[
Lock	CTRL/COMMAND+G

B

Unlock All	CTRL/COMMAND+SHIFT+G
Apply Last Filter	CTRL/COMMAND+E
Last Filter	CTRL/COMMAND+SHIFT+E

The shortcuts above apply to specific arrange or transform commands; the following apply to mouse and keyboard combinations while using various tools.

Set center with dialog box	Hold ALT/OPTION and click the mouse with Scale, Reflect, or Shear tools
Apply transform to copy	Hold ALT/OPTION and drag while transforming with Rotate, Scale, Reflect, Shear, or Reshape tools (add SHIFT to constrain transformation)
Transform pattern	Hold TILDE (~) and drag while transforming with Rotate, Scale, Reflect, or Shear tools

 The Adobe Illustrator Quick Reference Card and Help documentation say the Twirl tool transforms patterns independent of objects when the TILDE (~) key is held down. This is true for the other tools, but not the Twirl tool.

Painting Shortcuts

Toggle Paintbrush and Eyedropper	Hold ALT/OPTION
Sample gradient color	Hold SHIFT key while using Eyedropper

Path and Mask Shortcuts

Join	CTRL/COMMAND+J
Average	CTRL/COMMAND+SHIFT+J
Repeat Pathfinder	CTRL/COMMAND+4
Make Mask	CTRL/COMMAND+7
Release Mask	CTRL/COMMAND+ALT/OPTION+7

| Make Compound Path | CTRL/COMMAND+8 |
| Release Compound Path | CTRL/COMMAND+ALT/OPTION+8 |

The shortcuts above apply to specific path or mask commands; the following apply to mouse and keyboard combinations while using path-related tools.

Select Convert Direction Point tool	Hold CTRL/COMMAND+ALT/OPTION while using Seletion, Direct Selection, or Group Selection tools
Select Convert Direction Point tool	Hold CTRL/COMMAND+ALT/OPTION while using the Pen tool
Toggle Add/Delete Anchor Point tools	Hold ALT/OPTION key
Select Add Anchor Point tool	Hold ALT/OPTION while using the Scissors tool
Choose Eraser tool	Hold CTRL/COMMAND while dragging back over path with Pencil tool

B

T

U

V

W

X

Z

FREE ILLUSTRATOR TIPS!